THE ROUTLEDGE COMPANION
TO ARTS MANAGEMENT

The Routledge Companion to Arts Management contains perspectives from international scholars, educators, consultants, and practitioners sharing opinions, exploring important questions, and raising concerns about the field. The book will stimulate conversations, foster curiosity, and open pathways to different cultural, philosophical, ideological, political, and generational insights.

Four broad thematic areas are used to organize current topics in the field of arts and cultural management. Part I introduces a mixture of perspectives about the history and evolution of the practice and study of arts management, the role of arts managers, and how arts management is being impacted by the digital age. Part II focuses on the dynamics of entrepreneurship, change processes, and leadership practices. Part III includes globally focused topics on cultural policy, cultural rights, and community building. Part IV examines a sampling of topics related to functional activities that are common to arts and culture organizations around the world such as marketing, planning, increasing diversity, hiring, fundraising, and sustainability.

This book builds a comprehensive understanding of what arts management can mean in an international context, creating an essential resource for students, scholars, and reflective practitioners involved at the intersection of business and the arts.

William J. Byrnes is Professor Emeritus in Arts Administration at Southern Utah University, USA.

Aleksandar Brkić is Lecturer at the Institute for Creative and Cultural Entrepreneurship (ICCE), Goldsmiths, University of London, UK, covering the fields of cultural/arts management and cultural policy.

Routledge Companions in Business, Management and Accounting

Routledge Companions in Business, Management and Accounting are prestige reference works providing an overview of a whole subject area or sub-discipline. These books survey the state of the discipline including emerging and cutting-edge areas. Providing a comprehensive, up to date, definitive work of reference, Routledge Companions can be cited as an authoritative source on the subject.

A key aspect of these Routledge Companions is their international scope and relevance. Edited by an array of highly regarded scholars, these volumes also benefit from teams of contributors which reflect an international range of perspectives.

Individually, Routledge Companions in Business, Management and Accounting provide an impactful one-stop-shop resource for each theme covered. Collectively, they represent a comprehensive learning and research resource for researchers, postgraduate students and practitioners.

Published titles in this series include:

The Routledge Companion to the History of Retailing
Edited by Jon Stobart and Vicki Howard

The Routledge Companion to Innovation Management
Edited by Jin Chen, Alexander Brem, Eric Viardot and Poh Kam Wong

The Routledge Companion to the Makers of Global Business
Edited by Teresa da Silva Lopes, Christina Lubinski and Heidi J.S. Tworek

The Routledge Companion to Accounting in Emerging Economies
Edited by Pauline Weetman and Ioannis Tsalavoutas

The Routledge Companion to Arts Management
Edited by William J. Byrnes and Aleksandar Brkić

For more information about this series, please visit: www.routledge.com/Routledge-Companions-in-Business-Management-and-Accounting/book-series/RCBMA

THE ROUTLEDGE COMPANION TO ARTS MANAGEMENT

Edited by William J. Byrnes and Aleksandar Brkić

Routledge
Taylor & Francis Group

LONDON AND NEW YORK

First published 2020
by Routledge
2 Park Square, Milton Park, Abingdon, Oxon OX14 4RN

605 Third Avenue, New York, NY 10017

First issued in paperback 2021

Routledge is an imprint of the Taylor & Francis Group, an informa business

Publisher's Note
The publisher has gone to great lengths to ensure the quality of this reprint but points out that some imperfections in the original copies may be apparent.

British Library Cataloguing-in-Publication Data
A catalogue record for this book is available from the British Library

Library of Congress Cataloging-in-Publication Data
A catalog record for this book has been requested

ISBN 13: 978−1−03−208932−4 (pbk)
ISBN 13: 978−1−138−49222−6 (hbk)

Typeset in Bembo
by Apex CoVantage, LLC

CONTENTS

Contents

FIGURES

TABLES

CONTRIBUTORS

Daniela Aliberti is a PhD student in Management at Università Cattolica del Sacro Cuore (Milan, Italy). She is studying creative and cultural industries from different perspectives. Her research work focuses on the role of social evaluation of personal and organizational conduct in the film industry, while she is also interested in exploring the benefits of contemporary art for organizations.

Julianne Amendola is Chief Advancement Officer at the Minneapolis Institute of Art, leading fundraising strategy through oversight of major and individual gifts and stewardship, corporate and foundation relations, information management and operations, and events. She has more than 25 years of experience in fundraising management and has launched many collaborative partnerships as well as Mia's innovative membership model.

Ruth Bereson, PhD, is Professor and Dean, Engagement (Creative Arts), Griffith University (Australia), and has held senior positions in higher education and the arts and cultural sector internationally. She researches in the fields of arts management, cultural policy, cultural diplomacy, and leadership and actively contributes to the field as a speaker and through a wide range of books, edited volumes, and articles.

Jean E. Brody is Teaching Professor and Program Director of the Online Arts Administration and Museum Leadership program at Drexel University. Along with her work as an arts administrator and educator, she has worked in arts for social change, as a dramaturg, stage manager, and director.

Renate Buijze, PhD, is a researcher at the Erasmus School of Law (ESL) and Disbursement manager at the Erasmus Trustfonds. Her research focuses on cross-border philanthropy for the arts and the tax incentives involved. With a master's degree in cultural economics and entrepreneurship and a PhD degree in tax law, she has an interdisciplinary scope on research.

Piergiacomo Mion Dalle Carbonare is SDA Fellow at SDA Bocconi School of Management and PhD Candidate in marketing at the University of Valencia. He teaches courses on place branding, territorial marketing, and cultural policies and his research interests are mainly on management of cultural institutions. He is a visiting PhD student at SMU, Dallas.

Josephine Caust, PhD, is Associate Professor and Principal Fellow (Hon) at the University of Melbourne. She is the author of *Arts Leadership in Contemporary Contexts* (Routledge 2018) and the editor of *Arts and Cultural Leadership in Asia* (Routledge 2015). She has published extensively on arts and cultural policy and worked in the arts sector in many different roles.

Farooq Chaudhry, a former professional dancer, is Co-founder and Producer of Akram Khan Company. The French Ministry of Foreign Affairs acknowledged Chaudhry in a list of the world's top hundred cultural actors and entrepreneurs in 2008. Chaudhry was awarded an honorary doctorate from De Montfort University for his services to dance and in 2019 was awarded an OBE for his services to dance and dance production.

Meggy Cheng is Director of Marketing with the Hong Kong Philharmonic Orchestra. With years of experience working in both the commercial sector and in the arts, Meggy has specialized in strategic planning, marketing, PR, communications, and fundraising. She is a 2018/19 Clore Fellow and is currently undertaking the Clore Leadership Programme in the UK.

Rebecca Wai In Chou is the General Manager of Macao Orchestra, a department of the Cultural Affairs Bureau of Macao S.A.R. Government. With years of experience as an arts manager in both private and public sectors, she has interests in organizational development, strategic planning, and human resources management. Rebecca also worked for the Macao Arts Festival and the Macao International Music Festival between 2013 and 2014.

Constance DeVereaux, PhD, is Associate Professor and Director of Arts Administration at University of Connecticut. Her expertise as a scholar, researcher, and consultant in cultural management spans 25 years. She works with universities, NGOs, and government agencies on cultural management and policy projects. Her research is published internationally. Her most recent work is *Arts and Cultural Management: Sense and Sensibilities in the State of the Field* (2018).

Kaywin Feldman was recently appointed Director of the National Gallery of Art in Washington, D.C. From 2008 to 2019 she led the Minneapolis Institute of Art as its director and president. She has served as President of the Association of Art Museum Directors and Chair of the American Alliance of Museums. She is a frequent speaker on reinventing the museum for the 21st century.

Brea M. Heidelberg, PhD, is Assistant Professor of Entertainment & Arts Management at Drexel University. Dr. Heidelberg investigates diversity, equity and inclusion, human resources, and professional development issues in nonprofit arts organizations. She currently serves as Vice President of the Association of Arts Administration Educators and on the editorial board of the *American Journal of Arts Management*.

Sunitha Janamohanan has been working in the arts in Malaysia since 1999 and has been an arts manager, curator, producer, venue manager, and heritage manager. She currently teaches in the Programme in Arts Management at LASALLE College of the Arts, Singapore. Her research interests include community and socially engaged arts practice, and local arts management models in developing Southeast Asia.

Rebekah Lambert is Senior Vice President with Arts Consulting Group, Inc. In her work with arts and culture organizations across North America, she facilitates strategic planning and community engagement processes through which her clients create and take ownership of useful and actionable plans that evolve from in-depth stakeholder dialogue about their organization, role, impact, and future in their communities.

Boyi Li, PhD, is a lecturer in Management at the Business School of Exeter University. His research interests include creative cities, space of creativity, and digital economy. He received his doctoral degree from the London School of Economics.

Benny Lim, PhD, is Assistant Professor of Cultural Studies and Associate Director of the Master of Arts in Cultural Management programme with the Chinese University of Hong Kong. Since 2001, Benny has produced and directed over 70 theatre productions and arts festivals.

Justin Macdonnell is Executive Director of the Anzarts Institute, a cultural consulting agency and think tank, and is a leading arts manager holding executive roles in major organizations in Australia, NZ and the USA. He has produced numerous works in music, theatre, dance and physical theatre, toured internationally, undertaken consultancies for public and private arts organizations and published three works on arts history and policy.

Marta Massi, PhD, is an assistant professor at Università Cattolica del Sacro Cuore, Italy. She has been a visiting scholar at Deakin University, Australia and McGill University, Canada. Her research focuses on arts and culture marketing, management of arts organizations, and branding in arts and cultural organizations.

Nigel D Morpeth, PhD, is a research fellow at the University of Hull's Culture, Place and Policy Institute and is a visual artist. He previously worked for three other universities in the UK and in community-based leisure in three local authorities. During Hull UK City of Culture in 2017, he was a volunteer and worked with the Monitoring and Evaluation Team on the visual arts programme, which currently informs his research.

Guy Morrow, PhD, is head of the Arts and Cultural Management graduate program at the University of Melbourne, Australia. He is the author of *Artist Management: Agility in the Creative and Cultural Industries* (Routledge 2018) and co-author of *The New Music Industries: Disruption and Discovery* (Palgrave Macmillan 2016). He has worked extensively as an artist manager in the international music industries.

Oonagh Murphy, PhD, is a lecturer in Arts Management in the Institute for Creative and Cultural Entrepreneurship at Goldsmiths, University of London. Her research explores best practice on the scalability of emerging technologies for cultural organizations. Her work centers on critical praxis and working in partnership with cultural organizations to define and develop digital practice.

Rachel Parker is Director of Arts Administration at Southern Utah University. When not teaching, Rachel works as a consultant for nonprofit arts organizations and serves as the Arts Leadership Chair of the Kennedy Center American College Theatre Festival Region VIII.

Chiara Paolino, PhD, is an assistant professor of Organization Theory and HR Management at Università Cattolica del Sacro Cuore (Milan, Italy). Her research interests revolve around knowledge and learning dynamics at the workplace, diversity management, and the role arts-based methods in organizations.

Chiara Piancatelli, PhD, is a research fellow at SDA Bocconi School of Management, Milan. Her research activities focus on cultural marketing, consumer behavior, experiential marketing, and digital marketing. She worked as a visiting research associate at Deakin University, Australia, where she conducted research on the impact of digital technology on consumer behavior within the arts sector.

Marcin Poprawski, PhD, is Deputy Dean of the Faculty of Social Sciences of the AMU University in Poznan, Poland, and works in the Institute of Cultural Studies at the AMU and the ROK AMU Culture Observatory. His research interests, publication topics, and projects include cultural policies, cultural management and entrepreneurship, festivals management, aesthetics in management, organizational cultures in cultural & creative organizations, and heritage institutions.

Milena Dragićević Šešić, PhD, is the former President of the University of Arts, Belgrade, and is Chair of the UNESCO Cultural Policy and Management Department, University of Arts in Belgrade. She is the Director of the Research Institute of the Faculty of Dramatic Arts (Belgrade) and a board member of the European Diploma in Cultural Project Management (Brussels). She is a UNESCO expert, has published 18 books translated into 17 languages, and was awarded the Commandeur dans l'Ordre des Palmes Academiques in 2002.

Alex Turrini, PhD, is Associate Professor at the Department of Social and Political Science at Bocconi University and Visiting Chair of the Division of Arts Management and Arts Entrepreneurship at SMU Meadows School for the Arts, Dallas. His research activities center on public policies and management in the arts and cultural sector and public sector leadership and change.

Marilena Vecco, PhD, is Associate Professor in Entrepreneurship at Burgundy School of Business, Dijon (France) and associated to the Carmelle and Rémi Marcoux Chair in Arts Management, HEC Montréal. Her research focuses on cultural entrepreneurship and management with a special focus on cultural heritage and art markets. Marilena has over 17 years of academic and professional experience as a researcher, lecturer, and consultant for different international organizations.

Anmol Vellani is the Founder and former Executive Director of India Foundation for the Arts and Co-founder of Toto Funds the Arts, which support the arts across India. He has directed over 40 theatre productions. His essays and talks have covered arts entrepreneurship, intercultural dialogue, culture and development, cultural mapping, arts collaboration, and transgressive art, among other subjects.

Ben Walmsley, PhD, is an associate professor in Audience Engagement in the School of Performance and Cultural Industries at the University of Leeds (UK). Prior to his academic career, he worked as a producer at the National Theatre of Scotland. Ben is the Co-editor of *Arts and the Market* and has published widely on arts management, audience research and cultural policy. Since 2014 he has directed the National School for Arts Fundraising and Leadership.

Matthew Welch, PhD, is Deputy Director and Chief Curator at the Minneapolis Institute of Art. He has been with the museum since 1990, and currently plays a key role in charting the museum's strategic vision. He presently oversees an initiative to optimize the visitor experience through compelling, accessible narratives and welcoming in-gallery experiences. At the same time, he is committed to advancing the museum's national and international reputation through scholarship, exhibitions, and important acquisitions.

Audrey Wong is Head, School of Creative Industries, LASALLE College of the Arts, where she also leads the MA Arts and Cultural Leadership programme. She was formerly Artistic Co-director of independent space The Substation, served on the boards of the Singapore Art Museum and National Arts Council, and from 2009–2011, was a nominated member of Parliament representing the arts.

Yong Xiang (Hardy), PhD, is a professor at the School of Arts at Peking University and vice dean of the Institute for Cultural Industries at Peking University, where he is working in the Art Management and Cultural and Creative Industries Program. He is a co-editor of *China Cultural and Creative Industries Reports 2013* (Springer 2013).

Mio Yachita assumed her position as a research associate at the Graduate School of Global Arts, Tokyo University of the Arts in October 2016. She previously served in the Japan Foundation and was appointed to the Malaysian office from 2012 to 2016 as a deputy manager. She specializes in culture in external relations, community-engaged arts, and cultural policy of Japan.

INTRODUCTION TO *THE ROUTLEDGE COMPANION TO ARTS MANAGEMENT*

The field of arts management as a practice and as an area for research and study continues to grow. The number of books published, e-newsletters circulated, and blog sites dedicated to helping arts managers try to do their job more effectively continues to expand worldwide. Colleges and universities are graduating more aspiring arts managers, and the scope of research and scholarship in the field has become more diverse and sophisticated. Service organizations in the performing and visual arts are also providing professional development, conferences, training, and resources designed to build skills and to advocate for the arts to policymakers, legislators, and funders. With all this growth comes the challenge of how best to serve the varied needs of students, researchers, scholars, and practitioners seeking ideas, insights, and examples of how arts managers are engaging in managing the arts. Taking all of these factors into account, we have compiled what we think will be a helpful resource for this growing constituency.

This book offers examples of case studies and research that demonstrate how creativity and collaboration in the cultural sector can change lives, enhance communities, and help artists and arts organizations thrive. However, we are also raising questions through international perspectives about arts management practice and research. This book features a diversity of experiences in different cultural environments and contexts while at the same time finding common ground in a practice coming from the perceived Other. Europe, the U.S., and Australia are not the only centers for the new ideas and challenging questions in the field of arts management – China (including Hong Kong and Macau), India, Singapore, Malaysia, and many more environments are widening the scope and coverage of topics. We see this book as one more step in the direction of building a more substantial understanding of what arts management can mean in the international context.

Four broad thematic areas are used to organize current topics in the field of arts and culture management. Part 1I introduces a mixture of perspectives about the history and evolution of the practice and study of arts management, the role of arts managers, and how arts management is being impacted by the digital age. Part 2II focuses on the dynamics of entrepreneurship, change processes, and leadership practices. Part 3III includes globally focused topics on cultural policy, cultural rights, and community building. Part 4IV examines a sampling of topics related to functional activities that are common to arts and culture organizations around the world such as marketing, planning, increasing diversity, hiring, fundraising, and sustainability.

We have assembled a mixture of international scholars, educators, consultants, and practitioners to share their opinions, explore important questions, and raise concerns about the field of art management. Our goal was to create a book that would stimulate conversations, foster curiosity, and open pathways to different cultural, philosophical, ideological, political, and generational perspectives. That means that we, as editors, did not necessarily always agree with all the points of view presented or the way they were argued. As a matter of fact, we didn't always agree with each other about some of these varied viewpoints. However, we strongly believe that we need more dialogue and platforms from which we can critically discuss and debate the issues in the field to help promote more understanding and to be able to advance and expand the field further. We think our contributors have provided readers with a distinctive mix of topics that will help broaden the reader's knowledge and perspective; will help the educators and students in providing valuable insights, reflections, cases, and questions; and that will spark curiosity and interest about how the field of arts management is continuing to evolve and grow.

William J. Byrnes and Aleksandar Brkić

Co-editors

William J. Byrnes is Professor Emeritus in Arts Administration at Southern Utah University. He has a longstanding interest in cultural leadership, organizational development, strategic planning, marketing, and fundraising. Byrnes has lectured and presented on topics in arts management such as leadership, fundraising, planning, and organizational development in America, Europe, and Asia. He is the author of *Management and the Arts*, which is in its 5th edition.

www.linkedin.com/in/billbyrnes
https://managementandthearts.com/5e

Aleksandar Brkić is Lecturer at the Institute for Creative and Cultural Entrepreneurship (ICCE), Goldsmiths, University of London, covering the fields of cultural/arts management and cultural policy. Aleksandar has a significant international experience as an educator, an arts manager, and creative producer working in the intersections of performing arts, visual arts, and design in Europe, US, Asia, and Africa.

www.gold.ac.uk/icce/staff/brkic-aleksandar/

OVERVIEW OF *THE ROUTLEDGE COMPANION TO ARTS MANAGEMENT*

Part I: The evolving field of arts management and the expanding roles of arts managers

The first six chapters in the *Companion to Arts Management* explore a wide range of topics in the field of arts management. Questions are raised about the efficacy of arts management, what are the roles and functions of arts managers, and what ethical framework should artist managers function within. A methodology is proposed for arts organizations facing pressures exerted by governmental policymakers, the pros and cons of digital media as a force for opening arts organization to more diverse voices in communities is assessed, and the impact of big data on artist management practices is researched and evaluated.

In Chapter 1 contributors Justin Macdonnell and Ruth Bereson offer a provocative review of the evolution of arts management and the impact of managerialism on the field in recent decades. They are questioning the way the relationship between the artist and arts manager has become influenced by forces that have reframed the arts as being a part of the cultural and creative industries. They see that proscriptive government funding, an ever-increasing bureaucracy, undue influence by private donors and foundations, overemphasis on entrepreneurialism, and narrow conformist views and behaviors by arts manager are undermining the collaborative foundations of the arts. Theirs is a call to question assumptions about what arts management has become and how it is taught in universities, constantly challenging the position of the arts in the practice, teaching, and research in the field of arts management.

Constance DeVereaux extends many of the topics introduced in Chapter 1 by posing ontological questions about the role of the arts manager. DeVereaux unfolds the layers of management functions and tasks often connected to what the role of an arts manager is and drills down to examine issues related to values, ethics, and ultimately asks what an arts manager can or should be.

Anmol Vellani adds to the themes of the opening chapters by sharing his philosophical reflections on the role of the artist manager as it relates to artists who span a continuum from being self-directed to more audience led. His chapter differentiates the behaviors and functions of artist managers responding to the needs of the artists at each end of the spectrum. He likens the artist manager for the self-directed artists to a social entrepreneur who is mission-driven and who is guided by an ethical framework designed to enhance the value of the artist's work.

Milena Dragićević Šešić argues that cultural organizations in Europe face pressures from national and supranational cultural policies and the demands placed on them from arts audiences and communities. She offers the framework of adaptable quality management as a way for cultural organizations to respond to these pressures. Adaptable quality management could be deployed by arts organizations in the form of laboratories generating innovative work, or activist organizations using socio-political programming, or organizations that take a transdisciplinary research approach directed toward knowledge creation, or lastly, organizations could take a transfer of knowledge role which can help build a general love for the arts. The overarching goal is to create an autonomous public cultural system capable of being a force of its own.

Oonagh Murphy discusses how technology is changing societies and influencing cultural organizations and arts managers. Murphy notes these are fundamental changes that are impacting how patrons interact with and relate to the arts. Innovative approaches to audience and art form development are reviewed, and examples of organizations that have successfully engaged with the public using new technology are shared.

The final chapter in this section looks at the arts management practice of artist management. Guy Morrow is interested in concepts related to how access to big data might modify the arc of an artist's career and their working relationship with an artist manager. Morrow notes access to more information about audience interests may impact or be shaped by artists as they communicate with the public and seek support and funding.

Part II: Entrepreneurship, leadership, and transformation change

This section starts with a historical review of the changing definition of cultural and creative entrepreneurship and the rise of the artist-entrepreneur. In addition, the rise of a dance company is evaluated in the context of the roles of cultural entrepreneurs and artist managers, and a large producing theatre in the UK helps provide a case study for how change can be implemented and managed. Interviews with arts leaders navigating through their first year on the job demonstrate how two different approaches to managing change processes in organizations can be undertaken, and a review of the adaptive leadership model, assessed for its applicability to arts organizations, concludes this section of the book.

Marilena Vecco offers a detailed history and comprehensive overview of the evolving definition of the term entrepreneur and cultural and creative entrepreneurship. Vecco builds upon this history in exploring the concept of the "artpreneur" which combines the artist with the entrepreneur. The intersection of the processes used by artpreneurs and arts management is also discussed.

Farooq Chaudhry focuses on the roles of a cultural entrepreneur and the artist manager as it connects with his personal experience as a producer of the contemporary dance company under the artistic direction of Akram Khan Company. The chapter covers the growth of the dance company, the role of the producer in enhancing the artist's work, and the need to go beyond traditional business models.

Change and the change process is touched upon in many chapters in this book. Ben Walmsley focuses on arts leadership and how it can become more effective in deploying change in cultural organizations. Walmsley uses The Yorkshire Playhouse in the UK as a case study of how the change process supported the theatre transitioning to a creative development hub and center.

Rachel Parker also looks at the change process by comparing how two arts leaders approached their new jobs in cultural organizations. A new museum director and a new executive producer of a theatre company tackled change in organizations that were at very different points in their life cycles. Parker also uses concepts from cognitive restructuring to demonstrate how this psychological approach can be used in the change process.

Lastly, the adaptive leadership model has been around for about 25 years, and William J. Byrnes offers an assessment of its applicability to arts organizations. The basic structure of the model is reviewed, and examples are offered to demonstrate its potential application to different organization change circumstances.

Part III: Developing communities and evolving cultural policy

The next nine chapters explore a range of topics that cover the changing arts and culture ecology worldwide. The labyrinth created by the growth of cultural networks is examined within the context of an expanding universe of information and the potential for these networks to help arts organizations solve strategic problems they face is explored. The cases of Japan and the city-state of Singapore offer examples of how government policies can influence cultural production. The concept that people have cultural rights as part of their human rights is examined through the lens of government funding priorities and practices. The impact of cultural collectives is highlighted in Malaysia, and the sustainability of these non-organizations is assessed. Volunteers play key roles in arts organizations around the world, and the city of Hull in the UK offers a platform from which to examine the impact volunteers as cultural mediators have on museums and the public. The worldwide growth of arts festivals is examined in light of new practices and management schemes. Poland has seen a significant shift in its cultural ecology with its membership in the EU. The impact and sustainability of new arts venues on the cultural environment of the country are investigated. Lastly, the evolution of concepts surrounding creative cities and cultural economics is explored using Beijing as a backdrop.

Aleksandar Brkić explores the topic of cultural networking and its role in leveraging cooperation and development across disparate types of cultural organizations. These networks include associations designed to advance learning in arts management and in developing cultural policy. Questions are posed about the proliferation of these networks and how they could be better aligned to support collaboration and advocacy, as well as questioning their future in the "times of quantum reality."

Audrey Wong shares the distinctive evolution of government support for the arts in Singapore as it seeks to be known as a "global arts city." Wong explores the occasionally bumpy relationship between the state, artists, and arts managers through the several decades of leadership changes and programming at an arts center known as "The Substation."

Meanwhile, in Japan, Mio Yachita documents how cultural policy resulted in the creation of often-redundant cultural facilities across the nation. Yachita argues this policy has had an influence on approaches to the education and training of arts managers and has also led to extensive discussions about how other elements of cultural policy have had an impact on programming in facilities.

Jo Caust does a comprehensive review of the variances in how governments provide funding support for the arts while posing questions about the degree to which citizens across the globe have cultural rights – meaning access to and the ability to participate in the arts. Caust points out that while UNESCO has promoted cultural rights for several decades, and many countries and local governments have endorsed the concept, she finds political, economic, and social gaps in realizing these rights.

Sunitha Janamohanan explores how a free informal outdoor library known as Buku Jalanan in Malaysia, which has been created by volunteers, has become a force for creating community and building cultural agency across the country. The author also explores how Buku Jalanan, as an art collective with its specific organizational model, deals with the question of sustainability of an arts organization.

Volunteers also played a big part in the success of the United Kingdom's Hull City of Culture 2017 program. Nigel D Morpeth offers insights on how a year-long series of cultural programs was greatly facilitated by volunteers and assesses the impact of these activities on building civil society. Morpeth's detailed case study of the City of Culture program demonstrates how volunteers were essential in fostering a broader engagement with the public across the city.

Arts festivals are a growing phenomenon around the world. Benny Lim profiles four Asian global cites engaged in producing numerous types of arts festivals. Lim assesses the impact of curating and managing festivals that include examples such as the Shakespeare 400 Festival in Kuala Lampur, the Bangkok Theatre Festival, and the West Kowloon Cultural District of Hong Kong "Freespace Happening."

Marcin Poprawski shares detailed research on the significant growth in the number of arts and culture institutions in Poland (almost 300 in less than a decade) which has created an impact on the arts ecology that is still being assessed. Case studies include the Gdansk Shakespeare Theatre, the philharmonic hall in Gorzow, a heritage center in Poznan, and an arts center in Wloclawek. In addition, Poprawski examines four other arts and cultural institutions. This research informs a series of recommendations targeted to arts managers and leaders, policymakers, and governing entities.

The concluding chapter on communities and cultural policy is a discourse on creative capital using a detailed research framework developed by the authors. Yong Xiang and Boyi Li suggest a rethinking is in order between culture, urbanism, and sustainable development. They also offer a case study using Beijing as an example of a city undergoing transformation driven by elements of the creative economy.

Part IV: Arts organizations: strategic management, marketing, and fundraising

The final nine chapters cover a broad range of topics related to functional activities of arts organizations that provide strategic support in mission fulfillment. Marketing, fundraising, planning, hiring, diversity, and staffing of arts organizations is examined using case studies to help illustrate the application of research and theory in the field of arts management. Differing international perspectives provide the reader with opportunities to reflect on techniques and tools used to connect with audiences and patrons and to cultivate sustainable fundraising.

Arts marketing is an often-contentious function in cultural organizations. Marta Massi and Chiara Piancatelli guide us through the transformation of marketing as a type of "third-wheel" to an essential tool in building relationships with audiences and the public. Arts marketing is seen as a useful strategic process to help build organizational identity and much more. Examples are provided of how different cultural organizations have used marketing techniques to engage with a wide range of stakeholders.

Next, the process and practice of planning is a core function in all types of public and private organizations. Consultant Rebekah Lambert takes us through a planning process used by many arts organizations in America. She contrasts two types of organizations – a small historical museum in a rural area and a symphony orchestra in a large metropolitan environment – and takes us through a step-by-step process supported by numerous diagrams and tables designed to provide the reader with a comprehensive planning framework from which to work.

We shift our attention to the topic of diversity, which has become a priority issue arts organizations are attempting to address across a wide span of disciplines. Jean E. Brody provides history, context, and examples of critical processes that arts managers and their organizations in America can deploy to meet the diversity, equity, and inclusion goals they have set. This chapter provides practical steps arts organizations can take to develop a mindset and policies that reshape their relationships with their community.

Brea M. Heidelberg methodically explores the details of staffing by demonstrating processes that can be used in small- and medium-sized arts organizations lacking a dedicated human resources department. An example of a task analysis process is used to demonstrate how arts organizations can create effective job postings which will attract and build a competent and diverse workforce. This chapter reinforces how diversity, equity, and inclusion goals, covered by Brody in the previous chapter, can be achieved.

The next chapter focuses on "artistic interventions," which is a process that can be employed by arts managers to help many different types of for-profit and nonprofit organizations create a more satisfying workplace. Daniela Aliberti and Chiara Paolino provide an overview of how artistic interventions have evolved over the last two decades and have been used successfully in corporate settings in Europe and Italy in particular.

The last four chapters examine various facets of fundraising and development from an international perspective. We start with Renate Buijze, who shares her research on how international fundraising is practiced in 36 arts organizations. The strategies and tactics used by these organization are reviewed, and the effectiveness of the fundraising campaigns are discussed. The level of engagement and strategies used by organizations as they go about fundraising is contrasted.

Alex Turrini, Piergiacomo Mion Dalle Carbonare, and Marta Massi focus on the evolution of fundraising from engaging donors through forms of private patronage to more democratic methods of fundraising, which now include activities such as crowdfunding. Country-based fundraising idiosyncrasies are discussed, public and private donor perspectives are explored, and the future importance of fundraising as a function in cultural organizations is highlighted.

Fundraising history for classical music organizations is reviewed by Benny Lim, Meggy Cheng, and Rebecca Wai In Chou, with a special focus on Hong Kong and Macau which are part of what is called Special Administrative Regions (SAR) in China. Case studies of five music organizations are provided to demonstrate how public and private funding play a part in supporting these organizations.

Lastly, the environment of philanthropic support of museums is explored from the perspective of the need to evolve programming and engagement practices to respond to the changing demographics in America. From the specific angle of museum managers, applying action research, Kaywin Feldman, Julianne Amendola, and Matthew Welch offer recommendations that can better position museums to meet the needs of future donors and museum-goers.

PART I

The evolving field of arts management and the expanding roles of arts managers

1

ARTS MANAGEMENT AND ITS CONTRADICTIONS

Justin Macdonnell and Ruth Bereson

Some pre-history

All too often in today's world subjects such as arts management are presented as if they have emerged fully baked and are universally understood. This chapter will examine some of the meanings and the concepts which underpin the term and make recommendations concerning current modes of education. It will ask the reader to consider in-depth, and against various contexts, the complexities inherent in this field of practice and study.

The study of arts management is a relatively new concept, but the practice goes back as far as any organised society. The moment a work is introduced to an audience by a third party, the practice of arts management occurs. In the Western World we might first describe the practice as having been undertaken by the Greeks where the Archons understood that it was their duty to finance and present theatrical work to the citizens of the state. This role has been undertaken in many forms since then, from philanthropic gesture, to royal patronage, governmental subvention, and various commercial modes through to contemporary crowd sourcing. The term itself in the Western World came into parlance in the latter part of the twentieth century where the study of arts administration initially observed the practices of governmental subvention post-WWII. It was also associated with only the virtues of the arts, Mathew Arnold's 19th century influential concept of Sweetness and Light (Arnold, 1865), whereas the arts do not only channel good as witnessed by the way in which they have been used in totalitarian regimes.

In the 1980s the new obsession with managerialism which affected English-speaking countries slowly saw the term 'administration' replaced by that catch-all 'management' (Protherough and Pick, 2003). Indeed, the term 'arts management' suggests an engagement with the notion of 'progress' – a way forward, a process of doing things, of 'managing the arts'. However we will argue that what we used to think of as the Western World has over the last half century constructed the concept and practice of arts management not from need but from a loss of nerve. We have built it out of the demands of our regulators, not out of the wants of the activity itself. And where all that was needed was skill, we have elevated it to a science based on a belief in how the arts needed to be shaped and financed rather than how they might emerge and grow. It is a classic case of form follows funding.

Odd obsessions

These are obsessions oddly of the English-speaking world and for a long time almost exclusively of the English-speaking world. Most of the structures that this managerialism has put in place have ensured that we only speak to each other within very confined circles, and for the most part in code, without looking to engage with what the rest of the world may have to offer. They emanate from a post-war Britain whereas even that country has moved on (Keynes, 1946; Tusa, 2014; Williams, 1989). Little by little that plague spread to other climes and now infects many nations and cultures that once knew better. Because of that imagined construct in which we have enmeshed ourselves a body of practice and a methodology has grown up and is ever more outdated. Today it verges on irrelevant to creating, producing and delivering the arts and thereby of ascribing value to them.

Yet the need to administer the circumstances in which art is made and in which we aim to support its practitioners and help them to thrive is not idle. It will not vanish merely because our current methods are starting to fail. What might we learn if we looked a little further afield beyond the holy family of the Anglosphere? What might we discover about our current dilemmas if we thought back to a time before John Maynard Keynes (1946) was deemed to have invented how we now administer the arts? Or how might those who want to join our ranks as producers and managers escape the sheltered workshop of the self-repeating academy as the preferred path to management training in the arts? Why have we paid so little attention to the role artists might play in designing both their own self-managed environment and management required from others? Above all, how in these circumstances, do we keep alive a healthy sense of critique in order to make fine and useful distinctions about who we are and what we aim to do? How do we shape a language that can more accurately describe what the arts represent at their best rather than one that just determines what we are expected to see and, in that unlovely usage, consume?

We would all agree that the arts aren't goods and services in any traditional sense and that their impact in society and upon society cannot be measured merely with the conventional social and economic criteria. Surely too much ink has already been spilt on that topic to need any more discussion. That 'the arts' – as generally if generously understood – are critical to humanity is also a view that presumably we would all share. Yet, 'management' especially as expressed as management of the arts, however broadly or narrowly defined, implies a kind of commodification. So, however tiresome it might seem, we need to make a distinction yet again between what 'the arts' are and how they are 'used' in various circumstances or societies. Policy about the arts, both public and private, more often than not focuses on how the arts intersect with agendas which go far beyond their specific domain. As a consequence, they progressively constrict the very arts they seek to support. But at the same time, we would argue that to emerge and prosper, artists and the arts demand maximum freedom. Yet every day they are subjected to bureaucratic processes that achieve the very opposite.

For instance, many of the systems we hold dear (arms-length distribution of funding, for example) are relatively new and anchored in political and economic times in which they arose. Yet for that very reason they are dated, and their datedness too often strangles invention and initiative. So conditioned have we been by these systems that we have come to accept that they are the only way management, governance and public oversight can be. Even thoughtful commentators such as David Throsby (2018) continue to argue, like Winston Churchill (UK House of Commons, 1947), that it's the best of a bad lot. Of course, his reference refers to the Australia Council for the Arts, but he and many others would make a similar claim for sibling bodies in other countries. Thus, we mistake the end for the means. But the ways in which arts meet their audiences have pre-dated and will outlive these rubrics and if we are bold, perhaps we can help them on their way.

A conundrum

Perhaps the notion we can manage the arts at all is philosophically problematic. It is undoubtedly a complex issue and the way we have chosen to do it over the decades may even have been destructive at some level. Part of the problem is that the boundaries keep shifting and the one between arts and culture is the most permeable of all.

So, at the outset it is important to frame what we are talking about. The arts has become a catch-all phrase invoked by various pundits to take on a variety of meanings; it has also been used interchangeably with that closely aligned word 'culture'. We are used to an invocation of Raymond Williams' (1976) now famous dictum 'culture is one of the three most complex words in the English language' and then conflating that complexity to refer to the arts. But in order to make fast a very big distinction we should perhaps go back in time, revert to Kluckhohn and Kelly's (1945) seventy-year old landmark anthropological definition: 'By culture we mean all those historically created designs for living, explicit and implicit, rational, irrational, and non-rational, which exist at any given time as potential guides for the behaviour of men'. However, the arts, and by extension their management, are something else. In particular, what can we ever mean by 'the arts' – to be managed or otherwise – assuming there is a collective usage to begin with?

We would distinguish the arts as consciously and formally constructed artefacts in whatever medium, having value independent of their symbolic significance, and able to be exchanged or traded in and across society. Their management (be it production or distribution) thereby becomes a specialised activity with its own value but not of itself having greater social worth than similar activities in other economic spheres.

We would also distinguish the arts as different from cultural expressions which may result in artefacts of equal aesthetic quality, but which lack the formal intention in their creation. We would claim too that everywhere and in every age the arts – in the preceding sense – are a product of the surplus economy and thus may, strictly speaking, only arise in urban society. Only cities can produce and sustain the arts.

While non-urban societies may produce and benefit from surplus, with rare exceptions they have not historically provided the division of labour necessary to support the making of art (artists in our understanding) as a conscious, independent social activity. Accordingly, whereas ceremony, in whatever sense one cares to consider it, may occur anywhere, only the city could transform it into theater and so on.

In managing all of this we are then talking about a modern urban phenomenon. Of course, there is artistic practice throughout urban and non-urban environments but the places where the arts are managed are the festivals, houses of performance, galleries, museums and institutions which have been the prime features of the metropolis on and off since Maecenas held a salon and Caracalla built his Baths.

Industrial action

There has more recently been the notion that something had emerged called an industry about the arts rather than a profession or indeed a vocation. In adopting that usage, we consider that we downgraded and ultimately deceived ourselves. In that curious commodifying description, practitioners of the arts tried to persuade the powers that be, and maybe even themselves, that there was something bigger, more significant than the mere historical practice of music, theater, literature, painting and sculpture that could be taken seriously and needed to be reckoned with. Strength in numbers perhaps? Size matters after all? To go further: it is strange, when one considers it, that the term 'hybrid' arts is now widely used, as though the concept of the arts was not already hybrid. We have, of course, progressed of late to the even more *jejeune* usage of the 'creative industries' and thus from inventing such categories have evolved into patterns of official categorising and judgment about them resulting in a vicious cycle of self-delusion that it all somehow means something. We do well to remind ourselves of Hans Christian Anderson's (1837) parable about the emperor.

That observation brings us by slow degrees to the way in which policy and ultimately sub-vention occurs and is linked to the ways in which states perceive the arts. It draws attention also to how we have allowed those perceptions to shape and reshape awareness of what we in the arts do and why. For example, much emphasis has conventionally been placed on Keynesian thought and the post-war language of the Welfare State, roughly translated in our small terrain into the concept of the 'Arts Council arms-length distribution model'. This is a view seen almost always through the antique lens of a faded British *oikoumene*, i.e. United Kingdom, Australia, Canada, New Zealand (Keynes, 1946). How – if at all – did the American world catch the same bug and all the administrative and attitudinal paraphernalia that accompanied it? But so it did and not only catch it but propagate it into a host of post-graduate taught degrees with associated organising bodies to provide accreditation for the tertiary education market and to distribute the low communion of its managerial cult before returning it to its British originators purified and elevated into Holy Writ (Protherough and Pick, 2003).

All this was, in turn, weighted down by the idea of a non-profit ethos in which many if not most of the arts have been trapped as though not-for-profit somehow was or ought to be an end in itself, the wonder of our age and glory of our priesthood. Or worse, it has grown the notion that 'profit' could be construed solely in financial terms. Certainly, we aim for 'profit' in the sense of the realisation of the dreams of artists and how that dreaming profits us all. We do or should distribute our profit (or dividends) to those shareholders (our audiences) across the country or the world. But please let us have no more talk of non-profit because that implies we are for loss. Yet loss metaphorically is the very thing which our modern arts management has largely settled for and has done so step by step: loss of self-worth; loss of status; loss of an ability to imagine any other reality; loss of integrity; and finally loss of face before the world we hoped to persuade.

Why manage?

Of course, the question is not so much is there such a beast as arts management or even should there be, but rather: is it worthwhile? Since society first moved beyond a subsistence economy and specialised division of labour became possible, most tasks have required something that the modern world would recognise as management. The marketplace, literally in the Neolithic era and long after, to the 'markets' figuratively in the present day, have always required a degree of organisation and even regulation. Religion too rapidly transformed itself from ritual to elaborate administration whether of belief or tithes. After priesthood and pottery, prostitution was an early starter in the field of economic specialisation and arguably one of the most enduring. Whether by barter or buying and selling, all of these services involved a product and a consumer and all in varying degrees offered an aspect of entertainment. As the product (or production) become more elaborate someone or something was needed to mediate between it and its customer or, if one prefers, the audience. Someone had to spruik the wares, collect the dues and pay the piper, and someone had to promise that a good time could or even would be had by all. It might be the finest food and drink, exotic dancers, a fight to the death, the most lyrical teller of tales, a human sacrifice or merely eternal life. You paid your money and you took your chance. But there had to be a go-between – a promoter, or if you will, a pimp.

For the best part of ten thousand years no one thought there was anything remarkable about this. Indeed, as late as the nineteenth century nothing much had changed. In that respect, art or entertainment was no different from other commodities. Some of those providing the intermediary functions were now called impresarios, though instead of gladiators or dancing girls they now offered recitals by superstars of the day like Franz Liszt and Jenny Lind or lecture tours by Charles Dickens. After all, impresario was once only Italian for businessman; not much different from the chap who sold dress material or later, the horseless carriage. The Uffizi was likewise once just some banker's offices.

The crucial part of all this was that each and every one aimed to make a buck. From the man who supplied the lions for the Colosseum to Salomon bringing Haydn to be lionised at the King's Theatre, it was a business transaction (Nalbach, 1972). The men who organised the companies of players in Elizabethan and Jacobean London were doing it not just for the love of art or storytelling but for money. Happily, in some cases art triumphed and survived the fashion of the day. But actors, actor/writers like their touts and urgers, all had to eat. Entertainment was the aim but the oil that greased the wheels was always lucre. One might extrapolate this into a duke or pope buying the services of an artist as hired help to design a dome or adorn a chapel, write a mass or produce a masque. There, however, was undoubtedly also the exercise of taste. Those Renaissance and Baroque customers knew what they wanted and what it was worth. Equally later, be it P. T. Barnum, known to some as the father of modern marketing or the dissemination of 'humbug' (Barnum, 1855), or Diaghilev, the great Russian Impresario who brought the Ballet Russes to Europe, each believed he was seeking and selling the best the world had to offer.

Now none of this is to suggest that the role of the intermediary or manager is not and cannot be a creative one. Or that it is or has always been simply horse-trading. There are too many examples to the contrary. Nonetheless, in identifying them we may be at the vexed crossroads between managing and producing. Once upon a time to be a producer or indeed a curator meant something – and something quite specific in the world of the arts and entertainment. Perhaps curators needed a little more producing skill and producers could on occasions have done with more curatorial care, but at least we knew where we were with both. Today, it would seem, that everyone in the performing arts is a 'producer' of something. And 'curating' has become as common as cooking programmes and often less interesting.

Who are or were we trying to convince and about what with a term like 'arts management' or even the concept of the professional arts manager? That the arts somehow unleashed if left to artists needed to be corralled? That we could shield the political and bureaucratic classes and thereby society itself from the worst excesses of artistic willfulness or extravagance if everyone conspired to accept what were originally a few simple rules in exchange for some pieces of silver? The rules have expanded hugely but somehow the pile of silver has remained oddly static.

It all seems from a distance of years very much a product of the managed economy, the concern it was that the end of charity (or was it capitalism, as then understood?) and thus there was a clear need to control. Or was it perhaps that in Britain, at least, God's work and running the Empire having evaporated as career prospects there was surplus to requirements of those who were capable of doing this great task or had the prospect of becoming so? Or that art or the arts like the 'natives' would be easy to manage? Now there's a thought.

The paradox is that the belief that the addiction to arms-length and peer assessment was freedom actually put creativity into the straitjacket of compliance fenced about with arcane terminology and bags of dubious evaluative criteria. Some may recall that it was mostly about trying to persuade the powers that be that we were serious players in the self-management field, when what we actually did was open the door to top-down determination.

Stewardship

The question arises then, did we become guides or guards of the sacred arts cow? Arts management and thereby arts managers became complicit in the dumbing down of that which they sought to protect and preserve. Or did we become the new traitor to the arts, like Octavio Paz's depiction of La Malinche, the Mayan woman who learnt the new trick of speaking Spanish and thus became the Cortés's mistress, interpreter and secret weapon against the Aztecs? (Octavio, 1961).

We would argue that we have glibly adopted and are now conditioned by the vocabulary of our managerial overlords, having surrendered governance to those who know nothing of art. Above all, we have failed to evolve a language of our own in which we could shape and argue the principles on which artists wish to live and work not as bureaucracy has determined. All this has become the death by a thousand cuts. No wonder we have been reduced to being a 'sector'!

Not content with adopting the dreaded practice of the management apparatchiks, the arts have (as with education, health and other professions that once also held their heads high) adopted their linguistic contortions. Health has become 'case management'; education is largely viewed as a transactional commodity and valued only by training outcomes; welfare is seen not as a right in a civilised society but as an annoyance to Treasurers. For this is not just the world of 'stakeholders' 'due diligence' 'core competencies', 'skill set' and the boorish 'win-win'. It is also the happy hunting ground of Orwellian Newspeak in which we have 'efficiency dividend' and 'value engineered out' for cut and 'downsize' for getting the sack. Though less sinister, we might add: 'put on the backburner' for delay, 'brainstorming' for discussion and facilitating and mentoring for what used to be called guiding and teaching or the tired and tiresome sporting metaphors 'level playing field', 'punching above one's weight', 'kicking goals', 'hole in one', 'moving the goal posts', 'raising the bar' and now the dreaded 'doubling down'.

Perhaps the real problem is that we think too shallowly about management in seeing it as a kind of one-dimensional handmaiden to the arts. How often have we heard 'my role is to create the circumstances in which artists can thrive' or words to that effect. Orson Welles perhaps got it right in *The Third Man* (Greene, 1949). As Harry Lime noted:

> Like the fella says, in Italy for 30 years under the Borgias they had warfare, terror, murder, and bloodshed, but they produced Michelangelo, Leonardo da Vinci, and the Renaissance. In Switzerland they had brotherly love – they had 500 years of democracy and peace, and what did that produce? The cuckoo clock.

More accurately of arts managers it might be said: 'I have built a cage in which artists will do as they're told'. Or is it: 'like the Delphic Oracle I will sit on my tripod inhaling the incense of business plans and budget arcanery and interpret for the adoring crowds the gibberish of the gods'. And I will charge a fee for it. So, is it then a priesthood? Or an enclosed order? The Sisters of Perpetual Compliance perhaps?

We might do well to take heed at C.S. Lewis' remarks which remind us of the unintended consequences of our nanny states:

> Of all tyrannies a tyranny sincerely exercised for the good of its victims may be the most oppressive. It may be better to live under robber barons than under omnipotent moral busybodies. The robber baron's cruelty may sometimes sleep, his cupidity may at

some point be satiated, but those who torment us for our own good will torment us without end, for they do so with the approval of their own conscience.

(Lewis, 1970)

Maybe our shallowness consists in having reduced what was once a creative profession in which manager and producer were in effect one into two-dimensional guardianship, where we act as lofty stewards, accompanying hapless artists through a trail of local administrivia. On one side there is the obsession with finance and on the other the household gods of what is laughingly known as Human Resources, as though humanity formed any part of their dread practice. We say nothing of so-called governance knowing how few arts managers can put their hand on their hearts and swear that that is or ever has been an enjoyable experience, still less a productive one.

Interestingly, the competing political system of the time did not subject the arts to such assumptions or such language. Previous states, étatist France for example and those nations – notably in Latin America – which took their tone from France saw the arts as in service of the state (Isherwood, 1973). All these perforce would need to be managed differently to achieve the higher state outcomes; ministers such as Jacques Lang and presidents such as François Mitterrand got that as assuredly President Emmanuel Macron does today, and the irony was that artists did conspicuously better financially there and achieved higher status than in the more allegedly demotic models of the Anglosphere. The French author/convicted smuggler of cultural goods and Cultural Minister, André Malraux, who in part drew up the French post-war Arts Ministry model observed 'The artist is not the transcriber of the world, he is its rival' (Malraux, 1976) by which he reminds us of the French State's view of higher service.

In today's world there are other factors which intervene. Our shifting and increasingly unreliable notions of democracy (narrowed by a kind of NATO–speak to be co-extensive with elected parliamentary government), audience, advocacy and benefit and now the politics of correctness and identity have come to exercise a qualifying role. So where in all of this might we make a case for the role of the arts as an ethical as opposed to moral force? And how then shall we seek to manage (in both senses of the word) our obligation to hold that honoured mirror up to our times and manners? And perhaps more to the point, how many of us will dare?

For it is not only politics that censors and self-censors cultural discourse. The subtle and at times not so subtle pressures and persuasions of donors, sponsors and the newly anointed media of fake news all play their part in the mixed business of our new Babylon. Raulston Saul (1999) has thoughtfully considered these dilemmas both as they apply globally in our time and as they have designed the modern manager in both the public and private domains.

We must note too that because politics and public administration, in particular over the last half century, have moved inexorably into a domain that is almost exclusively economic, public discourse has little other frame of reference. Our thinking about the arts and thus the terms in which we express them are dominated almost exclusively by that crude second-hand and ill-adapted terminology.

There may have been a time, though most would have only a receding memory of it, when the arts in our society spoke on their own terms and their practitioners were proud to proclaim that what they did and what they produced had value in their own right and needed no economic or industrial justification (Carey, 2005). But now the arts, and in particular their managers, recast and regurgitate the language framed by so called 'funding agencies' like so many gulls feeding their ravenous chicks – though they are at least nourishing to their young. By contrast, ours has become a sterile exchange in which 'excellence', and 'innovation' and horror of horrors 'vibrancy' are mindlessly chanted as though something of worth was being sung (Pick, 1984).

Because of the almost entirely artificial barrier that has been erected between the allegedly subsidised and commercial, we have created not a vocation or a profession but a ghetto, or perhaps several ghettos. There is one which is success-averse and has turned to increasingly miniature forms (no wonder it's called the small to medium sector. What a terrible ambition to make oneself ever more invisible!). And on the other we have one that is averse to artistic exploration. But is that distinction real? Cushioned by the comfort of ongoing government subvention the supposed non-profit risk is often lower than in the for-profit jungle.

Making meaning

So, we write all this to ask: what does arts management mean in both these circumstances? Is it mainly a commodity to be borrowed, bought, grown, displayed, admired, sold? Are those of us who practice these dark arts merely the distributors of product and, necessary and significant as that may be, is it more than any skilled shopkeeper or restaurateur might accomplish in their chosen fields? Can all of this or any of this be housed safely under the umbrella of arts 'management'? Does it help or hinder that we struggle to draw this spectrum of activity together into a body of teachable or learnable skills and terminology? Is it helpful or destructive that the state attempts to intervene in this marketplace and evaluate it through the lens of those pedestrian criteria?

Robert Protherough and John Pick (2003) suggest that just as the business schools have increasingly shaped and distorted business itself and because they have propagated a cult of following only the money – qualifications in exchange for cash – so they have produced generations of graduates for whom greed is the only criterion of advancement. That very nineteenth-century notion of 'progress' has dictated the direction of travel. Similarly, those business schools, and to some extent even our arts schools that uncritically walked into the language of creative industries, ostensibly to please the piper, without inquiring about the distinction between creation of art and distribution systems, that for all their courses in supposed 'critical thinking' have created a cohort of managers who do not think, do not question, but who believe that leadership consists largely in heroic transformation.

So, the education of the arts manager more often than not is conducted these days within the confines of those same business schools, produces graduates unconcerned with doubt that the top-heavy, compliance-ridden, jargon-saturated organisations weighed down with the logos of their dubious partnerships in the not-for-profit cultural domain may be on other than the right track. The fact that for the most part they do not contain even the smallest component of aesthetics or any history of the subject prior to the invention of Keynesian Arts Funding says it all (Keynes, 1946). That they do not attempt to hold an argument about the nature of the subject impoverishes us all.

At its core there is an aesthetic contract formed between the artist and audience. This contract is a complex arrangement of bringing the best art to the best possible audience and the arts manager must create the circumstances to fulfil this. It does not rely on quantity but on criticality – on transmission of meaning and interaction between the artist and the audience. The manager is a conduit to this process (Pick, 2009). These days, however, we are more likely to hear from arts managers who have not engaged in critical distinction, to whom the arts may be lumped together in an inaesthetic amalgam. They will tell you they are 'passionate' about their genre (more likely they will say artform) but be singularly incapable of providing a succinct critique of what they do within it that reaches beyond the platitudinous. As the singer Peggy Lee (Leiber and Stoller, 1969) asked: Is that all there is? If so, go and run a golf club. It is less stressful and probably better paid.

But then there is the hidden curriculum of these schools which varies from country to country even within the liberal democracies but whose essential if unspoken creed is that the subsidised world is *ipso facto* good and desirable and is the only real model for the creation of art, and the for-profit world is if not bad then undesirable and essentially uncreative. Schools in the US might (publicly at least) claim otherwise and are quick to avail themselves of donations from a Broadway star among their alumni, but not far below the surface that essentially covert belief is the same.

Equally, however, does throwing one's hands in the air and declaring it all somehow unhelpful but unfixable take us anywhere? In a way it is reminiscent of the journalistic *bien pensant* obsession with the 'sensible centre' in politics as though any change of worth had ever been driven from the middle. Is then all we can hope for a type of arts management that represents a dreary centrist compromise between conflicting aims? And when we observe the slough into which both management and governance have fallen virtually worldwide one cannot help but think that like Cardinal Wolsey we are already 'at the mercy of a rude stream that must for ever hide' us (Shakespeare, 1623).

We know that many of the solutions we propose are not peculiar to the arts. Other areas of human endeavour that society cherishes like education and health demand fresh response to their management. We need urgently to grow a class of managers who are not the indentured servants of the state at one remove but rather the *agents provocateurs* of their cause, pushing back against the sterile bureaucracies that seek to cramp our artistic style and indeed for fifty years have succeeded in doing so. We need to procure change-makers who will act not just as barriers against intrusion by those who try to anatomise and assess and measure and subdivide art and artistic practice but take the fight to them and compel governments, private trusts, public institutions and ultimately the public itself not to pursue their way but to adopt ours.

A very large part of that will be to find ways to teach emerging managers, producers, enablers, call them what you will, how to shape the conversation to their own ends not merely to be shaped by what our self-styled masters chose. Thereby, they need to be able to manoeuvre elegantly, respectfully but decisively around the obstacles of excessive compliance and regulation and eventually demonstrate their lack of worth in the artistic world.

Maladjustment

One of the uglier signs of the great economic trade-off in the arts has been the phenomenon of title creep. In a procession of *follies de grandeur* cultural operatives believe themselves to have gone up in the world because those who were once simply managers or administrators became by inexorable degrees general managers, executive directors, managing directors and now CEOs or COOs. By the same token, in a two-person administration the erstwhile accountant is now the CFO. Chief of what? One asks. Clearly of insufficient workers. The sometime publicity officer is now Director of Marketing. All too often no more tickets are sold, but the job sounds more impressive. We need to abandon this rubbish and return to reality and recognise this frippery for what it is — a bribe to make the arts feel significant by those who believe they are not but can be bought off by grandiosity. And since everyone who receives any kind of public award or recognition is now 'humbled' by the experience, perhaps the time has come for some genuine humility.

These changes might imply a method of education in which we learn how to lead by delegating so that everyone in this new management has a real and dedicated investment in the process and in the result. That might also extend to considering that management is not just a closed circle but must include all who care about the cause in question. This tendency has also infected the international conferences and regulating bodies best known by their acronyms where IFAACA (the International Congress of Arts Councils and Cultural Agencies) holds its embracing large aspiration of 'World Summits', and the regulation and accreditation of the subject is run by associations such as AAAE (Association of Arts Administration Educators in the United States), ENCATC (European Network on Cultural Management and Policy) or the more recently formed ANCER (Asia Pacific Network for Cultural Education and Research) and dominated by a management discourse in bi-annual conferences such as AIMAC (International Conference on Arts and Cultural Management) and ICCPR (International Conference on Cultural Policy Research). To be in the centre of these is to maintain the dominant discourse but to interrogate them is tantamount to heresy. The question remains: after the advent of all these bodies, have 'the arts' been advanced or rather does this accretion of bureaucratic platforms indicate the inflated creep of administration over artistic outcome?

Whatever the case, the question remains, what happened to the parties we understood to be central to artistic creation, distribution and reception, simply put: the artists, producers and audiences? We have come to call those who join or support an enterprise by that other grotesque term 'stakeholders'. So be it. Let us then give those stakeholders in the arts some emotional satisfaction and psychic ownership in what they invest in and what they derive from their association with not just the art but the process of making and sustaining the art. That would suggest as well the use of new and emerging technologies to effect change in the way we work together and make decisions and create solutions rather than pandering to the narcissism of ill-named 'social' media. As we move more and more into digital collaboration, most of which remains remote and increasingly alienating, it will be vital for those who guide and guard the arts to be the leaders rather than the slavish followers of trends; to be at the forefront of finding new and better pathways to make that experience personal and emotive rather than isolating and divisive. Let us offer the prospects of technological solutions which can bring things together in new and previously unheard-of ways but also offer the prospect of human solutions which can match these and even outpace them.

So how in practice might this immense change occur? We consider the only realistic means is to pursue collaborative development through bringing different minds and contrasting sensibilities together to build ideas, work on projects and create solutions. Especially in education we would argue exploring methods away from the artificial and increasingly tepid environment of the ill-served, under-theorised classroom, especially at undergraduate university level where individuals with no experience are instructed didactically. Or at least to incorporate a strong aesthetic and historical understanding of the complexities of the subject into the instruction with an emphasis on the interrogative. The question: why manage the arts? should be at the heart of the inquiry (Bereson, 2005). In this context we would advocate for the symposium as a core place for debate and engagement. This would mean putting small groups together with differing backgrounds (whether their careers aim at the artistic or the administrative) mentored by individuals with first-hand knowledge and a good theoretical grasp of the subject who can present them with a project or a problem in an intensive bubble. That would allow them to structure their form and relationship and their solutions in their own way. This will vary with each group and the inputs of those in it. Maybe we need to look back to the Socratic dialogue and see what it teaches us not only about ideas and how to share them but about the courtesy of intellectual relations – a rare commodity in modern management.

The so-called creative or now more commonly termed 'cultural' industries have become over-attached to the notion of entrepreneurship, and the term and its associates tend to be employed loosely for all sorts of supposedly stimulating ventures. In the process they have confused our understanding of the arts. Cultural industries refer to modes of innovation, production and distribution whereas the arts above all are concerned with creation. It is perfectly possible in any event to have a successful creative industry with no artistic merit. Consider the manufacture and successful distribution of a book, but if no one has read what is between the covers, then no artistic exchange has taken place however many bucks there are in the bank. In 1964 Umberto Eco presciently described this term:

> Take the fetish concept of 'culture industry'. What could be more reprehensible than coupling the idea of culture – which implies a private and subtle contact of souls – with that of industry – which evokes assembly lines, serial reproduction, public distribution and the concrete buying and selling of objects made into merchandise.
>
> *(Eco, 1995)*

Let us in our mode of education not impose hierarchy or frameworks on those who seek to join us. Successful business needs rapid but considered decision making; it needs to be lean and agile; but it does not require high jumping to demonstrate that. Successful business also cannot endure too many tiers of decision making or eventually it will slow down and eat itself. It needs to be able to seize new opportunity and run with it but not so fast that it cannot learn from history. We need processes that inculcate the notion that successful enterprise needs to be always questioning itself. Asking why? and how? It is easy to become the victim of its own assumptions without testing them. Thus, its practitioners have to be able to challenge each other. How do you know? What's the evidence? How can we collect the evidence and keep it before us? How do we use the evidence?

This ongoing spirit of inquiry and self-interrogation is of course hard to do in bureaucracies where people spend a lot of time covering their backsides and where challenge and open criticism are not generally encouraged. Hence our government agencies are glued to the past and paradoxically defend a seventy-year-old Council model of oversight (which in its original form was not designed to be inclusive of all arts) (Keynes, 1946; Leiber and Stoller, 1969) when everything else in public and private administration has moved on. We have to find a way in which something can start small and grow and learn by failing how to meet challenges and overcome barriers and execute effectively.

This chapter has been written in the spirit of engagement with an important topic, often relegated to rule following and management speak. The invitation to set out some of the incongruities concerning that amalgam of 'Culture, Arts and Management' in a compendium devoted to management and the arts was an irresistible offer to engage with some of the larger problems facing the subject in its theory, practice and pedagogy. We are here making a call to turn the subject from the narrow defiles into which it has been channelled and let it flow and nourish a broader landscape and give a more ample meaning to the nature and value of the arts which we cherish.

References

Anderson, H.C. (1837). *The emperor's new clothes*. Denmark: Pook Press.

Arnold, M. (1865). *Essays in Criticism*. London: Dent. pp. 18.

Barnum, P.T. (1855). *The life of P.T. Barnum*. Redfield, IA.

Bereson, R. (2005). *Why manage the arts?* Kenmore, NY: Merrill Press.

Carey, J. (2005). *What good are the arts?* New York: Oxford University Press.

Eco, U. (1995). *Apocalypse postponed*. London: Flamingo, p. 31.

Greene, G. (1949). *The third man*. [screen play] London: British Lion Film Corporation.

Isherwood, R.M. (1973). *Music in the service of the King: France in the seventeenth century*. Ithaca, IA: Cornell University Press.

Keynes, J.M. (1946). The arts council: Its policy and hopes. Text of BBC broadcast. Reprinted from *The Listener*, 12 July 1945.

Kluckhohn, C. and Kelly, W.H. (1945). The concept of culture. In: R. Linton, ed., *The science of man in the world crisis*. New York: Columbia University Press, pp. 78–105.

Leiber, J. and Stoller, M. (1969). *Is that all there is?* [Record] Los Angeles: Capitol Records. [Performed by Peggy Lee].

Lewis, C.S. (1970). *God in the docs*. London: William B. Eerdmans Publishing Company.

Malraux, A. (1976). *La métamorphose des dieux, tome 3: L'Intemporel*. Paris: Gallimard. [*The Metamorphosis of the Gods, Volume 3: L'Intemporel*].

Nalbach, D. (1972). *The king's theatre, 1704–1867: London's first Italian opera house*. London: The Society for Theatre Research.

Octavio, P. (1961). *The labyrinth of solitude*. New York: Grove Press.

Pick, J. (1984). *The modern newspeak*. London: George G. Harrap & Co Ltd.

———. (2009). *The aesthetic contract*. Kenmore, NY: Merrill Press.

Protherough, R. and Pick, J. (2003). *Managing Britannia: Culture and management in modern Britain*. London: Imprint Academic.

Saul, J.R. (1999). *The unconscious civilization*. New York: Simon and Schuster.

Shakespeare, W. (1623). *Henry VIII*. London.

Throsby, D. (2018). *Platform papers 55: Art, politics, money: Revisiting Australia's cultural policy*. Sydney: Currency House.

Tusa, J. (2014). *Pain in the arts*. London: I.B. Tauris.

United Kingdom, House of Commons. (1947). *HC Deb* (11 November) vol. 444, col. 207. Available at: https://api.parliament.uk/historic-hansard/commons/1947/nov/11/parliament-bill

Williams, R. (1976). *Keywords a vocabulary of culture and society*. London: Croom Helm.

———. (1989). *What I came to say*. London: Hutchinson Radius.

2

ARTS MANAGEMENT

Reflections on role, purpose, and the complications of existence

Constance DeVereaux

"What is the role of the arts manager?" is a good question guaranteed to elicit conversation at any gathering in the field – some of it fruitful in coming to terms with the existential complications of a job role/function/purpose forever wedged into the in-between (between art and public, art and artist, artist and public, government and art . . . the list goes on). I call it a good question because it suggests the need for reflection apart from the exigencies of daily arts management life. Reduced subsidies, diminishing audiences, and the commodification of art experience take their toll on the time needed for contemplating what it all means – that is, what does it mean to be an arts manager? Without the opportunity to reflect, arts management risks reduction to rote performance of tasks as ends unto themselves and as activities distant from the value of the arts, undeserving of commendation or consideration in the process of ensuring that art remains present as a human and societal good.

This chapter is premised on the conviction that there is an important and beneficial role that arts managers play in the world of the arts and beyond. What that means is that there is an identifiable part to be played by the arts manager in a society where the arts are present, whether or not they receive full acknowledgement of their value by policymakers and the public. What that role is, however, is not entirely clear. I do not conjecture about any inverse relation between the perception of arts' value and the necessity of arts managers' role in society. A more important point is that like other societally determined roles – teacher, doctor, artist – arts managers are more than the sum of the tasks they perform, and the responsibilities assigned to them. Unlike these more familiar roles, however, it is far less clear what the role of arts manager is and what value it does, or should, deliver. To illustrate, here is a simple experiment in the form of a pop quiz.

Fill in the blank:

The role of a teacher is to educate.
The role of a doctor is to heal.
The role of an arts manager is to _____.

A response such as *to manage the arts* or *to manage an arts organization* does not seem quite right. Too much appears to be left unsaid in a way that the responses to the other examples do not. But why? The relative newness of the field may be one reason. Another may be that we lack the sustained conversation, research, or scholarship that can help us (or a lay public) with the answer. While we understand the value of education and of health, there is less standard agreement about the values of managing the arts, even among artists who might be taken as prime beneficiaries.

Although the functions of arts managers – that is the kinds of tasks they perform in organizations – has been explored in the literature, in particular through the lens of training – little has been written about their role in organizations or in larger society. Dubois and Lepaux (2019) note that "if there is little sociological research on arts management" there is even less to be found that focuses "on arts managers apart from the seminal studies by Paul DiMaggio and Richard Peterson looking at the United States thirty years ago" (39). The same is true for other fields of study that might investigate the role of arts manager as a phenomenon, such as political science, management studies, and even the field of arts management.

The aim of my chapter is to examine the question of this role from a few perspectives that are intended to cast a waxing light on its nature, along with some potential answers. My method is exegetical, lyrical, and polemical in combination. What I hope to outline is a direction and some methods that a future exploration of the role of arts manager might take.

First, I stipulate that although *role* speaks to *function*, they are not the same thing. Roles, according to Pacheco and Carmo (2003), cannot be reduced to their deontic characterization. That is, they are more than a "mere set of obligations, permissions or other normative concepts" (152). Function, in contrast, relates to tasks, permissions, acting and interacting, and similar types of activities. A listing of the functions of arts manager, for example, does not explain why it is important to perform these functions except for the most immediate of gains – writing a grant, for example, to fund a project; or designing an advertising campaign to attract an audience. Recalling the case of a teacher: in order to educate, the person demonstrates to students how to perform the functions of math, science, music, or other subject, explains ideas, and models a correct action, for example, "here is the correct way to position your legs to perform a plié." But these teaching actions are not coterminous with what it means to be a teacher. The role or part the teacher plays in a school and in society goes beyond these things. Some suggestions are that a teacher's role is to inspire and to encourage – proposals that are not alien to most readers because of a shared conception of what teachers do that is not premised on any individual teacher, but on accepted conventions for how *teacher* is understood. In other words, role is an abstract notion that is defined, in good measure, by agreed-upon conventions.

Biddle (1979) emphasizes context as an important part of defining role. To compare again to my common examples, although the role of a teacher is to educate, and the role of a doctor is to heal, these functions can also occur outside of the "teacher" and "doctor" contexts. For example, a parent may do both. The point, once again, is that to discover the role played, we have to go beyond the mere tasks performed by teacher, doctor, parent, and arts manager. In this chapter I further explore the distinctions between role and function in the context of arts manager, provide historical context, examine how the role of arts manager might emerge, and conclude with thoughts on some directions the conversation on roles might take for future benefit.

What lies beyond

Arts management has been described as a fragmented field. By this it is often meant that its roots and borrowings from other fields are multiple and varied; there is no well-identified or agreed-upon canon that documents its development. In the context of practice, William J. Byrnes' *Management and the Arts* and Art Extension Services' *Fundamentals of Arts Management* have earned the status of canonical guides to the functions of arts management and as providers of strategies for carrying them out. Full disclosure: Byrnes' books had an important influence on my own development as an arts management practitioner at the helm of a regional arts council in the Western United States many years ago. The latest edition of the book includes much more theory than earlier versions; a welcome addition for reinforcing that any task, no matter how applied, is backed with theory. These books, and many others designed to provide readers a grounding in arts management practice, proceed from the assumption that arts management is more like management than it is to other fields. Definitions of management, and often of arts and culture, preface advice on how to integrate the operations of the first into the demands of the second. Early books in the field were part of establishing this trend. *The Arts Management Handbook* (Reiss, 1962) leads with economics and sociology but is strongly informed by a management perspective. *Arts Administration and Management* (Shore, 1987) begins with an overview of management and its concepts, then proceeds to show how these principles may be applied to the case of managing arts organizations. Many years later, Rosewell's *Arts Management: Uniting Artists and Audiences* (2013) continues the trend including several chapters on the historical development of management from the late 18th to early 21st centuries (with an additional reference to ancient Egypt and Sumeria). Her book's title comes close to identifying a role for arts managers – that of bringing artists and audiences together. But no special attention is paid to the role of arts manager beyond the functions they perform.

In contrast, John Pick and Malcolm Anderton, who co-authored *Arts Administration* (1996), make much deeper inroads into exploring the nature of arts management (or administration, in their terms) with a statement, echoed in my own, that the role "cannot be adequately described simply by offering the conventional description – 'arts administrators are people who administer the arts'" (1). They explain that "those who administer the arts are quite different from those who administer more conventional activities" (Ibid). Referring to the management aspects of arts administration, the authors state that these are the "commonest parts" (2) of the work that arts administrators do. While it is unclear if they mean to say that these are the most typical or the more prosaic aspects of the job, their point is to show that arts administrators serve some higher purpose, which contrasts sharply with the more mundane activities of preparing a budget or plotting the details of a project plan. To this end, Pick and Anderton explain that the practices of the field "are based on values extrinsic to their system" (Ibid) so that when viewed from the perspective of management or economics "good arts administration" will appear "confused, too much concerned with imprecise questions of human values" (Ibid). In other words, an outside observer familiar with the operations of mainstream management will not recognize arts administration practices as being of the same kind or order as their own.

A discussion of role theory by Masolo et al. (2004) emphasizes patterns of relationships dependent on external properties as an ontological characteristic of *role*. In comparison, Pick and Anderton suggest a multiplicity of relationships and external properties that serve to construct the role of arts manager. More than just "office routines" the arts manager must understand and be involved in the arts, arts criticism, politics, psychology, and several other areas of knowledge. Arts managers are a unique mixture, according to the authors, of teacher, conventional manager, entrepreneur, and other roles. Aside from the enormous demands this would put on any individual arts manager, the point is to suggest that a role emerges out of the connections among these various entities and the relationships, of all of them, to the arts. To this mix of connections is added the idea that arts managers or administrators are an intermediary bringing artists and public together, but are also the bridge between art and publics, and very often, too, between artists and art. During my days as an arts manager, I was often interviewed by the media, called upon to explain my own and other arts managers' role relative to the arts. My stock answer was, "Arts managers make the arts happen." Filling in the gaps, I would explain that artists sometimes lacked the means (economic, political, or social) to create, display, or disseminate their work and needed the assistance of someone like an arts manager. Arts managers have a role to play in making sure that artists have both opportunity and means to create and display their work. At the same time, arts managers help ensure that the public has an opportunity to experience the arts. Despite a tradition, originating in the Romantic era, of artists as lone genius, "artistic work is not autonomous: the role of artists arises from the collective undertaking of artistic work" (Segers, Schramme, and DeVriendt, 2010). Within this collective is a role for the arts manager.

Even so, a question remains whether the work of the arts manager is categorically different, in some way, from non-arts managers. That is because exploring a societal convention, such as the role of arts manager, is a pursuit into the conceptual. Arts managers exist. They perform functions. But, does that take us any closer to understanding their role? A follow-up question is, in a world (like ours) where the arts exist, do arts managers play a part that is important, necessary, identifiable, or valuable in any way? In other words, while the perspectives developed previously move toward a clarification of the arts manager's role it is yet an incomplete idea.

Context is another important element. Davis and Barrett (2002) see roles as extrinsic features of an entity (such as an arts manager) that are linked to modalities of participation. "A musician is still a musician while sleeping" (Masolo et al., 2004, p. 268). While the example here seems to suggest that it is the function (playing music) that counts, in fact not all people who strum a guitar are counted as musicians. In another context I have quoted Aristotle's views on human excellence using the example of a lyre player. The philosopher's view is that the person who plays the instrument badly "is not properly called a lyre player" (DeVereaux, 2009, p. 159). The difference between knowing how to perform a function (whether it is done well or imperfectly) and being the thing that the function describes is significant. Elsewhere, I have pointed to the context differences between the couple dancing to the music of a club DJ and the same individuals performing a choreographed ballet on stage (DeVereaux, 2011). In this sense, roles are understood to be dynamic properties. In other words, entities can change their roles – I am a ballet dancer for my job but when I go dancing with my mates I am just a person dancing in a club. The difference is not in the actions performed *per se* but in the

> Organizational discourses, along with discursive practices such as training, appraisal and information systems [that] shape the identity . . . by recognizing specific actions and behaviors. You have to make choices about what to do and which identity to take at any particular moment in time.
>
> *(Ibid, 41)*

It is, therefore, my particular participation in the context of the ballet world including rehearsing, performing, training, employment as a dancer with a ballet company, and attendant discursive practices that define my role as a ballet dancer. The same should be true of arts managers in the arts management world. But, what is the arts management world and how does it emerge?

There is some suggestion that arts management in the United States emerged with the creation of the National Endowment for the Arts. Consider, then, the declarations and purposes espoused in the United States' National Foundation on the Arts and Humanities Act which recognizes that

> While *no* government *can call a great artist* or scholar *into existence*, it is necessary and appropriate for the Federal Government *to* help create and sustain *not* only a climate encouraging freedom of thought, imagination, and inquiry but also the material conditions facilitating the release of this creative talent.
>
> *(20 United States Code 951, 1965)*

18

Although the statement concerns the role of government, its relevance to arts management emerges in the notion that artists may lack the material conditions for producing artistic work, and someone like an arts manager may be useful in providing assistance. In other words, *arts manager* begins to exist as an identifiable entity under conditions where artists risk disadvantage for being artists under conditions where the appropriate material conditions do not exist.

I persist nonetheless in wondering if making the arts happen in this way constitutes a role, or is it just a wider conception of function? One might state, for example, that the business manager in a shoe factory makes shoes happen. Or, to broaden the scope, that she makes it possible for people to walk without undue harm to their feet. She connects shoe designers (a kind of artist, in fact) to people who need and wear shoes. In contrast, it is clear that Pick and Anderton see a unique role for arts managers that is beyond the simple function of connecting people to a product or service – one, in fact, that concerns human values. In this, they allude to the special role of the arts, which has also been said to concern human values. The same connection is not typically (if ever) made about shoes.

The connection to human values noted in Pick and Anderton is also echoed in many mainstream ideas about the arts. The authors raise "the awkward truth that artists shape the way we live and the value we put on human experience, much more than do economists or management theorists" (3). One could reasonably argue, however, that Pick and Anderton are quite wrong. Human history, of late, has demonstrated just the opposite. Science, industry, marketing, and managerialism are far more evident in determining many aspects of human life. Putting their views into context however, Pick and Anderton proceed from a perspective with distinctly Romantic roots – the idealized notion connecting art and nature, nature and mankind, and the primacy of both individual and human value. The Romantic movement arose in reaction to the Industrial Revolution, in contraposition to the increased dominance of science, industry, and mechanization characteristic of the industrial era. The same factors were responsible for the advent of managerialism as the brief account in the next section shows. The history of both these movements have influenced the contemporary idea of arts manager.

Historical perspective on management

Although some observers may claim that the "history of management is as old as human history" (Buble, 2015, p. 2), its contemporary form is said to have its start as a 19th-century offshoot of the field of economics (Keulen and Kroeze, 2014). In other words, the organizing of activities to get things done is something that humans have probably always engaged in (organizing a hunting party for example, or a search for nuts and berries to add to the winter store). It is quite imprecise, however, to suggest that organizational or business management originated in early human history. What we mean by "management" is a child of the late 19th century, and the concepts "business" and "management" were first connected at that time. Business (that is, the operation of a commercial enterprise) before the Industrial Revolution was typically a small-scale affair, for example, the small apothecary shop or trade store. The cognate in the arts and culture sector is the small community theater, dance troupe, or gallery. "Beyond a few kinds of organization – the church, the military, a smattering of large trading, construction, and agricultural endeavors (many unfortunately based on slave labor) – little existed that we would recognize as managerial practice" (Gunther McGrath, 2014). The growth of larger scale organizations after that time seemed to require a different manner of getting things done; hence new practices demanding standardization, specialization of labor, workflow planning, and optimization of outputs (Ibid). Given that business organizations were the primary target in these developments, *business management* as a coalescing term came to dominate our thinking about the concept of management. In time, managerial strategies were more widely applied to the extent that managerialism "is an increasingly prevalent modern-day phenomenon. Its influence is said to have extended far beyond the organizational setting into economic, social, cultural and political spheres and to have become so pervasive" that it now affects all aspects of human life (Shepherd, 2017, p. 1). The "management boom" that came about after World War II "changed society permanently" (Cunliffe, 2009, p. 17) largely because management had become a familiar term and had been legitimized through social practice (Ibid).

Management as a concept and set of strategies has evolved since the Industrial Revolution. Since then, increased use of technology and ensuing new economies have changed some of our thinking. A difficulty, however,

> stems from the fact that management is an applied science [resulting in a] lack of coherent theoretical concepts. Management theorists have adopted and applied the concepts from other disciplines. Thus, the theory of management evolved in symbiosis with its supporting disciplines such as mathematics, statistics and behavioral science, depriving itself of the motivation to find its own conceptual framework independent of the respective disciplines.
>
> *(Buble, 2015, p. 3)*

The commentary may sound familiar to arts management scholars who wonder about finding a unique conceptual framework for their field as well. For our purposes, the point is that business enterprises needed managerial strategies beginning in the era of large-scale corporations in order to promote production efficiency and effectiveness. Quoting the scholar Stanley A. Deetz, management expert Ann L. Cunliffe states that managerialism was the product of the management boom. It describes "a kind of systematic logic, a set of routine practices and an ideology ... a way of doing and being in organizations which has the ultimate goal of enhancing efficiency through control" (Cunliffe, 17). Although Cunliffe sees a connection between theory and practice, theory does not help, necessarily, in discovering the role of manager, and thus, for our purposes may not be helpful in the context of arts manager either. If not from theory, do the same exigencies, ideologies, and need for control apply to the arts as they do to business enterprises, whether in the case of large-scale enterprises (the Vienna Philharmonic in Austria or the Rijksmuseum in the Netherlands) or the small theater company in Manchester, or dance troupe in Cincinnati? The question is valid if one is hesitant about the continued efficacy of management as necessary, or advised, for organizational success, and if one sees the role of arts manager as adhering to principles (human values, for example) outside of the norm for non-arts business managers.

Contrasting pairs

The preceding brief historical overview is intended to highlight some of the identifying characteristics of the arts and of management that emerge in their socially constructed contexts and to examine the connecting threads between management and the arts that may contribute to the formation of *arts manager*. Contemporary arts managers, I argue, are inheritors of two traditions that in many ways are diametrically opposed – on the one hand, the notion of the arts as Romantic enterprise and, on the other, managerialism as inherited from the Industrial Revolution. What is it that reconciles them to produce the entity called arts managers and that is different from manager proper, if indeed it is?

In the case that Pick and Anderton are correct and arts administrators, as an entity, are somehow unique, what their claim lacks is concrete proof. Recent work from sociologists Vincent

Dubois and Victor Lepaux, however, may provide the needed evidence gleaned from their research on characteristics and motivations of applicants to university-level arts management programs in France. The authors are careful to note the limitations of their study – respondents are uniquely French university students applying to degree programs in France. The authors' comparisons to the United States and United Kingdom permit some extension beyond the case of France. Significantly, for the discussion of the role of arts manager (or cultural manager, in their terms), the authors state that choice of career "cannot only be explained on grounds of individual motivation. What is usually called a career choice, hinges on social conditions" (2019, p. 40). Were it only an individual choice, we could not rely on societal context or relationship patterns to discover the role we seek.

Notable among Dubois and Lepaux's findings is the suggestion that applicants to arts management programs differ from those who apply to other kinds of university degree programs, which could lead to the expectation that these differences will persist at the end of their education and into their careers. While Dubois and Lepaux do not make this latter claim, there is yet merit in examining the differences they identify. According to the authors, students applying to cultural management degree programs in France are primarily women from affluent backgrounds who have "accumulated high levels of educational capital" (47) before submitting an application to the degree program. They have a "personal taste for culture and intense cultural practices" (48) and desire to work exclusively in the cultural sector. Socialization and upbringing have a great deal to do, therefore, with the choice of cultural management as a career. This is significant because it is consistent with the principles of role theory as described here. Further, it suggests that much like the concept of management, arts management is constituted in the expectations and performative behaviors of the people who engage in it, as well as in the legitimacy given to the performative behaviors from outside the system of management or arts management.

Another contrast is worthy of mention however, which problematizes the concept of arts manager. That is the contrast between arts manager and artist. Anecdotally (including in my own career), I have observed that artists may look upon arts managers through the lens of an unspoken play on words: they aren't artists (one might say), they are something akin to an "art official," which if pronounced quickly sounds more like *artificial*. The slur was immortalized in a slightly different context by American artist Robbie Conal in a poster featuring the late Republican Senator, Jesse Helms, a prominent leader in the conservative movement in the United States, and responsible for an agenda during the Culture Wars period that opposed government funding of the arts. Jesse Helms was the Art Official/Artificial in question. The slur has been used, as well, to suggest that arts managers are inauthentic participants in the process of art production, display, and dissemination. In this view, their role is not assistive, but rather apart from and, in some cases, contrary to the aims of artists. It is a perspective, therefore, that questions the need for arts managers and thus denies them a special or useful role.

Interviews conducted by Ivonne Kuesters with arts managers, are an attempt "toward a more accurate perception of arts managers" (2010, p. 43). She finds it

> remarkable that the characterization of the role of the arts manager is not made with reference to its functions or its position or in distinction to similar roles; rather, it is made entirely in contrast to the role artist . . . arts manager is seen as opposed to the artist, and that their functions are unconnected and complementary. The difference between the artist and the arts manager is emphasized so strongly that any influence of the arts manager on the art itself seems impossible.
>
> *(Ibid)*

While recognizing the complementarity of arts managers' role to artists, Kuester also states that the common conceptualization of arts manager duplicates "conceptualizations of art and economy/finance as strictly separated spheres" (44). Such conceptions may be in contrast to the notion of arts manager as an intermediary or bridge, a view that is reinforced by Segers, Schramme, and Devriendt (2010) in their study on the professionalization of arts management in the context of Flemish arts policy. Citing previous research, they note that following substantial investments in marketing and organizational management in the European cultural sector in the 1980s and 1990s,

> efforts on the level of marketing and changes in organizational structure have not been effective in achieving the cultural objectives of increasing audience attendance and creating cost efficiencies. On the contrary, the professionalization of arts management has had the paradoxical effect of increasing overhead costs.
>
> *(58)*

More plainly stated, the overhead costs of running organizations and managing performances goes largely to salaries of arts managers. Segers et al. state that "Although there was a substantial increase in subsidies [in the period studied], this has not been to the benefit of the individual artists working in performing arts organizations . . . The money seems to have been spent rather on growing overhead costs" and "the strong focus on overhead structures, organizational management, and even corporatization within subsidized arts organizations, threatens to clash with the ideal of the autonomous artist" (Ibid). The relevance of these studies is that they seem to define a negative role for arts managers in opposition to the aims or benefits to artists. More damningly, the study suggests that rather than serving the aims of art, public, or artists, increased subsidies may do little more than create paid positions for people who call themselves arts managers.

As Cunliffe states, ways of talking and framing management bring about "ways of acting and forms of managerial identity into being" (10). If so, this can occur in the negative sense – a role for arts managers that delegitimizes their role – as well as in the positive sense of arts manager playing an integral, and welcome part, in making the arts happen.

What emerges is that patterns that join arts managers and artists in an environment of economic exchange may have limited value in fostering greater understanding of the role of arts managers. In discussing motivations for creativity among artists, for example, Klamer and Petrova state that in the case of "economic assumptions that individuals primarily respond to monetary incentives (a rational choice), mounting empirical evidence shows that a rational-choice model may have limited value if we want to understand artists' creativity" (2007, p. 245). Instead,

> It is crucial for the artists to work in the social environments in which they belong, where they can learn and share knowledge, ideas, and inspirations with others, and where they have common ground. Researchers are thus challenged to detect the peculiarities of social environments that foster creativity. One perspective is to examine how the art world sustains itself based on peculiarities of the arts domain and fields.
>
> *(250)*

Such claims reinforce that social environments are the birthplace of the roles an individual plays in her career. A social environment where rational choice dominates may create a very different arts manager than one in which other principals and conditions prevail. Concerning the artist, Klamer and Petrova state that processes "by which creativity turns from a trait to achievement embodies interactions between the creative personality and the creative environment that evoke the creative act and later the creative product" (253). Might the same be true of arts managers? In other words, role may reside in the unfolding of processes and in the interactions between arts manager/artist, arts manager/art, arts manager/public, and the like.

A word on globalization

Although several of the studies cited here focus on arts management and managers in the national context, they suggest possibilities for a more universal concept. My first attempt to address this issue was from the perspective of globalization and what its realities might mean for arts management practice. I co-organized a symposium that gathered together a small group of scholars, educators, and practitioners for facilitated discussion about the role of the cultural manager as global citizen. A description of the published proceedings reads:

> The selection of this theme by the symposium organizers was to respond to debates about the effects on the field of cultural management as the result of globalization/ transnationalism, enlargement of the EU, perceptions about the US relating to cultural hegemony, perceptions and realities relating to cultural identity and cultural citizen-ship, as well as the effect of these factors on the role of cultural managers in the 21st century.
>
> *(DeVereaux and Vartiainen, 2008)*

At the time, the idea of cultural managers needing to be aware of global issues was still new and sometimes disputed. The symposium produced a set of recorded and transcribed discussions that represented views of the collected individuals on the question: Is there a special role for cultural managers within the dimension of global citizenship? Referencing the work of Colin Mercer, we wrote,

> if culture and cultural policy . . . are about human development then cultural man-agement must have something to do with it as well. One way to understand cultural management is that it has to do with managing cultural activities in a way that allows for – maybe even contributes to – human development.
>
> *(11)*

Pick and Anderton would clearly agree. While the focus of the symposium was on the cultural manager as global citizen, placement in the global context might reveal arts managers' role more concretely and universally. For example,

> the global citizen, in very general terms, is conceived of as someone who is engaged, globally, in a way that is embracing of the diversity of cultures the world has to offer, and is in some sense, someone who supports the value of diversity, and even contrib-utes to its flourishing or development in the cultural sphere.
>
> *(DeVereaux 9–10)*

This description of global citizen aligns well with the concept of arts manager today – a person who performs her functions in a multicultural context. In the words of one symposium participant,

> You can't put a moat around your culture, even if you thought that was a good idea. So, I thought that the cultural manager had to mediate between so-called cultural

imperialism, or globalization, which is sometimes called Americanization, and the local national cultural that defines one's personal identity.

(DeVereaux and Vartiainen, 33)

Of note is that in the global context, the notion of arts managers as intermediary is expanded to require negotiation more so than bridging or connecting, in this case against such forces as imperialism and globalization. The concept of identity is also raised. As one participant states, "it is important for the cultural manager as a social manager to be concerned with one's identity; what we are" (33). Cultural hegemony is a pervasive threat to local cultural identity as indicated by a participant who comments that cultural managers have a great deal of power, which should be used "very carefully" (56).

Affluence was also addressed as a factor. Characteristics such as being well-traveled, educated, and speaking several languages tend to attach to those who have the financial means to bring them about. The difficulties of attaining the status of global citizen in the role of cultural manager may depend on financial ability. Finally, the symposium raised the ethical attributes of cultural management. To engage in the issue, one participant provocatively observed that when

> we speak of the cultural manager, we talk in that way that the manager will be a kind of positive person. . . . Does it necessarily have to be that way? . . . Is it necessary for the person to be aware of ethics? Can a bad person be a good cultural manager?
>
> *(75)*

"Perhaps" another participant responded, "but not a good global citizen," adding, "the idea with the concept of global citizenship is just that. It's a concept. It's almost like arts management; value driven, mission driven. It's not a tangible thing. It's an idea" (Ibid).

The role not taken

What emerges in my account is a sense, I hope, of some agreement about what an arts manager (arts administrator, cultural manager or administrator) is and the part, in an arts management world, that such a person plays. Pick and Anderton claim that *arts administrator* is an unfortunate term because it emphasizes administrative functions over other higher purposes that emerge from relationships with the arts, culture, and with artists. Elsewhere, I have written that transition of cultural management from the practices of isolated individuals carrying forward the work of their organizations – often in ad hoc ways – to an organized profession with recognized centers of training has not resulted in development of a common set of theories and practices (DeVereaux, 8). The dual traditions of post-industrial revolution and romantic idealism may have served as foundational myths for ways of thinking about the role of arts manager. On the subject of management, again, Keulen and Kroeze (2014) reflect that foundation myths "even if historically inaccurate, can still serve the conceptual function of grounding the culturally transmitted chain of institutions and conventions in history." In other words, the precise origins of arts manager may be less important than how we think it occurred, and where that places us now. To that end, I have lately come to think that more than theory and practice, arts management is a matter of legitimization in their own world, and the world outside of their domain of practice, one in which their contributions are recognized and valued. Legitimization is still being earned, however. My recommendation for trainers of arts managers and for emerging arts managers themselves is to look beyond the given traditions of management and the arts. While each has influenced arts managers' role, the rapid changes in the arts world, in management, and in the world outside of both pose possibilities to proactively embrace. Rather than ask what an arts manager is, I prefer the question: what can an arts manager be?

References

Biddle, B.J. (1979). *Role theory. Expectations, identities, and behaviors.* New York: Academic Press.

Buble, M. (2015). Tendencies in evolution of 21st century management. *Management: Contemporary Management Issues,* 20(special issue), pp. 1–17.

Byrnes, W.J. (2014). *Management and the arts.* 5th ed. Waltham, Massachusetts: Focal Press.

Cunliffe, A.L. (2009). *A very short, fairly interesting and reasonably cheap book about management.* Los Angeles: Sage.

Davis, A. and Barrett, L. (2002). Relations among roles. *Proceedings of OntoLex,* 2. Las Palmas, pp. 9–16.

DeVereaux, C. (2008). Cultural citizenship and the global citizen. Artists and Marketing – The beginning of a rewarding friendship: C. DeVereaux and Pekka Vartiainen, eds., *The cultural manager as global citizen.* Cultural Management and the State of the Field Series. Helsinki: HUMAK University Press, pp. 9–24.

———. (2009). In a Ross: Artists and Marketing – The beginning of a rewarding friendship, S. Bekmeyer-Feuerhahn et al., eds., *Forschung im kulturmanagement.* Berlin: Lehre e.V. Verlag, Bielefeld, pp. 155–167.

———. (2011). Is art a fruit or a vegetable? On developing a practice-based definition of art. *Studia UBB, Philosophia,* 56(3), pp. 7–25.

DeVereaux, C. and Vartiainen, P. (2008). *The cultural manager as global citizen.* Cultural Management and the State of the Field Series. Helsinki: HUMAK University Press.

Dubois, V. and Lepaux, V. (2019). Towards a sociology of arts managers. Profiles, expectations and career choices. In: C. DeVereaux, ed., *Arts management: Sense and sensibilities in the state of the field.* London: Routledge.

Keulen, S. and Kroeze, R. (2014). Introduction: The era of management: A historical perspective on twentieth-century management. *Management & Organizational History,* 9(4), pp. 321–335.

Klamer, A. and Petrova, L. (2007). Financing the arts: The consequences of interaction among artists, financial support, and creativity motivation. *The Journal of Arts Management, Law, and Society,* 37(3), pp. 245–256.

Kuesters, I. (2010). Arts managers as Liaisons between finance and art: A qualitative study inspired by the theory of functional differentiation. *The Journal of Arts Management, Law, and Society,* 40(1), pp. 43–57.

Masolo, C., Vieu, L., Bottazzi, E., Catenacci, C., Ferrario, R., Gangemi, A., and Guarino, N. (2004). Social Roles and Their Descriptions. Laboratory for Applied Ontology, ISTC-CNR, Trento & Roma, Italy & IRIT-CNRS, Toulouse, France.

McGrath, R.G. (2014). Management's three eras: A brief history. *Harvard Business Review.* Available at https://hbr.org/2014/07/managements-three-eras-a-brief-history

National Foundation on the Arts and Humanities Act. (1965). 20 United States Code 951.

Pacheco, O. and Carmo, J. (2003). A role based model for the normative specification of organized collective agency and agents interaction. *Journal of Autonomous Agents and Multi-Agent Systems,* 6(2), pp. 145–184.

Pick, J. and Anderton, M. (1996). *Arts administration.* London: Routledge.

Reiss, A. (1962). *The arts management handbook.* New York: Law-Arts Publishers.

Rosewell, E. (2013). *Arts management: Uniting artists and audiences.* Oxford: Oxford University Press.

Segers, K,. Schramme, A., and Devriendt, R. (2010). Do artists benefit from arts policy? The position of performing artists in Flanders (2001–2008). *The Journal of Arts Management, Law, and Society,* 40(1), pp. 58–75.

Shepherd, S. (2017). Managerialism: An ideal type. *Studies in Higher Education,* 43(9), pp. 1668–1678.

Shore, H. (1987). *Arts administration and management: A guide for arts administrators and their staffs.* New York: Quorum Books.

3

THE DESIRE OF THE ARTIST AND THE DHARMA OF THE ARTIST MANAGER

Anmol Vellani

I heard someone from the music business saying they are no longer looking for talent, they want people with a certain look and a willingness to cooperate . . . I thought, that's interesting, because I believe a total unwillingness to cooperate is what is necessary to be an artist – not for perverse reasons, but to protect your vision. The considerations of a corporation, especially now, have nothing to do with art or music. That's why I spend my time now painting.

—*Joni Mitchell in Hilburn (2004)*

Introduction

There are artists who prefer to be self-directing and produce work free of external influences and concerns. There are also artists who consider audience tastes and preferences as paramount in shaping the art they produce. This chapter will paint a portrait of these two types of artists, opposite in temperament and inclination, and discuss what is practically and ethically at stake for artist managers who work with one or the other.

It is not my claim that all artists can be placed in either one of these two categories. There are art makers who are an amalgam of the two types of artists I will describe, displaying features and propensities of both. And there are artists who, though they create work that follows the voice that speaks to them from within, are alert to the need to reassess their work in response to voices they hear from the outside. The reaction of audiences and critics may induce them to take a fresh look at their work. Visual artists may heed the advice of curators, and playwrights the counsel of dramaturges or directors. The two kinds of artists I will describe, moreover, need not remain forever riveted to their ways of producing art: artists can turn, for instance, from being self-absorbed initially to becoming more audience-sensitive later in their careers. Fixing the spotlight single-mindedly on the previously mentioned pair of starkly contrasting artists, however, better fulfils the purpose of this chapter, because it throws into sharper relief what might be missing in the received understanding of artist managers.

The literature on artist managers is often written, understandably, for the benefit of artists and describes the preferred traits, qualifications, skills and capacities of artist managers, the scope of their work and the set of functions they can be expected to perform (Simpson and Munro, 2012). Here artist managers are viewed from the standpoint of the artist: what can or should she demand from artist managers to advance her career and protect her interests? But even when artist managers are addressed directly, they are described in broadly the same way (Allen, 2007). What we are told, I believe, is an incomplete story about artist managers. This chapter strives to fill the gaps in that narrative by looking at the manager–artist relationship more thoroughly from the artist manager's perspective.

The artist manager and the desire of the artist

Imagine a manufacturing company that specializes in dental hygiene products such as toothpaste, toothbrushes, dental floss and mouthwash. Since profit for the promoters and shareholders is the only bottom line for a business enterprise, managers in this company and the people who design or make its products are not expected to take decisions based on any emotional, sentimental or other personal investment they might have in whatever the company manufactures. Their singular and overriding concern must be to ensure that the products attract enough buyers to turn a profit over time. If, for example, sales figures for its tongue scraper are declining, and there is little hope of arresting the trend, the company's response will and must be either to modify the product or withdraw it from the market altogether. Any attempt to 'save' the product – because, say, the promoter is attached to it, or because it is an important part of the company's legacy – would make little business sense. Similarly, a shopkeeper will stop selling Coca-Cola if it sits on the shelf for too long. Should he keep it in stock because he likes to drink it himself, instead of clearing space for faster-moving products, he would be acting in a manner contrary to his interests as a retailer. For a manufacturer, a service provider, a wholesaler or a retailer, the driving incentive, I repeat, is profit, and it trumps all other considerations.

For the artist manager, the producer is the artist (or the arts group or collective) and the product is the art she creates. Whereas a corporate manager focuses entirely on making profits for his company by helping to meet, create or anticipate the needs and preferences of actual or potential clients and customers, an artist manager must respect the *desire* of the artist, certainly if he is working with the kind of modern or contemporary artist who is primarily 'absorbed in relating expression to self rather than to the market' (Vellani, 2014, p. 32). The self of such an artist might be expressed in the ideological commitments of her art, or its aesthetic sensibility, or in how it is impelled by her inner disquiet or responds to her experience of her social and political milieu. The artist manager, aware of this profoundly intimate relationship between the artist and her art, cannot ask her to modify or jettison what she creates in order to satisfy market tastes and preferences. Instead he must rise to the challenge of finding acceptability for what the artist desires to create in the public imagination (Colbert, 2003, p. 31). This is exactly what Farooq Chaudhry, who manages the Akram Khan Company, has committed himself to doing. In his eyes, Akram Khan's dream must come first, and his job is to 'take risks and look for opportunities to translate this dream into an actual project' (Chaudhry, 2019, Chapter 8, this volume). 'Throughout my career,' he further writes, 'I have always let art have the first say in any action I have taken . . .' (Ibid). And it is hard to imagine that Chaudhry would be driven to let Akram Khan's dream have the 'the first say' and take on the immense challenges and risks associated with trying to monetise that dream, unless he felt strongly drawn to his art, the meaning it held for him.

The kind of artist I have described does not, however, create art for its own sake. She hopes that her art will find an audience. If she is a novelist, she will want readers; if she is a performing artist, she will want spectators; and if she is a filmmaker, it is very unlikely that she makes films for the exclusive purpose of screening them in her home theatre. Indeed, it is quite natural for her to intend her art to have such an outcome. In its absence, her practice could, with justification, be called self-indulgent. If she is a novelist, she is not driven to write her books principally *because* she wants to be read (or become famous or rich), but neither does she write fiction entirely for her own pleasure. This thought has been captured pithily by the poet Vijay Seshadri, who has been quoted to say, 'I don't write for the market. I don't even write for me. I write for the poem' (Ramdev, 2018, p. 2). Hirschman (2013, p. 253) has observed that

> any sustained activity, with the possible exception of pure play, is undertaken with some idea about an intended outcome. A person who claims to be working exclusively for the sake of the rewards yielded by the exertion itself is usually suspect of hypocrisy: one feels he is really after the money, the advancement or – at the least – the glory, and thus is an instrumentalist after all.

Hirschman would characterise a self-expressing artist as someone who is not driven by narrowly instrumental reasoning but is nevertheless someone who endeavours 'with some idea about an intended outcome.' The realisation of the intended outcome of her activities, however, is far less predictable than the result of a whole range of routine activities (such as using boot polish to shine shoes):

> (T)here are many kinds of activities, from that of a research scientist to that of a composer or an advocate of some public policy, whose intended outcome cannot be relied upon to materialize with certainty. . . . From their earliest origins, men and women appear to have allocated time to undertakings whose success is simply unpredictable: the pursuit of truth, beauty, justice, liberty, community, friendship, love, salvation, and so on. . . . (A)n important component of the activities thus undertaken is best described not as labor or work, but as *striving* – a term that precisely intimates the lack of a reliable relation between effort and result. A means-end or cost-benefit calculus is impossible under the circumstances.
>
> (Hirschman, 2013, p. 254)

In fact, the self-driven artist strives with two outcomes in mind, neither of which can be realised with certainty. The first is to attain what she strives to create, although there is no assurance that she will not, in her own eyes, fall short of realising what she envisions or aspires to create. Some artists, forever dissatisfied with their art, may even believe more strongly that between the striving and the attainment falls an unbridgeable chasm, that the intended outcome is not just uncertain but beyond reach, an *impossibility*. Samuel Beckett, the playwright of despair, may have regarded this condition as essential to being an artist, as suggested by his haunting lines, 'Ever tried. Ever failed. No matter. Try Again. Fail again. Fail better' (Beckett, 1989, p. 101). But even if those lines were intended to be no more than self-referential, it would nevertheless be true that he believed that this condition was essential to being Samuel Beckett.

The second intended outcome of the artist's striving is to attract an audience for her work. Whether she will succeed in doing so is unpredictable, unless there exists, fortuitously, a ready audience for her work. The artist manager would have a distinctive reason for existence when there is a gap between what the artist desires to create and what the market is prepared to consume, provided the artist feels or discovers that she herself is ill-equipped or disinclined to close that gap (henceforth referred to as the 'g-a-p'). His special responsibility would be to overcome that g-a-p, or at least reduce the uncertainty associated with the second intended outcome of the artist's striving, while accepting that what the artist desires to create is non-negotiable.

The artist manager, if he joins forces with the kind of artist I have described, faces the challenge of reconciling the artist's striving with its second intended outcome. If the artist's work causes discomfort or offence, or produces cognitive dissonance, or demands that people re-examine their deep-seated prejudices, or calls for a radical shift in hitherto uncontested ways of seeing, there might be a greater incongruity between her practice and its intended outcome.[1] The artist manager must help to create the material conditions that enable the artist to live by her choices; at the same time, he must create and expand the audience for what her desire produces. His success in narrowing or closing the g-a-p could potentially support her practice because the net income generated in the marketplace can create the means to enable her to focus solely on her creative aspirations. He might try to conquer this problem by finding investors, donors or corporate sponsors to underwrite her artistic process and production, but this might be as challenging as finding an audience for her work, and for the same reason: her art might be seen as too edgy, too disturbing, too provocative, too avant-garde. Donors might not want to risk their reputation by associating with her art; investors might not want to risk their money on work whose 'market-friendliness' is untested; and corporate sponsors, being inherently risk-averse, will be forthcoming only after the artist has acquired a standing and an audience (Chaudhry, 2019, Chapter 8 in this volume).

My argument will be that the artist manager stands out from the rest of the crowd of managers when he partners with self-expressing artists for whom their own dreams and visions brook no compromise. For it is then that he confronts forces that pull in different directions, such as those I have described here. When he volunteers to face the pressure to manage and overcome these contrary forces, he can be said, as I shall argue, to have a mission and an ethic that is exceptional and dissimilar from managers in other fields.

I will say a lot more about the relationship between the artist manager and the self-driven artist in the ensuing sections. But even the brief account I have provided thus far might be thought to be inapplicable to modern and contemporary art that does not bloom entirely from the creative urge of an individual. For example, theatre and dance work is often configured through processes of give-and-take and collaboration. The self of the creative individual cannot possibly have license to rein freely in these contexts of artistic production if collaboration is to have any meaning. Here the artist manager, it might be urged, does not confront the autonomous desire of an individual artist and the particular challenges associated with it. My response to this demurral would be that the kind of desire that the artist manager encounters might be no different in the case of a performing arts company which adopts a collaborative mode for developing productions, except that the desire would now pertain to the *company* and not to this or that individual in the company. In other words, the company too may desire, like the individual artist I have described, to pursue an independent practice and create work free of the influence of external non-artistic considerations.

I can anticipate another objection to what I have said earlier – that I am wedded to a romantic idea of the artist. I am not perturbed by that complaint as long as no one makes the silly claim that such artists are an extinct species. Furthermore, it is not my view that they are the only breed of artists in the world. The next section will be concerned with drawing a contrast between two types of artists – the self-driven artist and the entertainer – and I will propose that it is only in relation to the former that an artist manager shoulders a distinctive mantle of responsibility.

Artists and entertainers

The domain of the entertainment industries is vast, spanning popular film and music, television sitcoms and reality shows, musical and comedic theatre, gaming and much else besides. In what follows, I will talk only about one category of artists in the entertainment industry – namely magicians, ventriloquists, stage hypnotists, stand-up comics, circus clowns and the like – who perform for the amusement of others and are called entertainers.

There are many tendencies and traits that distinguish an entertainer from a self-directed artist. The entertainer's primary preoccupation is with gratifying revealed or anticipated public tastes and preferences. If an act fails to grab the audience, she will modify or drop it from her repertoire. For the self-directed artist, this is inconceivable because she measures her worth as an artist from within, not on the basis of its public acceptability. She does not regard the public as the final authority on the value of her art; rather she decides for herself whether her work lives up to or falls short of what she had set out to do as an artist and what she imagines to be the purpose of her art. The self-driven artist and the entertainer think of failure differently. The former does not aspire to fail in the eyes of the public, but her primary anxiety is related to the *uncertainty* of the result of her striving (will I create work that is true to what I want to express?). For the latter, how the public receives her art is the key measure of its value and, therefore, of failure and success. Her chief anxiety is related to the *desirability* of the result of her striving (will the public accept my work?).

I may be faulted for advancing a view that unduly polarises these two categories of artists. Entertainers do not invariably behave as if they were slaves to audience tastes and expectations. Stand-up comics, for instance, might have moral qualms about telling racially charged jokes or stories that demean women, despite being told that such material is lapped up by audiences. My view, however, is that audience acceptability is the *paramount*, though not always the *overruling* consideration, for entertainers. Another objection could be that artists driven by the need for self-expression are not disinclined to participate in events and activities to promote their art (book launches, media interviews, sneak-peeks, etc.). This is true, of course, and for an obvious reason: they desire, as I have indicated, to have their work read, seen or heard, but reaching audiences is the *secondary*, not the *primary* aspiration for such artists.

Instrumental reasoning decides which acts the entertainer will present to her audience. She reasons, in other words, in this way: if audiences are thirsty, I will give them water, unless they prefer beer. The only limit to the dictates of instrumental reasoning (which relies on facts) might be urged, as I have suggested, by her moral conscience (which would be informed by her values). If, however, she is a neoliberal market fundamentalist, who recognises only economic value and rejoices in the victory of means-ends reasoning, she will anaesthetise her conscience, assuming she has one, to enlarge her market appeal and maximise the inflows from her performances. For then, attracting the greatest possible number of spectators to her performances would matter above all else, including the means by which she gets to her goal. Neoliberal thinking, far from being able to take a stand against pornography, for example, demands that pornography be encouraged if it has the potential to capture a larger market (Vellani, 2015, p. 18).

In contrast, instrumental thinking does not exert sovereignty over the artist for whom 'the audience is not the starting point but the end point' of the work she creates. The entertainer's fundamental interest is in generating economic value, specifically financial rewards for herself, by creating work that is relished by the audience. It is, therefore, perfectly possible and of little consequence that she might in fact have a low opinion of the work she performs. Such distancing from her art is impossible for the self-expressing artist. For her, there is no profit, as the Bible instructs, in gaining the whole world and losing her soul, because she is principally spurred to create art that she sees as being of value and meaning for *herself* as much as for others. That value may reside, in her view, in the aesthetics of her work, or its perspective on the human predicament, or its attempt to give voice to the voiceless or provoke people to reappraise the world in which they live, and so on.

What is uncertain is whether the value that she is striving to create will delight, move, inspire or transform her intended audiences or be received with indifference or incomprehension. If the g-a-p exists, will *they* find or discover value in her work? And if that g-a-p is to be narrowed or closed, the prevailing public taste for art must either *enlarge* or *change*. In other words, success in overcoming the g-a-p would be achieved if public taste either begins to accommodate or is supplanted by a preference for the kind of work that the artist in question creates.

One source among the many that can lead to changes in public preferences is particularly interesting, and to explain its nature, I will begin by narrating a true story. A school friend of mine was a fan of Elvis Presley and I would quarrel with him about his taste in music. Some years later, after he had discovered Bob Dylan, he said to me, 'You were right. I can't think what on earth I saw in Elvis Presley.' He was obviously not telling me that his taste in music had enlarged, that now he liked both Elvis Presley and Bob Dylan. And while he was indicating that his taste in music had changed, he was telling me not only that he had lost interest in Elvis Presley, but that he now disliked his music. What he said next, however, is especially notable: 'If I hadn't been so obsessed with Elvis, I might have discovered Dylan earlier.' This claim is not so much about the aversion he had developed to Elvis Presley as it is about regretting that he had been fond of his music in the first place. It is not about his dislike for Elvis; it is about disliking his liking for Elvis.

My friend's last remark introduces us to the idea of second-order desires, first proposed by the philosopher Harry G. Frankfurt (1971, p. 7):

> Besides wanting and choosing and being moved to *do* this or that, men may also want to have (or not to have) certain desires and motives. They are capable of wanting to be different, in their preferences and purposes, from what they are. . . . No animal other than man . . . appears to have the capacity for reflective self-evaluation that is manifested in the formation of second-order desires.

Hirschman's elegant articulation of Frankfurt's position is worth recounting:

> 'men and women have the ability to step back from their "revealed" wants, volition, and preferences, to ask themselves whether they really want these wants and prefer these preferences and, consequently, to form metapreferences that may differ from their preferences.
>
> *(Hirschman, 2013, p. 250)*

My friend's second-order desire took the form of deploring his earlier liking for Elvis Presley and was, therefore, an act of 'reflective self-evaluation'. The formation of a second-order desire does not necessarily indicate a change in taste (because I could dislike my fondness for aerated beverages and yet find myself unable to resist the temptation to drink them) but it certainly signifies a change in values.

> A taste is almost defined as a preference about which you do not argue. . . . A taste about which you argue, with others or *yourself*, ceases ipso facto being a taste – it turns into a *value*. When a change in preferences has been preceded by the formation of a metapreference, much argument has obviously gone on within the divided self; it typically represents a change in values rather than a change in tastes.
>
> *(Hirschman, 2013, p. 251)*

To explore the further implications of second-order desires, consider an example from outside the arts – the dumping of lighters manufactured in China into the markets of South and Southeast Asia. Imagine an Indian who buys these lighters because they are cheaper than lighters made in his country. One day, however, he begins to have misgivings about his preference for Chinese-made lighters because he has come to believe, one, that it is important to encourage local industries and, two, that Chinese dumping constitutes an unfair trade practice. Having developed this meta-preference, he lets go of his first-order desire for 'Made in China' lighters and commits himself to buying only lighters made in India. The sacrifice he would make because of this commitment might be insignificant in the case of lighters, but the hole it would burn in his pocket would certainly get bigger, and cause him more distress, if the cost-differential between dumped Chinese products and their Indian equivalents becomes larger.[2] Should, moreover, most of his compatriots take a similarly principled stand, it will no longer profit the Chinese to dump lighters and other products on the Indian market.

Likewise, products of the entertainment industry will have to be withdrawn from the market if they, like the dumped Chinese products in our fabricated story, come up against widely shared second-order desires. Consider the following scenario: a stand-up comic has captured a devoted audience, which is especially attracted to her routine of homophobic jokes and stories. At some point, though, appreciable numbers of her loyal following develop a distaste for their taste in the politically incorrect content of her performances. Not only do they stop attending her shows, they begin staging protests outside the venues where she performs. Television channels, ever mindful of public opinion, are no longer willing to offer her a platform. Confronted with sharply declining audiences and revenues, her manager advises her to excise those portions of her performance which have begun to cause widespread offence. She may choose to spurn his advice because she genuinely believes that homosexuality is unnatural and wrong. But if she takes this decision, despite facing the imminent threat of being kicked out of the market altogether, she would be behaving in a manner expected of a self-absorbed artist, not an entertainer. The alternative would be to heed his advice, a decision which might sadden her in view of her moral stance but would be consistent with the fundamental dharma of the entertainer. In the given circumstances, this is the right choice for an entertainer to make: it profits her to lose her soul to gain the world, which simplifies the job of her manager.

The self-driven artist might also be homophobic or misandrous, her views writ large in her art. What if in time she confronts a conscientious objection to her art from audiences that previously loved her work? Her manager might say that her (primary) desire to produce art with content that a growing public is finding objectionable has begun to undermine his efforts to fulfil her (secondary) desire to acquire an audience for her work. His task is complicated by the structure of her motivation: unlike the entertainer, she sees no profit in losing her soul to gain the world.

The influence of second-order desires on the public taste for an artist's work need not be negative, causing an extensive turning away from her art, as my examples seem to suggest. The influence may also be positive, attracting growing audiences for her art. This is because second-order desires can take two forms that have the potential to modify behaviour: one, people can dislike their liking for X; two, people can dislike their dislike for, or failure to like, X.[3] Consider an example that elucidates what can happen if you develop a meta-preference which takes the form of disliking what you dislike. Your girlfriend loves Picasso. You, on the other hand, dislike him. You can tell, however, that it upsets your girlfriend that you do not share her passion for the artist. As a result, you develop a distaste for your aversion to Picasso, a second-order preference which pushes you to strive hard to overcome your antipathy to his work. You read books and attend talks on his life, his work and his influence on twentieth-century art. In time you begin to appreciate Picasso and you are finally able to relate to what your girlfriend sees in him. The outcome of your efforts is not only a newly acquired preference in art but an altered way of viewing and assessing art. Since your preference change has been preceded by the formation of a meta-preference, this implies, as Hirschman suggests, that your values with respect to art have changed.

It should be noted, however, that a reversal in your preference for, say, Hindi film music over Indian classical music may indicate, but does not require, the prior formation of a meta-preference. There could be many reasons why you might have turned from disliking to liking Indian classical music. For example, the reason why *my* resistance to this genre of music broke down, in fact, was this: I was subjected to unavoidable and prolonged exposure to classical music during my growing years, since my mother learnt and practised it at home.

What, however, has changing disliking into liking have to do with the artist manager? Very little for a manager who 'takes care of business' for an entertainer. His job is to advise the entertainer to *avoid* being disliked and focus solely on serving up what the public is known or can be expected to like and keep working on her material to widen its appeal and attract new audiences. For an artist manager associated with a self-driven artist, though, the presence of the g-a-p might require active engagement with what the public dislikes. Indeed if the g-a-p is severe, and the artist's work is widely misunderstood or detested, the need to convert disliking into liking might be a matter of life-and-death, obliging him to create multiple opportunities (both face-to-face and on various online and offline media platforms) for educational, value-shaping interfaces *between* the artist and the public or engagements *about* the artist *for* the public. He must consistently strive to push against ingrained perceptions and preferences in order to generate greater interest in what the artist has to offer. This is an indispensable endeavour if resistance to the artist's work is to be broken down, though the gains from it may take a long time coming if they come at all. Peter Bendixen (2000, p. 8) believes that

> one of the managers core functions is that of establishing a secure and effective position for his client within the relevant environment. He must firmly plant reputation and distinction in the minds of customers, audiences and consumers, as well as in the media . . . and among the experts, critics and whomever else may be of importance. Seen from this perspective, a manager creates public reputation and distinction as a kind of cultural capital.

My point is that serving this function becomes far more vital and urgent for a manager who has to counter pervasive disregard for or hostility to the work of a self-driven artist.

Although I have spilled much ink on distinguishing between the self-regarding artist and the audience-led entertainer, ground realities, as I said at the start, do not support the idea that all artists can be parked in either one or the other of these two categories.[4] For instance, a playwright who sees her writing for the stage as motivated from within may also work for the entertainment industries – writing skits for commercial radio stations, scripts for television serials, and screenplays for profit-oriented films. Without any feeling of discomfort or conflict, she may be able to compartmentalise her artistic life, creating work that she regards as self-expressive on the one hand, and churning out stuff primarily with an audience in mind on the other. For her, writing plays is a very personal undertaking, unlike the rest of her artistic output, which she accepts will be guided by market considerations.

Just as an artist with a 'divided' identity compartmentalises her working life, an artist manager who teams up with her can be expected to compartmentalise his efforts on her behalf, setting one set of goals for the self-directed side of her artistic personality and another set of objectives for the audience-directed side of her creative identity. This is a natural conclusion to draw if there is any truth in my submission that an artist manager's challenges and concerns are different when he assists an entertainer as against a self-expressive artist. But a manager who works exclusively in this compartmentalised fashion for an artist who traverses both entertainment and self-expression may serve her interests only up to a point. He might fail to pick up on opportunities that exist for leveraging one aspect of her artistic practice for the benefit of the other. If she is a reputed playwright who has undersold her skills in the entertainment industry, her manager could and should flaunt her achievements in one area to win her greater access to the other. Or he might have to work in the opposite direction because her playwriting has attracted less recognition than the work she has done for commercial radio, television and cinema.

One obvious point that these examples drive home is that a management professional would be ill-advised to enter the arts field with a fixed or preconceived understanding of the artist manager's functions and responsibilities, since the *kind* of artist or arts group with whom he joins hands will be a key determinant of the challenges he will face, the aims he will need to pursue, and the tasks he will need to perform. One can also safely conclude that managers who take care of the needs and interests of pure entertainers discharge more or less the same responsibilities as corporate managers in fields outside the arts, because both rely solely on cost-benefit computation to achieve the same ultimate goal – to maximise the buy-in and profit margin for whatever they put out on the market.

The artist manager's mission and ethic

Are an entertainer's manager (M1) and a self-directed artist's manager (M2) any different in how they might respectively relate to the arts in general and to the art of the creative person that they take responsibility for espousing and monetising?

M1 is not required to have any interest in the arts at all. He will need at best some familiarity with the world of the arts, enough to be effective in utilising his skills to advance the entertainer's career. And if he does have an interest in the arts, and personal responses to the entertainer's artwork – be it joy, indifference, disapproval or repugnance – he must have the objectivity to put these feelings aside and let instrumental reasoning decide which parts of the entertainer's repertoire will find less or more purchase with the audience. Profit is the only bottom line for him, as it is for the corporate manager described earlier, and if he allows his personal views about the entertainer's work to interfere with his decision-making, he would be failing in his responsibility to further the interests of the entertainer. Indeed, both the entertainer and her manager must share the same relationship of *distance* to her art, recognising that their respective feelings or opinions about it count for nothing if their profit-directed goals are to be advanced. Of course, as I have indicated earlier, there may be instances where scruples about certain parts of the entertainer's repertoire overrule profit-maximising considerations.

By contrast, except when no g-a-p exists, it is scarcely credible that M2 could have no interest in the arts, and no penchant for the art produced by the self-driven artist he manages. The higher the mountain he is ready to climb to gain audience traction for the artist, the more difficult it is to doubt that he derives his motivation and job satisfaction from something that goes beyond achieving success in closing the g-a-p. If he has taken a path of greater resistance in his choice of assignment – one that, moreover, carries an enormous risk of failure – it is natural to suspect that this is because the assignment holds a larger meaning for him personally, a feeling, perhaps, of connection or empathy with the artist's striving and the kind of work she dreams of producing. When M2 volunteers to support a self-driven artist, it must be because he cherishes the art she strives to bring *into* the world, and he signs, in effect, an unwritten contract to uphold her art and bring it *to* the world. The self-driven artist and her manager, therefore, must share the same relationship of *closeness* to her art. One or the other might have reservations about this or that piece of work that she produces, but both would be equally and firmly convinced about the larger significance and purpose of her art. Indeed, if M2 does not share the artist's belief in her work, one might wonder if he would be capable of the necessary resolve and perseverance to beat the odds that may be stacked against him and effectively protect and advance the interests of the artist.

It is helpful to translate this dissimilarity between M1 and M2 into the language of values: M1 need not believe that the entertainer he manages is producing something of (non-financial) value, let alone value with which he identifies, whereas M2 must believe that the work of the artist he manages is producing (non-economic) value to which he relates. This unlikeness matches the divergence in how they see their fundamental role: M1's is to generate profit as an end in itself, while M2's is to secure capital and assets (whether through angel investors, grant makers, individual donors, sponsorship or/and the market) as a means to promoting and sustaining the creation of value. Filipe M. Santos (2012, pp. 337–340) would say that M1 is capturing (or appropriating) value and M2 is creating value, and this contrast between M1 and M2 parallels the seminal distinction that J. Gregory Dees (2001) has made between business entrepreneurs and social entrepreneurs:

> Social entrepreneurs . . . are entrepreneurs with a social mission. . . . Mission-related impact becomes the central criterion, not wealth creation. Wealth is just a means to an end for social entrepreneurs. With business entrepreneurs, wealth creation is a way of measuring value creation. This is because business entrepreneurs are subject to market discipline, which determines in large part whether they are creating value. If they do not shift resources to more economically productive uses, they tend to be driven out of business.

M2 is like a social entrepreneur (SE) in being mission-driven, except that his mission is to create and sustain *artistic* rather than *social* value. This formulation, however, does not capture the full scope of M2's mission, as it fails to take into account his role in *enhancing* value creation. His mission, in other words, should be understood as extending to creating opportunities for the artist to *enrich* her practice and creativity, should she express a desire to gain broader exposure to the artistic environment or genre in which she works; or feel the need to collaborate with other artists; or simply want to share knowledge, ideas and processes with her counterparts and draw inspiration from them.

For M2, moreover, the commitment to sustaining value creation implies taking actions of a kind that also do not form part of SE's mission. What is the nature of this special commitment? The answer lies in understanding that M2 and SE create value in contrasting ways. SE leverages the market as a means for supporting the creation of social value. The first undertaking is not directly related to the second. This lack of interdependence between SE's two endeavours means that the fate of the former can have no more than an instrumental effect on the latter, either enabling, restraining or defeating the mission to create social value. M2, however, must create value by directly linking art to the market because artistic value is created only when art is validated by public acceptance and appreciation.[5] For this reason, failure or success can have a non-instrumental effect on value creation in the arts. Whereas a coalition of forces (such as NGOs, municipalities and advocacy groups) more usually creates social value, an artist alone gives birth to art and, in consequence, to artistic value. It is thus only natural, especially as the self is folded into her practice, that she should be deeply and personally affected by how her work is received – whether it attracts public and critical acclaim, whether it is widely dis-seminated and consumed, and whether it brings in financial rewards or other honours. An artist's practice, therefore, can be derailed by the cause-effect relationship between the creation and reception of art. The response to her art can be self-affirming or produce self-doubt. If her work is received badly, she may begin to question the value of her art and even decide to abandon her practice. But even when the artist's work is received well, it can have a negative impact on her practice.

Consider how differently M1, M2 and SE might view success. Success for M1, as for enter-tainers, is measured solely in terms of revenue generation and is never seen as a problem: the more of it the better. For SE as well, success in the market is always welcome because it gener-ates the financial resources for mission-directed activities. For M2, however, market success for the artist, which is often accompanied by fame and adulation, can pose problems and he must be alert to its potentially corrupting influence. The trappings of success once made Indian theatre directors cautious, formulaic and repetitive, unwilling to take risks for fear of losing hold of the audiences they had established and the state support they had attracted (Vellani, 2008, pp. 138–39). To abide by the instruction to 'meet with Triumph and Disaster/And treat those two impostors just the same' (Kipling, 2000, pp. 134–135) is daunting for anyone, and an artist is no different in being affected equally by success and failure, often reacting to both in the same way – by losing her edge, leaving the dream behind. And when the artist's will to live by her desire weakens, M2 is called upon to be the jealous protector of her dream – urging her to resist erosion of purpose; reigniting the flickering flame of self-belief; and rousing her to recommit to her artistic vision. He must exhort her to 'rage, rage against the dying of the light' (Thomas, 2000, p. 148), become the fire that once burnt brightly in her, the torch she once held to illu-minate her path.

To sustain value creation, therefore, M2 must not only secure the material conditions that enable the artist to pursue her practice but also safeguard and fortify her original desire to create work on her own terms, should triumph or disaster threaten to weaken it. Could it be said, in protest, that the latter should not be seen as a commitment that forms an essential part of M2's mission, but as a practical step he is required to take to remove an obstruction on the road to his mission? This objection, however, does not withstand scrutiny. There is a fundamental differ-ence between surmounting a hurdle to a quest and preventing the foundation of a quest from crumbling. A social entrepreneur generates capital to change the world for the better in one way or another. Whether his mission is to reduce income inequality, improve sanitation or gain recognition for the rights of marginalised groups, his striving to create social value is likely to encounter various social, cultural, economic or political obstacles, but these are clearly barriers standing in the way of his mission. M2 might also confront such extrinsic challenges, but he also comes across, as I have suggested, a different kind of threat to sustaining the creation of artistic value: the failure or success in securing market/public support for what the artist desires to cre-ate can itself diminish the artist's will to live by her desire. The artist's withering desire is not an external hindrance to value creation because her desire is the *source* of value creation. If M2's mission includes a commitment to sustain the artist's practice, he also has an obligation to secure the footing on which that practice rests. Recall also that M2's mission is to seek public validation for the artist's work without compromising its integrity – a commitment which enjoins him to try to arrest the artist's own temptation to imperil the integrity of her practice.

To speak about commitments and obligations is to enter the field of ethics, and I will end by looking explicitly, if briefly, into the question of the artist manager's ethics. On the one hand, an artist manager's personal ethics and politics (apart from his tastes, interests and leanings in the arts) may underpin the professional choices he makes. Both M1 and M2 may be inclined to represent and assist an artist or arts company whose ambitions and preoccupations are aligned with their own political and ethical views. M2's politics, for example, may explain his preference for allying with an anti-capitalist and pro-poor group of artists rather than one exclusively concerned to push a feminist agenda. He might have scruples about accepting assignments with artists obsessed with portraying gratuitous violence against women or encouraging young people to take up addictive drugs. Then again, he might have a zeal for performance art but refuse to work for those artists who cause injury to themselves or traumatise spectators, because he finds such acts to be morally indefensible or personally offensive. M1, who favours working with entertainers, may be wholly concerned with extracting economic value from the arts, yet he may be keener to accept an assignment with an entertainer whose politics, which finds expression in her art, resonates with his own. He could also have moral compunctions about associating with an artist whose performances, in his view, are unacceptably transgressive or too littered with mindless sexual innuendos. As in all personal matters, artist managers will differ about what they will stand for or stand up for in the arts.

On the other hand, it is possible to speak about the ethics of artist management and not just about the ethics of an artist manager. Different professions adopt a code of ethics, listing obligations and responsibilities (to employers, clients, consumers, co-workers, society and so on) to which their members are expected to adhere. Ethical standards might likewise be articulated for the profession of artist management. 'Do not misrepresent the work of an artist to the public' might be a precept that the profession could befittingly embrace, for it is general enough to be applicable not only to M1 and M2 but across the field.

There is room, however, to ask a final question about ethics – which is neither as relative as the personal ethics of the artist manager, nor as general as the professional ethics of artist management: does an artist manager have an ethic which springs from the nature of the artist he is managing and is inscribed in the role he plays for her? I believe that M2 does have such an ethic and M1 does not, and the specific nature of that ethic is strewn across the earlier pages of this chapter. To repeat in a nutshell what I have already said: M2 must uphold the artist's desire and the integrity of her art; he must never, therefore, allow her art to be compromised, degraded or disrespected while pursuing support for her practice or opportunities to present or disseminate her work; he must champion and help to enrich the (non-financial) value of her art; and he must also strain to lift the artist from any gathering darkness in her soul, any weakening of will to live by her desire. He would then and only then be true to his own desire and larger purpose to share with unnamable others the meaning and value that he sees in her art. That is his challenge. That is his dharma.

Notes

1 Not always, though: the marketability of shockingly transgressive art is illustrated by the careers of many artists, among them singer-songwriter G.G. Allin and performance artist Marina Abramović.

2 Sacrifices are often exacted by a commitment to a larger cause. As Ann E. Cudd (2014: p. 37), citing Amartya Sen (1985: p. 187), writes: 'To be an agent is to form a conception of the good, which may . . . also at times involve sacrificing one's well-being for something else that one values.'

3 The two other possibilities – the liking of one's dislike for X and the liking of one's liking for X – are not of interest because they do not motivate a change in taste or preference. If one is satisfied with one's likes and dislikes, one is not spurred to alter one's preferences; it is only when one is dissatisfied with one's likes and dislikes that one might try to change them.

4 This distinction does not hold true also for some entertainment industries of recent origin. The Video-on-Demand (VoD) services (Netflix, Amazon Prime Video) produce and buy content with an eye to popular demand while carrying material of niche interest as well – material which might have been created by self-directed artists. Because VoD strives to maximise revenues by catering to the widest possible

range of audience preferences, it operates with the same impulse as the entertainer but not with the same business model.

5 This does not apply to pre-modern art, which creates emotional, social, ritualistic, symbolic and sacred meanings in a community setting.

References

Allen, P. (2007). Principles of management for the artist manager. In: *Artist management for the music business*. 1st ed. Oxford: Focal Press, pp. 1–9.

Beckett, S. (1989). Worstward Ho. In: *Nohow on*. 1st ed. London: John Calder, pp. 101–128.

Bendixen, P. (2000). Skills and roles: Concepts of modern arts management. *International Journal of Arts Management*, 2(3), pp. 4–13.

Colbert, F. (2003). Entrepreneurship and leadership in marketing the arts. *International Journal of Arts Management*, 6(1), pp. 30–39.

Chaudhry, F. (2019). More than the sum of its parts: Dance, creative management and enterprise in collaboration. In *The Routledge companion to arts management*, Chapter 8 in this volume.

Cudd, A. (2014). Commitment as motivation: Amartya Sen's theory of agency and the explanation of behaviour. *Economics and Philosophy*, 30(1), pp. 35–56. Available at: http://dx.doi.org/10.1017/S026 6267114000030 [Accessed 8 Nov. 2018].

Dees, J. (2001). *The meaning of "social entrepreneurship"*. [online] Duke Innovation & Entrepreneurship. Available at: https://entrepreneurship.duke.edu/news-item/the-meaning-of-social-entrepreneurship/ [Accessed 18 Nov. 2018].

Frankfurt, H. (1971). Freedom of the will and the concept of a person. *Journal of Philosophy*, 68(1), pp. 5–20.

Hilburn, R. (2004). An art born of pain, an artist in happy exile. [online] *Los Angeles Times*. Available at: http://articles.latimes.com/2004/sep/05/entertainment/ca-hilburn5 [Accessed 12 Feb. 2019].

Hirschman, A. (2013). Against parsimony: Three easy ways of complicating some categories of economic discourse. In: J. Adelman, ed., *The essential Hirschman*. 1st ed. Princeton: Princeton University Press, pp. 248–264.

Kipling, R. (2000). If. In: P. Keating, ed., *Rudyard Kipling: Selected poems*. London: Penguin, pp. 134–135.

Ramdev, D. (2018). Vijay Seshadri: In the glow of a splendid, silent sun. *Deccan Chronicle*, p. 2. Available at: https://deccanchronicle.com/lifestyle/books-and-art/101118/vijay-seshadri-in-the-glow-of-a-splen did-silent-sun.html [Accessed 13 Nov. 2018].

Santos, F. (2012). A positive theory of social entrepreneurship. *Journal of Business Ethics*, 111(3), pp. 335–351. Available at: https://dhriiti.com/wp-content/uploads/2017/11/Positive-theory-of-SE.pdf [Accessed 19 Nov. 2018].

Sen, A. (1985). Well-being, agency, and freedom: The Dewey lectures 1984. *Journal of Philosophy*, 82(4), pp. 169–221.

Simpson, S. and Munro, J. (2012). The manager. In: S. Simpson, ed., *Music business: A musician's guide to the Australian music industry*. 4th ed. London: Omnibus Press, pp. 74–97. Available at: https://simpsons.com. au/wp-content/uploads/Music-Business-Chapter-5-The-Manager.pdf [Accessed 24 Jan. 2019].

Thomas, D. (2000). Do not go gentle into that good night. In: W. Davies and R. Maud, eds., *Collected poems 1934–1953*. 1st ed. London: Phoenix, p. 148.

Vellani, A. (2008). How not to commodify the arts: Exemplary entrepreneurial practice from India. *UNESCO E-Journal*, 1(2), pp. 133–148. Available at: www.academia.edu/35290199/ [Accessed 26 Nov. 2018].

———. (2014). Success, failure and cultural entrepreneurship. In: A. Vellani, ed., *Enabling crossovers: Good practices in the creative industries*. 1st ed. Singapore: Asia-Europe Foundation, pp. 27–32. Available at: www.asef.org/images/ASEF_Publication_EnablingCrossovers.pdf [Accessed 20 Oct. 2018].

———. (2015). The creative economy, cultural policies and the arts. In: N. Piplani, ed., *Asia-Europe network of urban heritage for sustainable creative economies*. 1st ed. New Delhi: Indian National Trust for Art and Cultural Heritage, pp. 15–19. Available at: www.asef.org/images/docs/AE_NetworkUrbanHerit age_report.pdf [Accessed 20 Oct. 2018].

4

CONTEMPORARY ARTS IN ADAPTABLE QUALITY MANAGEMENT

Questioning entrepreneurialism as a panacea in Europe

Milena Dragićević Šešić

Contemporary systems of cultural institutions, its programmes and policies of operation are under great pressure from new public policies and the economic demands of its boards, which are limiting institutions' already questionable autonomy.[1] Due to austerities in public budgeting and influences of globalization, cultural institutions are becoming mutually competitive, closely looking at each other's (market) achievements and development trends instead of developing according to their values and the specific needs of their communities and environments. Quantitative criteria became the key "benchmark" of development, thus making cultural institutions' projects bigger and bigger (spectacular) and often populistic. Projects have to become competitive on the global market, attracting an audience and tourists from different countries that could make each programme profitable or at least (financially) sustainable (Kotler and Kotler, 2008; Chong, 2002).

At the same time, at the end of the twentieth century, cultural institutions have contributed a lot to the changes in the cultural sector by engaging a new generation of artists and mediators (connectors) aware of socio-political and cultural contexts through integrating critical issues in their programming. For the first time in their history cultural institutions started to be inclusive, still keeping their main programming process based on excellence and quality while introducing certain openness in making programmes widely accessible, even sometimes opening to participation processes that would address those from de-privileged social backgrounds or migrant communities.

However, the new millennium has brought different challenges as cultural policies turned more to sustainable cultural development, markets and sustainability of art institutions (Dessein et al., 2015; Balta and Dragićević Šešić, 2017; Hristova, Dragićević Šešić, and Duxbury, 2015; UNESCO, 2018a), thus asking cultural operators and artists to behave accordingly using managerial and marketing techniques in governance and audience development. These demands have made it necessary for the cultural system to introduce an entrepreneurial approach in those organizations that are keeping their nineteenth-century structures (museums, libraries, national theatres) and which has resulted in them adopting a more "intrapreneurship[2]" mode of operation.

This new approach demanded refocusing of the institutional arts management that was standardized since the beginning of New Public Management[3] toward entrepreneurialism that, besides creativity and openness to innovation, demands transversal skills (skills related to communication, persuasion, fundraising, teamwork, etc.) from a majority of employees, especially those having important leading positions in programme design (content and methods of implementation).

Thus, in contemporary Europe, arts and cultural institutions are under pressure to become service providers, to be marketable and to attract as many visitors and different sorts of users as possible (treated often as customers).

Suggesting adaptable quality art management (Dragićević Šešić and Dragojević, 2005) as a possible solution, this chapter will explore possibilities to integrate its methods and premises in the creative sector. The major issue to consider is the role of entre/intrapreneurship in the

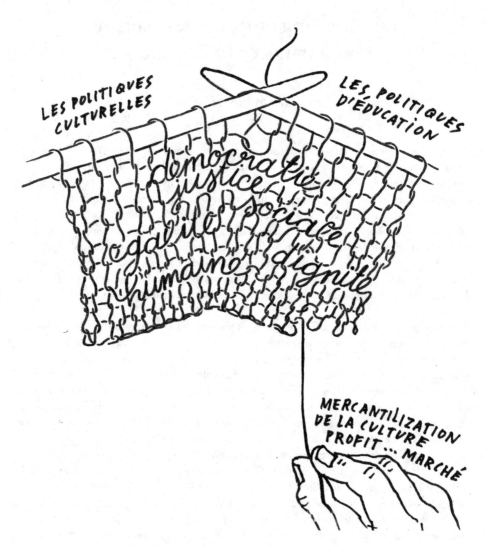

Figure 4.1 Vahida Ramujkić's illustration for the book: *Vers les nouvelles politiques culturelles*, Milena Dragićević Šešić, Belgrade: University of Arts and Clio, 2014

Source: Courtesy Vahida Ramujkić

management of arts institutions: its values, beliefs and myths in contemporary Europe. The main research question: is entrepreneurialism (or the intrapreneurialism) the ONLY way to make a cultural institution sustainable?

The research starts with the thesis that in this situation cultural institutions have two-fold pressures: national and European cultural policies on one side and arts audiences and community needs and demands on the other. Can a cultural institution keep its profile and mission, its values, beliefs, and integrity – its autonomy – having to respond on both managerial and populist (market) pressures and be accountable to both sides? (Protherough and Pick, 2002).

The research will use a qualitative and evaluative approach, analyzing the impact of different policy recommendations (transfer from policy recommendations to programmes and projects), using methods of empirical research: narrative and discourse analysis, content analysis of major project activities, focusing on the extent of changes in programming and methods of mediation. Impact studies, which are usually created in Western Europe to offer advocacy arguments for a desired cause (or to prove to a funder how successful the project was in achieving its aim, especially when financed through Creative Europe program or national ministries), are misused in policy making in an undeveloped country to justify budget cuts, pushing institutions and festivals more and more towards the market. All of this shows to what extent cultural community has accepted imposed instrumentalization of the arts.

The issues that are going to be questioned include: the consideration of entrepreneurialism as an ultimate skill of expanded professionalism (Danhash and Lehikoinen, 2018); the role of cultural institution as an implementer of cultural policies; whether they can fulfil their missions as corporations managed by CEOs with the crucial perspective of income and profit; and, is adaptable quality management and intrapreneurialism a possible response?

Policy-informed practices

In recent years numerous theories had been developed with the purpose to justify public investment in culture by its contribution to GDP development or to different developmental processes through its "spillovers". Even UNESCO contributed with its Convention 2005 (Convention on the Preservation and Promotion of Diversity of Cultural Expressions) to economic reconsideration of contemporary arts (the original name of the convention was Preservation and Promotion of Contemporary Arts and Cultural Contents, which truly reflects its intentions). The aims of this convention were: to support sustainable systems of governance for culture; achieve a balanced flow of cultural goods and services; integrate culture in sustainable development frameworks and to promote human rights and fundamental freedoms. Three out of four aims are linked to better governance, management, efficiency and sustainability of the art sector around the globe while only one is trying to protect the autonomy of artist and art field (Anheier, 2015).

Limiting contemporary arts to its economic values and "cultural expressions" to those that can be protected by copyrights and easily sold on the world market (popular culture vs. folkloric, traditional culture) this convention stressed that support should be given to those that can make further benefits from those investments. Thus, it was heavily influencing national cultural policies that used to finance mostly public institutions and not for-profit projects. Today, analyzing the UNESCO web site, which presents selected innovative examples of national cultural policy measures (UNESCO, 2018b), it is obvious that most of it relates to the national film, book and music industry development (Brazil, France, Denmark), export and access to foreign markets (Argentina, Denmark) and to entrepreneurial endeavors that are supposed to be self-sustainable or socially responsible (Peru, Portugal).

These policy measures of the Convention 2005 and its potentials, besides the scope of crea-tive industries, in the domain of contemporary arts production and among the public cultural sector, have yet to be explored although this is a legal instrument that still has more potential to be used in spite of "very few resources and even fewer sanctions with which to set against a world order dominated by global finance and the corporations with which it is intertwined" (Justin O'Connor, email to the UNESCO technical assistance community, 2015).

The Convention 2005 obtained the most important outcomes in developed countries such as Canada, Germany and France where coalitions for cultural diversity had been created, stimulating development of art entrepreneurialism both in the cultural institutional sector as well as in private creative industries. It influenced a lot of the policies of granting: usually the producers of commer-cial film projects have not asked public bodies for donations – now the projects with commercial perspectives have more chances to get funding as the aim of the convention (implemented through different measures of national cultural policies) is to support sustainability of cultural organizations.

The new challenges within the implementation of the convention are related to the market changes in the digital era. Thus, the ECCD (the European Coalition for Cultural Diversity) devoted its attention to the promotion and funding of European works, particularly with regard to Video-on-Demand services (most of whom are non-European service providers).

> The rapporteurs have therefore drafted measures that protect and support cultural diver-sity, namely by implementing a mandatory quota of 30% and prominence of European works online. These measures also provide for Member States to prevent online services from circumventing national investment obligations designed to ensure a virtuous circle of investment in a diversity of audiovisual films and programmes online.
>
> *(Coalition française, 2018)*

It is obvious that both coalitions and national governments are concerned with the protection of European creative industries' markets, thus leaving measures for contemporary "non-profit art" outside of their interest, only supporting it through the networks of public cultural institutions and festivals. It is through these networks that contemporary artists can gain some support for produc-tion and distribution and thus it is important to enable changes in the public cultural system that would embrace innovations and experiments that are not easily hosted within creative industries.

The European Research Partnership on Cultural and Creative Spillovers conducts and com-missions research that aims to advocate and influence public policies for strategic development of arts and cultural organizations across Europe. Their main thesis is that through spillover effects of the arts, culture, and the creative industries, society and the economy are affected (Fleming Creative consultancy, 2015). The group is underlining how arts influence growth and develop-ment of places, community and social life, local as well as the national and regional economy. This theory is one that mostly had influenced European policies such as: European Agenda for Culture in a Globalizing World (2007), Cultural participation and inclusive societies (CoE), EU strategy for international cultural relations, etc.

> This research partnership defined cultural and creative spillover effects as the pro-cess by which an activity in the arts, culture and creative industries has a subsequent broader impact on places, society or the economy through the overflow of concepts, ideas, skills, knowledge and different types of capital. Spillovers can take place over varying time frames and can be intentional or unintentional, planned or unplanned, direct or indirect, negative[4] as well as positive.
>
> *(Fleming Creative consultancy, 2015)*

Figure 4.2 A sculpture designed by New York artist Mirko Ilić (from former Yugoslavia) to be given as an award to the best company – art sponsor by the Ministry of Culture of the Republic of Serbia (2005–2007) as part of support of the development of active art sponsoring policies

Source: Courtesy Mirko Ilić

Further up, this report identified three types of spillovers: knowledge spillovers (when ideas and narratives enter in wider society and economy), industry spillovers (referring to effects of arts and culture on different elements in cross-sectorial value chains, i.e. innovative forms of organization, communication, etc.) and network spillovers (creating cultural quarters, creative clusters, etc.). Both Fleming and Vickery had studied how value extend out of these spillovers and who benefits in society and economy, but it is important to underline that they support cultural autonomy as a principle and do not believe "that spillover necessarily equals instrumentalism" (Vickery, 2018, np).

However, spillover research developed "defensible claims based on the kind of evidence that policy makers can accept" (Vickery, op. cit.), but by developing them it turned the attention of policy makers only to those values of art that can be measured, compared and used in other public policies such as health, housing and urbanism, crime and justice, etc.

In similar way theories of creative class (Florida, 2014), creative industries (Hartley, 2005; Bilton, 2007), creative economy (Kong and O'Connor, 2009), cultural entrepreneurialism (Varbanova, 2016), etc. had fueled cultural policy discussions, leading more and more toward managerialism in the cultural field, imposing not only transparency and accountability to the creative sector, but also a strategic approach in inter-sectoral development, trans-sectoral partnership (with health, justice and other social institutions as well as with economy: tourism, gastronomy, agriculture, fisheries, etc.).

All of that, through different public debates, policy measures on European and national levels and numerous programs of all three sectors (public, private and civil), especially through private–public partnerships, created a situation where cultural institutions and artists were expected to develop intrapreneurial (if within cultural institution) or entrepreneurial commercial projects (artists are expected to create, as entrepreneurs, jobs for themselves). The European Capital of Culture programme is only one among many that promotes strategic and business approaches in city development, using culture – institutions, arts and artists – as a key engine.

Different expectations still exist for cultural institutions such as contributing to safeguarding national and city identity, offering a platform for contemporary artists to produce new art works, offering to the cultural community new and challenging sensations while at the same time being more inclusive and welcoming to wider communities, providing entertainment and enjoyment, and ultimately earn a new box office income in order to fulfil its budget. These demands are often contradictory, as classical dramaturgy pieces or artefacts from the past might not be interesting for wider audiences unless "nationalized" and/or "spectacularised" or contemporary arts forced to limit its production expenses as producers could foresee lack of audience interest for experimental and innovative art pieces. Inclusion in itself is demanding extra investments that often cannot be justified by market revenue as those vulnerable communities usually cannot pay high cost of entry tickets.

For cultural institutions to develop all kinds of programmes to fulfill these diversified demands a new type of professional is needed, a professional that besides having skills linked to his major profession (curator, theatre producer, librarian, etc.) also has those skills and abilities to design new types of programmes, projects, methods, or to create even his or her own company or a job outside the institution. This cultural professional needs to be an entrepreneur, manager, mediator, connector, and networker who could be termed a cultural operator who ideally can succeed in the situation of diminishing public funds and the rise of big, spectacular or complex (consortium, network) projects that are demanded by public donors such as Creative Europe.

Adaptable quality management: cultural organizations' response

Numerous theories of arts management tried to find their response to demands that cultural policies started to impose on cultural organizations. Taking as a starting point general business management theories, many authors focused on strategic management and planning (often connecting non-profit as such and arts), introducing, mostly through case studies, issues that are relevant for art organizations (Byrnes, 2003; Varbanova, 2013; Kaiser, 1995; Dragićević Šešić and Dragojević, 2005). The other group (most of them economists) found entrepreneurialism and creative industries as their focus of research, from Baumol and Bowen's most famous book (1968), through the works of Haghoort (2003, 2007), Thomson (1999), till Galenson (2006), Duxbury (2004), and Justin O'Connor who is critically approaching the issue (2010). An important body of work related to the question of introducing marketing in the cultural sector has been developed (Colbert et al., 1994; Kotler and Scheff, 1997; etc.), as well as research related to fundraising and financing of the arts (Bodo et al, 2004; Bonet and Donato, 2011; Ginsburgh and Throsby, 2006), etc. Recently, a new body of research appeared related to arts and cultural leadership (Kay and Venner, 2010; Dalborg and Lofgren, 2016; Caust, 2012). All of these academic efforts were focused to offer a diversified set of tools to improve the management of cultural institutions or to raise capacities of small cultural organizations in the independent sector. Thus, issues of strategic development, planning, marketing and fundraising are prevailing while themes related to quality programming and artistic achievements were rarely seriously tackled (probably under the assumption that these professional skills are already developed, and that art managers need only transversal skills of expanded professionalism to make their organizations successful and sustainable on the market).

Adaptable Quality Management (Dragićević Šešić and Dragojević, 2005) tried to offer a framework where both artistic achievements and strength and importance of cultural content will be taken into account together with strategic planning, financing and fundraising, marketing and audience development. Ethics and aesthetics of an art organization are a key basis for the development of its strategic management and marketing where entrepreneurialism (mostly in fact intrapreneurialism) is *spiritus movens* for opening of the new artistic horizons and new dimensions of operations. Philosophy of development is in the heart of the critical self-reflection that starts with values and aspirations (artistic ambition and social responsibility) of an art organization, having intrapreneurship as a major strategy. This approach opposes those developed under the pressure of cultural policies to be more income generating and sustainable that introduced managerialism (Protherough and Pick, 2002): strategic planning with "SMART goals", market assessments, fundraising methods, often neglecting its own organizational culture and values. Thus, creative leadership has been replaced by managerial leadership focused on its visible and measurable results (mostly quantifiable as income or number of audiences).

The perspectives of adaptable quality arts management directly relate to mission, goals and vision of the organization, based on its specific operating philosophy and organizational culture. Several types of organizations can be identified that each demand different strategies and ways of management that had to be logically created from within and not applied as a learned technique. Of course, even this typology is a tentative one as each institution is a case in itself, thus shared participatory management is a precondition for a successful application of adaptable quality arts management.

Arts organizations might be created as *laboratories* that generate and discover new content and processes and create innovative art works; *activist organizations* choose to become a meeting ground of ideas that would lead and inspire socio-political changes through art achievements and processes; an art organization can be a *transdisciplinary research ground* oriented to creativity and exploration that leads to knowledge creation; it can devote its mission to *transfer of knowledge* or different ways of audience development, spreading enthusiasm and love for arts. Of course, there are many that can choose "only" to be "earning", commercial organizations based on good marketing adapted to the values of global society (art fairs or Broadway as paradigms), not accepting that art is a public value, created, above all, in the public interest. In creative industries, many organizations would consider themselves as trendsetting. These two in fact apply to the extreme what most art management books suggest – to research needs in an environment and create an offer that can easily be marketable and sold. Adaptable quality management tries to find a response for those who would never compromise their values and aspirations and that are focused on artists' needs and public interest, thinking about their products only as public goods. Often, solutions are linked to different types of intrapreneurial initiatives.

Laboratories (platforms, hubs,[5] art centers, etc.) place research and innovation in the center of their activities whether they are local or internationally oriented. Processes might differ, orientation toward context can be stronger or weaker (sometimes isolation is a prerequisite of creation), but all of them are ready to take artistic risks and to explore those areas of art that are not dominating either in the curatorial world or on the art market. Strategies of development differ, but in cases when they are internationally oriented, they have to rely on securing accreditation rights (as the most income might come from knowledge transfer realized through opening of art courses, residencies, etc.); strategic partnerships (with scientific research organizations or innovative social movements)[6] and networking (to strengthen their often very lonely position in local context).[7]

Activist organizations consider all of their members as social activists that tend to use the strength of arts for social and political changes. In the turbulent times at the end of the twentieth and beginning of the twenty-first centuries, when solidarity and empathy were socially neglected and non-desirable values,[8] different collectives of artists and intellectuals started to self-organize movements and platforms aiming to raise awareness about new socio-political processes and also to create art works and complex projects to give voice to those silenced by new political measures. These organizations cannot and should not apply general management and marketing tools as they are inherently opposed to their values. Thus, they have to develop adequate ways of operation to become sustainable but not lose their political or their artistic vision. Adaptable quality management offers for their development several types of strategies, such as linkage strategies and strategies of public action, and in cases of the bigger organizations, intrapreneurialism also can be implemented. The major sense of their existence is linked to the achievement of common goals, of creating a public dialogue and thus the use of public spaces is a prerequisite of their effectivity. It is very important for such organizations to have strong international lobbying that can advocate for them in times of repression and crisis. The Center for Cultural Decontamination in Belgrade (Dragićević Šešić and Stefanović, 2017) is a typical activist organization that uses the strategy of linkages and the strategy of internationalization to make its programmes more known and effective, often going with its projects in public spaces joining other social and political movements[9] in different intrapreneurial endeavors that are making organization always going with the time.

Organizations that act from a *transdisciplinary research ground* are usually based on values related to the importance of arts and culture for human development and knowledge creation. They were created in times where artistic and scientific research had been academically separated and platforms to connect them could appear only outside of standard institutional frameworks. Festivals such as Ars Electronica in Linz are typical examples of such organizations. Even institutions such as the European Cultural Foundation in Amsterdam act in this manner, using both academic research and researchers on one side and artist and artistic collectives on the other to produce programmes that connect both: Arts for Social Change, Arts + Science,[10] B/ORDERS (an open forum for the plight of the immigrant), Craftivism[11] (that enables one part of organization to act as an activist organization), Digital Cultures lab.[12] It shows a high level of intrapreneurialism within the organization that in the last twenty years was also under pressure to introduce managerialism in its operation (accountability not only for every spent penny but also for multiplication of their achievements regarding hardly measurable immediate effects). That motivated ECF not only to search for different methods of evaluation and assessment and their representation (plurennial and annual reports, conferences, books) – but also for new types of activities and programmes.

Learning organizations that put a learning process as well as *transfer of knowledge* in the heart of their operations are the most widespread among both cultural institutions and organizations of the civil sector. Libraries and museums to small organizations within civil society build their philosophy of development on the ability to understand needs and capacities of communities and contexts in which they operate, thus continuously changing themselves. The difference between organizations "managed to be market successful" and organizations "managed to be effective in its context" easily can be seen among museums. The global museum became a paradigm of the society of spectacle (Debord, 2004) and consumeristic society (Baudrillard, 1998) while most of the museums implicitly working within the framework of adaptable quality management kept their identity and values but changed their relations to the area of their work becoming more responsible and accountable to the context and new social needs. While the first group uses strategies of spectacularization and inter-sectorial sponsoring partnerships with big corporations by practicing corporate management and marketing strategies, the second group uses more subtle strategies of linkage (often with NGOs that promote social inclusion), networking (creating small sub-networks within ICOM), or public action (raising neglected historical issues on public agenda or giving visibility to women, migrants and other de-privileged social groups).

Although New Public Management demands contractual engagement of artists, practices of adaptable quality management demand a more stable form of employment in most of the cases. Developing an organization as a laboratory, as an activist organization, as a *transdisciplinary research ground* or as a learning organization focusing on knowledge transfer demands a permanent and committed team of artists and other professionals who can, through long term programmes and actions, develop effective and meaningful art and cultural activities. Artists can find their *raison d'être* and place in such institutional cultural systems by choosing to perform in orchestras like Berlin Philharmonics (Fulker, 2016) or Kronos Quartet that go beyond classical music performing, doing research in communities and creating music in a dialogue with other types of music not learned in conservatoires.

However, today, due to managerial pressures, there are fewer possibilities to work in such types of organizations and to be on permanent salary. Cultural institutions often cannot allow themselves to employ musicians, actors or cultural managers but have to find way to employ them project-based, especially if skilled for expanded professionalism, capable to perform several roles. Even orchestra musicians are expected today to be able to lead children's workshops, to work with the disabled or to be open for different kinds of contextual research. Adaptable quality management, by stimulating organizations to creatively approach re-design of their own organizational structure and to invent strategies that recognize community potentials and resources, might become a method that helps art organizations to safeguard their identity and at the same time develop original strategies to achieve their mission and goals.

In most of the cases, the strategy of internationalization, European networking, and cross-border partnership are very helpful for organizational development, but that demands from cultural professionals and artists one more skill – skill to speak a foreign language. However, it is not any language, but English – enabling cultural institutions to participate in international programmes in the time of globalization in spite of the fact that many of these organizations want to challenge globalization and its effects. In Creative Europe, strategic program of the EU, this is the key issue; but also in sub-regional cooperation, like in the case of Albanian-Serbian cultural and artistic dialogues. Thus, artistic statements: "An artist who cannot speak English is no artist" (Mladen Stilinović, Zagreb) or "I do not want to learn English language" (Alexander Brener) are pointing to the fact that internationalization of the work of cultural institutions does not always mean real internationalization but more westernization with an emphasis on Anglo-Saxon knowledge and trends. In the contemporary world cultural institutions and professionals cannot develop without being present at art world conferences, networks, fairs, biennials, festivals and residencies.

Figure 4.3 Mladen Stilinović: *An artist who cannot speak English is no artist*
Source: Courtesy Branka Stipančić

Globalization-informed practices: entrepreneurial response

The world of cultural work today has changed immensely within creative organizations in private and civil sectors, especially in creative industries where many jobs had been replaced by robots and software (cinematography), and many markets enlarged from local or domestic to "unexpected" world regions (popularity of K-pop in France; Turkish TV serials throughout the Arab world, the Balkans and Asia; Japanese literature around the world).

Cultural institutions make specific efforts (adaptable management) to understand those global processes and to introduce in their work relevant aspects to make their achievements known in wider communities through digital technologies, new media, professional information channels and networks, using also different forms of advertising and repackaging of their products to be communicative on a global market.[13]

These are efforts that are mostly implemented through intrapreneurial initiatives such as incubators, laboratories and hubs created within cultural institutions. These forms might have a short or long life as their existence depends heavily on their market success or on top management support, as they are created to earn money for the institution or to bring additional prestige and media attention (this second reason makes the endeavor "unpopular" when the management changes and it is often closed). There were numerous examples of those intrapreneurial initiatives within cultural institutions in Serbia. The National Theatre, as well as the Yugoslav Drama Theatre in Belgrade, has developed "scenes-studios" open to more experimental art projects and lesser-known artists. In Belgrade, museums instituted laboratories for professional education in conservation skills (Diana in the National museum) or specific departments and festivals (Teatroteka in the Theatre Museum; Open Graphic Atelier and the Festival of Archeological Films in the National Museum).

Creative hubs, a relatively new phenomenon in Europe, as most of them had been created after 2011, contribute to the diversification of opportunities for engaging professional artists – although mostly have a disciplinary approach. Hubs are mostly created around design and other creative industries while numerous artists in more conventional art disciplines hardly find their places in them. Most of the hubs are co-working spaces or incubators focusing on a single discipline or few related disciplines. Heinsius in his study (2018) estimates that there are probably thousands of creative hubs in Europe alone, mostly located in inner centers of the cities or creative districts (post-industrial buildings). Parts of hubs define themselves as "pre-incubators" or "accelerators": pre-incubators help transform an idea into a business plan while incubators develop a business plan into a working start-up; accelerators assist in further growth of start-ups. In every case, the point is in business entrepreneurialism and not about artistic development. In each moment of this process the initial mission and strategies have to be re-adapted according to the market; research has not discussed all ethical dilemmas that creatives are facing with keeping their artistic integrity during this process. Of course, most of them are privileged platforms for the development of a professional life offering, besides space, consultancy, training and marketing. However, most hubs reflect the composition of the founding group's disciplinary interest unless they are created by commercial property developers that are just offering spaces for a day, week or permanently. The language distinction might not be very clear as the term co-working space is mostly used by business developers while, often, co-working signifies practice used by bottom-up initiatives emphasizing values of cooperation and solidarity.

Within art schools, hubs are created with an aim to help artists transition from educational to professional life. Slowly professional challenges are introduced to graduates, but schools offer a protected environment where the absence of results does not lead to bankruptcy – it is one more learning opportunity. More than 50% of art school hubs are publicly funded and one quarter has both public and private funding, while only 20% is privately funded. It is completely the opposite for independent hubs of which only 14% are publicly funded. It is interesting that, according to the research, 61% of the university hubs have not evaluated their activities and services (Heinsius, 2018, p. 40). It means that, although trying to teach art students entrepreneurial skills of which strategic planning, including evaluation, is one of the key competencies, the hubs themselves are not operating according to business logic.

Heinsius in his study underlines that all hub examples are just "snap shots of a certain moment in time . . . answering to specific needs of their constituent community, with no best model to follow" (Heinsius, 2018, p. 41). Heinsius made an interesting typology of hubs, starting with mono-hubs that include both incubators of entrepreneurial logic (Guildhall School of Music and Drama, London) and practice-based doctoral art schools (the Nida Art Colony, Lithuania) that hardly can be considered as hubs (preparing students only for artistic excellence and, eventually, giving them chance for larger networking). The second group relates to bottom-up hubs, mostly developed as a joint action of several cultural managers, entrepreneurs and artists (Nova iskra Belgrade and Poligon Ljubljana) and this group is the one that responds the most to the criteria of expectations that hubs have to offer entrepreneurial skills to emerging artists and cultural managers. The third type relates to general incubators and addresses only those with a business (start-up) idea and in reality, refer to music, media, and design, disciplines that are entrepreneurially minded (Heinsius, 2018, p. 49). Among them the research explored results of Factoria Cultural (Madrid), Makerversity (Amsterdam), HKU Expertized Center for Creative Entrepreneurship (Utrecht) and the Center for Knowledge Transfer (Vienna). The fourth group relates to start-ups specialists (Innovation RCA at the Royal College of Art in London) that offer consultancies and "business angels", potential investors in those start-ups.

The research has shown that, besides high diversity of approaches and methods of operation, most of the hubs are related to the creative industries stimulating those ideas that can be transferred in a business endeavor. Ideas that might lead towards not-for-profit NGOs creation or organizations that are needed but without possibilities to be funded, such as services for contemporary dance or creative writing or public art projects, can hardly expect to be hosted in those hubs unless developed within graduate art programmes and thus realized in university hubs. However, besides managerialism, hubs are offering consultancy and help, and those organized on the bottom-up principle even offer peer help and solidarity. This shows that strategies developed within adaptable quality art management might be used in different manners in entre/intrapreneurial endeavors of hubs and within creative industries that also have the responsibility for creating public good.

Conclusion

Cultural institutions today have different responsibilities and commitments. They have to be key platforms for art production, knowledge production, for the education of audiences for critical reflection and art participation but also to contribute to social and economic development realizing their own sustainability (designing "profitable" programmes and projects). All these demands are contradictory: how to do research both artistic and curatorial and develop active citizenship (Mercer, 2002) if the programmes are focusing on profit making?

Words like benchmarks, entrepreneurialism, sustainability, efficiency are creating frameworks that are introducing new values in public cultural sphere, values that are more oriented towards the "money making", entrepreneurial capitalist world. This world is not interested in artistic or curatorial research whose results are uncertain or clearly not immediately usable. In large parts of the world the corporate sphere links with politics in order to have access to large public projects – thus, critical thinking of the employees is not stimulated regarding both the social environment and inner organization of an enterprise (as those inner discussions reduce efficiency).

However, adaptable quality management and intrapreneurialism might be a good response for a cultural institutional system pressed by the demand of new public management, and even for the whole creative sector including civil society organizations in culture and those creative industries that have social responsibility embedded in their practices, to negotiate values and develop intrapreneurialism in public interest.

Cultural institutions are forced now to organize processes to enable continuous learning of its employees in both professional and entre/intrapreneurial skills (expanded professionalism). The world is changing so quickly; technologies change every day, needs and demands coming from the community and larger environment are bringing new challenges, so all of that asks for continuous learning and continuous professional development, which is the base of adaptable quality management (Dragićević Šešić and Dragojević, 2005, pp. 34–47).

But at the same time, cultural institutions have to advocate and lobby for culture as a public good, for an institutional cultural system with an autonomy to produce challenging and experimental art works but also to develop innovative cultural practices within communities, acting as transmedia and transcultural communicators. This public institutional cultural system, from museums and libraries to theatres and community cultural centers, has to develop, through different adequate strategies of linkage, broad systems of intertwined collaboration practices inside and outside the cultural sector, allowing intrapreneurialism to achieve its best results.

Speaking about distributive justice in a cultural realm, it is not fair to transfer all responsibilities on public cultural institutions. Public policies have to find ways to stimulate inclusion, such as Vienna Cultural Pass (2018), a pass allowing reduced or free participation in cultural events for persons with low income, and thus to support intrapreneurial initiatives of cultural organizations whether they relate to audience development, social inclusion or raising of their artistic and professional capacities and strengths. Through specific tailor-made educational programmes public cultural institutions should enable its managers and other professionals to become cultural entre/intrapreneurs that should act enabling different processes and different vectors to be engaged, making cultural institutions open to communities and new demands from the environment. At the same time, public cultural institutions have to embrace the existence of numerous forms of entre/intrapreneurship in the arts, enabling themselves to widen their own role toward different cultural functions – from production and exhibition space, dissemination agency, inclusive workshop, laboratory for transdisciplinary arts, memory dialogue space, hub for critical debate, etc.

Advocating for intrapreneurship in the public cultural sector (civil sector has the freedom to use adaptable quality management and entrepreneurialism) is bringing space for important cultural creativity (endorsed by the UNESCO Convention 2005); for achieving numerous spillovers such as a job market for artists; establishing a relation to the city branding; supporting trans-sectoral endeavours and sustainable regional and national development. That would need structural reform of public sector (supported by cultural policy) to enable them to establish different forms of hubs and incubators, in partnership with private or civil sectors or in partnership with other public cultural and educational institutions, achieving economic results but not losing their main sense of purpose and mission.

To conclude – the public cultural system has to become an autonomous sphere – not to accept policy pressures to foster values of competitivity, efficiency and profitability, thus accepting the exclusion of public responsibilities for arts and cultural development but accepting its duty to respond to new needs with adequate intrapreneurialism and social imagination.

Notes

1 This chapter is partly based on data gathered through project: n. 178012 Identity and memory, financed by the Ministry of Education and Science, Republic of Serbia.

2 Intrapreneurialism is an innovative structural and programmatic change within cultural organization that introduces new programmes or services, capable to be self-financed or financed through donors committed to causes that intrapreneurial endeavor address (social change, art education, etc.).

3 New Public Management describes efforts to change governance of public administration and public institutions to be more "business-like": to use efficiently and effectively public funds. Citizens became customers of the public sector (Protherough, Pick, 2002).

4 The gentrification effects are usually considered as negative by the neighborhood and cultural community while political agents and tourism organizations see gentrification of neighborhoods as positive for city branding. Lots of books and texts had shown how Manhattan had changed its face due to the number of artists that inhabited its poor neighborhoods.

5 However, the word "hub" that ten years ago was used for artistic platforms, today is more used for such centers that can earn money and live on the market (Heinsius, 2018: pp. 31–54). The word "creative hubs" is accepted globally for all those initiatives that are hosting design (commercial endeavors – business entrepreneurship) and art projects and initiatives linked to ideas of social inclusion and community development (Kapoor, 2016).

6 Organizations that experiment with relations of art and nature might find their natural collaborators in ecological movements, etc.

7 Wuppertal Theatre under leadership of Pina Bausch or Tadeusz Kantor Kriket Theatre in Cracow used to belong to this group of organizations and both were facing problems after a death of the leader. This

points to the typical weakness of those organizations that adaptable quality management should prevent demand for shared, participative leadership.

8 In both welfare countries where neoliberal economy and New Public Management introduced values of competitivity and profit making so that social policies developed in the sixties started to be abandoned; and in the countries of new democracies where transition was characterized with even more brutal rejection of social policies' measures.

9 When the organization was closed or threatened to be closed, they used their international friendship networks to prevent that from happening (Dietachmair & Gielen, 2017: pp. 279–303).

10 This lab explores how arts and sciences might be transformed through a Cultural Re-Think where artists and scientists work together. "What outcomes could be possible? What solutions might be found to big questions?"

11 Craftivism is addressing anti-capitalism, environmentalism, feminism or any other social issue or cause, centered on practices of handicrafts.

12 Exploring the digital revolution and information age, this lab wants to critically investigate the internet, new media and digital technologies and the roles they play in contemporary society, media, culture, politics and the arts.

13 Many ambitious theatre institutions besides titling their performances in English are rehearsing their "top products" in English language to facilitate their touring and festival presentations. Thus, a performance of *Isabella`s Room* (2004) of the Belgian Needtheatre (Brussels) had three versions: in Flemish for the local market, in French for the wider Belgium market and in English for the world market of theatre festivals. Each of the performances had a different rhythm according to the language used.

References

Anheier, H., (2015). Towards a monitoring framework. In: *Re-shaping cultural policies, a decade promoting the diversity of cultural expressions for development*. Paris: UNESCO, pp. 31–44.

Balta, J. and Dragićević Šešić, M. (2017). Cultural rights and their contribution to sustainable development: Implications for cultural policy. *International Journal of Cultural Policy*, 23(2), pp. 159–173.

Baudrillard, J. (1998). *The consumer society: Myths and structures*. London: SAGE Publications.

Baumol, W. and Bowen, W. (1968). *Performing arts – The economic dilemma*. Cambridge, MA: MIT Press.

Bilton, C. (2007). *Management and creativity: From creative industries to creative management*. Oxford: Blackwell.

Bodo, C. et al. (2004). *Gambling on culture: State lotteries as a source of financing*. Amsterdam: CIRCLE.

Bonet, L. and Donato, F. (2011). The financial crisis and its impact on the current models of governance and management of the cultural sector in Europe. *ENCATC Journal of Cultural Management and Policy*, 1, pp. 4–11.

Byrnes, W. (2003). *Management and the arts*. Waldham, MA: Focal Press.

Caust, J. (2012). *Arts leadership: International case studies*. Melbourne: Tilde University Press.

Chong, D. (2002). *Arts management*. London: Routledge.

Coalition française 2018. Available at: www.coalitionfrancaise.org/en/the-european-coalitions-for-cul tural-diversity-are-concerned-regarding-a-procedure-against-the-avms-cult-report-at-the-european-parliament/ [Accessed 17 Jul. 2018].

Colbert, F. et al. (1994). *Marketing culture and the arts*. Montreal: HEC Chair in Arts Management.

Dalborg, K. and Lofgren, M. (eds.) (2016). *Perspectives on cultural leadership*. Goteborg: Natverkstan kultur.

Danhash, N. and Lehikoinen, K. (2018). *Career in the arts: Visions for the future*. Amsterdam: ELIA.

Duxbury, N. et al. (2004). *Creating economic and social benefits for communities*. Vancouver: Creative City Network of Canada.

Debord, G. (2004). *Society of the spectacle*. Austin, TX: Rebel Press.

Dessein, J. et al. (2015). *Culture in, for and as sustainable development*. Jyvaskyla: University of Jyvaskyla.

Dietachmair, P. and Gielen, P. (2017). *The art of civil action: Political space and cultural dissent*. Amsterdam: Valiz.

Dragićević Šešić, M. and Dragojević, S. (2005). *Art management in turbulent times*. Amsterdam: Boeckman Stiftung.

Dragićević Šešić, M. and Stefanović, M. (2017). Activism as a leadership style: An independent cultural organization in a troubled context. *Forum Scientiae Oeconomia*, 5(1), pp. 35–42.

Fleming Creative Consultancy. (2015). *Cultural and creative spillovers in Europe: A preliminary evidence review*. London: Fleming Creative Consultancy.

Florida, R. (2014). *The rise of the creative class – revisited: Revised and expanded*. New York: Basic Books.

Fulker, R. (2016). *Three Berlin orchestras welcome refugees.* Deutsche Welle. www.dw.com/en/three-berlin-orchestras-welcome-refugees/a-19086225 [Accessed 19 Jul. 2018].

Galenson, D.W. (2006). *Analyzing artistic innovation: The greatest breakthroughs of the 20th century, working paper 12185.* Cambridge, MA: National Bureau of Economic Research.

Ginsburgh, V. and Throsby, D. (2006). *Handbook of the economics of art and culture.* Amsterdam: Elsevier.

Haghoort, G. (2003). *Art management: Entrepreneurial style.* 3rd ed. Delft: Eburon.

———. (2007). *Cultural entrepreneurship: On the freedom to create art and the freedom of enterprise.* Utrecht: Utrecht University.

Hartley, J. (2005). *Creative industries.* Wiley-Blackwell.

Heinsius, J. (2018). From education to professional practice: Are the creative hubs the answer?. In: N. Danhash and K. Lehikoinen, eds., *Career in the arts: Visions for the future.* Amsterdam: ELIA.

Hristova, S., Dragićević Šešić, M. and Duxbury, N. (2015). *Cultural sustainability in European cities: Imagining Europolis (Routledge studies in culture and sustainable development).* London: Routledge.

Kaiser, M. (1995). *Strategic planning in the arts: A practical guide.* Oakland, CA: Kaiser/Engler Group.

Kapoor, S. (2016). Arts hubs in urban landscapes: An essential ingredient to living cities. In: Mumbai first, ed., *The making of vibrant cities.* New Delhi: Rupa.

Kay, S. and Venner, K. (2010). *A cultural leadership reader.* London: Cultural Leadership Programme/Creative Choices.

Kong, L. and O'Connor, J., (2009). *Creative economies, creative cities: Asian-European perspectives.* New York: Springer.

Kotler, N.G. and Kotler, P. (2008). *Museum marketing and strategy: Designing missions, building audiences, generating revenue and resources.* San Francisco, CA: Jossey-Bass.

Kotler, P. and Scheff, J. (1997). *Standing room only: Strategies for marketing in the performing arts.* Boston: Harvard Business School Press.

Mercer, C. (2002). Towards cultural citizenship: Tools for cultural policy and development. http://dx.doi.org/10.2139/ssrn.2153304 [Accessed 8 Jul. 2018].

O'Connor, J. (2010). *The cultural and creative industries: A literature review.* 2nd ed. London: Arts Council England.

Protherough, R. and Pick, J. (2002). *Managing Britannia.* London: Edgeways.

Thomson, J. (1999). A strategic perspective of entrepreneurship. *International Journal of Entrepreneurial Behavior and Research,* 5(6), pp. 279–296.

UNESCO. (2018a). *Re-shaping cultural policies: Advancing creativity for development.* Paris: UNESCO.

———. (2018b). Available at: www.unesco.org/culture/cultural-diversity/2005convention/en/periodic report/goodpractices/# [Accessed 17 Jul. 2018].

Varbanova, L. (2013). *Strategic management in the arts.* London: Routledge.

———. (2016). *International entrepreneurship in the arts.* London: Routledge.

Vickery, J. (2018). The spillover effect. *Arts Professional,* 15 March 2018. Available at: www.artsprofessional.co.uk/magazine/article/spillover-effect

Vienna Cultural Pass. (2018). Hunger auf Kunst und Kultur ("Kulturpass"). Available at: www.wig.or.at/TU%20WAS!-PASS.1046.0.html [Accessed 17 Jul. 2018].

5

BY NOT FOR

Engagement strategies in a digital age

Oonagh Murphy

Introduction

In a digital age, everyone is a creative producer, a publisher and distributor – from Facebook posts to YouTube videos. Creative production and knowledge distribution has been changed forever by Web 2.0 technologies. This chapter explores how this new operating environment has generated both challenges and opportunities for the cultural sector.

The innovation and creativity writer, Charles Leadbeater argues that there is a notable cultural shift away from things being done *for* us towards a new model of things being done *with* us (Leadbeater, 2009). Describing how the age-old rhetoric of politicians working 'for us' is being cast aside by a new rhetoric of 'we did this together', he suggests that 'the spirit of with took Barack Obama to the White House as thousands upon thousands of volunteers organized over the web and took to the phones to get out the vote' (2009, p. 6). The principle of *with* is that knowledge is co-produced and comes from multiple diverse sources including traditionally qualified experts but also enthusiasts and professional-amateurs, so called – 'Pro-Ams'.

The challenge for arts managers is to create an open culture and to work with diverse voices rather than simply a self-appointed guild of geeks. As Gauntlett reminds us, 'social capital is a resource based on trust and shared values' (Gauntlett, 2011, p. 133). Trust is something which needs to come from both within and outside the institution, and understanding is central to creating a trusting relationship between patrons and institutions.

This chapter does not focus on social media practices per se, but instead on digital technologies and how they have created social changes in wider society, and in turn how these technologies have altered the operating context of arts organisations in the UK and US. A context that provides opportunities for increased diversity, engagement and new relevance, but one that also poses challenges for arts organisations.

The optimism of social media and a promised digital utopia has somewhat been curtailed by recent controversies that have seen social media data used to influence key elections in the UK and US (Cadwalladr and Graham-Harrison, 2018; Hand, 2018; Harris, 2018; Persily, 2017). These events, alongside the introduction of the *General Data Protection Act, 2018* in Europe, have made arts organisations and wider society more conscious of data, ethics and commercial use of personal information (Debatin et al., 2009; Richardson, 2017; Stutzman, 2016). Social media is after all not free, rather it is free at the point of use – users pay for these services by giving the companies access to their personal data.

In an increasingly digital world, technology and remix culture has opened up the avenues to participation. No longer do patrons need to be invited to participate, nor does participation necessarily need to exist within the scaffolded confines of the cultural organisation. Increasingly, participation is becoming self-directed, with patron-generated participatory practices existing in parallel to facilitated participatory opportunities offered by an institution. This chapter surveys innovative approaches to audience and art form development and the role that digital technologies and digital culture are having on the work of the contemporary arts manager.

Digital literacy and the arts manager

Digital culture and digital technologies have long been central to marketing campaigns engaging with audiences, education programmes and increasingly to art form development (Greffe, 2004; Kelly, 2010; Miles, 2017). However digital technologies have now become so pervasive that more than simply providing communication platforms, which replace traditional analogue modes of communicating with audiences, these technologies have created a wider cultural shift with audiences now seeking to enter into a reciprocal dialogue with cultural institutions.

Web 1.0, the first generation of World Wide Web technologies and user experience opened up access to information. However, with the birth of Web 2.0 and social media we have seen a move towards participatory engagement – web users rather than simply consumers of information are now active creators and participants in the development and analysis of available knowledge. When Tim O'Reilly and Dale Dougherty coined the term 'Web 2.0' in 2004, they defined it as a move towards the creation of software tools that would create a more participatory web (O'Reilly, 2005). However their initial emphasis on software and technology platforms has in recent years 'lost its tether to the web-programming models it espoused and has become closely linked to a design aesthetic and a marketing language' (Mandiberg, 2012, p. 4); as such Web 2.0 can best be defined as an 'ethos or approach'(Gauntlett, 2011, p. 5) rather than a defined technology platform.

The ethos and technologies developed since the birth of Web 2.0 has prompted cultural institutions to begin to develop new relationships with their audiences (Russo and Peacock, 2009). Social media has provided new ways to collect and share information, and harness 'collective intelligence' (O'Reilly, 2005). This approach is a significant value shift as it requires arts institutions to move away from the role of custodian of knowledge towards a more open model that recognises there is more talent outside of the institution than within it. While such technologies bring opportunities for arts organisations across many disciplines to become more efficient and relevant cultural institutions, they also present problems for senior managers and established arts managers who may not possess the necessary digital literacy and skills base to fully implement such technologies within their institutions (Stein, n.d.).

The term digital literacy was coined by Paul Gilster as 'the ability to understand and use information in multiple formats from a wide range of sources when it is presented via computers' (Gilster, 1997). Digital literacy is a term that emerged from the concept of literacy, which Jones and Flannigan argue has historically been used to distinguish between the educated and uneducated classes (Jones and Flannigan, n.d.). Literacy originally referred to the ability to read and write, however multiple more nuanced definitions have emerged in recent years from information to media to digital literacy. Hobbs for example speaks of the interplay between digital and media in their definition of digital literacy:

> People need the ability to access, analyze and engage in critical thinking about the array of messages they receive and send in order to make informed decisions about the everyday issues they face regarding health, work, politics and leisure.
>
> *(Hobbs, 2010)*

Perhaps then rather than a single definition of literacy, we are moving towards a world where multiple literacies are required to succeed in both personal and professional life. In a comparative analysis of digital literacy research from an international perspective, Pietrass notes that across the available definitions three prominent categories emerge, namely: media analysis, media selection and media production (Pietrass, 2007). This multiple literacy model centers on the need to be able to both create and consume information on a variety of digital and analogue platforms (Bawden, 2001). The New York City Department of Education provides us with a useful definition of digital literacy, which incorporates these three components and places an emphasis on production and collaboration alongside consumption

> Digital literacy is more than knowing how to send a text or watch a music video. It means having the knowledge and ability to use a range of technology tools for varied purposes. A digitally literate person can use technology strategically to find and evaluate information, connect and collaborate with others, produce and share original content, and use the Internet and technology tools to achieve many academic, professional, and personal goals.
>
> *("Enhancing Digital Literacies" NYC Schools Department,*
> *quoted in Murphy, 2014)*

This definition places an emphasis on the ability to find, connect, collaborate, consume and produce digital content and as such is wider ranging than the definition provided by Gilster in 1997. This definition outlines both the challenges and opportunities for arts managers in an increasingly digital age. The opportunity for authentic engagement with audiences on an audience's own terms, through new platforms and media, provides a foundation for art form development, new audiences, and new stories to be told.

Arts managers can look to their colleagues in museums for support when it comes to developing new digitally relevant systems, processes, missions, and visions for their institutions. Museums, perhaps more so than other, non-collecting arts institutions, have to date struggled with issues of authenticity, control and gate keeping. Writing in 2011, Robert Stein interviewed a series of museum innovators around what they saw were the challenges of digital culture. Across the research we see a number of familiar themes emerge. Ed Rodley, the then-Associate Director of Integrated Media at Peabody Essex Museum, cites authority as a key concern:

> Participatory culture doesn't do away with the need for authority, but it will privilege a different kind of authority, a more transparent, more engaged one.
>
> *(2012, p. 218)*

While Nancy Proctor, the then-Head of Mobile Strategy and Initiatives at the Smithsonian Institution, talks about the need to engage with participatory culture at the core of museum practice, perhaps even radically changing the structure of museums institutions to be more relevant, because superficial 'innovation' means that museums are simply putting a new face on an old body. She advocates that museums must undertake 'the much harder, less sexy, but ultimately more sustainable task of radically restructuring our museums and practices even as we work within those very institutions' (2012, p. 222). Here we see two key themes emerging, namely authorial control, the official voice of the institution and superficial change, projects which tick participation, outreach and engagement boxes, but fall short of engendering progressive organisational change. Stein sums up this dilemma well by asking 'whether or not we are ready to do the hard work of authentic engagement? Or, are we instead seeking the 'quick-hit' payoffs to be gleaned from the current crop of cultural fads?' (2012, p. 221)

Leadership is of course key to the success of arts institutions responding to and indeed thriving within this new technological and cultural landscape. The autocratic, top-down approach of leadership by a 'charismatic leader' as observed as being prevalent by Nisbett and Walmsley, sits in contradiction to the participatory ideals of Web 2.0 (Nisbett and Walmsley, 2016). The complexity of designing systems and structures that enable authentic participation across all segments of an organisation is not lost on the creator of the World Wide Web, Berners-Lee:

> I had (and still have) a dream that the web could be less of a television channel and more of an interactive sea of shared knowledge. . . . I imagine it immersing us in a warm, friendly environment made of things we and our friends have seen, heard, believe or have figured out.
>
> *(Tim Berners-Lee quoted in Rosen, 2012, p. 111)*

Whilst the web is increasingly becoming a complex and at times toxic place, the utopian vision of what the web could be, as proposed by Berners-Lee, does offer a useful vision for the contemporary arts manager, a vision that somewhat contradicts the charismatic leadership model that has become prevalent across the sector. Caust argues that 'models of leadership that have been associated with the arts historically may no longer have any validity in a post-modern world. Likewise, structures and organizational models of the past may no longer have relevance in the twenty-first century' (Caust, 2017, p. xi).

In the preface to his 2012 book *What You Really Need to Know about the Internet*, Naughton outlines the force at which this 'new' media ecosystems demand organisational and institutional change.

> Our new media ecosystem is immeasurably more complex than the one in which most of us were educated and conditioned. Yet complexity is something that we have traditionally tried to ignore or control. Since denial and control are no longer options, we need to tool up for the challenge. In particular, we need to pay attention to how complex systems work, and to how our organisations need to be reshaped to make them cope with the complexity that now confronts them.
>
> *(Naughton, 2012, p. 5)*

In a crowded media and content landscape, the quality of stories, content and art form becomes even more important, and arguably that quality will come from culturally relevant dialogue influenced in part by digital culture. Glocer argues that 'If you want to attract a community around you, you must offer them something original and of a quality that they can react to and incorporate in their creative work' (Tom Glocer quoted in Rosen, 2012, p. 15). Creative work is not confined to professional 'creatives' but in a digital age, everyone is a creative producer, a publisher and distributor, from Facebook posts to YouTube videos. Creative production and knowledge distribution has been changed forever by Web 2.0 technologies. Whilst this provides opportunities for arts organisations to become more diverse, it also presents challenges as we increasingly see a casualization in the workforce (Briziarelli, 2018; Drahokoupil and Piasna, 2017; Milland, 2017; Stewart and Stanford, 2017) and a devaluation of creative labour (Fisher and Fuchs, 2015; Gauntlett, 2011).

Web 2.0 and collaborative ideals

Leadbeater argues that one outcome of Web 2.0 technologies impact on wider society is that there is a notable cultural shift away from things being done for us towards a new model of things being done with us, like describing how the age-old rhetoric of politicians working 'for us' is being cast aside by a new rhetoric of 'we did this together' (Leadbeater, 2009). This new ethos, which is being facilitated by Web 2.0, is already breeding new kinds of organisations. From Net-Mums to Wikipedia, these organisations gain social capital not from the expertise of core voices, but from the diversity and multiplicity of voices that create content for them. Social capital is a term used to mirror financial capital; however social connections replace money in this system of capital (Gauntlett, 2011, p. 129). Although there are a number of writers who have sought to define social capital (Coleman, 1988; Putnam, 2001) it is Pierre Bourdieu's three-tiered model that provides us with the clearest insight into the complexities of capital within contemporary society (Bourdieu, 1986). Bourdieu defines capital as having three components: cultural, social and economic. Cultural capital refers to formal knowledge, education and an appreciation of high culture from opera to the fine arts. Social capital is based on one's network of friends, allies and associates, while economic capital is based on financial assets. In an increasingly networked world social capital has increasing importance for cultural organisations. Leadbeater suggests that arts organisations need to facilitate this new ethos and respond to the new modes of creation and engagement that Web 2.0 is prompting audiences to expect. In examining why people want to contribute to arts organisations he explains the intrinsic drive to seek 'the satisfaction of solving a puzzle' (Leadbeater, 2009).

Inviting people in is not as simple as opening the doors – Leadbeater points out that if that was the case 'Starbucks could claim to be the world's leading art business' (Leadbeater, 2009, p. 10). The challenge is to create an open culture and work with diverse voices rather than simply a 'self-appointed guild of geeks.' By only working with those who have advanced digital skills, social capital would replicate the power hierarchies of old and thus defeat the spirit of 'with' that Web 2.0 technologies have spawned.

Fleming also notes the move towards porous organisational structures in *Embracing the Desire Lines – Opening up Cultural Infrastructure (2009)*. This move towards open and porous cultural organisations is a radical affront to these traditional temples of power, those grand Victorian buildings that 'for so long have stood steadfast as examples as symbols of cultural continuity and comfort' (Fleming, 2009, p. 1). For him the need to become more open and porous is centred on the issue of relevance; cultural organisations need to appeal to the public if they are to survive. In a broad sweep he cites approaches ranging from 'co-commissioning and co-curating, connecting the knowledge, content and tastes of different communities' and suggests that this should happen throughout the institution both onsite and online (Fleming, 2009, p. 13). However again we are reminded that openness, partnership and collaboration in any form is not easy 'to open the doors a little wider is to encourage vulnerability as much as innovation and opportunity' (Fleming, 2009, p. 20).

Govier also makes the link between the challenge facing museums and cultural organisations in *Leaders in Co-Creation? Why and How Museums Could Develop Their Co-Creative Practice with the Public, Building on Ideas from the Performing Arts and Other Non Museum Organisations* (Govier, 2009a), suggesting that focusing the co-creation debate on 'power' is a bit of a red herring. She suggests that museums are never going to relinquish all power to visitors so it is more beneficial to move the debate beyond one of democracy versus elitism towards an enquiry into how museums and their visitors can work together.

In tough economic times, we need to be relevant for and connected to our publics: letting them contribute to our future development makes sense on so many levels economic as well as ideological.

(Govier, 2009b, p. 5)

It is perhaps useful with reference to this quote to briefly revisit Guntaillike, as he also places the same emphasis on the importance of innovation: 'innovation is sometimes presented as a desirable extra, something that organisations might do when they have some spare cash ... innovation is much more basic that this: it is the condition for survival in a changing environment' (Guntaillike, 2008). In concluding her review of case studies and literature Govier states that 'the best collaborative work happens within a framework and that it does need management and leadership. You need to plan, design and reflect for effective collaboration' (Govier, 2009b, p. 17).

Simon notes how Web 2.0 technologies have ousted traditional knowledge structures, with users seeking reviews, opinions and comments from other, often-anonymous Web 2.0 users, rather than from traditional 'experts.' When buying online we read reviews and make purchasing decisions based on the content provided by other users, rather than solely the 'expert' reviews in a newspaper or on the sleeve of a book. Simon expresses the value of responding to the challenges posed by this new landscape through a helpful anecdote:

Consider the experience of cooking with a child. Under no circumstances is it easier or faster to bake a cake with an eight-year-old than to do it yourself. However, including the child builds your relationship with him, empowers him as a maker, and teaches him some basic cooking, scientific and mathematical concepts. And it produces a cake for everyone to enjoy.

(Simon, 2010, p. 14)

The value of stakeholders, be they audience, visitor or patron, is something that occurs in multiple studies (Boorsma and Chiaravalloti, 2010; Conway and Whitelock, 2007; Hsieh, 2009; Hsieh, Curtis, and Smith, 2008); however a key challenges that also emerges centres on the authenticity of such practices (Head, 2007; Rentschler et al., 2002). The Open Stage Project, initiated by The Theatre Royal Stratford East (TRSE), tested the concept of sustained engagement as a means to give up power and sharing it with 'people who want to come along to the party'; the project blurb describes dialogue as a founding principle of the project.

'The Open Stage project is dedicated to democratizing theatre, to listening to the voices and stories of those in the community who are not often heard, and to building a sense of empowerment and ownership of the theatre by the local community'(Glow, 2013, p. 131).

In order to truly open the gates, TRSE were required to relinquish their role as gatekeepers and consciously reflect upon the need to alter the status quo and move beyond 'policing the boundaries of taste'. Rather than developing an audience for existing work, this project sought to look beyond the parameters of the organisation's own understanding of theatre and provide space, permission, and authority to ideas developed outside the organisation. This involved asking the community what stories were of interest to them, rather than prescribing what narrative the community would be invited to respond to, as is often the case with outreach focussed work.

For many years now, arts institutions have sought to develop new audiences, to bring the people to them, to educate and help non-attenders understand art forms. However, Web 2.0 technologies have created a new phenomenon, with citizens asserting their rightful place amongst art forms and institutions in which they are not represented. In parallel to arts organisations gingerly opening the gates, through specific audience development programmes, we have seen social media serve as a platform to galvanise self-organising audiences who have stood up and staked a claim on arts organisations.

Bhaskar describes the traditional model of arts production as the 'broadcast model', and argues that this linear approach has begun to give way to a 'consumer-curated model' (2017, p. 207). This is in part due to an increasingly mass media, 24/7, always-on cultural landscape which means that for many, push notifications and subscription services deliver a constant feed of culture via the mobile devices in their pockets (Boyd, 2012). Today we are experiencing a cultural overload on a daily basis, with more 'content' than ever before, 'the power to decide who watches what and when has flipped from broadcasters to audience'(Bhaskar, 2017, p. 208). This has resulted in two major shifts of audience–institution dialogue.

Shift 1: embracing Web 2.0 principles of participatory design

Firstly, we see arts organisations embracing Web 2.0 technologies and culture as a means to tell the stories of the day, and in doing so are creating a dialogue with new and often more diverse audiences.

An early example of an organisation gaining the rewards of entering bravely into the unknown by applying the principles of Web 2.0 culture to their physical space, in 2012, was Walker Art Centre. *Open Field* was a three-year long project developed by Walker to challenge established ideas about what art and participation could look like. The project invited anyone (i.e. not just artists) to propose an activity, which would then take place on the lawn of their building with the least mediation possible. In an introduction to a book published as part of this project Sarah Schultz and Sarah Peters from Walker Art Centre explain Open Field's underlying principles:

> Grounded in the belief that creative agency is a requirement for sustaining a vital pub-
> lic and civic sphere, it nurtures the free exchange of ideas, experimentation and seren-
> dipitous interactions. Whether hosting a collective of artists building a schoolhouse, a
> pickling demonstration, or a raucous group of children rolling down a hill, Open Field
> attempts to break with a number of timeworn conventions about the role of museums,
> creativity and public life.
>
> *(Walker Art Center and Schultz, 2012, p. 19)*

Within the context of an organization-authored experience, this project is extreme in its open-ness and included activities as diverse as an Internet Cat Video Festival (Burgess, 2015), and a workshop called 'Car Theft for Kids' (which taught kids how to break into cars, and out of cars – should they find themselves in a hostage situation). It is an important project because it tested and pushed boundaries and moved beyond the superficial mode of participation described by Govier. In a publication associated with this project, Ippolito notes:

> It's a lot easier for museums to give lip service to the commons than to tear down
> the stanchions keeping the mummies and Monet's at arm's length. Yet museums must
> question their identity as gatekeeper, whether of the zookeeper or cashier variety, if
> they are to remain relevant in the age of the remix.
>
> *(Ippolito, 2012)*

This project used four guidelines and twelve rules to guide participation; these rules which sought to scaffold experience (for example encourage people to participate) but discourage reckless or dangerous behaviour were heavily debated within the museum. In a chapter called 'When Bad Things Don't Happen' Peters reflects on the development journey within the museum, and the positive outcomes of the project (hence the chapter title) (Peters, 2012). This project's value is drawn from its imperfections; it was diverse and eclectic, at times unrefined. It was the polar opposite of a curated exhibition with associated branding, but it was this imperfection and critical praxis that created a valuable dialogue about the role and purpose of Walker, a dialogue that happened not within the walls of the museum, but instead on its front lawn for all to see. Embracing the creative journey provides room for real dialogue to occur between those within the institution and those outside (Murphy, 2016).

The importance of dialogue is something that is echoed by Fuel Theatre Companies, Theatre Club, a concept that sits on the periphery of an organization and seeks to provide a safe space for outside voices. The concept for Theatre Club was derived from *Dialogue*, an event developed by Maddy Costa and Jake Orr. *Dialogue* was created as a platform to invite audiences to discuss the work they had just seen in a welcoming and unpretentious small group environment; intimacy is vital to ensure all voices are heard. The key to *Dialogue* is that no one from the production attends the group, allowing audience members to lead and reflect on the production, steering the conversation towards their own experience. This format gives agency to the audience and values their own lived experience as a respected contribution to interpreting work. It is a social media chat in real life. As Costa explains:

> Theatre is a communal activity, and sometimes the best fun in seeing a show is chatting about it afterwards in the bar or on the journey home. But what if you're in the sizeable minority of people who go to the theatre alone, aren't part of a theatre-making community, and don't have anyone with whom to share their opinions?
>
> *(Maddy Costa quoted in Theatre Club Handbook:*
> *New Conversations About Theatre, n.d.)*

Criticism is at the heart of Costa's work; having worked as a critic at a national newspaper, she was approached by theatre-maker Chris Goode to engage in a period of 'embedded criticism' with the work of his, at the time, new company. The brief for what this might look like, and the rationale behind it, is spelt out in an email from Goode to Costa.

> A cross between a dramaturg, an archivist, a documentary artist, and outreach officer, a brand manager and Jiminy Cricket. Someone whose job it is to remind us what we do, to explain to others who we are, to have a long memory, to relate that memory to the present instant and to what seems likely to happen tomorrow. . . . Not just an outside eye (and ear) but also a memory, a conscience, a nagging voice. A heart.
>
> *(Chris Goode quoted in Costa, 2016, p. 201)*

More than a dialogue between two, this email, now published in a book chapter by Costa in which she explores *The Critic as Insider*, provides a helpful foundation from which to reimagine the role of the audience to that of a vocal, active and critical participant. This email serves as perhaps a provocative, perhaps aspirational, but nonetheless instructive manifesto for what a critically engaged, digitally minded, contemporary audience might look like.

For Damian Martin, Costa's work, and *Dialogue* more specifically, represents a wider shift towards new forms of theatre criticism, including critics being invited to sit in writers' rooms or be embedded in an arts organization. However Martin also outlines how criticism has followed the academic trend of moving outside the ivory tower: 'The effect of these changes has been a looser boundary between the academy and the public arena, with distinctions less clearly demarcated' (Damian Martin, 2016, p. 199).

Shift 2: claiming space

Secondly, we see audiences stepping up and claiming space within arts organisations in which they do not feel represented, an approach that can be both challenging and enriching.

The *Black Ticket Project* (BTP) has many similar traits in terms of opening up new dialogue and creating new approaches to platforming audience experience; however it began outside the organization to which it speaks. Tobi Kyeremateng created the *Black Ticket Project* in 2017, as a means for herself and other people of color working in theatre to support people from their own community to attend culturally relevant theatre for the first time. Their first campaign supported people to attend *Barber Shop Chronicles* at the National Theatre, a work written by a black playwright, and performed by a racially diverse cast. Kyeremateng, a theatre producer, realised that whilst this work told a story that she and her friends could relate to, many of her friends felt that booking a ticket for the National Theatre was a big risk. The show became a sell-out success, and the result was that by the time many of those whose story was being told on stage grew the confidence to purchase tickets, only the most expensive were available. This was a major problem for Kyeremateng, who notes that 'Despite the international success of Barber Shop Chronicles, it felt like something was missing in the audience development of the show'(Kyeremateng quoted in "Black Theatre Live," 2018). As such BTP began as a radical intervention to the work of a national institution, the National Theatre in London.

Whilst audience development work often centers on providing affordable ticketing, BTP was able to go further in that it questioned traditional power structures from the perspective of those that do not attend. Kyeremateng argues that arts organisations need to go further than simply programming 'diverse' work. 'Programming 'diverse' . . . work is only one leg of bringing in 'diverse' audiences. A very important feat, but also think venues underestimate how much trust-building is involved in inviting in people you've alienated throughout your history'(Kyeremateng, 2018). In the spirit of Web 2.0, BTP was a project created completely independently of the organization it spoke to, The National Theatre. It challenged traditional cultural capital power structures, and through social media empowered social capital, the knowledge of one's own culture, connections and narrative, as a valuable and important new approach to defining what an audience for a national theatre could be. BTP was work that Kyeremateng and her peers felt needed to be done, and rather than wait on an institution to do it, they began a community campaign and through a crowdfunding campaign raised funds for 30 tickets. More than simply a ticket project, this scheme seeks to empower young black people to not only attend, but to enjoy, and perhaps even 'own' their experience. When young people attend an event with the BTP they are met by a volunteer facilitator who works with the project and are welcomed into the venue and supported through the rules of theatre. 'Accessing theatre isn't just about what you see, but also how you experience a venue once you're inside. The journey starts from your front door to your theatre seat' ("Black Ticket Project is creating opportunities for young Black people to access theatre. | Patreon," n.d.). Kyeremateng explained that not being able to go back to your seat if you go to the toilet, or sitting in the front row for a show, or not being permitted to bring a drink into the auditorium can all be confrontational experiences for the uninitiated. Since it began BTP has grown in its remit and has begun to partner with theatres (although it still maintains its position as a critical outsider), this alongside repeated crowdfunding campaigns has led to 1,000 tickets being made available for young black people to attend culturally relevant, exciting, and engaging theatre. Having operated completely independently to send young people to the *Barber Shop Chronicles* at the National Theatre for their first project, BTP have now partnered with the National Theatre. This has resulted in the National Theatre providing a quota of complementary tickets for their production of *Nine Nights* in 2018. The National Theatre also block-booked additional tickets which were offered at a discount rate, and thanks to a crowdfunding campaign by BTP, offered free at point of use to participants.

Both Open Field and Dialogue demonstrate ways that arts organisations are 'opening the gates' and creating new platforms for participation, exchange, storytelling and programming. BTP provides a more radical example of how underrepresented audiences are kicking open the gates and claiming space. However, what unites the three projects is that whilst different in their institutional relationships, they all seek to empower audiences and reassert the value, relevance and importance of the arts within a mass media, content-saturated world. As Kyremateng asserts 'It's important for young black people to know that this form of art exists and that they can reference it at some point' (Kyeremateng quoted in Akpan, 2018). It is perhaps fair to say that whilst Web 2.0 technologies and the cultures they have spawned have created many challenges for arts organisations, they have also provided new power structures that present the possibility of welcoming more diverse voices in, not to simply attend a performance or visit an exhibition, but to claim space and take ownership of their national institutions. As such arts managers must reflect upon how they can adopt born digital, participatory design into their everyday practices, in the work they programme and the audiences they engage with. Perhaps more challenging is the need for arts managers to engage with those seeking to claim space, to facilitate engagement, even if it is unexpected and uninvited. Authentic engagement may not derive from a strategic plan, but from a conversation on Twitter, or an interaction at an event. To be open to the unexpected is to welcome change, and as such it is both daunting and exciting, but ultimately in today's digitally saturated society it is also crucial to the continued relevance of our arts organisations.

References

Akpan, P. (2018). How one 23-year-old woman is making theatre accessible for black youth [WWW Document]. inews.co.uk. Available at: https://inews.co.uk/culture/arts/how-one-23-year-old-woman-is-making-theatre-accessible-for-black-youth/ [Accessed 15 Oct. 2018].

Bawden, D. (2001). Information and digital literacies: A review of concepts. *Journal of Documentation*, 57, pp. 218–259. https://doi.org/10.1108/EUM0000000007083

Bhaskar, M. (2017). *Curation: The power of selection in a world of excess*. London: Piatkus.

Black Theatre Live [WWW Document], (2018). Available at: www.blacktheatrelive.co.uk/news/black-ticket-project-creating-opportunities-for-young-black-people-to-access-theatre [Accessed 15 Oct. 2018].

Black Ticket Project is creating opportunities for young Black people to access theatre. | Patreon [WWW Document]. (n.d.). Patreon. Available at: www.patreon.com/blackticketproject/overview [Accessed 15 Oct. 2018].

Boorsma, M. and Chiaravalloti, F. (2010). Arts marketing performance: An artistic-mission-led approach to evaluation. *Journal of Arts Management, Law and Society*, 40, pp. 297–317. https://doi.org/10.1080/10632921.2010.525067

Bourdieu, P. (1986). The forms of capital. In: J.G. Richardson, ed., *Handbook of theory and research for the sociology of education*. Westport, Conn: Greenwood Press.

Boyd, D. (2012). Participating in the always-on lifestyle. In: M. Mandiberg, ed., *The social media reader*. New York: New York University Press, pp. 71–76.

Briziarelli, M. (2018). Spatial politics in the digital realm: The logistics/precarity dialectics and Deliveroo's tertiary space struggles. *Cultural Studies*, pp. 1–18. https://doi.org/10.1080/09502386.2018.1519583

Burgess, D. (2015). We can haz film fest!: Internet Cat Video Festival goes viral. *NECSUS European Journal of Media Studies*, 4, pp. 261–268. https://doi.org/10.5117/NECSUS2015.1.VAL4

Cadwalladr, C. and Graham-Harrison, E. (2018). Revealed: 50 million Facebook profiles harvested for Cambridge Analytica in major data breach. *The Guardian*.

Caust, J. (2017). *Arts leadership in contemporary contexts, Routledge advances in art and visual studies*. New York: Routledge.

Coleman, J. (1988). Social capital in the creation of human capital. *American Journal of Sociology*, 94, pp. 95–120.

Conway, T. and Whitelock, J. (2007). Relationship marketing in the subsidised arts: The key to a strategic marketing focus? *European Journal of Marketing*, 41, pp. 199–222. https://doi.org/10.1108/03090560 710718184

Costa, M. (2016). The critic as insider: Shifting UK critical practice towards "embedded" relationships and the routes this opens up towards dialogue and dramaturgy. In: D. Radosavljević, ed., *Theatre criticism: Changing landscapes*. London: Bloomsbury Methuen Drama, pp. 201–218.

Damian Martin, D. (2016). Unpeeling action: Critical writing, training and process. *Theatre, Dance and Performance Training*, 7, pp. 195–211. https://doi.org/10.1080/19443927.2016.1180318

Debatin, B., Lovejoy, J.P., Horn, A.-K. and Hughes, B.N. (2009). Facebook and online privacy: Attitudes, behaviors, and unintended consequences. *Journal of Computer-Mediated Communication*, 15, pp. 83–108. https://doi.org/10.1111/j.1083-6101.2009.01494.x

Drahokoupil, J. and Piasna, A. (2017). Work in the platform economy: Beyond lower transaction costs. *Intereconomics*, 52, pp. 335–340. https://doi.org/10.1007/s10272-017-0700-9

Fisher, E. and Fuchs, C. (eds.) (2015). *Reconsidering value and labour in the digital age*. London: Palgrave.

Fleming, T. (2009). *Embracing the desire lines: Opening up cultural infrastructure*. London: Cornerhouse.

Gauntlett, D. (2011). *Making is connecting: The social meaning of creativity from DIY and knitting to YouTube and Web 2.0*. Cambridge and Malden, MA: Polity Press.

Gilster, P. (1997). *Digital literacy, Wiley computer publishing*. New York: Wiley.

Glow, H. (2013). Cultural leadership and audience engagement: A case study of the Theatre Royal Stratford East. In: J. Caust, ed., *Arts leadership: International case studies*. Prahran, VIC: Tilde University Press, pp. 131–143.

Govier, D.L. (2009a). Leaders in co-creation? Why and how museums could develop their co-creative practice with the public, building on ideas from the performing arts and other non- museum organisations. Clore Leadership Report.

———. (2009b). Leaders in co-creation? Why and how museums could develop their co-creative practice with the public, building on ideas from the performing arts and other non- museum organisations. Clore Leadership.

Greffe, X. (2004). Artistic jobs in the digital age. *Journal of Arts Management, Law and Society*, 34, pp. 79–96. https://doi.org/10.3200/JAML.34.1.79-96

Guntaillike, R. (2008). Mission 2.0 advice for arts organisations and cultural organisations from the social web [WWW Document]. *Mission Models Money*. Available at: https://webcache.googleusercontent. com/search?q=cache:eYN0k8SsX2gJ:https://artsconnect.files.wordpress.com/2009/02/mission-20-advice-for-arts-cultural-organisationsfrom-the-social-web.doc+&cd=2&hl=en&ct=clnk&gl=uk [Accessed 6 Feb. 2018].

Hand, D.J. (2018). Aspects of data ethics in a changing world: Where are we now? *Big Data*, 6, pp. 176–190. https://doi.org/10.1089/big.2018.0083

Harris, J. (2018). The Cambridge Analytica saga is a scandal of Facebook's own making | John Harris | Opinion | The Guardian [WWW Document]. *The Guardian*. Available at: www.theguardian.com/commentisfree/2018/mar/21/cambridge-analytica-facebook-data-users-profit [Accessed 1 Aug. 2019].

Head, B.W. (2007). Community engagement: Participation on whose terms? *Australian Journal of Political Science*, 42, pp. 441–454. https://doi.org/10.1080/10361140701513570

Hobbs, R. (2010). *Digital and media literacy: A plan of action: A white paper on the digital and media literacy*. Recommendations of the Knight Commission on the information needs of communities in a democracy, Aspen Institute.

Hsieh, J. (2009). Strategic stakeholder orientations and performance consequences-a case of private non-profit performing arts in the US. *International Journal of Nonprofit and Voluntary Sector Marketing*, n/a–n/a. https://doi.org/10.1002/nvsm.364

Hsieh, J., Curtis, K.P. and Smith, A.W. (2008). Implications of stakeholder concept and market orientation in the US nonprofit arts context. *International Review on Public and Nonprofit Marketing*, 5, pp. 1–13. https://doi.org/10.1007/s12208-008-0001-x

Ippolito, J. (2012). Which commons: Market, zoo, or tribe? In: S. Schultz, ed., *Open field: Conversations on the commons*. Minneapolis: Walker Art Center, pp. 74–75.

Jones, B.R. and Flannigan, S.L. (n.d.). *Connecting the digital dots: Literacy of the 21st century*. https://er.educause. edu/articles/2006/1/connecting-the-digital-dots-literacy-of-the-21st-century

Kelly, L. (2010). How Web 2.0 is changing the nature of museum work: FORUM. *Curator: The Museum Journal*, 53, pp. 405–410. https://doi.org/10.1111/j.2151-6952.2010.00042.x

Kyeremateng, T. (2018). Programming "diverse" (sidenote: How do we get rid of this word?) work is only one leg of bringing in "diverse" audiences. A very important feat, but also think venues underestimate how much trust-building is involved in inviting in people you've alienated throughout your history. @bobimono.

Leadbeater, C. (2009). The Art of With. Cornerhouse, Manchester.

Mandiberg, M. (ed.) (2012). *The social media reader.* New York: New York University Press.

Miles, S. (2017). Do we have lift-off?" Social media marketing and digital performance at a British arts festival. *Journal of Arts Management, Law and Society*, pp. 1–16. https://doi.org/10.1080/10632921.2017.1366379

Milland, K. (2017). Slave to the keyboard: The broken promises of the gig economy. *Transfer: European Review of Labour and Resources*, 23, pp. 229–231. https://doi.org/10.1177/1024258917696233

Murphy, O. (2014). Increasing the digital literacy of museum professionals: Digital innovation and the museum sector in Northern Ireland (PhD). University of Ulster, Belfast.

———. (2016). Rethinking participatory practice in a web 2.0 world. In: K. McSweeney and J. Kavanagh, eds., *Museum participation. New directions for audience collaboration.* Edinburgh: Museum Etc.

Naughton, J. (2012). *From Gutenberg to Zuckerberg: What you really need to know about the internet.* London: Quercus Publ.

Nisbett, M. and Walmsley, B. (2016). The Romanticization of charismatic leadership in the arts. *Journal of Arts Management, Law and Society*, 46, pp. 2–12. https://doi.org/10.1080/10632921.2015.1131218

O'Reilly, T. (2005). What Is Web 2.0 [WWW Document]. Available at: www.oreilly.com/pub/a/web2/archive/what-is-web-20.html [Accessed 10 May 2018].

Persily, N. (2017). Can democracy survive the internet? *Journal of Democracy*, 28, pp. 63–76. https://doi.org/10.1353/jod.2017.0025

Peters, S. (2012). When bad things don't happen. In: S. Schultz, ed., *Open field: Conversations on the commons.* Minneapolis: Walker Art Center, pp. 127–144.

Pietrass, M. (2007). Digital literacy research from an international and comparative point of view. *Research in Comparative and International Education*, 2, pp. 1–12. https://doi.org/10.2304/rcie.2007.2.1.1

Putnam, R.D. (2001). *Bowling alone: The collapse and revival of American community.* 1st. touchstone ed. New York: Simon & Schuster.

Rentschler, R., Radbourne, J., Carr, R. and Rickard, J. (2002). Relationship marketing, audience retention and performing arts organisation viability. *International Journal of Nonprofit and Voluntary Sector Marketing*, 7, pp. 118–130. https://doi.org/10.1002/nvsm.173

Richardson, J. (2017). The National Gallery predicts the future with artificial intelligence. MuseumNext.

Rosen, J. (2012). The people formerly known as the audience. In: M. Mandiberg, ed., *The social media reader.* New York: New York University Press, pp. 13–16.

Russo, A. and Peacock, D. (2009). Great expectations: Sustaining participation in social media spaces | museumsandtheweb.com. Presented at the Museums and the Web.

Simon, N. (2010). The participatory museum. Museum 2.0, Santa Cruz, California.

Stein, R. (2012). Chiming in on museums and participatory culture. *Curator: The Museum Journal*, 55, pp. 215–226. https://doi.org/10.1111/j.2151-6952.2012.00141.x

Stein, R. (n.d.). Technology: The catalyst for change in the future of museums. Mus.-ID.

Stewart, A. and Stanford, J. (2017). Regulating work in the gig economy: What are the options? *The Economic and Labour Relations Review*, 28, pp. 420–437. https://doi.org/10.1177/1035304617722461

Stutzman, N. (2016). The Dallas Museum of Art Friends program – More knowledge by friends. [WWW Document]. www.artsmanagement.net. URL www.artsmanagement.net/Articles/The-Dallas-Museum-of-Art-Friends-program-More-knowledge-by-friends,3754 [Accessed 1 Aug. 2019].

Theatre Club Handbook: New Conversations About Theatre, (n.d.). Fuel Theatre.

Walker Art Center and Schultz, S. (eds.) (2012). *Open field: Conversations on the commons.* 1st ed. Minneapolis: Walker Art Center.

6

ARTIST MANAGEMENT IN THE AGE OF BIG DATA

Guy Morrow

Introduction

This chapter concerns artist management practices within the creative and cultural industries, specifically within the music, dance and film sectors, during the period 2009 to 2018. It therefore locates artist management practices within a time period that includes the present historical moment; a context in which there is increasingly prevalent discourse concerning 'big data' and 'automation' and the impact these will have on the lives and work of future human beings. The premise of this chapter is that we need thriving artists to have thriving arts organisations and a healthy arts sector overall. It is in this context that this chapter examines the question: in what ways does the data economy impact artist management practices? It presents a spectrum of engagement with data analytics services from what I will call 'small data' to 'big data' and asks an additional research question: can data analytics services that are specific to the arts help artists to thrive? In addition to an engagement with the data from in-depth semi-structured interviews with artist managers and self-managed artists, this chapter presents brief case studies of services such as Culture Counts, an Australian and United Kingdom-based company that believes in using data to inform arts management-related decisions; Capacity Interactive, a New York-based company that likewise believes in using data to inform arts management-related decisions; Next Big Sound, a New York-based company that believes in the power of data to transform the music industries; Music Glue, a London-based company that enables artists and other entities in the music industries to control their own data with a specific focus on direct artist-to-fan relations; and Facebook, the largest online social media and social networking service company in the world. This chapter considers the extent to which these services are automating artist management. In doing so, it examines what small and big data mean for the field of arts management.

In my earlier work (Morrow, 2018), I argued that artist management is organic, adaptable and diverse and that it contrasts with other forms of management that emphasize linearity, conformity and standardization. I also posited (following Hesmondhalgh and Baker, 2011) that the uniqueness of artist management stems from its subordination to artistic creativities and the fact that such symbolic creativities are artistically/aesthetically autonomous and "cannot be reduced to set rules or procedures" (Hesmondhalgh and Baker, 2011, p. 84). Of central concern to this chapter is the question of how the data deluge affects the artistic/aesthetic autonomy of the artist, and also the professional autonomy of the artist manager. Therefore, this chapter ultimately examines whether artistic creativity and managerial creativity are immune to metric power (Beer, 2016) or not.

This chapter draws on the theoretical notion that, for artists, there has been a paradigm shift from linear career progression, which was characterized by an initial dependency on the subjective, and therefore supposedly more autonomous, 'gut instincts' of gatekeepers such as artist managers, illustrated in Figure 6.1, to circular career progression (Hughes et al. 2016). Circular career progression in the arts, illustrated in Figure 6.2, involves artists initially connecting directly with audiences via digital means and then the still required gatekeepers or 'cultural intermediaries' (Bourdieu, 1993), reacting to (more) objective data and metrics that demonstrate a particular artist has some traction in a market already, before they invest time, money and energy.

Through this process, artist management-related decisions, initially at least, become less subjective or 'autonomous' and more driven by audience small data. In this way, circular career progression potentially undermines the notion of the 'liberal artist' (Wiseman-Trowse, 2008); in this paradigm the artist is potentially not as free to self-express because they are responding to audience data during the process of creating their work. This also potentially affects the artist manager's contributions to their client's artistic creativity. In my earlier work (Morrow, 2018),

Figure 6.1 Linear career progression

Source: Adapted from Hughes et al., 2016, p. 29

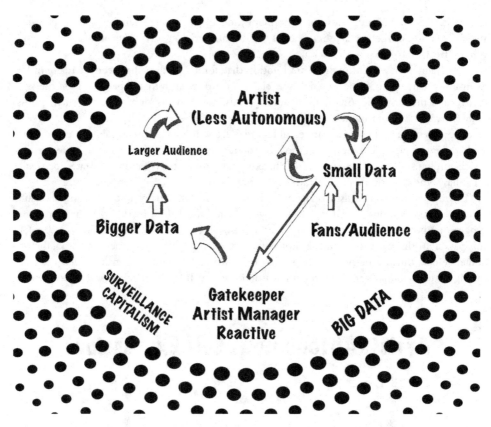

Figure 6.2   Circular career progression

Source: Adapted from Hughes et al., 2016, p. 30

I defined artist management as a form of group creativity that involves the interaction between artistic creativities and managerial creativities (see p. 8). I argued that defining artist management in this way enables us to pluralise this form of creativity and to conceptualise it as a dialectic between these two clusters of creativities, creativities that are at times in conflict, and at other times in harmony. And obviously artists and their managers each sometimes make contributions to each other's creativities. For example, The Rolling Stones' early manager Andrew Loog Old-ham's visual intelligence was pivotal in them being positioned as the antithesis to The Beatles; he is arguably responsible for the band's early visual (photographic) representation as 'bad boys' (see Oldham, 2000, 2003). Therefore, in such a way, artist managers sometimes make artistically creative contributions to their clients' careers and these contributions are also potentially going to be caught up in small and big data circulations.

While research to date into data analytics services that specialize in the cultural sector, such as Culture Counts, has focused on the potential incorporation of such data analysis into cultural policy assessment frameworks and arts organizations' existing evaluation capacities (Gilmore, Glow and Johanson, 2017; Moore, 2016; Phiddian et al., 2017; Wright, 2018), this chapter will examine their potential adoption within artists', and artist managers', evaluation capacities.

Big data

While acknowledging that there is no agreed definition of big data, Kitchin (2014), who is a professor at the National Institute of Regional and Spatial Analysis at the National University of Ireland Maynooth, has compiled some of the various attempts to articulate what big data are. According to him, they are:

- Huge in *volume*, consisting of terabytes or petabytes of data
- High in *velocity*, being created in or near real-time
- Diverse in *variety* in type, being structured and unstructured in nature, and often temporally and spatially referenced
- *Exhaustive* in scope, striving to capture entire populations or systems (n = all), or at least much larger sample sizes than would be employed in traditional, small data studies
- Fine-grained in *resolution*, aiming to be as detailed as possible, and uniquely *indexical* in identification
- *Relational* in nature, containing common fields that enable the conjoining of different datasets
- *Flexible*, holding the traits of extensionality (can add new fields easily) and *scalable* (can expand in size rapidly) (68)

Such a definition of big data needs to be accompanied with a discussion of the economic value of this form of measurement in the digital age. Regarding big data, Davis, who is the Vice-Chancellor of the University of Melbourne, noted:

> Today, the world's most valuable resource is no longer oil but data. Amazon, Apple, Facebook, Microsoft and Alphabet, Google's parent company, are the five most valuable listed firms in the world, collectively taking in over US$25 billion in the first quarter of 2017 alone.
>
> *(in Goldbloom and Davis, 2017)*

The age of surveillance capitalism (Zuboff, 2018) is therefore upon us and it presents some artists and their managers with a contradictory situation. The aforementioned circular career development model (see Figure 6.2 and also Hughes et al., 2016) necessitates artists attempting to engage an audience directly in order to demonstrate enough signs of exponential growth (by way of metrics) in order to attract various cultural intermediaries. Some cultural intermediaries are still needed because they are the ones who can harness the energy generated by direct artist to fan connections and, by adding resources, can help grow the artist's career. However, for artists, and to a lesser extent their managers, discussing their audience data and becoming surveillance capitalists themselves by monitoring their own audience in this way is the new 'selling out'.[1]

Selling out

The countercultural concept of selling out relates to the artistic/aesthetic autonomy of the artist and the way in which discussions of this form of autonomy help to construct (perceptions of) the authenticity of the artist. It therefore relates to the age-old art versus commerce dichotomy.[2] While authors such as Goodman (1998) have successfully outlined the way in which artists and countercultural figures such as Bob Dylan were able to, with the help of manager Albert Grossman, negotiate artistic freedom and construct an 'authentic' persona within the countercultural movement of the 1960s – all the while being very interested in his career and the market for his music – in the age of big data, the notion of 'selling out' has morphed from practices such as licensing music for use in an advertisement (arguably no longer selling out – see Hughes et al., 2016, p. 71), to discussions of the use of metrics by artists in attempts to understand their audience.

This notion of selling out therefore relates to the autonomy of the artist and the freedom artists have to create and to shape their own lives. This concept needs to be revisited in the age of big data. Historically speaking, Banks (2010) noted that autonomy in cultural production has been associated with freedom from commercial concerns since the late eighteenth century and was originally associated with Romanticism. The Romantics conceptualized the artist as a being a special, rare and unique individual who possessed a fragile 'gift' – a gift that could be undermined by rational calculation in the (then) modern era. Since this time however, there have been numerous critiques of the notion of autonomy in cultural work which Banks (2010) has astutely summarized (see pp. 254–259). In contrast to these critiques however, Banks engaged with the work of Ryan (1992) to argue that autonomy is in fact *guaranteed* due to the fact that creative labor resists the abstractness and alienation to which other forms of labor are subject under capitalism due to the 'named status' of the artist. The fact that there is a demand within the creative and cultural industries for original products that are generated by named artists and collectives such as bands impairs, and essentially blocks, the efforts of the capitalist system to standardize and depersonalize creative labor. Whether this remains the case in the age of surveillance capitalism, however is a specific concern of this chapter.

Small data

From the perspective of artists, the best way to understand contemporary versions of the practice of 'selling out' is to consider the relationship between 'small data' and 'big data' and to engage with Beer's (2016) notion of circulation. Banafa (2015) noted that "small data connects people with timely, meaningful insights (derived from big data and/or "local" sources), organized and packaged – often visually – to be accessible, understandable, and actionable for everyday tasks" (np), while Rouse (2014) argued that

> The term *small data* contrasts with *big data*, which usually refers to a combination of structured and unstructured data that may be measured in petabytes or exabytes . . . which combine to make big data very difficult to manage. Small data, in contrast, consists of usable chunks.
>
> *(np)*

When considering artist management practices, it becomes clear that the use of small data is nothing new. A single audience member's reaction to a piece of music, a dramatic work, or visual art in a cave could be considered to be a piece of small data. Further, discussing what has *not changed* within the music sector of the creative and cultural industries, rather than what *has changed* in the age of big data, Watson (2013) noted that some music entrepreneurs from the past used live performance to gauge audience interest and thus the potential size of the market for recorded music. He noted that they would "walk into a venue and look left, then look right, and if they couldn't see the walls of the venue past the crowd they would sign the band." However, while artist management has involved use of small data in this way, when the small data is gleaned via services such as Facebook and takes the form of micro moments of positivity reinforcement when a (so-called) friend likes a draft of an artistic idea, this small data-related interaction inevitably gets caught up in what Beer (2016) calls a process of *circulation*.

Metric power

For Beer (2016), circulation forms part of a tripartite theory of what he calls 'metric power'. In examining the linkages between metrics and power in the contemporary setting, Beer focused on the relations that exist between *measurement, circulation,* and *possibility.* In an age in which many significant developments will center around data, Beer examined how measurement links into power, governance, and control and argued that it is in the relations between *measurement, circulation,* and *possibility* that we can locate and understand metric power. Essentially, his neo-Foucauldian concept of 'metric power' involves an attempt to understand the power dynamics around and within big data. In relation to artist management practices, it is therefore important to consider how small data-related circulations and feedback loops that are generated when artists test artistic ideas via social media, for example, interweave into the power structures of big data through their circulation.

The concept of circulation relates to the way in which data that are produced feed back into the further production of data, and, according to Beer, the way in which they do so in different and unequal ways. Some measurements are more visible and powerful than others and they can also take on a life of their own. Of particular relevance to this chapter are the ways data moves feedback and circulation forward in the creative processes involved in cultural production. In an earlier work, Beer (2013) attempted to understand how data circulate back into culture and thereby transform the way in which culture is produced, disseminated and consumed. Referring to this earlier work in his 2016 book, he noted that:

> Culture has always had its circulations – of shared symbols, images, and trends – but these circulations of data and metrics represent an expansion and energising of these circulatory pathways. We need to understand the underlying politics of these circulations of data.
>
> *(87)*

Beer argued relating to the underlying politics that systems of measurement and data extraction are the means of *neoliberalization* (14), whereby almost everything within social and political life becomes defined through competition within markets.

In the context of the arts, what is most interesting about these systems of measurement and data extraction is their intolerance of ambiguity. The open-ended nature of artistic creativity and the ambiguity that often stems from attempts to answer questions relating to what art actually is, what it is for, and what 'good' it is,[3] means that, as Radbourne, Johanson, and Glow (2010) found, arts managers often find it difficult to articulate exactly what audiences get out of the experiences that they help to create. Both small and big data's hostility toward ambiguity has come to the forefront of current debates relating to data analytics services that have been specifically designed for the arts.

This is where the ambivalence of services such as Culture Counts and Capacity Interactive enters the frame. On the one hand, these services offer a tantalizing possibility of being able to move arts managers beyond the aforementioned ambiguity toward being able to measure artistic 'quality' and impact. This includes an ability to use metrics to articulate stories relating to the intrinsic/cultural value of the arts. On the other hand, according to some (such as Phiddian et al., 2017), they are a threat to the sector because they will undermine the artistic freedom and the open-ended and ambiguous nature of artistic creativity.

Culture Counts

In their provocatively entitled article 'Counting Culture to Death', Phiddian et al. (2017) provided an Australian perspective on the company Culture Counts, which is a "digital evaluation platform for measuring cultural impact" (Culture Counts, n.d.), and they extrapolated their perspective to make arguments relating to the use of quality metrics in the arts generally. It is through services such as Culture Counts that we see a head-on collision between the ambiguity stemming from understandings of art and systems of measurement and data extraction. In relation to this service, Phiddian et al. (2017) ultimately argued that "the quantifying turn in cultural policy is not delivering on its promises and . . . its unintended consequences are destructive" (1) and that while "statistical data, well channelled, may provide useful ancillary information . . . where questions of value are concerned, it cannot replace critical judgment" (Ibid). In contrast, Gilmore, Glow, and Johanson (2017) provided a more balanced analysis of Culture Counts' claim that the data collected using their tools can help arts managers and organisations "to produce richer stories about their unique impact and value, facilitate deeper engagement and interaction with audiences and communities, and build stronger cases for support and investment" (Culture Counts, n.d.). Their study concerned various arts organizations' use of this service in two different territories, namely, Australia and the UK, and in terms of their findings, Gilmore, Glow, and Johanson (2017) noted that:

> participating organisations experienced Culture Counts as an efficient mode of data collection in a standardised form that provided opportunities for networking with stakeholders . . . It reinforced their existing knowledge of their audiences, and produced data in a form that provides evidence of impact for Funders.
>
> *(292)*

Their research findings did not however provide evidence of a capacity to build public understandings of the qualitative meanings people derive from art; the service does not help to address the ambiguity stemming from attempts to articulate the 'value' of the arts. They also argued that Culture Counts does not promote the means for audiences to partake in artistic decision-making and that it has the effect of reinforcing pre-existing understandings of artistic value. As a consequence, it perpetuates art forms that are already prioritized by cultural policies and funding bodies and therefore reinforces the power of the status quo in the arts.

A question arises here as to whether Culture Counts data can be classified as big or small. While generally researchers such as Gilmore, Glow, and Johanson (2017), Crossick and Kaszynska (2014) and Gilmore, Arvanitis, and Albert (2018) have noted that big data is of interest to the arts sector and to cultural policy makers, they have also noted that to date this interest has merely been speculative and that their work only speaks to the *potential* use of big data. Essentially, according to Gilmore, Arvanitis, and Albert (2018), the data generated by Culture Counts is not big enough to be classified as big data. Therefore, in the context of a discussion of circulation in this chapter, and of the interrelationship between small and big data, Culture Counts can be classified as a small data organization. However, circulations of this data arguably do reverberate within the broader big data economy, and following Beer's (2016) argument that data analytics permeates an increasing number of areas within society, when considering artist management it is hard not to argue that the small data circulations obtained through services such as Culture Count impact artistic creativity.

It is in this context that the tendency of arts management research by authors such as Phiddian et al. (2017), Gilmore, Glow, and Johanson (2017), Crossick and Kaszynska (2014) and

Gilmore, Arvanitis, and Albert (2018) to focus on cultural policy and arts organizations is striking given that, in the arts sector in Australia for example, 77 percent of all artists identify as freelancers/self-employed artists, while 87 percent of visual artists identify as being freelance/self-employed (Throsby and Zednik, 2010, p. 53). Given these percentages, and the fact that the largest amount of funding allocated by the Australia Council during the 2013–14 financial year went to major performing arts organizations and key organizations (Australia Council, 2014, pp. 20–21), artists and artist managers are often left to their own devices. Yet we need thriving artists to have thriving arts organizations and a healthy arts sector overall.

This chapter therefore fills a gap within this body of literature by focusing on the ways in which artists, self-managed artist entrepreneurs and artist managers shape futures for themselves in ways that increasingly interact with the data economy. This is particularly important given that, as Segers, Schramme, and Devriendt (2010) noted, there is a paradox relating to arts policy: "although the arts have been largely embedded within organizational and management structures, the situation of individual artists has become more vulnerable" (58). This chapter therefore seeks to work towards addressing this gap in our knowledge.

Research design: selection of industries, cases and participants

This chapter reports on a subsection of a research project concerning artist management within the creative and cultural industries that was carried out in New York, London, Toronto, Sydney and Melbourne between 2009 and 2017.[4] I conducted semi-structured interviews with 22 artist managers and self-managed artists across three sectors of the creative and cultural industries: music, dance and film. This method was supplemented by analysis of the trade press associated with each industry and data analytics services such as Culture Counts, Capacity Interactive, Next Big Sound, and Music Glue as well as the social media platform Facebook. I selected these three industries because they involve two of the different circles that constitute Throsby's (2008) seminal concentric circles model of the creative and cultural industries. Throsby's concentric circles model has four layers or circles that are used to classify the industries that produce cultural goods and services:

Core creative arts

- Literature
- Music
- Performing arts
- Visual arts

Other core cultural industries

- Film
- Museums, galleries, libraries
- Photography

Wider cultural industries

- Heritage services
- Publishing and print media
- Sound recording
- Television and radio
- Video and computer games

Related industries

- Advertising
- Architecture
- Design
- Fashion

(Throsby, 2008, p. 149)

This research project primarily concerned the core creative arts, and, through a consideration of artist management strategies, the relationship between this core and the outer circles of this model. I selected the music industries and the dance industries because they form part of the core layer of this model, while I selected the film industries because they represent the second layer of this model.

All participants agreed to take part on the basis of anonymity and therefore names and organizations are not identified in order to protect the participants' identities. The interviewees' names that are used in this chapter are pseudonyms.[5] In this research project I employed a qualitative approach. The aim was to capture an aspect of the creative and cultural industries – artist management – as it is experienced, and interpreted, by the participants in this project. To this end, I employed an 'intensive' rather than an 'extensive' (Harré, 1979) research design. I investigated how artist management practices work in a small number of cases in order to generate explanations of the development of artists' careers and of the experiences involved in artist–artist manager relationships.

This project began with an examination of the extent to which the international music industries have decentralized, and whether this has shifted commercial control from monopoly companies, such as major record labels, to smaller artist–artist manager teams. The scope of this project was then broadened to include self-managed artists and artist managers working within the film and dance industries. This made the project unique as most other studies have tended to be confined to one cultural industry. The primary research questions for this project then became: what is it like to manage artists in the creative and cultural industries? Or if you are a self-managed artist, what is it like to manage your own career? Are agile management strategies used within the creative and cultural industries? Can agile methods be used for managing artists within the creative and cultural industries? In what way does the data economy impact artist management practices? Can data analytics services that are specific to the arts help artists to thrive?

When selecting interviewees in each industry, I made an effort to achieve a balance between male and female participants. However, an even split between the two sexes was not achievable due to the fact that the sector that was the initial focus of this project, the music industry, is still male dominated (see Henry, 2009, p. 143). In total, four females and 18 males were interviewed for this study. Balance was also sought in terms of the following dimensions: those well established in their industries, newcomers and mid-career workers; older and younger participants; participants working for larger artist management companies and those working on a freelance basis; those working in New York City and London, two central areas for Western cultural production, and those working outside of these cities. The recruitment of interviewees was guided by these efforts. However, I also made the most of serendipitous opportunities for interview leads provided by some of the participants.

Findings

Like the literature concerning Culture Counts, data analytics, cultural policy, and arts organizations (Phiddian et al., 2017, Gilmore, Glow, and Johanson, 2017 and Gilmore, Arvanitis, and

Albert, 2018), the arguments presented in this chapter relating to artist management in the age of big data are also speculative. While evidence relating to the use of small data by artists and artist managers has been obtained (see Hughes et al., 2016), the argument here – that by reacting to small data circulations artist managers and other types of gatekeepers are feeding the big data economy – primarily relates to possibilities and potentialities. This is because a limitation of this study concerns scale: big data is so big that it is beyond the scope of this chapter to be able to zoom out to that level. Therefore, rather than zooming out, the interview data relating to artist management practices will be used to zoom in to a discussion of these practices in relation to some key trends that have emerged relating to 'measurement' and 'labor' generally.

Measuring managerial creativities

A key question that emerged during the research interviews concerned the immeasurability of artist management labor. When considering how human capital, 'people data' (Deloitte, 2015) and analytics could inform the interrelationship between artists and artist managers, it is important to note that artist managers work for their artist clients. However, as they are most often service providers to artists, rather than direct employees, they are somewhat immune to new approaches that are being used in other fields to quantify human capital and reinvent Human Resources by utilizing new access to people data in order to measure performance. Discussing the immeasurability of artist management labor, one London-based artist manager in music and interviewee for this project, Jack, noted that artist management is:

> fairly intangible. . . . There's not always enough concrete stuff to show from a very busy manager to the client of what they've actually been doing with their time. . . . They know what their accountant does. They know what their lawyer does. They often don't know what the manager does . . . management is a huge pie of stuff you have to do. It includes managing the lawyer and managing the accountant.
>
> *(Interview 2)*

In this way artist management is intangible, adaptable and diverse and it contrasts with other forms of management, and labor generally, that may be more measurable. Managers are generalists by their very nature, whereas, within the music sector specifically, lawyers and accountants are specialists.

Similarly, regarding the issue of self-management in the contemporary dance sector, as well as in-kind support from friends and family, Sydney-based and self-managed contemporary dancer and interviewee for this research project, Anne, noted that this form of labor is even more immeasurable:

> If I was to do some sort of economic case study of how I've gotten to this point, the amount of resources, financial, 'in kind' from friends, family, from myself that have gone into my career, essentially supporting dance in Australia, are huge. Above and beyond the government funding. That is never accounted for and I think there's something to be said for acknowledging how much time people put into it where it is unpaid, where it is in kind, not to mention people around them who are supporting them and making it possible for them to do what they do.
>
> *(Interview 3)*

Therefore, self-managed artists and artist managers, due to the nature of their labor, may be immune from the emergence of people data to measure their performance as managers/self-managers.

However, in both the case where a separate artist manager is involved and when an artist is self-managing, the data economy has changed *how* they give advice, or *how* they strategize for themselves. Regarding how the cultural industries *used* to function, Williamson, Cloonan, and Frith (2011) noted that:

> The music industries . . . are organized around two givens that are considered to be essentially irrational (and therefore in a sense unknowable) – musical/artistic talent, on the one hand; public/consumer taste, on the other . . . one consequence is that a premium is put on what one might call experiential knowledge.
>
> *(460)*

In contrast to this however, according to Watson (2016), this reliance on experiential knowledge has lessened due to the increasing use of small data to drive decisions. According to him, the cultural industries now function in the following way:

> Industry intermediaries no longer have to just back their instincts – instead they can support whatever is already generating an exponential adoption curve within their audience. As a result, garnering the support of such powerful people now typically depends on pointing to proof of early reactivity rather than on appeals to gut feel or longstanding relationships. The gatekeeper role has largely shifted from a seemingly omniscient picking of 'winners' to a role of enabling and amplifying audience 'likes'.
>
> *(Foreword in Hughes et al., 2016, p. ix)*

The tension between advice that is based on data/evidence versus advice that is based on a vaguer reference to experience has come to the foreground when considering use of data generally within the creative and cultural industries (see Saintilan and Schreiber, 2018, pp. 130–138). Interestingly, one interviewee, London-based artist manager in music, Jack, noted that artist managers' typical reliance on a certain type of vague, experiential knowledge put them at a disadvantage when it came to dealing with 'professional advisors' such as lawyers and accountants:

> I think at the moment a lot of managers are at a big disadvantage. There's an authority on a lawyer's opinion that there isn't with a manager's opinion, even if the opinion is just, "Should we sign with Universal or Sony?" It's really not a technical legal thing. The manager's opinion would be less weighty than the lawyer's in general. Obviously, there's exceptions with very big managers.
>
> *(Interview 2)*

Arguably a lawyer's advice is also often based on experiential knowledge to the extent that they may refer to their experience of working with their entire client base with vague reference to 'previous cases', with the specific evidence substantiating their assertions not being able to be disclosed (often conveniently) due to issues of confidentiality. For interviewee Jack, the different weight of advice partly also stems from the fact that lawyers are regulated and need to be licensed, whereas, for the most part, artist managers are not regulated. This lack of regulation in turn relates to the immeasurability of artist management labor, a lack that sometimes works in managers' favor, and other times not. This lack of measurability and associated lack of regulation particularly works against artist managers when it comes to the level of risk to which their time investment in a client's career is exposed.

Interestingly, one London-based senior artist manager in music and interviewee for this project, Tom, discussed the issue of the duty of care that artist managers have to their clients and also whether artist managers in the future will more often be able to take out insurance in attempts to protect their speculative investment of time in developing a client's career:

> Many of our clients aren't easy to manage for various different reasons and one of them is that sometimes our clients can be very unstable individuals and at what point as a manager do you cease to be responsible? Or you are unable to be responsible because the recipient is unwilling or unable to take advice? So, there is a real area sitting in there and I somehow like the expression of a 'duty of care' and I wonder if it would be possible to turn it into a commercial application.
>
> *(Interview 1)*

In the age of data analytics, artist managers such as Tom could insist on using devices such as the Apple Watch to coach and monitor their clients. In their advertising, Apple boasts that the Apple Watch could become your personal trainer and it is through use of these technologies that metric power could directly impact the artist–artist manager relationship. As Beer (2016) noted: "Metric power is not just about such hi-tech devices, but these provide us with a visible marker how our bodies can be directly interfaced into the infrastructures of metric harvesting" (6). In this way, for better or worse, devices such as the Apple Watch could automate the exercise of a duty of care to clients for which managers are responsible. Interviewee Tom noted regarding the issue of insurance, that:

> I'm a manager, I manage one big act, my big act is very unstable, but I have to commit myself 100% to that artist, whether or not they perform . . . in certain circumstances . . . an artist has demanded that the manager is exclusive to them. . . . So, if as a manager you are reliant 100% on the performance of your client, then, if you're client can't perform, that's a problem. And to my knowledge there are levels of insurance you can take but they are hard to find and they only exist at the top end of the earning structure because they are all financed relatively. . . . What provision is there between an artist and a management representative in the event that the artist is unable to perform?
>
> *(Interview 1)*

According to Beer (2016), insurance companies increasingly "offer reduced premiums and other incentives if you are prepared to share the metrics from your wearable device with them" (7). The lifestyles of artists captured in such metrics could shape artist managers' decisions about where they invest their time, which client they prioritize and the extent to which they can insure their investment of time.

Measuring artistic creativities

While the performance of artist managers and self-managed artists in their managerial roles may be somewhat immune to metric power due to the intangible and generalist nature of what they do, there are numerous means for artist managers to access small data relating to their artist/client's performance, or their own artistic performance if they are self-managed. These include the aforementioned data analytics service Culture Counts, as well as Capacity Interactive, Next Big Sound, Music Glue, Facebook and many other services. While small data has arguably always been used by artists to test ideas and to garner general feedback, these services offer artists an opportunity to quantify this type of feedback more efficiently. As I have argued elsewhere (see Morrow, 2018), this means that theories and processes relating to agile project management are relevant here. This is because a number of participants in the broader research project from which this chapter draws noted that they do not use traditional planning and that the perceived tension between 'management' and 'artistic creativity' is partly due to the fact that, from their perspectives, management is trying to generate a rigid plan for something that is quite fluid, free spirited and agile. As one Sydney-based and self-managed contemporary dancer and inter-viewee for this project, Anne, noted:

> I'm starting this new work, and I know what some of the initial things are that I'm interested in, but I don't know what it is or what it adds up to. . . . I look for and respond to invitations and opportunities. I look for opportunities and go "oh yeah, I can do something for that." And by saying that it forces me to focus in and pull something together. So hopefully it will accumulate over the next couple of years so that I will be clearer in knowing what it is. So, looking for any performance opportu-nities and especially low-key ones, to test out ideas, to try images, and to see what the response is. (*Interview 21* cited in Morrow, 2018, p. 27)
>
> (Interview 3)

Therefore, rather than using more traditional project management approaches by pursuing pre-set goals or opportunities and assembling means after a goal is set, artists such as Anne work in ways that are more in line with agile project management (Morrow, 2018, p. 52). Through their artistically creative processes, they literally use build-measure-learn feedback through their engagement with their collaborators, and with their audience. For example, by enabling par-ticipants to respond to change, rather than follow a rigid plan, agile management often involves small teams that work autonomously so that they can be agile in their response to small data, with managers therefore managing for goals rather than micromanaging processes. Therefore, for Medinilla (2012), one of the key principles of agile management is self-organization. Dis-cussing this principle in relation to her collaborative process when dance making, interviewee Anne noted:

> I see a lot of dance people who hold on tightly to the ideas and the images and the aesthetic and within that the collaborators are serving the dance or serving that main thing. I always try not to have that heavy hold. I think maybe when I was younger I was a bit more prescriptive, but now I try to trust my collaborators that whatever they come up with, and then of course there's that next process of to-ing and fro-ing and working out the nitty-gritty, but I like to give them quite a lot of freedom.
>
> (Interview 3)

While a dancer's reaction to a dance maker's instruction is a form of small data, and such interac-tion during a collaborative process is certainly not a new phenomenon, what is new is the ability to use audience feedback concerning art works that are in the making at a much earlier stage of the creative process through engaging various data analytics services.

Of course, involving the audience in the artistically creative process goes against the historical baggage in the arts relating to notions of the liberal artist, authenticity, and selling out, and this is why arts-related data analytics services such as Capacity Interactive, Culture Counts, Next Big Sound and Music Glue use the following, arguably cautious, language on their websites:

Measurement: We believe in using data to inform decisions. If it's digital, measure something. Let data help decide, but don't let it take over (Capacity Interactive, n.d.).

Imagine a scenario where cultural organisations . . . are measuring the quality of their work using a standardised set of metrics that they themselves have shaped . . . to benefit from real-time data analytics. . . . Imagine they are using this data to make better cultural programming decisions . . . and grow audiences (Culture Counts, n.d.).

Artists, managers, labels, merchandisers and promoters use Music Glue to control their online presence and e-commerce with ease, owning their data and selling anything, to anyone, anywhere, via any device, in over 25 languages and currencies (Music Glue, n.d.).

We believe in the power of data to transform the music industry: Launched in 2009, Next Big Sound is the leading provider of online music analytics and insights, tracking hundreds of thousands of artists around the world (Next Big Sound, n.d.).

Clearly, these small-data–related services are cautious in their approach in this sector, alluding to notions of not letting data take control (Capacity Interactive) and to the idea that the arts sector itself is involved in shaping any standardized set of metrics that are being used (Culture Counts).

Conclusion

When considering Beer's (2016) notion of metric power and the extent to which the small data circulate via these services then in turn forms part of big data circulations, there are very real causes for concern relating to the freedom of artistic expression and the independence of 'liberal' artists. For example, data could potentially be used by arts organisations, artists and their managers in a way that is similar to how it is allegedly being deployed in political campaigning. In the context of a discussion of changes to advertising and political campaigning, Pesce (2017) is critical of influential data analytics firm Cambridge Analytica because it:

harvests every bit of data publicly available about a voter, cross-references it to generate a profile of that voter, then . . . purchases Facebook advertising targeted at the voter and designed to 'trigger' that voter into making a desired voting choice.

(6–7)

According to Pesce (2017), Cambridge Analytica founder Robert Mercer is friends with former United Kingdom Independence Party (UKIP) leader Nigel Farage and former US President Donald Trump adviser Steve Bannon (who also at one stage worked for the firm) and therefore he puts the question of whether the Brexit and Trump political successes had more to do with Cambridge Analytica's capacities to drive 'persuadable' voters to their desired outcomes, than to the widely touted anti-establishment revolt. According to the Australian Broadcasting Corporation (ABC News, 2018a), on the 20th of March 2018, a Cambridge Analytica employee turned whistleblower disclosed that a major privacy breach had occurred when Facebook enabled Cambridge Analytica to mine the data of 50 million users to use in targeted political advertising in their attempts to help Donald Trump win the 2016 US election. As a result, according to the Australian Broadcasting Corporation (ABC News, 2018b): "Facebook had its worst trading day in five years, in the wake of the report, with about $US35 billion ($45.38 billion) wiped off its total market value overnight".

Communication is fundamentally changing and the arts form part of many systems of communication and, partly thanks to data analytics services such as Culture Counts, Capacity

Interactive, Music Glue and Next Big Sound, artistically creative processes are arguably being impacted here. There is clearly potential for artists and artist managers to use data analytics services to design strategies that will persuade consumers to purchase or to fund their art over the art of their competitors. This arguably presents artists with a highly sophisticated and non-transparent means of 'selling out'. In this way, marketing would move much further forward in the creative process in a way that parallels the impact of big data on political campaigning. As Cambridge Analytica CEO Alexander Nix (2016) noted: "We can use hundreds or thousands of individual data points on our targeted audiences to understand exactly which messages are going to appeal to which audiences way before the creative process starts" (in Goldbloom and Davis, 2017). Furthermore, Pesce (2017) posits that deliberate emotional exploitation and monitoring are arguably central to Facebook's business model. Therefore, when artists post artistic ideas to this social media platform with a view to generating small data feedback loops that they can then use to inform their next creative direction, these small data circulations can potentially be swept up in Facebook's use of big data to generate revenue for its shareholders.

These concerns remain, despite the findings of this research that the immeasurability of artist management labor makes it somewhat immune to new approaches that are being used in other fields to quantify human capital. This also applies to self-management labor in the arts which, as we saw in the contemporary dance sector, is a form of labor that is even more immeasurable. While these managerial creativities are somewhat immeasurable, artistic creativity and an artist's wellbeing are potentially more measurable. The findings of this research suggest that artist managers in the future will more often be able to take out insurance in attempts to protect their speculative investment of time in developing a client's career. In this way, for better or worse, devices such as the Apple Watch could automate the exercise of a duty of care to clients for which artist managers are partly responsible.

Notes

1 For an in-depth discussion of the notion of 'selling out' within the music industries in the digital age, see Klein, Meier and Powers, 2017 and Hesmondhalgh, 1999.
2 See Hesmondhalgh and Baker, 2011, pp. 81–112 for a detailed discussion of this dichotomy.
3 For an in-depth discussion relating to what 'good' the arts are, see Carey (2005).
4 A larger subsection of the data from this research project has been published in Morrow (2018). See this publication for a longer outline of the research design for this project.
5 See Appendix A for a list of the interviewees and the pseudonyms used in this study.

References

ABC News. (2018a). *Australia's privacy commissioner demands answers from Facebook over data scandal*. Available at: www.abc.net.au/news/2018-03-20/privacy-commissioner-investigating-facebook-breach/9568552 [Accessed 20 Mar. 2018].
————. (2018b). *Cambridge Analytica boss caught on tape offering to set up honey trap with Ukrainian prostitutes*. Available at: www.abc.net.au/news/2018-03-20/facebook-under-pressure-as-eu-us-urge-probes-of-data-practices/9564988 [Accessed 20 Mar. 2018].
Australia Council for the Arts (2014). *Annual report: 2013–2014*. Strawberry Hills, NSW: Australia Council for the Arts.
Banafa, A. (2015). Small data vs. big data: Back to the basics. [online] *Datafloq*. Available at: https://datafloq.com/read/small-data-vs-big-data-back-to-the-basic/706 [Accessed 8 Mar. 2018].
Banks, M. (2010). Autonomy guaranteed? Cultural work and the "art – commerce relation." *Journal for Cultural Research*, 14(3), pp. 251–269.
Beer, D. (2013). *Popular culture and new media: The politics of circulation*. Cham: Palgrave.
Beer, D. (2016). *Metric power*. London: Palgrave Macmillan.

Bourdieu, P. (1993). *The field of cultural production: Essays on art and literature.* Cambridge: Polity Press.

Carey, J. (2005). *What good are the arts?* London: Faber.

Crossick, G. and Kaszynska, P. (2014). Under construction: Towards a framework for cultural value. *Cultural Trends*, 23(2), pp. 120–131.

Capacity Interactive (n.d). *Capacity interactive: About.* Available at: http://capacityinteractive.com [Accessed 8 Mar. 2018].

Culture Counts (n.d.) *Culture counts: We value culture.* Available at: https://culturecounts.cc [Accessed 4 Sep. 2017].

Deloitte. (2015). *Global human capital trends 2015: Leading in the new world of work.* London: Deloitte University Press.

Gilmore, A., Arvanitis, K., and Albert, A. (2018). Never mind the quality, feel the width: Big data for quality and performance evaluation in the arts and cultural sector and the case of culture metrics. In: G. Schiuma and D. Carlucci, eds., *Big data in the arts and humanities: Theory and practice.* London: CRC Press: Taylor and Francis Group.

Gilmore, A., Glow, H., and Johanson, K. (2017). Accounting for quality: Arts evaluation, public value and the case of "culture counts." *Cultural Trends*, 26(4), pp. 282–294.

Goldbloom, A. and Davis, G. (2017). Kaggle founder talks big data. *Pursuit*, 15 June. [online]. Available at: https://pursuit.unimelb.edu.au/podcasts/kaggle-founder-talks-big-data [Accessed 4 Sep. 2017].

Goodman, F. (1998). *The mansion on the hill: Dylan, Young, Geffen, Springsteen, and the head-on collision of rock and commerce.* Lexington, KY: Vintage.

Harré, R. (1979). *Social being: A theory for social psychology.* Oxford: Blackwell.

Henry, C. (2009). Women and the creative industries: Exploring the popular appeal. *Creative Industries Journal*, 2(2), pp. 143–160.

Hesmondhalgh, D. (1999). Indie: The institutional politics and aesthetics of a popular music genre. *Cultural Studies*, 13(1), pp. 34–61.

Hesmondhalgh, D. and Baker, S. (2011). *Creative labour: Media work in three cultural industries.* Abingdon, Oxon and New York: Routledge.

Hughes, D., Evans, M., Morrow, G., and Keith, S. (2016). *The new music industries: Disruption and discovery.* Cham, Switzerland: Palgrave Macmillan.

Kitchin, R. (2014). *The data revolution: Big data, open data, data infrastructures and their consequences.* London: Sage.

Klein, B., Meier, L., and Powers, D. (2017). Selling out: Musicians, autonomy, and compromise in the digital age. *Popular Music and Society*, 40(2), pp. 222–238.

Medinilla, Á. (2012). *Agile management: Leadership in an agile environment.* Heidelberg: Springer.

Moore, P. (2016). Big data and structural organisation in major arts bodies: An evolving ethnographic method. *Cultural Trends*, 25(2), pp. 104–115.

Morrow, G. (2018). *Artist management: Agility in the creative and cultural industries.* Abingdon, Oxon and New York: Routledge.

Music Glue (n.d.). *Music glue: About.* [online]. Available at: www.musicglue.com/ [Accessed 8 Mar. 2018].

Next Big Sound (n.d.). *Next big sound: About.* [online]. Available at: www.nextbigsound.com/ [Accessed 8 Mar. 2018].

Oldham, A.L. (2000). *Stoned.* London: Secker & Warburg.

———. (2003). *2Stoned.* London: Random House.

Pesce, M. (2017). The last days of reality. *Meanjin*. [online]. Available at: https://meanjin.com.au/essays/the-last-days-of-reality/ [Accessed 6 Feb. 2018].

Phiddian, R., Meyrick, J., Barnett, T., and Maltby, R. (2017). Counting culture to death: An Radbourne, R., Johanson, K., and Glow, H. (2010). Empowering audiences to measure quality. *Participations: Journal of Audience & Reception Studies*, 7(2), pp. 360–379.

Rouse, M. (2014). What is small data? *What is.com.* (online). Available at: http://whatis.techtarget.com/definition/small-data [Accessed 6 Feb. 2018].

Ryan, B. (1992). *Making capital from culture: The corporate form of capitalist cultural production.* Berlin: Walter de Gruyter.

Saintilan, P. and Schreiber, D. (2018). *Managing organizations in the creative economy: Organizational behaviour for the cultural sector.* Abingdon, Oxon and New York: Routledge.

Segers, K., Schramme, A., and Devriendt, R. (2010). Do artists benefit from arts policy? The position of performing artists in Flanders (2001–2008). *Journal of Arts Management, Law, and Society*, 40(1), pp. 58–75.

Throsby, D. (2008). The concentric circles model of the cultural industries. *Cultural Trends*, 17(3), pp. 147–164.

Throsby, D. and Zednik, A. (2010). *Do you really expect to get paid? An economic study of professional artists in Australia.* Surry Hills, NSW: Australia Council for the Arts.

Watson, J. (2013). Keynote Presentation, BIGSOUND Conference, Brisbane, 12 September.

Williamson, J., Cloonan, M., and Frith, S. (2011). Having an impact? Academics, the Music industries and the problem of knowledge. *International Journal of Cultural Policy,* 17(5), pp. 459–474.

Wiseman-Trowse, N. (2008). *Performing class in British popular music.* Basingstoke: Palgrave Macmillan.

Wright, D. (2018). Towards a computational cultural policy studies: Examining infrastructures of taste and participation. *International Journal of Cultural Policy,* online before print, pp. 1–15.

Zuboff, S. (2018). *The age of surveillance capitalism: The fight for a human future at the new frontier of power.* New York: Public Affairs.

Appendix A

The interviews

Interview No.	Pseudonym	Job Title	Industry	Location	Date
1	Tom	Artist manager	Music	London	15/12/09
2	Jack	Artist manager	Music	London	18/04/09
3	Anne	Contemporary dancer	Dance	Sydney	29/03/17

PART II

Entrepreneurship, leadership, and transformational change

7

THE "ARTPRENEUR"

Between traditional and cultural entrepreneurship. A historical perspective

Marilena Vecco

Introduction

The purpose of an art is not the release of a momentary ejection of adrenalin but rather the gradual, lifelong construction of a state of wonder and serenity

—*Glenn Gould*

This chapter discusses the concept of entrepreneurship in the artistic field by adopting a historical approach. Concepts of the history of entrepreneurship and of cultural entrepreneurship will be used to analyse the figure of the "artpreneur" (artist-entrepreneur), a concept that was raised recently within the field of cultural entrepreneurship. Within this chapter, we refer to artists involved in discovering and pursuing new artistic and cultural ideas, "using a multitude of artistic expressions and organisational forms as vehicles by which to express and convey these ideas to the public" (Scherdin and Zander, 2011, p. 3). The starting point of this analysis is represented by the comparison between the entrepreneur and the artist (Schumpeter, 1911). Joseph A. Schumpeter's *Theory of Economic Development* (1911) will be used firstly to define and develop the theoretical framework, and secondly to define the characteristics and behaviour that are common to both artists and entrepreneurs. We conclude by discussing the concept of the "artpreneur".

"We industrialists do not calculate. On the contrary, we learn to regard our ideas as truly crowned by success as something that laughs at calculations, a bit like an artist's success".[1] This is how Robert Musil (quoted) presented Arnheim, the great twentieth-century bourgeois protagonist of his *Der Mann ohne Eigenschaften*. This comparison with the artist reappears in Schumpeter (1911): "The entrepreneur is someone who carries out a creative action, adding an element of reality that places the figures in new contexts just like a great creative artist with the artistic elements at their disposal" (p. 74). The entrepreneur is somewhat an artist: there is a hedonism in his actions that goes beyond any ethos and/or routine will, but also beyond any pleasure of possession as in consumption (Zanini, 2013).

As Scherdin and Zander (2011) observe, although similarities characterising artistic activity and the entrepreneurial processes exist within the business context, these two fields have never converged in the academic research of the artistic process, and the dynamics of artistic activity have not been studied within the entrepreneurial framework; only a few cases can be quoted within the marketing (Hills and La Forge, 1992; Fillis, 2002; Lehman, Fillis, and Miles, 2014). On the other hand, entrepreneurship research has analysed economic phenomena as a core topic, focusing on the start-up phase of the entrepreneurial process (Cooper, 2003; Davidsson, 2005), without considering that "the creative setting of art and the artistic work must intersect with a number of phenomena dealt with by the traditional entrepreneurship literature, with ample opportunities for cross-fertilization between the two fields" (Scherdin and Zander, 2011, p. 2). This assumption is in line with the concept of consilience as unity of knowledge, introduced by Wilson (1999). Our positivist approach looks for distinction instead of unification within the domain of knowledge. As Einstein wrote to his friend, Marcel Grossmann: "It is a wonderful feeling to recognize the unity of a complex of phenomena that to direct observation appear to be quite separate things" (quoted by Wilson, 1999, p. 5).

The present chapter intends to cover this gap in the context of cultural entrepreneurship and shed some light on the "artpreneur" concept. The chapter is structured in four sections. After this introduction, we shall provide a brief presentation of the figure of the entrepreneur over time. No single definition of entrepreneurship or the entrepreneur exists as they are dynamic concepts that continue to be reconfigured as they adapt to the specific historical, social, cultural and infrastructural context. Throughout this historical excursus on the concept of entrepreneurship, we shall explore the common features attributed to the traditional entrepreneur. Afterwards, we shall present the concept and identity of the "artpreneur", stressing the similarities in the main features and characteristics outlined in the extant literature on the traditional entrepreneur. Furthermore, some attention will be paid to the points of intersection with the process of arts management and the artpreneur, proposing some reflections on the artpreneurs' lessons to arts and traditional managers. Finally, we will recap our main arguments and present our conclusions.

The image of the entrepreneur throughout history

If one is to understand the economic process and the role the entrepreneur has in this process, it is necessary to analyse its historical evolution. The Hebrew Bible states that economic welfare is heavily dependent on the respect of God's Ten Commandments. Only in such a case "The Lord will open the heavens, the storehouse of his bounty . . . you will lend to many nations but borrow from none" (Deut. 28, 12). The same concept is expressed by Joshua: "Keep this Book of the Law always on your lips; meditate on it day and night, so that you may be careful to do everything written in it. Then you will be prosperous and successful" (Joshua 1.8). Human energy is therefore not directed at the creation of economic enterprise, but at the development of the spiritual sphere. At the same time, however, it implies that the rich who show deference to God are regarded as figures of the highest respect.[2]

In Ancient Greece, the philosophers' attitude towards trade in particular was generally negative. Plato would have eliminated it from the activities that were allowed in the Crete colony that he hypothesised to create in *Laws*, since the search for profit leads to immoral practice (*Laws*, IV 705). Demosthenes, a politician, hated money lenders (Against Pantaneto, 37, in particular 37.52). Aristotle hypothesised a system of direct exchange between the producers of different goods without the exchange of money, defining a sort of exchange tax between a product/service and the other, calculated on the basis of demand or relative need (Aristotle, *Nicomachean Ethics*, V.3.1133).[3] The Greeks thought money destroyed the very essence of society.

In the Gospels, religious teachings regarding the rich was equally influential in the formation of the negative image of the entrepreneur throughout history, and still today. However, in the interpretation of Christ's speeches on the subject one forgets that he was referring to the rich of that time, not the modern-day wealthy, which is characterised by a different ethicality and societal dimension.

It was Johannes Messner (1891–1984) who pointed out how the Catholic economic ethics of the thirteenth century contributed to the 'discovery' of the entrepreneur. In other words, it had discovered the importance of the entrepreneurial function in the creation of the economic objective of the common good. The entrepreneur's function seemed to make sense since it was in the general interest and the matter of profits caused no moral scruples. On the basis of the mediaeval theory on money, usury was forbidden while profit on capital that came from any entrepreneurial activity was allowed. Several economic historians such as Werner Sombart (1863–1941) revived the importance of this distinction.

The aversion towards the entrepreneur creator also had a socio-psychological reason. Most people used to prefer the image of a creator working away peacefully in their own field, thus attaining the ideal of human existence. Their life underwent no fundamental change. Year after year, the pace unfailingly remained the same. It was the symbol of a peaceful society. The entrepreneur, on the other hand, was considered as one whose objective was to change the course of things, according to his abilities. Joseph A. Schumpeter (1883–1950) described this capitalist process as when the entrepreneur comprises the main driving force behind the process of 'creating destruction'. This was not at all surprising since for years the entrepreneur had been attributed with destructive powers.

The founding fathers of free economic thought conceded no space to the creator entrepreneur either. Although Adam Smith (1723–1729) made the discovery that the economic process should be seen as a cycle, he remained blocked within the mechanical vision of the eighteenth century and continued to interpret the economic process as if it were a law of nature. The theory of liberalism and of *laissez-faire* is derived from this, according to which pre-arranged harmony is maintained by an 'invisible hand'. David Ricardo (1772–1823) also believed the entrepreneur was superfluous; he regarded the economic process as something that was somehow automatic. These authors only saw the entrepreneur as a mere financer of capital, that is, a capitalist, as Karl Marx (1818–1883) would later explore.

The first clear outline of the entrepreneurial concept appeared in the works of Richard Cantillon (1680–1734), followed by Adam Smith in the late eighteenth and early nineteenth century. Jean Baptiste Say (1767–1832) went on to emphasise the entrepreneur's skill at creating value: "The entrepreneur shifts economic resources out of an area of lower and into an area of higher productivity and greater yield" (Say, 1803). It was at the beginning of the twentieth century that economists recognised the essential role of the creator entrepreneur to guarantee economic growth. To the three production factors (land, capital and work), Alfred Marshall (1842–1924) added a fourth: organisational skill. It was not until 1912, thanks to the publication of the *Theory of Economic Development* by Schumpeter, that a positive entrepreneurship theory made any progress. According to Schumpeter, the essence of the entrepreneur's specific function was to discover and implement new combinations of production in new practices. Schumpeter's model was that of a creator entrepreneur, a crucial driving force of innovation and as a consequence, also of economic growth. Later, the definitions of the entrepreneur and entrepreneurship were to proliferate. Every author tended to favour and emphasise one particular characteristic of the psychological figure and function of the entrepreneur. Table 7.1 shows a summary of these diverse definitions.

The "artpreneur": the artist and the cultural entrepreneur

Let us now look more closely at the parallel between the artist and cultural entrepreneur to define the concept of the 'artpreneur'. As Swedberg so perceptively observed (2006), some of the concepts in the first edition of the *Theory of Economic Development*[1] can be used to develop

Table 7.1 Summary of the main definitions of entrepreneur throughout history

Entrepreneurs buy at certain prices in the present and sell at uncertain prices in the future. The entrepreneur is a bearer of uncertainty.	Cantillon, 1755/1831
Entrepreneurs are **pro-jectors**.	Defoe, 1887/2001
Entrepreneurs attempt **to predict and act upon change** within markets. The entrepreneur bears the **uncertainty** of market dynamics.	Knight, 1921/1942
The entrepreneur is the person who maintains immunity from control of rational bureaucratic knowledge.	Weber, 1947
The entrepreneur is **the innovator** who implements change within markets through the carrying out of **new combinations**. These can take several forms: • the introduction of a new good or quality thereof, • the introduction of a new method of production, • the opening of a new market,	Schumpeter, 1911/1934
The conquest of a new source of supply of new materials or parts, and the carrying out of the new organisation of any industry.	
The entrepreneur is always a **speculator.** He deals with the **uncertain** conditions of the future. His success or failure depends on the correctness of his **anticipation** of uncertain events. If he fails in his understanding of things to come he is doomed.	von Mises, 1949/1996
The entrepreneur is **co-ordinator and arbitrageur.**	Walras, 1954
Entrepreneurial activity involves identifying opportunities within the economic system.	Penrose, 1959/1980
The entrepreneur recognises and acts upon profit opportunities, essentially an arbitrageur.	Kirzner, 1973
Entrepreneurship is the act of innovation involving endowing existing resources with new wealth-producing capacity.	Drucker, 1985
The essential act of entrepreneurship is new entry. New entry can be accomplished by entering new or established markets with new or existing goods or services. New entry is the act of launching a new venture, either by a start-up firm, through an existing firm, or via internal corporate venturing.	Lumpkin and Dess, 1996
The field of entrepreneurship involves the study of sources of opportunities; the processes of discovery, evaluation, and exploitation of opportunities; and the set of individuals who discover, evaluate, and exploit them.	Shane and Venkataraman, 2000
Entrepreneurship is a context-dependent social process through which individuals and teams create wealth by bringing together unique packages of resources to exploit marketplace opportunities.	Ireland, Hitt, and Sirmon, 2003
Entrepreneurship is the mindset and process to create and develop economic activity by blending risk-taking, creativity and/or innovation with sound management, within a new or an existing organisation.	Commission of the European Communities, 2003

Source: Author adaptation on Organization for Economic Co-operation and Development (OECD)/Ahmad and Hoffmann (2008).

a theory of cultural entrepreneurship. In fact, the assumption that the analysis of art may be contextualised in the same way as economic analysis may be more generically applied to culture.

The parallel between the artist and entrepreneur that Schumpeter used is extremely useful for our analysis. Both the artist and entrepreneur are agents of change. They are dynamic, active, full of energy and endowed with the qualities of leaders. According to this interpretation, the

Table 7.2 The conceptualisation of cultural entrepreneurship according to young Schumpeter

	Economics	Culture
Dynamic or entrepreneurial change	Economic development	Cultural entrepreneurship
Static or non-entrepreneurial change	Economic adaptation	Cultural evolution

Source: Swedberg, Journal of Cultural Economics (2006).

true artist is one who introduces something new (and innovative) in the arts, and so too does the entrepreneur. Both break with social conventions (in economic terms and with existing equilibriums) to put together new combinations of elements, materials, and production systems, and show no opposition to change. On the contrary, they seek opposition as a catalyst for their activity. Because of these particular marked characteristics, the artist and entrepreneur are opposed to the static majority that Schumpeter identified (see Table 7.3).

From this perspective, the concept of combination, which is fundamental in Schumpeter's thought, could also be adapted to the art world. The economic entrepreneur working in the creative sector can be conceptualised as someone who creates combinations out of disparate elements, of which art is one. Or, as Swedberg said (2006), the artist who is interested in economic and cultural success may be conceptualised as someone who is trying to link his work with other elements in a combination that works. Let us now look at the distinctive traits of the cultural entrepreneur (Table 7.4).

Table 7.4 clusters the definitions into three different groups. The first group is "The beginning. Making culture", which gather the first contributions rooted in the sociology and others more recent which are characterised by a sociological perspective and focus on defining and making culture. The second cluster collects definitions underlining the process of cultural and creative entrepreneurship within the market dynamics; the deployment of culture is outlined. The last group represents an advancement of the previous cluster as it goes beyond the market perspective. The emphasis is on the development and strengthening of intangible capitals of different forms.

This clustering is useful for three different reasons. First it allows to identify and understand different streams and waves of cultural and creative entrepreneurship over time; second, it creates a basis to identify points of convergence and divergence, and finally, it provides some insights on the present state of the art of the discipline as well as some potentially fruitful avenues for research.

Despite multiple attempts to define the cultural/creative or art-entrepreneur, no one agreed-upon definition has emerged, and two clearly different figures are often combined. Consider: the entrepreneur who is active in the cultural sector; and the entrepreneur, through a more holistic view, who creates culture regardless of the sector he is working in. The former may be an individual with little ability and inclination to innovation. The mission of the latter, on the other hand, is to create cultural value. They therefore carry out activities that can influence the attitude, thoughts, and behaviour of the public (Smit, 2011; Beckman, 2007), present and future cultural values, as well as contributing to changes of aesthetic paradigms (Rentschler, 2007). Recent literature dealing with concepts of artists (Harvie, 2013) reveals a slowly changing paradigm, shifting away from a purely aesthetic to a more economic and entrepreneurial focused perspective, considering the cultural/artpreneurs rooted in the socio-economic processes. This is particularly clear in many studies and analysis of the second cluster outlined in Table 7.4. This sounds as a clear claim of the positioning and function of the cultural entrepreneur as an

Table 7.3 Parallel between the entrepreneur and artist according to young Schumpeter

The entrepreneur/artist	The static majority
Disrupt the balance	Seek balance
Pursue innovation	Repeat what has already been done
Active, full of energy	Static, with little energy
Leader	Follower
Creates new combinations	Accepts conventional production methods
Feels no internal resistance to change	Feels strong internal resistance to change
Is convinced his actions are right and perseveres	Is hostile to new actions carried out by others
Makes intuitive choices when faced with a multitude of new alternatives	Makes a rational choice amongst existing alternatives
Motivated by the power and joy of creation	Purely motivated by needs and stops once they have been met

Source: Adaptation of Swedberg's presentation of Schumpeter's analysis, *Journal of Cultural Economics*, p. 250.

Table 7.4 Definition of the cultural and creative entrepreneurship and entrepreneur over time[1]

1. The beginning. Making culture

Bourdieu (1980)	"Thus, the opposition between 'genuine' art and 'commercial' art corresponds to the opposition between ordinary entrepreneurs seeking immediate economic profit and cultural entrepreneurs **struggling to accumulate specifically cultural capital,** albeit at the cost of temporarily renouncing economic profit. As for the opposition which is made within the latter group between **consecrated art and avant-garde art,** or between orthodoxy and heresy, it distinguishes between, on the one hand, those who dominate the field of production and the market through the economic and symbolic capital they have been able to accumulate in earlier struggles by virtue of a particularly successful combination of the **contradictory capacities** specifically demanded by the law of the field, and, on the other hand, the newcomers, who have and want no other audience than their competitors-established producers whom their practice tends to discredit by imposing new products-or other newcomers with whom they vie in novelty" (pp. 268–269).
DiMaggio (1982)	"the creation of an organizational base for high culture in America. . . . . The **cultural capitalists** were, in Lewis Coser's terms (1974), a greedy elite" (pp. 304, 306).
Aageson, Maule, and Filleul (1996)	"Cultural entrepreneurship involves a conception, an initial launch, and a transition to an established event. . . . The category of cultural entrepreneurs are **non-profit team of entrepreneurs who provide a cultural service with high value,** but because of transaction costs, has low revenue potential" (p. 54).
Spilling (1991)	"This kind of entrepreneurship [cultural-economic entrepreneurship] is aimed at **developing a business or institution based on a cultural concept,** and mainly based on a commercial or at least non-profit economic principles. . . . to launch some kind of cultural project or action in order to influence or change the frame of reference of the people in an area. Cultural entrepreneurship also can be aimed at improving more generally (cultural) standards of an area and creating more attractive environments for residential areas as well as the business community" (pp. 36, 37).

Banks (2006)	"In ideal type, the post-modern cultural entrepreneur operates unfettered by tradition; a **creative free spirit** driven by the desire to make money but also broker creative alliances, combine previously disparate aspects of production and consumption, and to contribute to, and be drawn by, the cosmopolitan, diverse city and its sense of place (Florida, 2002; O'Connor and Wynne, 1996; Wittstock, 2000) . . . are in part motivated by **a desire to contribute to the aesthetic 'vibrancy' of the city** (Wynne and O'Connor, 1998) or helping to **inspire 'creative' urban renaissan**ce (Florida, 2002), demonstrating the **political or social motivations of cultural workers** has generated limited interest" (p. 457).
Swedberg (2006)	"that economic entrepreneurship primarily aims at creating something new (and profitable) in the area of the economy, while cultural entrepreneurship aims at **creating something new (and appreciated) in the area of culture.** While moneymaking is often a crucial component of cultural entrepreneurship, it does not constitute its primary focus. Cultural entrepreneurship, as I see it, may therefore be defined as the **carrying out of a novel combination that results in something new and appreciated in the cultural sphere**" (p. 260).
Johnson (2007)	"'cultural entrepreneurship' which here refers both **to the creativity and initiative of the founder and to the constraint and opportunity** represented by the specific cultural schemas that structure the historical context in which the founder is embedded" (p. 99).
Rentschler (2007)	"The term cultural entrepreneur could apply to **an artist whose body of work has had a great impact on the changing perceptions of aesthetics and identity,** has produced for mass consumption for a wider audience than would normally have been the case and who has actively marketed their work" (p. 671).
Metze (2009)	"The 'cultural entrepreneurship' discourse provides an alternative interpretation [and] aligns entrepreneurship' with a counter-cultural or subordinate discourse of '**maintenance of cultural value**' that artists, residents and small business in the creative sector often express" (p. 2).
Scott (2012)	"Cultural entrepreneurs are a social group comprising mostly young people whose primary life goal is to build an artistic career. Their common characteristic is that **they make cultural products while undertaking other paid work,** within and outside the cultural sector, for they have yet to secure an income from their artistic production" (p. 238).

2. The process and the market. Utilizing culture

Lounsbury and Glynn (2001)	Glynn (2001) "We define cultural entrepreneurship as **the process of storytelling** that mediates between extant stocks of entrepreneurial resources and subsequent capital acquisition and wealth creation" (p. 545).
Ellmeier (2003)	"Cultural entrepreneurialism means **all-round artistic and commercial/ business qualifications,** long working hours and fierce competition from bigger companies" (p. 11).
Wilson and Stokes (2004)	"we follow Ellmeier´s definition of 'cultural entrepreneurialism' – encompassing all-round artistic and commercial/business qualifications, long working-hours and fierce competition from bigger companies. . . . the **particular ability of the cultural entrepreneur to coordinate artistic and managerial resources** . . ., can be seen as a defining characteristic of the use of the term 'entrepreneur'" (p. 221).

(Continued)

Table 7.4 (Continued)

Bovone (2005)	"*Cultural entrepreneurs*, through the products they offer, establish **links between their own experience/identity and the consumers' experience/ identity.** Therefore, they are **cultural intermediaries.** Almost at the end of his famous work *La distinction*, Bourdieu writes that 'new cultural intermediaries' are members of a new lower middle class acting as a 'drive belt' of the typical good taste of the upper classes; they are 'intellectuals . . . in charge of soft manipulation activities . . . in the big bureaucracies of cultural production, radios, televisions, poll/inquiry institutes, study offices, big newspapers and weekly magazines' (Bourdieu, 1979, p. 422)" (p. 362).
De Bruin (2005)	"Entrepreneurship in the creative sector may be defined as: *The process of adding value to creative inputs/creativity.* This value-adding process might not only entail combining creative inputs with humdrum inputs, but could also involve an 'entrepreneurial value chain' (de Bruin, 2003a)" (p. 145).
Rae (2005)	"creative entrepreneurship, which can be defined as the **creation or identification of an opportunity to provide a cultural product, service or experience**, and of bringing together the resources to exploit this as an enterprise (Leadbeater and Oakley, 1999)" (p. 186).
Yang (2005)	"Cultural entrepreneurs tapped into the new cultural market by offering CR **[Cultural Revolution] related cultural products.** . . . Cultural entrepreneurs understand the market and know how to negotiate political control" (p. 16, 22).
Wilson and Stokes (2006)	"we follow Ellmeier's definition of 'cultural entrepreneurialism' – encompassing all-round artistic and commercial/business qualifications, long working-hours and fierce competition from bigger companies. . . . This focuses attention squarely on the particular **ability of the cultural entrepreneur to coordinate and leverage artistic and managerial resources**" (p. 369).
Aageson (2008)	"Cultural entrepreneurs are **change agents** who leverage cultural innovation to create thriving economic systems. Cultural entrepreneurs are **risk takers**, change agents, and resourceful visionaries who **generate revenue from innovative and sustainable cultural enterprises** that enhance livelihoods and create cultural value for both producers and consumers of cultural products and services" (p. 92).
Lange (2008)	"Culturepreneur describes an urban protagonist who possesses the **ability to mediate between and interpret the areas of culture** and of service provision" (p. 116).
Dacin, Dacin, and Matear (2010)	"As do other types of entrepreneurs, successful cultural entrepreneurs appear to possess **certain individual aptitudes and skills.** These include social position and status-seeking motives (DiMaggio, 1982), creativity and alertness to opportunity (Aageson, Maule, and Filleul, 1996), and the ability to combine resources creatively (Peterson and Berger, 1971). In particular, cultural entrepreneurs must be able to **accumulate and manipulate cultural capital, the set of skills, knowledge, practices, and tastes that are rare, distinctive, and socially honored** (Bourdieu, 1984)" (p. 47).
Fillis (2010)	"Creativity enables the **entrepreneurial marketer** to act on these **opportunities in ways which can result in competitive advantage** for the organisation. It can provide the basis for innovation and business growth, as well as impact positively on society generally (Bilton, 2007). . . . The entrepreneurial marketer develops his or her own individualised version

	of planning and strategy formulation based on a combination of formal rational methods and more informal artistic approaches. A key ability of the entrepreneurial marketer is **to identify and act on opportunities before the competition can do so.** Works or acts of entrepreneurial marketing cannot be reduced to purely economic dimensions. It is the quality of these acts which ultimately impacts on behaviour and performance" (pp. 96–97).
Hausmann (2010)	"cultural entrepreneurs are identified as **artists undertaking business activities** within one of the four traditional sectors of the arts. . . . [They] **discover and evaluate opportunities in the arts and leisure markets** and create a (micro) business to pursue them" (p. 19).
Kavousy et al. (2010)	"Cultural entrepreneurs are **resourceful visionaries, generating revenues from culturally embedded knowledge systems and activities**; their innovative applications of traditions to markets result in economically sustainable cultural enterprises" (p. 228)
Konrad (2010)	"Cultural entrepreneurs are individuals who create **new organizations, products or activities within the cultural sector**" (p. 336).
Snyder et al. (2010)	"Cultural entrepreneurs a) **are visionary leaders** who have passion for creating cultural enterprises, b) drive the **creation of new cultural markets and industries**, c) leverage 'cultural capital' through innovation, thus furthering cultural values, traditions, knowledge and local livelihoods, d) create a 'whole cloth' of **cultural diversity and sustainability**, weaving together economic, social, environmental, and cultural values, and e) remain mission driven, market focused, creating both financial wealth and cultural value" (p. 7).
Lange (2011)	"The term 'culturepreneur' is a compound of 'culture' and 'entrepreneur' and was first suggested by Davies and Ford (1998, p. 13), following Pierre Bourdieu's typological notion of an entrepreneur as someone who embodies various forms of capital (Bourdieu, 1986, p. 241). 'Culturepreneur' describes an **urban protagonist who possesses the ability to mediate between and interpret the areas of culture and service provision.** He may be characterized, first and foremost, as a **creative entrepreneur**, someone who runs clubs, record shops, fashion shops, galleries and other outlets, as well as someone who closes gaps in the urban landscape with new social, entrepreneurial and socio-spatial practices" (p. 260).
Phillips (2011)	"*arts entrepreneurship* refers to the process whereby **tangible cultural capital is created**" (p. 20).
Preece (2011)	"performing arts entrepreneurship will refer to the process of **starting a not-for-profit organization** with the intent of generating artistic performances (creation and/or presentation)" (p. 105).
Smit (2011)	"The current discourse about the creative economy draws on different notions of cultural and creative entrepreneurs. These definitions differ. . . . However, they all concentrate on **economic activities dedicated to producing goods and services with mainly aesthetic and symbolic value**" (p. 170).
Towse (2011)	"They do much more than manage the activity [of producing cultural value for both producers and consumers]; typically, they **discover it and exploit its revenue potentialities.** They have the one quality that cannot be bought or hired, namely alertness to revenue generating arbitrage, involving either new products, new materials, new processes or all of these in some combination" (p. 157).

(*Continued*)

Table 7.4 (Continued)

Hagoort, Thomassen, and Kooyman (2012)	"The cultural entrepreneur is an **artist** who works in a project form with assistants and board members, and makes an idea viable" (p. 14).
Enhuber (2014)	"cultural entrepreneurship can be understood to refer to '**cultural change agents and resourceful visionaries** who organize cultural, financial, social and human capital, to generate revenue from a cultural activity' (Tremblay, 2013)" (p. 4).
Beltrán and Miguel (2014)	"The creative entrepreneurs analysed in this article share some features with the entrepreneurs described by economics theories, but there are also significant differences. In line with these theories, they do indeed make innovations, creating new products and generating new markets. However, the **economic risk they incur in doing this is reduced as the investments are made fundamentally in symbolic capital**" (p. 41).
Bujor and Avasilcai (2015)	"An entrepreneur in creative industries is a person that uses his/her **creativity, ideas, passion to realize economic activities, most of the time, as an individual**. This person does not differ at all from the stereotype entrepreneur as principles governing such business and the tools used to achieve it are the same. What differs is only people's conception of those who run such businesses. Though the entrepreneur in creative industries has a different structure, he/she will use the **creativity in his/her own business development as well** or can anytime to choose a business partner to complete him/her (the business manager), this matter being framed as a creative solution" (p. 1730).
Chang and Wyszomirski (2015)	"a possible general definition: 'arts entrepreneurship' is a management process through which cultural workers seek **to support their creativity and autonomy, advance their capacity for adaptability, and create artistic as well as economic and social value**" (p. 11).
Chen, Chang, and Lee (2015a)	"A creative entrepreneur is defined here as the founder of a company in one of the creative industries" (p. 900).
Chen, Chang, and Lo (2015b)	"Creative entrepreneurs in this paper are defined as the **founders** who establish and remain in charge **of a business in a creative industry**" (p. 906).
Essig (2015)	"Thus, in the arts and culture context . . . it may also be understood to include the **creation of new expressions of symbolic meaning by** individuals. . . . We can understand entrepreneurship, in the arts and culture sector and elsewhere, as **a process for converting means** to desirable ends through a mediating structure or organization that may be called a 'firm'" (p. 227).
Bujor and Avasilcai (2016)	"Entrepreneurship in creative industries, and information related to the development **of entrepreneurial skills** in these industries are not well known, or rather fully known. The term of creative entrepreneurship has become a term that refers to the business activity of entrepreneurs belonging to the creative industries. . . . Creative businesses are more active than other types of businesses in **promoting innovation**. The real challenge that those who dare to engage in a creative entrepreneurship must face, is the need to find a **balance between the artistic side, and the financing and the business development side**. From the term of entrepreneurship in the creative industries (creative/cultural entrepreneurship) derives the term of entrepreneur in the creative industries (creative entrepreneur), which deals with the realization of a strategy,

Bujor and Avasilcai (2016)	"Entrepreneurship in creative industries, and information related to the development **of entrepreneurial skills** in these industries are not well known, or rather fully known. The term of creative entrepreneurship has become a term that refers to the business activity of entrepreneurs belonging to the creative industries. . . . Creative businesses are more active than other types of businesses in **promoting innovation**. The real challenge that those who dare to engage in a creative entrepreneurship must face, is the need to find a **balance between the artistic side, and the financing and the business development side**. From the term of entrepreneurship in the creative industries (creative/cultural entrepreneurship) derives the term of entrepreneur in the creative industries (creative entrepreneur), which deals with the realization of a strategy, organizational design and leadership in a **cultural context**. This notion characterizes those talented and successful entrepreneurs, able to turn their ideas into products or services to society (UNCTAD; UNDP, 2010)" (p. 25).

Bujor and Avasilcai (2016)	"Entrepreneurship in creative industries, and information related to the development **of entrepreneurial skills** in these industries are not well known, or rather fully known. The term of creative entrepreneurship has become a term that refers to the business activity of entrepreneurs belonging to the creative industries. . . . Creative businesses are more active than other types of businesses in **promoting innovation**. The real challenge that those who dare to engage in a creative entrepreneurship must face, is the need to find a **balance between the artistic side, and the financing and the business development side**. From the term of entrepreneurship in the creative industries (creative/cultural entrepreneurship) derives the term of entrepreneur in the creative industries (creative entrepreneur), which deals with the realization of a strategy, organizational design and leadership in a **cultural context**. This notion characterizes those talented and successful entrepreneurs, able to turn their ideas into products or services to society (UNCTAD; UNDP, 2010)" (p. 25).

Calcagno and Balzarin (2016)	"These special professionals are well ingrained in the business world but – as artists – they also play **the role of gatekeepers** of their own language, looking for a realistic balance **between artistic goals and the sustainability of their entrepreneurial choices**. . . . The artists-entrepreneurs combine their artistic attitudes with a deep sense of business (Marinova and Borza, 2013), economically sustaining the cultural enterprise in coherence with their cultural vision (Zemite, 2010). . . . The ambiguity and complexity of a role that **combines entrepreneurial wisdom and artistic practices** (2004; Preece, 2011; Marinova and Borza, 2013) give great relevance to the artists-entrepreneurs observed in the **multiple dimensions of their role** (Jones, Svejenova, Strandgaard Pedersen, and Townly, 2016)" (pp. 29–30).

3. Beyond the market perspective. The intangible capitals

Klamer (2011)	"Cultural entrepreneurs are people who are geared towards the realization of **cultural values** . . . [Being] focused on the (cultural) content being about the art itself and the **creative process is a moral attribute of the cultural entrepreneur**. The economics has to be an instrument for them in order to realize cultural values. . . " (p. 154).
Kolsteeg (2012)	"Cultural entrepreneurs are **growth oriented** with growth strategies strongly connected with the artist identity and/or creative reputation" (p. 5).

(Continued)

Table 7.4 (Continued)

Konrad (2013)	"Culture entrepreneurs especially need to know how to build up the **right set of relationships** with external partners, and how to act in a complex social network" (p. 308).
Harvie (2013)	"Entrepreneurs and artists can generally be seen to share special capabilities for **risk-taking and innovation**, or what economist Jason Potts call the **'human capital' of creativity, novelty generation, new interpretations and meanings' and 'the creative skills** and abilities that enable humans to continually change and adapt' (p. 3).
Mokyr (2013)	"Cultural entrepreneurs, then, are defined as individuals that add to the menus from which others choose. . . . usually they build upon existing but diffuse notions, and formulate them in a sharp set of propositions or beliefs, which serve as a cultural Schelling focal point to their contemporaries. In that sense **they create something new**" (p. 3).
Kolsteeg (2013)	"Cultural entrepreneurs by definition work **in a social, political, economic and artistic discourse**" (p. 5).
Lampel and Germain (2016)	"the figure of the creative entrepreneur characterizes the **indeterminacy** of many activities in organizations that turns each individual into a kind of entrepreneurial venture. The structural and strategic context might support all **individual initiatives**, but attaining creative **consciousness in organization is also a question of 'performing the self'** in this context by merging the organizational discourse of entrepreneurship and initiative with the individual's 'inner self'" (p. 2330).
Beckman (2007)	"to approach professional employment in the arts in a creative manner that will **generate value for individuals and groups** inside or outside traditional arts employment domains" (p. 89).

Source: Author elaboration.

1 This table includes all articles published on ranked journals or highly quoted in the cultural and creative entrepreneurship literature (emphasis added).

economic agent. However, examples of "artpreneurs" are to be found in the history of art. First Hills (1992) and later Fillis (2002) recall several examples of entrepreneurial marketing practice drawn from the Italian Renaissance and from modern art history.

The creation of cultural values, which is demanded by both producers and consumers of cultural goods and services, is the core mission of both previously mentioned categories of cultural entrepreneurs (Aageson, 2008; Aageson, Maule, and Filleul, 1996; Klamer, 2011; Snyder et al., 2010). Moreover, their activity creates shifts in attitudes, beliefs and behaviours (Snyder et al., 2010; Smit, 2011), influences perceptions of aesthetics and identity (Rentschler, 2007) and creates "something new (and profitable) in the area of the economy" (Swedberg, 2006, p. 260).

Authors such as Towse (2011) have underlined that cultural entrepreneurs are mission driven and focused on the creation of both financial and cultural wellbeing. Similar to the second (b) model presented above, the cultural entrepreneur combines artistic qualities with an acute business sense. Cultural entrepreneurs are resourceful individuals (Aageson, 2008; Towse, 2011) c who identify and develop their cultural capital in the process of value creation (Snyder et al., 2010). According to this perspective the economic success or sustainability is of secondary or functional value (Klamer, 2011; Metze, 2009; Aageson, 2008) because it is a tool to create and to continue to create cultural value.

Within this chapter, the concept of the 'artpreneur' refers to artists involved in discovering and pursuing new artistic and cultural ideas, "using a multitude of artistic expressions and organisational forms as a means to express and convey these ideas to the public" (Zander and Sherdin, 2011, p. 3). According to Harvie (2013), these individuals can be considered an expression of the creative entrepreneurialism modelling supported by many funding regimes. They are interpreting their independence and ability to exploit opportunities, take risks, self-start, think laterally, problem solve, and adopt innovative ideas and practices, in order to be productive both aesthetically and socially. This perspective is rather distant from other more commerce-based entrepreneurialism models (Brink, 2012). All of these different approaches highlight how the process of artistic entrepreneurship can be interpreted as a condition of recognising and making the most of opportunities (reflecting Schumpeter's understanding); on the other hand, however, little attention is paid to the process as a form of social creativity understood as the ability to create opportunities (Gartner and Carter, 2003; Hjorth, 2003). This process is fundamental for a more holistic and comprehensive understanding of the figure of the cultural entrepreneur and/or artpreneur. Cultural entrepreneurship is a process of leadership, management, negotiation, networking, and the balancing of core skills. It can set out a product as different to the competition, lead to the invention of new products/services, create the conditions for a particularly creative working environment, or develop a real competitive advantage *à la Porter*. In a completely different context, Deleuze stated, "Life comes into being as becoming. . . . Life is desire, and desire is the expansion of life through creation and transformation" (Colebrook, 2002, p. 135 quoted in Hjorth and Johannisson, 2007). Using this perspective, we can say that with their projects and activities, the cultural entrepreneur fulfils this desire completely, maximising cultural values and actively shaping the aesthetic paradigm in the social and cultural context.[5]

The artistic entrepreneur is a facilitator, a gatekeeper, a change actor, a sort of *Mann der Tat* who, by subverting the artistic, cultural and socio-economic status quo, not only innovates and creates but above all acts, since the process is under their control. Considering the artistic process and work, the 'artpreneur' introduces novelty, which is a typical topic of entrepreneurship literature as we have already seen in the first part of this chapter. New, innovative ideas are developed through a non-linear process, in a context characterised by risk and uncertainty. To affirm their novelty and creativity, artists are obliged to change and innovate the artistic paradigm. The crisis generated by the inappropriateness of the existing paradigms and the shift to new ones are *sine qua non* conditions to deploy their artistic potential as intrinsic motivation. As Lindqvist (2011) points out, there is a parallel between the myth of the entrepreneur and the myth of the artist as a charismatic, visionary, undertaker and creator, thinking in and outside the box. Both of them are characterised as unique individuals, having a sort of 'divine talent' which allows them to be ahead of their time and foresee and shape future trends. This is an ability which correlates to their pro-activeness. As Klamer (2011) and Ripsas (1998) argue from different perspectives (artistic or non-artistic), the entrepreneur is an individual who takes risks to develop his or her initiatives, which requires vision and foresight. They are visionaries whose contribution is sometimes unacknowledged by present society and can play a role as economic agents in the cultural and art markets.

In this literature review, all authors are shown as trying to provide a definitive definition of the cultural entrepreneur and/or 'artpreneur'. Such definitions often stress the differences that separate cultural entrepreneurship from traditional entrepreneurship.

I want to adopt a different approach which enables us to bridge the traditional field of entrepreneurship and 'artpreneurship'. Despite the multiple analyses presented since, we agree with a comparatively early statement made by Spilling: "In most cases there is little reason to distinguish between cultural-economic entrepreneurship and the classical form of entrepreneurship – in both cases it is about having visions and perspectives, having adequate competence and networks, and transforming ideas into a going enterprise" (1991, p. 36).

The main point is to identify the shared attributes of these two fields – to show that being entrepreneurial is a mindset, a process, and a behaviour and that it implies specific features/skills and competences (Figure 7.1).

The core of this model is the shared entrepreneurial process (Shane, 2003), which focuses on entrepreneurial behaviour and on understanding entrepreneurial dynamics and processes. This can be applied to different disciplines and sectors. What makes it different for our purposes is the context or the socio-economic and cultural environment (this includes the market as well), characterised by its own dynamics and exchange models (Klamer and Zuidof, 1999). This system is characterised by different rules and logics that define a diverse ecosystem in which the cultural entrepreneur acts. Goals and values are culturally oriented; the cultural entrepreneur as the 'artpreneur' tries to maximise cultural values. They are primarily driven by a strong non-monetary internal motivation (Swedberg, 2006). The cultural entrepreneur is an innovator (Blaug and Towse, 2011) who creates something new to be appreciated in the cultural sphere (Swedberg, 2006). This is an individual and innovative act, which can potentially benefit all of society.

The preceding proposed framework is useful and can be utilised to distinguish cultural entrepreneurship from traditional entrepreneurship or from social entrepreneurship. To summarise,

Figure 7.1 The framework of (cultural) entrepreneurship

any distinction should not be merely based on the entrepreneur's features but rather than on the environment in which they act, which implies specific values and goals, which may differ from traditional entrepreneurship. This framework can bridge the different varieties of entrepreneurship and be used to comparative purposes within these varieties. Specially, it may serve as the basis for identifying several points of convergence and divergence, as well as some potentially interesting avenues for future cultural and creative entrepreneurship research. For example, the performance assessment within the entrepreneurship discipline is still more based on the tangible dimension; little attention is based on the intangible one while in the cultural and creative entrepreneurship this perspective is reversed. This will imply a deep reflection and revision of the performance assessment and the sustainability criteria of the business in the different varieties of entrepreneurship. Moreover, this framework can contribute to legitimizing the full status of this discipline face to traditional or social entrepreneurship. As it happens for cultural economics compared to traditional economics, cultural and creative entrepreneurship are considered as a second-order discipline. Finally, it can open up a cross-fertilisation process between cultural and creative entrepreneurship and the more traditional entrepreneurship. This can legitimise businessmen who try to distinguish themselves with the genius status historically attributed to artists and acknowledge the influence of artists' practices on their performances in guiding their thinking and actions.

Conclusions

This chapter analysed and compared the concepts of artist and entrepreneur with the aim of contextualising the figure of the 'artpreneur'. 'Artpreneurs' combine artistic qualities with business sense: they have a deep knowledge and feeling of art, creativity, and a strong inclination and pro-activeness in recognising and taking opportunities and risks in the cultural business environment (Klamer, 2011; Rentschler, 2007). Compared to managers in the art sectors, artpreneurs are more proactive and may potentially fully (it depends of course on the scale of the business) manage their value chain process. They developed specific skills and capabilities which allow them to survive and adapt themselves to an unstable environment (Vecco, forthcoming). These elements can be transferred from the artpreneurs, or more generally speaking from the arts to the traditional entrepreneurs and art managers, to achieve cross-fertilisation. These elements – such as an aesthetics-based behaviour to develop a more creative and innovative behaviour, artistic processes to boost extreme creativity and flexibility, and the aesthetic intelligence (Mucha, 2009; Goodwin and Mucha, 2008) – constitute some of the lessons to improve their human and professional sustainability in the medium and long term (Vecco, forthcoming).[6]

We presented a model which bridges traditional entrepreneurship and cultural/artpreneurship. The accent is not on the differences between them but rather the unification of the fields. Adopting a consilience-based approach, we can show that traditional entrepreneurship and cultural/artpreneurship are characterised by the same dynamics, processes, mindset and skills but applied in different environments, which implies different values and objectives to pursue.

Considering the artist as an entrepreneur also combines notions of risk-taking and paradigm-breaking behaviour. The concept of innovation and of breaking norms and rules, the concept of paradigm developed by Kuhn (1962), the ability and/or talent for innovation and to be the bearer of social and cultural meaning, are therefore central in the parallel between the artist and the cultural entrepreneur. As Lindqvist observed (2011), the artist and entrepreneur assume a fundamental role in our society and in the creation of wellbeing, although this role is difficult to quantify. For many authors (see Table 7.4), the concept of Schumpeterian innovation, which centres on breaking existing rules, is fundamental and represents their *raison d'être*. In many cases, these two figures become the precursors of their time, since they are able to take risks and make the most of the opportunities offered by the social, economic and cultural context in which they find themselves.

In conclusion, adopting this approach, we show that the artist has the potential to be an 'artpreneur'. Both are agents of change; they introduce something new and innovative. They are very positive to change as it represents their drive. Furthermore, they break with social conventions – in economic, social and cultural and/or artistic terms – to put together new combinations of elements, materials, and production systems and expressions within the arts. In this sense, their main objective is that of maximising artistic and cultural values, fulfilling completely Deleuze's concept of desire as an expansion of life through creation and transformation.

Notes

1 Translation of the author.
2 For example, in the discussion that developed during the first century AD regarding the leadership of the Sanhedrin, Eleazar ben Azarya was considered a suitable candidate to replace the disposed president Gamliel II, since he was wealthy and God fearing (*Talmud Babilonese*, Berakhot, 27b–28a).
3 See also the discussion in F. Miller "Aristotle and Business: friend or foe?"
4 Some concepts were to be modified in the second edition in 1934.
5 Since contemporary art expresses itself by using every kind of material and process, the creation of materials or innovative processes in any sector can contribute to the development of art if guided in the right way.
6 This article presents a detailed description of the artpreneurs' lessons. These lessons are divided into three different categories: behaviour, skills and process.

References

Aageson, T. (2008). Cultural entrepreneurs: Producing cultural value and wealth. *Cultures and Globalization: The Cultural Economy*, 2, p. 92.

Aageson, T., Maule, C.J., and Filleul, E. (1996). Cultural entrepreneurship and the Banff television festival. *Journal of Cultural Economics*, 20(4), pp. 321–339.

Ahmad, N. and Hoffmann, A.N. (2008). A framework for addressing and measuring entrepreneurship, OECD Statistics Working Papers 2008/02, Paris: OECD.

Banks, M. (2006). Moral economy and cultural work. *Sociology*, 40(3), 455–472.

Beckman, G. (2007). 'Adventuring' arts entrepreneurship curricula in higher education: An examination of present efforts, obstacles, and best practices. *Journal of Arts Management, Law, and Society*, 37(2), pp. 87–112.

Beltrán, G. and Miguel, P. (2014). Doing culture, doing business: A new entrepreneurial spirit in the Argentine creative industries. *International Journal of Cultural Studies*, 17(1), pp. 39–54.

Blaug, M. and Towse, R. (2011). Cultural entrepreneurship. In: R. Towse, ed., *A handbook of cultural economics*. 2nd ed. Cheltenham: Edward Elgar.

Bourdieu, P. and Nice, R. (1980). The production of belief: Contribution to an economy of symbolic goods. *Media Culture Society*, 2, pp. 261–293.

Bovone, L. (2005). Fashionable Quarters in the Postindustrial City: The Ticinese of Milan. *City & Community*, 4(4), pp. 359–380.

Brink, E. (2012). *The Artpreneur: Financial success for artistic souls*. London: Papy Publishing.

Bujor, A. and Avasilcai, S. (2015). Creative industries as a growth driver: An overview. Managing Intellectual Capital and Innovation for Sustainable and Inclusive Society, Management, Knowledge and Learning, Joint Conference, 2015, 27–29 May, 2015, Bari, Italy, pp. 1725–1731.

———. (2016). The creative entrepreneur: A framework of analysis. *Procedia – Social and Behavioral Sciences*, (22), pp. 21–28.

Calcagno, M. and Balzarin, E. (2016). The artist-entrepreneur acting as a gatekeeper in the realm of art. *Venezia Arti*, 25, pp. 29–36.

Chang, W.J. and Wyszomirski, M. (2015). What is arts entrepreneurship? Tracking the development of its definition in scholarly journals. *Artivate: A Journal of Entrepreneurship in the Arts*, 4(2), pp. 11–31.

Chen, M.-H., Chang, Y.-Y, and Lee, C.-Y. (2015). Creative entrepreneurs' Guanxi networks and success: Information and resource, *Journal of Business Research*, 68, pp. 900–905.

Chen, M.H., Chang, Y.-Y., and Lo, Y.-M. (2015). Creativity cognitive style, conflict, and career success for creative entrepreneurs. *Journal of Business Research*, 68, pp. 906–910.

Cooper, A. (2003). Entrepreneurship: The past, the present, the future. In: Z.J. Acs and D.B. Audretsch, eds., *Handbook of entrepreneurship research: An interdisciplinary survey and introduction*. Dordrecht: Kluwer Academic, pp. 21–34.

Dacin, P.A., Dacin, M.T., and Matear, M. (2010). Social entrepreneurship: Why we don't need a new theory and how we move forward from here. *Academy of Management Perspectives* (August), pp. 37–57.

Davidsson, P. (2005). *Researching entrepreneurship*. Boston, MA: Springer Science & Business Media, Inc.

De Bruin, A. (2005). Multi-level entrepreneurship in the creative industries New Zealand's screen production industry. *Entrepreneurship and Innovation* (August), pp. 143–153.

Ellmeier, A. (2003). Cultural entrepreneurialism: On the changing relationship between the arts, culture and employment. *International Journal of Cultural Policy*, 9(1), pp. 3–16.

Enhuber, M. (2014). How is Damien Hirst a cultural entrepreneur? *Artivate: A Journal of Entrepreneurship in the Arts*, 3(2), pp. 3–20.

Essig, L. (2015). Means and ends: A theory framework for understanding entrepreneurship in the US arts and culture Sector. *Journal of Arts Management, Law, and Society*, 45(1), pp. 227–246.

Fillis, I. (2002). Creating marketing and the art organisation/What can the artist offer? *International Journal of Nonprofit and Voluntary Sector Marketing*, 7(2), pp. 131–145.

———. (2010). The art of the entrepreneurial marketer. *Journal of Research in Marketing and Entrepreneurship*, 12(2), pp. 87–107.

Gartner, W.B. and Carter, N.M. (2003). Entrepreneurial behavior and firm organizing processes. In: Z.J. Acs and D.B. Audretsch, eds., *Handbook of entrepreneurship research*. Boston: Kluwer Academic Publishers, pp. 195–221.

Goodwin, C.A. and Mucha, R.T. (2008). *Aesthetic intelligence: What business can learn from the arts*. Available at http://www.cgoodwinassociates.com/assets/downloads/AIarticle.pdf [Accessed 25 Nov. 2017].

Hagoort, G., Thomassen, A., and Kooyman, R. (2012). *Pioneering minds worldwide: On the entrepreneurial principles of the cultural and creative industries: Actual insights into cultural and creative entrepreneurship research*. Delft: Eburon Uitgeverij BV.

Harvie, J. (2013). *Fair Play. Art, Performance and Neoliberalism*. Basingstoke: Palgrave MacMillan.

Hausmann, A. (2010). German artists between bohemian idealism and entrepreneurial. *International Journal of Cultural Policy*, 12(2), pp. 17–27.

Hills, G.E. and LaForge, R.W. (1992). Research at marketing interface to advance entrepreneurship theory. *Entrepreneurship: Theory and Practice*, Spring 1992, p. 33+.

Hjorth, D. (2003). *Rewriting entrepreneurship – for a new perspective on organisational creativity*. Copenhagen/Malmö/Oslo: CBS Press/Liber/Abstrakt.

Hjorth, D. and Johannisson, B. (2009). Learning as an entrepreneurial process. *Revue de l'Entrepreneuriat*, 8(2), pp. 57–78. doi: 10.3917/entre.082.0057.

Johnson, V. (2007). What is organizational imprinting? Cultural entrepreneurship in the founding of the Paris Opera. *The American Journal of Sociology*, 113(1), pp. 97–127.

Kavousy, E., Shahosseini, A., Kiasi, S., and Ardahaey, F. (2010). Cultural entrepreneurship strategies in Iran. *Serbian Journal of Management*, 5(2), pp. 227–241.

Klamer, A. (2011). Cultural entrepreneurship. *The Review of Austrian Economics*, 24(2), pp. 141–156.

Klamer, A. and Zuidhof, P.W. (1999). *The values of cultural heritage: Merging economic and cultural appraisal*. Los Angeles: Getty Conservation Institute.

Kolsteeg, J. (2012). Strategic practice in creative organisations. In: J. Hagoort, A. Thomassen, and R. Kooyman, eds., *Pioneering minds worldwide. On the entrepreneurial principles of the cultural and creative industries*. Utrecht: Eburon, pp. 42–45.

———. (2013). Situated cultural entrepreneurship. *Artivate: A Journal of Entrepreneurship in the Arts*, 2, pp. 3–13..

Konrad, E. (2010). Kulturunternehmertum. *Wirtschaftspolitische Blätter*, 57(3), pp. 333–348.

———. (2013). Cultural entrepreneurship: The impact of social networking on success. *Creativity and Innovation Management*, 22(3), pp. 307–319.

Kuhn, T.S. (1962/1997). The structures of scientific revolutions and comments on the relations of science and art. In: *The essential tensions: Selected studies in scientific tradition and change*. Chicago, IL: University of Chicago Press, pp. 340–351.

Lampel, J. and Germain, O. (2016). Creative industries as hubs of new organizational and business practices. *Journal of Business Research*, 69, pp. 2327–2333.

Lange, B. (2008). Accessing markets in creative industries: Professionalization and social-spatial strategies of culturepreneurs in Berlin. *Creative Industries Journal*, 1(2), pp. 115–135.

———. (2011). Professionalization in space: Social-spatial strategies of culturepreneurs in Berlin. *Entrepreneurship & Regional Development: An International Journal*, 23(3–4), pp. 259–279.

Lehman, K., Fillis, I.R., and Miles, M. (2014). The art of entrepreneurial market creation. *Journal of Research in Marketing and Entrepreneurship*, 16(2), pp. 163–182.

Lindqvist, K. (2011). Artist entrepreneur. In: M. Scherdin and I. Zander, eds. *Art entrepreneurship*. Cheltenham, Norhampton: Edward Elgar, pp. 10–22.

Lounsbury, M. and Glynn, M. (2001). Cultural entrepreneurship: Stories, legitimacy, and the acquisition of resources. *Strategic Management Journal*, 22(6/7), pp. 545–564.

Metze, T. (2009). Discursive power in deliberations: A case of redevelopment for the creative economy in the Netherlands. *Policy and Society*, 28(3), pp. 241–251.

Mokyr, J. (2013). Cultural entrepreneurs and the origins of modern economic growth. *Scandinavian Economic History Review*, 61(1), pp. 1–33.

Mucha, R.T. (2009). *Aesthetic intelligence: Reclaim the power of your senses*. Booksurge.

Musil, R. (2016/2017). *Der Mann ohne Eigenschaften*. 4 Bde. (im Rahmen einer Musil-Gesamtausgabe in zwölf Bänden). Salzburg: Jung und Jung.

Phillips, R. (2011). Arts entrepreneurship and economic development: Can every city be 'Austintatious'?. *Foundations and Trends in Entrepreneurship*, 6(4), pp. 239–313.

Preece, S. (2011). Performing arts entrepreneurship: Toward a research agenda. *Journal of Arts Management, Law, and Society*, 41(2), pp. 103–120.

Rae, D. (2005). Cultural diffusion: A formative process in creative entrepreneurship? *The International Journal of Entrepreneurship and Innovation*, 6(3), pp. 185–192.

Rentschler, R. (2007). Painting equality: Female artists as cultural entrepreneurial marketers. *Equal Opportunities International*, 26(7), pp. 665–677.

Ripsas, S. (1998). Towards an interdisciplinary theory of entrepreneurship. *Small Business Economics*, 10(2), pp. 103–115.

Say, J.B. (1803). *Traité d'économie politique: Ou, simple exposition de la manière dont se forment, se distribuent et se consomment les richesses*, Translation: *Treatise on political economy: On the production, distribution and consumption of wealth*. Kelley: New York, 1964 (1st ed. 1827).

Scherdin, M. and Zander, I. (2011). Introduction. In: M. Scherdin and I. Zander, eds., *Art entrepreneurship*. Cheltenham: Edward Elgar, pp. 2–9.

Schumpeter, J.A. (1911). *Theorie der wirtschaftlichen Entwicklung*. Leipzig: Duncker & Humblot.

———. ([1911] 2003). The theory of economic development. In: J. Backhaus, ed., Boston: Kluwer. This text constitutes chapter 7 of Theorie der wirtschaftlichen Entwicklung (1911) and has been translated by Ursula Backhaus.

Scott, M. (2012). Cultural entrepreneurs, cultural entrepreneurship: Music producers mobilising and converting Bourdieu's alternative capitals. *Poetics*, 40(3), pp. 237–255.

Shane, S. (2003). *A general theory of entrepreneurship. The individual-opportunity nexus*. Cheltenham: Edward Elgar.

Smit, A. (2011). The influence of district visual quality on location decisions of creative entrepreneurs. *Journal of American Planning Association*, 77(2), pp. 167–168.

Snyder, C., Binder, M., Mitchell, J., and Breeden, L. (2010). *Cultural entrepreneurship: At the crossroads of people, place, and prosperity*. (Publication). Santa Fe, New Mexico: Global Center for Cultural Entrepreneurship.

Spilling, O.R. (1991). Entrepreneurship in a cultural perspective. *Entrepreneurship and Regional Development*, 3, pp. 33–48.

Swedberg, R. (2006). The cultural entrepreneur and the creative industries: Beginning in Vienna. *Journal of Cultural Economics*, 30(4), pp. 243–261.

Towse, R. (2011). *A handbook of cultural economics*. Cheltenham: Edward Elgar Publishing.

Vecco, M. (forthcoming). Artpreneurs' lessons to traditional entrepreneurs. *International Journal of Entrepreneurship and Small Businesses*.

Wilson, E.O. (1999). *Consilience: The unity of knowledge*. New York: Vintage Books Edition.

Wilson, N. and Stokes, D. (2004). Laments and serenades: Relationship marketing and legitimation strategies for the cultural entrepreneur. *Qualitative Market Research: An International Journal*, 7(3), pp. 218–227.
———. (2006). Managing creativity and innovation: The challenge for cultural entrepreneurs. *Journal of
Small Business and Enterprise Development*, 12(3), pp. 366–378.
Yang, G. (2005). Days of old are not puffs of smoke: Three hypotheses on collective memories of the cul-
tural revolution. *The China Review*, 5(2), pp. 13–41.
Zander, I. and Scherdin, M. (2011). *Art entrepreneurship*. Cheltenham: Edward Elgar.
Zanini, A. (2013). *Principi e forme delle scienze sociali. Cinque studi su Schumpeter*. Bologna: Il Mulino.

8

MORE THAN THE SUM OF ITS PARTS

Dance, creative management and enterprise in collaboration[1]

Farooq Chaudhry

Creativity is just about connecting things. When you ask creative people how they did something they feel a little guilty because they didn't really do it, they just saw something. It seemed obvious to them after a while.

—Steve Jobs[2]

Introduction

This chapter focuses on dance making as business, examining the role of the cultural entrepreneur as well as the arts and artist manager in the dance world. It reflects on my personal experience as a producer of the contemporary dance company Akram Khan, to argue that business need not be a dirty word in the arts. Rather than putting forward a normative road map to success, I seek to share my work practices over the past fifteen years to contribute to an understanding of the tricks of the trade in dance management.

It is important to mention that contemporary dance, overall, is a niche performing art, and though practised worldwide, like many other niche activities it has a relatively small audience when compared to more mainstream arts like classical ballet or the dance shows found in London's West End and New York's Broadway. By definition, its expressions are of today or seen from current perspectives, and the creative process is highly experimental and fraught with risk. Over-protection of its inherent experimental nature has resulted in an unhealthy scepticism within the industry whereby contemporary dance framed as a 'business' leads to its core values being contaminated. This scepticism could be a throwback to a time when arts management lacked a professional framework and was primarily being administered by altruistic individuals who were passionate about the arts yet with little formal training or understanding of the industry needs.

It is reassuring that since the 1990s growing professionalism of arts management and leadership has had a larger number of arts organisations becoming business focussed to strategically advance creativity, growth and sustainability. As McNicholas (2004, p. 58) put it:

> A new field is evolving. Arts/culture and business relationships, always somewhat edgy or "something different", now act as on the edge innovative systems and dynamic

complex adaptive relationship systems, offering unique opportunities and powerful economic advantages for businesses and communities in the 21st century.

In this chapter I seek to demonstrate that only with a dynamic, resilient and enterprising framework artists, producers and cultural leaders can optimise creativity and add cultural value to their practices. There are three sections. The first maps out the trajectory of the company's growth. The second looks at the role of the producer and how it can enhance value and propel vision to an arts organisation. The final section discusses the need to re-think and go beyond traditional business models in the arts as this has proven to be an integral catalyst in the company's artistic success.

Trajectories: harvesting a dance company

I'm not interested in how people move. I'm interested in what makes them move.

—Pina Bausch[3]

Before analysing the nature, practices and learning of our contemporary arts organisation, it is useful to consider how it came into being and what the driving forces were behind its creation. I first met Akram Khan, choreographer and dance artist, in 1999 after retiring from dancing. I had just completed a master's degree in arts management and was working as a trainee manager for a small arts organisation in London. The job was temporary, and I was expected to find my own personal artistic portfolio with which I could continue working with once my contract expired. In the summer of that year I saw a young Akram Khan perform at the Southbank Centre in London. I knew instinctively that I had witnessed something special. His dance language was an intelligent blend of contemporary dance and a North Indian classical dance form called Kathak. This language enthralled me, and I wanted to know more about him and his art. We spoke. There was a good chemistry and in a matter of months we started working together albeit informally. Once the partnership was established, I told Akram that I was confident I could take him somewhere different and new but, equally, he could do the same for me. I needed an artist who could challenge me as much as I could challenge him. That was our first promise to each other and on this basis, we started our journey together.

More often than not, professional projects in the arts world begin as an amateur dream. Funds were very scarce. We worked unbelievably hard and invested any money we earned from one-off performances into starting up a company. My first useful piece of advice to Akram was that he needed to travel abroad and develop a broader international perspective. I managed to secure him a place on a European-funded choreography course in Belgium called the X-group. He came back after six months with an increased artistic appetite. I then asked him what his dream (vision) was. He said he wanted to create a small ensemble work with original production elements and have the time to explore his ideas deeply. As he was speaking my inbuilt calculator was working out the value of this ambition. It came to around £60,000. . . money we certainly did not have. But I wanted to do it the way he imagined and the way I believed would work, so I had no option but to sell my modest one-bed apartment to raise the capital we needed, which I did. It was at this moment that I realised that I was an entrepreneur!

The project (Rush) as I suspected had a big impact and very quickly attracted attention from the global dance community. This in turn brought a large number of performances, which generated revenue. This also started the process of converting talent, ambition, risk and hard work into the three key drivers of any enterprise that wants to stand out from the crowd – excellence, innovation and reputation. This naturally brought greater confidence, which was then used as fuel for larger, more ambitious, projects. Audiences began to like us very quickly and we were deemed successful.

Success and failure in dance

Success in contemporary dance is usually associated with validation through arts awards, sell-out houses, gaining access to the international touring circuit and getting to work with the most gifted creative collaborators. In turn, a 'successful' dance company or artist becomes a magnet for world-class dancers, generating further opportunities for collaboration. If success is consistent, the company might be rewarded by its National Arts Council with regular funding over a sustained period of time. In the case of the UK, the company can then become a National Portfolio Organisation (NPO).

However, I try hard to steer away from notions of success and failure. Aside from the dangers of complacency and myth-making, they can be misleading because success can make one feel that they are a lot better than they actually are, while failure can make one feel they are a lot worse than they are. If anything, being comfortable with the prospect of failure can be a more potent force for success as well as an opportunity for introspection as a company. This is because one asks tough questions when one fails and does this much less when one succeeds. Failure is the road to new insights and learning. As the leading American choreographer Twyla Tharp stated, 'to get the full benefit of failure you have to understand the reasons for it' (2006, pp. 215–217), whether it is failure of skill, of concept, of nerve, of repetition or of denial.

Our earliest actions began to delineate what then would become our company's core principles and rules:

*   Akram Khan must always start every project with a dream
*   As a producer I must take risks and look for opportunities to translate this dream into an actual project
*   There is an absolute commitment by us both to quality, excellence, innovation and the need to make ourselves better
*   We would learn from everything we do

Another challenge related to managing success and failure is the so-called second work syndrome. Usually applied to music artists, novelists and film directors who achieve critical acclaim with their first album, book or film, it occurs when the heightened expectation of their second outing bears down on them resulting in underachievement. This is equally so with dance and our company succumbed to this pressure leading up to the premiere of our second work, Kaash, in France in 2002. We produced work that was underdeveloped. We failed to impress key people in the industry, and we did not manage to secure international presentations of this work. After a crestfallen week we dusted ourselves off and examined our failure with a fine-tooth comb. We reinvested significantly to rework and develop this production by tightening up the structure and ensuring the lighting and choreography were clearer and more coherent. In addition, we added more interesting rhythmic articulation and variation to the movement language. Within six weeks we turned our fortunes around and put ourselves back on track. Those important people saw our work again and they liked it and have supported it ever since.

Parallel to this, another potentially damaging scenario can take place. It is what I call the inability to surf momentum skilfully. When perceived 'success' came quickly, we found ourselves bombarded with a multitude of opportunities. We felt tremendously wanted. The euphoria resulting from this seduction began to cloud our judgment. We were running adrift like a ship at sea without sails or a rudder being pulled in all directions. We were beginning to make wrong decisions and liaise with the wrong people; that is, those who were taking a short-term interest in our work or wanted to present it as a tokenistic representation of cultural identity as opposed to an artistic merit and a genuine interest in supporting a career trajectory. In the traditional business world, it is the time when companies are most prone to collapse as they are unable to maintain cash flow to support their unexpected quick growth. It is a scenario almost impossible to anticipate. When it happened to us a six-month organisational review with an established consultant helped us refocus and discipline our intentions. As a result, we developed a formal company structure with a strategic business purpose and plan.

Mission and vision

The organisational review we undertook laid the seeds for self-determination. From the process of deciding what we did not want to do we were left with three things we did want to do:

- Artist–to–artist collaborations[4]
- Ensemble/company work[5]
- Classical Kathak solos[6]

Developing a company's vision and mission is equally important and constitutes the first step in planning for organisational success in arts management (Rosewall, 2014, p. 46). It took about ten years for Akram Khan Company to formulate a clear and authentic vision. During our infancy we grew by becoming what emerged from doing what we did not want to do or be. Just like a sculptor taking away clay to reveal the statue within, the more we worked, the clearer our artistic identity became and what we cared most about doing. From this process of distillation, we were able to articulate our vision and mission statements:

Our vision

To produce thoughtful, provocative and ambitious dance productions for the international stage by journeying across boundaries to create uncompromising artistic narratives.

Our mission

To take human themes and work with others to take them to new and unexpected places – embracing and collaborating with other cultures and disciplines.

Each production, then, relates to these statements. The dance language used in our work is rooted in Akram Khan's classical Kathak and modern dance training and his fascination with storytelling. The work continually evolves to communicate ideas that are intelligent, courageous and new, bringing with it international acclaim and recognition as well as artistic and commercial success – a core element of our vision.

Vision in business represents a mental image of your future world and how you see yourself getting there; in other words, a goal or a desired result; the former suggests a journey, the latter, a destination. In the business of dance, process is as much the unique selling point as the final production. It is usually what differentiates one arts organisation from another. The continuum of vision is a highly dynamic concept that needs careful and creative attention at every point. Vision shapes identity as much as identity shapes vision and if this dynamic interacts at a consistent level over a sustained period of time, it then crystallises into what is normally called a brand.

What is a brand? It is not just a question of a logo. The brand includes a company's style, character and values. The organisation is built on these values, be they artistic, moral or financial. They usually mirror the ethos and personality of the founder(s). Moreover, an organisation is not just a name with a certain number of people on the payroll, but it is essentially the creation of a culture – a way of doing things and viewing the world in a particular fashion. Understanding who you are (your brand) and what you do (your culture) demands self-awareness and the ability to stand outside of yourself and observe yourself objectively. This process of self-reflection then becomes a tool for growth, change and internal accountability.

Once the brand has been defined, the question of how to move away from essentialist cultural views and reductionist classifications arises. Despite Akram Khan and myself being of South Asian origin and our work clearly influenced by Indian classical dance aesthetics, we both decided from the outset we would not let ourselves be confined by cultural pigeonholing. We both fiercely believed that what we did was more important than who we were and that being labelled as a South Asian dance company would be a limited representation of our artistic vision.

Furthermore, we believed focussing on cultural identity could seriously undermine our ambitions and growth. This was at a time when political correctness around issues of diversity in the arts was controversially splitting opinion, with one camp believing it allowed for artistic mediocrity; the other saying under-representation of minority groups did not sit well with the UK's liberal and democratic values. We aligned ourselves with the first group despite the fact that amplifying cultural identity was a fast track to funding and grants. We had to make our way on artistic merit and not by shouting from the margins about not being culturally recognised. In recent times a concern with 'diversity in the arts' has shifted away from social and political agendas and is now being championed on creative grounds, what the Arts Council England refers to as the 'Creative Case for Diversity' (ACE, 2018). Artistic excellence and innovation were, then, the foundations of our brand.

Establishing trust with audiences

The relationship an arts company establishes with its audiences also relates to how the company presents itself and what its core goals are. Unlike conventional consumer and product/service relationships whereby certainty and clarity are required to trigger a purchase, contemporary dance asks for a different type of transaction. The artist usually has only the faintest hint of what they will create when they embark on their artistic quest. All pre-premiere press and marketing will focus on the artist's inspiration and less so on the outcome of such artistic creation. What is sold to the audience is an element of surprise and mystery and the invitation to dream. The relationship between artist and audience, therefore, asks for a great deal of loyalty and trust because at times this transaction can be uncomfortable, provocative and disruptive; in other words, designed to throw the audience off balance, sometimes even undermining existing perspectives to create new ones. Colbert (2003, p. 30) sums this up succinctly by stating that 'high art has a product focus and popular art a market focus'. He expands this further:

> The fundamental concept in traditional marketing – meeting the needs of the consumer – does not apply in high art. The artistic product does not exist to fulfil a market need. Its *raison d'etre* is independent of the market, which is what makes it a particular marketing challenge. Instead of seeking to meet the consumers' needs by offering them a product they desire, the arts manager seeks consumers who are attracted to the product.
>
> *(Colbert, 2003, p. 31)*

Even with an audience attracted to the product this unusual and complex transaction is exacerbated even further as the audience tends to be the last thing in the contemporary dance artist's mind when they begin a new project or production. They do not start with the audience; rather, they finish with them. The audience is the final cog in the creative process. The audience can be considered the final collaborator as they complete the artist's work. This makes the level of risk far greater and treacherous than a conventional brand/consumer relationship, making the need for a robust, resilient and flexible business framework more pertinent. It acts as ballast, allowing what is being rooted to move as freely as it can without getting lost or buckling under the stress of uncertainty and the expectations of multiple stakeholders. Dance through enterprise requires a high degree of uninhibited innovative thinking and the artist requires a high degree of protection for them to be courageous with their ideas. As Tharp (2006, p. 5) puts it:

> I don't know what music I will be using. I don't know what dancers I will be working with. I have no idea what the costumes will look like, or the lighting or who will be performing the music. I have no idea of the length of the piece, although it has to be long enough to fill the second half of a full programme to give the paying audience its money's worth. . . . My dancers expect me to deliver because my choreography represents their livelihood. The presenters in Los Angeles expect the same because they've sold tickets to a lot of people with the promise that they will see something interesting and new from me. . . . That's a lot of people, many of whom I have never met, counting on me to be creative. . . . But right now I'm not thinking about this. I'm in a room with the obligation to create a major dance piece.

Ideas are an arts company's currency. They motivate and inspire us. Our ideas define who we are as a company and we are judged by whether they are clear, honest, authentic, accessible, interesting or innovative. We stand and fall by our ideas. The most exciting and meticulously crafted ideas can become innovations. They often begin without too many pre-set rules or structures. As they evolve organically and if we listen to them, they develop their own unique structures according to their needs. This is as necessary for organisational growth as it is for art making.

The art of collaboration

Of all the performing arts dance is probably the most naturally collaborative. This is the case because it does not use a recognisable spoken language, like theatre does. Dancers usually come from a range of different dance disciplines and cultures and this makes them creative collaborators too. Modern dance is a majority of the time an original creation and is not built on existing texts like theatre. It has to be written, devised and expressed. Aside from choreography and dancers, this art form requires music, lighting, costumes, scenery, sound engineers, technicians, and dramaturgy, among others. This collaborative process is one strategy for ensuring a high level of collective innovation and artistic protection. Following Rixhon (2008, p. 1) innovation involves:

> the successful implementation of creative ideas within a context. Individual or collective creativity is a starting point for innovation; it is necessary but not sufficient. The creative insight must be put into action to make a genuine difference, to introduce a modified business process or to provide an improved product. Creativity may be displayed by individuals, but innovation – the production of the creation – occurs only in an organised environment. Innovation, like many functions, is an organisational process that requires specific tools, methods and leadership.

The process of collaboration involves several steps: curiosity, conversation, connection, commitment, concept, exchange, constraint and innovation. Constraints are part of collaboration as much as uninhibited freedom can be a catalyst for new ideas. The path to greater creativity and hence innovation involves recognising and working with the constraints that are inherent within the art form or area of activity. Obstacles 'increase the possibilities of perception' and 'expand our conceptual scope' (Lehrer, 2011). Instead of seeing them as troublesome, barriers that may cause us to quit or to become overly pragmatic, they can, if embraced with an open and engaged mind, foster new thoughts and ideas and allow us to trespass on the boundaries of familiar thought to a better end. In my experience, the biggest constraints have been time, funding, lack of imagination and fear.

Collaboration can be thought of as a very specific process that follows different stages to fulfil an objective. Each artist has their own working methods and spends their formative years refining this as much as their artistic voice. By the time our company had entered its tenth year, our process had transformed from a conventional ten- to twelve-week continuous creation period to one that was spread out over eighteen months of work. This would begin with blue-sky brainstorming by the core creative team to establish a collective vision rooted in Akram's initial inspiration. With the vision now seeded, each collaborator could go off and develop their individual areas of responsibility, remaining in contact with Akram throughout.

The second stage is to 'cast' the dancers and musicians according to the needs of the project. This is followed by a month of 'play' in a rehearsal studio. Play with no thought about an outcome is a highly effective creative tool to source new ideas in the most unlikely places. It functions as a doorway to new thinking and new content through combinations free from the logical mind. Collaborators would then be invited into the tail end of the play period after which the company would take a break to reflect and absorb what happened. A few months later everyone would reconvene and begin the process of generating content and laying down a structure. The company would then take another short reflection break and spend the final few weeks on stage refining and editing structure and material until it was ready for the world premiere. The transference to an extended period on stage ensures that scaling up from the studio has sufficient time to adjust and find its own internal logic.

In short, my recommendations for successful collaboration in the arts involve:

- Be prepared to 'kill your sacred cows'
- Balance selfishness and selflessness
- Enjoy the risk that is inherent in the process
- Don't try to over control the process to make it efficient. It's creative so there is no linear approach
- Be prepared to make it up as you go along
- Choose the right people and not the best people
- Know the difference between doing it right and doing the right thing
- Enjoy being lost and the change that will come from it
- Act, don't think
- If you think, do it like a pioneer
- Discover the meaning and don't start with it
- Give more than you take
- Avoid saying 'it is mine'

This could be called our dance company's manufacturing process through which we create the optimum conditions for our dance creations. It affords us the choice as to when we could put up and take down the 'scaffolding' through which we could build our artistic product. If managed poorly and by giving way to pragmatism and compromise the scaffolding would remain, diluting the theatrical experience and demonstrating how the work was made rather than what it is seeking to convey.

This optimum process is very expensive. Our early productions cost between £150,000 to £250,000 to produce. This upgraded process took our costs up to £500,000–£600,000. Yet, this raising of the artistic bar resulted in us being invited to create for the London Olympics 2012 and added considerable reputational value. It proved to be an investment in our intangible values and showed how important the role of the producer was in such process.

The rise of the dance producer

You can't cross the sea merely by standing at the water. I have to become my own version of an optimist. If I can't make it through one door, I'll go through another door – or I'll make a door.
—Rabindranath Tagore[7]

In many aspects, a dance producer is a lot like conventional business entrepreneurs. They thrive from taking risks, live from their passions, love problem solving and are inherently creative learning machines. They cannot be shackled to a desk. They tend to be individualists, rule-breakers and non-conformists. Producers drive growth and ambition. Managers bring stability and protection. Producers are difficult to define and therefore many studies are of individuals or a mindset as opposed to a particular skillset that one acquires through training or education. Often what they do and who they are is ingrained in their identity. Therefore, to understand what kind of dance producer I am, it would be useful for the reader to know where I have come from.

In 2011 I was invited to speak about my role as a producer of Akram Khan Company at an arts conference in Palestine. After listening to my presentation, an Austrian journalist described me as a curious mix of a businessman, artist, philosopher and street kid. I am a Pakistani immigrant who arrived with my family to the United Kingdom in 1963. In the next twenty years, firmly rooted in a working class background, a range of experiences would leave a mark in my life: I was the top of my class at primary school and also, being the leader of a local council estate criminal gang, I was put into care in 1974 after my parents divorced; I was incarcerated in juvenile delinquent centres for two short spells; and then found a way out of my early life troubles by being placed into a 'therapeutic' community called Peper Harow. The philosophy of the school was that by having access to regular psychotherapy and an enriched creative environment, emotionally damaged boys could restore their self-esteem and create new identities forged in self-awareness and hope. On leaving Peper Harow in 1981 I studied English Literature in the School of African and Asian studies at Sussex University. On taking my very first contemporary dance class, without hesitation I quit university to train as a professional dancer. I graduated in 1986 and enjoyed a virtually non-stop professional dance career until 1998. I then went back to university to study MA Arts Management at City University in London. In 1999 I met the British choreographer and dancer Akram Khan and we founded the Akram Khan Company in October 2000. I am still working with the company today.

In the past fifteen years, dance productions have become more sophisticated with higher production values. This is as much to do with advances in theatre technology as increased support from national funding agencies. Consequently, artistic directors have become more demanding to the point that the traditional responsibilities of general manager or executive director are no longer adequate to meet raised expectations. In addition, an expanded market through globalisation meant access to a wider pool of resources and opportunities. A void was appearing within dance organisations that needed a new enterprising mindset that could meet these new challenges and exploit new opportunities. With this came the rise of the dance producer.

In the case of the Akram Khan Company the dance producer role has been instrumental in driving its growth and ambitions in service of the vision. It emerged as a new force in contemporary dance. Considering entrepreneurship, there is little that separates a business entrepreneur from a cultural entrepreneur aside from the market context in which they work and the outcomes they seek. Both will seek to increase market presence and maximise customer experience by the quality of their product. One may define value or reward by increased share price; the other, by generating high-quality intellectual property. They are both powerful and dynamic enterprising forces for introducing new ideas and for transforming old ones. Bridgstock (2013, p. 126, following Duening) lists some of the attributes of successful arts entrepreneurship which can be found in the business literature:

- The opportunity recognising mind
- The designing mind
- The risk managing mind
- The resilient mind
- The effectuating mind

However, there is no formula to be a successful producer. Having worked on both sides of the stage, my understanding and experiences are the elements that play a big part in my judgment and decision-making. It is a highly individualistic role and requires as much instinct as intellect, since often a producer is dealing with intangible invisible forces as tangible ones.

In this sense, a producer can be described:

> Like a quiet magician who makes the near impossible possible, gathering resources in such lean times, never losing integrity and making it look deceptively simple when it isn't, it isn't at all.
>
> *Karthika Nair (personal correspondence, 2013) – co-founder*
> *and former producer of Eastman in Flanders*

> One of the producer's greatest tasks was to conjure up the circumstances by which artists can create their best work
>
> *Glen Berger (2013, p. 9) – Song of Spiderman: The Inside Story*
> *of the Most Controversial Musical in Broadway History*

It is interesting to see how both quotations refer to magic and conjuring as key elements in the producer role. Magic aside, my daily work as a producer comprises:

- Being involved in the conception of our projects
- Helping source and assemble creative teams
- Managing communications lines between creative teams
- Being the chief negotiator with all stakeholders
- Scouting for future projects
- Finding the right investors for our work
- Finding the right distributors for our work
- Finding the right platforms for performance

- Protecting integrity of artistic vision/priorities
- Being an architect of ideas that further artistic and company growth

Currently there are many manifestations of the producer role, ranging from a brilliant production manager, a forward-thinking efficient administrator, to an out-of-the-box thinking entrepreneur. When I first adopted the title in 2004, which was a time when such role was virtually unheard of in contemporary dance, I likened it to the type of producer found in filmmaking and traditional theatre. These producers spend a majority of their time interfacing between the creative process and the resources that help shape the project vision. Quite simply, as a producer one divides attention between the art and the money.

Having to work with a range of stakeholders, producers need to be fluent in many languages so that things do not get lost in 'translation'. For instance, the agenda of a funder who may face the higher authorities that allocate their budgets will be too far away from the choreographer facing his or her creative team. Yet they need each other, and it is the producer's task to ensure that their needs are understood. The fact that a producer has to listen to as much as they have to talk offers them a doorway to never-ending learning.

Our business is dance making. Etymologically, the term business refers to 'the state of being busy', although earlier meanings in old English defined the word as 'anxiety' and later on, a difference was made between busyness and having a 'business' to attend to (Cresswell, 2010, p. 65). With this logic, (dance) business can be associated with industry as it involves an exchange of services and skills to the mutual benefit of the parts involved.

A good producer, thus, is also the master of such exchange. From my experience, it is the process and not the outcome that is the most stimulating aspect of the job; in other words, the skill of solving a puzzle not just with a solution but also with another more audacious question. Producers can be as visionary as artists with similar amounts of fearlessness, craziness and passion. In a more connected and globalized world, new partnership opportunities emerge but with them, the complexities of working across borders. At the same time, in recent years there has been greater emphasis from national governments on the value of the cultural and creative communities as important contributors to GDP and economic growth. Both the producer and the arts company need to adapt to these ever-changing times and a good strategy, in our case, has been developing an innovative business model.

Beyond traditional business models

By three methods we may learn wisdom: first, by reflection, which is noblest; second, by imitation, which is easiest; and third, by experience, which is the most bitter.
—Confucious[8]

Although strategies are important in the business world, we did not have one. We made it up as we went along, particularly in the early years. Strategies are difficult to plan and are multidimensional; as Mintzberg's (1987) classic 'five Ps' approach has suggested, there can be multiple definitions and a strategy can be approached as plan, plot, pattern, position or perspective. Even with our burgeoning business model we were still a micro economy, and micro economies tend to be more tactical than strategic. The fact that we were relatively small meant that we could be agile and grow fast, unlike large companies. Akram Khan Company operates as a 'bamboo business', a metaphor that suggests strength, flexibility, prolific growth and space down its centre for new ideas.

Strategy in most cases was applied retrospectively to show that we knew what we were doing even though this was not always the case. It allowed us to conveniently forget mistakes, luck, poor judgment, the bad decisions that went well and the good decisions that went bad. It joined all the good dots and turned a blind eye to the bad ones, leaving behind legacies of incompetence, lousy judgment and abject failure. At the heart of growth there is both vulnerability and strength, the feeling of being exposed, but also the unique opportunity to stretch and grow in novel and unpredictable ways (Sheehy, 2006).

Difficulties render an arts organisation stronger. As we started with a spirit of enterprise it was important that our artistic growth was underpinned by a robust and clear sense of commercial discipline. We were not seeking only to protect, conserve and consolidate our company's value, but rather, the capacity to respond to change was a necessary skill. Embracing change proved crucial to develop our organisational confidence, reminding us that business models change every time a crisis hits. In recent years, the Arts Council England has shifted the emphasis of their funding rhetoric to that of 'investment' as opposed to subsidy. A study was commissioned (Langley and Royce, 2016) to develop good practice business planning in the arts and cultural sector. The key emphasis of this study was how to prepare and write a business plan to both mitigate risk and encourage a clear vision for growth.

Essentially, to remain an ambitious enterprise we needed a flexible and very responsive business structure. Many organisations in the UK's arts funding sector tend to adopt the model of a limited company with charitable status (not for profit). It allows organisations to access funds from trusts and foundations, be tax exempt and ensure charitable aims are prioritised over commerciality. However, they come with a high degree of accountability and can inhibit a more ambitious mindset. In 2003, after a six-month organisational review with an experienced consultant it was concluded that a charity structure would best serve our company's artistic aspirations. Despite this very sensible recommendation, as an entrepreneur it did not feel right so I rejected this direction. As an alternative I chose a for-profit structure which was a company limited by guarantee (Akram Khan Company). At the time it was an uncomfortable decision for some board members, particularly as it would mean paying corporation tax on revenue, but I assured them it was the ideal way forward towards sustainability, independence and most importantly, artistic excellence. As profits increased, I decided to set up a charity (AKCT) to which we could gift aid some of the profits to support and fund the work of the dancers with whom we worked.

We resisted the urge to adopt the traditional business model used by many established dance companies whereby dancers are employed on a full-time basis. We wanted the artistic flexibility to cast our projects, rather than our productions being determined by the number of dancers on the payroll. We believed it could limit ambition and place enormous pressure on operational efficiency. It also brought with it the danger of the vision serving the organisation rather than the organisation serving the vision. Hence it was important that the business plan functioned as a tool to use in planning our future activities and operations, as 'the story of the future that your organisation wishes to create; a route map but not a straitjacket' (Langley and Royce, 2016, p. 7).

In 2006, as our reputational value started to gain traction, we were receiving more commercial opportunities such as Akram to co-direct and create a duet with the Oscar winning French film actress Juliette Binoche (In-I). These projects garnered more popular interest as well as high-level sponsorship (Hermes Foundation and SG Private Banking). This resulted in an increased volume of performances with higher performance fee guarantees. Despite Akram Khan Company being a for-profit structure, it was receiving public monies from the Arts Council England and, therefore, we felt high levels of revenue could be a conflict of interests, so a new company limited by shares was formed: Khan Chaudhry Productions (KCP), of which Akram

Khan and myself were shareholders. We would, however, employ the Akram Khan Company's (AKC) operational structure to produce and manage this project, therefore generating further revenue for the company. KCP also gift aided some of its profits to AKCT to support younger artists. AKC would do the experimental *avant-garde* work, KCP would respond to commercial opportunities that helped to strengthen the company brand, and AKCT would support a new generation of artists.

Though legally independent, this ecology of three business structures is set up to support and serve each other's interests without getting the money mixed up in one pot. It is virtually the same talent pool maximising its value and assets without stepping on different agendas and confusing things. The original idea for this model first came to me when sitting in an airport lounge on tour. I scribbled it down (Figure 8.1) and then articulated it more clearly in a formal diagram (Figure 8.2).

Business models reflect and are closely aligned to the arts company's organisational priorities. At the same time, priorities need to be translated into specific objectives. In the case of Akram Khan, our priorities – growth, independence, stability and flexibility – have informed the following objectives:

- Continue to make high-quality, innovative work
- Establish ourselves as an international brand
- Ensure our work is accessible to as many diverse cultures and audiences as possible
- Develop alternative income streams
- Continue operations with no more than one quarter income dependency on public subsidy

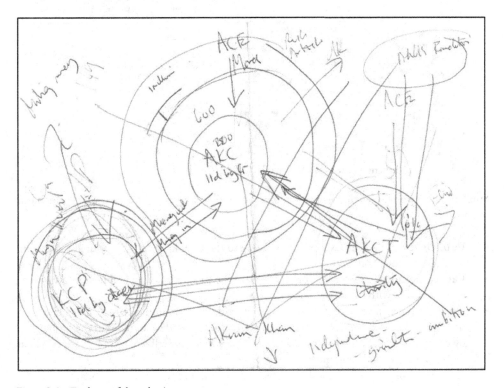

Figure 8.1 Ecology of three business structures

- Expand and create a supportive and flexible structure for artistic and administrative personnel
- Develop professional training opportunities for artists
- Implement modern business practice to support/propel artistic work
- Establish a strong and generous work culture and ethos
- Continue to work with high-profile artists in other genres
- Identify alternative performance opportunities
- Ensure that at least 15% of our work is seen in less privileged markets

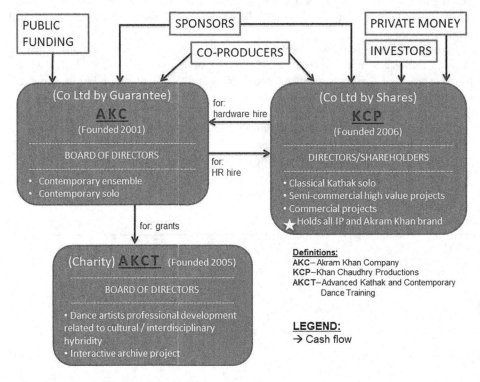

Figure 8.2   Formal structure of the three companies (AKC, AKCT, KCP)

Similarly, these priorities and objectives reflect the funding sources and partners with which our organisation works:

- **Public subsidy:** a least favourite source due to the high levels of accountability based on social and political outcomes
- **Earned income:** a favourite source in view of the satisfaction of spending your own hard-earned money with a degree of independence
- **Co-producers:** invest not only in produced works but also in the artist's career. These are usually long-term relationships and often participate in the development of the production by offering physical resources such as theatres or studios as well as cash. They are excellent feedback providers during the creative process.
- **Commissions:** not so artistically satisfying. We do not set the artistic agenda.

- **Sponsors:** usually have a role when company value, reputation and quality are proven. It is a partnership often based on the alignment of values, ideals, brand and reputations. With our current sponsor for instance, the French road construction company Colas, we are bound together by our commitment to diversity and to connect the world through talent.

	03/04	04/05	05/06	06/07	07/08	08/09	09/10
Akram Khan Company	328,905	696,587	637,376	525,703	717,051	743,438	646,048
AKCT	-	-	10,527	31,327	99,625	40,010	246,964
Khan Chaudhry Productions	-	-	-	-	690,967	2,226,560	577,366
Total	**328,905**	**696,587**	**647,903**	**557,030**	**1,507,643**	**3,010,008**	**1,470,378**
Public Funding	40,267	98,235	195,000	184,950	190,036	195,166	200,435
% of AKC turnover	12%	14%	31%	35%	27%	26%	31%
% of total turnover	12%	14%	30%	33%	13%	6%	14%
International income	229,193	444,001	294,565	328,710	1,074,116	2,140,131	1,014,544
% of total turnover	70%	64%	45%	59%	71%	71%	69%

	10/11	11/12	12/13	13/14	14/15	Average last 5 years
Akram Khan Company	1,326,135	1,554,051	935,885	1,913,028	837,608	1,313,341
AKCT	35,774	17,685	68,615	90,518	98,218	62,162
Khan Chaudhry Productions	349,482	63,320	121,632	245,450	894,500	334,877
Total	**1,711,391**	**1,635,056**	**1,126,132**	**2,248,996**	**1,830,326**	**1,710,380**
Public Funding	204,817	190,684	225,000	220,322	215,610	211,287
% of AKC turnover	15%	12%	24%	12%	26%	16%
% of total turnover	12%	12%	20%	10%	12%	12%
International income	1,148,901	1,232,622	776,081	1774,669	1,249,125	1,236,280
% of total turnover	67%	75%	69%	79%	68%	72%

Figure 8.3   Financial footprint of the three companies (AKC, AKCT, KCP) between 2003 and 2015

Dealing with such a range of funding sources can be demanding. It is not necessary for the artistic director, though, to be overly concerned with financial and organisational matters. Some awareness is needed, but many feel hamstrung and inhibited by day-to-day management. When artistic directors lose their artistic focus and energy by being side-tracked with operational burdens, their work almost invariably suffers. Artistic directors have a great deal to lose – they lose their reputations. The producer loses the trust and faith of their spider web of stakeholders. In the slipstream of both lies the success of the arts organisation.

In just over fifteen years Akram Khan Company has established itself as one of the leading contemporary dance companies in the world. A highlight in the company's trajectory was featuring prominently in the opening ceremony of the London Olympic Games in 2012. Our historical narrative in numbers can be summarised as follows:

- 21 productions
- 1560 performances (one performance every 3.5 days continuously for 15 years)
- 398 venues
- 61 countries
- 910,215 audience members (not including the Olympic Games)
- 82% average attendance
- Over 300 jobs created for artistic and administrative personnel
- Average reliance on public subsidy – 12%

Being a non-verbal art form, dance has a fantastic capacity to cross borders and reach diverse groups of people and audiences. This explains why dance companies of all scales can tour prolifically. This, in effect, makes them export enterprises. Yet, there is much to consider when working in this business model. Aside from the obvious pressures of global currency fluctuations being an 'export' company, we also must be culturally sensitive and diplomatic when we work with different countries. Ignorance and a lack of respect for different business practices can be damaging to international opportunities and partnerships. As human beings we may all want the same things but our processes and drivers for choice and decision-making can vary dramatically. The case of how a large Chinese company chose a contract that had inferior technology from a French company rather than a vastly superior technology offer from an American company has been documented by *Time* magazine a few years ago. When asked about the rationale behind their decision, the Chinese company stated that the French spent most of their time listening to them and did not make them eat their food unlike the Americans.

A final major challenge is that dance as an activity cannot benefit from modern technologies to become cheaper and more efficient. For instance, a composer can download software that allows him to access hundreds of instruments from all over the globe at the push of a button. Dance still requires real bodies for eight to ten hours a day, in a warm, well-lit dance studio for an average of ten to twelve weeks' creation. Year on year inflationary pressures raise these costs, placing further pressures on the dance companies and choreographers.

Conclusion

You can only lose something that you have, but you cannot lose something that you are.
—Eckhart Tolle[9]

In this chapter I have shared some of the lessons learnt as part of my role as a creative producer in a contemporary dance company. A good producer resembles a good artist in that they see things before other people see them or they simply see things that other people cannot see. Then they make it happen.

I also discussed why dance needs to be seen and approached as enterprise and what this means in terms of strategies and tactics, funding sources, working with others, relating to audiences and touring. I also discussed some of the issues and opportunities that lie at the heart of creating, organising and managing an arts organisation operating both locally and internationally in a highly globalised world.

Particularly, dance making/touring in an international context comes with inherent difficulties and challenges that can threaten and impair growth. The first is selling original work to the market before it is made. This is where reputation is of a premium. We also work in a financial model where revenue generation is limited beyond live performance. We only make money when we are on stage because of the ephemeral character of the performing arts. Composers, writers, visual artists can make money 'while they sleep'. As we build up repertoire there is also the danger of being in competition with ourselves in what is essentially a limited market.

Through years of trial and error, risk-taking, embracing change and adopting a creative and flexible approach, an innovative model has emerged in the management of dance business. This is not necessarily a template to be imitated but an insight into a mindset where learned abilities married to innate human qualities such as endurance, perseverance, passion, conviction and the desire to be one's best has allowed our vision to fulfil its potential.

Lauded for consistently producing imaginative and inventive works, Akram Khan Company has received numerous prestigious national and international arts awards. International touring is the company's 'bread and butter' business with a prolific ongoing presence at many of the world's high-profile arts festivals and venues. The company's business model is nowadays studied alongside Cirque Du Soleil (in organisations such as the London Business School and Goldsmiths, University of London) as an example of success in the arts and entertainment industry.

Our first company business plan in 2005 was entitled 'journeys not destinations'. This is a timely reminder that there are still many challenges ahead and questions for the artistic leaders of today and the future. Such as what does a win/win look like when negotiating in a highly globalised world at war with increased parochialism? Is it enough to have a single bottom line when success is hinged on so many interlocking factors? Can we have multiple bottom lines – artistic success, financial success, moral success and a happy company? Can leaders access greater power and creativity by being more playful, disruptive, transparent and vulnerable?

Throughout my career I have always let art have the first say in any action I have taken, and, in this chapter, I would like it to have the last word. My teenage daughter recently asked me: 'When do you know you are in love?' After reflecting on it for a minute or two, I answered 'it is not how you feel about that person when you are with them, it is how you feel about yourself when you are with them. If you contract, you know you are with the wrong person, and if you expand, you know you are with the right person'. This, I believe, is also the purpose of art. It is how we feel about ourselves when we engage in cultural experiences, and the purpose of our dance and its business model is to expand so that these experiences are deeper, last longer and when at its very best, remain in our hearts and minds for our lifetime.

Acknowledgment

The author would like to thank Cecilia Dinardi for her support, assistance and encouragement when writing this chapter and to Aleksandar Brkić, Akram Khan, Akram Khan Company, Karthika Nair, Su-Man Hsu, Tian-Lan Chaudhry, Melvyn Rose, Clifford Summers and Jiaxuan Hon for their love, trust, inspiration and friendship throughout my career.

Notes

1 This chapter is based on a previous text entitled "Business of Dance", originally published on the Akram Khan website in 2011.
2 Steve Jobs, taken from Wolf (1996) Steve Jobs: The next insanely great thing, *Wire Magazine*, available online: www.wired.com/1996/02/jobs-2/

3 Pina Bausch, taken from Eichenbaum, R. (2017) *Inside the Dancer's Art*, Middletown, Conn.: Wesleyan University Press, p. 112.
4 Such as in the productions of *Zero Degrees*, *Sacred Monsters* and *In-I*, where Akram Khan was collaborating and performing with celebrated artists (e.g. Sylvie Guillem, Juliette Binoche).
5 As in the case of the works of Kaash, Ma, bahok, Vertical Road, where professional dancers were chosen to perform in works larger than a duet.
6 Where Akram Khan was performing alone in work heavily influenced by his classical Indian dance training, such as in Polaroid Feet, Ronin and Gnosis.
7 Rabindranath Tagore (1954) *Three plays: Mukta-dhara, Natir puja, Chandalika*. Oxford: Oxford University Press, p. 115.
8 Phrase attributed to the Chinese philosopher Confucius, taken from *Confucius Says: First 100 Lessons*, by Graeme Partington (2017: 62), published online by Lulu.
9 Tolle, E. (2006) *A New Earth: Create a Better Life*. New York: Penguin Books, p 221.

References

Arts Council England. (2018). *Equality, diversity and the creative case: A data report, 2016–17*. Manchester: ACE.
Berger, G. (2013). *Song of Spiderman: The inside story of the most controversial musical in Broadway history*. New York: Simon and Schuster.
Bridgstock, R. (2013). Not a dirty word: Arts entrepreneurship and higher education. *Arts and Humanities in Higher Education: An International Journal of Theory, Research and Practice*, 12, pp. 122–137.
Colbert, F. (2003). Entrepreneurship and leadership in marketing the arts. *International Journal of Arts Management*, 6(1), pp. 30–39.
Cresswell, J. (2010). *Oxford dictionary of word origin*, Oxford: Oxford University Press.
Langley, D. and Royce, S. (2016). *Business planning guidance for arts and cultural organisations*. London: Arts Council England.
Lehrer, J. (2011). Need to create? Get a constraint. *Wired.com*. Available at: www.wired.com/wiredscience/2011/11/need-to-create-get-a-constraint/
McNicholas, B. (2004). Arts, culture and business: A relationship transformation, a nascent field, *International Journal of Arts Management*, 7(1), pp. 57–68.
Mintzberg, H. (1987). The strategy concept I: Five Ps for strategy. *California Management Review*, 30(1), pp. 11–24.
Rixhon, P. (2008). Innovation leadership: Best practices from theatre creators. In: L. Becker, et al. eds., *Führung, innovation und wandel*. Kissing: Symposion Publishing, pp. 197–215.
Rosewall, E. (2014). *Arts management: Uniting arts and audiences in the 21st century*. New York: Oxford University Press.
Sheehy, G. (2006). *Passages: Predictable crises of adult life*. New York: Ballantine Books.
Tharp, T. (2006). *The creative habit: Learn it and use it for life*. New York: Simon & Schuster.
Wolf, G. (1996). Steve Jobs: The next insanely great thing. *Wire Magazine*. Available at: www.wired.com/1996/02/jobs-2/.

9

MANAGING CHANGE AND THE IMPLICATIONS FOR LEADERSHIP

Ben Walmsley

Introduction

The contention that change is now the only certainty for arts and cultural organizations has almost become a cliché. This is largely because different external drivers of change have combined to create a perfect storm for arts managers and leaders. For example, the financial drivers for change (caused largely by the global financial crisis of 2008–09 and the ensuing public and private funding cuts to the arts) are being compounded by the increasingly complex expectations of audiences (for example to participate and co-create) and by the proliferation of digital technologies and the dazzling opportunities that they present.

Despite these disruptive external factors, very little research has been conducted into change management in the arts, and even less into how leaders can shape and lead a change initiative. As Darren Peacock (2008) argues, there is "a gap in our understanding about how change happens and how we can shape its outcomes" (p. 334). This means that arts and cultural organizations tend to embark on change initiatives in the dark, often reinventing the wheel or repeating the same old mistakes. The lack of insight into how change happens also means that managers and leaders can feel unsupported and isolated when tasked with leading and implementing change in their organizations. But perhaps even more worryingly, arts and cultural organizations often put their heads in the sand and hope in vain that the need to change will magically disappear. It has justifiably been argued that this reaction has created a dangerous state of inertia that is now damaging the sector and holding it back (Bolton et al., 2011).

There is therefore a significant management gap in this key area of organizational activity. The aim of this chapter is to address this gap by providing an overview of the core theories pertaining to change management and applying them critically to the arts and cultural sector through a case study of a large regional theatre in the United Kingdom. The chapter will explore the core drivers and processes of change and discuss the implications of these for arts managers and leaders. It will highlight the importance of a clear vision and the need for open communication during a change initiative and conclude with a call for a more professional focus on this increasingly vital area of management activity.

Why managing change is important

Not-for-profit organizations are undergoing a radical transformation across the globe and this shift is forcing arts and cultural organizations to become much more responsive to change (Cohen, 1999). There are several factors driving this transformation, including

- Public funding cuts and pressure to diversify income streams
- The need to fund the arts and culture through innovative models
- The imperative to collaborate with a diverse range of external partners
- The rise of participatory culture, co-production and co-creation
- The need to engage with audiences in a relational way rather than market to them in a transactional way
- The rise of sophisticated interactive digital communications technologies
- The ominous reality of ageing audiences and the need to attract younger/future audiences

One of the most significant challenges facing the arts and cultural sector is therefore the urgent need to develop effective strategies to ride this wave of change. Indeed a number of scholars and industry commentators are starting to argue that only the most adaptive organizations will survive. This is a sobering assessment of the current state of play, and it highlights the imperative to inculcate a culture of change. These kinds of wake-up calls should focus the minds of arts managers and leaders and galvanise their organizations into action, because it is becoming ever more apparent that the status quo is not an option. Change doesn't just happen magically in an organization: if it is to culminate in a positive outcome and endure then it needs to be planned and managed very carefully. We will now move on to consider how change happens and what it looks like in action.

Change as a complex process

There is an ongoing argument amongst academics about whether change is evolutionary and internally motivated, or revolutionary and externally driven. Freeman (1994) argues that both types of change are valid, and that the choice of approach should depend on the organization's circumstances and strategic objectives: where evolutionary change "acts to reinforce and refine the organization's existing vision, strategy, structure, and processes", revolutionary change "acts to transform them" (Freeman, 1994, p. 214). We have noted that a number of external factors are driving change in the arts and cultural sector. But sometimes, change can occur from within, perhaps motivated by the vision of a transformational leader, or by the recruitment of a new staff member. Increasingly, change is happening organically through processes of action research, where organizations evolve by doing something different – by collaborating with a new strategic partner, for example. What we can appreciate from theoretical and practical insights is that change sometimes needs to be *both* evolutionary *and* revolutionary – it needs to keep nudging an organization's strategy forwards while allowing for a new and transformative vision and a proactive response to new external drivers.

In the past, change was often equated with, and indeed believed to be dependent on, a state of crisis (Welch and McCarville, 2003) or on a sudden environmental change (Fouts and Smith, 1999). But nowadays there is a degree of theoretical consensus around the idea that change is a *process* rather than an end in itself; that it is *emergent* and never finished or complete. The emergent model of change reflects a post-modern, post-structuralist understanding of organizations as "systems of flux and transformation" (Morgan, 1997; Peacock, 2008, p. 338). To reflect the development from the revolutionary towards evolutionary theory, Peacock (2008) distinguishes three different models of organizational change (see Figure 9.1), which depict what he refers to as reactive, proactive and emergent change.

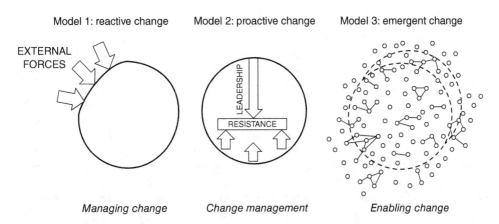

Figure 9.1 Three models of change in organizations

Source: Peacock, 2008, p. 336. Used with permission.

As you can see, in Model 1 change is occurring in a reactive way: the organization is creaking under the pressure of this change, which is imposed suddenly and violently from outside. This might, for example, be in response to a funding cut or to new legislation on protecting audience data. This model represents a typical process of change in a non-agile organization that is not ready for change. In Model 2, you can see how change is happening in a more proactive way, although this is being met with resistance from some staff members or maybe from volunteers or even the board of directors. A common example of this might be the arrival of a new CEO who joins the organization with a new artistic vision or leadership style which generates conflicts amongst those who prefer the status quo. This again illustrates a typical model of change that is often encountered in the sector; but in this case, although many people in the organization are still not ready for change, its leaders are trying desperately to push it through. The problem here is that they have not prepared the organization for change in advance, and the culture is therefore not receptive. In the third model, change is *emerging*; it is being *enabled*, perhaps via a distributed leadership style, and it is messy and contingent. Perhaps most significantly, you can see here how change is occurring beyond the walls of the organization, involving external stakeholders such as audiences, community leaders, schools, funders and philanthropists. This is, at least in theory, the ideal change scenario, because it requires organizations to be in a constant state of readiness for change, to be *change-ready*. This vision again perceives organizational change as a process rather than a one-off outcome or project.

Although change can often appear to be imposed on us, seemingly out of the blue, it is important to consider organizational change as an internal collective process because change is never finished or complete. Peacock thus advocates the emergent model of change as the most appropriate one for modern organizations, which, he argues, must remain in a constant state of readiness to respond to new drivers for change. In this respect he agrees with Alain Rondeau (1999), who contends that cultural organizations are subject to a combination of internal and external forces that compel them to change in order to survive, and with Chris Bilton (2007, p. 118), who defines organizational change as "a process of incremental adaptation to external changes and internal intentions". Bilton argues that an evolutionary, incremental model embeds change into an organization's culture and encourages "the agents of change and the agents of continuity to work together" (p. 126). Indeed Bilton goes on to claim that tensions such as these are what actually drive organizations forward and enable them to evolve. We can see here how change can act as a kind of fuel that propels organizations towards their future strategic goals. Accordingly, organizations that don't change or actively resist change soon run out of fuel and end up stuck in the sand as they are overtaken by their competitors.

When we consider change as a process, it can make it appear messy and contingent, and therefore a little intimidating and even chaotic. The skills required to manage change thus challenge some of the existing thinking on arts management, which traditionally involves achieving stated objectives via the activities of planning, organising and controlling (Byrnes, 2009). So it is maybe disconcerting to managers when scholars depict organizational change as "a pattern emerging from chaos" (Bilton, 2007, p. 116). If arts managers need to control, how can they possibly manage chaos? Bilton means here that sometimes things need to get worse before they get better, especially in a scenario of transformational change. A prime example of this from outside the arts and cultural sector would be a political demonstration or even a riot which ultimately culminates in a positive social outcome. So it is important to remember that as well as planning, organising and controlling, effective arts managers also need to *lead* (Byrnes, 2009). We will explore the relationship between leadership and change later in the chapter, but suffice to say for now that change requires significant leadership skills, including the ability to manage people and processes, which as we all know can sometimes be very messy indeed! As Stacey (2003) argues, the management theories of organizational change are generally flawed by two misconceptions: the assumption that organizations exist separately from employees, and their inability to deal with paradox.

Some further reassurance about the positive aspects of chaos is provided by chaos theory itself, which informs us that behavioural patterns that might appear to be random can actually be integral to the effective development of natural ecosystems, including organizations. Complexity theory also provides some useful insights into processes of change, offering a useful post-structuralist framework for enabling change based on a "dynamic, interdependent, contingent and unstable view of reality" (Peacock, 2008, p. 339). Some scholars argue that perceiving industries and organizations as complex systems enables managers to improve their decision-making and find innovative solutions (Levy, 1994). Others go even further, claiming that applying complexity theory to organizational change can actually produce a "quasi-equilibrium state, just short of the point where a system would collapse into chaos, at which the system maximizes its complexity and adaptability" (Grobman, 2005, p. 370). This suggests that arts managers should actually embrace complexity and chaos, and interpret them as preconditions of positive change.

Managing change

It is all very well for academics and other external commentators to argue about structures and processes of change; but even when the right preconditions for positive change are in place, there are myriad reasons why change initiatives often fail in reality. Many organizations lack the necessary vision or confidence for change, while others are overly complacent about their public funding or shy away from any kind of organizational conflict. As Welch and McCarville (2003) note: "Change suggests a loss of control, increased uncertainty, as well as a threat to traditional procedures, values, and status levels" (p. 23). So there are many reasons *not* to engage positively with change and this is what can lead to a state of inertia.

Because managing change is inherently complex and chaotic, generally involving a diverse range of unpredictable stakeholders and outcomes, it is important to appreciate what tends to go wrong and to troubleshoot likely problems in advance. Every change process is unique because every organization and staff member is unique. This means that change is contingent and needs to be managed in a different way in different contexts in different organizations; there is not a one-size-fits-all solution to managing change. Although existing studies and theories of managing change can be very useful, for example by highlighting common issues and providing tried-and-tested strategies for success, ultimately it is incumbent on managers to determine the right way to manage change in their own particular situations and organizations.

The change management literature focuses heavily on leadership, and this is often to the detriment of middle managers and other line managers, who play a vital role in organizational change by communicating regularly with frontline staff (Lewis et al., 2006). This is where Robert Hewison and John Holden's (2011) work on distributed leadership comes to the fore, illustrating how leadership (and therefore change management) is the responsibility of everyone in the organization. Or, as Bilton puts it: "Rather than directing change, managers provide a climate within which change can occur" (2007, p. 134). You can see here how a 'change-ready' organizational culture is a vital pre-condition for positive and enduring change.

The challenge for leaders and managers, however, is that organizational culture is not always easy to manipulate. Scholars are divided into three camps here:

1   Those who maintain that culture is manageable
2   Those who claim that culture can sometimes be manipulated
3   Those who insist that culture is immune to management action

(Ogbonna and Harris, 1998).

The truth presumably lies somewhere in the middle of these positions, but because every organizational culture is different, some will inevitably be more flexible and manageable than others. Ogbonna and Harris argue that the goal of organizational change is to effect genuine *value-level* change, which they define as employees' "authentic willingness" to change rather than "resigned compliance" (1998, p. 285). So another important consideration for managers is how to garner active buy-in from their colleagues. A further challenge, which is related to the need for organizational buy-in, is the need to manage the positive and negative roles that organizational sub-cultures can play in supporting or resisting change initiatives. Existing studies highlight, for example, how the cultures of individual departments can often shape the identity and engagement of employees more than the wider organizational culture itself (Smollan and Sayers, 2009). Getting middle managers on board is certainly one important key to success.

Peacock's model distinguishes between 'managing change', 'change management' and 'enabling change', suggesting that there are three common approaches to dealing with change amongst arts and cultural managers. According to the model, 'managing change' refers to a reactive management response to an unanticipated or uncontrollable event. This little confusing, as managing change is a generic term commonly deployed to describe how those in positions of leadership deal with aspects of change. Peacock's point here, however, is that effective change managers need to be *proactive*; they need to anticipate change and integrate it into everyday working practices. Likewise, 'change management' in the model seems to refer to the act of implementing change or pushing a change initiative through (or perhaps even down) an organization. Again, this is a little ambiguous, as change management is another umbrella term invoked generally to cover the same activities and issues as managing change. So we could argue that these distinctions are predominantly semantic. However, 'enabling change' represents a particular approach to managing change; it implies a distributed and relational leadership style and a more post-modern perception of organizational behaviour. The different characteristics of traditional and change-ready managers are outlined in Table 9.1.

Table 9.1 Change and organizational characteristics

Traditional organisations are . . .	Traditional managers and leaders . . .	Change-ready organisations are . . .	Change managers and leaders . . .
reactive	React	emergent	enable
rigid & resistant	Control	flexible & adaptive	facilitate & adapt
opaque	Conceal	transparent	communicate
managerial	tell & order	participatory	consult & develop
directional	Direct	motivational	motivate
hierarchical	harness power	flat	devolve power
closed	Hide	open	disclose
insular	maintain relationships	networked	build relationships
impermeable	Introspect	porous	scan
backward-looking	conserve	forward-looking	disrupt
risk-averse	restrict & limit damage	innovative	innovate & take risks
reflective	re-tell old stories	visionary	invent new stories
logical & structured	maintain order	paradoxical & chaotic	embrace complexity
transactional & contractual	manage employees	relational & dialogic	lead people
static	Preserve	dynamic	transform

Communicating change

Another vital prerequisite to managing change effectively is sophisticated communication, and there is a general consensus in the academic literature that successful change management is dependent on the following factors:

- Open, participative discussion
- Regular, planned and honest communication
- Full and early disclosure of relevant information

According to Welch and McCarville (2003), communication of change should aim to:

- Crystallize the need for change
- Relate the change initiative to common objectives
- Clarify employees' roles in creating change
- Promote new behaviours to facilitate its implementation

However, despite all the best efforts of managers and leaders, some employees will always react negatively to change and try to preserve the status quo, whilst others will seek reassurance and support. To minimize resistance to change and maximize employee engagement, change managers have been counselled to listen as much as possible and create an environment where employees can "vent" (Lewis et al., 2006, p. 123). Lewis et al. also highlight the benefits of informal, succinct, motivational and jargon-free face-to-face communication, whilst emphasizing the need to manage employees' negative emotions and highlighting the positive role that stories and metaphors can play in the change process. This last point is echoed by Macaulay, Yue, and Thurlow (2010), who claim that the story of change itself can help an organization make sense of itself and construct its new identity. Stories help to build or redevelop an organization's identity and have a powerful impact on both the internal cultural and the external brand, so if change leaders can (re)create positive stories during a change initiative, this can rally staff around the mission and provide positive momentum.

Like stories, metaphors can also act as powerful symbols, and they can be deployed by managers to visualise the need for change and provide a positive image of what change might deliver. Peacock (2008) claims that people's beliefs about organizations are embedded in the metaphors they use to describe them. In order to illustrate his claim, Peacock cites Morgan's (1997) eight common metaphors to construe organizations: machines, organisms, brains, cultures, political systems, psychic prisons, flux and transformation, and instruments of domination. We can see here how potent some of these metaphors are and how they might impact (positively or negatively) on people's perceptions of an organization. Just ask yourself: would you want your organization to be perceived as a brain or as an instrument of domination?! We can also appreciate here the connections with the theories of change explored earlier in the chapter: change-ready organizations are more likely to be perceived as organisms, brains, cultures, flux and transformation. Some of these metaphors may appear a little abstract, but they illustrate how imagery and metaphor can be harnessed by change managers to create positive mental constructs of organizations in other people's minds. They are thus an effective tool to adopt when undertaking a significant change initiative and can help managers to not only make, but also to crystallise and illustrate the case for change.

It is important to acknowledge, however, that there are sometimes very valid reasons for resisting change, such as fear of redundancy, of losing control, or being overworked, and sadly change does not always result in a better outcome. Managers and leaders need to understand and deal with these anxieties; existing studies of change have revealed how exploiting informal networks can allow change leaders to access the knowledge of key stakeholders and thus head off potential resistance and mitigate against the rumours and misinformation that can proliferate during periods of change. Another acknowledged tactic is to actively seek out sceptical stakeholders or 'blockers' of change, who can provide a constructively critical, objective and sometimes external perspective. This can reduce the risk of leaders pursuing whimsical or self-interested change and/or adopting a blind position of advocacy. Most arts and cultural organizations can find these knowledgeable and sceptical stakeholders amongst their funders, donors, boards and audiences, as well as, of course, amongst their own staff.

Implications for leaders and leadership

We have seen already that managing change requires a specific approach and skillset that supersedes what is traditionally expected of arts managers. This is because enabling change actually demands sophisticated leadership skills. Scholars are increasingly considering leadership as a process and an interpersonal quality, rather than something that is embedded exclusively in senior people. So there is no reason why managers (or anyone else for that matter) cannot embody the requisite leadership skills to enable organizational change. Indeed as we have seen, departmental managers are often the key facilitators (or blockers) of organizational change because they have an influencing role in sub-cultures. Having said this, effective change management requires a holistic organizational approach based on the strategic alignment of values and key stakeholders around a clear and relevant vision, mission and rationale for change. Organizational leaders are therefore generally in the best position to enable change, as they possess the strategic overview of the organization and act as temporary custodians of its vision, mission and values. Staff members in particular need to understand why they should personally engage with the initiative and what's ultimately in it for them, and again, leaders are generally best placed to provide this high-level guidance and support. It is inevitable that change will involve staff working in different ways, and leaders are usually the only people who are fully empowered to put in place appropriate support mechanisms (such as dedicated time, training and development) to actively support this operational evolution.

Often the main challenge leaders face during a change initiative is dealing with resistance. Welch and McCarville (2003) argue that employees' resistance to change is inevitable because it upsets their professional equilibrium; raises unwanted questions about their roles; and ultimately threatens their job security. For many employees, change is correlated with pain and their reaction to it can fluctuate from apathy to active resistance (Sharma, 2008). Effective change leaders therefore need to be adept at managing conflict, just as they also need to be able to empathise with their colleagues' concerns and anxieties. However, leaders often struggle to deal effectively with resistance, sometimes precisely because they lack the requisite interpersonal skills to listen, communicate, empathise and manage conflict. These are the kinds of skills that are often learned the hard way, on the job, and they tend to come with experience, but there are simple tactics that leaders can deploy to deal more effectively with blockers. For example, Lepine, Colquitt, and Erez (2000) propose three simple strategies for dealing with resistance to change:

1   Replace resistant employees
2   Invest in training and development
3   Recruit 'change-ready' individuals

The first of these options should really be a last resort and only implemented once other avenues have been explored. There are significant legal implications involved in removing or replacing staff, which is why major change initiatives are often accompanied by organizational restructures. Making people redundant is a painful and complicated process, and it can often involve expensive compromise agreements and culminate in damaging staff morale. It can also often mean that redundant posts cannot be replaced like-for-like, which might leave a vacuum in a key strategic or operational area of the organization. As we have seen, bringing resisters on board as critical friends, or even winning them over, can be a highly effective strategy and this is therefore a preferred option to replacing or removing them entirely.

The second option of investing in training and development is perhaps an obvious one, but it is a strategy that is often overlooked. As change involves adapting to new ways of working, training, development, mentoring and coaching can all help colleagues to make a smoother transition to the new model while simultaneously developing their skills, expertise and morale. So this can be a win-win strategy. However, these first two options highlight the fact that change can be expensive and require leaders to carve out or make the case for significant investment in what, as an often intangible, internal process, can constitute a difficult sell to a board, funder or donor.

The final option – the strategy of proactively recruiting change-ready individuals – is what I would consider a game-changer. Recruitment can be a nefarious activity, which is often compromised even further in the arts and cultural sector by nepotism, poor HR processes and the notorious lack of diversity in the field. Job and person specifications are often predominantly skills- and experience-based and fail to take account of personal values and qualities such as people's propensity for risk, novelty, innovation and change. The advantages of recruiting change-ready individuals to an organization in such a fast-moving sector are readily apparent, and this smart preventative strategy can ultimately save leaders a lot of heartache, time and money.

The conception of change-ready organizations as paradoxical, complex, chaotic and conflictual that we discussed earlier in the chapter also has significant implications for leadership models and organizational structures. Recent research in the cultural industries (e.g. Hewison and Holden, 2011; Taylor, 2011) has advocated conceiving of organizations as networks, perhaps building on Deleuze and Guattari's notion of the 'rhizomatic network', where organizations function from and across the centre rather than from the top down (Yu, 2004). The significance of organizational structure in facilitating change is not only related to its role as an enabler of change; it also determines how change is communicated across an organization and provides a platform for its style and model of leadership. Modern leaders increasingly need to lead across networks rather than down traditional hierarchies: with the rise of strategic partnerships, co-productions, crowdfunding, co-creation and consultancy, traditional authority that flows down from a leader via a hierarchy is less important than the ability to operate as part of a network through persuasion, compromise and focusing energy (Holden, 2011). The role of the cultural leader is to act as an "intermediary", bridging creativity and administration, and integrating, mediating or even exacerbating conflict (Glynn, 2006, p. 61). The ability to manage (or invoke) conflict is a core aspect of change management, and it is another reason why relational and transformational leaders are often the most effective agents of change. This is because relational leaders are "enablers", who lead others through delegation and empowerment; they draw on their strong delegation and communication skills as well as on their colleagues' talents to ensure that a shared vision is achieved (Hewison, 2004).

Despite the increasing focus in the change management literature on participatory and distributed leadership (Holden, 2011), there is a general consensus that it is leaders' responsibility to create a strong vision and lead their organizations through change (Lewis et al., 2006). In other words, most commentators agree that leaders should act as 'change agents', whose role is to promote participation and communication, and facilitate the change process. In this sense, leaders need to act as entrepreneurs (or intrapreneurs) because it is their role to envision, drive and implement change. However, some scholars regard leaders' role in initiating change as much less proactive. For example, Peacock (2008) contends that change often comes from outside the organization and argues that leaders should enable change rather than become the instruments of it, while Bilton claims that if leaders are "locked into a single strategic vision, it becomes much harder for them to respond to change" (2007, p. 117). Stanziola (2011) goes even further, suggesting that leaders are limited in their ability to promote change because organizations' attitudes to risk and innovation are shaped essentially by their location, size and sector. This is an interesting challenge that is certainly open to debate. Whilst location, size and sector clearly have an influence on underlying cultures of risk and innovation, it would be disingenuous to claim that these are the predominant cultural drivers in any single organization. Table 9.1 summarises the core theories we have explored so far in this chapter regarding managing change in the arts and cultural sector. It suggests that what separates traditional organizations and their managers and leaders from change-ready organizations are essentially structures, models, attitudes and behaviours rather than art forms, location and size.

Let's now see how these theories about managing and leading change play out in the real world of a large and busy arts and cultural organization.

Case study: West Yorkshire Playhouse

Introduction

West Yorkshire Playhouse (WYP) in Leeds is one of the largest producing theatres in the UK. Its mission is to create world-class, relevant and compelling theatre and to transform people's lives by the power and vitality of its work (West Yorkshire Playhouse, 2018). Back in 2011, as part of a strategic change programme called Transform, which was designed to develop the 'resilience' of five of its regular funded organizations that it felt faced immediate opportunities or challenges, Arts Council England (ACE) awarded WYP £1.47m to explore how a regional theatre could operate most effectively in the 21st Century. Based on my own extensive mixed-methods evaluation of this major change initiative, which comprised document analysis, surveys, depth interviews and focus groups, this case study provides an account of West Yorkshire Playhouse's two-year action research project. It reflects in particular on the synergies and gaps between theories and practices of managing change in the context of the arts and culture.

Drivers of change

The drivers of change for WYP were both internal and external. Back in 2008, one of the reasons the then-chief executive, Sheena Wrigley, had applied for her post was that she felt that WYP was an organization in desperate need of change: "I've always been really excited by the idea of reinventing things . . . and the role had been created with the idea of that person agitating change. . . . I'm always interested in what's its next reinvention" (Wrigley, 2012). This sentiment was echoed by the new artistic director, James Brining, who joined the theatre halfway through the process and reflected: "Transformation is a crucial thing for me to deliver" (Brining, 2012). So from the outset, even though the impetus for change had come from outside the organization, it was clear that both leaders took a proactive approach to change and perceived themselves as transformative change agents.

Interviews with senior staff at both ACE and WYP indicated that there was an agreement that change at WYP was non-negotiable and that there was an incontrovertible need to re-vision. Indeed this is why WYP was expressly *invited* by ACE to apply for the Transform fund. ACE's regional manager argued that the Transform funding allocated to WYP was not a luxury because the consequences of *not* funding change were too unpalatable: "It was our one opportunity to really have a proper engagement with the organization for substantial change; we couldn't have done it without that money and that investment" (Arts Council England Officer, 2012). But there was also a strong internal acknowledgement of the pressing need for change. WYP's external change mentor, Richard Watts, described his first staff workshop as follows:

> Most people talked about how they tried to create change and had kind of given up. They felt like they were tired and there was quite a passive perspective about what they could do, but a real consensus about what the need was (Watts, 2012).

This consensus was shared by everyone, Watts felt, except by some long-standing board members. Interviews with Brining (2012) and with the change initiative's project manager, Owen Roberts (2012), highlighted WYP's core strength as producing a "well-made play", but conveyed the sense of staff "running nowhere on a treadmill", of a theatre without an artistic vision or purpose, which Wrigley (2012) visualized as "a donut without a centre".

The change mission

WYP's mission for the initiative was to "refresh and revitalise our theatre in a way that opens up creative opportunity and opens out our buildings, talent and resources" (West Yorkshire Playhouse, 2012). This mission was translated into six strands, which were articulated in the project plan as follows:

1 Produce four creative pilots or experiments
2 Implement artistic succession
3 Create a new business model
4 Develop audiences and communications and re-brand
5 Develop people and internal culture and strengthen operational processes
6 Plan for capital investment

Chiming with ACE's view that WYP needed to broaden its audience base, both Wrigley (2012) and Brining (2012) named a key goal as "porosity", which Brining visualized as the theatre becoming a "crossroads" and Wrigley described as "opening up avenues through which people can pass, whether that's artists, audiences or participants" (ibid.). Wrigley (2012) defined resilience as "having some confidence in what the future's going to look like, driving that future and being more in control of it, rather than always responding to circumstance".

Process, structure, empowerment and barriers

The theatre's decision to take an action research approach quickly revealed inherent strengths and weaknesses. Brining's view (2012) is that it helped the organization to "crash into the ice flow" whilst Watts (2012) argued that it encouraged "a process-vision rather than an end-vision", which made the initiative more "iterative" and "experiential". This was partly inevitable because there was no clear end-vision at the start of the project, but also a deliberate choice influenced by the appointment of a new artistic director (Brining) halfway through the process. However, although the action research approach secured the active participation of around half of the 60 permanent staff members (engagement in the entire initiative was controversially voluntary), Watts felt that this created a false impression of democratic decision-making which caused tension when top-down decisions were subsequently made regarding departmental restructures and redundancies. Wrigley's view is that while the matrix structure implemented especially for the initiative produced some innovative ideas, which subsequently fed directly into artistic and strategic planning, it also encouraged some ambitious blue-sky thinking which might never be realised because of the loss of around £0.5m in core funding, leading to a potential sense of disillusionment amongst the staff.

Wrigley and Brining identified the main barriers to change as fear, complacency, inertia, intransigence, passive resistance, false prioritisation and evolution. This confirmed the key barriers to change identified in previous studies but also highlighted how an evolutionary approach to change can actually act as a barrier, as well as an enabler. In this case, this evolutionary approach was interpreted as a complacent belief that change would happen organically and without any proactive interference, whereas the leadership team were convinced that a more revolutionary approach was required. Although Watts felt that 50% of staff engagement was a healthy level of participation, other interviewees were less convinced and some staff members blamed the lack of engagement on the negative leadership of certain line managers and on the lack of clarity regarding the exact role and power of participants. This view was borne out by the change programme's project manager, who identified a problem with powerful sub-cultures or "kingdoms", which gave him the impression of working across several organizations (Roberts, 2013).

Communication

The communication strategy changed quite quickly from a balanced internal and external focus to an exclusive concentration on internal change, and this reflected a general acceptance that the first phase of the initiative had to be about "getting our house in order" (Wrigley, 2012). In Watts's opinion, communicating change is always challenging because "it's not about what you say, it's about what's heard" (Watts, 2012). Perhaps for this very reason, the communications manager identified her key message as "we are *all* the change" and listed her core objective as effecting a positive shift in culture (Loveday, 2012). According to Wrigley (2012), one quick win was indeed a palpable cultural shift, with staff "responding to each other differently and treating other people's ideas differently".

However, the focus groups revealed a lack of shared understanding of the project's goals across the organization. Participants agreed that one of the aims of the initiative was to explore new working practices internally, but there were differences of opinion about whether this aim was a desirable one. Whilst some participants acknowledged a desire to see internal change as a vital refreshment to prevent "mission drift" and make the organization more cutting edge, others felt that they didn't have time to learn to work in a different way because "it just screws up all the other projects that we're working on" (focus group participant, anonymous). In terms of external focus, while some participants acknowledged and supported the aim of "beginning to change artists and theatre-makers' perceptions of West Yorkshire Playhouse" (West Yorkshire Playhouse, 2012), others felt that the internal focus was self-indulgent and thought the project should focus more externally on audience development.

Action learning and impact

When questioned about the creative pilots, most participants felt that they *had* encouraged staff to work in different ways, but many felt that it was just a case of two weeks of working differently and then everyone returning to their old ways of working. There were some concerns that the focus on new ways of working ignored the expertise that existing staff already had, and several participants felt they could have contributed more if they had been given the opportunity but that "management makes all the decisions, there's no involvement from the rest of the staff that may have an interest" (focus group participant, anonymous). Two respondents said they felt forced, rather than encouraged, to participate and work in different (and in their opinion worse) ways.

Over 70% of survey respondents had engaged with the creative pilots, which indicated a high participation from staff in this new area of activity. Most participants were excited by the work they had seen and 73% of respondents were interested in taking part in future ventures of this kind, even though 89% felt that the pilots had not provided them with any opportunities for professional development. Most respondents felt that one legacy of the pilots was that people were already starting to talk to and about the theatre in different ways. Ticket sales for the Transform Festival were up significantly on the previous year, suggesting that audiences were getting more familiar with the theatre producing and presenting such work. The festival's associate producer reflected the views of many when she claimed that the pilots "marked a milestone" and proved that "change is possible"; but at the same time, "when you come in on Monday it's like nothing ever happened, everyone is just sunk back into their routines" (Letman, 2013).

A recurrent sentiment in the interviews with employees was a frustration with the matrix structure adopted for the change initiative. Staff had generally engaged with the so-called houses in good faith and held high expectations of their potential legacies, but were disappointed at the end of the project that their collective thinking seemed to have disappeared with little acknowledgement of any legacy or follow-through into strategic planning. Another problem transpired to be the chairing of the houses by senior managers, some of whom were overly dominant and/or lacked the requisite facilitation skills. This highlighted the theoretical focus on the importance of professional development to support a change initiative. However, participants did commend the matrix structure for facilitating internal communication and improving the culture by breaking down the "corrosive sub-cultures" and diluting what one employee referred to as "the weed-choked well" (Roberts, 2013).

Legacy

The most dramatic legacy of the initiative seemed to be the re-conceptualization of the role and model of a regional theatre as an open, creative development hub which should provide a home for a diverse range of artists and wider stakeholders. As the associate producer expressed it:

> It's not just about being able to present – because if the theatres went, there'd still be places to present shows. So it's about training and development and it's about

our social spaces, our role within the community, the people that we work with, it's almost like being an arts centre meets a club or entertainment space, meets a community centre, meets a theatre that presents shows every night. And I think that's what theatre needs to be. I think that's what we're heading towards – and that's what I've learnt which I didn't know when I got here . . . a theatre can act as a development agency and lab (Letman, 2013).

This re-visioning seemed to emerge both as a direct result of the action research – particularly as a legacy of the creative pilots – and through the necessity of the funding cuts, which required the theatre to become leaner and produce less work. This has now led to a revitalized artistic vision, based partly on a greater reliance on and positive embracing of co-productions with a range of artistic partners, which in turn has required an acceptance of the different and more flexible ways of working that were trialled through the creative pilots.

Discussion

Although the academic literature generally advocates internal, evolutionary change, the case study of West Yorkshire Playhouse illustrates that in practice, major change is often driven by external forces and funded in moments of crisis. This is perhaps particularly the case in the not-for-profit arts sector, where funding is short-term and subject to whimsical shifts in cultural policy; and it was interesting to note that both Wrigley and Brining listed evolution as a *barrier* to change at WYP. What they meant by this was that there had never been a rupture in artistic policy or funding, and this had inhibited change and engendered a sense of complacency. One key finding from the case study is that intelligent funding can buy vital time for organizational change to take place and support its development; but because of short-term funding patterns, fear and/or inertia, arts organizations often fail to embrace change unless they are forced to. This confirmed the findings of existing studies.

There were clear areas of consensus between theory and practice regarding barriers to change and the vital roles that culture, process, communication, management and leadership all play in a change initiative. The financial barriers to change highlighted in the literature were also visible in the case study: WYP could not embark on its change programme until specific funding had been secured, and ACE conceded that they had learned the importance of funding change properly. The psychological barriers of fear and uncertainty evident in the theory were also reflected at WYP (and indeed were borne out as redundancies started to occur); but complacency, inertia and resistant managers and board members also emerged as key barriers to change, reflecting perhaps the covert power held by voluntary directors and the un-dynamic career structure that characterises the arts and cultural sector (several managers had been at the theatre for over ten years).

Another area of convergence between theory and practice emerged to be the role that stories and metaphors can play in facilitating and underpinning organizational change. Peacock's (2008) claim that people's beliefs about organizations are embedded in the metaphors they use to describe them was borne out in the interviews, with participants referring to WYP variably as a juggernaut, a donut, a treadmill and a buoy. Wrigley and Brining's approach to leadership reflected Hewison's (2004) definitions of relational and transformational leadership and responded to Peacock's call for leaders to enable rather than dictate change – at least until the funding cut forced the leaders to enact a redundancy programme. The case study also confirmed Lewis et al's (2006) theory about the significant role that middle managers can play in supporting or blocking change: the evaluation highlighted the potentially significant impact of sub-cultures reflected in the academic literature, but it also demonstrated that a positive organizational culture can create the right environment for change to occur. However, the extent to which the organizational culture was managed or manipulated remained unclear, and it remains to be seen whether negative sub-cultures will prevent durable change or whether 'value-level change' will ultimately be secured.

Conclusion

In a period of unprecedented funding cuts and shifting audience demands, change must be a priority for both arts and cultural organizations. However, because of short-term funding patterns, fear, complacency, weak leadership and inertia, many organizations fail to embrace change unless they are forced to. The case study of West Yorkshire Playhouse has shown how evolutionary and revolutionary change can combine to produce a positive change legacy, but one uncomfortable truth emerging from the case study is that crisis and rupture are sometimes prerequisites of positive change. However, change can also evolve incrementally through visionary leadership, through an adaptive structure and culture, and through positive stories and metaphors.

There appears to be a consensus surrounding the increasing need for arts and cultural organizations to become more adaptive and resilient by reassessing their business models and re-visioning their relationships with artists, audiences, funders, businesses and communities. The case study of West Yorkshire Playhouse highlighted the changing role of the regional theatre from a repertory producing playhouse to an open, creative development hub where multiple stakeholders can co-create and co-produce. Substantive redevelopment of this nature demands significant change and investment, and arts organizations need to be supported in this by their funders and other key stakeholders, including their professional networks, donors, audiences and boards.

There remains a significant knowledge gap in the sector about how change happens, why it needs to happen and how to lead it. This chapter has provided a critical overview of the core theories of managing change in the arts and culture, and discussed the implications for leaders and leadership. It has critically applied these theories to a case study of a major change initiative at West Yorkshire Playhouse in Leeds in the hope that current and aspiring leaders will embark on change programmes with greater insight and confidence and instil the structures, models, values and attitudes required to develop change-ready organizations fit for the 21st century.

References

Arts Council England Officer. (2012). Interview with Ben Walmsley. 25 April, Leeds.

Bilton, C. (2007). *Management and creativity: From creative industries to creative management*. Oxford: Blackwell.

Bolton, M., Cooper, C., Antrobus, C., Ludlow, J., and Tebbutt, H. (2011). *Capital matters: How to build financial resilience in the UK's arts and cultural sector*. London: Mission Models Money.

Brining, J. (2012). Interview with Ben Walmsley and Leila Jancovich. 25 May, Leeds.

Byrnes, W.J. (2009). *Management and the arts*. 4th ed. Oxford: Elsevier.

Cohen, M. (1999). Commentary on the *Organization Science* special issue on complexity. *Organization Science*, (10), pp. 373–376.

Fouts, P.A. and Smith, A.W. (1999). Shaken and stirred: Arts organizations reacting to radical environmental change. *International Journal of Arts Management*, 1(3), pp. 10–21.

Freeman, S.J. (1994). Organizational downsizing as convergence or reorientation: Implications for human resource management. *Human Resource Management*, 33(2), pp. 213–238.

Glynn, M.A. (2006). Maestro or manager? Examining the role of the Music Director in a symphony orchestra. In: J. Lampel, J. Shamsie, and T.K. Lant, eds., *The business of culture: Strategic perspectives on entertainment and media*. London: Lawrence Erlbaum, pp. 57–69.

Grobman, G.M. (2005). Complexity theory: A new way to look at organizational change. *Public Administration Quarterly*, 29(3–4), pp. 351–384.

Hewison, R. (2004). The crisis of cultural leadership in Britain. *International Journal of Cultural Policy*, 10(2), pp. 157–166.

Hewison, R. and Holden, J. (2011). *The cultural leadership handbook: How to run a creative organization*. Farnham, Gower.

Holden, J. (2011). Current issues in cultural and strategic leadership. In: B. Walmsley, ed., *Key issues in the arts and entertainment industry*. Oxford: Goodfellow, pp. 179–193.

Lepine, J.A., Colquitt, J.A., and Erez, A. (2000). Adaptability to changing task contexts: Effects of general cognitive ability, conscientiousness, and openness to experience. *Personnel Psychology*, 53(3), pp. 563–593.

Letman, A. (2013). Interview with Ben Walmsley. 26 March, Leeds.

Levy, D. (1994). *Chaos theory and strategy: Theory, application, and managerial implications*. London: John Wiley & Sons.

Lewis, L., Schmisseur, M., Stephens, K., and Weir, K. (2006). Advice on communicating during organizational change: The content of popular press books. *Journal of Business Communication*, 43(2), pp. 113–137.

Loveday, J. (2012). Interview with Ben Walmsley. 25 May, Leeds.

Macaulay, K.D., Yue, A.R., and Thurlow, A.B. (2010). Ghosts in the hallways: Unseen actors and organizational change. *Journal of Change Management*, 10(4), pp. 335–346.

Morgan, G. (1997). *Images of organization*. Thousand Oaks, CA: Sage.

Ogbonna, E. and Harris, L.C. (1998). Managing organizational change: Compliance or genuine change? *British Journal of Management*, (9), pp. 273–288.

Peacock, D. (2008). Making ways for change: Museums, disruptive technologies and organizational change. *Museum Management and Curatorship*, 23(4), pp. 333–351.

Roberts, O. (2012). Interview with Ben Walmsley. 25 May, Leeds.

Roberts, O. (2013). Interview with Ben Walmsley. 25 April, Leeds.

Rondeau, A. (1999). The transformation of cultural organizations: Applications of a model. *International Journal of Arts Management*, 1(3), pp. 29–43.

Sharma, R. (2008). Celebrating change: The new paradigm of organizational development. *The Icfai University Journal of Soft Skills*, 2(3), pp. 22–28.

Smollan, R.K. and Sayers, J.G. (2009). Organizational culture, change and emotions: A qualitative study. *Journal of Change Management*, 9(4), pp. 435–457.

Stacey, R. (2003). *Strategic management and organizational dynamics: The challenge of complexity*. Harlow: Pearson Education.

Stanziola, J. (2011). Some more unequal than others: Alternative financing for museums, libraries and archives in England. *Cultural Trends*, 20(2), pp. 113–140.

Taylor, C. (2011). Performance, organization, theory. In: J. Pitches and S. Popat, eds., *Performance perspectives: A critical introduction*. Basingstoke: Palgrave Macmillan, pp. 191–201.

Tushman, M.L. and O'Reilly, C.A. (1996). Ambidextrous organizations: Managing evolutionary and revolutionary change. *California Management Review*, 38(4), pp. 8–30.

Watts, R. (2012). Interview with Ben Walmsley and Leila Jancovich. 18 May, Leeds.

Welch, R. and McCarville, R.E. (2003). Discovering conditions for staff acceptance of organizational change. *Journal of Park and Recreation Administration*, 21(2), pp. 22–43.

West Yorkshire Playhouse. (2012). *Action research business plan.* Leeds: West Yorkshire Playhouse.

West Yorkshire Playhouse. (2018). *Who are we?* [Internet]. Leeds: West Yorkshire Playhouse. Available at: www.wyp.org.uk/about/about-us/who-are-we/ [Accessed 27 Feb. 2018].

Wrigley, S. (2012). Interview with Ben Walmsley and Leila Jancovich. 18 May, Leeds.

Yu, J.E. (2004). Reconsidering participatory action research for organizational transformation and social change. *Journal of Organizational Transformation and Social Change*, 1(2–3), pp. 111–141.

10

LEADING CHANGE

Two executive leadership transitions through the lens of cognitive restructuring

Rachel Parker

Introduction

Change can be difficult and painful, but change is necessary; the adaptable organization is the successful one. While managing change is one of the most important jobs of the arts administrator, dealing with resistance to change is perhaps the most crucial step of that process. Leaders must learn to understand the implications of the change required, focusing on "who is going to have to let go of what . . . and what people *should* let go of" (Bridges and Mitchell, 2002, p. 40, emphasis added). Leaders must be able to shepherd the organization through the complex transition process, which hopefully leads to meaningful change.

This chapter will first explore the concept of cognitive restructuring and the change process, and then use it to analyze the first year of the new Executive Producer of the Utah Shakespeare Festival and the new Director/Curator of the Southern Utah Museum of Art. This unique opportunity presented itself when these two arts organizations in the small town of Cedar City, Utah, hired individuals around the same time from outside of the community to guide them through a period of great transition and change.

While a comparison of each organization and leader is apples to oranges, the study of how two different people stepped into the leadership role of organizations with unique histories and cultures can perhaps inform future arts leaders on how to be effective agents of change; to lead rather than manage through the inevitability of change. "We understand by now that organizations cannot be just endlessly 'managed,' replicating yesterday's practices to achieve success" (Bridges and Mitchell, 2002, p. 33).

Introduction to change

The uncertainty that comes with change can be very difficult to navigate. It is a time when all logic and reason can fly out the window, and emotions trump everything. In the chapter "Leading Transition: A New Model for Change' from the book *On Leading Change*, contributors William Bridges and Susan Mitchell state that:

> "thousands of books, seminars, and consulting engagements purporting to help 'manage change' often fall short. These tools tend to neglect the dynamics of personal and

organizational transition that can determine the outcome of any change effort. . . . In past years, perhaps, leaders could simply order change. Even today, many view it as a straightforward process: establish a task force to lay out what needs to be done, when, and by whom. Then all that seems left for the organization is . . . to implement the plan. . . . But then, why don't people *Just Do It?*

(Bridges and Mitchell, 2002, pp. 33–34)

The answer can be found in that often-neglected transition phase of change. "Transition is the state that change puts people into. The *change* is external . . . while the *transition* is internal" (Bridges and Mitchell, 2002, p. 34). To effectively enact change, a leader must first understand what needs changing, second uncover and manage the reasons behind resistance to the change or uncertainty, and third help those affected by the change through the sometimes-painful transition process. It is, frankly put, a minefield. So how does the successful arts administrator navigate transitions without causing more damage?

Cognitive restructuring as a vehicle for change

The root of resistance to change is found in loss and how people perceive it; loss of comfort, loss of some benefit, loss of 'How we've always done things.' In *Understanding and Changing Your Management Style*, which will be the focus of this chapter, author and multidisciplinary behavioral scientist Robert Benfari details the concept of *cognitive restructuring*. In it, the goal "is to identify internal monologues that are related to the stressful event, to evaluate this self-talk for its rationality and influence on behavior, and then to produce new self-talk to modify the original cognition and the undesired behavioral pattern" (Benfari, 2013, p. 17). If the leader can usher stakeholders along this path of cognitive restructuring, the external change can be accomplished because the internal transition has been carefully managed.

Recognition

"Becoming aware of our assumptions, perceptions, and feelings is the first step in cognitive restructuring" (Benfari, 2013, p. 35). In a single stressful situation, there can be 100 different reactions. The key is figuring out what those reactions stem from. As change leaders, we must first recognize our assumptions, perceptions, and feelings towards the situation before we can help other stakeholders recognize their own and start cognitive restructuring. We must assess what 'loss' is at stake; what need is being taken away or not met. "Needs are the forces that organize the perceptions, judgments, and actions that we use in our drive toward competence. . . . Because these assumptions and beliefs in part determine our needs structure, becoming conscious of them can help us modify these underlying elements and lead to change" (Benfari, 2013, p. 127).

Analysis

"Deeply rooted assumptions can distort our perceptions such that they reinforce the old assumptions. By opening up our perceptual field with 'floodlight' vision rather than 'spotlight' vision, we have the opportunity to alter these assumptions" (Benfari, 2013, p. 19). This is a common task in the critical thinking process, to try to see things from all sides, acknowledging bias. As change leaders, once we have checked our own bias, we must analyze the assumptions, perceptions, and feelings brought to the surface in Step 1, assessing the validity of such.

139

Correction

"Understanding and correctly interpreting the underlying patterns of our own and others' needs are essential to any change effort" (Benfari, 2013, p. 127). Once the assumptions, perceptions, and feelings have been recognized and analyzed, it is time to make the course correction. Whether or not the resistance is valid, this is the point where the leader must ask "Where do we go from here?" It is up to the individual to decide if the barrier to change is too high and if staying or leaving is the right call. The leader cannot make that decision for the individual. The leader can only make sure all decisions are made with all available information. The leader must continue moving forward.

The case studies: an historical context

With an understanding of change and the role cognitive restructuring can play in the transition process, the historical context and analysis of the leadership shift of both the Utah Shakespeare Festival and the Southern Utah Museum of Art can begin.

> **The Utah Shakespeare Festival** presents life-affirming classic and contemporary plays in repertory, with Shakespeare as our cornerstone. These plays are enhanced by interactive festival experiences which entertain, enrich, and educate (Utah Shakespeare Festival, 2018).

With a desire to capitalize on the thousands of tourists visiting the many National and State Parks in the area, to combat the ease being created by the construction of new Interstate 15 to "just pass through" the town, and with a love of the arts, the Utah Shakespeare Festival (USF) was founded in 1961 by Fred Adams and his wife, Barbara, in Cedar City, Utah. Under the umbrella of the College of Southern Utah (now Southern Utah University), the first productions were performed over two weekends in July. *The Taming of the Shrew* and *Hamlet* "drew 3,726 visitors and over $2,000, enough to prove to the College of Southern Utah and the community that this could be a profitable venture" (Paul, 2011, p. 9).

By the second decade of operation, USF "had grown into an impressive and noteworthy regional theatre. The season had expanded, and the need for new facilities had become apparent" (Paul, 2011, p. 11). In 1977, the Adams Memorial Shakespearean Theatre was dedicated. The 1970s also saw an increase in performances and attendance; increasing ticket sales allowed USF to begin hiring more staff, increase production budgets, and add special events. In 1981 USF began offering Actors Equity Association contracts, increasing the quality and professionalism of the company. In 1989, USF opened a second venue, The Randall L. Jones Theatre. In 2000, the Tony for Outstanding Regional Theatre was given to USF.

In June of 2016, USF

> celebrated the biggest event of its history with the ribbon cutting for the Beverley Sorenson Center for the Arts, including two new theatres for the Festival:

the Engelstad Shakespeare Theatre (which replaced the aging Adams Shakespeare Theatre) and the Eileen and Allen Anes Studio Theatre (a new, flexible theatre which seats about 200 playgoers). These two theatres join the existing Randall L. Jones Theatre to give the Festival three very different performing spaces for the future (Utah Shakespeare Festival, 2018).

The arts center also houses the administrative offices and a rehearsal/education hall for USF, as well as the Southern Utah Museum of Art. This Tony Award-winning festival has become a jewel of the state, and one of the most well-regarded regional theatres in the country.

Today, USF annually welcomes approximately 100,000 guests and produces more than 300 performances across three theatres during a 16-week season. The annual budget for the 2017 summer season was 7.4 million dollars. USF has 30 full-time and eight part-time staff, five graduate students working in assistantships, and 250–300 seasonal staff (depending on the season) including actors, designers, technicians, and audience services staff. Volunteers number above 200 annually and the board currently stands at 18 members, though the bylaws allow up to 25. USF has an education touring company, and during the regular season offers a free nightly Greenshow, literary seminars, facility tours, and workshops, among other things, to complete the USF experience (Utah Shakespeare Festival, 2018).

There is also much that has not changed at USF. Founder Fred Adams is still a fixture in the halls of the festival administration building. His influence is felt throughout each meeting, theatre space, and performance. Like most arts organizations, USF has experienced both success and struggle, and through both there permeates a deep sense of tradition. Honoring the past is something that is very important to many who work there.

In 2017, R. Scott Phillips, USF's first full-time employee, stepped down as Executive Director, a position he had held since it was created in 2005. After an exhaustive national search, Frank Mack was named as Phillip's replacement, with a title change to Executive Producer. Mack came to Cedar City from the University of Connecticut where he was the founder of Graduate Programs in Arts Administration. He had an extensive and impressive resume in theatre management and had been the managing director at such places as California Shakespeare Theatre, Connecticut Repertory Theatre, Geva Theatre Center, and the New Jersey Shakespeare Festival. Mack received his BGS in acting from the University of Kansas, Lawrence, and his MFA in directing from Virginia Tech.

The Southern Utah Museum of Art strives to foster engagement and experiential learning for students of Southern Utah University, as well as communities across the region through its permanent collections, diverse exhibitions, and participatory experiences (The Southern Utah Museum of Art, 2018).

Also on the campus of Southern Utah University is the Southern Utah Museum of Art (SUMA). Housed in a brand new, $10 millionbuilding (as part of the Beverly Taylor Sorenson Center for the Arts, which is also the home of the Utah Shakespeare Festival theatres and Administrative Offices), SUMA is an education-focused facility that is itself a work of art, inspired by the region's famous slot canyons.

The museum, which opened in 2016, is 20,500 square feet, with 6,600 square feet of that space dedicated to exhibitions. The remainder of the space is used for administration, education, conservation, and special events. Students and faculty of SUU's College of Performing and Visual Arts utilize SUMA for experiential learning. SUMA is the "Teaching Hospital" attached to the SUU Arts Administration Graduate Program "Medical School." Operating on a $450,000 budget, SUMA is free and open to the public (The Southern Utah Museum of Art, 2018).

While SUMA itself is a very new entity, it evolved from the Braithwaite Fine Arts Gallery, also on the campus of SUU. The Braithwaite first opened its doors in 1976 in the basement of an academic building. There was a small exhibition space, as well as storage for the permanent collection. In its last year (FY16), the Braithwaite had approximately 5,000 visitors.

In 2009, Reece Summers, former director of the Braithwaite, approached beloved landscape artist, Jimmie Floyd Jones, about a retrospective exhibition for the Braithwaite Fine Arts Gallery. The discussion led to a much grander idea: an art museum for SUU and Cedar City. As a Cedar City native and lover of the arts, Jimmie had a vision of what an art museum could bring to this campus and community: the opportunities that he missed during his childhood. The university agreed to work toward the creation of a museum, which is now known as the Southern Utah Museum of Art (SUMA). For the new museum, Jimmie left his home and studio near Zion National Park, his collection of art, and 15 new landscape paintings created in 2009, the year of his death. Many in the community consider SUMA as "The house that Jimmie built."

Since opening, SUMA has welcomed over 40,000 visitors to see its temporary exhibitions and the works of Jimmie F. Jones. The museum is dedicated to featuring the artwork of regional artists, faculty, and students from the SUU Department of Art & Design, as well as emerging and distinguished artists from around the country.

Strengths of the nearly 2,000-object permanent collection include the body of work by Jimmie F. Jones that exemplifies his notable career in the region, as well as a robust collection of prints featuring well-known artists such as Pierre-Auguste Renoir, Salvador Dalí, Katsushika Hokusai, Thomas Hart Benton, and others (The Southern Utah Museum of Art, 2018). The SUMA staff is comprised of two full-time and four part-time positions, six graduate students working in assistantships, four work-study undergraduate students, 25 volunteers, and an eight-member board.

Shortly after the doors opened, Reece Summers retired, and Jessica Farling was hired after a national search to serve as the Director/Curator of the museum. With several years of demonstrated expertise in developing new audiences, donor cultivation, and board and volunteer management, Farling came to SUMA from the Fred Jones Jr. Museum of Art, located on the campus of the University of Oklahoma, where she had worked for several years. An emerging museum leader, Farling had the potential to be the visionary needed to bring SUMA out of the dream stage and into a working reality.

The case studies: interviews and observations

Both new leaders were asked the same questions separately. Following are the responses to those questions, coupled with observations of those responses through the lens of both general leadership theory and cognitive restructuring.

What is your leadership philosophy?

Frank Mack (FM): I try to live by a quote I once read: "A good leader is a person with integrity who is committed to the organization and the people who work together to accomplish the organization's mission; this person leads by example, communicates without ceasing, and shows care, concern, and consistency in all dealings" (International Association of Administrative Professionals, 2009).

The reason I picked this philosophy was because it recognizes that the success of the organization is not just one person's job. Collaboration is a key component in how we produce theatre and how we need to come together administratively. It's pretty straightforward. It's all about communication and respect and working together.

Jessica Farling (JF): I've been the middle management employee that was discouraged from empowering my colleagues. I came into this position with the determination to create a culture of empowerment. In fact, when I interviewed for this position, I made it a point to go beyond empowering the staff and discussed a vision statement that displayed a sense of empowerment for the community.

Rather than a traditional leader, I strive to be a creative leader by being interactive (rather than one way), concerned with being real (rather than being right), able to learn from mistakes (rather than avoid mistakes), open to unlimited critiques (rather than limited feedback), and able to take risks (rather than sustaining order). I don't just believe in creativity because we are an art museum. I think these are qualities that make any leader a stronger, more transparent, and more successful.

At the end of the day, I pulled myself up through the ranks, starting as a part-time student employee in an art museum. I worked my way through middle management and hoped to be in a leadership position that could make real positive change. Those qualities are hard to teach and are easier when you've experienced it for yourself. I try to regularly reflect on past experiences to help manage current situations. In some cases, they help me understand my past supervisors. In other cases, they help me to not make the same mistakes.

Observations: The quote Mack uses to steer his leadership style like a personal leadership mission is, as he puts it, "pretty straightforward." It succinctly describes a good general leader. But a one-line philosophy can only do so much when in the thick of managing change. A leader must know how he or she reacts to many different situations and conflicts and personality types. He or she must know what pitfalls to avoid because of personal leadership weaknesses, and he or she must have a plan to discover why a person is reacting to change adversely.

Farling goes much deeper with her answer. Where a person comes from and what situations that person experiences inform how that person responds when given a leadership role. Farling knew what worked and did not work in her past dealings with leaders, she knows how she responds to conflict and stress, and she knows how to listen to others when they are experiencing similar conflict and stress. She uses this knowledge and experience to curate her leadership philosophy, which she acknowledges is constantly changing and evolving. She recognizes she too must be agile like the organization she leads.

Upon your hiring, how did you begin assessing the current state of USF/SUMA?

FM: Through documentation and through conversation. What documentation I could find, I would study. And when I arrived in Cedar, I set up a system for meeting with the staff, board members, stakeholders, and university administrators. In those meetings, I would listen. I would keep a list for every person or department of the things I wanted to learn more about or didn't understand or was interested in possibly changing, and I would refer to that list every time I met with that person or department.

As I listened and asked questions, I began to see the big picture; what was working and what wasn't. I told people what I thought we could do, which was generally pretty well received. People were ready to do things differently.

JF: I did a good amount of research before I arrived in Cedar for the interview process, but there was a lot of stuff I couldn't figure out by just looking online. There were a lot of holes and things I didn't necessarily put together. So, when I started, it was mostly observing and listening.

One of the first shocks I received was walking into an exhibition before I was on contract and seeing prices on the labels and the little red dot stickers symbolizing that the piece was sold. It really surprised me. I thought 'Where am I?' This was supposed to be a museum, not a gallery, so it did alarm me. This is not what a museum does. So, with that history of the Braithwaite Gallery and even with SUMA as a new organization, that has been a big piece, realizing that we still have to transition from gallery to museum. But I also understood that the museum had been open and then everyone was "So. How are we going to fund this?" So, the first conclusion they came to was selling art.

My first day on the job I was preparing the budgets and I saw that SUMA had not made that much selling art. If they had made $300,000, then that would have been a different story, but that wasn't the case. This led me to start thinking about different sustainable strategies, and what ultimately led me to think about restructuring the board to focus more on fundraising. I wanted to come up with ways of making up for the money lost by not selling artwork.

Just observing in those first few weeks gave me a better idea as to what was happening, but the second part of assessment needed to be conversations and discussions and finding out what people wanted. In the first six months I had conversations with every staff member (part-time undergraduate students, part-time graduate students, and part-time community members) one-on-one where I didn't have an agenda or questions, just "Tell me about your job" and "Tell me what your vision is for SUMA." That was really helpful and showed me that these part-time employees have really great ideas and perceptions of SUMA because they are in the trenches. They know what SUMA and its potential is.

Then it was about building relationships outside of the staff with stakeholders and community members, asking "What is SUMA to the community?" "What are the community needs that SUMA can meet?" There is still a lot of work left to do there, as there were a lot of misconceptions about the purpose of SUMA, but it all goes back to the basics of communication, which isn't that complicated.

Observations: Before one can understand the path to change implementing cognitive restructuring, one needs to know the state of the organization, or how cognition is currently structured. When they stepped into the leadership role at USF and SUMA, both Mack and Farling observed and listened to discern what was working in their respective organizations, and (perhaps more importantly) what was not.

Through these meetings and observations, both leaders also had a chance to get to know the personalities of those with a vested interest in their respective organizations, from staff to patrons. This would theoretically allow each leader to anticipate any perceived loss to any changes that would need to be made.

Farling in particular took this time to get to know the people beyond the structure of the museum. She asked how stakeholders felt about SUMA, and what they envisioned for the future of the organization. While Mack focused on the business, Farling folded in the human factor. This would prove invaluable later as she managed a great deal of resistance to changes she wanted to implement.

How did you identify what needed to change?

FM: Having come from a professional theatre company in a university setting, I quickly understood how this one was structured, as it was very similar. It is very clear; it was not mysterious. But how people managed that structure was mysterious. The basic administrative structure of the festival is just plain as day: It's an auxiliary unit of Southern Utah University, it receives no direct financial support from the university, it's expected to pay for itself and generate a surplus that is maintained in reserve accounts by the university. But how you actually do that successfully is a whole other story.

Knowing that USF had lost in the last two seasons about 1.65 million dollars, it doesn't take an MFA in arts administration to look at that and think "Something isn't working here." So the first change was that we needed to stop hemorrhaging money. The 2017 budget was 7.4 million and going into the 2018 season it is about 6.5 million. We had to make a lot of deep and painful cuts. And for the first time in my life, I proposed a budget at a deficit of $424,000 to the board. They approved it, knowing that it is a process to get us to the point we need to be. The goal is to have a balanced budget for the 2019 season. We're almost there.

JF: I don't know that I consciously was prioritizing changes that needed to be made, but I knew we needed to start with our foundation, which is the board. It needed to be restructured and focused in on raising money. We are in the middle of that process right now and I think it has gone very well. Before, SUMA had two boards, an Advisory Board and the Friends of SUMA Board, which was problematic. The solution was merging the resources, moving some people from the Friends Board to the Advisory Board, and then changing the Friends Board into a committee under the umbrella of the Advisory Board which is working very well. I need the board out there building relationships and seeking new funding sources, I don't need them overseeing the day-to-day operations, which is what SUMA had in the beginning.

Once the transition of the board restructuring is complete, then we can start thinking about a strategic plan. That is the big change slated for my second year. Now all those opportunities that were identified in my first six months that needed to be changed but weren't pressing can be formalized through this strategic planning process.

Observations: Both Mack and Farling were able to understand what needed to change in their respective organizations rather quickly. Perhaps this was because they were both new to the organizations and did not have the preconceived notions or revisionist histories influencing decisions. Again, both listened and observed. It is important to do both because perceptions and reality can often be drastically different.

Mack's situation was black and white: USF needed to stop losing money. That was clear, perhaps even from Mack's interview for the job. There was no question: running in the red called for changes in how the money was both earned and spent.

At SUMA, it was not as clear. Being a new museum (though it had evolved from another entity with its own history), the best place to look for opportunities for improvements and course corrections was in the foundational documents, such as the policies and mission. Farling combed through the organizational structure and found those areas to adjust, specifically the board setup. She knew once that foundation was solid, she could shore up and improve the rest of the museum, changing the cognitive structure of the stakeholders.

How receptive has the Board been to the needed changes?

FM: The structure of the board for USF is a little different. It is established by the university as an Advisory Board. Members do not have any fiduciary responsibility to the festival because all fiduciary responsibility lies with the university. The Executive Producer reports directly to the President of SUU, who performs the functions of oversight on behalf of the SUU Board of Trustees and the Utah State Board of Regents.

The board is set forth in policies 13.22 and 13.23, which exist in the official Southern Utah University Policies and Procedures (Southern Utah University, 2018). These policies hadn't been updated in probably ten years, so we are currently in the process of doing those updates. Most of the changes were just cleaning up language and clarifying gray areas, but there were a few substantive changes. For example, we are adding a one-year, ex officio student position on the board. It makes sense to have student representation. It adds a dimension to the board that was badly needed.

As far as I'm aware, there has been no board resistance to any of the changes we have made. Most of the changes make sense, for example the tightening of the budget. It was a large amount of little changes or adjustments that all added up to a gigantic decrease in the budget and the proposing of the deficit I mentioned earlier. We fine-tuned every line item on that budget, and the board understood. The board members see the writing on the wall in terms of the cuts we've had to make and the restructuring we've had to do. So as far as the board goes, they are actually ready for change and ready for USF to get back to full financial health.

JF: First of all, let me reiterate that the board was initially called an Advisory Board, but it did more than just advise. But it wasn't a governing board, either. It was somewhere in the middle. Before the doors were open, we needed people to be really hands-on to even get those doors open. And in the first year, we had to have those people helping to keep the place running. We don't need that anymore. The board itself is being changed and restructured. What is important is getting those people who have been so involved over the past three years or so through the process of change; through the transition.

Usually board members don't have time to be involved in the day-to-day, nor do they want to. But here, they were very involved. I came in to a group of retirees that wanted to fill all their time with SUMA, and they were going to run it all. That was so foreign to me and I knew that if anything had to change, this was a priority.

One thing I noticed immediately was how the structure of the board was not healthy in regard to its board/staff relations. Staff, because they were part-time and/or students, were not valued. Board members were running the show, and without a foundation of empowerment. SUMA is a university-based museum. Since our university's mission lies in experiential learning, we have a unique opportunity to provide these students, both graduate and undergraduate, with the chance to gain meaningful hands-on experience that can translate to galleries and other non-profit models.

How I approached the board changes, how I framed it, was that roles were changing, but everyone still had a role to play. I think that helped with their reception to change, and I tried, over time, to plant that seed, and water it, so it wasn't as painful as it could have been. We are now approaching the end of our transition. The change is almost complete, and it has been very positive.

Observations: The next phase Mack and Farling went through was to get buy-in regarding the identified changes from everyone in the organization through recognizing assumptions, perceptions, and feelings related to those changes, and to help key players recognize those factors as well. They also ventured into analysis, trying to see the reactions to change from all sides. Recognition and analysis are the first two phases of the cognitive restructuring process.

The board of USF was ready for changes in the financial structure of the organization. Mack did not have to sell the drastic cuts in the budget to the USF Board; they knew these painful changes were necessary.

Farling, on the other hand, had to do a great deal of selling of her ideas for changing the board. A good portion of the changes necessary at SUMA involved the board itself, and she needed to really be diplomatic with each conversation and each relationship. After much strategic maneuvering, Farling has arrived a point where the change has happened with a great deal of support from the newly restructured board, and those who were not supportive have self-selected out of service. It is important to note here that losing team players is absolutely all right. Organizations change, and so do the people involved.

How receptive have other stakeholders been to the needed changes?

FM: When there is a lot of change, there are a lot of questions to answer. And me being hired wasn't the only change. The festival moved into this new, state-of-the-art facility, away from the beloved Adams Theatre. We also moved from two Artistic Directors to one, we had our General Manager move on, we had our Development Director retire, we had to replace our Marketing Director (because she replaced the GM), so there have been a lot of changes in general at USF over the past few years.

There were some people who were concerned about some of the decisions that were being made, like the drastic cutting of the budget, but that is to be expected. There were audience members that were concerned that the festival wouldn't have the same "feel" as it did in the past. The feedback that we have been getting is that the plays are as good as they ever were and there is no change in the artistic quality. As for donors, we did get some pushback on decisions. There are donors that are in the wait-and-see mode, and some that support us fully, and some that have withdrawn support. But those are predictable reactions based on the degree of change we've had. We just deal with it as it comes. We've tried to rebuild relationships and build confidence. I think that is where I spend the majority of my time.

JF: It's all about seeing the big picture and the end goal, and then work backwards from there. So, if there are stakeholders that I need to finesse, I'm not just going to tell them what they want to hear, but I'm not going to blindside them, either. Open and honest communication is the key.

A good example would be the Art Auction. It was a fundraising event the Braithwaite had done in the past, but it didn't get implemented when the transition was made to SUMA. I wanted to try it at least one time to see how it would go, but I suggested we have the event at SUMA rather than the restaurant they had held it in for 20 years. It was like I poisoned them. It was blasphemy. The graduate students here have very strong opinions and great ideas about how we could do it better, and then we have stakeholders who can't see the auction any other way than it has been for the last 20 years. I'm in the middle of that right now. And I've been the staff person telling my director that we really need to push for change, and him not at least try to bring everyone together. He didn't like conflict, he just maintained the status quo. So, I've tried to be a different kind of leader. It just takes time and finesse. It won't come from one meeting. It will come from lunches and visits and conversations, always looking to the big picture. For the 25th annual Art Auction, we will be moving the event location to the museum. I finally had to tell them, "You're just going to have to trust us."

Observations: As to shepherding stakeholders through the transitions necessitated by the changes they both knew needed to happen, Mack and Farling continued to work on the first part of the cognitive restructuring process, recognition. This phase is perhaps the most important since one cannot fix a problem of which one is not aware.

Both also continued into the analysis phase of cognitive restructuring. With the stakeholders, both "learned to describe the change and why it must happen" succinctly (Bridges and Mitchell, 2002, p. 40). Additionally, they were both transparent in the processes leading to change. This increased "the degree to which the change agent the organization members are willing to hear, respond to, and be influenced by one another" (Lunenburg, 2010, p. 4).

How did you manage resistance to the needed changes?

FM: The way to figure that out was the only way I know how, and that is collaborative. I was trained as a theatre director, and what I know is the way we worked in rehearsal, which is everybody sits down and contributes to making the show successful. So actors and designers and crew have to come in with their ideas, their choices, they have to do their homework, and they have to contribute to the creative process. You can't get anywhere in a rehearsal if someone is not willing to explore choices. The only way we make progress creatively in rehearsal is by collaborating. It kind of sounds touchy-feely, but it's hard.

Ultimately, we have to think strategically, or we're all going to fail. Ultimately, you have to get over your obstacle or ego or whatever it is, or the show is going to fail. We know when it's going to open, and we know the financial universe the show has to live in, but beyond that, we have to solve stuff on our own. I don't know another industry that has a better on-time delivery than ours. Opening night is an unforgiving deadline.

There are certain fallbacks in rehearsal, where you are in a scene and you don't really know what the next step is, you can always tap into basic acting training and think "What does my character want? What is the objective? What are the obstacles that are preventing my character from getting what he wants?" You can always default to that and you're going to make progress creatively, by asking those questions. And the same is true in arts administration.

The worse the situation is, the easier it is to get people to change. When the (financial) circumstances were as dire as they were at the festival, everyone knew that there needed to be change. Again, in a rehearsal, if the scene is dull and boring, you don't have to convince the actors that something needs to change. Everyone can feel it. And everyone at the festival knew that there needed to be change. There was not a constituency that said it needed to stay the same. Running a 1.65-million-dollar deficit over two years is evidence that something is very wrong. We all knew there needed to be cuts, but we also all wanted to make sure those cuts didn't damage the artistic integrity of the shows.

JF: I think I came into a situation where most were ready to change. As far as a search committee and a board goes, in museums, they can see a new director as a sort of savior; they're going to solve all of our problems and they're going to give us a vision. But the goal is to make sure that everyone is on the same page so that the vision and the mission are being fulfilled, no matter who is sitting in the director's chair. So for the most part, I have been very supported and trusted, and I have the right experience that I can bring to SUMA. So usually, if I talk through the resistance, it turns out fine and people understand the need for the change.

It is also important for the director to empower the staff, and I think in the past the staff had not been appreciated or heard as much as they should be. There has been a bit a resistance there to put trust in these students. It gets frustrating when board members are working with staff members and don't have that mutual respect for them because they are students. That is something I have been working on. But how do I fix that? How do I get the board to value and respect these people as professionals, particularly the arts administration graduate students? They know what to do, and they shouldn't have to check with me to do something. And it's just as valid for them to try something new and to fail. Let them learn from that experience.

Observations: Once the assumptions, perceptions, and feelings were recognized, Mack and Farling began to differ when they became fully immersed in the analysis phase of cognitive restructuring. Both treated the resistance which stemmed from the assumptions, perceptions, and feelings discovered in phase one, differently.

Farling worked to uncover the cause behind resistance to the changes needed in the organization. She compromised and negotiated and stuck to her convictions when needed.

Mack, on the other hand, had hard data to back up the need for change and felt that if anyone was resistant to that data, they needed to get over it.

Both ran into several types of biases, including the In-Group Bias ("overestimating the abilities and value of our immediate group at the expense of people we don't really know") and the Status-Quo Bias ("the unwarranted assumption that another choice will be inferior of make things worse"), but both were able to manage those biases with communication and transparency (Dvorsky, 2013).

How do you maintain the transition process until the changes are complete?

FM: The first thing that was different was that I was very open. Here was an organization where people were very accustomed to not knowing about the financial operation of the organization. Transparency wasn't a thing. And I was very transparent in everything. Transparency is a very important objective.

The second thing was staying neutral on everything that had happened before. So I didn't criticize the people who were there before me, I didn't praise them either, except to say we wouldn't be here without them. When it came down to individual decisions they had made, I stayed neutral. And I also knew I couldn't fairly judge any of that stuff. I wasn't there.

JF: A lot of it is knowing where the resistance is coming from, and not avoiding or ignoring it. For example, I know a lot of the artists in the community are not happy with SUMA because of misconceptions back at the creation of the museum. Can I ignore that? Sure! Is that the right thing to do? No! Therefore, we're doing the total opposite by putting together an artist committee, and people who I know are going to say things that I don't agree with are going to be on that committee. I want to face it head-on. Let's have a formal way that this can be a discussion. There will be both resistance and buy-in on that committee, but what is past, is past. I wasn't here when promises were made, and the person that made those promises isn't here anymore. The conversation needs to keep going.

One of my goals is to be better about knowing what to do in the moment. I can reflect on situations and figure out what happened, but I'd like to be better prepared to address change and resistance and transitions right when it happens. I plan on applying to the Utah Division of Arts and Museums' Change Leader Program. I also plan on doing some more listening sessions like I did when I started this job. I want to ask about what worked and what didn't and try to continually improve. If we don't build in times for reflection, as leaders or staff or boards, then we won't have a good assessment of where we are as an organization.

Observations: Correction, or the third phase of cognitive restructuring, was also handled differently by both leaders. As mentioned, during the transition stage, or the process to achieve the desired change, leaders need to be advocates, mediators, and facilitators (Stagl, 2011).

Farling was all of these things. She allowed people to go through the transition process much like one experiencing grief: A mourning period for what is being lost, a neutral ground where the individual can sit in that loss and contemplate next steps, and then a period of getting back to work.

Mack treated those in the transition process with the adaptive leadership embodiment of "relentless realism" (Bernstein, 2016, p. 50). He encouraged his staff to solve the problems as a group, ensuring everyone had stock in the change. Farling opted for the more human-centered focus when dealing with transition, while Mack had his eye on the bottom line.

At the end of your first year, what did you learn (or re-learn) about managing change?

FM: I will say that it's harder now than it was when I first got here. I'm not new anymore, I can't credibly say "I don't know anything about that" because I do now. So, it gets harder, but you just have to focus on the things that are going well, on the things that are succeeding, and communicating that. I try to keep the focus on the benefits of all those hard decisions we made in my first year, and how they are propelling us into the future.

JF: This past year has reaffirmed the importance of communication. Not just *that* you communicate with staff, board members, volunteers, community members, but *how* you communicate with them. It helped that I took the same message and tailored depending on the audience. And that communication is a two-way street. I have to be open and willing to listen to our various stakeholders, even if I know I'm not going to like what I hear or agree with them.

Observations: Both Mack and Farling have learned a lot about themselves in the past year. They both recognize that there is still much to do in their respective organizations, and much to learn as leaders. And that, really, is the key to change leadership: knowing yourself and making an effort to know those you lead.

"Being an effective leader begins with understanding yourself. Knowing what motivates you, what your strengths and limitations are and how you respond in different situations all contribute to self confidence as you lead change. Along the same line, understanding and learning about those with whom you interact also contributes to your effectiveness as a leader" (The Utah Division of Arts and Museums, 2018).

It is also interesting to note that both Mack and Farling mentioned the importance of communication. Both had this seemingly obvious bit of knowledge reiterated and validated during their first year of leadership at USF and SUMA.

Conclusion

The change process is very hard for many, but to be able to change is necessary if one wants to succeed. As arts administrators learn to manage change, special care needs to be given to the transition part of the change process, and that care is found in the steps of cognitive restructuring.

The leader must understand what needs changing, manage the resistance created, and help those affected by the change through the transition process. "The advantage of cognitive restructuring is that it fully accounts for not just behavior, but also for thoughts and perceptions. . . . Cognitive restructuring makes us acutely aware of the role of our perceptions in determining our behavior" (Benfari, 2013, p. 35).

The new leaders at the Utah Shakespeare Festival and the Southern Utah Museum of Art were able to enact a great amount of change in their first year. As staff and stakeholders at both organizations become accustomed to the new normal, it will be interesting to see if both leadership styles were the ones needed for their respective organizations. I believe they were.

USF needed a person to put the company back on track financially; a person willing to make the tough (sometimes very painful) decisions that needed to be made. USF needed a person with no ties to the history of the organization, who could scrutinize it from a bottom-line point of view, without any baggage tainting actions taken. The USF staff members and stakeholders were there to speak up for tradition through the change process, but their new leader needed to challenge them with hard facts. I believe they found that person in Frank Mack.

However, while bottom lines are indeed important, so is the human factor. Emotions trump everything when it comes to change, and the key part of cognitive restructuring requires the leader to try to understand what the team members are thinking and feeling. While Mack made some effort to get to know the humans behind the structure and to be transparent with the decisions, there was little finessing when it came to managing resistance to change. Farling, on the other hand, was all about finesse.

SUMA needed a person to shepherd it into its new life as a university museum. With a new and beautiful building, they needed a person to help fill it with both art and organization. SUMA needed someone equipped with museum best practices, with new ideas and energy, and with creativity and practicality, to help guide the organization into its potential. Farling certainly was this person. She has been able to accomplish much cognitive restructuring in her first year through transparency, communication, collaboration, and strategy. SUMA is fortunate to have her.

Comparing two very different types of arts organizations at two very different points on their evolutionary arc might seem folly, yet observing two leadership styles at organizations in the same small town in Southern Utah can perhaps open up the possibilities of what will work in our organizations. What is certain is this: change is inevitable, and arts administrators must learn to navigate those rough waters effectively.

References

Benfari, R. (2013). *Understanding and changing your management style*. San Francisco: Jossey-Bass.

Bernstein, M. and Linsky, M. (2016). Leading change through adaptive design. *Stanford Social Innovation Review*, pp. 49–54.

Bridges, W. and Mitchell, S. (2002). Leading transition: A new model for change. In: *On leading change*. San Francisco: Jossey-Bass, pp. 33–46.

Dvorsky, G. (2013). *The 12 cognitive biases that prevent you from being rational*. Available at: https://io9.gizmodo.com/5974468/the-most-common-cognitive-biases-that-prevent-you-from-being-rational [Accessed 15 May 2018].

International Association of Administrative Professionals. (2009). *Leadership theories and styles*. Available at: www.academia.edu/22211238/Leadership_Theories_and_Styles_IAAP_2009_Administrative_Professionals_Week_Event_Event [Accessed 12 September 2018].

Lunenburg, F. (2010). Managing change: The role of the change agent. *International Journal of Management, Business, and Administration*, 13(1), pp. 1–6. Available at: National Forum. Available at: https://naaee.

org/sites/default/files/lunenburg_fred_c._managing_change_the_role_of_change_agent_ijmba_v13_n1_2010.pdf [Accessed 7 June 2018].

Paul, R. (2011). *Celebrate 50 years*, The Utah Shakespeare Festival, Cedar City.

Southern Utah Museum of Art (SUMA). (2018). *History*. Available at: www.suu.edu/pva/suma/about.html [Accessed 13 April 2018].

Southern Utah University. (2018). *Policies and procedures*. Available at: https://help.suu.edu/policies [Accessed 19 October 2018].

Stagl, H. (2011). *Seven roles of a change agent*. Available at: www.enclaria.com/2011/01/06/seven-roles-of-a-change-agent/ [Accessed 15 May 2018].

Utah Division of Arts and Museums (UDAM). (2018). *Change Leader Program*. Available at: https://heritage.utah.gov/arts-and-museums/resources-arts-museums/resources-prof-dev-change-leaders [Accessed 15 May 2018].

Utah Shakespeare Festival (USF). (2018). *About us*. Available at: www.bard.org/about/ [Accessed 13 April 2018].

11

GETTING ON THE BALCONY

Deploying adaptive leadership in the arts

William J. Byrnes

Introduction

The need for effective leadership and management in the arts has never been greater. Whether it is an intimate poetry reading or a huge city-wide music festival, there are expectations that leadership will be practiced which will routinely fulfill outcomes and achieve desired impacts. The process of creating and sharing visual and performing arts experiences that engage, educate, enthrall, and maybe even unsettle people occurs within increasingly complex and evolving social, political, economic, and technological environments. Boundaries are blurred between art forms and artists are exploring a variety of entrepreneurial pathways that continually change. Worldwide, cultural organizations are trying to adapt, change, and meaningfully respond while continuing to be creative forces for new ways of thinking and living (Caust, 2018, pp. 5–8).

What leadership methods and styles might be appropriate to help arts organizations thrive in these evolving environments? Does it make sense to focus on being a servant leader (Greenleaf, 1997, 1991, 2002) who uses a mix of transformative (Bass, 1990) and authentic leadership techniques (George, 2015)? Or, is using a combination of Path-Goal Theory (House and Mitchell, 1974) and Situational Leadership (Hersey, Blanchard, and Johnson, 2013) going to be more effective in meeting the needs of organization and stakeholders? Leading using mindfulness techniques has been suggested as an option (Lippincott, 2016). Maybe using collaborative techniques embedded in the process of creating theatre, dance, or opera productions will produce the best results (Foster, 2018).

As an alternative to these leadership approaches, this chapter will explore whether the adaptive leadership model could be employed to assist cultural organizations to meet the challenges they face. Developing adaptive leadership practices could help cultural organizations thrive and become more resilient. The basic tenets of adaptive leadership will be explained and tested in situations often found in the arts. Lastly, the efficacy of adaptive leadership will be discussed in light of complexity theory, leader training limitations, the difficulty in identifying adaptive challenges, and the personal limitations leaders must confront when attempting to deploy this leadership model.

Overview of the adaptive leadership model

Adaptive leadership involves implementing a series of carefully planned interactions between leaders and followers as they confront difficult situational challenges their organization faces (Heifetz,

155

Grashow, A. and Linsky, 2009, p. 32). After assessing the types of challenges (i.e., technical, technical and adaptive, or adaptive), a leader engages in facilitating behaviors designed to help followers learn, adapt, and change their thinking, values, beliefs, and work patterns. Peter G. Northouse created a schematic of Heifetz's adaptive leadership model to depict the interaction of the situational challenges with leader behaviors designed to engage followers in processes that solve problems, and that can lead to lasting change within organizations (Northouse, 2019, pp. 260–271).

The six leader behaviors that are part of a diagnostic framework include:

- Get on the balcony
- Identify the adaptive challenge
- Regulate distress
- Maintain disciplined attention
- Give work back to people
- Protect leadership voices from below

These six behaviors are used to create opportunities for leaders and followers to work together to tackle the difficult issues that surround adaptive change. The leadership model calls for establishing a holding environment which is deemed a safe space to allow followers to work through potential solutions to the challenges being faced (Northouse, 2019, p. 261).

Adaptive change and leadership deconstructed

Let's explore in more detail the concepts that are central to this change process by starting with a definition of adaptive leadership. Heifetz describes adaptive leadership as "the practice of mobilizing people to tackle tough challenges and thrive" (Heifetz, Grashow, and Linsky, 2009). That may mean the leader stands back and lets conflict and disagreements surface so that they can be addressed from the followers' perspective. The assumption is if the followers are not part of the adaptation process the organization will not be able to change successfully.

Adaptative organizational change is likened to the biologic processes of altering DNA. The organization preserves most of its core DNA needed for its survival, but the change process may require discarding or rearranging other parts of its DNA. This new DNA arrangement should enable the organization to adapt to changing environments. Those organizations not effective at adapting risk becoming extinct or stuck operating at a suboptimal level. Heifetz describes the use of the DNA overlay as a way to promote change, build on the past, and adapt as a result of trial, error, and experimentation (Heifetz, Grashow, and Linsky, 2009, pp. 13–17).

Adaptive change and cultural organizations

An example of a difficult adaptive challenge faced by an arts organization and which requires it change and adopt new behaviors might be how it goes about becoming more diverse, equitable, and inclusive. Arts organizations aspire to be more diverse, but demographic research indicates that this is not the case (Cuyler, 2015). The challenge to become more diverse may be technical (where the job openings are advertised) and adaptive (attitudes and implicit biases make the organization seem unwelcoming to minorities).

A second example of an adaptive challenge could involve a regional symphony orchestra with a traditional programming approach that is resulting in dwindling audiences. The leadership team (e.g., the music director and executive director) sees there is a need to change the organization to better meet the programming interests of a broader cross-section of the community. The leaders may conclude that to connect more deeply with people in the community, the orchestra players, staff, and board need to adapt and change attitudes about what it means to be a classical music organization in the 21st century. These adaptive changes may include rethinking the mission and values of the orchestra, developing empathetic perspectives about who is being served (or not) by their programming, and exploring alternative concert schedules and formats. If the leaders try to force change from the top down, it would likely result in resistance by orchestra members, the staff, board members, and people in the community. However, by using adaptive leadership, the music director and executive director could engage everyone in a process that results in changing the orchestra in ways that make it more flexible and responsive to its community.

Change or status quo?

Adaptive change starts with an assessment of the status quo. Organizations develop cultures and social systems which constitute the norms and ways of doing things that align with the type of business it operates (Byrnes, 2015, p. 105). Therefore, before deploying adaptive leadership, the leader first must understand the current state of an organization. Typically, the impetus that drives planning and change is the perception that there are dysfunctions that need to be addressed in the organization. However, Heifetz notes that:

> There is a myth that drives many change initiatives into the ground: The organization needs to change because it is broken. The reality is that any social system (including an organization or a country or a family) is the way it is because the people in that system (at least this individuals and factions with the most leverage) want it that way. In that sense . . . the system is working fine, even though it may appear to be "dysfunctional" in some respects to some outside observers.
>
> *(Heifetz, Grashow, and Linsky, 2009, p. 17)*

Examples of status quo situations that seem impervious to change could include the programming mindset of the previously mentioned symphony orchestra or an arts organization that says it values fiscal responsibility but continues to operate with a structural deficit. This same organization may publicly express the value it places on education and community engagement, but when requests are made for additional staff and budget resources to increase the impact of these activities, the funding never seems to be available. The point is, organizations create narratives to explain away and rationalize their shortcomings.

Technical problem and adaptive challenges

Heifetz originally proposed a framework for assessing the types of problems organizations face, tactics that might be employed to solve the problems, and whether the problems the leader had to confront were technical (clear solutions) or adaptive (requires learning) in *Leadership Without Easy Answers* (1994). This framework is still used and helps guide leaders in their initial assessment of the challenges faced by an organization. In an arts organization, an example of a technical challenge might be a data management software system that is difficult to use, and that is not providing the information needed to manage the organization effectively. The ticketing or membership software system may require a convoluted workaround to connect to the bookkeeping and finance software and, to make matters worse, neither system is connected to the software used by the fundraising staff. The solution to the problem will likely be costly but, in the end, a technical challenge like this can be overcome.

The previous example of the software problem demonstrates how a challenge could also be both technical and adaptive. For example, each of the current systems will likely have a staff member or manager who possesses expert knowledge of how the software works. The new software will need to be acquired, and then training will be required across multiple departments in the organization. However, some members of the staff may see the change as a loss of control. Heifetz notes, "Habits, values, and attitudes, even dysfunctional ones, are part of one's identity" (Heifetz and Linsky, 2002, 2017, p. 27) and resistance to change often becomes a broader concern about a loss of what is familiar. The current system may not work well, but the staff has become very adept at making it function. The system may be "broken," but there is pride among the staff that they make it work.

Switching to a new software system will typically involve creating a request for proposals (RFP) which requires managers and staff to work together developing their needs and requirements. In this case, technical and adaptive leadership will be required by the project leader if all the interested parties are to collaborate and complete the process of acquiring and deploying the new software. Followers (staff) will need to actively engage with each other by exchanging ideas and sharing the problems they are trying to solve with the new system. Learning about how work is done in other departments can provide new insights among the staff. The goal is to use this cycle of learning and collaboration to diffuse the anxiety that often accompanies change.

A recent real-world example of facing technical and adaptive challenges by an arts organization likely occurred when three different opera companies changed their performance schedules from a typical fall and spring season to a summer season. For example, in 2016 the Portland Opera changed to a 12-week summer schedule after 50 years of operating a more traditional performance schedule (Stabler, 2014). Ft. Worth Opera also made a similar change to a summer festival season in 2007 (Bailey, 2009) and more recently, Opera Philadelphia presented its first summer festival in 2017 (Cooper, 2015). In all three situations, these opera companies had to grapple with adaptive and technical challenges that would be felt within the organizations, and that would impact audiences, donors, and their communities.

When reading about theses dramatic programming adjustments, there was a common adaptive challenge each organization was trying to address: financial pressures that threatened their sustainability. Each faced adaptive challenges that required they make significant changes in how they operated. The 2009 magazine article *Darren Woods Leads Fort Worth Opera to New High* offers a glimpse into the process used in making change. The process was described by General Director Darren Woods as "a bonding experience for the staff, too, who had a real say in the company's future" (Bailey, 2009). While there was no evidence of systematic use of the adaptive leadership model by these opera companies, the changes being made required adaptation and had an impact on the DNA of each company.

Adaptive leader behaviors

Let's more closely examine the six behaviors that are part of the diagnostic framework a leader needs to use in assessing how to meet the adaptive and technical challenges an organization may face (Heifetz, Grashow, and Linsky, 2009, p. 74). Each of these behaviors seems to align well with how cultural organizations function.

Get on the balcony

For the leader to gain perspective about how the organization is functioning, they need to take the step of "getting up on the balcony" (Heifetz, 1997; Heifetz, Grashow, and Linsky, 2009; Heifetz and Linsky, 2002, 2017). This leader behavior aligns well with an actual practice used frequently in the arts. If a director, choreographer, or designer wants to see what is going on onstage, they will often go to the balcony or move to the rear of the auditorium to gain perspective. Or, a conductor may ask the assistant to step up to the podium, so they can move to the balcony to hear how the ensemble sounds. A curator and the artist may step back and assess if the desired impact of the exhibit installation has been achieved.

Heifetz writes "achieving a balcony perspective means taking yourself out of the dance . . . even if only for a moment" (Heifetz and Linsky, 2002, 2017, p. 53). Being on the balcony "can include such things as taking some quiet time, forming a group of unofficial advisers . . ., or simply attending meetings as an observer" (Northouse, 2019, p. 263). Using the example of the software transition mentioned earlier, the leader might sit in on the RFP planning meeting to gain perspective about conflicts and divisions that may exist among the staff related to the software change.

Identify adaptive challenges

Adaptive challenges typically involve problems connected to values, beliefs, and attitudes held by people in the organization. For example, the leader may identify that the status quo of an arts organization (e.g., the symphony) is causing it to fall into programming patterns that are no longer exciting and that do not engage audiences. To better assess the nature of the adaptive problems, Heifetz identifies four archetypes associated with adaptive challenges (Heifetz, Grashow, and Linsky, 2009, pp. 77–86).

Archetype 1: gap between espoused values and behavior

An opera company may have established its identity and reputation through high-quality programming of the "standard repertory." However, attendance and sales have been slipping over three decades. To address the problem, the company adds Broadway musicals to its schedule. After another decade it finds that more than half its schedule is now musicals. However, the company continues to represent itself as an "opera" company. When a new music director is hired, they push for programming more modern operas and want the company to perform fewer musicals. The music director (MD) thinks the opera company has lost its focus by chasing ticket revenue and feels strongly that the organization needs to take a different programming direction. The diagnosis is that the opera company's current programming conflicts with its core purpose.

Archetype 2: competing commitments

The opera company music director makes a compelling case to the artistic director (AD) that the company needs to be performing more modern operas and doing premieres of new works. They agree that the company needs to be doing more to develop future composers, singers, and audiences. They begin pondering from "the balcony" how to go about making this programming shift. However, some of the staff and a few of the board members are less certain that this change is worth the risk. The advocates for keeping the programming pattern that has worked for years (mix of opera and musicals) become concerned that the proposed changes will financially hurt the company. At the same time, the artistic leadership and a few of the staff and board members are expressing interest in going in this new direction. The advocates for change and for keeping the status quo are beginning to solidify, and competing commitments are coming into focus.

Archetype 3: speaking the unspeakable

No one has been speaking up about the fact that the opera company is performing more musicals than operas. The status quo seems to be working fine. However, the music director is questioning what the mission really is. The most important thing the artistic leadership can do at this point is to encourage "speaking the unspeakable" (Heifetz, Grashow, and Linsky, 2009, p. 82). Is opera central to the core programming of the company? If the opera company is to be a company, then the staff and board members need to be able to have an open dialog amongst themselves about the idea of changing the programming mix. Conflicting beliefs, values, and attitudes need to be discussed and addressed by the leadership. This is a critical time in the change process. The notion that *qui tacet consentit*, or silence assumes consent, can make the change process more difficult.

Archetype 4: work avoidance

If the leadership team is not careful, the adaptive change process may veer off course, and staff and board members who oppose the changes will slip into behavior patterns identified as "work avoidance" (Heifetz, Grashow, and Linsky, 2009, p. 84). Signs of this type of behavior include not speaking up at meetings and the formation of subgroups or individuals who engage in disruptive passive-aggressive behaviors. For example, the marketing director may think that performing unknown opera premieres is folly and as a result, they dial back their creative contributions on how they might go about marketing and communicating about a new season of programming. Alternatively, there may be board members who are not committed to this programming change, and as a result, they might consider making smaller annual donations, or they may feel less passionate about advocating for the company when out in the community.

Regulate distress

The fictional opera undergoing adaptive change shows the need of the leadership team to regulate elevated levels of distress among the staff. Some mix of the four adaptive challenge archetypes is not uncommon in arts organizations. For example, the changes being contemplated would likely require an adjustment to the mission and vision statements. Disagreements about wording changes to the mission could derail the entire change process. The adaptive leadership model offers three methods for the leader to manage this expected distress: "(1) create a holding environment, (2) provide direction, protection, orientation, conflict management, and productive norms, and (3) regulate personal distress" (Northouse, 2019, p. 265).

Holding environment – The idea of creating a holding environment makes a great deal of sense if the leader is trying to keep the change process from turning toxic.

These types of organizational "safe spaces" have their origin in the field of psychology and counseling. (Modell, 1976) Heifetz describes the concept of a holding environment in an organization as "all those ties that bind people together and enable them to maintain their focus on what they are trying to do" (Heifetz, Grashow, and Linsky, 2009, p. 155). A holding environment might be created at an offsite meeting space, (i.e., neutral territory). The important thing for the leader to do is to articulate this "space" is for experimenting with ideas, disagreeing, and even arguing but with the end goal of working toward solutions (Heifetz and Linsky, 2002, 2017, pp. 102–107).

Safe Space – A safe space for the opera company would be where staff and board members can express their differences and seek points of agreement. For example, if there are concerns about performing operas that are less familiar to the staff and board, then the leadership team might stage a short excerpt from one of these works and discuss it. Overcoming a lack of knowledge about new works and composers can be part of the learning process for everyone in the opera company.

Regulate Personal Distress – If adaptive change is going take place, the leadership team needs to be willing to listen and engage its stakeholders even if it means there are moments of discomfort. The holding environment may be messy and noisy at times, but if people in the organization value open communication, the potential for meaningful learning and change to take place is enhanced. The leader needs to help build consensus and diffuse conflict.

Maintain disciplined attention

The adaptive leader also needs to facilitate followers staying focused during the change process. For example, there could be three or four work groups organized to tackle various parts of the change process for the opera company. One group might be working on drafting revisions to the mission and vision statements and, in coordination with the marketing and development areas, they could be gathering feedback from key stakeholders in the community about the changes being considered. There could be another working group tasked with researching new operas that are influencing the repertoire around the world. The adaptive leadership team should be coordinating all these workgroups to make sure they are productive and are working toward meeting agreed-upon deadlines.

Give the work back to the people

The adaptive leader uses disciplined attention to also give work back to the opera company staff and board to engage them in the adaptive change process. If change is to be meaningful and lasting, the people who are part of the opera company need to feel and believe they are a necessary part of making these changes. New behaviors, attitudes, and beliefs do not come easily to people. If the staff and board do not feel they have a substantial part to play in re-envisioning the opera company, then the change process will be superficial. The leaders need to be willing to step back and let the followers grapple with the problems and arrive at solutions. The staff, for example, need to be able to say, "We helped write the new mission statement, and others of us wrote a marketing plan that supports our new mission and our programming direction." The idea of "placing the work where it belongs" (Heifetz and Linsky, 2002, 2017, p. 127) may be a big leap to make if an organization has a history of being led by a top-down leadership team. Giving work back requires a level of trust that also must be cultivated and nurtured.

Protect leadership voices from below

The last leader behavior includes providing the opportunity for people without authority in the organization to be heard. If the leader is going to give back work to followers, they then must recognize that the authority and power structures in their organization may inhibit this process. If the leader says they want to hear from everyone, but the staff witnesses negative consequences befalling those who speak up, then the adaptive change process will be undercut. Heifetz offers a description of how a leader can go about protecting the "troublemakers" while at the same recognizing organizational structure may keep alternative points of view from surfacing. Troublemakers tend to be isolated and are often ignored in organizations, but Heifetz notes that they may be "the only ones asking questions that need to be asked and raising issues that no one wants to talk about" (Heifetz, Grashow, and Linsky, 2009, p. 168).

Creating and managing disequilibrium

As we have seen, adaptive leadership is multi-layered, and adaptive challenges demand the leaders and followers stay alert, engaged, and focused on the problems that go well beyond making technical changes to internal processes. Tackling adaptive challenges requires putting the organization in what is describe as a "state of disequilibrium" (Heifetz, 1997). The adaptive leadership model posits there is a Productive Zone of Disequilibrium (PZD) created when addressing adaptive and technical challenges and that a leader monitors and constantly tweaks the zone so that "enough heat [is] generated by your intervention to gain attention, engagement, and forward motion, but not so much that the organization (or your part of it) explodes" (Heifetz, 1997). The metaphor used is that of a pressure cooker with the idea that the heat setting needs to be constantly adjusted during the adaptive change process (Heifetz, Grashow, and Linsky, 2009).

The adaptive leader's job is to start conversations and pose tough questions and create disequilibrium that will be unpleasant for a time. The PZD of the fictional opera company would allow for the pros and cons of producing fewer musicals and doing more modern operas and world premieres to be discussed without creating so much conflict that it becomes divisive. There could be several discussion threads about ways these adaptive challenges can be addressed. We saw that by regulating distress, using holding environments, by giving work back to peoples, and so forth, the leader can guide the followers through the PZD to reach the adaptive changes required to help the opera company address the existential issues it faces. The outcome of successfully navigating the PZD might be the reaffirmation the company's commitment to fostering creativity and artistic excellence.

Sustaining and thriving as an adaptive leader

An adaptive leader needs to be highly self-aware and connected to their purpose and values. We have looked at the processes used by an adaptive leader, but there is value in looking at what it takes to put this leadership model into practice. Heifetz notes that:

> There is no reason to shoulder the difficult work of leadership if you do not have compelling, higher purposes to serve, whether saving the world, renewing your organization, or helping your community meet long-standing challenges and thrive through tough times.
>
> *(Heifetz, Grashow, and Linsky, 2009, p. 233)*

Mission and vision-driven arts organizations seem an ideal environment in which to deploy a leadership model and system designed to engage people who share values shaped by a belief that the arts are a force for good and bettering the world. Adaptive leadership stresses followers need to do more than follow; they must engage in helping realize the potential of the organization through the adaptive work everyone must do (Northouse, 2019). Also, the adaptive leader needs to be courageous, inspiring, and willing to experiment continually while taking take care of themselves in order to personally thrive and survive (Heifetz, Grashow, and Linsky, 2009, pp. 233–255).

Purpose

An adaptive leader, or any leader for that matter, needs to be monitoring and strengthening the shared purpose of the people in the organization. For example, if a leader sees the need for an intervention to build a stronger culture in an organization, there would still need to be work done to sustain this change. Constant communication about the shared values and instituting new rites and rituals in the organization would need to be done to reinforce the new values and beliefs (Heifetz, Grashow, and Linsky, 2009, p. 237). For example, the Portland Opera general director would have likely needed to stress the mission-driven reasons for changing to the summer season to help focus the staff on the positive aspects of the new schedule.

Courage

Heifetz points out that adaptive leaders need to refashion working relationships with people in the organization. Getting on the balcony may mean a leader will need to alter expectations colleagues may hold about them (Heifetz, Grashow, and Linsky, 2009, pp. 248–251). Sticking to an agenda that is driven by change will not be easy or painless. Heifetz warns that the change process "calls for building the stomach for the journey" (Heifetz, Grashow, and Linsky, 2009, p. 260). The personality trait of being a people pleaser, for example, is not likely to produce adaptive change.

Inspiring people

Developing and strengthening communication and listening skills are important if an adaptive leader is going to build trust and inspire people in the organization to take risks and make the technical and adaptive changes needed to help the organization fulfill its purpose. Some of the suggestions offered by Heifetz and his colleagues for inspiring people echo concepts offered by Robert Greenleaf in his book *Servant Leadership* (Greenleaf, 1977/2002). Various techniques that can be explored include authentically sharing ideas with followers and being open to input. Being nonjudgmental and engaging in deep listening can help inspire trust (Heifetz, Grashow, and Linsky, 2009, p. 266).

Experiment

"Everything you do in leading adaptively is an experiment" (Heifetz, Grashow, and Linsky, 2009, p. 277). Leaders are often placed in situations where they are expected to have all the answers. However, some of the paths taken in the change process may fail to achieve results. The fear of not being right and of failing makes leaders and managers risk-averse. Therefore, being open with followers about why choices are being made can help mitigate the anxiety generated when trying out new ideas and processes.

Thrive

If a leader is personally struggling with too much to do and is suffering from burnout, the time and energy needed to be effective in the role of an adaptive leader is going to be difficult to find. Heifetz and his colleagues offer suggestions to achieve a work-life balance. They also suggest the leader have a few confidants to confer with when grappling with the repercussions of the change process being managed. The idea of creating a personal holding environment is explored along with balancing being realistic and optimistic (Heifetz, Grashow, and Linsky, 2009, p. 292).

Looking at adaptive leadership from a different balcony

Adaptive leadership, as we have seen, is a complex process with many moving parts. There is much to learn if one is to be effective and successful leading an organization through a cycle of change. Using a basic understanding of adaptive leadership as a process and the expectations placed on an adaptive leader, let's "move up to the balcony" for another author's perspective on adaptive leadership.

Four types of organizations

Juan Carlos Eichholz's 2017 book *Adaptive Capacity – How organizations can thrive in a changing world* expands on Heifetz's model. Eichholz creates a grid diagram to depict how four general types of organizations go about the process of adaptive change. Communal, Innovative, Bureaucratic, and Action-driven organizations reside at each corner of a grid which is framed by a horizontal continuum that spans from participatory to hierarchical processes and orientations that vertically span from internal to external in their focus (Eichholz, 2017, p. 58). For example, communal organizations can include NGOs and NPOs which tend to be driven by a "sense of belonging" as expressed by values such as "inclusion, caring, and consensus" (Eichholz, 2017, p. 62). Innovative organizations, which could include those in the arts, are driven by creating an "impact," and their values may include "creativity, "collaboration," and "meaning" (Eichholz, 2017, p. 62).

As an adaptive leader of an arts organization, it would seem wise to analyze and assess where the organization tends to function within Eichholz's framework. For example, a state-run arts or cultural heritage museum would likely have the driving forces and values associated with more bureaucratic organizations (e.g., "safety" and values such as "formality, tradition, and regularity") (Eichholz, 2017, pp. 59–61). Therefore, a starting point for building adaptive capacity is going to be different from a more communal or innovative organization. Eichholz notes that "not all companies and institutions are expected to be equally adaptive, and he adds "organizations should all try to be more adaptive or increase their adaptive capacities within the limits of their nature" (Eichholz, 2017, p. 66).

"A second useful barometer of an organization's adaptive capacity is the way in which authority is exercised" (Eichholz, 2017, p. 112). The same grid is used to align authority with the four types of organizations. Communal organizations tend toward the use of "conciliatory" authority with a goal to make sure everyone "feels included and heard." Meanwhile, bureaucratic organizations may use authority more paternalistically, and action-driven organizations often use directive authority (move fast and seek results). Innovative organizations tend to use authority "in a facilitative way, by providing space and resources for people to deploy themselves and generate impact" (Eichholz, 2017, p. 112). The key insight here is that "observing the mode in which the authority is exercised in an organization is a simple and effective way of analyzing its adaptive capacity" (Eichholz, 2017, p. 113). For example, the leader of a state-controlled bureaucratic cultural heritage museum could use directive authority to nudge people toward taking more responsibility for elements in a change process.

Getting on the balcony to assess the realities of being an adaptive leader

The concluding section of this chapter will move up on the balcony to examine various obstacles that an arts manager may face when contemplating deploying the adaptive leadership model. The model will be briefly assessed by looking at four critical areas that could be obstacles to deploying it: the complexity of the process, training an adaptive leader, identifying adaptive challenges, and what leader attributes and personal skills are required to be an adaptive leader. A case study (see Box 11.1) describes how the leadership team of the Sacramento Ballet is going about exploring elements of adaptive leadership as an approach to chart a path of change.

Complexity

Heifetz, Grashow, and Linsky have created a leadership model that has been described as a "subset of Complexity Leadership Theory" (Northouse, 2019, p. 259). Arts organizations are complex adaptive systems (CAS) and fit the description of "neural-like networks of interacting, interdependent agents who are bonded in a cooperative dynamic by common goal(s), outlook(s)," and "need(s), etc." (Uhl-Bien, Marion, and McKelvey, 2007, p. 299). Being an adaptive organization implies there is an awareness among all the stakeholders (leaders and followers) of the overlapping systems and subsystems that power it. Without this self-awareness, the adaptive capacity of the organization, as Eichholz pointed out, will be reduced and change and adaptation will come more slowly, if at all.

An arts manager using the principles of adaptive leadership will be required to make a significant commitment to learning how all the systems and subsystems work (or don't) in their organization. The mindsets and habits driving operating processes will need to be confronted, and changed and traditional top-down bureaucratic structures may need to be mitigated. There may be fewer levels of management in an arts organization, but there is still structure and hierarchy that can be resistant to change. There also may be an underlying culture of conflict between the aspirations of an artistic director and more risk-averse followers and board members.

Box 11.1   Ballet Company Leaders Learning and Implementing Adaptive Leadership

The Sacramento Ballet, founded in 1954, recently underwent a leadership change that afforded the organization the opportunity to confront its status quo and increase its adaptive capacity. In the spring of 2017 the board of directors moved ahead with replacing its long-time co-artistic directors (Crowder, 2017). The new artistic director Amy Seiwert and executive director Anthony Krutzkamp took over the leadership of the ballet company for its 2018–2019 season (Browing, 2018). At the urging of board president Andrew Roth, this leadership team undertook the study of adaptive leadership. Roth first encountered adaptive leadership through an executive development program offered by his employer, the California State Teachers Retirement System (Roth, Seiwert, and Krutzkamp, 2019). Roth proposed that the three of them undertake a year-long collaborative reading of *The Practice of Adaptive Leadership (2009)*. The trio met to discuss the concepts of adaptive leadership and as a way to bond as a team. Reading and discussing adaptive leadership unfolded through a process that allowed them to shape a framework for change that was a good fit for the ballet company. For example, the Seiwert and Krutzkamp focused on aligning staff functions and breaking down autonomous work groups that were in place. Dealing with issues of loss and change (the previous co-artistic directors had been there for 30 years), and the need to turn up the heat on new ways of doing and thinking among the staff were slowly introduced. Adaptive leadership was being implemented in a way that allowed for it to take root organically. The leadership team took a strategic, or what could be described as a choreographic approach, to implementing the adaptive leadership by testing and assessing (rehearsing) it before considering an organization-wide rollout of the full process.

Leader training

The Practice of Adaptive Leadership (2009) is a comprehensive, practical guide to the leadership model, but it is questionable if one would attempt to adaptively lead without intensive preparation, training, and coaching. Heifetz and his colleagues have created a consulting firm which offers support services and workshops on how to implement and engage in adaptive leadership. Lacking the resources to hire a consultant, an arts manager would need to undertake a lengthy period of self-education before trying to use this complex and multi-level model. For example, a new self-taught adaptive leader might start with testing and demonstrating various elements of the adaptive leadership process. They might work with the staff and board to teach them how to use the diagnostic tool of observing and interpreting what is really going on inside the organization. Then the focus could shift to exploring the types of challenges the organization may face.

In some respects, adaptive leadership could be viewed as yet one more prescriptive methodology for leading that is part of what Harvard professor Barbara Kellerman calls the "Leadership Industry" (Kellerman, 2012, p. xiii). Kellerman is skeptical about the ability of most leadership training programs to deliver on their promises. However, she does note that Heifetz is among those experts who have "developed ways of teaching how to lead that had particular resonance" (Kellerman, 2012, p. 181). However, Kellerman also notes that teaching leadership has "too many competing experts offering too many competing pedagogies, most of which are based neither on empirical evidence nor on a well-established theoretical tradition" (Kellerman, 2012, p. 174).

The challenge of identifying adaptive challenges

The diagnostic method described by Heifetz for identifying the types of challenges is dependent on the leader and the leadership team being astute and willing to ask tough questions. Trying to ascertain if there is a collective will to solve problems that require making substantial changes can be equally daunting. The comfort zone created by the status quo can be hard to break out of. Heifetz's notes that "yesterday's adaptations are today's routines" (Heifetz, Grashow, and Linsky, 2009, p. 49). The opera company example mentioned earlier at some point decided to add musicals to its schedule, and now that is the norm. This means that uncovering the true nature of the type of challenges an organization faces is going to take a significant amount of effort because it will also involve breaking through the routines that are deeply ingrained in the organization's culture.

In addition, getting up on the balcony to do this kind of assessment can be easier said than done. The people in artistic and strategic leadership roles often are also enmeshed in operations. For example, an artistic director of a theatre company may be directing one or more shows in a season which can then lead to extended periods where strategic questions are put on hold. It is difficult to get up on the balcony and assess the whole organization when one is already on a different balcony looking at things such as how the staging is working in a scene. That is not to say it cannot be done, but realistically, every leader has their limits when it comes to where they will be able to concentrate their time.

The adaptive leader's attributes

The last set of issues that need to be faced include the capabilities and skills of the person in the leadership role. Being adaptable is often cited as a highly valued management and leadership skill (Basadur, Gelade, and Basadur, 2014, Northouse, 2019). Heifetz, Grashow, and Linsky offer a series of strategies, recommendations, and practices that a person can use to develop and sustain themselves as an adaptive leader (Heifetz, Grashow, and Linsky, 2009, pp. 181–203). For example, they suggest a leader needs to see themselves as a "system" and to be aware that "you are actually made up of several role identities," and that you need to manage "multiple and not always clear or consistent values, beliefs, ways of being, and ways of doing" (2009, p. 182). They also focus on the personal aspects of being an adaptive leader and offer suggestions on how best to "deploy yourself" (2009, pp. 230–231). The suggestions to "stay connected to your purpose," "engage courageously," and "inspire people" (Heifetz, Grashow, and Linsky, 2009, pp. 233, 247, 263) are seen as behaviors to cultivate to be an effective adaptive leader. While all these practices seem reasonable, even Heifetz and his colleagues admit that "many of the techniques we suggest may be outside your own behavior norms" (Heifetz, Grashow, and Linsky, 2009, p. 231).

This observation introduces an interesting dilemma. How does one behave as an adaptive leader? If the process for deploying oneself requires behaving outside your norms, then there is another layer to the process of becoming an adaptive leader which would need to be addressed – the adjustments needed in a leader's identity and personality. If for example, a person assesses themselves as not being well-versed in engaging people "courageously," or if they feel they lack the communication skills to "inspire people," then what steps will need to be taken to strengthen these behaviors?

Changing behavioral patterns is difficult and is often unsuccessful. For example, trying to improve how you "deploy yourself" could entail using the techniques found in the *control-theory model* of the self. This model "proposes that people regulate their behavior by making a series of comparisons against preexisting standards until the behavior matches the standards" (Carducci, 2015, p. 429). For example, if a leader wants to be able to inspire people, they would first need to examine the impact their current communication style is having on followers. Based on their analysis of their ability to inspire followers, they might need to seek outside coaching to hone their communication skills.

It is beyond the scope of this chapter to explore the many processes and techniques needed to develop one's readiness level, regulate behavior, and to lead adaptively. This leadership model assumes that an adaptive leader will self-assess and then work to close the gaps that might undercut their efforts. However, these behavior patterns may be easier to envision than to do. Helen Delaney noted in an article entitled "Identity Work in Leadership Development" that:

> The majority of identity and leadership development research tends to offer a largely positive and unproblematized picture of doing identity work in leadership development. Perhaps this positive bias is symptomatic of a trend in leadership studies whereby many leadership scholars are also directly involved in facilitating or designing leadership development initiatives, which may make it difficult to gain critical distance.
>
> *(Delaney, 2017)*

In some ways, *The Practice of Adaptive Leadership* follows a similar positivist bias. Ultimately, trying to build an organization that can be truly adaptive seems destined to be a frustrating process given the realities of organizational complexity and the exigencies of human behavior. Enormous will, stamina, and a great deal of practice would be required of someone attempting to lead adaptively.

Conclusion

This examination of the theory and practice of adaptive leadership was motivated by an interest in investigating options arts managers and leaders might explore when seeking to build the capacity of cultural organizations to change. While not a definitive study, it is hoped that further research can be undertaken to explore the efficacy of adaptive leadership and cultural organizations.

One obvious area that needs further analysis is how an arts manager attempting to deploy adaptive leadership might go about mobilizing followers who may be part-time staff or members of a bargaining unit. An arts leader could be dealing with followers made up of at-will employees, independent contracted artists (e.g., designers, directors), union employees (actors, musicians, dancers, stage-hands, and so forth), part-time seasonal staff, and volunteers. It is not hard to imagine a circumstance in an arts organization in which follower subgroups would conflict with each other. Therefore, building an adaptive culture in an arts organization would likely entail working with multiple interest groups and in some cases, followers with sporadic engagement and who might never be part of the change process.

Regardless of the change and adaptation process used by the leadership team, it is important to remember that understanding what the tolerance level is for change in the cultural organization is critical. Expanding the adaptive capacity of an organization is demanding work that will take considerable time and effort. It is essential that there is ongoing diagnostic work being done to understand how the organization really works (or doesn't).

Overall, the collaborative leader-follower foundation of the leadership model seems suited for the cooperative and creative framework found in arts organizations. Empowering people to question the status quo can become the status quo. Building a creative organizational culture which makes the practice of regularly getting up on the balcony to see what is really going on seems to be an achievable goal and one that can help organizations thrive.

References

Bailey, M. (2009). *Culture feature: Darren Woods leads Fort Worth opera to new highs.* [online] Available at: http://digital.360westmagazine.com/article/Culture+Feature%3A+Darren+Woods+Leads+Fort+Worth+Opera+To+New+Highs/128499/13966/article.html [Accessed 28 Sep. 2018].

Basadur, M., Gelade, G., and Basadur, T. (2014). Creative problem-solving process styles, cognitive work demands, and organizational adaptability. *Journal of Applied Behavioral Science*, 50(1), pp. 80–115.

Bass, B.M. (1990). *Bass & Stogdill's handbook of leadership*. 3rd ed. New York: The Free Press.

Browing, K. (2018). *Sacramento Ballet introduces new artistic director, pledges innovation*. [online] Available at: www.sacbee.com/entertainment/arts-culture/article211755624.html [Accessed 11 Jan. 2019].

Byrnes, W.J. (2015). *Management and the arts*. 5th ed. Burlington: Taylor & Francis.

Carducci, B.J. (2015). *Psychology of personality – view points, research, and applications*. 3rd ed. Hoboken, NJ: John Wiley & Sons, Inc.

Caust, J. (2018). *Arts leadership in contemporary contexts*. New York: Routledge.

Cooper, M. (2015). *Opera Philadelphia's new seasonal structure caters to bingeing*. [Online] Available at: www.nytimes.com/2015/10/21/arts/music/opera-philadelphias-new-seasonal-structure-caters-to-binge-ing.html [Accessed 28 Sep. 2018].

Crowder, M. (2017). *Big changes announced for Sacramento Ballet*. [online] Available at: www.sacbee.com/entertainment/arts-culture/article125760194.html [Accessed 11 Jan. 2019].

Cuyler, A. (2015). *An exploratory study of demographic diversity in the arts management workforce*. [Online] Available at: www.giarts.org/article/exploratory-study-demographic-diversity-arts-management-workforce [Accessed 12 Oct. 2018].

Delaney, H. (2017). Identity work in leadership development. In: J. Storey, et al. eds., *The Routledge companion to leadership*. New York: Taylor & Francis, p. 574.

Eichholz, J.C. (2017). *Adaptive capacity – how organizations can thrive in a changing world*. 2nd ed. London: LID Publishing Ltd.

Foster, K. (2018). *Arts leadership: Creating sustainable arts organizations*. New York: Routledge.

George, B. (2015). *Discover your true north*. Hoboken: Wiley & Sons, Inc.

Greenleaf, R.K. (1977/2002). *Servant leadership: A journey into the nature of legitimate power and greatness*. New York: Paulist Press.

Greenleaf, R.K. (1997/1991/2002). *Servant leadership*. Mahwah: Paulist Press.

Heifetz, R.A. (1997). *Leadership without easy answers*. Cambridge: Harvard Press.

Heifetz, R. and Linsky, M. (2002/2017). *Leadership on the line*. Boston: Harvard Business Review Press.

Heifetz, R., Grashow, A., and Linsky, M. (2009). *The practice of adaptive leadership*. Boston: Harvard Business Press.

Hersey, P.H., Blanchard, K.H., and Johnson, D.E. (2013). *Management of organizational behavior*. 10th ed. Boston: Pearson.

House, R.J. and Mitchell, R.R. (1974). Path-goal theory of leadership. *Journal of Contemporary Business*, 3, pp. 81–97.

Kellerman, B. (2012). *The end of leadership*. New York: Harper Collins Publishers.

Lippincott, M.K. (2016). *A study of the perception of the impact of mindfulness on leadership effectiveness*. Philadelphia: University of Pennsylvania.

Modell, A.H. (1976). The 'holding environment' and the therapeutic action of psychoanalysis. *Journal of American Psychological Association*, 24, pp. 285–307.

Northouse, P.G. (2019). *Leadership theory and practice*. 8th ed. Los Angeles: Sage Publications.

Roth, A., Seiwert, A. and Krutzkamp, A. (2019). Adaptive leadership at the Sacramento Ballet [Interview] (4 January 2019).

Stabler, D. (2014). *Fort Worth opera to Portland opera on changing to a summer festival: Expect higher costs*. [Online] Available at: www.oregonlive.com/performance/index.ssf/2014/10/portland_opera_can_take_a_less.html [Accessed 28 Sep. 2018].

Uhl-Bien, M., Marion, R., and McKelvey, B. (2007). Complexity leadership theory: Shifting leadership from the industrial age to the knowledge era. *The Leadership Quarterly*, August, 18, pp. 298–318.

PART III

Developing communities and evolving cultural policy

12

ROLES OF CULTURAL NETWORKS IN THE TIMES OF QUANTUM REALITY[1]

Aleksandar Brkić

Introduction: Times of "Quantum Reality"

. . . whilst we work tirelessly to reduce the amount of information in our reality, there is a fundamental argument that suggests that the amount of information in the Universe as a whole, if understood correctly, can only ever increase.

(Vedral, 2010, p. 11)

Vlatko Vedral proposes that the quantum of information in our universe is an ever-increasing fact. There has been, since Lord Keynes came up with the notion of an Arts Council in the United Kingdom, and the United Nations concerned themselves with the notion of collective culture, a proliferation of organisations which concern themselves with artistic and cultural practice and the way they intersect with national and international policy. This chapter will explore that notion in terms of organisations which have been set up to facilitate the international exchanges in the field(s) of culture/arts, mostly focusing on the arts management and cultural policy networks, and the roles they play in the field today.

Arts/cultural management, often joined together with cultural policy, is a field nurtured in challenging post–WWII geopolitical times that asked for a lot of efforts to connect the actors in the same field of practice on the international level. Challenges were numerous – lack of sources of information; high travel costs; limited ways of communication; political and ideological simplified binary divides (i.e. East-West; Developed-Underdeveloped; Communist-Capitalist); cultural and language specificities, and many other. Geopolitical seismological shifts triggered by the fall of the Berlin Wall in 1989 have challenged concepts about the nature of our world, where these divides were very soon broken, and diluted rather than "fixed". The world became much more interconnected, faster, closer and – unevenly balanced.

A new binary conundrum of parallel spaces rose to the surface – one cosmopolitan and other national. These parallel tracks, like siblings trying to find their own independence, seem to be inextricably bound together and we observe how they play out in the distinct and different ways in which they influence our lives, creating something that we can metaphorically call a "quantum reality" (Vedral, 2010). On one side, there would appear to be an attempt on the part of the global elite to promote "methodological cosmopolitanism" (Beck and Grande, 2007). On the other, as an apparent counter-reaction, we witness a proliferation of nationalism and revival of "methodological nationalism" (Wimmer and Glick Schiller, 2002) on a global scale. The contradiction is inherent and yet not mutually exclusive, for we live in a world in which we can be at the same time in two distinct and different places. While networks were going outwards, national cultural policies were getting more and more confused, mostly going inwards. There are often different criteria of success from the perspective of global/cosmopolitan network communities in the field of culture compared to the priorities of national cultural and education policy agendas (i.e. the paradox of the Creative Europe collaboration projects on the level of EU, balancing between national and supranational success indicators).

Vedral's proposition about an ever-increasing universe of information certainly would seem to describe the ways in which there is an ever-increasing rise of (cultural) networks. The emphasis he makes however is on "information" rather than "meaning". Does 'more' mean better? Can those networks stay in the relatively same frameworks as the ones with which they started?

Mobility was always an intrinsic factor of actors in the cultural sector. In fact, mobility was one of the crucial strategies used by all ancient empires to both acquire and disseminate their ways of life (intangible elements), as well as to promote their cultural artefacts (tangible elements). This strategy expanded radically with the industrial revolution as new forms of increasing speed and scope impacted world trade.

However, since the 1990s, as the culture of individualism became more dominant than the traditional ideas of communities (shift from the traditional communities to so-called communities of interests), and the expansion of low-fare travel and democratization of the Internet, cultural exchanges became much easier. Low barriers to entry to the world of networking gave rise to a new generation of individuals-as-networks. This shift made it much easier for networks to expand in many different ways, and different kind of forms.

Just as the landscape for networks is complex, so too are the ways in which frameworks for cultural policy connected with the culture/arts, and the field(s) of arts management and cultural policy. These frameworks function on the local (i.e. city policies), micro regional (i.e. region within a nation-state), national, macro regional (wider regions beyond nation-state borders) and international level, with the networks ideally being positioned on the intersection of different layers of inquiry. Figure 12.1 demonstrates how these networks purpose interlock. These different levels on which cultural networks operate tend to cross over, and there is often a debate on the borders between the standards and priorities between them (i.e. local vs. national; national vs. international).

These overlapping spaces are far from being the only ones that make the context for cultural networks complex. As Colin Mercer was warning us, these spaces, described by Bruno Latour with metaphors such as levels, layers, territories, spheres, categories, structure, systems . . . as well as art forms, genres, and silo-based funding and policy agencies are now rather exchanged with a "fibrous, threadlike, stingy . . . capillary character" (Latour, 1997, p. 2; Mercer, 2010, p. 37).

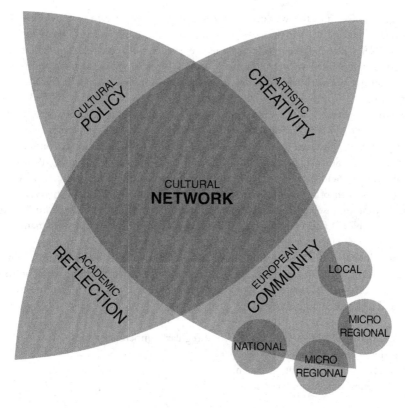

Figure 12.1 Positioning a cultural network in a European context

Source: Brkic, 2014

Exploring the labyrinth of cultural networking today

a network is a self-generating, self-organizing, self-sustaining system. It works through multiple feedback loops. These loops allow the system to monitor and modulate its own performance continually and thereby maintain a state of homeostatic equilibrium. At the same time, these feedback loops induce effects of interference, amplification, and resonance. And such effects permit the system to grow, both in size and in complexity. Beyond this, a network is always nested in a hierarchy. From the inside it seems to be entirely self-contained, but from the outside, it turns out to be part of a still larger network.

(Shaviro, 2003, p. 10)

It is not easy to define a cultural network today. Since Manuel Castells (2001, 2004, 2009) and Richard Florida (2012) published their highly influential, but from many angles contested work (i.e. Peck, 2005; Hoyman and Faricy, 2009), cultural networking and networking in general became a popular notion of academic discourses. At the same time, networking became an integral element of the "creative class" – mobile individuals with the high levels of social and economic capital (Florida, 2012), a concept that was used as the priority of number of cultural policy documents around the world (i.e. The Arts and Culture Strategic Review – ACSR in Singapore, launched in 2010, giving the cultural policy vision, mission and goals for Singapore until 2025) (NAC, 2012). Everyone, everywhere, every day . . . is networking. Still, this is happening in the world filled with conundrums, and as Leger is saying in his polemical book – "someone can not network and continue to network in the same way that Marxist professors sell their books and anarchist artists apply for government grants" (Leger, 2018, p. 3).

If we define a network simply as a group of people interacting in a certain way with each other, we can then say that "cultural network is an organization of people and/or institutions of similar professional interest or role performed in their respective cultural communities or a given form of art" (Sternal, 2013, p. 8). Position of these networks has changed in the life of professionals in the field of culture/arts – from being one of the main sources of information and experiences from other communities, cities, countries, regions, cultural networks are now trying to position themselves in the space of information overload that is at the same time dealing with the problem of attention scarcity. There are now a number of many-to-many tools that are there to support cultural cooperation.

Pehn saw the cultural network as a "virtual place of exchange" that is creating a philosophy "out of the sum of its members' philosophies, which must be reflected in it", with "notions such as rivalry and competition as alien" (1999, p. 29). He listed these four features as most important for a cultural network as an organization:

- Strong interpersonal ties, which go beyond regular competence issues
- Non-hierarchical relations
- Openness for development and change
- Innovativeness of structure and activities

Entering a cultural network may resemble one's experience in a labyrinth, balancing between the local, national, regional, global views. Pozzolo, Bacchella, and Agusto (2001, p. 14) discuss this kind of experience relating it to the myths deeply engrained in us:

> In any type of labyrinth, from the one represented by Ariadne's thread to Tarry's Theorem, the strategies for finding one's way through are characterized by the impossibility of attaining a global view. Decisions are conditioned exclusively by "local vision," and are made one after the other (as in an algorithm) based on "local attention". Even Daedalus, who was imprisoned in the labyrinth of his own design, managed to escape only after taking to flight. From above, he was able to recognise the structure of the labyrinth and to identify solutions to the problems which had remained unresolvable while he remained on foot.

Cultural networking can be a confusing process and it does take some kind of a system to be applied so that the individual or an arts organization can find the way through different potential paths. One of the pioneers of cultural networking in Europe, Mary Ann DeVlieg, defined cultural networks as "a form of organising and not organisations per se" (DeVlieg, 2001).

In that sense, conceptually, we can approach cultural networking through four basic categories:

- Organizational (institutional) model (*network as an organization*)
- Strategic direction of an existing organization (*networking as a strategic direction*)
- Form of communication (*networking as a trait or a skill*)
- A way of organizational behaviour (*networking as an ecology of an organization*)

Network as an organization is a legal entity that usually has its own structure, secretariat (centre), some kind of governing body, general members assembly and different kind of projects that are produced on an annual or periodic level.

Networking as a strategic direction is a way of operating in a highly connected world that one arts/cultural organization can decide to take for one or more strategic cycles. This decision can be a result of the impossible position that the organization has in a relatively closed local/national environment. By applying this strategy, an organization can still be active and influential on the local/national level, but getting its strength from the validation, projects, image and funding it received from the partners connected through the network.

Networking as a trait or a skill became one of the core elements of arts/cultural management as a field. It is on the one side promoted by the rapid technological developments and the concept of individuals-as-networks on one side and on the other by communication as a classical trait of arts/cultural managers.

Networking as an ecology of an organization became a way of functioning related to the culture of collaboration and co-creation instead of the culture of competition. It is a specific way of looking at the ecosystem in which the organization is positioned, in which every organization is a node in a network of potential collaborators and partners.

According to the statement, or "manifesto document" called "The Value of International Cultural Networks" (2016), signed by 20 cultural networks based in Europe,[2] cultural networks exist

> to promote and facilitate all forms of international collaboration, and improve the access to arts and culture; build trust and nurture relationships across national borders; to connect and bridge realities, coordinate joint efforts (advise, host, mediate inside respective fields and beyond); promote cultural equity, defend the intrinsic value of the art.[3]

This kind of sharing produces a culture of shared awareness, shared creation and shared responsibility (Shirky, 2008).

However, because of the history of the development of organizations like ENCATC or AAAE, we are mostly thinking of cultural networks as organizations that have their "secretariat" and members. Depending on their motivations to be in these cultural networks, Vellani (2010) categorized members into Leaders, Participants, Freeloaders, Floaters and Cynics, emphasizing that the healthy network would need to focus on the active participants, trying to "minimise floaters and cynics, without maximising leaders" (p. 3). One of the questions that become important is: what really motivates the professionals in the field to be the Participants in the cultural/arts management education network today, compared to the period 1960–2000?

Most of the best known, highly visible and influential international networks, which concern themselves with education in arts and cultural management and cultural policy, such as for example Association of Arts Administration Educators (AAAE), The European League of Institutes of the Arts (ELIA), and European Network on Cultural Management and Policy (ENCATC), were initiated either in United States or Europe at the end of the "Age of Extremes", in the fractured times of late 20th century (Hobsbawm, 2013). They became some of the most significant pillars of the ecosystem of what will later be defined as a field of arts/cultural administration/management and cultural policy education. These networks continue to be active today, although at this juncture in their history they appear to be jostling amongst themselves as they search for new ways in which to reposition their membership and reshape their frameworks from their Eurocentric or Northern Americentric beginnings towards a more global embrace and approach.[4]

Looking into the survey done with more than 50 cultural networks and organizations based in 32 countries in Europe, Asia Pacific, the Americas and Africa, as part of IFACCA's "THRIVE:

Networking Culture Leaders" platform (Laaksonen, 2016), representatives of cultural networks defined the purpose of their organizations in various ways, that were summed in the report (Laaksonen, 2016, p. 20):

- Advocacy for the arts and culture and their role in building a sustainable, fair and harmonious society and transparent, accountable governance
- Accessibility of the arts and culture to all through education, training, awareness-raising, information sharing and creative experiences
- Building bridges and connections between sectors, disciplines and stakeholders
- Promotion of cultural diversity and values, understanding, peace and dialogue
- Promotion of specific art form sectors, cultural institutions, creative industries and national or regional art scene
- Strengthening and facilitating cultural dialogue, exchange and cooperation
- Resourcing and strengthening local communities, civil society and grassroots involvement
- Fostering sustainability, equality and harmonious co-living
- Supporting capacity-building, improving the working conditions of cultural professionals, and defending their rights
- Strengthening the role of members and serving their needs
- Strengthening communication and cooperation between cultural networks and other stakeholders

Most of these goals, directions, and strategies seem like elements of well-structured organizations, with clear and rooted missions and reasons for existence. Nevertheless, the fluid character of a network as a form, where members are continuously joining and leaving, make the cultural networks "structures of low formality, constantly under development" with the members having a number of options to choose from when it comes to the level of their commitment (Sternal, 2013, p. 9).

Examining the profiles of cultural networks across Europe in his insightful report for Culture Action Europe, Ivor Davies identified a number of general characteristics that are shared across the sector positioning them in different ways as:

- Learning spaces and awareness-builders – providing services to members and others, to increase understanding of shared issues – both internally and externally focused
- Meeting spaces for people with shared interests – providing physical (and virtual opportunities to enable members and others in their sector to meet, share new experiences and ideas and gain mutual strength
- Meeting places for people with diverse interests – as above but reaching out to connect with more diverse, interests and perspectives (e.g. culturally, geographically, disciplinary etc.)
- Event promoters – bringing together groups of artists from diverse backgrounds to make and share work internationally
- Intercultural resources – providing services and environments that enable people from diverse cultural backgrounds to interchange, build lasting relationships and cooperate in their practice
- Vehicles for inter/transdisciplinary practice – exploring and building connections with ideas and practice across diverse, complementary (or apparently contradictory) disciplines
- Partnership consortia – enabling members to work together to form partnerships based in their own specialist fields
- Project developers and partners – working centrally or with partners to devise, develop, and deliver cooperation projects

- Communication media (internal) – researching and disseminating news and information services for members and to their own specialist sector of interest
- Addressers of issues in or with related fields – seeking out and working with others, in order to connect with and impact on important wider social and economic issues
- Special interest mouthpieces (external) – being the voice of a specialist sector in wider debates about social and economic life, whether individually or collaboratively, as part of a wider 'movement'
- Special interest "ears" (external and internal) – being an observatory that brings into and enhances the dissemination across the network of specific and wider intelligence, knowledge and awareness
- Advocacy agencies – devising and delivering strategies, towards and on behalf of their own specialist sector, to increase reach and impact, solicit support and recognition or argue for progress and change
- Self-promoters – pursuing own interests of growth and sustainability, by increasing reach and impact and developing sustainable organizational and financial models
- Non-profit distributing enterprises – providing a range of specialist services generating income that can, in turn, be reinvested into the wider objectives of the network (2016, p. 26).

These characteristics can be considered to be only invitations for further debate about the roles and the positions cultural networks have in the wider cultural/artistic ecosystem. Networks became an organizational form for collaboration in a complex and globalized world, and we will discuss some of the trending issues that come out from the roles they (can) play.

Trending issues for cultural networks

There are a number of trending issues that came out as a consequence of the lack of shared supra-semantics – the ways of understanding and defining, meaning and position of a cultural network in a wider cultural/educational ecosystem. Some of the most recurring ones will be examined in this section, and they came up from the author's engagement as the co-ordinator (together with Audrey Wong) of Asia Pacific Network for Cultural Education and Research (ANCER) as well as from the activities of the "THRIVE: Networking Culture Leaders" conference co-organized by International Federation of Arts Councils and Culture Agencies (IFACCA), Asia-Europe Foundation (ASEF) and Asia Pacific Network for Cultural Education and Research (ANCER) in Singapore, 29–31st August 2015.

Lifecycles of cultural networks

When some of the cultural networks were formed, no one was thinking about their lifecycle. They were constantly evolving and were existing as flexible, informal and emergent structures (Staines, 1996). Now, for most of the cultural networks that are existing for more than 20–30 years, one of the prevailing dilemmas are related to the questions of their sustainability. And when the issue of sustainability is being discussed, very soon you understand that we are talking about a very tangible organizational sustainability – there are some employees, their families, offices, contracts, as well as the legacy of the founders. And in this struggle for survival and sustainability, a number of them start overlapping with each other, being forced to create alliances and partnerships with other networks (i.e. ENCATC and AAAE, TACPS and ANCER).

Who would have the courage to pull the plug, even if we all agree that the mission of the network has been fulfilled, or there are some other platforms, organizations, or networks that are covering that mission better than us? We can even talk about a version of a "family trap" when it comes to some of the cultural networks, and the fear of failure in the face of the history/ founders as well as the wider society that would see the closure of a network tragically, as some kind of death. This position takes us back to the myth of Atlas – a Titan condemned to hold up the sky on his shoulders for eternity. Some of the pioneering cultural networks are often having discussions about their position – if we stop existing will the world still be spinning? Can we walk away and stop holding the heavens "by ourselves"?

Another reason that triggers the self-questioning of the need for the existence of some of the cultural networks is the efficiency questions, so typical (and equally problematic) for the arts organizations. Cultural networks are criticized for not being representative enough, not having enough active members, not affecting certain kind of change, not having enough "outputs". This criticism directed towards the lack of "strategic efficiency" misses the reasons for the existence of a cultural network – being efficient was never their primary purpose or strength (Davies, 2016, p. 17). Cultural networks should be able to rely on the "spillover" or "network effect", kicking off and nurturing initiatives in a specific networking space, and then – let them go. Because of the way arts organizations are usually evaluated, and cultural networks often go under the same criteria, the main question remains – how do we monitor the "effectiveness" of the network and trace the impacts of the "network effect"?

The governance confusion and the institutionalization of networks

Cultural networks today can be found on different positions of this 'scale' – from ENCATC that is actively following Castell's idea of networks becoming new institutional forms (Castells, 2001) to ANCER (Asia Pacific Network for Cultural Education and Research), that can loosely be defined as a goal directed, 'serendipitous' or tactical network (Uzelac, 2011). However, lines between the individual-as-network, network as a process and network as an organization are blurred and defining them became completely useless. Consequences of this burred state can be clearly observed through the issues of accountability in the network – in these mixed structural spaces, who actually decides and takes responsibility for the governance structure or directions that networks will take? As much as we saw that cultural networks were from some point becoming new dominant forces (Provan and Kenis, 2008), it becomes more difficult to figure out the nature and real purposes of these forces.

More than ever, the question of the most appropriate models of governance that make international cultural networks more effective and sustainable are being asked. Whether the cultural network is a participant-governed, lead organization-governed or network administrative organization (Provan and Kenis, 2008), we get closer to another dilemma of cultural networking – when we discuss about the sustainability of cultural networks, are we thinking about the sustainability of the organizational model (Provan and Kenis, 2008) or sustainability of ideas (Antariksa, 2016)? Cultural networks came to a point where they are dealing with a number of issues connected with the stage of organizational maturity, they reached leaving behind the romanticised myths of organically created flows of people and ideas that most of them have in their stories of creation.

One of the questions that influence the governance models is the legitimacy of the representation of members. Who do the members represent – themselves as individuals/professionals, their organizations, cities, countries, regions, continents? This problem of so-called non-representativeness of members was raised by Fondazione Fitzcarraldo (IETM/Fondazione Fitzcarraldo, 2001) almost 20 years ago, and it seems that today nothing happened that helped to get us closer to some kind of resolution. There are some innovative examples of diversifying and delegating power and responsibility amongst the members of the cultural network that helped the network stay relevant and dynamic (Višnić, 2007, p. 31). In this case, the members of the cultural network are only those that are active at that moment. They have all the rights and responsibilities. At the same time, any of the passive members can be re-activated and become a member with her/his engagement in some of the initiatives, platforms, or projects.

Another element of the reality of the everyday life of cultural networks is that most of the members are simply not interested in governance. And while they all support the democratic and participative ways of governing a cultural network, when the moments of participation come, only a small percentage of them are part of so-called active membership. And it is relatively easy today to coordinate a young network with the ambition to be part of some kind of imaginary post-hierarchical paradise, but problems start when the network starts growing – then the need for management and some kind of coordination becomes a reality (Leger, 2018, p. 54).

There are examples of organizations that started as projects, grew to become platforms and then some kind of version of a cultural network. One of those is "On the Move",[5] Cultural Mobility Information Network, that started in 2001 as a project of another network – Informal European Theatre Meeting (IETM) and funded by European Cultural Foundation (ECF). Project-based logic of governance is still at the core of "On the Move", backed by the pressures to "survive" as an organization, as a structure, that needs to fund its existence, staff, website, and other costs. Model of networking in this case becomes a secondary issue, eaten by the tactics of the survival of the cultural network as a project-based organization. This fluctuation between the project-based organization and network, as a mode of operation, became one of the survival strategies.

Still, the question of redundancy remains – why are we calling some of them cultural networks if they are in their substance project-based arts organizations? One of the core differences when it comes to the (organizational) culture of these two different frameworks is that the arts organizations tend to be consensus driven institutions, while cultural networks should be the spaces of dissonance. Cultural networks are in their nature more tolerant when it comes to differences and are not there to strive towards the structural/organizational stability. As "learning organizations", they are in a "constant process of change and adaptation", making "constant readjustments to their working methods as the world in which they operate throws up new challenges and conflicts" (Staines, 1996). We need to constantly re-evaluate what are the initiatives/roles that are in the domain of the cultural networks and to distinguish them more clearly from the ones that can be better executed by the arts organizations. If not, some of the cultural networks may continue competing with some of their members for attention, funding and a place in the ecosystem.

Enhancing the voices: inside/outside paradigm

One of the important characteristics of the cultural networks in their earlier days, was that they were important validating/accreditation bodies for their members – either on the organizational or personal level. Membership of a certain network like ENCATC contributed to your professional reputation on the national or a regional level in the face of your stakeholders. In the same way as was happening at the Occupy Wall Street, cultural networks have a "human microphone" effect in the wider field –certain voices that would not be heard at the international level become more prominent, even if they are sometimes coming from the "small" nations or markets (Finland, Serbia, etc.).

From another angle, because of the exposure on the international networking platform, these voices are taken more seriously at "home". The cultural network becomes a form of "accreditation body", branding an individual or an organization as legit, validated and respected on an international level by the professional community it is a part of.

However, this aspect of cultural networking has significantly changed in recent years. Cultural networks became just one of the layers of the significantly expanded cultural field that now consists of a number of actors that are playing this role – individuals, institutions, whole industries, online portals, mobile applications, new networks that are not necessarily "cultural". These changes are calling for a serious re-questioning of the role that the cultural networks actually play in enhancing the voices of their current and future members.

Advocacy strategies

Today, the importance of the cultural networks as advocacy platforms is questioned in relation to the individual-as-network type of attitude nurtured by the "always connected" society. Here the question Eugene Tacher asked in 2004 becomes even more interesting – "are we connected because we are collective or are we collective because we are connected?" (Tacher, 2004). Unfortunately, even in the guidelines of "Creative Europe", the flagship programme of the European union, there is no emphasis on advocacy as the criteria for funding successful applications. At the same time, very well-designed propaganda/cultural diplomacy/soft power initiatives delivered through the foreign cultural centres and EUNIC are still flourishing.

An individual arts/cultural organization is often not strong enough to lobby for a certain issue or a cause and mobilize people on the local, national, regional and international level. Throughout the whole 20th century, citizens were using different kinds of social networks, circles of friends, parties, associations, unions, clubs . . . to be able to share and more effectively deal with their problems/issues (Bennet and Segerberg, 2013).

One of the distinctions that is often blurred today is the one between the idea of promoting a cause and advocating for one. With the development of NGO's, volunteer associations and numerous online communities of interests powered by the disruptive character of technology and new media, advocacy initiatives became significantly more spread out, effective and visible. This radical technological development also shifted the understanding of advocacy and the role cultural networks played. At the end of the 20th century, these networks were part of the "collectivist" movement, while we are still not sure how to understand the "connectivism" as a movement that is adopted by new generations that grew up with the new media and technology (Bennet and Segerberg, 2013).

Future of cultural networking

> *Maxwell's demon: a hypothetical being imagined as controlling a hole in a partition dividing a gas-filled container into two parts, and allowing only fast-moving molecules to pass in one direction, and slow-moving molecules in the other. This would result in one side of the container becoming warmer and the other colder, in violation of the second law of thermodynamics.*
> —*Oxford Dictionary, 2016*

With arts/cultural organizations being consensus driven organizational models, networks should be representing non-spaces of dissonance that not only tolerate, but actively support and encourage differences. Cultural networks have the potential to be in the center of a new social framework that goes beyond the construct of nation (Anderson, 1991) and in a similar way like Maxwell's demon from the perspective of quantum physics, play the role of the in-between-space that nurtures the dialogue between different players in the field. There is a large potential in a better interconnectedness of culture/arts with other areas/sectors, through networks as a communication channel (Brkić, 2014). Cultural networks will need to create more heterogeneous stakeholder alliances going beyond the like-minded individuals, organizations, institutions and agencies they have been confined to for a long time (Mercer, 2010, p. 32).

Low cost of communication in the times of "social media platforms as ideology" (Lovink, 2016) made the formation and development of new cultural networks "ridiculously easy" (Paquet, 2002). That is already leading towards cultural networks in the "clouds" in the wave of "mass amateurization" of the process of group creation (Shirky, 2008, p. 54). Being the creation of the 20th century, cultural networks as we know them are slowly fading away – "the transformation of very open and rather general cultural networks into more localized and more specialized ones is underway" (Švob Đokić, 2011, p. 28). Or, the transdisciplinary ones, such as Agenda 21 for Culture,[6] related to the topics and agendas that are in a need for a different kind of approach to networking.

Will cultural networking become just one of the dymensions of digital networking, with all its social and political issues we are trying to deal with? Lovink (2016) cynically reflects on our current position:

> Under this spell of desire for the social, led by the views and opinions of our immediate social circle, our daily routines are as follows: view recent stories first, fine-tune filter preferences, jump to first unread, update your life with events, clear and refresh all, not now, save links to read for later, see full conversation, mute your ex, set up a secret board, run a poll, comment through the social plug-in, add video to your profile, choose between love, haha, wow, sad, and angry, engage with those who mention you while tracking the changes in relationship status of others, follow a key opinion leader, receive notifications, create a photo spread that links to your avatar, repost a photo, get lost in the double-barrel river of your lifetime, prevent friends from seeing updates, check out something based on a recommendation, customize cover images, create 'must-click' headlines, chat with a friend while noticing that '1,326,595 people like this topic'.

To juxtapose this cynism with the pinch of romanticism, there is a chance that the concepts of friendship and hospitality (Budhyarto, 2015) are a good new starting point for cultural networks, 'to explore what it means to be part of a common that is not merely a resource management exercise, but an alternative to treating the world as a made up of resources' (Hine, 2016). Although Lovink (2011, p. 164) believes that we need to "abandon the 'friends' logic and start to play with the notion of dangerous design".

Maybe the existence of cultural network does not depend on the questioning of the format, structure or the way they are organized, but from the topics and debates they select to deal with in a world that has more of "one-way dialogues" than at the end of the 20th century (Davies, 2016, p. 57). The solution may lie in the focus on the "sustainability of ideas" (Antariksa, 2016), rather than sustainability of structures (Hagoort, 2016). These two roles, connected with activism and pragmatism are often in tension, and it is not an easy task to reconcile them, especially for a sector whose "core values embrace experimentation and innovation – in both form and content" (Davies, 2016, p. 80).

Davies (2016, p. 26) posed some of the questions that could be reflection points for most of the cultural networks today, to help them clarify their roles and potential future:

- How well do stakeholders understand this complex profile, why it is important and what brought it about?
- How well do networks' own publics (members and users) understand their own profile, and why and how it came about?

- Which of these characteristics are driven, respectively, by internal demands (e.g. from members, officers, users) or by external pressures (e.g. from stakeholders, funders)?
- How does the complexity and level of responsibility attached to the profile match to the resources and financial structure of these networks?
- How do networks balance the competing pressures imposed by the relative demands of each within the whole?
- Who (outside 'the core group' of officers and board) really understands the nature and implications of this challenge?
- In a context of change, and of a receding public European investment, what strategies, if any, are available today to networks to address these issues?

Cultural networks are facing a serious challenge in the coming period and most of these questions need to be raised and discussed with some clearer strategic focus as a result. They will probably have to embrace and own the new technology that supports a dialogue and empowers the processes of co-creation. Some of the examples that are presenting the possibilities of the creative blurring of the lines between real and virtual space are collaborative platforms Hitrecord,[7] co-founded by the actor Joseph Gordon-Levitt and Daisie,[8] co-founded by the actress Maisie Williams. These platforms, which are connecting creative people from all over the world through the work on collaborative projects, could be interesting case studies that can be used for the new frameworks of the cultural networks. In some way, cultural networks need to figure out what this fluid space for encounters and collaboration can look like in the next period.

Because of the character of the world we live in today, where we are becoming more aware that information is in the center of our universe, as Nunes recently concluded – "whatever solution to organizational and strategic problems can be expected today will in all likelihood come from within networks" (Nunes, 2014, p. 11). Will they be informal or formal, virtual and viral? We will not have to wait for a long time to see. And participate.

Notes

1 This article partly came out from the research project "Ontology of Arts and Cultural Management Education" generously supported by Research Committee of LASALLE College of the Arts, Singapore.
2 Cultural networks that signed "The Value of International Cultural Networks" document are: ARRE – Association of European Royal Residences; CAE – Culture Action Europe; ECHO – European Concert Hall Organisation; EMC – European Music Council; ELIA – European League of Institutes of the Arts; ETC – European Theatre Convention; EMCY – European Union of Music Competitions for Youth; Eurozine; Res Artis; OTM – On the Move; ECA-EC – European Choral Association – Europa Cantat; ENCC – European Network of Cultural Centres; IMC – International Music Council; IETM – International network for contemporary performing arts; TEH – Trans Europe Halles; RANN – Réseau Art Nouveau Network; FACE – Fresh Arts Coalition Europe; NEMO – The Network of European Museum Organisations; Triangle Network and RESEO – European Network for Opera, Music and Dance Education.
3 This quote is edited from the original document, which can be accessed at http://on-the-move.org/files/last-%20The%20Value%20of%20International%20Cultural%20Networks%20-%20copie.pdf (Accessed 16 Mar. 2017).
4 The oldest active cultural network in Europe is European Festivals Association, formed in 1952 in Geneva.
5 www.on-the-move.org
6 www.agenda21culture.net
7 www.hitrecord.org
8 www.daisie.com

References

Anderson, B. (1991). *Imagined communities: Reflections on the origin and spread of nationalism.* London: Verso.

Antariksa. (2016). Keynote speech at ANCER Research camp 'Collective Creative Practices in Southeast Asia', Singapore, Lasalle College of the Arts, 18–20 November 2016.

Beck, U. and Grande, E. (2007). Cosmopolitanism: Europe's way out of crisis. *European Journal of Social Theory*, 10, p. 67.

Bennett, W.L. and Segerberg, A. (2013). *The logic of connective action.* New York: Cambridge University Press.

Budhyarto, M. (2015). Hospitality, friendship, and an emancipatory politics. *Seismopolite: Journal of Art and Politics.* Available at: www.seismopolite.com/hospitality-friendship-and-an-emancipatory-politics [Accessed 20 Jan. 2019].

Brkić, A. (2014). *Cultural policy frameworks (re)constructing national and supranational identities: The Balkans and the European Union.* Amsterdam: European Cultural Foundation.

Castells, M. (2001). *The rise of the network society, the information age: Economy, society and culture.* Vol. I. Oxford: Blackwell.

———. (2004). *The power of identity, the information age: Economy, society and culture.* Vol. II. Oxford: Blackwell.

———. (2009). *Communication power.* Oxford: Oxford University Press.

Davies, I. (2016). *Cultural networking in Europe: Today and tomorrow. A reader.* Brussels: Culture Action Europe.

DeVlieg, M.A. (2001). *Evaluation criteria for cultural networks in Europe.* Brussels: EFAH.

Florida, R. (2012). *The rise of the creative class, revisited.* New York: Basic Books.

Hagoort, G. (2016). Keynote speech at ANCER Research camp 'Collective Creative Practices in Southeast Asia', Singapore, Lasalle College of the Arts, 18–20 November 2016.

Hine, D. (2016). *Friendship is a commons in build the city: Perspectives on commons and culture.* Amsterdam: ECF.

Hobsbawm, E. (2013). *Fractured times: Culture and society in the twentieth century.* London: Little, Brown.

Hoyman, M. and Faricy, C. (2009). It takes a village: A test of the creative class, social capital, and human capital theories. *Urban Affairs Journal*, 44(3).

IETM/Fondazione Fitzcarraldo (2001). *How networking works.* Helsinki: Finnish Arts Council.

Laaksonen, A. (ed.) (2016). *D'Art report 48: International cultural networks.* Sydney: IFACCA.

Latour, B. (1997). *On actor network theory: A few clarifications.* Available at: www.nettime.org/Lists-Archives/nettime-l-9801/msg00020.html [Accessed 10 Feb. 2019].

Leger, M.J. (2018). *Don't network: The Avant Garde after networks.* New York: Minor Compositions.

Lovink, G. (2011). *Networks without a cause: A critique of social media.* Cambridge: Polity Press.

———. (2016). On the social media ideology. *e-flux Journal*, #75 (September 2016). Available at: www. e-flux.com/journal/on-the-social-media-ideology/ [Accessed 17 Jan. 2019].

Mercer, C. (2010). Culturelinks: Cultural networks and cultural policy in the digital age. In: B. Cvjetičanin, ed., *The evolving aspects of culture in the 21st century.* Culturelink. Zagreb: IRMO.

NAC. (2012). The report of the arts and culture strategic review, 31 January 2012. Singapore: National Arts Council. Available at: www.nac.gov.sg/dam/jcr:1b1765f3-ff95-48f0-bbf9-f98288eb7082 [Accessed 15 Feb. 2019].

Nunes, R. (2014). *Organisation of the organisationless: Collective action after networks.* London and Leuphana: Mute Books and PML Books.

Paquet, S. (2002). *Making group-forming ridiculously easy.* Available at: http://radio-weblogs.com/0110772/2002/10/09.html#a426 [Accessed 7 Feb. 2019].

Peck, J. (2005). Struggling with the creative class. *International Journal of Urban and Regional Research*, 29(4), December 2005.

Pehn, G. (1999). *Networking culture: The role of European cultural networks.* Brussels: Council of Europe Publishing.

Pozzolo, L., Bacchella, U., and Agusto, G. (2001). Study on the effects of networking. In: IETM/Fondazione Fitzcarraldo, ed., *How networking works.* Helsinki: Finnish Arts Council.

Provan, K.G. and Kenis, P. (2008). Modes of network governance: Structure, management, and effectiveness. *Journal of Public Administration Research and Theory*, 18(2).

Shaviro, S. (2003). *Connected, or what it means to live in the network society.* Minneapolis: University of Minnesota Press.

Shirky, C. (2008). *Here comes everybody: The power of organizing without organizations.* London: Allen Lane.

Staines, J. (1996). *Working groups: Network solutions for cultural cooperation in Europe.* Brussels: EFAH.

Sternal, M. (2013). Cultural cooperation networks – What are they, how do they form and operate?. In: *Closer look: European cultural cooperation networks in practice*. Warsaw: Cultural Contact Point Poland and Adam Mickiewicz Institute.

Švob Đokić, N. (2011). Cultural networks and cultural policies: A missing link. In: B. Cvjetičanin, ed., *Networks: The evolving aspects of culture in the 21st century*. Zagreb: Institute for International Relations Culturelink Network.

Tacher, E. (2004). Networks, swarms, multitudes. In: *CTHEORY*, http://ctheory.net/ctheory_wp/ networks-swarms-multitudes-part-two/

The Value of International Cultural Networks. (2016). Available at: https://cultureactioneurope.org/ news/communication-on-the-value-of-cultural-networks/ [Accessed 15 Feb. 2019].

Vedral, V. (2010). *Decoding reality: The universe as quantum information*. 1st ed. Oxford: Oxford University Press.

Vellani, A. (2010). Networking: Motivations and challenges. Conceiving connections: A network seminar, New Delhi.

Višnić, E. (2007). Mreža clubture. In: D. Vidović, ed., *Clubture: Kultura kao proces razmjene 2002–2007*. Zagreb: Clubture.

Wimmer, A. and Glick Schiller, N. (2002). Methodological nationalism and beyond: Nation-state building, migration and the social sciences. *Global Networks*, 2(4), pp. 301–334.

13

RULES OF ENGAGEMENT IN THE GLOBAL ARTS CITY

The case of The Substation in Singapore

Audrey Wong

The emergence of arts management as a profession and course of study, at least in Europe and the US, paralleled the need for "arts organizations . . . to be accountable to different kinds of patrons – from private donors to foundations and government agencies" (Paquette and Redaelli, 2015, p. 19). In his classic text on arts administration, Pick observes that "the arts administrator appears as the middleman in a three-way transaction between artist, audience and the state" (1980, p. 1) and elaborates on how the state influences the work of presenting artistic works in public. The state is a patron of the arts through the provision of grants, and exerts an influence in other ways, through the law and policy actions in adjacent spheres such as education, heritage preservation and so on.

In Southeast Asia, systematic and transparent state funding of the arts, particularly contemporary arts, has generally been low or intermittent, with the exception of Singapore where state patronage of the arts accelerated in the 1990s when the government explicitly recognized the economic potential of arts and culture. A national-level strategy for developing the arts sector was spurred by the convening of a government-level Advisory Council on Culture and the Arts in 1988, which released a seminal report in 1989. Two years later, the government established the National Arts Council as the statutory agency with responsibility for promoting the growth of the arts in the nation-state. The state conceived of the desirability of the arts in two particular dimensions: as a contributor to the nation's continued economic growth which included the aspiration for Singapore to be a global arts city, and as a tool for citizens' social bonding in a multi-ethnic, multi-religious society (Report of the Advisory Council on Culture and the Arts, 1989; Renaissance City Report: Culture and the Arts in Renaissance Singapore, 2000). With the state keenly embracing its role as patron, it was inevitable that the arts sector expanded, with the establishment of arts and cultural institutions, non-profit and commercial companies, and ancillary service providers throughout the 1990s and 2000s, leading to a corresponding demand for arts managers.

Anderton and Pick elaborate on the definition of arts administration as

> the ability, using every legitimate social, political and managerial skill, and with the fullest and most up-to-date political, legal and economic circumstances in mind, to forge the best available aesthetic contract, bringing together the arts and the largest and most appropriate audience in the best possible circumstances.
>
> *(1996, p. 3)*

Thus, a significant aspect of the arts manager's work involves engaging with the state and its conception of the value of the arts to public life. The presence of "patrons" and the "state" in definitions of arts administration suggest two critical and related areas of knowledge for arts managers: the know-how to manage relationships with patrons who provide the artist with resources (particularly of a financial nature), and awareness of the "political, legal, and economic" environment for artistic work. The latter would include knowledge of policies and policy making concerning arts and culture, and how the structures and institutions of law and government function. These of course, vary from country to country. Each system of cultural governance that has been established, the power hierarchies and relations between players, as well as the values, ideology and justifications underlying state support of the arts result in particular rules of engagement within the arts sector and between artist and patron that may be either explicit or unspoken. There is a body of context-specific tacit knowledge concerning how artists engage with state patronage.

In a study of the Singapore theatre sector and its relations with the state, Chong notes that "the sociology of art has demonstrated that, far from being economically or politically disinterested, artists as social agents have always had to engage within a specific social economy in order to achieve some degree of fame or success" (2011, p. 2). Both the state (the governing) and arts practitioners (the governed) have agency and it is their interrelations which produce the peculiar characteristics of the arts world they inhabit and influence the modus operandi of artists and the organizational and institutional structures that have evolved for the production of art.

Over time, patterns of engagement between the state, arts practitioners, institutions and patrons in the sector become entrenched as new participants entering the arena learn and internalize these rules and habits through experience or by working alongside seasoned arts professionals. The patterns of behavior establish a certain tone to the way that the arts are managed in a particular environment and may privilege certain aspects of management or managerial skills. In each context, there are assumptions and values that underpin the habits of doing. A particular "culture" or character of cultural governance emerges that is distinct to each society or arts ecosystem, which may need to be articulated for the benefit of new entrants into the system. Hence, a case could be made for including such tacit knowledge in the training of aspiring arts managers.

In what follows, I will elucidate the explicit and unspoken norms of engagement in Singapore between the state (which is the main patron of the arts) and arts managers and practitioners and describe the particular "character" of cultural governance in the city-state that is shaped by these norms. The norms of engagement will be illustrated through the case of one arts organization in particular: The Substation, a non-profit arts center founded in 1990. The oldest continuously existing independent arts center in Singapore, The Substation has weathered the various arts policy shifts introduced by the state since the 1990s.

Before proceeding to an analysis of The Substation, an account of cultural governance in Singapore and the "political, legal and economic circumstances" in which The Substation operates is necessary. The context for managing the arts is discussed using existing literature on Singapore's cultural policy and its political landscape. This is followed by a brief history of The Substation, drawn from documentary sources. Here, the patterns of the center's engagement with the state which is at once its patron and landlord as well as the enforcer of the law, will emerge. Finally, specific examples from different times of The Substation's history are discussed to illustrate the artist-state relations.

Action research has been employed as I was a participant in the organisation's interactions with the state, having been a former artistic co-director of the arts center (from 2000–2009). Some of my experiences and observations during this period have been published. These and other published interviews with significant players in The Substation's history, as well as accounts by individuals who were proactive and bona fide participants in incidents recounted in this chapter, were useful sources of information for the analysis. Bona fide participants' narratives were drawn from either their written accounts or in found texts produced by third-party publishers.

As published research pertaining to the management of arts organisations in Singapore is sparse, at present there is much that can be mined from practitioners' accounts. Given the lack of published research and historical accounts about Singapore's arts sector, newspaper reports also serve as a means of record-keeping. Hence these have also been referenced particularly for specific events in The Substation's history.

The tone of cultural governance in the "developmental state" of Singapore

In 1969, in the early years of Singapore's independence, founding Prime Minister Lee Kuan Yew pronounced that poetry was a "luxury we cannot afford" (Tay, 2017, p. 65), voicing the prevailing view then, that the arts ought to be pursued only after the nation-state had attained economic stability. The nation-state's official perspective on the arts changed over its 53 years of independence as the country prospered. By the early 1990s, Singapore officially aspired towards becoming a "global city for the arts" as stated in a report published by the Ministry of Information and the Arts and the Economic Development Board (Wee, 2012, p. 1; Kong, 2012, p. 282; Peterson, 2001, p. 202; Velayutham, 2007, p. 130). The rules and patterns of engagement between the governing and the governed have correspondingly evolved throughout Singapore's political and economic development – a direction determined by the sole ruling party in this parliamentary democracy since independence, the People's Action Party.

Most scholarly literature on the arts in Singapore focuses on its arts and cultural policies, particularly analyses of the state's cultural policy iterations since the 1990s (see for example, Kong, 2000; Kwok and Low, 2002; Tan, 2007; Lee, 2007; Chong, 2005, 2010; Ooi, 2010; Kong, 2012). Given the government's strong hand in most aspects of life in the small nation-state, it is unsurprising that much of the literature examines the dilemmas in policy making and implementation, particularly the often fraught relationship between the soft authoritarian state's desire for global city status and a thriving creative economy versus the need to maintain tight political control, often wielded through the blunt instrument of censorship. Lee and Lim, for example, comment that "on one hand the government seems to accommodate greater socio-cultural plurality, but on the other it suppresses the emergence and development of an independent civil society" (2004, p. 159).

To some extent, the tension between creativity and control can be explained through Singapore's historical and geographical circumstances, which have influenced its political development and governance. The high degree of state control in Singapore is aided by its small geographical size (720 square kilometers) and population density (around 5.7 million people on the island). A former British colony governed as part of a larger territory with Malaya, Singapore's legal and political systems were partly inherited from the British. Singapore's independence was originally predicated on its future as part of the Federation of Malaya, but differences between the two territories led to Singapore's sudden exit in 1965. The circumstances of its birth – a tiny island with no natural resources, thus placing its survival in peril – set the tone for the political leadership's cultivation of a "continual sense of crisis and urgency amongst the population" (Perry, Kong, and Yeoh, 1997, p. 6) and explains the priority accorded to economic development which persists to the present day. The political leadership emphasized that sacrifices were necessary to achieve political stability and higher living standards. These sacrifices include political freedoms that are taken for granted in western liberal democracies, such as media controls, curbs on public assembly, and outlawing of trade unions apart from those affiliated to the government-controlled National Trades Union Congress. The leadership also saw that political division would threaten the nation's prospects of survival and took action in the early days of independence to eradicate what it saw as the communist threat and opposition to its rule, detaining or sending into exile many political opponents.

Scholars have called Singapore a "developmental state" due to the emphasis on economic development as "a means to larger goals, as well as being an end in itself" (Perry, Kong, and Yeoh, 1997, p. 7). The "developmental state" is characterized by the government's control over the economy and a tendency towards state intervention (Low, 2001; Stubbs, 2009). This description has been applied to Singapore and the East Asian "tigers" of South Korea, Taiwan and Hong Kong which underwent rapid economic development in the 1980s.

In the developmental state, the ruling government constructs a powerful state apparatus to ensure its policy goals are achieved. Though the strong hand of the state in such countries should recede as economic development is attained, this has apparently not been the case in Singapore (Pereira, 2008). Tan characterizes the strong hand of the state in Singapore thus:

> powerfully ensconced in a dominant party system and hegemonic state, the PAP government has effectively propagated the idea that it is more important for a small country with limited resources to have meritocratic, pragmatic and economically-oriented government than one that is limited by principles of accountability, transparency, and checks and balances.
>
> *(2017, p. 41)*

In Rodan's (2004) analysis of the PAP government's moves towards transparency reform after the 1997 Asian financial crisis, it is noted that while government liberalized the financial sector, it retained a large degree of control through a state apparatus that included legislation and a structure of government-linked companies (GLCs) and statutory agencies, as well as a system of political co-option of private sector interests and grassroots activity. The state apparatus includes a network of grassroots organisations such as Residents' Committees that extend into the daily lives of ordinary Singaporeans, particularly within the environment of the highly planned, extensive public housing system where 80% of the population reside.

Rodan further observes that "the regime remains adept at blocking avenues of mobilization and collective action among social and political actors" (2004, p. 82) even though in recent years, it has refrained from the use of "blatantly repressive" (p. 83) laws, preferring instead to apply "administrative law" (p. 84). An example of the application of administrative law cited by Rodan is the government taking out criminal or civil lawsuits for defamation against journalists who were deemed to have overstepped the boundaries in their criticism of the government, judiciary or political figures.

In the arts, the application of "administrative law" often takes the form of revocation of funding based on contractual guidelines in arts grants which, among other clauses, require artists and arts groups to refrain from explicitly advocating or promoting LGBTQ causes and alternative "lifestyles", and from making work that could create conflict between ethnic and religious communities or call into the question the legitimacy and integrity of the government and its agencies. There are also laws that govern the presentation of arts and films in public spaces. Organizers of public arts events are required to obtain an "arts license" administered by the IMDA (Info-communications Media Development Authority) while all films screened in public venues have to be given clearance (that is, a classification) by the IMDA and Board of Film Censors. This ensures that content presented in public conforms to what the state deems appropriate for public consumption. For example, Tan Pin Pin's 2014 documentary film on Singapore political exiles, *To Singapore With Love*, was rated "not allowed for all ratings" by the IMDA which prevented the film from being screened in its home country. Accounts of national history presented in film and artwork which present opposing views to orthodox accounts are deemed particularly sensitive by the government, as demonstrated in the government's response to Tan's film. The Minister for Communications and Information stated in Parliament that it gave a "misleading account" of Singapore history (Nur Asyiqin Mohamad Salleh, 2014).

The political style of the government rests on a set of assumptions and values which include meritocracy and pragmatism as principles of the government's modus operandi (Tan, 2017). These effectively construct a ruling orthodoxy that is learnt by those (including arts practitioners) engaging with the state and its agencies.

Meritocracy – loosely speaking, the idea that individuals rise in society through his/her own talent and achievements rather than by dint of an inherited socioeconomic background or family connections – creates an "aristocracy of talent" (Tan, 2017, p. 22) at the helm of government. In the Singapore context, the prized qualities determining merit are "academic and professional qualifications" (Tan, 2017, p. 24) which means a government of "technocrats" and politicians who possess a high level of technical and professional expertise to administer government functions.

The technocratic government functions on the basis of pragmatism and objectivity, where decisions are made on the basis of "objective" criteria derived through impersonal study or a scientific method (Tan, 2017, p. 60). This institutionalizes a "bureaucratic rationality" (Koh, 2008).

In addition, pragmatism privileges economic rationality and quantifiable statistical data and places less emphasis on social values (Tan, 2017), particularly those associated with western liberal notions of democratic participation such as freedom of the press and freedom of speech. Tan (2017) also contends that the state is uncomfortable with expressions of the intangible and with abstract notions. In this light, the Singapore government's interest in developing Singapore's cultural and creative economy can be interpreted as a pragmatic strategy aimed at attracting the globally mobile elite and further investment to ensure Singapore's economic growth (Kong, 2000, 2012; Ooi, 2010). The pragmatism and bureaucratic rationality of Singapore's style of governance implies a divide between the government and arts practitioners who are comfortable with abstraction and are often driven by a striving for ideals and artistic integrity rather than monetary gain (Chong, 2011, p. 49).

The Substation: a history between the center and the margins

The contrast between the Singapore government's pragmatism and artists' striving for artistic freedom can be seen in Chong's 2011 study of the Singapore theatre sector cited earlier. Chong adopts Bourdieu's concepts of field and habitus in his analysis of artist-state relations and demonstrates that the theatre sector is "also a political organization of resources and an economic network of players aligned along the many contours of power and ideologies where individuals struggle against each other, as well as against the state, to achieve their goals" (2011, p. 2). Theatre practitioners both contest against and collaborate with the state. Chong describes the habitus of the English-language theatre community which is middle-class, highly educated and which, he contends, deploys the cultural capital from these characteristics in the struggle for artistic freedom and in securing resources from the state. In doing so, theatre practitioners at times reinforce the orthodoxy of the state's stance on the role of arts in Singapore's development and at other

Figure 13.1 The Substation in 2017

Source: Courtesy of The Substation

times, resist the heavy hand of the state. Both the artist community and the state bring into their engagement with each other certain assumptions and patterns of thought and action.

Chong's account offers a useful entry point into an analysis of The Substation, which has dealt regularly with the heavy hand of the state throughout its history. To begin with, an introduction to The Substation is necessary:

> A visiting friend from Malaysia recently shared her amazement at how a space like The Substation is able to persist in such a meticulously engineered environment. She especially noted the rapid erasure of familiar places and the diminishing sense of rootedness, and how the whole neighbourhood had transformed almost overnight into an exclusive playground for the affluent . . . she mourned the loss of common spaces, lamenting the uprooting of neighbours such as the National Library, S11 [street hawker centre], MPH [bookstore], Hock Hiap Leong [local 'coffeeshop' or traditional street corner café]. . . . Yet, in this ubiquitous gentrified landscape, The Substation continues to seek out the tiny cracks and stresses that naturally emerge. – Noor Effendy Ibrahim
>
> *(The Substation, 2011)*

This quotation illustrates the contrast between Singapore's economic pragmatism and the idea of cultural rootedness and community spirit symbolized by The Substation, as perceived by artists who have a long association with it. The Substation was an early example in Singapore of adaptive re-use of a disused building in Singapore. It was also one of the first examples of a government-directed cultural re-purposing of an old building where the operations of the new entity would be devolved to non-governmental groups, albeit still tied to the state through grants and other forms of subvention.

The building itself was in the city center, next to the former Tao Nan School. It was a power substation from the 1920s but by the early 1980s had outlived its purpose. In 1986, the Ministry of Community Development which then held the cultural affairs portfolio, approached some arts groups with an offer to them to lease it for a nominal monthly rent; however, the groups would have to cover the cost of renovation, estimated at $500,000 or more (Leong, 1986, p. 13). Two arts organisations responded to the Ministry. One was Practice Performing Arts School, led by theatre director and playwright Kuo Pao Kun, who rallied support for his idea of an arts center that in his own words, would be dedicated to the pursuit of "creative, pluralistic, artistic ventures" and "an honest pursuit in search of a transcendence, reaching for a new sensitivity raising ourselves above crass consumerism and short-term material success" (1990, cited in Wong, 2015, pp. 12–13). The government then agreed to fund the renovations and appointed Practice Performing Arts as the manager of the center.

The Substation opened in September 1990 with a Minister presiding over its official opening ceremony. Its premises included an art gallery, a small black box theatre, rehearsal/workshop rooms, and an outdoor tree-lined courtyard known as the Garden. In 1995 its operations were separated from Practice Performing Arts and a new non-profit corporate entity, The Substation Limited, was established. The site and building are leased to The Substation Limited – the landowner is the Singapore government through the Singapore Land Authority and the lease is managed by the National Arts Council. Thus, from the start, The Substation was already entwined with the state and continues to deal with the state as landlord and funder. Currently it is a Major Grant recipient, the highest tier of arts funding available from the Arts Council.

Kuo (1939–2002) is one of Singapore's most beloved artists, who wrote and worked in Chinese and English and introduced ideas and forms of contemporary experimental theatre to Singapore. With his wife Goh Lay Kuan, Kuo established the Practice Performing Arts School

Figure 13.2 The Substation in 1991

Source: Courtesy of The Substation

in 1965. In the 1960s and 1970s, Chinese activists in Singapore were under scrutiny by the government because of suspected sympathies for the communist cause, and in 1976 Kuo was detained without trial. Released in 1980, he was later awarded the Cultural Medallion – Singapore's highest honor for artists. Kuo was a mentor to many artists and an inspirational figure for championing artistic expression: in the words of the Esplanade arts center's tribute to Singapore arts pioneers, he was "the strength of Singapore theatre in the 80s and 90s and forged a body of work built on humanistic ideals" (The Esplanade, n.d.). Kuo was also a pioneering institution-builder – the three organisations he founded, Practice Performing Arts, The Substation and The Theatre Training and Research Programme, occupy significant roles in the ecosystem of Singapore arts.

Kuo's vision for the new arts center was to be an "open space" where different art forms and artists mingled and anyone stepping in from the street could encounter art. At that time, there were few independent venues in Singapore. As theatre director Kok Heng Leun observed, it provided a welcoming space for a wide range of art forms "from the refined to the raw, the well-made productions to experimental ones, and the popular to the esoteric" (Kok, 2015, p. 45). It quickly built a reputation as a space for nurturing young Singapore artists, experimental art, and artistic collaborations across disciplines (Wee, 2012). Multidisciplinary thematic arts festivals and events such as the ecologically themed Tree Celebration in 1991 featuring visual and performing artists, writers and storytellers, were a distinctive programming feature.

Over the next two decades, The Substation evolved as Singapore's arts scene developed. The year after its founding, the National Arts Council was set up. Young artists went on to establish their own arts companies and produce festivals under their company banner. Under the second Artistic Director T. Sasitharan (1996–2000), The Substation's programming was streamlined as

Figure 13.3 The Substation in 2010

Source: Courtesy of The Substation

activities, exhibitions and performances were planned around specific seasons or art form plat-forms. Sasitharan paid attention towards how The Substation could best serve the needs of artists and support them in developing artistic rigor (cited in Wong, 2015, p. 55). The third generation of Artistic Directors, myself and Lee Weng Choy (2000–2009), focused on maintaining the his-torical strength of the center in terms of incubating artists and artworks, and in cultivating depth as well as dialogue in the arts (Yap, 2008). This artistic strategy was a response to the Singapore arts sector undergoing a period of expansion immediately after the publication of the Renais-sance City policy report in 2000. The policy direction at this time released additional funding for the arts which, among other effects, created flagship local arts companies who could share the work of sector development alongside the state's arts institutions and agencies.

The 2002 opening of the showpiece arts center for the nation, the Esplanade – Theatres on the Bay, was a game-changer that presented both opportunity and threat to The Substation. As opportunity, many artists who started their practice at The Substation had their works presented by the Esplanade, which boosted their careers and maturing artistic practice. As threat, the Esplanade's capacity to present on a larger and an international scale, along with the continuing expansion of events and festivals in the country, meant that The Substation was overshadowed and received less public and media attention.

In the late 1990s to mid-2000s, the Esplanade was the focal point for the arts commu-nity's suspicion of the state's desire to "subject the arts to market logic" (Chong, 2011, p. 41). They worried about the establishment of a hegemonic center that would privilege global, internationalized arts and negate the "plural margins" and raw, local voices (Wee, 2012; Kong, 2000). As early as 1993, the tension between the center and margins, or state orthodoxy and alternative voices, and the Esplanade – then known as the "Singapore Arts Centre" and yet to be constructed – was debated in The Substation's first arts conference, entitled Art vs Art (Lee, 1995). The Substation had become a site for the "margins" to gather and a node where the artistic community and civil society met. However, in the absence of a major non-governmental institution offering artistic leadership, The Substation became the de facto "center" for championing artists. This was to some extent due to Kuo's charismatic leadership, but The Substation's deliberate multidisciplinary artistic programming which made it an artists' hub was also a factor.

The ideal of supporting "alternative" voices who offered other perspectives to state ortho-doxy contrasted with the pragmatism underlying governance in Singapore. Art forms connected to marginal voices in society such as the punk and metal music scenes also found in The Substa-tion a "spiritual home of sorts" (Martin, 2017). The alignment of The Substation's mission to the idea of giving voice to the "alternative" can be contextualized against the broader development of Singapore arts since the 1980s. Since that decade, theatre – and English-language theatre in particular – had become a "vibrant site of production concerned with the critical exploration and expression of postcolonial Singapore culture, politics, and identity" (Chong, 2011, p. 77), due to stringent media controls which meant that perspectives that were different from state orthodoxy could be expressed on the stage rather than on television, radio, or the news media. At the same time, a new, younger generation of visual artists experimented with conceptual art, installation art, performance art, "happenings", site specific and interdisciplinary interventions (Wee, 2003). The symbolic significance ascribed to The Substation as a champion and safe space for the arts took on greater urgency in the mid-1990s with the state's revocation of funding from Forum Theatre and performance art, which effectively banished these forms and their practitioners to the margins.

Resistance to the hegemonizing effect of the market orientation implied in the global arts city project, and the tension between the margins and the center, returned during the tenure of the Artistic Director who served from 2010–2015, Noor Effendy Ibrahim, who sought to make The Substation "a meeting place for the known and the unknown . . . for the points of intersection and collision that form the very heart of interdisciplinary practice and community building" (Noor Effendy Ibrahim and Wee, 2012). Artists noted that his tenure was marked by "a sense of inclusivity" and the "indie spirit" (Martin, 2014). At this time, the streetscape around The Substation building rapidly gentrified while the Singapore Management University, with its cohorts of business students, expanded around it, as attested by the experience of Effendy's friend from Malaysia cited earlier. Nearby, the former Supreme Court and City Hall were being converted into the massive new National Gallery of Singapore which opened in 2015 – the state's latest jewel in the crown and a site to show off the art of Singapore and its neighbors while staking a claim to art and museum leadership in the region. As an indicator of how the arts landscape had changed since the days when Kuo helmed The Substation, the National Gallery reportedly drew 1.5 million visitors in its first year of operations (Huang, 2016). The Substation certainly could not compete with such an institution, whether in terms of the scale of projects, international profile, or visitor numbers.

In September 2015, the 25th anniversary of The Substation and two months before the opening of the National Gallery, the center announced that visual artist and curator Alan Oei would be its next Artistic Director. Oei had plans to take The Substation in a different direction. Oei was responding to the changes in the Singapore arts landscape as much as Effendy, Wong and Lee had, stating that The Substation had to review the role it would play in the arts as other art spaces and galleries that had opened in the past decade were now performing similar roles in artistic incubation and presenting experimental work (Martin, 2015). Oei went as far as to state that "the public doesn't really care about The Substation" (Fang, 2016) which could be interpreted to mean that The Substation needed refreshing to appeal to a new generation that had never experienced the halcyon days of Kuo's tenure. As will be discussed later, Oei's announcement of artistic programming changes provoked opposition among the artists who had been long-term regular collaborators, an indication of the deep attachment that this community felt to the space and what The Substation stood for – the values of openness, collaboration and social commitment that the arts center had communicated since Kuo's leadership.

The sense of attachment felt by this segment of the arts community to The Substation was reflected in the amount of press coverage of the appointment of its last two artistic directors (Effendy and Oei). Indeed, in 2009 when co-directors Wong and Lee stepped down, the Board of Directors and General Manager felt the need to involve the artistic community that had called the center "home" in the search for a new artistic director. Dozens of regular artistic collaborators, representatives from partner artistic and civic organizations and former Board members were invited to a closed-door meeting with the candidates who were on the final shortlist. The Substation's management set up a website specifically to communicate information about the progress of the search (The Substation, 2010), the first Singapore arts organization to do so, acknowledging a certain social responsibility to the arts communit(ies).

The Substation's history can be mapped against developments in Singapore's cultural policy and the global city project, which is why it is useful for illustrating the rules of engagement between the arts sector and the state. To do this, specific incidents that occurred at The Substation at different points in its history will now be discussed.

Rules of engagement: negotiating a space for artists and 'alternatives'

From the preceding discussion, three factors can be identified as being of significance to The Substation's existence:

- Space (physical as well as a more abstract notion of space for creative expression)
- Economics and the increasing market orientation of the arts in Singapore as the global city project has taken shape
- Ideals linked to civic and democratic participation reflected in The Substation's championing of minority voices, the inclusivity of its programming, and its search for new artistic leadership

The following discussion on rules of engagement between the arts organization and the state is framed in terms of these three interrelated factors.

In late 2015, artistic director Oei announced his proposed plans for The Substation where programs would be almost entirely curated in-house according to an annual theme and venue rentals would be phased out. This would mean the end of many activities organized by artists and arts groups not employed at the center, such as arts classes, artist-organized exhibitions and independent music gigs. Oei's plans provoked passionate responses from artists and organizers who had been regular venue hirers or artistic collaborators of The Substation (Fang, 2016). Some acknowledged that The Substation had lost some of its dynamism and been overshadowed by newer, better-equipped arts spaces like the Esplanade or newer "arts housing" enclaves like Aliwal Arts Centre and Goodman Arts Centre (set up by the National Arts Council) which provided office or studio spaces as well as venues, based on a cluster concept.

Despite this acknowledgment, there was still palpable anxiety that Oei's plans would shut out long-term creative networks which had gathered around The Substation (Fang, 2016), and dilute the values of inclusivity and civic participation associated with the center. There were concerns that it would be less friendly to the possibility of "failure", or art that is not accepted by the public at first viewing – one of Kuo Pao Kun's most-cited quotations had been about the value of "worthy failures" over "mediocre successes" (Havan and Chan, 2012, p. 139). Among those responding was Shaiful Risan, an independent punk organizer who argued for the need to have a space in Singapore that was sympathetic to the raw and alternative. Such spaces would let "new bands that sucked take the stage, but then allowed them to keep playing until they actually become significant" (Atmos, 2016). These spaces would also have room for communities and subcultures like punks who are perceived by more pragmatic mainstream communities as being messy and potentially subversive.

Others saw the impending change and the artists' responses as a sign of the failure of those artistic communities who claimed The Substation as a home – their failure to act collectively and "take part in shaping and nurturing this open home, a civic or common space" (Koay, 2016). The debates led to a town hall being convened by The Substation, as much to defuse pent-up anxiety as to hear out the artists, filmmakers, gig organizers, and other stakeholders (Fang, 2016), and eventually Oei decided to reverse part of his plan.

The struggle over "space" illustrated here can be read as symbolic of the Singapore condition, where land and property are expensive and the use of every pocket of land is tightly planned and regulated by the state. This means that the cost of producing and presenting the arts may be beyond the reach of subculture communities who do not enjoy state patronage. These communities on the margins such as punks and independent musicians typically include a large number of the Malay ethnic minority. In other words, "space" is a political matter. As a city center space, The Substation brought the "margins" to the "center", making them visible.

The Substation's openness to communities less visible in mainstream Singapore had regularly brought it into confrontation with state orthodoxy. In the early 2000s, The Substation – which saw itself as a node for artists and civic actors to meet – provided space for meetings of a group of activists for the gay community who called themselves People Like Us (PLU). Their gatherings attracted police attention. It was not always clear to the center's management whether the police were concerned that the meetings contravened the laws on public assembly – a matter of public security – or if the authorities frowned upon these gatherings as promoting "alternative life-styles" that went against state orthodoxy (Singapore still has a law criminalizing homosexuality). Eventually, The Substation's management received a communication over the telephone from the Arts Council that it should not host PLU activities, citing the terms on which the building had been leased – it was for "arts use" and these meetings did not fall within the definition of "arts". This was an example of the application of "administrative law" (Rodan, 2004).

Other incidents of a similar nature recurred in the early 2000s and eventually the Arts Council informed The Substation's management that it should not be involved with "politics" and that politics and arts should be separated. One may trace the state's characterization of what constitutes "politics" to the 1990s, when then Prime Minister Goh Chok Tong stated a clear position about media adopting particular stances in relation to social or political issues: "if you want to set a political agenda, then you have to be in the political arena" (Rodan, 2004, p. 96). As noted earlier, the government often acts as if it "knows best" (Tan, 2017, p. 25).

In the first days of Effendy's tenure as Artistic Director in 2010, while I was still employed at The Substation as an associate director to assist with his transition into the leadership role, another phone call from the Arts Council requested that The Substation stop hosting a meeting of another group of activists and artists because of the group's affiliations to a particular political cause. Neither PLU nor this particular group was a formally registered organisation; they were more akin to self-organized networks. A member of the group who was an artist had rented a room under the center's open rental policy, and The Substation's management had not been aware of the subject of the meeting. As it was not a public event, the hirer did not apply for a license from the relevant authority. The Arts Council had received information from sources that were better-informed than the venue, and it was not clear who their source was.

In this instance, The Substation was informed that it might lose its lease on the building should the meeting take place. Balancing the needs of the many against the few, The Substation management decided to ask the hirer not to hold the event at The Substation, reasoning that it was more important to keep the arts center open to as many arts groups as possible given the scarcity of alternative venues in the city. The staff also assessed that the group was likely to understand this rationale. However, a few group members were critical of the decision and expressed their views strongly on social media and in emails, resulting in The Substation staff having to dialogue extensively with concerned parties in face-to-face meetings and online, taking criticism and explaining as best as it could.

It can be argued that The Substation could have taken a tougher stance with the state, refused to cancel the meeting and test the limits of the state's willingness to proscribe the arts sector. That might have been a missed opportunity, similar to an earlier, tense meeting of artists described by Wee (2012) after the proscription on performance art in 1994. At the meeting, there was enthusiasm for an idea proposed by a participant to place an advertisement in The Straits Times querying the state's decision. The enthusiasm simmered down when Kuo Pao Kun, who was present, commented that such an act might worsen the situation for the artist who had set things in motion, as he was then being charged with committing an obscene act. After this, according to Wee, the meeting ended inconclusively.

Decisions made at such times by arts managers and curators in such circumstances could take on symbolic or social significance; the case in 2010 certainly placed The Substation at risk of losing its reputation as a space welcoming to those on the margins and hence, its symbolic capital. These could, however, be necessary decisions for those managing contemporary art in Singapore.

The assumption that a clean line can be drawn between "arts" and "politics" is obviously, faulty and thus difficult to enforce, particularly when contemporary art frequently critiques developments in the global economy and capitalism. This proved to be the case for The Substation's presentation of Australian artist Deborah Kelly's 2009 performance project *Tank Man Tango*. This project commemorated the 1989 Beijing Tiananmen incident, memorializing the moment when a lone man carrying two plastic shopping bags stood in front of a tank about to enter the square to disperse the protestors. The art project re-choreographed the movements of the "tank man" into a dance which was video recorded; the video was supposed to be played during the event and the public invited to follow the "dance". This was a networked performance to be staged simultaneously in cities around the world including Auckland, Hobart, Brisbane, Belgrade, Brussels and Singapore (Wong, 2009). The Substation's programming team assessed the risks of this event, aware of the potential for the authorities to interpret this performance negatively; however, the spate of documentaries on television and articles in the local press about the 20th anniversary of Tiananmen reassured them that it would be safe to present the project. Nonetheless, The Substation decided to adopt a bureaucratic-rational approach and obtained an arts license from the relevant authority (then called the Media Development Authority). The day before the performance and after publicity about the event had been disseminated, The Substation received a phone call from the Arts Council to say that the event should be cancelled because of political sensitivities, though no specifics were given regarding the nature of the "sensitivities". Hence, even when the prescribed legal-administrative protocols (obtaining an arts license) are followed and permission granted, the authorities could still intervene at the last minute. It appeared that the state's interpretations of what was "sensitive" were not always consistent, hence the arts practitioners' reading of risks may not always be accurate.

The governing authorities' message to shut down these activities were delivered through a telephone call, where there is no visible trace of the communication. This is an example of the "back door" channels also described by Chong (2011), where censorship happens to some extent behind closed doors before the artistic presentation is staged. This type of censorship is less overt. Although the back-door channel provides some room for the artist to negotiate and to gather the grounds of the state's objection, the arts presenter cannot rely on documentary evidence concerning the authorities' objections when explaining the situation to others, including its audience. It is thus placed in the difficult position of having to speak for the state to some extent. As in the case at The Substation in 2010, the state's way of dealing with these cases might lead to divide-and-rule of the artist communities. Furthermore, the use of back-door channels is an example of how the state apparatus demonstrates its adeptness at "blocking avenues of collective action" among specific communities as previously noted (Rodan, 2004, p. 82). As no documentary evidence exists of the state's direct intervention apart from the artist's account, and the state continues to influence what the public sees, the unequal power between the artist and the state is reinforced.

These incidents reveal a precarity in the artist's position in relation to space for free artistic expression in Singapore, a fragility that is also seen in the fragmented responses of the artistic community to Oei's announcement of programming changes. To one art writer, this is symptomatic of the powerlessness of the artist to act in the face of entrenched state interests in pursuing the global arts city project, and how artists' paths are increasingly shaped by "an arts bureaucracy and its cultural policy"; this in turns leads to a "Singapore marked by intense specialization and atomization" (Koay, 2016). In other words, the artist communities are atomized and unable to act collectively.

Occasionally, adopting a bureaucratic-rational approach to a potentially contentious activity can produce a different outcome. This was seen in the authorities' different response to the *Candlelight Concert for Peace* held in March 2003 when I was still Artistic Co-director. The concert was organized by a group of artists in response to the US-led military action in Iraq and hence could be interpreted as an activity where art and politics were intertwined. It is not known why the authorities permitted the event to proceed, though the decision might have been prompted by the need to alleviate tension among the populace who were concerned about Iraq (a few individuals had been arrested for staging a protest outside the US Embassy), or in response to the ripple effects of public anxiety from the SARS epidemic that year. Originally conceived as an anti-war event, the organizers made a discoursal twist to frame it as an event promoting peace instead. The event featured performances, songs, readings, spoken word, a printmaking station, stalls promoting social causes and distributing mementoes. Participants were invited to write messages of peace on a wall in The Substation Garden and take photographs of themselves to post on the wall next to a photograph of the US embassy in Singapore – a symbolic "protest", as it were.

The concert attracted 600 or more participants, possibly the largest number of visitors to a single Substation event (Davis and Lee, 2004). The event had a proper license from the authorities, and organizers had met the police to discuss security arrangements and give assurances on the theme and types of performances. The organizers did not doubt that there was police surveillance of the event; in fact, for the sake of security, they recorded the event on video. This could be viewed as an instance where the English-educated, middle-class, arts professionals leveraged their cultural capital (as described by Chong, 2011) to negotiate a space for an activity which the state might have opposed. Unfortunately, the fallout from this (and other events) extended years into the future for at least two of the organizers, who were eventually denied a renewal of their permanent residency status in Singapore. Once more, this may have been a case of the state applying "administrative law" to reinforce political control.

Conclusion: implications for arts management training

Chong (2011, 2005) notes that, in the era of the global arts city, the artists who benefitted most from the state's largesse in Singapore were the English-language theatre practitioners with the requisite cultural capital. As the state became more interested in the arts, it also demanded more accountability from artists receiving grants, with the result that arts groups with a professionalized setup and stronger administrative ability were more likely to attract state and private patronage.

From its early days, The Substation had a programming and management team that included well-educated professionals. It developed organizational protocols to manage the center's activities, including programming and technical teams and in the 2000s, one staff member for each of the functions of marketing, facilities rental and accounting. In a country where bureaucratic rationality and decisions based on data and management science are prized, having a professional team of arts managers may have helped it survive the contestations with the "strong state".

The Substation's staff and board had to be adept at anticipating the state's responses to potentially contentious artworks and each generation of arts managers at the center inducted younger, incoming staff into the process through working together. However, the knowledge and experiences gained are not recorded or documented, leading to the question of whether and how such tacit knowledge about the rules of engagement can be systematically transmitted to aspiring arts managers.

The challenges faced by The Substation illustrate the character and modalities of managing the arts in Singapore, where the tone and style of political governance has a strong influence on the actions of arts practitioners. It would appear that the attributes of flexibility, risk-taking, and negotiating skills together with knowledge of how the governing authorities operate and communicate the state's desires are necessary for arts managers here. It will be useful to document the experiences of artists and arts managers who have gone through processes of negotiation with the state and to incorporate the tacit knowledge that they have accumulated as well as the histories of significant local arts organisations such as The Substation, in the training of future arts managers in Singapore.

References

Advisory Council on Culture and the Arts. (1989). *Report of the Advisory Council on Culture and the Arts.* Singapore.

Anderton, M. and Pick, J. (1996). *Arts administration.* London: E & FN Spon.

Atmos. (2016). *Perspectives: The substation.* Available at: www.atmos.sg/perspectives-the-substation. [Accessed 2 Jun. 2018].

Chong, T. (2005). Singapore's cultural policy and its consequences. *Critical Asian Studies*, 37(4), pp. 553–568.

———. (2010). The state and the new society: The roles of the arts in Singapore Nation-building. *Asian Studies Review*, 34(2), pp. 131–149.

———. (2011). *Theatre and the state in Singapore: Orthodoxy and resistance.* London and York: Routledge.

Davis, L. and Lee, W.C. (2004). The substation candlelight concert for peace. *FOCAS: Forum on Contemporary Art and Society*, Singapore: Focus, pp. 390–391.

Fang, J. (2016). The substation's Alan Oei reverses some decisions on its revamp plans. *Today*, Singapore, 5 April.

Hava, D. and Chan, K.B. (2012). *Charismatic leadership in Singapore: Three extraordinary people.* New York: Springer.

Huang, L. (2016). National gallery welcomes over 1.5 million visitors. *The Straits Times*, Singapore, 9 November.

Koay, G. (2016). We never owned this space. *Medium.com*, 8 February. Available at: https://medium.com/@godwinkoay/we-never-owned-this-space-8f864dc05eed [Accessed 20 May 2018].

Koh, G. (2008). Bureaucratic rationality in an evolving developmental state: Challenges to governance in Singapore. *Asian Journal of Political Science*, 5(2), pp. 114–141.

Kok, H.L. (2015). The place of the substation: A space and a place for a beginning. In: A. Wong, ed., *25 years of the substation: Reflections on Singapore's first independent art centre.* Singapore: The Substation and Ethos Books, pp. 38–47.

Kong, L. (2000). Cultural policy in Singapore: Negotiating economic and socio-cultural agendas. *Geoforum*, 31, pp. 409–424.

———. (2012). Ambitions of a global city: Arts, culture and creative economy in 'post-crisis' Singapore. *International Journal of Cultural Policy*, 18(3), pp. 279–294.

Kwok, K.W. and Low, K.H. (2002). Cultural policy and the city-state: Singapore and the 'new Asian renaissance'. In: D. Crane, N. Kawashima and K Kawasaki, eds., *Global culture: Media, arts, policy, and globalization.* New York: Routledge, pp. 151–168.

Lee, T. (2007). Industrializing creativity and innovation. In: K.P. Tan, ed., *Renaissance Singapore? Economy, culture and politics.* Singapore: NUS Press, pp. 45–68.

Lee, T. and Lim, D. (2004). The economics and politics of 'creativity' in Singapore. *Australian Journal of Communication*, 31(2), pp. 149–165.

Lee, W.C. (ed.) (1995). *Art vs art: Conflict and convergence – the substation conference 1993.* Singapore: The Substation.

Leong, Weng Kam. (1986). PUB station turns arts centre. *The Straits Times*, Singapore, 30 September.

Low, L. (2001). The Singapore developmental state in the new economy and polity. *The Pacific Review*, 14(3), pp. 411–441.

Martin, M. (2014). Substation AD Noor Effendy Ibrahim to step down after 5 years. *Today*. [online] Available at: www.todayonline.com/entertainment/arts/substation-ad-noor-effendy-ibrahim-step-down-after-5-years [Accessed 2 Jun. 2018].

———. (2015). The substation's new director Alan Oei announces big changes for the arts centre. *Today*. [online] Available at: www.todayonline.com/entertainment/arts/substations-new-director-alan-oei-anounces-big-changes-arts-centre [Accessed 2 Jun. 2018].

———. (2017). Punk museum opens as part of the substation's new exhibition on city spaces. *Channel News Asia*. [online] Available at: www.channelnewsasia.com/news/lifestyle/punk-museum-opens-substation-new-exhibition-city-spaces-9149646 [Accessed 2 Jun. 2018].

Ministry of Information and the Arts. (2000). *Renaissance city report: Culture and the arts in renaissance Singapore*. Singapore: Ministry of Information and the Arts.

Noor Effendy Ibrahim and Wee, C.J.W-L. (2012). The real world, interdisciplinary arts and the community: an interview with the artistic director of the substation - a home for the arts. *Performance Paradigm: A Journal of Performance and Contemporary Culture*, 8. Available at: www.performanceparadigm.net/index.php/journal/issue/view/14 [Accessed 9 Aug. 2018].

Nur Asyiqin Mohamad Salleh. (2014). Parliament: 'To Singapore with love' has 'distorted and untruthful' accounts of past history: Yaacob. *The Straits Times*. [online] Available at: www.straitstimes.com/singapore/parliament-to-singapore-with-love-has-distorted-and-untruthful-accounts-of-past-history [Accessed 11 Jun. 2018].

Ooi, C.-S. (2010). Political pragmatism and the creative economy: Singapore as a city for the arts. *International Journal of Cultural Policy*, 16(4), pp. 403–417.

Paquette, J. and Redaelli, E. (2015). *Arts management and cultural policy research*. London: Palgrave Macmillan.

Pereira, A. (2008). Whither the developmental state? Explaining Singapore's continued developmentalism. *Third World Quarterly*, 29(6), pp. 1189–1203.

Perry, M., Kong, L., and Yeoh, B. (1997). *Singapore: A developmental city state*. New York and Singapore: John Wiley and Sons.

Peterson, W. (2001). *Theatre and the politics of culture in contemporary Singapore*. Middletown, Connecticut: Wesleyan University Press.

Pick, J. (1980). *Arts administration*. London: E & FN Spon.

Rodan, G. (2004). *Transparency and authoritarian rule in Southeast Asia: Singapore and Malaysia*. London: Routledge Curzon.

Stubbs, R. (2009). What ever happened to the east Asian developmental state? The unfolding debate. *The Pacific Review*, 22(1), pp. 1–22.

Tay, E. (2017). A luxury we cannot afford: The poetry of Yong Shu Hoong, Toh Hsien Min, and Boey Kim Cheng. In: A. Poon and A. Whitehead, eds., *Singapore literature and culture: Current directions in local and global contexts*. New York: Routledge, pp. 62–81.

Tan, K.P. (2007). New politics for a Renaissance city? In: K.P. Tan, ed., *Renaissance Singapore? Economy, culture and politics*. Singapore: NUS Press, pp. 17–36.

———. (2017). *Governing global-city Singapore: Legacies and futures after Lee Kuan Yew*. London and New York: Routledge.

The Esplanade. (n.d.). *Tribute SG, performing arts, Kuo Pao Kun*. Available at: www.esplanade.com/tributesg/performing-arts/kuo-pao-kun [Accessed 2 Jun. 2018].

The Substation. (2010). The search for an artistic director of the substation. Available at: http://thesearchforanartisticdirector.blogspot.com/2010/ [Accessed 13 Aug. 2018].

———. (2011). *What's on – January to March 2011*. Singapore: The Substation.

Velayutham, S. (2007). *Responding to globalization: Nation, culture, and identity in Singapore*. Singapore: Institute of Southeast Asian Studies.

Wee, C.J.W-L. (2003). Creating high culture in the globalized 'cultural desert' of Singapore. *The Drama Review*, 47(4), pp. 84–97.

———. (2012). Introduction: Practicing contemporary art in the global city for the arts, Singapore. *Performance Paradigm: A Journal of Performance and Contemporary Culture*, 8. Available at: www.performanceparadigm.net/index.php/journal/issue/view/14 [Accessed 9 Aug. 2018].

Wong, A. (ed.). (2015). *25 Years of the substation: Reflections on Singapore's first independent art centre*. Singapore: The Substation and Ethos Books.

Wong, M.E. (2009). Tank man tango (with Peter McKay, Frank Motz, Teik-Kim Pok, and Yao Souchou). *Broadsheet: Contemporary Visual Art + Culture*, 38(3), Adelaide: Contemporary Art Centre of South Australia, pp. 190–194.

Yap, June. (2008). In contemporary Singapore: An interview with Audrey Wong and Ho Tzu Nyen. *C-Arts: Asian Contemporary Art and Culture*, March-April, pp. 89–90.

14

CULTURAL FACILITY DEVELOPMENT IN JAPAN AND ITS IMPACT ON CULTURAL POLICY, COMMUNITY, THEATRE AND ARTS MANAGEMENT

Mio Yachita

Introduction

The main aim of this chapter is to reconsider the impact of overwhelming construction of "municipal cultural facilities"[1] to the ecosystem of Japan's arts and culture, including such development of the research and education of arts management. Despite the fact that lack of a comprehensive cultural policy resulted in the redundancy of cultural facilities throughout the country, this chapter will argue that municipal cultural facilities consequently shaped the arts management studies in Japan to be in today's form, as well as aided in shaping the national cultural policy by invigorating the discussion of the public role of the arts. This chapter will first identify the background of Japanese society in the 1980s: how the overwhelming construction of municipal cultural facilities happened and how it influenced the discussions such as the role of community programs, the necessity of the professional staffs (especially in theatres and music halls), and the fundamental relation of the arts to the society. It will then argue that the over-constructed public cultural facilities that mostly resembled the modern western style of architecture, triggered the discussion of the accountability of cultural policy amidst the dichotomy of "foreign" (Western) and "original" (Japanese) culture. Finally, this chapter will reflect the influence brought by municipal cultural facilities to arts management research and education, as well as the reciprocal impact to the national cultural policy.

In a country that has a rapidly developing economy, it is not rare to find the excessive construction of cultural facilities, among other infrastructures, in order to bring economic benefit and demonstrate country's prosperity. The situation of Japan discussed in this chapter could be used as a reference for those countries that share comparable situations and a similar cultural base. In today's world where arts management research tends to be Euro-centric or US-centric, it is crucial to have diverse case studies from various cultural backgrounds when making international comparisons. Analysis of cases such as Japan could contribute not only to make the comparative study more relevant, but also to the understanding of how to deal with the complicated nature of culture in a globalized world, as some examples that may seem peripheral to one may be unexpectedly closer and relevant to many others.

Dramatic upsurge of municipal cultural facilities

Japanese culture is known for many things – manga, anime, robots, and food – but one thing that is hardly known even within the country is the overabundance of cultural facilities. There are thousands of high-grade cultural facilities all over the country. While some towns built small-scale community theatres that cater to local theatre groups, other larger cities and prefectures decided to establish prodigious cultural centers.

To name a few of these municipal cultural facilities, the Shimane Arts Center was founded in 2005 by the Shimane prefectural government, home to 700,000 people. The center is equipped with a large hall of 1,500 seats, a small hall of 400 seats, a museum with four full-fledged exhibition halls, and an inner court with a carefully designed square pool of water that becomes a natural mirror. The architecture of 36,000 m² was designed by the award-winning architect Hiroshi Naito. The construction is said to have cost about 13.6 billion yen (136 million USD)[2] (Asahi Shimbun, 2003), while the overall annual budget of the Culture Foundation of Shimane Prefecture (CFSP), who manages the art center as well as three other venues and programs, is about 940 million yen a year (9.4 million USD) (CFSP, 2017). A second example is the Morioka Civic Cultural Hall, established by the Morioka city government, with a population of 300,000, located 500 km north of Tokyo. Cultural Hall was built in 1998 with a large theatre hall of 1,516 seats and a small concert hall of 356 seats. While the architecture was not featured greatly as it was built within the business complex, the city decided to install a 10 m-high pipe organ in a small hall, custom-made by the French organ builder Marc Garnier. Morioka Foundation for Cultural Activity (MFCA), municipal foundation who manages the cultural hall as well as 10 other halls and museums, operates under the annual budget of 940 million yen (9.4 million USD) (MFCA, 2016). The last example is the Hibiki Hall established by Shōnai town in Yamagata prefecture. Shōnai is a charming town of 21,000 people near the coast of northeast Japan. The region is known as a major agricultural production area famous for its fruits and rice, and the hall is literally surrounded by beautiful rice paddy fields. The large hall of 504 seats is carefully designed to have acoustic excellence created by the respected consulting firm for classical music halls, Nagata Acoustics. It opened in 1999 with a performance by the late internationally renowned pianist Hiroko Nakamura with an all Chopin program, who advised on the selection of the Steinway piano for the hall (Nagata Acoustics, 1999).

There exist several statistics compiled by different organizations, but a study by JAFRA suggests that as of 2014, there are over 3,588 of such public cultural facilities all over the country, only counting those that were established by local municipalities, not by the national government (JAFRA, 2015). This study classified cultural facilities into four categories: (1) concert halls and theatres (specialized and general), (2) fine art museums (excluding educational museums), (3) studios for visual and performing arts, and (4) cultural complexes that combine at least two of these criteria. Specialized facilities include fully equipped theatres suitable for operas, ballet, and large-scale theatre performances; concert halls with superb acoustics and full-size pipe organs; and museums with large exhibition halls and storage rooms with highly precise temperature and humidity control. Other general facilities include studios for visual and performing arts, community spaces, conference halls and multipurpose sports facilities that are permanently furnished with the ample equipment for the purpose of hosting staged performances.

As Yoshimoto uncovered in his detailed study *Reconsidering the Expanding Role and New Paradigm for Japan's Cultural Policy* (2008), the 1990s saw the pouring of 3.8 trillion yen (approximately

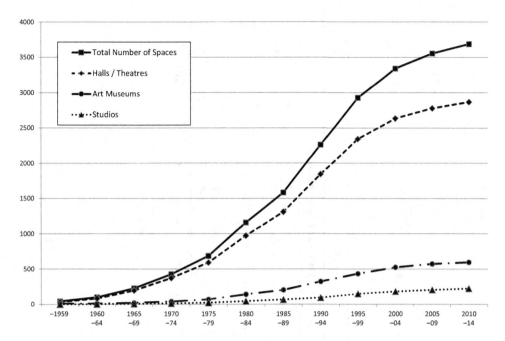

Figure 14.1   Number of municipal cultural facilities built from 1959 to 2014 in Japan

Source: JAFRA, 2015

38 billion USD) into construction of such municipal cultural facilities aided by Japan's massive economic growth, resulting in the opening of an average of two theatres every week and one museum every two weeks (Yoshimoto, 2008). Since there are 47 prefectures, 20 designated cities and 1,558 smaller municipalities (non-designated cities, towns and villages) at the time of the survey, in theory there are more than two cultural centres in every city, town and village on average. Although the construction rush peaked in the 1990s, municipalities have been continuing to build more cultural facilities to this day.

Metaphorically speaking, many of these cultural facilities were created similarly to how host countries of the Olympic games rush to make massive, world-class stadiums and swimming pools, except that world-class programs were not planned in advance in all of these places. Furthermore, it did not just happen in one host city, but in almost every municipality in Japan. How did this massive cultural construction effort happen, and how did it affect the ecosystem of the arts in Japan?

"Age of Culture" and the commencement of cultural policy in municipalities

The Japanese economy began to rapidly grow in the middle of the 1950s. When the Gross National Income per capita exceeded its highest pre–WWII figure in 1956, the Economic White Paper declared that it was officially "the end of the postwar era" (EPAJ, 1994). This remarkable economic growth continued into the 1970s, in what was called the "Japanese Miracle," seeing Japan take its place as one of the strongest economies in the world (The Brookings Bulletin, 1976). The miracle finally hit the roof in the 1980s, followed by the so-called economic bubble that abruptly burst in the 1990s, leaving the country with a severely depressed economy over the following decades. Preceding the economic crisis, then-Prime Minister Masayoshi

Table 14.1 Data table of Municipal cultural facilities built from 1959 to 2014 in Japan

	No. of Valid Responses	Years											
		–1959	1960–64	1965–69	1970–74	1975–79	1980–84	1985–89	1990–94	1995–99	2000–04	2005–09	2010–14
Total Number of PCF buildings	3,338	43	50	115	186	241	425	385	632	592	371	180	118
Total Number of Spaces	3,687	45	56	127	199	259	474	424	678	665	414	214	132
Halls/Theatres (total)	2,866	35	50	113	176	218	381	338	533	500	290	143	89
Specialized	1,432	21	38	75	93	90	160	153	296	270	124	60	52
General	1,434	14	12	38	83	128	221	185	237	230	166	83	37
Art Museums	596	10	3	10	17	31	72	63	118	111	90	48	23
Studios	225	0	3	4	6	10	21	23	27	54	34	23	20

Source: Japan Foundation of Regional Art-Activities (JAFRA). 2015. Report of the Current State of Public Cultural Facilities in 2015. Tokyo: JAFRA. Used with permission.

Ōhira stated in his first policy address before the National Diet in 1979 that Japan had reached the "Age of Culture (*Bunka no Jidai*)," leaving behind the age of economy that sought for endless economic prosperity (Aoki, Kawamura, and Makita, 2006, Ōhira, 1979a). This and his following policy address are said to have brought about the commencement of the decades of governmental investment in culture (Yoshimoto, 2008).

Neki and Kobayashi both claim that until around the 1980s, there was an implicit, unwritten agreement among Japan's policy makers to avoid politicizing culture. It was considered a gesture of repentance for the censorship, restriction, and oppression inflicted on arts and culture as well as the coerced labor to create propaganda materials during World War II (Kobayashi, 2014, pp. 139–140; Neki, 2001, p. 23), not to mention that the country was more focused on re-building its society from the aftermath of the war. Due to this implicit understanding, the government's approach to culture has long been referred to as *Bunka Gyōsei* (administration of culture), not *Bunka Seisaku* (cultural policy), keeping its role to a minimum, and focusing mostly on cultural heritage. Therefore, it is said to be only after Prime Minister Ōhira's policy speech in 1979 that national and local policy makers started to consider cultural administration within a broader framework of policy, as they came to widely use the term the "Age of Culture."[3]

Another point that the prime minister emphasized at that time was "the age of culture is also the age of regions," stating that the government will "lay a foundation of nation-building" by "bolstering the local regions to be more diverse, vital, and autonomous," and will "actively advance policies for cultural activities in the regions, as well as reformation and reinforcement of the existing policies" (Ōhira, 1979b: Translation by author), promising the commitment to transfer more power and autonomy to the local government. Subsequently, governors and mayors of local municipalities have initiated reforms utilizing the idea of "Age of Culture." Terms such as "culturalization of public administration (*Gyōsei no Bunka-ka*),"[4] the opposite of "administration of culture," were coined to describe that cultural policy should not be about the administration of the department in charge of cultural activities, but rather it should provide a comprehensive strategy for the entire municipality that ties into other areas such as education, community, tourism, economy, and social welfare. Academics such as Keiichi Matsushita and Tadao Umesawa have particularly contributed to advocating the idea that culture is the key to bring sophistication to the community and administration. Local policy makers and researchers in municipal administrations competed with each other to figure out what this new "Age of Culture" would look like in their regions, as they enthusiastically welcomed encouraging opinions such as Umesawa's "Faucet Theory," that claimed culture would "flow out" even in remote areas, like water from the faucet, once an abundant cultural infrastructure was developed throughout the country (Kobayashi, 2018a).

Encouraged by the idea that culture is the key to bring sophistication to municipal administration, many took the chance to invest in the construction of infrastructure. These projects were hugely aided by regional development bonds, a national government scheme to stimulate municipalities' public works by balancing out the debt with national subsidy. Since the development bond only covered construction costs, after the completion of the facility and the following economic crash in the late 1990s, many municipalities were left with barely enough of a budget to operate the buildings, let alone any capacity to create a vision, artistic direction, or simply, better programs (Yoshimoto, 2008). Criticism mounted that the expensive running costs of government-built empty and visionless cultural facilities were dragging down municipal budgets, while relatively short-term public projects such as building cultural centers helped governors and mayors bring some achievement before their election (Yamamori, 1999). As the excessive construction did not only happen in culture but also in other sectors, it was commonly called "public policy of empty building (*Hakomono Gyōsei*)" as a satire for the municipal public policy that was heavily focused on construction without management vision (ibid).

Issues of professional staffs and legislative ground

At the time, government regulations obligated municipal governments to manage those facilities directly on their own or through foundations or organizations founded by the local government for the purpose. As a result, general local government employees, who typically only stay in one department for about three years before getting transferred to another, were put in charge to decide how to run these extravagant cultural facilities. Many of these cultural facilities, especially music halls and theatres that lacked professional staff, filled their schedules by simply renting the spaces out to citizens. Local piano teachers or retired amateur chorus singers booked these facilities, as well as a few commercial production companies who toured programs such as popular music shows or children's shows based on anime, TV programs or games. In other words, many music halls and theatres built to be able to cater to the world's finest performances were used almost merely as rental community halls.

Many cultural centers, especially music halls and theatres, were criticized for being too luxurious without a strategic plan to utilize them. This problem was caused by a lack of professional staff in governance, management and programing (Ito et al., 2001). Except for museums (and libraries, which are not included in the survey mentioned in the previous section), there were no legislations that provided basic conditions for theatres and music halls at the time. The National Museums Act (1951) under the Social Education Act (1949) defines the role of curators as a specialist, and obligates museums, including fine art, history, and natural museums as well as zoos and aquariums, to hire certified curators. Although there are considerable discussions relating to the legislation, such as on the reliability of the curator's qualification, it has been the firm regulatory base for municipalities to employ educated professionals in the cultural facilities. In comparison, legal definition for music halls and theatres could only be found under the Local Autonomy Act (1947) that defines the responsibility of municipalities for the construction and maintenance of "public facilities", including schools, hospitals, public transportation, and even streets and sewage systems (Ito et al., 2001, pp. 58–29). Some municipalities choose to establish local cultural ordinances to clarify the aim, role, and governing strategy of cultural centers, while others remain to manage without. Kobayashi argues that in the 1980s and 1990s, the municipal effort of promoting arts and culture, especially through music halls and theatres, was based in a "legislative vacuum" that lacked the control of national laws (Kobayashi, 2018b, p. 171). It was only after the national government passed the Basic Act of Culture in 2001 that clarified the municipalities' responsibility to promote culture and became a legal ground for municipal government to develop cultural policy. While the lack of professional staff caused inefficient usage of the centers, she claims that in certain municipalities, this "legislative vacuum" somehow created freedom to develop cultural policy without instruction and restriction from the national government (ibid).

Arts intermediaries for the municipal cultural facilities

Amid mounting criticisms, municipalities and managing organizations of cultural facilities were urged to develop strategies to improve their programs. However, due to scarce knowledge and experience of managing cultural centers, some simply thought of improving the programs by purchasing a few programs a year from commercial companies based in the capital. In addition, there was also a major concern that passive rental halls in regional areas are only feeding the cultural content created in central Japan, instead of contributing to a creation of diverse culture in each area (Inayama, 2003). To address these challenges, a research committee of the development of regional culture formed under the Ministry of Internal Affairs, suggested to create a system to foster proactive, original and creative management and programming as well as mutual cooperation between the cultural centers. Based on the suggestion, the Japan Foundation of Regional Art-Activities (JAFRA) was established in 1994, in order to support creative development of regions through arts and culture, by responding to the needs of the municipalities. Since its establishment, JAFRA has created a number of training programs and research projects to encourage robust utilization of these public halls, based on the request of the municipality and advice from specialists in each field. Through training specialists, developing programs and publishing research and articles, JAFRA encouraged and guided municipal cultural centers to make their own initiatives to be more creative, inclusive, and efficient.

By the virtue of the municipality being close to stakeholders and citizens, many local governments prioritized community engagement as well as artistic appraisal. Upon such requests, JAFRA dispatched specialists as trainers to each region, to start initiatives such as outreach programs to schools, communities and hospitals, original performing arts production with citizens through workshops and artist-in-residencies, and helped building programs for volunteers, supporters and members. These programs not only functioned as a training for staff in cultural centers and municipal government, but also contributed to advocate artists, especially those in classical music, contemporary dance and theatre, to commit to community programs. Through its training, support and publication, JAFRA hugely contributed to instill the new ideas and key terms such as "outreach", "workshop", "artist-in-residency", and "volunteering" into public cultural sectors. These attempts to support cultural facilities that were over-constructed in the absence of cultural policy, consequently brought about the strong development of community-oriented programs across Japan.

Privatization of cultural facilities and establishment of art NPOs

As the society's interest in public facilities grew, two new laws were introduced in 1998 and 2003 that consolidated the tendency of community-oriented programs among regional cultural centers. The first is the Non-Profit Organization (NPO) Law that was established to authorize the official status for volunteer citizen rescue groups after the devastating Hanshin Earthquake in 1995, which marked the end of a plutocratic society supported by economic growth. This and subsequent revisions of related regulations regarding non-profit status allowed arts and cultural groups a new legal status apart from limited companies and foundations.[5] Interestingly, the very first organization that obtained NPO status in Japan, among all the other areas such as environment, social welfare, community development, education and sports, was the Hokkaido based theatre company, Furano Theatre Factory. This news encouraged the art industry, as some practitioners were skeptical about applying for the status in the beginning due to scarce and vague benefits for tax exemption, although many were seeking a better governance and management framework (Yoshimoto, 2017).

This newly introduced NPO law stimulated a new discourse regarding the social role of the arts, as civil organizations and companies who try to obtain the status are required to explicitly explain their missions and public role, for the first time for many. Faced with this new change, about 250 art practitioners gathered from all over Japan in 2003 to attend the very first "Arts NPO Forum," which was held at Kobe Art Village Center, the very place hit by the earthquake.

After the enthusiastic discussion, participants agreed to publish a statement at the end of the two-day conference, which started:

> In this forum, we confirmed that art is indispensable for solving the problems of modern society. Based on the recognition that art is an extremely societal existence, and very powerful in creating diverse values and moving the society forward, we are determined to advocate the power of art to our society.
>
> *(Art NPO Link/Yoshimoto, 2017: Translation by author)*

After the second forum held in the following year, the network itself established an intermediary organization, Arts NPO Link, and started a nationwide survey of arts-related non-profit organizations as well as continuing the forum and frequent discussions. According to their first published survey, Arts NPO Link has identified 1,742 arts and cultural related organizations among those registered as NPOs and received around 200 responses from them for the survey (Art NPO Link, 2006).[6] These organizations varied from artists' own companies, community arts organizations, arts spaces, artist-in-residencies, and intermediary organizations, to name a few. The number of non-profit cultural organizations has steadily increased since, as the most recent study in 2016 shows an identifiable total number of 4,272, with responses received from 527 organizations (Art NPO Link, 2017). The term "Arts NPO," which was originally fabricated at the first forum, became quite common after a decade, and is now widely used even in major newspapers without an annotation (Yoshizawa, 2018).[7] Arts NPOs were expected to be the new partners for the public cultural sector by representing the arts sector and civil society of the region.

The second legislation that influenced municipal cultural centers was the introduction of the Designated Manager System (DMS, or *Shitei Kanri-sha Seido*) in 2003. It was brought in as an amendment of Local Autonomy Law as a part of governmental reformation and privatization. For the first time, the new system allowed local municipalities to outsource the operation of public facilities to the private sector to seek more cost-effective management without losing their public purpose. Some of these facilities included parks, sports facilities, social welfare centers, libraries, museums, halls, and educational centers. Prior to this policy, local municipalities such as prefectural or city governments had little choice but to operate public facilities either directly as a department of the local government, or through public organizations such as foundations and public corporations established for the purpose. For cultural facilities, it was commonly the municipal cultural foundations that were in charge of day-to-day management.

Kobayashi (2014) and Yoshimoto (2008) both described this major shift as a "new paradigm" for Japan's cultural policy, as not only the introduction of the DMS shook the monopoly of municipal-founded organizations in the management of public facilities in general, but also the combination of the two legislations opened up the new possibility for the civil society to participate in it. At the same time, it came as shocking news for the municipal cultural foundations, whose sole purpose of existence was to manage the municipal cultural facilities. Municipal governments were faced with the decision whether to call for an open bidding, appoint someone under an unpublicized entrustment, or manage the facilities directly within the government administration. In the JAFRA's first research after the introduction of DMS, 70% to 80% of the public cultural facilities built by prefectural or large city governments adopted the DMS, while the figure was less than 30% in smaller municipalities (smaller cities, towns and villages) (2007). Within the 70% of those adopted DMS, over 60% of them appointed the "designated manager" through open bidding, while the rest of them were appointed in closed selection. Appointing the existing cultural foundation as a new designated manager without open bidding seemed as a compromise between adopting the new system and not dissolving municipal foundation immediately, however, it was undisputedly necessary to show the rigid evidence that the foundation was the most effective, one-and-only organization who could operate the cultural center. These reformations invigorated the discussions of the social role of arts, as municipal governments and their cultural centers confronted with the heavy pressure to explain their accountability, especially for the citizens of the region.

Traditional arts, national theatres and acceptance of western-style theatre

In comparison with the municipal effort to rapidly build cultural centers in the 1990s, the national government had begun the development of infrastructure for culture several decades earlier. The first national theatre in Japan was built in 1966, 20 years after the end of World War II, to cater primarily to traditional Japanese arts such as Noh, Kabuki, and Japanese traditional music. The National Engei Theatre[8] was opened in 1979, the National Noh Theatre in 1983 and the National Bunraku Theatre in 1984. Apart from this "hardware," Japan's traditional performing arts sector has an established support system, including subsidized regular performances in designated theaters,[9] yearly countrywide tours, and outreach programs to public schools among many others. The national theatre also founded a 2-year professional training program in 1970 to provide opportunities for committed young performers to enter the sector, as the arts has long been only inherited under the centuries-old hereditary system and decades of strict apprenticeship.

These programs were carried out based on the Law on National Theatre (1966) and the Act on Protection of Cultural Properties (1950). New National Theatre, which was planned after the update of the Law of National Theatre in 1990, was built in 1997 to be the first national theatre to host modern theatre, dance, western classical opera and ballet. Needless to say, it was not the first western theatre built in Japan. As early as the mid-19th century, successful tycoons and elites preceded the government to import and practice western culture as soon as the start of Japanese modernization.[10] Teikoku Gekijō (Imperial Theatre), which is said to be the first full-scale western-style theatre in Japan, was built in 1911 by a group of successful members of the business elite. Even Kabukiza Theatre,[11] the home of Kabuki built in 1898, originally had a western façade that reflected the modernity of that time. Numbers of western music halls had also been built during this time as western classic music education became more popular among the elites. Considering the upsurge of public theatres in the 1990s also primarily resembled the western style, these theatres and halls, together with the contents, manners and customs, were suddenly introduced into Japanese society only about 150 years ago and had especially spread explosively nationwide in the last 30 years.

Of course, the custom of social gatherings at the theatre and enjoying the performing arts existed long before the modernization and westernization of the mid-19th century. The oldest existing Noh theatre, in Nishi-Hongwanji Temple in Kyoto, dates back to 1581. The current style of Noh performance itself is said to have established in the 14th century, and its origins could date back as far as the 7th century. What these facts suggest is that the construction of the National Theatre in 1966 and the National Noh Theatre in 1983 were merely a modern upgrade of an infrastructure that has existed for many centuries, to meet regulatory and commercial necessity. On the other hand, the construction of western-style theatres marked the first introduction of western high culture into Japan at this scale. To this day, these two types of theatres, western halls and Japanese traditional-style theatres, have different roles, social impacts, and cultural importance, and their trajectories have been almost completely in parallel.

It could even be argued that part of the reason local municipalities in Japan competed in building western-style cultural centers after the 1980s was to show off their modernity, scale of economic development, and cultural sophistication, not primarily to promote the arts. Therefore, budgets were spent on bigger facilities, expensive equipment, and a modern look, rather than on the contents to be shown there. On the other hand, traditional arts have always been a subject of conservation, education, and archive, demanding advice from specialists. In addition, traditional arts and cultural heritage have been quite thoroughly protected by the national government since the end of WWII, leaving little space for the local municipalities to make autonomous decisions.

The problem of over-constructed, under-utilized cultural facilities did not happen only due to the lack of explicit cultural policy, but also due to the lack of collective cultural knowledge of the west. Despite nurturing top-class musicians and dancers in classical music and ballet at the national level, as well as having a remarkable amount of non-professional performers all over the country, the management of the western-modeled cultural center was still new to many, compared to traditional cultures that have been rooted for hundreds of years.

In the 1980s, many local policy makers simply believed that new, modern, and sophisticated culture would flourish once it was provided with ample amount of proper venues. For the majority of citizens, their first-hand encounter with culture, especially western culture, came from taking lessons for piano or ballet, or participating in culture clubs at school, not by attending concerts and shows by professionals. Thus, the well-equipped cultural centers in the region seemed like great places to present their own performances. In some places, the schedules of the rented-out public theatres quickly filled up with an abundance of non-professional citizen performers. In such a situation, on what ground would one choose to bring in professional artists instead of enthusiastic community performers? Why shouldn't amateur performers deserve to perform in the finest music halls? Who is more important to the community, a professional performer passing by as part of their tour or a passionate resident musician? Diligent and hardworking civil servants who are in charge of municipal cultural centers raised these kinds of questions, when specialists in arts or cultural policy were dispatched to suburbs to advocate for artistic programing and professional management of the centers. One can easily question the lack of knowledge, experience, or appreciation of the quality of the arts produced by professionals; however, it is also easy to assume that these questions would have been formed quite differently should the subject be replaced from western music to Japanese traditional arts. Traditional arts are firmly rooted in the community in general, and as controversial as it is, authenticity of the masters, rigid hierarchy of professional performers, rules, manners and customs are very well understood. For better or worse, managing a *western* cultural center did not burden policy makers, government officers nor citizens with such pressures.

The lack of resources, specialized staff, as well as in-depth knowledge towards the ecosystem of cultural centers modeled from the west caused inept management of highly designed halls in many municipalities. At the same time, however, the "legislative vacuum" for music halls and theatres created certain freedom for municipalities and citizens to consider their own unique way to manage them. Consequently, numbers of distinctive community-oriented programs have emerged through the struggle, inside and outside of the public cultural centers, precisely because people were comparably free from the regulations and the pressure of questioning the authenticity of the established arts. Since the rushing construction of cultural centers peaked in the 1990s, hundreds of case studies regarding community-oriented arts programs have been introduced and analyzed in numerous publications: JAFRA's periodical *Chiiki Sōzō* that has been published twice a year since 1995; some publications dedicated for the exceptional example of public cultural centers (Ei, 2000, Kobayashi, 2003, Kakiuchi, 2012); and other publications focused on the social role of the arts that expanded beyond museums and theatres (Fuji and AAF Network, 2012, Kumakura, 2015, Morishita, 2016). The struggle of fulfilling the accountability of supporting non-traditional, non-indigenous arts in society by public money also contributed to strengthen the fundamental argument of the public role of the arts. The accumulation of knowledge and the practice regarding the community-oriented arts could be considered as one of the most significant assets in arts management in Japan partly created under the influence of the development of cultural facilities.

Impact on arts management education and national cultural policy

Responding to the needs from many regions, universities have started to establish formal education of the arts management from the beginning of the 1990s. It is no exaggeration to say that this explosion of cultural facilities drove arts management and related fields through their developing phase. Professor Miyama, who created the first arts management curriculum in higher education in Japan at Keio University in 1991, recalls that in Japan the field was associated "closely to the issues of the public cultural facilities, especially after the recession" (Miyama, 2010). Professor Yasuo Ito also recalls that at the beginning of the 1990s, the primary focus of the education of arts management was especially on those regarding municipal cultural facilities (Ito, 2016). Masao Katayama, who created a fellowship program at the Saison Foundation[12] for arts managers to take post-graduate courses abroad, recalls the situation in the 1990s as follows:

> In order for non-profit performing arts to survive, we needed more than artists, sponsors and presenters. We needed people who can define and explain the role of arts within society.
>
> *(Katayama, 2016)*

As a result, cultural policy and the social role of the arts were much more vigorously discussed compared to strategic management of organizations. When the long-awaited textbook for arts management, *Introduction to Arts Management (Ātsu Manejimento Gairon)*[13] was published in 2001, it covered policy-related topics in five out of eight chapters, ranging from cultural rights in the constitution, management of the governmental cultural centers, and cultural policy of the municipalities (Ito et al., 2001; Kobayashi and Katayama, 2015).[14] In fact, other publications[15] and academic journals[16] also covered popular topics such as community engagement, local revitalization, social inclusion, arts in education and municipal cultural policies as their main subject. In comparison, areas such as organizational management were not given high priority (Nakao, 2015).[17] Considering the fact that many experts were more than well acquainted with the arts management education in western countries,[18] it is evident that the managerial element was not dismissed by ignorance, but as a conscious choice in the early years.

Development of public cultural facilities also impacted on the formation of the national cultural policy. In the midst of the inevitable reformation and the privatization of the management system of public facilities, Oriza Hirata, a renowned playwright and cultural policy specialist, actively advocated for the Theatre Law, which was successfully established in 2012. The Act on the Vitalization of Theatres and Music Halls (*Gekijō, Ongakudō tō no Kasseika ni kansuru Hōritsu*), commonly known as the Theatre Law, was a long-awaited piece of legislation designed to define the roles and status of public halls. Despite not including Hirata's original intention of accrediting theatres based on the creative capacity, nor obligating hiring specialists, the law acknowledged the issues of excessive construction and inept usage and became the first legal foundation for local governments to vitalize theatres and music halls.

Preceding the enactment of the Theatre Law, the national government passed its first foundational law for culture, the Basic Act of Promotion of Culture and Arts (*Bunka Geijutsu Shinkō Kihon Hō*) in 2001, encouraging both national and municipal governments to create a vision and take action for the establishment of cultural policy. The Act was recently amended in 2017 and updated to be the Basic Act of Culture and Arts (*Bunka Geijutsu Kihon Hō*). The amendment was influenced by several factors: *Washoku*, or Japanese traditional cuisine, being designated an intangible cultural heritage by UNESCO, the launch of the Cool Japan Policy to export intellectual property, and the successful bid to host the Olympics and Paralympics in Tokyo in 2020. Although the Act still remained mainly conceptional, it is significant that the amendment expanded the scope from promoting cultural activities to a wider perspective on the role of culture in society, namely community building, social welfare, education, international exchange, tourism, and the fostering of cultural industry. With the new amendment, there is a possibility of inter-ministerial efforts to support, promote, and develop the culture and arts sector to be more interdisciplinary, inclusive, and vibrant.

Accumulation of studies and practice, especially regarding the analysis of municipal cultural policies, development of community programs, and studies that explored the wider role of the arts in society had influenced the expansion of the policy measure (Kawamura and Ito, 2018). The upsurge of public cultural facilities consequently helped the development of arts management education, and at the same time advocated for the change of national cultural policy.

Conclusion and new challenges

Overwhelming construction of municipal cultural facilities has become an unavoidable issue when discussing about Japan's arts management and cultural policy after the 1980s. The policy heavily inclined towards construction of cultural infrastructure happened in the aftermath of rapid economic growth, aided by the national government's initiative to increase policy measures based on culture after WWII, as well as an effort to bolster the autonomy of municipalities. Based on the idea that culture will vitalize the local community and bring sophistication, municipalities built well-equipped, carefully designed luxurious public cultural centers throughout the country, only to find them in need of specialized, long-term management that became an economic burden to the local government. As a result, many of them, especially music halls and theatres that were lacking a legislative base, were simply rented out to use. Arts management and cultural policy research had developed rapidly under such circumstances, to fill the gap between the visionless high-quality cultural halls and its inefficient use. In addition, privatization of the public-funded facilities and the enactment of the NPO law accelerated the concept of involvement of civil society into the governance and management of public cultural centers. Consequently, such effort incubated unique development community-oriented programs inside and outside of the cultural centers, and later influenced national policy.

After almost 40 years since Prime Minister Ōhira's speech of "Age of Culture," the situation surrounding Japanese society has drastically changed. The economy once so strong that it was called the second largest in the world is now faced with severe problems such as depopulation, economic recessions, and increasing national debt. In this social climate municipal cultural centers are now faced with new challenges. One of the recent guidelines created based on the Theatre Law stated that public theatres now must aim for more effective management and are encouraged to diversify their income source. Following this, the Association of the Public Theatres and Halls (Zenkoku Koubunkyō)[19] recently published a handbook on fundraising for public cultural institutions (Zenkoku Koubunkyō, 2016). This was a startling change, as operations of public halls have been understood as part of the public service and not appropriate to gather funding elsewhere except for charging minimum amount for venue rental, tickets, and a lease from cafés and shops. Fundraising is still a comparably new concept in Japan, especially from individuals,[20] however, there are numbers of new attempts to encourage the action. Among encouraging legacy donation, utilizing dormant deposits, and introducing social impact investment, what has been so far the most successful is the *Furusato Nōzei*, or Hometown Taxation (Japan Fundraising Association, 2017, p. 26). The system enables individuals to pay some part of the residential tax to a municipality of their choice, apart from the place of their current residence. Together with the iconic "return gift" from the municipalities (such as a package of fresh vegetables from a farm in your home town), it skyrocketed from just above 8 billion yen (80 million USD) in 2008 to 365 billion yen (3.65 billion USD) in 2017 (MIC, 2018). Kōbunkyō's fundraising handbook encourages the use of Hometown Taxation as a new means of fundraising for the local cultural facilities (Zenkoku Koubunkyō, 2016). In fact, numbers of municipalities have already designated the usage of the tax income for cultural programs, festivals, heritage conservation, tourism, and educational programs. Kani Public Arts Center is an outstanding case of a municipal cultural facility directly endorsing the system. If one chooses to donate to the center through this system, the amount will be directly used for art programs hosted at the center. Although such examples are still rare, it shows great potential as a new fundraising strategy for municipal cultural centers.

Despite their original expectations, art NPOs, on the other hand, faced inextricable challenges especially in terms of employability[21] and sustainability. While some successfully developed into established organizations, the situation for many smaller arts NPOs did not improve, and the term art NPO has "always been associated with the negative connotation of being vulnerable" in terms of management (Arts NPO Link, 2017). However, research suggests that municipal cultural facilities that have adopted the Designated Manager System, NPO took over the management of 44 out of 834 music halls and theatres, or 83 cultural centers out of 1,526 (including museums) (Zenkoku Koubunkyō, 2017; JAFRA, 2015). While two of the well-known arts NPOs, Art Network Japan and BankART 1929 have dissolved their long-term partnerships with the local governments to manage the local art centers in 2016 and 2017, cases such as ZA-KOENJI Public Theatre (managed by Creative Theatre Network), Kadoma Lumiere Hall (managed by TOYBOX), and Toyo'oka Shimin Plaza (managed by Community Art Center Platz) still seem to exemplify successful models of partnership. In addition, there are increasing numbers of examples of NPOs becoming designated managers for revitalizing programs for abolished schools (Sasaki et al., 2015). Some arts NPOs are also taking other forms of partnership with the government, by being partners to regional arts festivals and biennials/triennials in provincial regions (Yachita, 2016). Also considering the fact that some of the most successful art spaces such as Arts Chiyoda 3331 apply social business models as limited companies and other forms of non-profit status, the potential of civil society and partnerships with local government seem to be expanding.

Though the danger of when policy inclines too heavily toward merely the construction of facilities is to be taken very seriously, the development of infrastructure in Japan did lay some groundwork for culture to flourish. Municipal cultural facilities stimulated a number of significant discussions that formed an essential part of Japanese arts management today and aided the creation of better relationships between arts and the country's society. In an ever uncertain and changing society, it is the socially engaged practices of the arts created with the influence of municipal cultural centers that holds shed of light in Japan's future.

Notes

1 Commonly known in Japanese as *Kōritsu Bunka Shisetsu* (公立文化施設), which directly translates to "public cultural facilities". The term is commonly used to refer to public museums, theatres, concert halls, art studios, and artist-in-residences that are established by the government, especially by local municipalities. This chapter uses the term "municipal cultural facilities" interchangeable to cultural centers, but especially when differentiating them from national or private ones, and when emphasizing the issue that many of them were regarded merely as "facilities" without professional management.

2 For the purpose of simplifying the comparison, amount shown here is calculated by 100 JPY for 1 USD within this chapter.

3 After his speech at the Diet on January 1980, the prime minister gathered a "Working Group for the Age of Culture" to discuss the vision of cultural policy. The final report published in July of the same year is considered to be one of the earliest comprehensive cultural policy reports, leading to today's cultural administration, including international cultural relations (Aoki et al. 2006). Unfortunately, the prime minister suddenly passed away during the election campaign in June, before seeing the final report from the working group.

4 Originally coined by Yawara Hata, former governor of Saitama Prefecture. The term seemed to have remained popular until the term "cultural policy" became commonly used in public administration.

5 Preceding this law, not-for-profit status was limited to foundations and associations. The strict conditions and requirements for the establishment of these organizations prevented many small arts organizations from obtaining nonprofit status. In addition, further administrative reformation in 2008 greatly eased the conditions of establishing foundations and societies, while at the same time mandating existing foundations and societies to choose between taxable general status and non-taxable public status. This reformation further blurred the distinction of municipal-funded cultural foundations and private organizations, as some municipal-funded foundation became taxable while other private foundation gained non-taxable status.

6 Art NPO Link has been hand-counting NPOs with activities related to culture, as official government statistics only provide information based on their designated mission, which contains research, arts, culture, and education as one sector.

7 Founder and manager of Arts NPO Link, Sadayuki Higuchi described this achievement of national-level recognition as one of the biggest contributions over the last ten years.

8 *Engei* is a form of traditional Japanese performance, which includes *manzai comedy, rōkyoku* storytelling, paper cutting performances and so on.

9 Municipalities that host National Theatres and Museums such as Osaka, Kyoto and Okinawa also subsidize their maintenance and programing. National Bunraku Theatre and its national resident company recently faced significant budget cuts and reformations for support from Osaka City, as the governor vigorously called it a "vested interest" (Mukai et al 2018).

10 To focus on the government initiative, private initiatives for creating cultural centers are not comprehensively discussed in this chapter, however, corporations have also played a crucial role in supporting the arts in Japan after 1980s as well. Those private theatres and museums not only paved the way for inviting top-class artists, but also created a standard for the fine service and management of cultural centers. Apart from owning halls and museums, a few corporate cultural foundations also created some of the most innovative cultural support programs. In 1990, the Association for Corporate Support of the Arts (Kigyo Mécénat Kyogikai: KMK) was established. As Yoshimoto (2008) and Kawashima (2010) argue, through their program KMK created a discourse that supporting the arts is not only an act of charity but also a way to enhance creativity and innovation within the corporation, and many of their initiatives influenced national and local cultural policy.

11 Despite some government support, Kabuki has always been managed under a private corporation, and is a registered trademark of Shochiku Co., Ltd.

12 Katayama describes the foundation as a place for "social experimentation" to fill the gaps in government support, by taking challenges that are difficult for governments. The idea of the fellowship was later taken by the national government and continues to this day as the Fellowship of Japanese Government Overseas Study programme for Emerging Art Professionals (Katayama 2016).

13 It is worth mentioning that the term *Āto (or Ātsu) Manejimento* is directly taken from its original English word to Japanese, indicating that it maintains as a foreign word and concept. Direct Japanese translations such as *Geijutsu Keiei* (芸術経営), or other terms such as Arts Administration, did not receive the same popularity despite the very first textbook edited by Akihiko Sasaki in 1994 being titled *Geijutsu*

Keiei. Muto argues for the similar development of foreign terms adopted as new Japanese words in his presentation (Muto 2014).

14 As Kogure (2001) anticipated, the textbook became widely accepted not only by lecturers in increasing numbers of arts management courses in universities, but also for professionals working in theatres, museums, cultural foundations, and civil servants in culture-related departments.

15 The situation was more or less the same in other publications that introduced the term arts management around the same time, including S. Kobayashi (1994), M. Ito et al. (2003), and Hayashi (2004). An exception was *The Art Industry* by Shin (2008), which is also one of the earliest publications. It addressed practical management topics, including the preparation of portfolios and fundraising, as it was based on her lectures designed for young artists.

16 Such as journals published by the Japan Association for Cultural Economics (established in 1992), the Japan Association for Arts Management (since 1998), and the Japan Association for Cultural Policy Research (since 2005).

17 After 14 years and three major revisions, the formerly mentioned textbook of arts management now has a chapter on organizational management, including fundraising. Nakao, the author of this new chapter, mentions that traditional management is sometimes considered a "narrow definition of arts management" in Japan.

18 Taisuke Katayama, professor at Shizuoka University of Art and Culture, an economist and researcher, dedicated a book on arts support in the United States, while Mari Kobayashi, a cultural policy, law and management professor at Tokyo University has published numerous comparative studies on the Japanese and European systems. S. Kobayashi, Hayashi, and Shin have graduate degrees from the United States, while M. Ito and his fellow contributors have a long experience working with European institutions.

19 The Association of the Public Theatres and Halls in Japan (Zenkoku Koubunkyō) was originally established in 1961 as a voluntary network for sharing information on tours, co-productions, and training. Reacting to the sudden increase of its potential members in the 1990s, in 1995 the group decided to advance its activities as a registered association. The association also conducts statistical research studies, consultation for management, sharing resources for programing, capacity development, and most significantly, now provides shared insurance for accidents and cancellations of shows. As a membership organization, the association has represented the needs and demand of public theatres and halls, especially after the 1990s.

20 A research study suggests that while private individual donations have seen a steady increase, especially after the 2011 Tohoku earthquake and tsunami, the largest motivator for donations still lies in the social pressure of traditional community habits (such as community bonds, support for local temples and/or shrines, or being asked by acquaintances) (Japan Fundraising Association 2017).

21 Yoshizawa's research proved that micro arts NPOs could only provide salaries far below the average starting salary of private corporations, making it impossible for staff to live without support from family members (Yoshizawa 2018). On average, a person with a high school diploma receives 161,300 yen (1,613 USD) in monthly income (MHLW 2016). On the other hand, according to Yoshizawa's interview, some employees of arts NPOs were receiving much less, ranging from 70,000 yen (700 USD) to 150,000 yen (1,500 USD).

References

Aoki-Okabe, M., Kawamura, Y., and Makita, T. (2006). *The study of international cultural relations of postwar Japan.* IDE Discussion Paper. Institute of Developing Economies, Japan External Trade Organization (IDE-JETRO). Available at: http://hdl.handle.net/2344/311

Arts NPO Link. (2006). Art NPO databank 2006. Tokyo: Arts NPO Link.

———. (2017). Art NPO databank 2016–17. Tokyo: Arts NPO Link.

Asahi Shimbun. (2003). Rekihaku geibun sentā kensetsu de ken keizaikokuka wo shisan/Shimane [Shimane Prefecture Estimates Economic Outcomes of Construction of History Museum and Cultural Center]. Asahi Shimbun. 17 September 2003. P32.

Association of Public Halls and Theatres in Japan (Zenkoku Koubunkyō). (2016). *Fundraising handbook.* Tokyo: Zenkoku Koubunkyō.

———. (2017). *Gekijō, ongakudō tō no katsudō jōkyō ni kansuru chōsa hōkokusho* [*Research report on the activities of public halls and theatres in 2017*]. Tokyo: Zenkoku Koubunkyō.

Brookings Bulletin. (1976). Understanding the Japanese 'economic miracle'. *The Brookings Bulletin*, 13(1), pp. 4–7. Available at: www.jstor.org/stable/23780983

Culture Foundation of Shimane Prefecture (CFSP) (2017). Annual report for Heisei 29 (2017). Available at: www.cul-shimane.jp/disclosure/

Economic Planning Agency of Japan (EPAJ). (1994). *Shōwa 31nendo-ban keizai hakusyo* [Economic white paper 1956]. Available at: http://www5.cao.go.jp/keizai3/keizaiwp

Ei, K. and Motosugi, S. (2000). *Chiiki ni ikiru gekijou* [*Theatre that lives with the region*]. Tokyo: Geidankyō Publishing.

Fuji, H. and AAF Network (2012). *Chiiki wo kaeru soft power* [*Soft power that changes the region*]. Tokyo: Seigensha Art Publishing.

Hayashi, Y. (2004). *Shinka suru āto manejiment* [*Revolving art management*]. Tokyo: Reirain Publishing.

Inayama, H. (2003). Chiiki kara no hassō – zaidan houjin chiiki sōzō no jigyou gaiyou ni tsuite [Inspiration from the region: Overview of the programs of JAFRA]. *Arts Policy & Management*, (19). Tokyo: Center for Arts Policy & Management, Mitsubishi UFJ Research and Consulting. Available at: www.murc.jp/_archives/artspolicy/newsletter/no19/19_05.pdf

Ito, M., Okabe, A., Kato, Y., and Niimi, T. (2003). *Āto manejimento* [*Art management*]. Tokyo: Musashino Art University Press.

Ito, Y. (2016). Chapter 19: Art management. In: Japan Association for Cultural Economics, ed., *Bunka Keizaigaku* [*Cultural economics: Trajectory and visions*]. Kyoto: Minerva Shobo.

Ito, Y., Katayama, T., Kobayashi, M., Nakagawa, I., and Yamazaki, T. (2001). *Ātsu manejimento gairon* [*Introduction to arts management*]. 1st ed. Tokyo: Suiyosha Publishing.

Ito, Y., Matsui, K., and Kobayashi, M. eds. (2010). *Kōkyō gekijō no 10 nen* [*The decade of the public theater in Japan*]. Tokyo: Bigaku Shuppan.

Japan Foundation of Regional Art-Activities (JAFRA). (2007). *Shitei kanrisha seido dounyuu jōkyō tou chousa* [*Research on the adaptation of Designated Managers System*]. Tokyo: JAFRA.

———. (2015). *Heisei 26 nen chiiki no kōritsu bunka shisetsu jittai chōsa hōkokusho* [*Report of the current state of municipal cultural facilities in 2015*]. Tokyo: JAFRA.

Japan Fundraising Association. (ed.) (2017). *Giving Japan 2017: The annual report on giving and volunteering for the year 2016*. Tokyo: Japan Fundraising Association.

Kakiuchi, E. and Hayashi, N. (2012). *Ticket wo urikiru gekijou* [*Full-house theatre: Trajectry of Hyogo performing arts center*]. Tokyo: Suiyosha Publishing.

Katayama, M. (2016). *Saison bunka zaidan no chōsen: tanjō kara tsutsumi seiji no shi made* [*Challenges of the Saison Foundation: From its birth to the death of Seiji Tsutsumi*]. Tokyo: Shosekikobo Hayama Publishing.

Kawamura, T. and Ito, S. (2018). *Geijutsu kihon hō no seiritsu to bunka seisaku* [*Establishment of the basic act of culture and arts and cultural policy*]. Tokyo: Suiyosha Publishing.

Kawashima, N. (2010). The importance of the business sector in cultural policy in Japan – a model of complementary relationship with government. In: J.P. Singh, ed., *International cultural policies and power*. Basingstoke: Palgrave Macmillan, pp. 140–151.

Kobayashi, M. (2003). *Koidegō bunka kaikan monogatari* [*A story of Koidego cultural center*]. Tokyo: Suiyosha Publishing.

———. (2014). The paradigm shift in local cultural policy in Japan. In: Lee, H-K. and Lim, L., eds., *Cultural policies in East Asia: Dynamics between the state, arts and creative industries*. Basingstoke: Palgrave Macmillan, pp. 139–152.

———. (2018a). Chapter 5: Jichitai bunka-gyōsei-ron saikō [Reconsidering municipal cultural administration]. In: M. Kobayashi, ed., *Bunka seisaku no genzai 3: Bunka seisaku no tembō* [*Cultural policy studies Vol. 3: Expansion*]. Tokyo: University of Tokyo Press.

———. (2018b). Chapter 10: Shitei kanrisha seido jidai no bunka shinkō zaidan no kadai to tenbou [Challenges and opportunities of cultural foundation in the era of designated manager system]. In: M. Kobayashi, ed., *Bunka seisaku no genzai 2: Kakuchō suru bunka seisaku* [*Cultural policy studies Vol. 2: Domain*]. Tokyo: University of Tokyo Press.

Kobayashi, M. and Katayama, T. (eds.) (2019). *Ātsu manejimento gairon* [*Introduction to arts management*]. 3rd ed. Tokyo: Suiyosha Publishing.

Kobayashi, S. (1994). *Bunka wo sasaeru – Āto manejimento jinzai, zaisei, kikaku* [*Supporting culture: Arts management – human resources, finance and programming*]. Tokyo: Asahi Press.

Kogure, N. (2001). Review of *Ātsu manejimento gairon* [Introduction to arts management], by Yasuo Ito et al. *Journal of Cultural Economics Japan*, 10, 2(3).

Kumakura, S. and The Art Project Research Group. (2015). *An overview of art projects in Japan: A society that co-creates with art*. Tokyo: Arts council Tokyo. Available at: https://tarl.jp/wp/wp-content/uploads/2017/01/tarl_output_38-1.pdf

Ministry of Health, Labor and Welfare (MHLW). (2016). *Chingin kōzō kihon tōkei chōsa* [*Statistics on the basic wage structure*]. Available at: www.mhlw.go.jp/toukei/itiran/roudou/chingin/kouzou/16/01.html.

Ministry of Internal Affairs and Communications (MIC). (2018). Furusato nōzei ni kansuru genjō chōsa kekka [Research results on the current status of the Furusato taxation]. Available at: www.soumu.go.jp/main_sosiki/jichi_zeisei/czaisei/czaisei_seido/furusato/topics/20180706.html

Miyama, Y. (2010). Āto manejimento kyouiku no kadai [Challenges of arts management education]. In: Y. Ito and S. Fujii, eds., *Geijutsu to kankyo* [*Art and environment*]. Tokyo: Ronsosha.

Morioka Foundation for Cultural Activity (MFCA). (2016). Annual report for Heisei 28 (2016). Available at: www.mfca.jp/about/business_report.html

Morishita, S. et al. (2016). *Social Art: Shōgai no aru hito to āto de syakai wo kaeru* [*Social Art: Changing the Society with Arts and Challenged People*]. Tokyo: Gakugei Shuppan Sha.

Mukai, D., Sakamoto, J. and Kaneko, M. (2018). Hashimoto-ryu, Bunraku, Kyōikuni Kyousou Genri; Hojokin minaoshi, kyōsōno yukue-ha [Hashimoto's way to introduce competition for Bunraku and Education: Subsidy overhaul and the fate of competition]. *Asahi Shimbun*. 21 February 2018, p. 32.

Muto, D. (2014). *From Butoh to Kontemporarii Dansu: The Asian perspective*. Presentation at: BUTOH SEASON: International Butoh Conference and Performance.

Nagata Acoustics. (1999). Nagata acoustics news '99(2) (144). Available at: www.nagata.co.jp/news/news9912.htm

Nakao, T. (2019). Chapter 5: Geijutsu bunka to soshiki keiei [Arts, culture and organizational management]. In: M. Kobayashi and T. Katayama, ed., *Ātsu manejimento* [*Introduction to arts management*]. 3rd ed. Tokyo: Suiyosha Publishing.

Neki, A. (2001). *Nihon no bunka seisaku-bunka seisakugaku no kouchiku ni mukete* [*Cultural policy of Japan: Towards establishment of cultural policy studies*]. Tokyo: Keiso Shobo.

Ōhira, M. (1979a). *Shisei hōshin enzetsu* [*Prime ministerial addresses*]. 25 January 1979. Available at: http://worldjpn.grips.ac.jp/documents/indices/pm/index.html

———. (1979b). *Shoshin hyōmei enzetsu* [*General policy speech*]. 3 September 1979. Available at: http://worldjpn.grips.ac.jp/documents/indices/pm/index.html

Sasaki, A. (1994). *Geijutsu keiei-gaku kōza* [*Textbook for arts management course*]. Vol. 1–4. Tokyo: Tokai University Press.

Sasaki, K., Shibata, H., Ito, R., Haneda, T. and Min, J. (2015). *Haikō wo katsuyō shita geijutsu bunka shisetsu niyoru chiiki bunka shinkō no kihon chōsa* [*Basic research on regional cultural development through the cultural centers utilizing abolished schools*]. Sapporo: Kyodo Bunkasha.

Shin, M. (2008). *Āto indasutorī – kyūkyokuno komoditi wo motomete* [*The Art Industry – Searching for Ultimate Commodity*]. Tokyo: Bigaku Shuppan.

Yachita, M. (2016). *Communities, projects, and festivals of the arts: Case studies and trajectories in Japan*. Paper Presentation for the Conference of Cultural Policy at Taiwan National University. Available at: www.academia.edu/30685896/

Yamamori, E. (1999). Hakomono sodai gomi ka sekai isan ka [Public Facilities: Oversized Garbage or World Heritage? *Asahi Shimbun*. 17 July 1999, p. 11.

Yoshimoto, M. (2008). Saikō, bunka seisaku – kakudai suru yakuwari to motomerareru paradaimu shifuto [Reconsidering the expanding role and new paradigm for Japan's cultural policy – from supporting arts and culture, to promoting inspired innovation]. *NLI Research Vol. 51 Autumn 2008*. Tokyo: NLI Research Institute.

———. (2017). Āto NPO no koremade to korekara [Before and Ahead of Arts NPOs]. In: *Art NPO Databank 2016–17*. Tokyo: Arts NPO Link, pp. 7–16.

Yoshizawa, Y. (2018). Chapter 12: Āto NPO no tenkai to jittai [Development and Reality of Art NPOs]. In: M. Kobayashi, ed., *Bunka seisaku no genzai 2: Kakuchō suru bunka seisaku* [*Cultural Policy Studies Vol. 2: Domain*]. Tokyo: University of Tokyo Press.

15

THE ARTS FUNDING DIVIDE

Would 'cultural rights' produce a fairer approach?

Josephine Caust

Introduction

It seems that the funding of arts practice is always a contested domain, whatever political view or system is dominant. In some contexts, for example, there is no government support for the funding of arts practice, while in others there are different interpretations of what this entails. In most forms of government, several sectors of society (agriculture, mining, manufacturing and sport) receive government subsidies. In a capitalist state this is sometimes described as 'welfare capitalism'. However, those opposed to the government funding of arts practice believe the arts should not be included in this framing because they are regarded as 'non-essential' (Bell and Oakley, 2015; Brabham, 2017; Brooks, 2001). Thus, in this framing the arts and cultural sector is not seen as a fundamental component of society and government support of the arts is seen as an indulgence and not a necessity.

Nevertheless, government funding of the arts occurs in many countries – sometimes as direct support and at other times indirect. In some instances, though, the cost involved in accepting government support can be challenging. For instance, in one party or autocratic states, government support is provided if the artist relinquishes the right to their freedom of expression. In the modern democratic state arts funding approaches arguably reflect less state intervention or censorship. However, there may still be a price to pay by the artist for that government support. The relationship between government and the arts is also often experienced as a legal transaction. This can mean that governments relate to the arts through regulations, tax concessions, censorship or even by acts within a nation's constitution. It is this last framing that is of interest here.

In this chapter relationships between government and the arts are explored with a particular emphasis on the issue of 'cultural rights'. This discussion encompasses what is understood by the term, how it might be realised within a national structure, the potential impact of its existence and how it might be applied in contemporary contexts.

Different approaches

It is difficult to get an accurate comparative picture of how much governments around the world spend on the arts because of different models of funding, different models of reporting and different ways of describing what is supported. While there is knowledge about how much one country might give to the arts and cultural sector in direct support, this spending might relate to different areas. For example, it is recorded that in 2013 the US Federal government spent US$6.13 per capita on the arts at a national level (The Statistics Portal, 2018). In the same year in Germany the per capita spending is recorded as around 117 Euros or around US$ 145 per capita and in Sweden 278 Euros or around US$344.93 per capita (Council of Europe, 2017). In Australia the amount spent directly on the arts at both state and federal level by government in the period 2015–16 was recorded as AUD$106.33 per capita or around US$80.17 (MCM, 2017). However, the combined total of all Australian government expenditure on arts and culture in 2015–16 was AUD$243.97 per capita or US$183.95 per capita (MCM, 2017). Thus, the amount nations spend per capita on the arts varies dramatically. But how the spending is framed also varies. There are caveats in doing direct comparisons because, as noted earlier, what is included and not included, may differ.

There are philosophical differences too in how governments approach the funding of the arts. While some countries believe that arts funding is part of a nation's identity and a fundamental government provision, other countries see arts funding as an area that they do reluctantly and with limited funds. Some governments directly fund the arts through a Ministry of Culture and others employ an 'arm's length' approach, such as the 'arts council' model, where funding is seen to be separate from political views/processes. Others believe that funding for the arts should be provided by the private sector through philanthropy, patronage and sponsorship. There are also views that the arts sector should be entirely dependent on the marketplace.

When John Maynard Keynes argued for the establishment of the Arts Council of Great Britain after World War II, he saw it as a necessity so that artists could make their work without the intervention of the state or the market place (Upchurch, 2004). In fact, it is noted that Keynes tried to ensure that governments had no direct role in decision making about arts funding by separating the allocation of money from the government of the day (Hetherington, 2015). This model of arts funding was replicated in other Commonwealth countries, including Canada and Australia. This framing of arts funding was known as 'arm's length' funding and usually involved a peer assessment system where arts funding was determined by a group of artists who were deemed 'peers' of the applicants. The notion of 'arm's length' was seen at the time as an important tenet of western democracy (Hillman – Chartrand and McGaughey, 1989). Cummings and Katz saw government support for the arts in the West as a continuation of a western tradition which 'encouraged the flowering of Western culture' (Cummings and Katz, 1987, p. 3).

In the 1980s the models of government engagement with the arts were described within four different framings. These were Patron, Facilitator, Architect and Engineer (Hillman – Chartrand and McGaughey, 1989). The Patron model is the arts council's model which provides funding at arm's length from government (e.g. the British, Australian and Canadian models). The Facilitator model is where various government 'tools' such as taxation and regulation are enabled to facilitate the donation of money for the arts through donation etc., but without direct engagement by government in the arts practice (the US model). The Architect model is where arts funding occurs through a Ministry of Culture with government bureaucrats tending to make the major funding decisions (the French model). The Engineer model is where arts funding is designed to directly further the ideas of the state and so the intent of the funding is more political rather than artistic (say the Chinese model). All these models of arts funding are imperfect in various ways. The delineation between them has also changed over the past few decades, with most states demonstrating aspects of each model in their approach.

More recently though the impact of a neoliberal ideology has had an effect internationally. It is argued within neoliberalism that every aspect of society is economic and because of this, should be in competition with each other (Monboit, 2016). A government's role in this framing is to stay out of any activity that can be left to market forces. This is an extension of the facilitator model but with further caveats. In this model, the arts should be allowed to flourish or founder as they wish – but without the input of any government money (Cowen, 2000). If the marketplace determines that certain arts practices do not survive, it is argued that this is the natural order of things. Further there is a view that the arts should be in the private domain, not the public domain (Livingstone, 2017).

The funding of arts practice by government has been hotly disputed when religious and political overtones about arts practices are introduced. Some US politicians have argued for example for the total defunding of agencies such as the National Endowment for the Arts because they believe that they support left wing or alternative views that do not reflect what they believe are mainstream American values (Brooks, 2001; Kidd, 2012; Livingstone, 2017). This argument was evident in the United States through the 90s and again more recently (Kidd, 2012; Livingstone, 2017). In 2017 while President Trump recommended zero ongoing funding for the National Endowment for the Arts, both the House and the Senate ignored this and recommended a small budgetary increase. Nevertheless, President Trump has continued to recommend zero funding for the NEA in the 2019 budget (Johnson, 2018). Recent changes in US tax legislation passed in December 2017 are likely to significantly reduce the amount that is donated to charitable organizations, and thereby arts organizations, by American citizens across the country from 2018 (Rooney, 2017). In addition, the tax changes will affect how much corporate organizations are willing to give to get tax breaks (Rooney, 2017). Hence, philanthropy as the backbone of support for arts and cultural activity in the US will be severely undermined. If President Trump were to successfully defund the NEA in 2019, the situation for arts funding in the US is likely to be bleak.

Those that do not support direct arts funding by government are suspicions of the motives of governments that do provide arts funding. For example, they might argue that governments are providing arts funding to support information control or to subsidise arts practice that supports their government's point of view. In one-party governments for instance there is certainly a history of direct government intervention in arts and cultural practice to pursue political objectives (Chong, 2015; Wang, 2014). This has led to some arts practice being framed negatively and others lauded, depending on the way the practice is viewed by the political leaders. In a fascist state such as Nazi Germany books were burnt, pictures destroyed, and artists killed to support the views of those in power (Carey, 2005). Contemporary visual art in particular was seen as 'degenerate' during the Nazi period (Adam, 1992). In autocratic regimes every artistic activity is likely to be subject to some form of direct and indirect censorship, including self-censorship. Scripts are read before production, exhibitions vetted, and artists given official approval before they receive state support. In countries such as Turkey, Ethiopia, Egypt, Iran, Russia and China there have been several cases of individual artists being 'black listed' or even imprisoned because their work is deemed unacceptable to the state (Plipat, 2018). The work of female artists has been particularly targeted for example in the states of Iran, Saudi Arabia, Egypt, India and Pakistan (Plipat, 2018). It is observed in other cases that artists have been generously supported, if they toe the party line (Li, 2014).

The justifications for government funding of the arts in the West has changed much over recent periods of time. For example, Canada is a western democratic state that would be seen to have a relatively generous and benign arts funding system operating at both a national and regional level. Yet it is noted that

> though the peer review process is supposed to be free of government influence, it continues to be shaped by the priorities of the government of the time.
>
> (D'Andrea, 2017, p. 254)

Thus, the modern reality of government funding for the arts might suggest that whatever form of government exists, there is likely to be some form of direct or indirect influence in terms of funding priorities. The government provides the money, so it then expects its own priorities to be reflected in the giving. Governments do not necessarily equate the needs of their citizens with their own political ideologies or preferences. The concept that government money is really taxpayers' money is usually remote from the thinking of a government in power. Peer systems for decisions about arts funding are seen as providing an 'arm's length approach' that distances the giver from the receiver, but even so, there are likely to be restrictions already in place that ensure certain activities can be funded and others not. There are some attempts to change that relationship by distancing the process even more from the government of the day and encouraging policy and decision making from the 'bottom up' rather than the 'top down'. For example, the Croatian cultural network *Clubture* has tried to control funding to its members by creating a separate peer body within the Croatian Ministry of Culture (Višnić and Dragojević, 2008). Nevertheless, there is always likely to be tension between providers of funds and those wanting to use them.

It is well recognised that governments can and do insert their own agenda into the decision-making process (Caust, 2017; D'Andrea, 2017; Feder and Katz-Gerro, 2015). This agenda might be about meeting particular performance outcomes, or it might relate to the integration of particular government priorities in the activities to be funded. Governments expect their financial contribution to achieve 'outcomes' and 'targets' (Mirza, 2006; Protherough and Pick, 2002). Arts practice is there to deliver economic and political outcomes rather than artistic revelations (Belfiore, 2004; Gray, 2007). Holden observed how government intervention in the United Kingdom became entirely instrumental in its expectations of artists and arts organisations during the years of New Labour (Holden, 2004). In an 'instrumental' framing, arts as an independent activity has no value, unless it is contributing to the needs of the state or the funder.

Further while direct intervention is unusual in an arts council model, it does occur. In the Canadian example it is recorded that governments interfered in the arts decision process in 1979, 1984 and 1992 (D'Andrea, 2017). In Australia, which has a similar arts funding model to Canada, direct government intervention in arts funding decisions occurred as recently as 2015 (Caust, 2017). Usually direct intervention is connected with a change in political priorities, usually heralded by a change in government, but indirect intervention exists, as already noted in relation to economic, political and social priorities (Bertelli et al., 2014; Caust, 2003; D'Andrea, 2017).

What is funded?

In most national contexts the funding of large arts institutions is favoured over the funding of say community arts or individual artists. In addition, heritage arts practices are usually preferred over contemporary or newer arts practices. In the case of western democracies for example, which have had a long history of arts funding, such as the United Kingdom, Australia or Canada, the major proportion of funding generally goes to support heritage arts practices and very little proportionately is given to contemporary arts practice (Bertelli et al., 2014; Feder and Katz-Gerro, 2015; Getzner, 2015). This pattern is replicated in European countries such as Germany and France which have been traditionally generous in arts funding support. It seems that in all government arts financing models, in whichever way it is delivered (see the discussion earlier re the Hillman Chartrand models) most of the money goes to the arts heritage area and what might be regarded as the 'high' arts (Harvie, 2015).

There are issues around always seeing the arts in a hierarchical model. This then privileges the 'high' arts and frames arts practice as always engaged in a movement towards reaching a pinnacle exemplified by the 'high' arts. It is argued that this framing fails to understand the basis of much contemporary or newer arts practice which is not driven by a desire to be part of an institutional framing or desirous of being accepted and lauded by an élite cognoscenti (Eltham and Verhoeven, 2015; Sparrow, 2015). The preferencing of heritage and the high arts seems to be also related to definitions of 'art' and the lack of recognition about the value or importance of arts practices in peoples' daily lives.

An Australian survey published in 2017 observed that the arts play a role in the lives of 98% of the Australian population (Australia Council, 2017). That is, the majority of Australians from all walks of life – different ages, genders, cultures and backgrounds – say they participate and engage with the arts on some level (Australia Council, 2017). Thus, from this evidence it can be concluded that arts practice has general acceptance and support amongst the Australian population. The cultural economist David Throsby argues further that there is bi-partisan political support for funding arts practice in Australia, if the funding support refers only to the major national arts or cultural institutions (Throsby, 2018). In other words, both sides of the political fence support the funding of the major cultural institutions. It is other aspects of arts practice, such as contemporary or community arts, that demonstrate differences in the political approach, particularly, say, when notions of 'excellence' are introduced. For instance, conservatives might see the term 'excellence' as reflecting size and hierarchical position whereas those in the middle and on the left might see 'excellence' as reflective of any good arts practice wherever it originates (Eltham and Verhoeven, 2015). Thus, the term 'excellence' refers to the values of the user and not to something that is objective or fixed.

Nevertheless, it is also recorded in Australia that there has been an increase in ambivalence towards public funding of the arts. In 2013 around 13% of the Australian population were negative or ambivalent about public funding of the arts but this increased to 25% by 2016 (Australia Council, 2017). This changing perception is seen as possibly reflecting a particular framing of the 'arts' – that is, if the arts are interpreted only as the 'high' arts. Funding of the arts is seen then as rewarding élite arts practices. While it is evident that arts practice is generally embraced by the majority of the population, the 'high' arts are not necessarily understood as the kind of arts practice that the majority support (Australia Council, 2017). If this is the case, there may be a need for further work around how the 'arts' are defined, as well as more consideration of skewed funding patterns versus broader popular cultural preferences.

Another issue related to the distribution of arts funding is the lack of perceived equity in terms of class, ethnicity and region. For example, it has been noted that the challenges in making a living as an artist is compounded if the artists are new immigrants (Grant and Buckwold, 2013). This might mean that regions where new immigrants are living are likely to be less equipped with cultural facilities and other cultural resources, including the provision of arts funding. In a recent study undertaken by this researcher with others in the West of Sydney it was noted that there was a feeling of frustration and disappointment about the current lack of cultural facilities in the Greater West Sydney region (Stevenson et al., 2017). The Greater West houses more than 50% of the population of Sydney (which is currently about 4 million), but most of the present cultural facilities are located in the east or the north of the city. It is recorded for instance that in 2014 while the Greater West Sydney region's population represents 30% of the state of NSW, it received only 5.5% of cultural funding allocated by the NSW Government (Psychogios and Artup, 2015). Further while housing 9.5% of the nation's population, the region received only 1% of Federal arts funding (Psychogios and Artup, 2015). A visual artist noted,

> the equity between how much funding the galleries and the institutions in Sydney get as opposed to Western Sydney – there's quite a huge gap. A huge divide.
>
> *(Stevenson et al., 2017, p. 12)*

In a response to the challenges present in the West of Sydney, activities are developing that are trying to address cultural, social and economic differences. One, which is designed particularly for women and children, is a bookstore founded in 2013 in Fairfield called *Lost in Books*. It stocks adults and children's books that are written in many different languages to reflect the diverse community that lives in the region. It also hosts artist in residency programmes that encourage activity that reflects other cultures and is hosting a festival that coincides with the UNESCO International Day of Mother Language to celebrate different languages within the community.

> Lost in Books is a social enterprise structured around a principle of accessibility – a place for people to access books in their own language "without feeling shamed, without having money to spend.
>
> *(Convery, 2018)*

However overall the challenges of Western Sydney (and other residential areas that are economically, socially and culturally deprived) demonstrate that social and political equity have not been comprehensively addressed in terms of arts funding distribution. Lack of access and provision of arts and cultural facilities does not allow large communities of people to express their arts practice or practice their culture in any meaningful way. This inequity in terms of funding and resources may relate to several issues. This may include artform, class, ethnicity and place of residence but it particularly seems to reflect economic differences. For example, it can be argued that at present the ratios of arts funding rewards the 'rich'. Yet the 'rich' are already privileged in terms of access to cultural facilities as well as in their economic capacity to participate. This is perhaps where the imbalance in arts funding, and the privileging of some sectors over others, is problematic, as it is clearly not democratic, equal or just. It is for this reason that it is important to consider how the introduction of the concept of 'cultural rights' might change how governments and communities address these issues.

What are cultural rights?

There has only been recent recognition that citizens of a country should have 'cultural' rights as much as they should have political or social rights (UNESCO, 2005). Cultural rights in this context are seen as basic human rights.

> Cultural rights comprise an aspect of human rights in that they are universal in character and guarantee all persons the right to access their culture.
>
> *(Barth, 2008, p. 79)*

Cultural rights can be a broad framing, but they do include the notion that all citizens should have access to and be able to participate in various forms of artistic and cultural practice of their choosing. It is also an acknowledgement that a community may have distinctive cultural practices based on cultural beliefs and traditions that define their community. Thus, ignoring or disregarding these practices potentially destroys the framework of that community. Further there is recognition that the protection of cultural rights is an important public interest issue which is in the long-term interest of humanity (Francioni, 2008). This is described also as an affirmation of one's own identity and need for autonomy (Barth, 2008, p. 80). It is noted within the theme of Cultural Rights and Ethics in the *Compendium of Cultural Policies and Trends in Europe*, a web-based information and monitoring site, that cultural rights are seen as part of civil rights relating mainly to:

- freedom of expression;
- right to and responsibility for cultural heritage;
- right to free practice of art and culture and to creative work;
- right to protect the intellectual and material benefits accruing from scientific, literary and artistic production;
- right to participate in cultural life and right to equally accessible and available cultural, library and information and leisure services;
- right to choose one's own culture;
- right to the development and protection of culture;
- respect for culture and its autonomy and for cultural identity (Johnson ed., 2018).

At the international level, there have been three important conventions passed by the UNESCO to protect cultural practices and heritage. These are the:

- Convention concerning the Protection of the World Cultural and Natural Heritage (UNESCO, 1972)
- Convention for the Safeguarding of the Intangible Cultural Heritage (2003)
- Convention on the Protection and Promotion of the Diversity of Cultural Expression (2005)

In 2001 UNESCO passed its Universal Declaration on Cultural Diversity (UNESCO website). This declared that all peoples had the right to experience and practice their own cultures. In the 2003 Convention it was observed that intangible cultural heritage was 'a mainspring of cultural diversity' defining it as,

> means the practices, representations, expressions, knowledge, skills – as well as the instruments, objects, artefacts and cultural spaces associated therewith – that communities, groups and, in some cases, individuals recognize as part of their cultural heritage.
> *(UNESCO Article 2, 2003)*

Further the 2005 UNESCO Convention recorded that cultural diversity is in the long-term interests of humanity and notes that achieving cultural diversity and the affirmation of cultural rights depends on freedom of expression being allowed and encouraged. Principle 1 of the Convention states,

> Cultural diversity can be protected and promoted only if human rights and fundamental freedoms, such as freedom of expression, information and communication, as well as the ability of individuals to choose cultural expressions, are guaranteed. No one may invoke the provisions of this Convention in order to infringe human rights and fundamental freedoms as enshrined in the Universal Declaration of Human Rights or guaranteed by international law, or to limit the scope thereof.
> *(UNESCO Article 2, 2005)*

This recognition that cultural diversity and by direct association, cultural rights, are dependent on the recognition and guarantee of human rights, is critical to seeing what is required legally to ensure that these principles are applied. Further within the UNESCO convention is the recognition that to enable the enactment of cultural diversity requires equal access. Principle 7 notes therefore,

Equitable access to a rich and diversified range of cultural expressions from all over the world and access of cultures to the means of expressions and dissemination constitute important elements for enhancing cultural diversity and encouraging mutual understanding.

(UNESCO Article 2, 2005)

Thus, unless a nation-state or nations combined, provide and allow equity of access, then the capacity to experience cultural diversity or express one's cultural rights is not possible. So, this suggests that legal intervention is necessary for cultural rights to be enacted. It is becoming recognised too that cultural rights are a basic human right that are critical if a society is to function in a free, just and democratic mode (Portolés and Šešić, 2017). This means that nations need to address constitutional issues that embrace human rights to allow for cultural rights. As Wang notes,

governments have a role to play in ensuring the production and circulation of a diversity of cultural products reflecting the different values and meanings comprising the makeup of civil society.

(Wang, 2014, p. 26)

This recognition has been embraced by the international organization United Cities and Local Governments (UCLG), a global network of cities, local and regional governments. Their Agenda 21 for Culture has 67 articles, divided into three sections: principles, undertakings, and recommendations (Agenda 21, 2008). The "Principles" include core values such as cultural diversity and human rights and culture itself is described as an essential part of constructing citizenship for people of all ages. The intent of this document and program is to embed principles for cultural development at the local level. This can be seen as a grassroots movement that may influence policies and programmes at the state and national level. It is noted in Agenda 21 that,

Cultural rights are an integral part of human rights. 'No one may invoke cultural diversity to infringe upon the human rights guaranteed by international law, nor to limit their scope.'

(Agenda 21, 2008, p. 5)

It is recorded on the UCLG website that by 2015 internationally over 500 local governments and regions had committed themselves to undertaking Agenda 21 for Culture in their locality.

In addition, some nations have also started this process. In Taiwan for example there has been an embrace by government of the need for a citizen's cultural rights (Hsin-Tien, 2015; Wang, 2014). When Taiwan had a national election in 2012, all the major parties addressed the need for cultural rights (Hsin-Tien, 2015). This has been an affirmation too of human rights. An important tenet of the approach in Taiwan is the recognition that governments should not be determining the kind of culture the community wants, but it should be an issue that is determined by the broader community. Taiwan has long had issues around cultural identity given its colonisation by Japan in the first part of the 20th century and its difficult ongoing relationship with mainland China. Hence Taiwanese identity has been a volatile and contested space over many years. The recognition of a citizen's cultural rights became a grassroots populist movement from the early 2000s. Power sharing with the community at large is a complicated mission for any governmentality and Taiwan is still challenged by many of the issues around this, but nevertheless there has been much progress in acknowledging and reflecting the cultural rights of its citizens (Hsin-Tien, 2015).

Other nations have embedded cultural rights in their approach to cultural policy for many years. For example, it is noted that Sweden's

> national cultural policy formulated in 1974 and reviewed in 1996 combine elements from several international human and cultural rights conventions. These aims also underpin the central cultural administration and the allocation of state subsidies.
>
> *(Koivunen and Marsio, 2007, p. 6)*

Thus, Sweden has been allocating arts funding on the basis of cultural rights for many years. In 1999 Finland also embedded cultural rights into its constitution, referencing values such as 'equality, liberty, freedom of expression, freedom of religion and right to education' (Koivunen and Marsio, 2007, p. 6). Nevertheless, both countries have been challenged by definitions relating to culture and cultural identity as an outcome of the growth of nationalism. In the case of Sweden for example, traditional folk heritage, once the domain of the political left, has become a field for demonstrating 'Swedishness' by the nationalist right (Kaminsky, 2012).

Governments certainly have an obligation to ensure that their citizens are treated fairly and equitably. In addition, modern societies are complex, multi-layered and diverse. There is not a homogeneity of culture or monoculture that may have been evident or perceived within some nation states 100 years ago. Migration is now a reality for all countries, and this has ensured that many different cultural communities exist alongside each other. To assert therefore that there is a *homogenous* national culture is likely to be naïve, possibly élitist or reflects a nationalist/populist agenda. As new migrants bring different cultures and practices with them, there is a necessity to recognise that a cultural diversity exists. This diversity then needs to be acknowledged, celebrated and reflected in national approaches to culture and the arts. Schafer (2015) argues that 'culture' is the missing link to deal with the present complexity of our world. Thus, recognising a citizen's cultural rights is an acknowledgement of the importance of culture for our future.

How can cultural rights be applied – the Australian case?

When considering cultural rights in the context of western democracies there are several issues that arise. On an international level it can be argued that many western democracies are already in a privileged position economically. However, it is also true that within every nation-state there are significant gaps between the sectors of the population that are privileged and economically successful and most of the population who are likely to be less advantaged. As noted already in the Western Sydney example, whole sectors of a community can be disadvantaged, although it might seem that the country itself is prosperous. This ongoing social and economic inequity brings many outcomes that are not positive. While the introduction of cultural rights might seem a utopian concept, it does enshrine legally the importance of access to artistic and cultural expression for everyone. If cultural rights are a basic human right, they then cannot be ignored or treated as non-essential. In fact, it can be argued that they would then be seen as part of the human condition and resourced adequately.

In the case of Australia there are challenges for including 'cultural rights' in the constitution. Australia's constitution does not include a Bill of Rights as the United States does for example (see Australian Federal Register of Legislation). It should be noted though that the

American Bill of Rights while allowing for 'freedom of expression' does not refer to cultural rights (see The US Bill of Rights). The Australian Constitution focuses primarily on the structural arrangements between the Federal body and the states bodies, in terms of jurisdictions and decision-making responsibilities, as well as the powers of parliament. There is no mention of human rights within that document. However, there are Parliamentary Acts that cover aspects of human rights such as the Racial Discrimination Act of 1975. Through various Acts of Parliament, fairer and more equitable policies and legislation have been introduced over time that clarify the rights and responsibilities of Australian citizens.

In addition, there is the Australian Human Rights Commission which is a government statutory authority that reports to Parliament through the Attorney General (see Australian Human Rights Commission website). It was established on the 10th December 1986 (International Human Rights Day) and is there to support and review human rights in all aspects of Australian law and practice. The Australian Human Rights Commission notes that while there is no Bill of Rights in Australia, the Australian Government has agreed to uphold and respect many of the United Nations' human rights treaties including the:

- International Covenant on Civil and Political Rights
- International Covenant on Economic, Social and Cultural Rights
- Convention on the Elimination of All Forms of Racial Discrimination
- Convention on the Elimination of All Forms of Discrimination against Women
- Convention Against Torture and Other Cruel, Inhuman or Degrading Treatment or Punishment
- Convention on the Rights of the Child
- Convention on the Rights of Persons with Disabilities

(Australian Human Rights Commission, 2018)

While it is acknowledged here that the Australian government has agreed to 'uphold' these conventions, there are many instances where Australian law is 'lagging behind' in terms of practice. In early 2017 for example there was a concerted attempt in the Australian Parliament by the government to modify the Racial Discrimination Act so that terms such as 'insult', 'offend' and 'humiliate' were replaced by the simple term of 'harass' in section 18C of the Act (McGhee, 2017). While the motion was defeated, the action demonstrates the vulnerabilities around human rights in the current legislation. In fact, the Australian Human Rights Commission argues that Australia should adopt a national human rights law (commonly called a charter of rights) as a means of addressing the anomalies and gaps that presently exist in the Australian Constitution and Acts of Parliament (Branson, 2010). The Commission notes further that at present Australia is the only Western democratic country that does not have a Bill or Charter of Rights. The Commission argues that if Australia had a Human Rights Act it would significantly improve the protection of human rights in Australia. An example they cite is that, 'it would make public servants consider human rights when making decisions and delivering services' (The Australian Human Rights Commission website). In addition, the Australian Human Rights Commission has produced a publication called the "Rights to Enjoy and Benefit from Culture" which outlines why cultural rights are an important aspect of human rights (see Australian Human Rights Commission website). However, as with many other aspects of human rights, the implementation of cultural rights as set out in the Commission document, is yet to be acted upon by the Government. If there was an Australian Bill or Charter of Rights that included cultural rights, then the enforcement of cultural rights would be more likely. Further there would be the capacity to enforce greater equity in the distribution of arts funding, as well as the provision of cultural facilities currently provided by governments at all levels. While it is recognised that there are never any perfect answers for ensuring equity and fairness, the presence of a constitutional intervention might provide a greater incentive.

Final comments

It is evident that while many countries provide funding for the arts and support the construction of cultural facilities, the rationale, methods and distribution of this funding is usually based on historical precedence rather than social, economic or cultural equity. This means that the way arts funding is distributed does not reflect necessarily the best or most interesting arts practice, nor does it reflect population demographics, or economic and cultural needs. Instead it reflects a hierarchical approach based on several criteria such as government priorities, institutional framings and privileged cultural preferences. A legal intervention that might be effective in changing this approach is the introduction of a citizen's cultural rights.

Cultural rights are part of a larger framework of human rights that should be available to all citizens in the world. While there is much greater economic prosperity in the world than say, 50 years previously, there are also major inequities in the way that prosperity is distributed. This inequity is reflected both between different nations and within nations. UNESCO and other national and international bodies have recognised that cultural rights are a significant human rights issue. It is important that individual countries take on this issue within their own constitutions or alternatively through their Bill of Rights, if we are to see future global change. If this occurs, then it is likely that we could see a fairer approach to arts funding because it would be embedded within a 'citizen's cultural rights' in a national constitution, rather than reflect sectional or ideological interests.

While some countries such as Sweden, Finland and Taiwan have made progress towards the acknowledgement of a citizen's cultural rights, many have not. In the case of Australia there is, as yet, no Bill of Rights for its citizens, so the issue of cultural rights is not high on the national agenda. But there is plenty of evidence that the current approach to arts funding and provision of cultural facilities is out of date and does not reflect the artistic, economic and cultural needs of its population.

Recognition and discussion of this issue has been limited globally, and when occurring, has usually related to cultural identity. If the issue of cultural rights was embraced more broadly, then it is possible that the huge disparities that we see in terms of arts funding distribution and access to arts facilities and practice might change. If a citizen's cultural rights were embedded in a country's constitution, then it is more likely that governments and political parties would take notice. It is also likely that a fairer or more equitable distribution of arts funds could occur, because it would be a legal and human rights issue, rather than an issue related to artistic preference or political ideology.

References

Adam, P. (1992). *Art of the third Reich*. New York: Harry N. Abrams.

Agenda 21 for Culture (2008). *Committee on culture – United Cities and Local Governments – UCLG*. Available at: www.agenda21culture.net

Australia Council (2017). *Connecting Australians: Results of the national arts participation survey*, 27 June 2017. Available at: www.australiacouncil.gov.au/research/connecting-australians/

Australian Human Rights Commission. (2018). *Rights to enjoy and benefit from culture*. Available at: www.humanrights.gov.au/rights-enjoy-and-benefit-culture

Barth, K.W. (2008). Cultural rights: A necessary corrective to the nation state. In: F. Francioni and M. Scheinin, eds., *Cultural human rights international studies in human rights*. Leiden: Martinus Nijhoff Publishers, pp. 79–90.

Belfiore, E. (2004). Auditing culture: The subsidised cultural sector in the New Public Management. *The International Journal of Cultural Policy*, 10(2) July 2004, pp. 183–202.

Bell, D. and Oakley, K. (2015). *Cultural Policy*. Oxfordshire: Routledge.

Bertelli, A.M., Connolly, J.M., Mason, D.P., and Conover, L.C. (2014). Politics, management, and the allocation of arts funding: Evidence from public support for the arts in the UK. *International Journal of Cultural Policy*, 20(3), pp. 341–359.

Brabham, D.C. (2017). How crowdfunding discourse threatens public arts. *New Media & Society*, 19(7), pp. 983–999.

Branson, C. (2010). *Media release: Important steps to better protect human rights but substantial gaps remain.* Australian Human Rights Commission, Wednesday 21 April 2010. Available at: www.humanrights. gov.au/news/media-releases/2010-media-release-important-steps-better-protect-human-rights-substantial-gaps

Brooks, A.C. (2001). Who opposes government arts funding? *Public Choice*, 108, pp. 355–367.

Carey, J. (2005). *What good are the arts?* London: Faber and Faber.

Caust, J. (2003). Putting the arts back into arts policy making: How arts policy has been 'captured' by the economists and marketers. *International Journal of Cultural Policy*, 9(1), pp. 51–63.

———. (2017). The continuing saga around arts funding and the cultural wars in Australia. *International Journal of Cultural Policy*. Available at: http://dx.doi.org/10.1080/10286632.2017.1353604

Chong, T. (2015). Deviance and nation building. In: J. Caust, ed., *Arts and cultural leadership in Asia*. Routledge advance in Asia Pacific Studies series. Abingdon: Routledge, pp. 15–25.

Convery, S. (2018). The many tongues of Lost in Books, the only bookstore in Fairfield. *The Guardian*, 22 February 2018. Available at: www.theguardian.com/books/2018/feb/22/the-many-tongues-of-lost-in-books-the-only-bookstore-in-fairfield

Council of Europe (2017). Monitoring public cultural expenditure in selected European countries 2000–2013. *Compendium: Cultural policies and trends in Europe*. Available at: www.culturalpolicies.net/web/statistics-funding.php?aid=232&cid=80&lid=en

Cowen, T. (2000). *In Praise of Commercial Culture*. MA: Cambridge, Harvard University Press.

Cummings, M.L. Jr. and Katz, R.S. (eds.) (1987). *The Patron state*. New York: Oxford University Press.

D'Andrea, M.J. (2017). Symbolic power: Impact of government priorities for arts funding in Canada. *The Journal of Arts Management, Law, and Society*, 47(4), pp. 245–258.

Eltham, B. and Verhoeven, D. (2015). Philosophy vs evidence is no way to orchestrate cultural policy. *The Conversation*, 29 May 2015. Available at: https://theconversation.com/philosophy-vs-evidence-is-no-way-to-orchestrate-cultural-policy-42487

Feder, T. and Katz-Gerro, T. (2015). The cultural hierarchy in funding: Government funding of the performing arts based on ethnic and geographic distinctions. *Poetics*, 49, pp. 76–95.

Federal Register of Legislation /Australian Constitution. Available at: www.legislation.gov.au/Details/C2013Q00005

Francioni, F. (2008). Culture heritage and human rights: An introduction. In: F. Francioni and M. Scheinin, eds., *Cultural human rights international studies in human rights*. Leiden: Martinus Nijhoff Publishers, pp. 1–15.

Getzner, M. (2015). Cultural politics: Exploring determinants of cultural expenditure. *Poetics*, 49, pp. 60–75.

Grant, J.L. and Buckwold, B. (2013). Precarious creativity: Immigrant cultural workers. *Cambridge Journal of Regions, Economy and Society*, 6, pp. 113–126.

Gray, C. (2007). Commodification and instrumentality in cultural policy. *International Journal of Cultural Policy*, 13(2), pp. 203–215.

Harvie, J. (2015). Funding, philanthropy, structural inequality and decline in England's theatre ecology. *Cultural Trends*, 24(1), pp. 56–61.

Hetherington, S. (2015). Arm's-length funding of the arts as an expression of Laissez-faire. *International Journal of Cultural Policy*, 3(4), pp. 482–494.

Hillman-Chartrand, H. and McGaughey, C. (1989). The arm's-length principle and the arts: An international perspective. In: M. Cummings and M. Schuster, eds., *Who is to pay? The International search for models of support for the arts*. New York: American Council for the Arts, pp. 43–77.

Holden, J. (2004). *Capturing Cultural Value: How culture has become a tool of government policy*. London: Demos.

Hsin-Tien, L. (2015). Interlocution and engagement: Cultural policy sphere and culture policy in Taiwan. In: J. Caust, ed., *Arts and cultural leadership in Asia*. Routledge Advance in Asia Pacific Studies Series. Abingdon: Routledge, pp. 48–58.

Johnson, H. (ed.) (2018). *Compendium of cultural policies and trends in Europe*. The Netherlands: Boekman Foundation. Available at: www.culturalpolicies.net/web/index.php

Johnson, T. (ed.) (2018). Arts advocates optimistic about NEA funding despite Trump's call for cuts. *Variety*, 14 March 2018. Available at: http://variety.com/2018/biz/news/national-endowment-for-the-arts-funding-trump-cuts-advocates-optimistic-1202725613/

Kaminsky, D. (2012). Keeping Sweden Swedish: Folk music, right-wing nationalism, and the immigration debate. *Journal of Folklore Research*, 49(1), 2012.

Kidd, D. (2012). Public culture in America: A review of cultural policy debates. *The Journal of Arts Management, Law, and Society*, 42, pp. 11–21.

Koivunen, H. and Marsio, L. (2007). *Fair culture? Ethical dimension of cultural policy and cultural rights*. Ministry of Education Finland. Available at: www.culturalpolicies.net/web/files/47/en/FairCulture.pdf

Li, Z. (2014). China sets up $70 million national arts fund, but what will it promote? *ArtNetNews*, 21 November 2014. Available at: https://news.artnet.com/art-world/china-sets-up-70-million-national-arts-fund-but-what-will-it-promote-176276

Livingstone, J. (2017). Why are Americans so hostile to state-funded art? *The New Republic*, 26 May 2017. Available at: https://newrepublic.com/article/142925/americans-hostile-state-funded-art

McGhee, A. (2017). 18C: Proposed changes to racial discrimination act defeated in senate. *ABC News*, 31 March 2017. Available at: www.abc.net.au/news/2017-03-30/18c-racial-discrimination-act-changes-defeated-in-senate/8402792

MCM Working Group. (2017). *Cultural Funding by Government 2015–16 Report*, Prepared by a consultant from the Australian Bureau of Statistics on behalf of the Meeting of Cultural Ministers July 2017, Commonwealth of Australia 2017.

Mirza, M. (ed.) (2006). *Culture vultures Is UK arts policy damaging the arts?* London: Policy Exchange.

Monboit, G. (2016). Neoliberalism – the ideology at the root of all our problems. *The Guardian*, Friday 15 April 2016. Available at: www.theguardian.com/books/2016/apr/15/neoliberalism-ideology-problem-george-monbiot

Rooney, P. (2017). The pall that the tax law is casting over charities. *The Conversation*, 21 December 2017. Available at: http://theconversation.com/the-pall-that-the-tax-law-is-casting-over-charities-89440

Schafer, D.P. (2015). *The secrets of culture*. Oakville, Canada: Rock's Mill Press.

Stevenson, D., Rowe, D., Caust, J., and Cmielewski, C. (2017). *Recalibrating Culture: Production, Consumption, Policy*. Institute for Culture and Society, Western Sydney University, Sydney.

Sparrow, J. (2015). Captain's call and cultures wars: The future of Australian Arts. *The Guardian Australia*, 28 May 2015. Available at: https://www.theguardian.com/commentisfree/2015/may/28/captains-calls-and-culture-war-the-future-of-australian-arts

Throsby, D. (2018). *Platform papers 55: Art, politics, money: Revisiting Australia's cultural policy*. Sydney: Currency House, New South Books.

Plipat, S. (2018). *The state of artistic freedom 2018*. Freemuse. Available at: https://freemuse.org/wp-content/uploads/2018/05/Freemuse-The-state-of-artistic-freedom-2018-online-version.pdf

Portolés, J.B. and Šešić, M.D. (2017). Cultural rights and their contribution to sustainable development: Implications for cultural policy. *International Journal of Cultural Policy*, 23(2), pp. 59–173.

Protherough, R. and Pick, J. (2002). *Managing Britannia: Culture and management in modern Britain*. Harleston: Edgeways.

Psychogios, T. and Artup, B. (2015). *Building Western Sydney's cultural arts economy – a key to Sydney's success*. Deloitte: Sydney.

The US Bill of Rights. 2018. Available at: www.constitutionfacts.com/us-constitution-amendments/bill-of-rights/ *The Statistics Portal*. Available at: www.statista.com/statistics/192454/arts-and-culture-us-federal-spending-per-capita-since-2002/

UNESCO. (1972). The general conference of the United Nations Educational, Scientific and Cultural Organization meeting in Paris from 17 October to 21 November 1972. Available at: https://whc.unesco.org/en/convention/

UNESCO. (2003). UNESCO Convention for the Safeguarding of the Intangible Cultural Heritage, Paris, 17 October 2003. Available at: UNESCO, UNESCO Convention on the Protection and Promotion of the Diversity of Cultural Expressions Paris, 20 October 2005. Available at: http://portal.unesco.org/en/ev.php

UNESCO. Available at: www.unesco.org/new/en/culture/themes/culture-and-development/the-future-we-want-the-role-of-culture/culture-and-human-rights/

Upchurch, A. (2004). John Maynard Keynes, the Bloomsbury group and the origins of the arts council movement. *International Journal of Cultural Policy*, 10(2), pp. 203–218.

Višnić, E. with a contribution by Dragojević, S. (2008). *A bottom up approach to cultural policy making Clubture Zagreb*. Available at: http://clubture.org/izdavastvo/a-bottom-up-approach-to-cultural-policy-making

Wang, L.-J. (2014). Cultural rights and citizenship in cultural policy: Taiwan and China. *International Journal of Cultural Policy*, 20(1), pp. 21–39.

16

MANAGING CULTURAL ACTIVISM

A case study of Buku Jalanan of Malaysia

Sunitha Janamohanan

Introduction

Every fortnight in a public park in a suburban Malaysian neighbourhood about 25 km outside of the capital city of Kuala Lumpur, a mat with books is laid out, art materials for children stationed nearby in plastic containers, and a group of young men and women in their early twenties settle down to talk, swap stories, and engage with anyone interested in stopping by. A plastic banner is unfurled and posted next to them: Buku Jalanan Shah Alam (Street Books, Shah Alam) – the pop-up free 'library' that has become a nationwide phenomenon with chapters throughout the country. Reading is optional.

Buku Jalanan,[1] which literally translates as 'Street Books' was founded in 2011 by Zikri Rahman, together with Azrie Ahmad and Mohammad Idham, when they were students at the Universiti Teknologi Mara (UiTM), a large public university in the city of Shah Alam,[2] Selangor, Malaysia. Conceived as a free, outdoor library, by a group of friends simultaneously interested in engaging with intellectually challenging ideas as well as in community service, Buku Jalanan has taken on the characteristics of a youth movement, inspiring lookalike chapters across the country, as well in countries as far afield as France and China. The Shah Alam Buku Jalanan was the first and longest running initiative and consists of about 15 members. They self-identify as a collective and have no formal organizational status yet have managed to not only survive for over seven years but have also continuously inspired others to launch similar initiatives, extending a reach and ideology that seems unhampered by institutional constraints of either a physical or organizational nature.

The pop-up library acts as both symbol and medium/conduit for cultural activity and, in fact, forms of activism. The members of Buku Jalanan Shah Alam are not practicing artists, and most do not come from any kind of art or creative background, and what they do does not fit neatly into an immediately recognized category of art making or production. There is, in fact, very little to no 'art' being made in this case, in the sense of tangible or performative outputs that conform to conventional and formalistic definitions of art. The realm of art in this context is instead taken to encompass a broad range of cultural expressions and grassroots action and civic engagement.

How and in what exact form the original Buku Jalanan has functioned, and indeed, seemingly thrived, is the main focus of this chapter. As shall be shown, the collective is not completely unique in the cultural landscape of Malaysia, but is, in fact, part of a rising trend of socially engaged practice in the country and which shares characteristics with others in the region of Southeast Asia. However, its rise and longevity in Malaysia is remarkable given its particular circumstances, which merits further study. The looseness of its organizational structure and behavior will be analyzed with reference to management theory and also against a rising global trend of cultural activism and socially engaged arts and cultural activity. The case study is necessarily situated within the socio-political landscape of Malaysia and also within a particular time period of about ten years, from the late noughties till the present, 2018. The point of temporality is mentioned here for two reasons: first, insofar as it relates to specific moments in time that affect the social and political realities in the country; and, second, in relation to the question of organizational sustainability over time.

The investigation of Buku Jalanan is done in three parts. The first looks at its purpose or mission with an overview of the inception of Buku Jalanan and attempts to identify the factors that drive its members to volunteer their time and energy to this endeavor. This author takes the view of Buku Jalanan as a collective of cultural agents (Sommer, 2006) and will offer a range of perspectives by which to contextualize the nature of their work. Part two looks at how they organize and the functional roles of its members, where an attempt shall be made to construct an understanding of the collective as an activism-led and horizontally organized group. The data on Buku Jalanan is compiled from several sources: media reports, printed materials provided by Buku Jalanan, published articles, a personal interview with three members, and a number of exchanges with Zikri Rahman over the course of 2017 through activities of a network of community-engaged arts practitioners administered by myself and researcher and arts education specialist Janet Pillai.[3] Lastly, the question of sustainability that is often central to so many arts groups will be tackled, and it will be argued that the notion of sustainability is both complicated and potentially resolved by the specific nature of the structure and purpose of Buku Jalanan.

Buku jalanan: from idea to movement

Buku Jalanan, as initiated by Zikri Rahman, Azrie Ahmad and Mohammad Idham, was an outdoor pop-up library that in 2011 started appearing in a local park by a lake on a Saturday evening every two weeks. The rules were simple: anyone could borrow books, with no identification required and no penalties for anyone who failed to return a book. The reading matter was equally egalitarian: any kind of reading matter – it could be literary fiction, pulp fiction, historical texts and nonfiction, popular magazines or anything anyone wanted to contribute. The collection began with members' own personal books, but gradually came to grow and include more and more diverse contributions. Costing very little to execute, the impedimenta required are mats for laying on the grass, books, arts materials for children to draw with, and banners with their name, Buku Jalanan. At 5 pm as the sun starts to descend and the often stifling equatorial heat abates, books are neatly laid out on the ground and Buku Jalanan members settle down for the next two hours. Children are enticed by the drawing materials and the '*conteng-conteng*' (scribbling) activity is a fun way to engage young parents, while making their temporary occupation of their corner of the park more visible and expanding their use of public space.

Buku Jalanan Shah Alam (henceforth referred to as BJSA) was the first and founding chapter, and Zikri Rahman has been its most visible spokesperson and advocate. He is also one of the most explicit and articulate in his views on society and politics and the need to reclaim public spaces and to create alternative and necessary spaces for discourse. Zikri[4] describes their founding thus:

> We would like to raise awareness and create alternatives for discourse. Books and the act of reading can be seen as neutral, but to see a group of students converge and take

part in different activities and sharing sessions within the realms of books, arts, culture and activism helps us to fill the void within university discourse and reimagine what we can do together . . . it is our desire to allow the culture of discourse and most importantly, the culture of dissent, to take place within our community.

(2017, pp. 51–53)

The void that Zikri describes is the result of specific controls and restrictions imposed on public life in Malaysia. At the time of Buku Jalanan's founding and until the time this article was written, university students have been prevented from engaging in any kind of political activity, and the formation of student bodies deemed "unsuitable to the interest and well-being of the students or the University" is prohibited by law (University and University College Act 1971, p. 18; Educational Institutions (Discipline) Act 1976).[5] A further number of acts exist that impinge on freedoms of expressions for all citizens, such as the Printing Presses and Publications Act 1984 (PPPA), used to limit the number of news media outlets; the Communications and Multimedia Act 1978 (CMA) used to control and censor media content; and the Peaceful Assembly Act, meant to be a reformed version of the Police Act 1967 which controlled the right to assembly and frequently executed with the notorious Internal Security Act's (ISA) right of detention without trial, but has instead been wielded in ever more oppressive ways. Several laws were rescinded in the first term of then Prime Minister Najib Razak from 2009–2014, drastically eroding Malaysian civil and political rights and freedom of expression, while promises of reform instead materialized into new laws that have further infringed on human rights, leading to a steady decline in Malaysia's global human rights ranking (Human Rights Watch, 2018).

This context is attributed as one of the significant motivating factors for Buku Jalanan members, alongside other factors such as community and solidarity. Within the first year of BJSA's founding, a second Buku Jalanan chapter was set up in Ipoh, the capital city of the state of Perak, just north of Selangor, and also home to another large UiTM campus. The number of chapters then grew rapidly with nine more established in 2012, followed by a swell of 21 in 2013 and 14 in 2014, bringing up the number of total chapters to 45. To date over 90 chapters have been set up, though how many truly active chapters remain is unclear. The rise in numbers in 2013–2014 is attributed by the members themselves to the socio-political conditions of the time. Sharifah Nursyahidah, a Buku Jalanan Kota Kinabalu member, refers specifically to the climate pre and post the general elections of 2013 which led youth to various acts of activism, and also describes the year as one that saw the rise of many non-governmental bodies and arts collectives as a response to a political situation that was increasingly oppressive, "*situasi politik yang semakin menekan*" (translation by author) (*Buku Jalanan – Simposium Buku Jalanan: Sebuah Catatan*, 2017, p. 12).

However, not all members profess overt political agendas, neither do they necessarily identify as activists. Buku Jalanan Shah Alam founding member, Azrie Ahmad, and two other current and active members, Asdani Saifullah Dolbashid and Fahmi Fadzil, state clearly that Buku Jalanan as a network or coalition of chapters does not label itself a leftist organization, despite what appears to be seemingly leftist leanings (2017, pers. comm., 27 December). This is reinforced by other chapters from the country as recorded in the transcripts of the Buku Jalanan Regional Symposium, held at the Ilham Gallery in Kuala Lumpur in August 2017 under the auspices of the 'Ilham Contemporary Forum Malaysia, 2009–2017'. Buku Jalanan was 'exhibited' as a cultural project with its organization and ethos showcased as a sort of living artefact in itself. A total of 45 members attended the symposium and also provided data prior to the gathering via email and a Google form survey. In the survey Buku Jalanan members were asked to choose whether they identified as an 'activator' (*penggerak*[6]), volunteer (*sukarelawan*) or activist (*aktivis*).

Although the majority selected activist, there were others who made their nonpolitical stance clear and others who preferred to describe themselves as an "active member" (*perserta aktif*), a term which seems to suggest not just being a member who is active versus inactive, but a member who is *pro*-active and motivated (emphasis added). (*Buku Jalanan – Simposium Buku Jalanan: Sebuah Catatan*, 2017).

This blending of art and activism, the testing of boundaries of public space and forging a sense of community characterizes but also complicates Buku Jalanan as it defies easy categorization. Their founding mission was very much driven by the realities faced by the populace, and which materialized as a subtle form of resistance particular to the cultural context of Malay mostly urban and suburban, college-educated youth. The members demonstrate a recognition of the failures of their government and a reaction against oppressive controls, describing the need to take matters into their own hands rather than depend on official institutions. However, their activities are not in the vein of agitation or direct lobbying for change, but instead are a carving out of political and social space, an exercise in expressive cultural democracy (Juncker and Balling, 2016).

Some elaboration is necessary here on the state of cultural and civic institutions in Malaysia. In terms of arts and culture, state museums and galleries exist throughout the country, but these are not well funded or managed. Although it is possible that schoolchildren might visit such institutions at least once in their lifetimes, a culture of arts-going is still not yet ingrained. Most Malaysian states do not have performing arts centres, though in the 1970s and 80s civic centres were built in a number of cities in Malaysia, and for some time were venues for performances and community activities from cultural shows to weddings. Smaller community centres were also built in suburban neighbourhoods. However, by the 1990s most of these centres started to decline in their popularity, and new strategies for youth engagement were introduced by the government such as the Rakan Muda (Young Friends) scheme accompanied by the building of new centres – Kompleks Rakan Muda – in towns around the country. Rakan Muda was launched in 1994 and in 2015 underwent a millennial-targeted make-over and "rebranding" with a new website sporting a distinctly un-governmental look; a focus on creativity and urban youth culture; as well as a programme of mentors that include designers, dancers and visual artists, as well as a young TV celebrity chef and urban farmers (*The Star* 2015, *Rakan Muda*, n.d.).

Libraries are also part of the cultural infrastructure, with state, municipal and community centre libraries in some shape or form throughout the country. Literacy rates have been improving steadily over the years and amongst youth aged between 15 to 24 years, it is reported as nearly 100% (UNESCO, n.d). Despite such encouraging facts and statistics, however, news reports point to a decline in reading and question the criticality of reading materials being consumed, while the heavy censorship laws of Malaysia that result in frequent, and often quite controversial, book banning makes regular headlines (*The Sun Daily* 2006, *The Star* 2012, *The Straits Times* 2015, *Zan Azlee* 2016, *Malaysian Insight* 2017). Given such conditions it is arguable that most state-sponsored institutions tend not to be viewed by a critical populace as spaces for discourse or an open exchange of ideas.

In terms of careers in the arts, it is mainly in the urban capital of Kuala Lumpur and the surrounding Klang Valley where there are sufficient possibilities for regular or full-time employment, whether as artists/creators or as producers/managers/promoters. Since the 2000s, however, secondary cities in Malaysia have been developing their cultural infrastructure or investing in "creativity" as part of global shifts towards creative industries and the economic benefits of culture for tourism, city branding and creative enterprises. Cities like George Town and Ipoh in peninsular Malaysia and Kuching in Sarawak, Borneo, boast annual arts festivals and city centres with commercially exploitable architecture and creative possibilities. This has led to a rise of new arts and culture workers in such cities, as well as in the capital, but there are still limited opportunities to find or create sustainable, full-time work in the field.

The arts and cultural landscape, thus, is one of limited arts infrastructure and funding mechanisms (Yong et al., 2016), underdeveloped systems of accountability and governance, as well as underdeveloped civic life within a tradition of top-down public administration. Any examination of an arts ecosystem – if one can even call it such – has to be considered within its economic and socio-political context, and this context, while specific to Malaysia, needs also to be considered in relation to regional and global influences and parallel developments.

Intersections of art, culture and society

Despite less than encouraging conditions for earning a living through the arts, or, possibly also a result of this and a manifestation of economic and social discontent, there has been a discernible emergence of artists, designers and other culture workers initiating or running projects in or with specific communities around the country. In 2014, a survey conducted to document community-based arts practice in Malaysia provided basic profiles of practitioners engaged in a range of work from using the arts to engage with at-risk youth, to neighbourhood beautification projects; cultural mapping exercises to inculcate heritage and cultural awareness, to acts of cultural resistance to prevent forcible relocation (Arts-ED, 2014). Though responses were limited and only 22 profiles were obtained at the time, it led to the founding of an informal network of practitioners who have continued to stay in touch through social media, and occasionally connect in person through workshops or other events. Unlike the United Kingdom or Singapore where the arts have become incorporated into social services under a neoliberal agenda, such state instrumentalization of the arts for social benefit has not yet developed into a full trend in Malaysia. Hence, many if not most projects are initiated by independent individuals or collectives of individuals, and, are often, spurred by a sense of social responsibility and justice.

The practice of artists or people using culture to affect social change is seen across Southeast Asia in various forms. Examples include the Jatiwangi Art Factory, an artist residency programme located in the tile-making village of Jatiwangi, West Java, Indonesia, and integrated into the cultural life of this specific community; the D Jung Space Project of Thailand, bringing creativity and the arts to rural communities for social cohesion and identity building; and the festivals in pagodas, initiated by a young group of friends led by 26-year old filmmaker Lomorpich Rithy in Phnom Penh, Cambodia, a project that simultaneously reclaims a traditional practice while creating new traditions and developing tastes for contemporary arts.[7] Examples of Malaysian collectives working with communities that predate Buku Jalanan include Lost Gens, an artist collective and residency based in Kuala Lumpur who sporadically focus attention on issues such as urban heritage and habitat loss; and Sabahan collective Pangrok Sulap known for their woodblock prints and activist statements on social issues affecting their community such as illegal logging and environmental degradation, to messages of ethnic pride.

In Southeast Asia, the line between art and social engagement is a blurry one. Indonesian curator Grace Samboh asserts that artists in Indonesia have never been separated from their social surroundings and asks "What is *not* socially-engaged? Without an existing and working system, everyone depends on each other anyway" (Samboh, 2016) (emphasis added). Iola Lenzi describes the relationship between artist-artwork-audience in Southeast Asian contemporary art as a trope developed "not for the sake of promoting a collective relationship or identity, but for conveying information and provoking thought through involvement", whereby "practitioners don't convene audiences as an experiential end-in-itself, but rather are driven by social objectives wherein audience-inclusiveness is a means of co-opting resistance" (Lenzi, 2014, p. 12). In his discussion of pioneering Indonesian artist Moelyono among others, Japanese curator Junichi Shioada high-lights the concern for community and how artists can build a better future for that community using art, making a distinction of Southeast Asian art practices from Western practice because of this (1997, cited in Lenzi, 2014, p. 11). Indonesian urbanist Marco Kusumawijaya is a vocal advocate in the region for the role of communities as laboratories for urban experimentation for ecological sustainability or as critics against the market (Kusumawijaya, 2012, 2014, 2015).

The type of cultural activity mentioned here and certainly the nature of the work of Buku Jalanan, whether by design or indirectly, tends to challenge or completely ignore the market authority in the arts and instead serves to destabilize and address imbalances of power: artists or individuals using creative or cultural means to engage with society around them for social change rather than economic gain. Such practice has been discussed increasingly in the past two decades, and goes by various terms: cultural activism, cultural resistance, community-engaged or socially engaged arts; in the visual arts socially engaged art is discussed as participatory, dialogical, or collaborative art (Bishop, 2006; Kester, 2004; Helguera, 2013); while in the performing arts, often in the realm of applied theatre, the work of pioneering figures such as Brazilian theatre practitioner and political activist and founder of the Theatre of the Oppressed, Augusto Boal, has been far-reaching in its influence, and forum theatre and theatre of the oppressed continued to be practiced today. In recent years socially engaged arts practice has also become a topic of interest for urbanists and geographers. British researchers Buser and Arthurs (2012, p. 3) place cultural activism in the context of urban planning, spatial politics and civil society, describing it as a form of organization of the intermingling of art, activism, performance and politics, and framing it according to three broad concepts that: (1) challenge dominant constructions of the world; (2) present alternative socio-political and spatial imaginaries; and (3) disrupt relationships between art, politics, participation and spectatorship. Focusing on the relationships between artists and works of art with publics, between civic leaders and citizens, and between the humanities and its engagement with the world, Doris Sommer of the Cultural Agents Initiative at Harvard University terms these practitioners, or activators, to borrow a Buku Jalanan term, as 'cultural agents': people who are not necessarily artists but individuals who use a variety of cultural means to lead towards collective change (Sommer, 2014). Recognizing small acts as well as grand interventions, culture does its 'work' when art meets accountability.

Returning to Southeast Asia, the intersection of art and society, as we have seen, is not new and the discourse goes beyond a conceptual avant-garde turn in contemporary art, with the artist or cultural initiator seen to be an integral part of their community or society. In the case of Buku Jalanan we find groups of young people seeking to *create* community, whether amongst each other, or as cultural citizens participating in democratic life. Borrowing the language of Sommer, we apply the term cultural agents to the activators of Buku Jalanan: cultural acts by agents who are not necessarily artists, seeking to engage with members of society through purposeful and symbolic organization. Buku Jalanan is a free library that uses literature and books to create a platform for community engagement. Through the situating of their activities in public space they exercise their rights as citizens and through its sustained and regular recurrence, make a symbolic statement about power, access and the democratization of space. For each individual participant, through the interactions with each other and with the materials they read, they engage in discourse and learn to respect alternative points of view, while developing critical political and civic sensibilities. Their ideology is propagated through their sustained activities and inspires other youths to similar action. Yet, all this is done in a purely voluntary and seemingly unsustainable manner.

Most literature on socially engaged art tends not to intersect with questions of organization, and certainly not with the language of management. From its early days of inception as a recognized field of management, in many parts of the world the role of the arts manager has traditionally been associated with either the nonprofit framework supported by arts or cultural policy and government and private philanthropy; or as a function of the art market where consumption drives creation. In either framework, the idea of enabling the creation of artistic outputs and ensuring that it reaches an audience has been increasingly discussed using business terms of management and administration, and, in fact, the link between management and the arts has been seen as a 'mark of respectability' (Chong, 2000, p. 296). Even in countries with less advanced infrastructure and support for the arts, the concept of art management is linked to the professionalization of the field. With socially engaged art and cultural activism a growing feature in the landscape of art and culture, however, it is increasingly likely that there are and will be arts managers and students of arts management who choose to apply their energies to work that is more integrated with their social constituents, and which affect or call for social change. It is imperative, therefore, that we seek new models that go beyond the binary of non- or for-profit organization, and that fall outside or somewhere in between the categories of public, nonprofit; and private, for-profit. This will be discussed further in the next session on the operational characteristics of Buku Jalanan.

Managing a 'non-organisation'

By 2014, as Buku Jalanans sprouted around the country, the founding members discovered that not all new chapters necessarily conformed to the same shared values. As a response to this, they produced a set of guiding principles written out as a manifesto that was and is made available to all members in the form of a zine. Zines are a popular form of literature in Malaysia (Wang, 2017) and punk aesthetics and the DIY (do-it-yourself) ethic are a common identifier amongst Malaysian youth subcultures regardless of their actual music or tribal affiliations. Indeed, a hand-made, photocopied form of self-publishing expresses effectively the ideology conveyed in Buku Jalanan's manifesto. The growth and rapid spread of Buku Jalanan, while recognized as needing to be managed somehow, was also recognized as a close result of its ethos, and it was therefore vital to not disrupt or restrict the autonomy each chapter was meant to have. The principles are not meant to be prescriptive but serve to underline their core values and make more tangible members' collective and shared identity.

The manifesto's four principles are as follows (translated from the Malay by the author):

- Reading materials for all/all types of things may be read
- Mobilized/operated freely, independently and with full autonomy
- Committed to a process of knowledge culture through B.A.C.A[8] (Books, Art, Culture, Activism)
- Celebrating (claiming) public space as a space for the culture of knowledge (*Panduan Berbuku Jalanan*, n.d.)

Included also in the zine are the following recommended readings: *Guerilla Warfare* by Che Guevara, *Hungry for Peace – How you help end poverty and war with Food not Bombs*, by Keith McHenry, and *Tactical Urbanisn: Short-term Action, Long-term Change, Vol. 2* by Mike Lydon, texts which further proclaim the ideology that informs their activities (*Panduan Berbuku Jalanan*, n.d., p. 5).

The founding Buku Jalanan of Shah Alam is neither an incorporated company nor a registered society and has no formal source of regular funding. In Malaysia, it is not, in fact, common for arts and culture organizations to be registered as nonprofits; and what type of an organisation

Buku Jalanan could be, in any case, which would be met with approval by the necessary approving government agency, is unclear. Even amongst the different chapters, there is variation in sense of self and purpose. It is also precisely because of this fluidity, however, that Buku Jalanan is so attractive to would-be members.

Most if not all Buku Jalanan chapters were started by students or recent graduates who returned to their hometowns after university and felt the need for similar activity in their hometowns. Only eight chapters receive external funding, and one, Buku Jalanan Chow Kit has formally registered as a nonprofit organization and is currently planning to expand their services to become a school for undocumented children, Sekolah Buku Jalanan. All the other chapters run on a wholly voluntary basis and this is something that has been recognized by members as a problem for sustainability. The absence of formal registration furthermore raises questions of governance, leadership, and accountability. Nevertheless, although systems of control may be deemed necessary for best business practice and organizations' compliance required in accordance with country-specific legislation, it is questioned here whether this lack of organizational structure also results in an agility which can be advantageous; a lack of structure can, in fact, permit a nimbleness and responsiveness to one's environmental context and any changes that may and inevitably do arise.

That different chapters have different ideas about what they are, or what collective form they take, is less relevant to the members than the working processes that they adopt. With the range in identifications – from a book club to a space for ideas, to a space for community engagement to a cultural movement – all members agreed that there was no need, in fact, to agree on a singular definition or form (*Buku Jalanan – Simposium Buku Jalanan: Sebuah Catatan*, 2017). This is one of the strengths of Buku Jalanan – their flexibility and malleability enough for others to take on and make it their own. They offer a basic philosophy and ideals, and the rest is up to anyone who shares their basic ideology. Some chapters have even renamed themselves, and this is acceptable. One member summed it up thus: "to me, the name Buku Jalanan is just a label. It doesn't matter whether a movement (chapter) does not use the Buku Jalanan name but the strategy is the same to spread knowledge to society" (translation by author) (*Buku Jalanan – Simposium Buku Jalanan: Sebuah Catatan*, 2017, p. 37). Buku Jalanan, therefore, becomes a tool, an approach, a methodology or strategy. It is not a thing in itself – but how does one govern a strategy?

Accepting that Buku Jalanan is an approach, but that each individual chapter has an identifiable form through which it executes its ideology, it is arguable that a framework of management can be applied to offer a semblance of organizational structure. However, arts management as a field of study and practice tends to focus on issues of survival and of sustainability centred on either funding or in organizational management, and the efficient running of arts organizations like businesses. The notion of success is too often viewed through the lens of financial success and efficiency and productivity are given assumptions and natural presuppositions of a business or entrepreneurial framework. The terms 'management' and 'administration' with its connotations of systems and execution of tasks seem far removed from the notion of agency, which implies autonomy and empowerment. Thus, it is questionable whether such systems are compatible with the collective practice of this study. Nevertheless, in an attempt to answer this, four basic functions of management are applied to Buku Jalanan Shah Alam (BJSA): planning, organizing, leading and controlling (Byrnes, 2014; Rosewall, 2014). Incorporated under leading and organizing are questions of staffing and supervising, and we start with this first.

BJSA has a flat, non-hierarchical structure and they do not have a designated leader. Although Zikri Rahman has been more visible than other members of BJSA, both he and the other members interviewed make it clear that this is not a leadership role. This has immediate implications for planning and organizing. According to the members interviewed, Azrie, Fahmi and Asdani, all decisions are made collectively (2017, pers. comm., 27 December). The bulk of their communication is via WhatsApp and they also use social media forms such as Facebook and Twitter to complement face-to-face communications; a majority vote for consensus is practiced responding to any issue that is put forward. Their manifesto already sets a very open and inclusive platform for participation which requires very little decision-making on a daily basis: no themes or parameters are set for books; therefore, nothing is rejected; the actual programme is simple and repeated each fortnight, thus there is little need for discussion or that can lead to potential disagreement. Other tasks involve designing posters and flyers, and this, like everything else, is done on a voluntary basis. According to Azrie, Fahmi and Asdani, this was how they successfully operated in the first three years without any issue. The main occasions in which they most often have to exercise collective decision-making is when they engage in activities beyond their core park and reading programme; examples of this include responses to incidents in their community that compel demonstrations of solidarity, or in the taking up of social causes.

While there is no hierarchy, each member is described as having a 'niche' and the trio insist that each member is sufficiently self-motivated to do their part. They say that there are rarely occasions where no member is able to deliver and there are always 'back-ups' in the event this might happen. All that is required for each session is a single individual with the necessary commitment. Each has skillsets that they make known and roles they fill. However, these roles are not considered "static" and are also rotated as described by Fahmi:

> We were thinking that we need to push each other with what we do and try to experience different things so that we understand how to manage ourselves properly/ . . . It started ad hoc, but then it became something quite regular. (If) the number of members who are active becomes less, the other people who are not used to the roles that they were used to are able to pick up. They understand the picture of what they are supposed to do.
>
> *(Fahmi, 2017, pers. comm., 27 December)*

The members, thus, are operating within a shared understanding dependent on mutual respect and responsibility. There is no hierarchy of supervision, but in effect, they all supervise each other.

Once a year, BJSA organizes a trip outside of their city, a "getaway", where they reflect on what they've been doing and "discuss directions for the next year" (Fahmi, 2017, pers. comm., 27 December). This is when planning occurs, and it is at one of these company retreat style trips that their 2014 Manifesto was drafted. From these reflections they also began to see the potential for greater impact though their activities. While the annual getaway results in a goal or objective for the year, perhaps a series of themes of issues of importance, the day-to-day operations is still loose and organic. Things may be suggested as and when they arise, and the group members respond accordingly.

From this, we can see that BJSA conforms in some ways to the workings of a more conventional organization. There is planning and decision-making, executed at a collective level. There are roles that are defined yet flexible. What they lack in terms of systems for control they seem to compensate with trust and faith in their fellow members. To examine this more deeply is beyond the scope of this chapter and necessitates approaches that draw more on the social sciences and humanities than of business and management. However, there are also regional scenarios that offer some basis of comparison.

Indonesia, with its vibrant grassroots organizations and artist collectives offers a valuable and culturally familiar point of reference. Nuraini Juliastuti, a scholar and herself a co-founder of the

Jogjakarta-based collective KUNCI Cultural Studies Center, outlines the characteristics of what she describes as 'alternative spaces' in Indonesia: youth initiated, often in multi-purpose spaces, utilizing electronic media for communications, and marked by a flexibility in the activities they run as well as operationally. She further stresses an openness to networks:

> with their inherent non-formal character, a particular activity of an alternative space is building collaboration with another space not necessarily working in the same field. . . . The strength of alternative spaces to form a new cultural movement lies in the combination of the capability to build a network with other creative spaces, and their potential to form cultural communities.
>
> *(Juliastuti, 2008)*

In a dialogue with Ade Darmawan, Director of Ruangrupa, a Jakarta-based visual arts collective founded in 2000, the two compare notes on collective and horizontal organization in Indonesia and on art infrastructure models that differ from that in the West (Juliastuti, 2012). Ade describes alternative spaces as a type of response to the context in Indonesia where the state has failed or neglected to produce adequate support for the arts.

> I prefer to look at the works of (artist initiated) spaces as 'contextual responses. Performing a series of experiments in their local environments, they develop an applicable model to respond to local needs. Such contextual responses, occurring in different places and sometimes short-lived, develop into local survival strategies. In the absence of formal art infrastructure, they work to improve the local system. They attempt an ideal system, even if that is only an illusion.
>
> *(cited in Juliastuti, 2012, p. 121)*

There is an emphasis on process in the work of Ruangrupa, and the term 'social practice' is used to describe the collaborative nature of their projects, not just within the members of the collective but with other partners and the community beyond. Networks are defined as being a precondition: 'it is like the idea of building a friendship. It is organic, spontaneous and open. Often, building a network also means a political act' (cited in Juliastuti, 2012, p. 124).

It must be noted here that the actual function of management is never explicitly talked about. The members of the collectives perform various tasks and may perform specific roles that may be fixed or changing, and this is a normal function of their organization with a recognized 'tension between structure and non-structure in organizations', organizations that are deliberately horizontal in structure and practice ("Curating Organizations Without Form", 2015). Crucial also to the conversation of collectives in Indonesia is the concept of friendship (Budhyarto, 2015; Samboh, 2016), which also figures prominently in the foundation of BJSA. The founding members were well acquainted with each other prior to their coming together to form BJSA, and it seems their friendship is a vital though easily overlooked factor in what binds them together and steers their productivity in the absence of formal structures. These intimate relationships, based on shared values and experiences, and navigated within personal and not professional boundaries stands in marked contrast to the contractual relationships based on formal transactions that are the norm in conventional organizations.

Buku Jalanan shares several features with their Indonesian counterparts: flexibility; an openness to networks and the leveraging of these networks to achieve their goals; and a specific response to a specific need in their local environment. This response is a fluid and adaptable one, and it appears that BJSA has evolved in response to the needs of members and of the community in which they have a presence. In inquiring into the groups longevity and what was presently in their future, the responses turned inevitably to a discussion on sustainability.

The sustainability conundrum

Between 2013–2015 the members of BJSA rented a physical space together with another collective and ran their activities from this new location. Now, in 2018, they are exploring ideas to again attempt a more structured 'home' for BJSA. The members interviewed described their current state as being on a 'down', after their rapid ascent in 2013, followed by a period of relative stability which they view more or less as a plateau, and they are now facing a potential decline (Fahmi, 2017, pers. comm., 27 December).

To obtain this new space, a physical 'home' for BJSA, their first step is to come up with a financial strategy to make this possible. As is typical for the group, there is no clearly defined way to go about this. It is a goal to work towards in whatever way each member works. Despite acknowledging that it is a resource heavy undertaking, Asdani explains the rationale and need:

> (Perhaps) we don't need to have a space. We can have our events anywhere. But for the long term, I don't think (going without a space is) sustainable. Because it involves a lot of effort and . . . we don't want everything to be so random, so ad hoc. Because you can say now that maybe you can have a workshop once or twice a month, but how long can you (continue like this). If you have a space, we can really organize ourselves, have a proper space, have proper events and have people really committed to the group.
>
> *(Asdani, 2017, pers. comm., 27 December)*

The members speak with conviction. They feel a need to make greater and more sustained contributions and believe that a physical space enables this. They see the place that they would set up as another step in the counter-narrative of public space and hope to see how their 'private' space can be truly more 'public'. By recognizing the increased privatization of public space and how what is conventionally thought of as public spaces are never truly public, they are able to reconcile their move to a physical and fixed location and continue an intellectual engagement with these concepts of power. What emerges here is not so much an issue of public space reclamation but the vital creation of common space: 'common space as a property that is fundamental to a community's existence as a body' and that fulfils the need for citizens to engage in common space in order to fully realize their fullest potential as cultural beings (Kusumawijaya, 2014). Buku Jalanan is significant for its ability to offer such a common space, whether it be an open public park with its spatial boundaries redefined and politicized through temporary claiming, or a bricks and mortar, walled enclosure that allows them to experiment with ideas of private and public.

Conceptually this may be resolved, but the cold, hard reality of financing a space remains to be addressed. The members of BJSA are currently exploring co-operative models in search of a viable business structure that would enable them to retain their independence and autonomy as a private entity not beholden to funders, while neither being a fully commercial venture, free from what they view as a potentially corrupting influence of money. One member, Azrie, has recently ventured into a business selling screen-printed t-shirts and apparel by local independent labels, and they are considering the feasibility of such creative enterprises. As is the trend with youth spaces, it is likely that the hybrid space they envision will be one the incorporates youth culture of DIY make culture, music, fashion and café culture (Juliastuti, 2008).

Seeking funding in the form of grants or sponsorships is not an option for Buku Jalanan both in practicality as well as ideologically. However, it is necessary to consider what the lack of receptive support structures means for groups that do not possess a defined organizational structure therefore setting them outside most systems of support, and whom engage in acts of subversion, regardless how subtle; and when culture is not offered for consumption but is instead a matter of *participation*. Such a scenario is increasingly less of a rarity, and it is proposed that increasingly hybrid spaces will become the norm versus the exception. Charles Esche, referring to the Rooseum Center for Contemporary Art in Sweden, proposes a new way of thinking about arts organizations:

> Now, the term 'art' might be starting to describe that space in society for experimentation, questioning and discovery that religion, science and philosophy have occupied sporadically in former times. It has become an active space rather than one of passive observation. Therefore, the institutions to foster it have to be part community center, part laboratory and part academy, with less need for the established showroom function. They must also be political in a direct way, thinking through the consequences of our extreme free market policies.
>
> *(Esche, 2004)*

We can begin to recognize some of this in an organiszation like Buku Jalanan: a space for experimentation, for discourse, for active participation and community, and a direct expression of political and social ideology and practice.

Buku Jalanan: what next?

While in Indonesia the movement of alternative spaces occurred in the post–New Order era of the late 1980s, it seems in Malaysia this is a movement that is currently picking up momentum in a 21st-century incarnation, and particularly in the form of library/reading room alternative spaces. In addition to Buku Jalanan, independent 'library' spaces have been emerging in recent years in the greater Kuala Lumpur area, as well as in other parts of the country. The Rumah Atap library and collective which hosts discussion events, and the Malaysia Design Archive which started as an online archive of design and has evolved into a physical reading room and discussion space as well as archive of visual culture, are both residents in the Zhongshan Building in Kuala Lumpur, a community of independent arts, culture and design initiatives that also includes an independent publisher. In other parts of Kuala Lumpur are Booku, an architect-initiated library and book space; and the Little Giraffe Book Club in Cheras that focuses on activities for young children. The newly set up Ruang Kongsi (literally Shared Space) in George Town, Penang, aims to be a community library as well as 'a center for social transformative knowledge and holistic learning with community courses on philosophy, social studies, human rights, democracy, and practical skills', as described on their crowdfunding start-up webpage (mystartr | Ruang Kongsi).

Buku Jalanan is both part of a youth movement and is also a movement in itself. Like their cohorts above, they are cultural agents who are activating new spaces for imagination, new possibilities and values. They are neither a nonprofit nor a for-profit, and their lack of a clear mission or organizational structure enables a sense of fluidity and freedom to choose to be whatever the members collectively want Buku Jalanan to be. Though concerned about matters of sustainability, their perspective of sustainability is in sustaining their energy and commitment to run their activities first, and only then on that of financial sustainability. The question of viewing themselves as staff of an organization is not even part of the discussion. Their autonomy and independence are not just for the organization but for each individual within it. The friendship amongst members is an extremely strong binding factor, one which is not untypical for collectives. They are not answerable to a board or any kind of supervisory committee, but are accountable to each other, and their communities will also hold them accountable; the clearest measure of their worth is in whether anybody seeks to engage with them through their activities.

The challenge is in maintaining this freedom, both ideologically and operationally, while bound to a physical space and the technical requirements in running it, or, to use a term by Buku Jalanan, in activating it. Charles Esche (2004) uses the term 'political imagination forum' which captures the possibilities of the kind of spaces that groups like Buku Jalanan aim to be, but also outlines the conditions needed: 'Creating possibility is not a fixed point of view but a slippery and changeable condition made of spatial, temporal and relational elements. In other words, for possibility to emerge there needs to be a site, a moment and a group of people' (para. 5).

Whether they go by the term of activists, activators, or cultural agents; or are viewed as a contextual response, a methodology, or a social practice, Buku Jalanan is a response to a specific felt need, at a specific moment in time. Buku Jalanan and collective cultural agents like them, as both process and an entity, offer possibilities for reimagining new relationships and structures for the organization or activation of cultural activities for social impact. Their flat, horizontal organizational structure depends on networks of support and bonds of friendship, while social relevance and their social relationships are both motivations and rewards. The workings of cultural agency and socially engaged arts do not fit into standard fields of study, and this chapter puts forth an argument for further context-specific and interdisciplinary research to identify and propose new frameworks for better understanding work of this nature. In the meantime, the activists and activators of Buku Jalanan will continue to act as free agents in their communities, and in the imagining of new realms of possibility.

Notes

1 *Buku* is the Bahasa word for 'book'; *jalanan* is a noun for streets or a network of streets, from the root word *jalan* which can mean road or street. But *jalanan* can also mean 'street' as in 'street artist' with its rebellious connotations. An English translation fails to convey this effectively, therefore we maintain the Bahasa name throughout.
2 UiTM was first founded as a training centre in 1956 around the time Malaya was moving towards independence from the British. It was founded on nation-building goals through indigenous and accessible education, and it offers low tuition rates for *bumiputera* students (ethnic Malay and indigenous youth). In 1967 it became the MARA Institute of Technology (ITM) and by the late 1990s transitioned into a university recognized by the Ministry of Education. Its name was changed to the MARA University of Technology/Universiti Teknologi MARA, with an 'i' retained in its acronym UiTM as a signifier of its history and to distinguish it from UTM, Universiti Teknologi Malaysia, one of the oldest engineering colleges in the country. Today it is the largest public university in the country and the Shah Alam campus is its main and original campus, with over 21 state satellite campuses across the country, and over 500 academic programmes on offer.
3 The Community Engaged Art Network Asia is an informal network of practictioners initiated by myself and independent researcher and founder of art education organization Arts-ED, Janet Pillai, in 2015. In 2017 with funding from the Krishen Jit Astro Fund, we ran two workshops to connect further with practitioners and facilitate knowledge sharing as a community of practice. A brief funders report summarizes the activities, of which Zikri and other members of Buku Jalanan was a part, and an article on the first workshop by Mark Teh (2017) is available at http://ceaasia.wixsite.com/home/malaysia.
4 As is the convention of Malay names, all individuals will be named in full and henceforth referred to by their given names.
5 In December 2018 amendments to the UUCA Act 1971 and other restrictive acts on students in higher education institutions were tabled in the Malaysian Parliament under the newly elected government of Pakatan Harapan following the May 2018 results of the 14th General Election. www.thestar.com.my/news/nation/2018/12/04/no-uuca-repeal-but-three-new-bills-tabled/#bL8S7sqGmlp0Ce8X.99

6 The translations are by the author. An alternative translation of the word *penggerak* would be mover, the
   root word *gerak* being move, and there is a correlation with Buku Jalanan being described as a movement
   (*gerakan*) by the members themselves as well as in this paper. However, the word 'activator' is preferred in
   this context as in English it captures more accurately the essence of someone who makes things happen.
7 All of the examples mentioned here are projects and activities that the author has learned of through
   contact with the founding or coordinating members of the initiatives. More information on Jatiwangi
   can be found through their social media accounts, as well as http://jatiwangiartfactory.tumblr.com/.
   They are also discussed in Mitha Budhyarto's article "Hospitality, Friendship, and an Emancipatory
   Politics", *Seismopolite: Journal of Art and Politics*, December 2015. For information about D Jung, see the
   report of the CEA Regional Exchange Meeting & Roundtables 2016 at http://ceaasia.wixsite.com/
   home/malaysia. Information on the Cambodian festival is only available in Khmer but can be seen on
   Facebook at www.facebook.com/bonnphum
8 The acronym spells out the Bahasa word for 'read' – *baca*

References

Arts-ED (2014). Survey report. *Community based arts & culture workers in Malaysia: A documentation project and resource site*. Available at: www.communityarts.my/survey-report [Accessed 1 Jan. 2018].

After movie, Malaysia also bans Fifty Shades of Grey books. *The Straits Times*, 27 February 2015. Available at: www.straitstimes.com/asia/se-asia/after-movie-malaysia-also-bans-fifty-shades-of-grey-books [Accessed 10 Jan. 2018].

Azlee, Z. (2016). Here we go banning books again. *Malaysia Today*, 8 January 2016. Available at: www.malaysia-today.net/2016/01/08/here-we-go-banning-books-again/ [Accessed 10 Jan. 2018].

Bishop, C. (2006). The social turn: Collaboration and its discontents. *Artforum*, February, pp. 178–183.

Budhyarto, M. (2015). Hospitality, friendship, and an emancipatory politics. *Seismopolite*, 13, December 2015. Available at: www.seismopolite.com/hospitality-friendship-and-an-emancipatory-politics [Accessed 10 Jan. 2018].

Buku Jalanan. (2017). *Buku Jalanan – Simposium Buku Jalanan: Sebuah Catatan*. Buku Jalanan Symposium, Ilham Contemporary Forum (Malaysia 2009–2017), Kuala Lumpur, 5 August 2017.

Buser, M. and Arthurs, J. (2012). Cultural activism in the community. *Connected Communities*, [Accessed 1 Jan. 2018].

Byrnes, W.J. (2014). *Management and the arts*. 5th ed. Burlington, MA: Focal Press.

Chong, D. (2000). Re-readings in arts management. *The Journal of Arts Management, Law, and Society*, 29(4), pp. 290–303.

Esche, C. (2004). What's the point of art centres anyway? – possibility, art and democratic deviance. *European Institute for Progressive Cultural Policies*. Available at: http://eipcp.net/transversal/0504/esche/en [Accessed 1 Jan. 2018].

Juliastuti, N. (2008). *Alternative space as new cultural movement: Landscape of creativity*. Paper presented in Indonesia 10 Years after, Amsterdam, 22–23 May 2008. Available at: <http://kunci.or.id/articles/alternative-space-as-new-cultural-movement-landscape-of-creativity/ [Accessed 2 Dec. 2017].

———. (2012). Ruangrupa: A conversation on horizontal organisation. *Afterall: A Journal of Art, Context and Enquiry, Volume 30 | Summer 2012*, Central Saint Martins, University of the Arts London, pp. 117–125.

Helguera, P. (2013). *Education for socially engaged art: A materials and techniques handbook*. New York: Jorge Pinto Books.

Home Ministry bans Irshad Manjis Book. (2012). *The Star*, 24 May 2012. Available at: www.thestar.com.my/news/nation/2012/05/24/home-ministry-bans-irshad-manjis-book/ [Accessed 10 Jan. 2018].

Human Rights Watch. (2018). Malaysia. *World report 2018*. Available at: www.hrw.org/world-report/2018/country-chapters/malaysia [Accessed 10 Feb. 2018].

Juncker, B. and Balling, G. (2016). The value of art and culture in everyday life: Towards an expressive cultural democracy. *The Journal of Arts Management, Law, and Society*, 46(5), pp. 231–242.

Kester, G. (2004). Conversation pieces: The role of dialogue in socially-engaged art. In: Z. Kucor and S. Leung, 2005 *Theory in contemporary art since 1985*. Chichester, West Sussex: Wiley-Blackwell, pp. 153–165.

Kusumawijaya, M. (2012). Arts between the state and the community: The problem of consumption in/of the city. Presented at Lasalle College of Arts, Singapore, 27–28 March 2012. Available at: https://mkusumawijaya.wordpress.com/2012/06/30/arts-between-the-state-and-the-community-the-problem-of-consumption-inof-the-city/ [Accessed 10 Jan. 2018].

———. (2013). Common space and public space in contemporary urbanization. In: W. Lim, ed., *Public space in Asia* 2014. Singapore: World Scientific, pp. 138–153.

———. (2015). Community as an alternative way of life towards ecological sustainability, or: Community as a critique towards state, market and desire. Presented at San Art, Ho Chi Minh City, June 2015. Available at: https://mkusumawijaya.wordpress.com/2015/07/20/community-as-an-alternative-way-of-life-towards-ecological-sustainability-or-community-as-a-critique-towards-state-market-and-desire/ [Accessed 10 Jan. 2018].

Lenzi, I. (ed.) (2014). *Concept context contestation: Art and the collective in Southeast Asia.* Bangkok, Thailand: Bangkok Art and Culture Centre.

'Ministry will bar 'offensive' publications', *The Sun Daily*, 4 December 2006. Available at: www.thesundaily. my/node/171950 [Accessed 10 Jan. 2018].

Panduan Berbuku Jalanan. (n.d.). Buku Jalanan. N.p.

Rahman, Z. (2017). Buku Jalanan's politics of the street: Zikri Rahman in conversation with Elaine W. Ho. In: H. Bashiron Mendolicchio and S. Bosch, eds., *Art in context: Learning from the field – conversations with and between art and cultural practitioners.* Berlin: Goethe Institute, pp. 50–59.

Rakan Muda (n.d.). Available at: http://rakanmuda.my/ [Accessed 10 Feb. 2018].

'Rakan Muda rebranded, with focus on creativity' (2017). *The Star,* 17 February. Available at: www.thestar. com.my/news/nation/2015/02/17/rakan-muda-rebrandinig/ [Accessed 20 Feb. 2018].

Rosewall, E. (2014). *Arts management: Uniting arts and audiences in the 21st century.* London, Oxford: Oxford University Press.

Ruang Kongsi (2017). Transform a space. *mystartr.* Available at: www.mystartr.com/projects/kongsi [Accessed 10 Jan. 2018].

Samboh, G. (2016). Taking and giving: Friendship as a way of thinking and doing. *ST. PAUL St Curatorial Symposium* 2016, Auckland, New Zealand, pp. 25–29.

Sommer, D. (2006). *Cultural agency in the Americas.* Durham, NC: Duke University Press.

———. (2014). *The work of art in the world*: *Civic agency and public humanities.* Durham, NC: Duke University Press.

'Turkish author slams Malaysia again for book ban', *The Malaysian Insight*, 14 October 2017. Available at: www.themalaysianinsight.com/s/18550/ [Accessed 10 Jan. 2018].

UNESCO. (n.d.). Malaysia. UNESCO Institute for Statistics. Available at: http://uis.unesco.org/country/ MY [Accessed 1 Jan. 2018].

Wang, G. (2017). A study of publishing in Malaysia, by OOMK magazine. *Stack.* Available at: www. stackmagazines.com/art-design/study-publishing-malaysia-oomk/ [Accessed 5 Jun. 2018].

Yong, B., Khairuddin, N.H., Joseph, R., and Tengku, S.I.(eds.) (2016). *Infrastrutures: Narratives in Malaysian art vol. 3.* Kuala Lumpur: RogueArt.

17

THE ROLE OF VOLUNTEERS IN FOSTERING SOCIAL INCLUSION IN A UK CITY OF CULTURE

Expressing new narratives of the visual arts in the city

Nigel D Morpeth

Introduction

This chapter provides key insights into the cultural mega-event of Hull 2017 UK City of Culture and their vision of a programme of 365 days of transformational cultural activities. It specifically identifies how volunteers were instrumental in helping to make more accessible the visual arts as an everyday experience for both residents of the city and visitors alike. In doing so, I explore whether volunteers created a sense of social inclusion by helping fellow residents to encounter new experiences in the visual arts and help to foster the broad benefits of cultural participation as force for social good in the city.

I argue that through their 'interventions' as cultural mediators, using the medium of the visual arts, volunteers enabled people to discover new narratives of the city beyond the grand narratives of senses of loss and decay that have previously been expressed. These old narratives of the city expressed mainly by external audiences, caricaturing Hull as a 'crap town' and in more poetic historical terms, the phrase: "Dear Lord save me from Hull, Hell and Halifax," set a grim and brooding scenario, in advance of people visiting the city. Over time the historical layering of images of the city has established an imagined geography of a city 'on the edge'; struggling to come terms with the destruction of World War II bombing; and in more recent times, the near terminal loss of a fishing industry (see Starkey et al., 2017). I argue that Hull City of Culture volunteers have been instrumental in their capacity as cultural mediators, in establishing narratives of the city, based on the cultural distinctiveness of the city. This cultural distinctiveness has been communicated through active volunteering community members, rather than based on a stifling distorted imagined geography imposed on the city.

Hull 2017 Ltd were the independent company and initial architects of both the volunteers programme and also the curators of the 365-day cultural programme. As the overarching company responsible for the delivery of the City of Culture year, Hull 2017 Ltd put in place organisational structures, which included a coordinating role in offering training and ongoing educational programmes. This enabled volunteers to be a crucial part of how members of the public encountered and experienced the visual arts and other cultural activities, in a range of venues and public spaces, during Hull's time as UK City of Culture.

So, what has happened in Hull to enable volunteers to be positioned as cultural mediators in the visual arts and is this the strongest indication that Hull has been able to develop a legacy from the staging of a cultural mega-event in the city?

In discussing this, it is crucially important to not lose sight of the need for critical insights on the contemporary manifestations of volunteering. There is a growing body of evidence that volunteering has been subsumed in neoliberal projects, in a UK context expressed through Big Society and in an age of austerity (See Lowndes and Pratchett, 2012). This neoliberal project has also extended to the increasing sense of competition between destinations, in gaining access to resources, to support what might be considered the everyday necessities of life. I argue that cultural expression and celebration is part of the vital components of everyday life (see Goffman, 1969) not exclusively, but not least through different expressions of the visual arts. In examining the concepts of volunteering, I consider comparative insights from volunteering in cultural and sporting mega-events, the concept of cultural mediation in the visual arts and the amorphous concept of social inclusion. I then apply insights from these concepts to the context of Hull 2017 UK City of Culture.

As a note of caution, the claims of what 'culture' can do, as an ameliorating force for good and curing of ills in society, might be overblown, not least in so-called policies for social inclusion. Therefore, the academy has a responsibility to make sense of these claims, not least that the vehicle of a UK City of Culture can automatically be a panacea for the structural excesses of the neoliberal project. The development of the City of Culture programme might be characterised by the imposition of cultural expressions 'from above,' rather than the development of cultural expression 'from below'. In borrowing the words of Boland, Murtagh and Shirlow: 'Fashioning a city of culture' or '12-month party?' (2016). City and Capital of Culture competitions might at best offer an overload of cultural celebration concentrated temporally, but at a cost. This cost is potentially an over attribution of more far-reaching social benefits to accrue from events, festivals and activities whose metier might well be contained within the realms of entertainment and 'in the moment' transient satisfaction. That these transient moments of satisfaction might then lead to more permanent legacy benefits requires thorough scrutiny and analysis. What is clear from my observations is that there are many different learning points to emerge, from the intersection between a developing visual arts infrastructure and the role of volunteers in cultural mediation with different types of audiences in Hull, during the UK City of Culture celebrations.

The complex phenomenon of volunteering

The UK Office for National Statistics (ONS) (2016) cites the International Labour Organisation (2001), in defining volunteering as "unpaid non-compulsory work: that is, time individuals give without pay to activities performed either through an organisation or directly for others outside of their household". They offer a caveat to this definition, recognising that there are formal and informal types of volunteering. Formal in the sense that it takes place in institutions, groups or organizations while informal volunteering relates to situations where people help friends and family perhaps in the role of childcare or adult care (2016, p. 2). The Office for National Statistics reveals that in terms of volunteering trends between 2005 and 2015, in the UK, there was drop in the total time that people volunteered, whilst conversely there was an increase in the number of people volunteering. This duality between formal and informal forms of volunteering requires further distinction, in the light of for example

Lyons, Wijkstrom, and Cary (1998), who argued that volunteering can be viewed from different perspectives, which include the *dominant paradigm, the non-profit paradigm*, the *civic society paradigm* and as *serious leisure*. Each of these perspectives has a type of motivation, an area of activity, organisational context and a mix of volunteer roles. The *dominant paradigm* includes motivations as altruistic acts, where people offer the 'gift' of their time to help people 'less fortunate' than themselves. The area of activity is the broad field of social welfare and might be based in organisations that are involved in statutory provision, involved in health care or education. The work done by volunteers is prescribed within a framework of 'human resources,' where staff are managed within recruitment and training framework, which is similar for full-time staff. The *non-profit paradigm* relates to agencies that increasingly are helping the state (both national and local) to deliver services, characterised as third-sector organizations or the volunteering industry. A profession of volunteer management has emerged and has led to the development of a *National Training Strategy for Volunteer Management* by the UK government (2010, p. 11). Rochester, Payne, and Howlett (2010) cite the work of Lyons, Wijkstrom, and Cary (1998) to identify how the *civil society paradigm* acts as a foil to the *non-profit paradigm*, and is based on voluntary activism, which is designed to encourage people to work together to respond to shared needs. Whilst there might be engagement with the not-for-profit organisation, they are more likely to be engaging in campaigning for better areas of provision in their sector. Lyons, Wijkstrom, and Cary (1998) identify areas of activity that are not restricted to social welfare but might include transport, town planning and the environment. Organisations involved in this form of volunteering are self-help groups and grassroots groups, now part of the 'community sector' according to Lyons, Wijkstrom, and Cary (1998); volunteers are not recruited but are inspired to take leadership roles, based on experience and a desire for self-growth. It is argued that these groups serve the interests of a membership rather than society as a whole.

In highlighting the launch of a *Manifesto for Volunteering in Europe* (European Volunteer Centre, 2006) as evidence of the importance of volunteering across a range of societies in Europe, Rochester, Payne, and Howlett (2010) cite the work of the European Volunteer Centre. In this context, volunteering is viewed as a form of "voluntary action (which) is an important component of the strategic objective of the European Union of becoming the most competitive and dynamic, knowledge-based economy in the world" (ibid.). Rochester, Payne and Howlett argue that this utilitarian application of volunteering is evidence that it forms a priority for government action, and an important policy stream for government. They view the importance for governments to maintain an infrastructure for volunteering *and* indeed a volunteering 'industry' (2010, p. 2). This 'industry' includes "national and local infrastructure organizations; an emerging body of professionally trained volunteer managers, quality standards and performance measures, all adopted to improve the quality of the volunteering experience" (2010, p. 8). Rochester, Payne and Howlett's (2010) appropriation of the paradigm *serious leisure*, is borrowed from the work of Stebbins (2004) and characterises volunteering as a form of leisure activity. In turn this type of volunteering is split into three categories; casual volunteering in local community events; project-based volunteering involved in the organisation of sporting, cultural or other events. *Serious leisure* as a hobby might mimic the development of skills and knowledge and acquisition of experience akin to developing a non-work career (Rochester, Payne, and Howlett, 2010, p. 14).

Neoliberalism and the concept of volunteering

Nichols and Ralston (2011) whilst acknowledging the "overlapping rewards of employment, leisure and volunteering," argue that volunteering should not always be viewed as the obverse of paid work or as the preparation to develop skills, that would enable people to become more employable. In citing the work of Levitas (2005), Nicols and Ralston noted how "the dominant discourse emphasising inclusion through employment, has undervalued unpaid work and volunteering and ignored more transformative possibilities involving rethinking the centrality of paid 'work'" (2011, p. 902). Rosol (2012) in her observations of community volunteering as a neoliberal strategy in the context of Berlin, argues that:

> The task for critical urban research is thus to analyse these processes of neoliberalization in the practice of urban development. For this purpose, not only "classical" neoliberal strategies such as privatisation, re-regulation and liberalisation in the transformation of cities must be studied, but also the seemingly "soft" strategies of involving civil society actors in urban governance.
>
> *(2012, p. 239)*

She added that: "This is connected to a changing understanding of the state and changing relation between state and citizens, usually described as a change from a welfare or providing state to an activating state" (ibid.).

An example of an activating state and volunteering, in a contemporary UK context, particularly emerged through the activating state-brand of "so-called" Big Society. This set the role of volunteering against the broader societal context of what utility political institutions such as government can extract from volunteering. Some commentators consider that volunteering can be a manifestation of exploitation, in the sense of extracting economic value from volunteers. In line with this thesis, Warren (2014, p. 228) highlights the work of Hardhill and Baines (2011, p. 7) who identified the "troubled rhetoric of the Big Society, which have threatened to devalue all non-monetised labour". Warren reminds us of the credo of Big Society, through the then-Prime Minister David Cameron, who identified "a new culture of voluntarism, philanthropy and social action" under the banner of Big Society (2010). Warren reminds us that this was perhaps just an example rebranding of an active civil society branding, which had emerged under former-Premier Tony Blair in 1997. The wider context of the brand of 'Big Society' under the Conservative-Lib-Dem coalition of 2010–2015 within the UK was that it was set against the broader societal branding of "austerity Britain". This had particular relevance for the cultural and creative industries, and the role of volunteers within them and offered some insights into how volunteering under the banner of Big Society, could offset diminished budgets, within the cultural sector, and those working in the creative labour force.

Co-production and creative labour

In highlighting the characteristics of creative labour, Warren suggested that geographical research "has tended to characterise it either in terms of 'cool' jobs in 'buzzing' places (Florida, 2002; Pratt, 2002) or precarious often poorly paid working conditions" (Watson, 2013; Reimer, 2009; Oakley, 2006). With these considerations in mind Warren highlighted that the purpose of the article

> argues for a subtler consideration of the complex combination of factors at play within the cultural ecology of art-making. Specifically, it focuses on the role of unpaid labour and volunteering, a form of work that has largely been ignored in geographical scholarship on creative labour. This constitutes an important oversight, given that volunteering is often relied upon – if not factored in economically – for large-and small-scale cultural organizations alike.
>
> *(2014, p. 278)*

Warren identifies that volunteering in arts organizations, viewed in a contemporary sense, "is gifted as non-monetary form of support in hard times." It can also be characterised as a 'helping out' 'gifting' or 'pitching in'. In highlighting this link between volunteering for the arts in times of austerity, Warren uses the example of the Yorkshire Sculpture Park, which lost 12% funding between 2011 and 2012. The fact that the workforce has an equal number of volunteers and paid members of staff was a further example of the increasing significance of volunteering in 'hard times' of austerity. Furthermore, Boland, Murtagh, and Shirlow (2018) suggest that City of Culture competitions are part of what they consider to be 'neo-liberal place competition' (also dubbed 'place-wars') and applied this thesis to Derry-Londonderry, who were UK City of Culture in 2013. The kernel of their argument is that, "Neoliberal urbanism generates fierce inter-city competition to host major cultural events, conditioning the actions of local stakeholders who produce bid documents resulting in excessive targets for impact and legacy *i.e. impact inflation*" (2018, p. 1). Given that they consider that these competitions might be fuelled by hype, it is perhaps at a more micro-level, to over-inflate the role of volunteers (and indeed as with the Yorkshire Sculpture Park, fill the role of paid members of staff) in carrying out the responsibilities of a winning city.

Warren suggests a more holistic role for volunteers, when working in an arts organisation, and suggests it should be seen as a form of "emotional and embodied acts of philanthropy" and that "volunteers in the arts can be viewed as philanthropist arts who give their labour, passion and time to place-making" (2014, p. 279). Warren further identifies that: "While under-addressed in geography, the role of volunteers in the production of art and tourism destinations more broadly is integral to the functioning of the creative and cultural sector" (2014, p. 279). In citing the work of Flew (2012, p. 105) and Menger (1999, p. 558), Warren emphasises that the "lure of artistic and creative work can be explained by a complex mix of monetary and non-monetary rewards: intrinsic motivators of personal satisfaction and social status; risk-taking despite the comparatively low probability of personal success" (2014, p. 279). Warren (2014) argues that volunteering is also seen as having "important implications for place-making; a social construction of meaning that helps to create a shared local identity" (2014, p. 280). Warren cites the work of Massey (2004) to identify how the individual agency of the volunteer can play a role in the ongoing dialectic of a place and the "re-assemb(ling) of the social and material elements of a place" (ibid). Arguably, volunteering for mega-events, both sporting and cultural, can contribute to a sense of place-making through individual agency creating elements of civic pride. This notion of civic pride emerged as a tangible feature of the positive response to the hosting of UK City of Culture 2017, in Hull.

Volunteering and mega-events

In providing observations of how the concept of volunteering is linked to mega-events, Nichols and Ralston (2011) noted that the legacies that are attributed to mega-events such as an Olympic Games tend to focus on economic benefits. They argue that volunteering can provide benefits of social inclusion, beyond considerations of employment, and that broader benefits might include benefits of active citizenship. Their research focused on the volunteering experience at the Manchester Commonwealth Games of 2002, with the hope that these insights could inform the benefits to be accrued by volunteers at London 2012. They highlighted through in-depth research the views of volunteers from the Commonwealth Games, that:

> Volunteering has provided integration into society. It has allowed volunteers to express active citizenship by 'giving something back', and to express an affinity with their

home town. Volunteering has provided a sense of worth and status independent of material worth.

(2011, p. 912)

Volunteering and the visual arts in the UK

Silva identified that in a UK context "in debates about participation in the arts, it is well accepted that a choice of going to a museum or art gallery, like that of going to the theatre or the opera, doesn't exist for a vast number of people. Some enjoy art, others feel something for art but feel disenfranchised and excluded from art" (2008, p. 267). Therefore, the plethora of voluntary and volunteering organizations throughout the UK such as Voluntary Arts play a vital role in making the visual arts more accessible to communities. Voluntary Arts highlight that they "work across the UK and the Republic of Ireland, with everyone who gets creative purely for the love of it. We also work with anyone who helps facilitate creative participation, those who fund it, provide space for it to happen and the people who work alongside communities to support them in their creative endeavours."

Writing in the Voluntary Arts newsletter, Kevin Murphy, presented an argument for *'How Creative Citizens are Building Hope in Local Communities'*. To support this supposition contained within the title of the article, he provided a catalogue of creative initiatives across the UK and Ireland, including; *Re-Tune* in Glasgow, where people with mental illnesses help to repair and rebuild stringed musical instruments, to a *Feather of Angels in Rotherham* where hundreds of interpretations of angels were on show throughout the town (Murphy, 2018). Both the celebration of the performing and visual arts form is a key part of the programmes of UK Cities of Culture, and the next part of the chapter focuses on Hull as UK City of Culture, and the role volunteers in the programme, and their engagement with residents and visitors through the visual arts.

Hull UK city of culture 2017

Research on the role of the volunteers during Hull City of Culture captured a range of both quantitative and qualitative data, which highlighted a number of statistical and personal insights as to what it meant to be a volunteer and their important role to the success of Hull 2017 City of Culture and also the social impacts of volunteering. The Cultural Transformations: The Impacts of Hull UK City of Culture 2017 – Preliminary Outcomes Evaluation report (2018) confirmed some of the headline features of the Information by Design Hull 2017 – Volunteer Programme End of Year Evaluation Report (2018). The Cultural Transformations evaluation report (2018) provided compelling statistical evidence of the number of people who were attracted to volunteer on Hull 2017 City of Culture. This report stated that "4,500 individuals expressed an interest in becoming a volunteer, with over 2,400 (set against a target of those going on to apply and successfully be trained and deployed" (2018, p. 198). This report revealed that for nearly 20% of volunteers, this was the first time that they volunteered and "across the project, 84,000 shifts took place, equating to 337,000 volunteering hours". The report also noted that in addition to volunteers coming from a range of different cultural backgrounds, 71% volunteers were women, 51% were in employment, 28% retired, 11% in full-time education and 10% "living with a long-term illness or disability or unemployed". In terms of diversity, 8% were BAME and 92% white British. The age profile revealed that the dominant age bracket was 55 to 64 at 27%, 17% of volunteers were 65–74 (2% over 75). With 19% of volunteers in the age bracket of 45–54, this meant that over 63% of volunteers were in the combined age brackets of 45–75. So, 10% were 35–44, 11 % 25–34 and 14% aged 16–24. Generally, the older demographic of volunteers mimicked the older demographic of audiences. 84,000 shifts took place and 98% of volunteers said that "their overall experience of volunteering has been good or excellent" (2018, pp. 199–200).

Hull UK City of Culture 2017: volunteering and the visual arts

Hull was the second city after Derry in Northern Ireland to receive the accolade of UK City of Culture and it will be followed in 2021 by Coventry. The UK has previously had two cities representatives as European Capitals of Culture – Glasgow in 1990 and Liverpool in 2008. In 2013, the city of Hull received the news that in 2017, it would represent the UK in 2017 as UK City of Culture. In 2015, Hull 2017 Ltd, an independent company, was established to deliver a mission of 365 days of transformational culture. This vision was organised and co-ordinated by six directorates, one of which was the Communications, Government and Stakeholders Directorate, which contained the team which co-ordinated the volunteering programme.

The City of Culture programme was set within four seasons, *Made in Hull, Roots and Routes, Freedom* and *Tell the World* and these seasons provided a thematic backdrop to the 300+ venue spaces, 2,800 events, cultural activities, installations and exhibitions which contained 465 new commissions. Overall, there were 5.3 million audience visits and more than 9 in 10 residents engaged in at least one cultural activity (*The Cultural Transformations: Preliminary Outcomes Evaluation report*, 2018, p. 11). This report also highlighted that "in the end of year residents' survey, almost three-quarters of residents (74%) stated that they had liked or loved the UK City of Culture 2017 in Hull, with only 4% saying that they disliked it or hated it" (2018, p. 142). Furthermore, "over half of audiences reported that the event they attended introduced them to a new art form or subject to the first time" (ibid.).

Overall, there were five impact areas, which included Arts and Culture, Place-Making, Economy, Partnership and Development and Society and Wellbeing which the *Preliminary Outcomes Evaluation* report analysed. There were a variety of aims within the programme which included the aim: 'To raise the aspirations, abilities and knowledge of residents through increased participation and learning' (Aim: 8). The volunteering programme was one of the 'vehicles' to help achieve this aim, and there was an emphasis on volunteers being involved in projects which would be able to deliver long-term benefits. It is important to acknowledge that there is a long-standing existing commitment to volunteering in Hull and as such an established infrastructure for volunteering. This infrastructure has been in place well before Hull 2017 and did not have any direct role in the establishing of arrangements for volunteering during Hull UK City of Culture.

The volunteering programme was launched in March 2016, and it was recognised that "with the scale and diversity of the project, volunteers roles varied greatly from practical event support to visitor welcome and even mass participation cast roles for major outdoor spectacles" (*The Cultural Transformations: Preliminary Outcomes Evaluation report*, 2018, p. 58). The first volunteers were recruited at an 'interview' stage, where they had the opportunity to opt for certain types of activities and events. Depending on the menu of events activities, available on a daily basis, each volunteer would be able to volunteer for events which corresponded to personal interest and expertise. With Arts and Culture as one the five main impact areas of the programme, opportunities to volunteer in the visual arts were plentiful.

Building on an existing visual arts infrastructure within the city

It is important to emphasise that there is an established and long-lineage of visual arts provision in Hull, from the avant-garde, to the more traditional representations of the visual arts. The work of *Cossi Fanni Tuti* and *Hull Time Based Arts*, from the 1970s onwards, offered a more radical representation of the visual arts, sitting alongside community-based provision at *Art-Link*, to a range of public sector art galleries, curating and exhibiting contemporary visual arts. Arguably, Hull 2017 UK City of Culture, enlivened the existing visual arts locations and provided the opportunity to show-case well-known formal visual arts spaces but also allowed the freedom and the scope to experiment and open up engagement for less traditional audiences for the visual arts. For example, as part of the Creative Communities Programme, *I Wish to Communicate with You*, was a high-profile public art project by the Goodwin Development Trust, in the Thornton Estate of Hull, involving local residents working with international lighting consultants and artists. (*The Cultural Transformations: Preliminary Evaluation report*, 2018, p. 55). This involved the residents choosing a coloured filter which covered the outside light on their outdoor corridor. Likewise, the *No Limits* programme brought artistic residencies to both primary and secondary schools in Hull. Hull 2017 Ltd. in conjunction with a private developer was able to open the Humber Street Gallery, a new contemporary art gallery (initially for 2017 and now for another 3 years), which provided a venue for more unconventional art performances, best exemplified by the Rotterdam based *Worm* avant-garde collective, 'taking-over' the gallery for a weekend in August 2017. The University of Hull's Brynmoor Jones Gallery staged a series of prestigious exhibitions, with the *Lines of Thought* exhibition which included drawings by Leonardo da Vinci and Michelangelo and attracted over 20,000 visitors (as indicated below the visitor total for 2016 was 6,000).

In terms of audience development in the visual arts and at a local level, a vehicle for social inclusion, the City of Culture year in Hull, saw the growth of audiences in galleries and museums in the city. For example, the Ferens Art Gallery, which hosted the *Turner Prize 2017*, had 519,000 visitors which was an increase in 309% from 2016 to 2017. Likewise, the Brynmoor Jones Library Art Gallery, went from attracting 6,000 visitors in 2016 to 55,000 in 2017, an increase in 785%. The newly opened Humber Street Gallery had 121,000 visitors in 2017. The Maritime Museum which also had visual arts exhibitions, had an increase of 393 % in 2017 with the audiences increasing from 70,000, in 2016, to 346,000 in 2017 (*The Cultural Transformations: Preliminary Evaluation report*, 2018, p. 84). Although there were criticisms that audiences might have been more diverse and included more 'hard to reach' audiences within the city, undoubtedly audience engagement with the visual arts was made more accessible by the interventions of volunteers as community *animateurs* and cultural mediators.

In the field of arts management there are potentially complex processes involved in ensuring that audiences have the greatest opportunities to be able to engage and understand representations of the visual arts, which might be difficult 'to read'. In that sense multi-sensory interpretation techniques might be employed to offer more opportunities to make work more accessible. Whilst within the context of Hull these techniques are prevalent in gallery spaces, what has been missing until Hull 2017 City of Culture is the addition of cultural mediators beyond the role of gallery staff 'policing' work. Hull 2017 volunteers have successfully carried out this role.

In proving a broader understanding of the concept of cultural mediation, *Pro Helvetia, the Swiss Arts Council*, from a continental European context, has developed an impressive bank of knowledge on cultural mediation, for those working in the professional field of the visual arts. Whilst they acknowledge that there are cultural variants as to what cultural mediation is, they identify that it is "evoking questions of negotiation which are at the heart of working between artistic objects, institutions, their social contexts and the people who encounter them" (Prohelvetia, 2018, p. 14). It is also interesting to note that the Liverpool Biennal, a 5-month festival of contemporary art is partly 'staffed' by volunteers and it is revealing in the advertisement for volunteers, that a job description to work on the Liverpool Biennal, 2018, includes reference to the role of cultural mediation.

For Hull 2017 City of Culture, volunteer shifts included working in different indoor and outdoor venues in the city, and Hull 2017 Ltd also instigated a *Look-Up programme*, of 10 art installations throughout everyday spaces in the city, beyond valorised gallery and museum spaces. These public spaces included car parks, shopping centres, the railway station and various refurbished city squares. The artwork ranged from the large and imposing *Blade* (effectively an artistic representation of a wind-turbine blade) to a series of artistic images of trans-migration, applied to windows in the entrance area of the railway station. Volunteers were on hand to meet and talk with members of the public and to discuss the artwork with them. As with the indoor visual arts venues of the Ferens Art Gallery and the Humber Street Gallery, volunteers played a pivotal role in adding their contribution to the experience of the public in their encounter with the artwork. Part of the aim of the *Look-Up programme* in the commissioning of potential artists, was to inspire to look at the city in a different way. *The Look-Up evaluation report* completed by Hull 2017 Ltd highlighted that: "The vision for Look Up was to challenge people's perceptions and experience of Hull. It sought to present a series of new artworks to intrigue and inspire throughout 2017, created in partnership; inviting people to 'look up from your phone, look out of our window, look around you–who knows what you'll see'" (2018, p. 8).

In some ways the aims of the project were redolent of John Berger's notion of 'Seeing with New Eyes' (1973) and the notion of an aesthetic approach to the visual arts, as part of everyday experiences. In a sense, this incorporates the wider notion of the democratisation of the visual arts, as something that is opened up to a wider audience and does not require crossing the physical or symbolic threshold of the entrance of a gallery or museum. Seeking permission from 'tastemakers' to engage in art or rather wondering whether you have permission to cross cultural thresholds, can be divisive, in who feels 'included' in a codified visual language, which is mainly for the domain of cultural elites. Arguably, art in public spaces potentially has created sense of accessibility, in freely allowing audiences to engage with it. This could be viewed as an approach to social inclusion and links with Hull 2017 Ltd broader 'Society and Wellbeing' aims, which acknowledged the generational disconnect of lack of engagement in the visual arts.

In making greater sense of this conundrum of social exclusion, it is helpful to apply the work of Bourdieu (see *Distinction*, 1984) and the concept of habitus. Authors such as Silva (2008) identify that: "Bourdieu's thesis identified a correspondence between class position and taste for legitimate culture, which resulted in a dominant class claiming and reproducing social privilege as a concomitant of its superior cultural competence" (2008, p. 268). Silva applied ideas related to Bourdieu's work to understanding the linkages between the visual art field and broader cultural processes and in particular how "cultural capacity affects the structure of social inequality," adding that "the field of visual art appears as one of the most distinctive fields of cultural practices, and one where the intensity of participation is highly relevant for social position" (2008, p. 267).

Hull (as had Derry in 2013) received the accolade of hosting the annual Turner Prize, in a key gallery space at the Ferens Art Gallery run by Hull Culture and Leisure Company, which is an offshoot of Hull City Council. As part of and complementing the City of Culture programme, the gallery had hosted a range of exhibitions, events and activities with volunteers 'shadowing' staff on staff shifts. Anecdotal evidence suggests that without volunteers carrying out shifts, which included face-to-face engagement with the public in various gallery spaces, the gallery would have struggled to remain open to the same extent with only paid members of staff. This was also the case in the latest new gallery to open in the city, the Humber Street Gallery, which was staffed through funding provided by Hull 2017 Ltd. As with the Ferens Art Gallery, the Humber Street Gallery was staffed by volunteers on a daily basis and volunteers were not restricted to roles of courtliness and information providers but carried out more extensive roles of cultural mediation.

For each of the *Look-Up* installations Hull 2017 Ltd employed an external peer assessor to give both quantitative and qualitative feedback on the artwork, partly through the application of the Arts Council quality metrics, to assess different elements of the installations. In addition to responding to 10 criteria, to assess the quality of the artwork, peer assessors also had the opportunity to offer views on Hull in general, and their perceptions of the city. Without exception peer assessors and artists singled out volunteers, not only for their courtliness and 'welcome' to the city but for many of the peer assessors they felt that volunteers were able to enrich the experience of viewing artwork. Volunteers appear to have gone beyond the role of city ambassadors and information providers and have engaged in a way with arts professionals that was refreshingly innovative and engaging. Their interpretations of the artwork were valued by the peer assessors. Peer assessors included artists and arts administrators, sourced regionally and nationally, and included national museums, such as the Victoria and Albert Museum.

In the words of one peer assessor when assessing the *Turner Prize 2017* at the Ferens Art Gallery, Hull that:

> I have been in the 'trade' for a long time and I thought the volunteers were quite impressive. Somewhere else they might have been 'super-annoying' because they were so enthusiastic. But it seemed to fit because it was of the place and so on. They were so enthusiastic and it really coloured your view of what the place was like. It was not just the *Turner Prize* but generally when I arrived they offered you something they thought you might have missed and it was so impressive. It was very good and it did change and colour the way I thought about the *Turner Prize* as well. They diluted and normalised it a bit and made it 'backdoor' so to speak.

This peer assessor had attended many of the previous *Turner Prizes* and sounded pleasantly surprised at the impact that the volunteers had had in their experience of this addition of the exhibition.

Another peer assessor, from a senior curatorial role in a national museum, came to evaluate one of the last of the 10 *Look-Up* projects, in the autumn of 2017, sited in the newly refurbished Trinity Square, next to Hull Minster, on the edge of the old town in the city. *A Hall for Hull* by Chile-based architects Pezo von Elrichshausen in collaboration with Swiss-based artist Felice Varini, was described by RIBA who had a hand in commissioning the work as "a hypostyle monumental room open to the immediate surroundings" (Royal Institute of British Architects, 2017). It consisted of 16 tubular open-top towers, made from perforated galvanised steel, that were accessible for people to enter them. The art work of Varini, was added to the towers, as a geometrical illusion which could best be seen from a so-called sweet-spot in the square. The peer assessor observed that:

> The volunteers were helping people stand at points where you can see Varini's work quite clearly as you need to find the 'sweet-spot' on the columns. Varini's optical illusion on the columns you can see from the perfect spot and this was not clear to people. The volunteers were helping people to see it and it was critical volunteers were there to help people understand the dimensions of the work because it was possible to pass by and not see it, as there was not a hoarding. You can figure it out for yourself but having the volunteers there was great and they were able to give more understanding to it too and you could have a chat with them. They were super really, helping people to understand all the City of Culture projects and everywhere I went everyone was incredibly informative and wanted you to find out about things.

The volunteers' skills as cultural mediators might in part have emerged from their initial training course; volunteers engaged in 'arts appreciation' in a pop-up mock gallery space in a training centre. Additionally, there were specific training sessions both to work in galleries and museums or specifically for events such as the Turner Prize. Hull 2017 Ltd. also provided a series of master classes which include a variety of visual arts appreciation sessions. *The Cultural Transformations; Preliminary Outcomes Evaluation* (2018) reported that "478 volunteer masterclasses were run across 110 different subjects, with 12,352 attendances. 84% of volunteers felt that they had gained skills from Hull 2017 training, and 76% from volunteer shifts, which they could use in other parts of their life" and furthermore "over 2,400 volunteers contributed 337,000 hours of social action, equivalent to 38.5 years. For 1 in 5 volunteers, it was their first experience of volunteering" (2018, p. 184).

Two quotes from volunteers who attended Volunteer Focus Groups during 2017 provide an understanding of the social impacts of volunteering. 'Volunteer One' described:

> I was the type of person who couldn't go anywhere on my own, and I knew that if I did this, I would have to make that step and go out there on my own and meet people and talk to people I never would, and it worked. I got more confidence.
>
> *(2018, p. 195)*

Volunteer Two described:

> I've enjoyed every time you go on a shift, you never know who you're going to meet, who you're going to talk to. I've had wonderful conversations with other volunteers and visitors. Just lovely, lovely conversations, which I wouldn't have had normally. It gives you extra confidence and pride.
>
> *(ibid.)*

Conclusions

Clearly, there are judgements to be made from the range of points raised within this chapter, on the context of cultural mega-events and the roles of volunteers who work alongside organizations with a paid workforce. The expanding scope of volunteer in contemporary society has seen the emergence of a volunteering industry, in which volunteers are subsumed into the wider organisational workforces. With diminishing budgets, in an age of austerity, organizations can choose to employ volunteers as a cost-cutting exercise. In the rhetoric of so-called Big Society, this might be viewed as 'culture on the cheap', where volunteers are used instrumentally to fill gaps in programmes. These interpretations have credence, if one accepts UK Cities of Culture are part of 'neoliberal place competition,' where destinations are partly chosen because of the existing scarcity of resources, in terms of funding streams for arts and culture. Arguably, this is intensified by destinations that are associated with economic decline, poverty and unemployment, such as Hull.

Anecdotal evidence from the programming of the visual arts in the 365 days of transformational cultural events in Hull, suggests that venues such as the Ferens Art Gallery and the Humber Street Gallery were reliant to a certain extent on volunteers to enable extended opening hours to be enjoyed by visitors. The implication is that without volunteers both venues could not have fully benefitted from extensive programmes and opening hours. Therefore, one interpretation of the role of volunteers in this context was that they were used instrumentally, redolent of the *non-profit paradigm*. However, in the broader application of the work of Lyons,

Wijkstrom, and Cary (1998) to the role of Hull City of Culture volunteers, one could argue that the *civic society paradigm* or the paradigm of *serious leisure paradigm* best explains their volunteering profile.

The role of volunteers went beyond 'staffing spaces', to employing a level of expertise that enabled volunteers to engage in cultural mediation and add their knowledge and expertise to the experience of enjoying the visual arts. Volunteers have had a unique part in delivering an extensive UK City of Culture programme and particularly in the role that they have played in quality arts and cultural events. They, as exemplified through the views of peer assessors, have demonstrated an expertise in cultural mediation, which goes beyond the sum of the parts of training and 'master class' development, initiated by Hull 2017 Ltd. This has led to a greater sense of social inclusion within the city, in which the visual arts have been the meeting point for social engagement.

Arguably, arts management has been transformed by the organic development of an infrastructure for arts and cultural activities, with volunteers at the heart of audience engagement and development. If we accept Bourdieu's (1984) central ideas about the accumulation of cultural capital thesis, volunteers have succeeded in playing a vital role in the democratisation of visual arts engagement. This has arguably led to an extended range of people who enjoy art, and it has been possible to 'move' people from the groups of the disenfranchised and the excluded, into the group of the culturally engaged. Arts management might have become a process of expressions from 'below,' as much as taste-making views expressed 'from above'.

However, Boland et al.'s interpretation of a CoC competition as a competitive contest suggests that it is not necessarily the most productive and equitable way of planning for cultural provision. This in turn ushers in a wider debate on a 'destination competition', with a winner able to leverage further resources for a city and losing candidate destinations having to fund and manage the visual arts with diminishing budgets. There is scope within further research in academy to compare the existing and long-term developments of infrastructures for the visual arts to understand the role played by 'Culture Competitions', in transformational elements within destinations.

Whilst winning destinations might boast a more high-profile series of arts and cultural events, perhaps of a magnitude that without increased budgets, a destination would not be able to afford, this raises questions as to how a programme of events is created, either dominated by cultural taste-making judgements 'from above' or from a greater blend of home-grown talent and expertise. There might in-part be an 'opportunity cost' for hosting destinations having a displacement effect, in displacing arts and cultural people and organizations from cultural programming. Furthermore, City of Culture programming might not have benefitted from their long-term involvement in everyday cultural expression in that locality. Additionally, there needs to be a breadth in cultural programming that incorporates diverse art forms.

The balance of the final iteration of a City of Culture (or ECOC) arts and cultural programme will have supporters and dissenters, in equal measure, and the conundrum of over-filling a programme to achieve a 365-day target of activity, is pitched against fewer arts and cultural events but perhaps introducing more high-profile quality events. It is interesting to note that the evaluation of Hull UK City of Culture 2017 saw positive responses from audiences about the quality of events. In fact, the *Preliminary Outcomes Evaluation* report (2018) noted that in terms of average audience ratings for events and activities: "Across all domains, audience tended to rate the Hull 2017 programme activities higher than the average rating seen across the 400 Arts Council England benchmark projects, which is a strong endorsement of the overall quality of the programme" (2018, p. 71).

It is possible to speculate that engagement in the visual arts within the city of Hull has changed significantly, within the context of the unique staging of the City of Culture event. The notion of a traditional infrastructure for the visual arts, in which communities may or may not have engaged with the visual arts, has seen a latent demand for a visual arts experience emerge. Furthermore, volunteers in 2018 remain an empowered group of workers, with a developing specialist knowledge of the visual arts enjoyment, to share both with community members and visitors to the city. As such they provide tangible evidence of power of the visual arts to offer positive strategies for social inclusion.

It is hoped that this chapter adds to the developing understanding of the role of volunteers in cultural-mega events and specifically within the field of the visual arts. It demonstrates that future research evaluating the role of volunteers in this type of cultural mega-event requires finding ways of capturing the complexity of how volunteers engage with community members and visitors to have a heightened experience of the visual arts. Furthermore, Hull City of Culture 2017 experiences of volunteering provides evidence that whilst there are common elements of learning points that might be applied to similar cultural mega-events, it is the elements of *uniqueness* that require careful deliberation and articulation. This *uniqueness* might be particularly related to the multi-layered aspects of the cultural features and accumulation of distinctive historical aspects of the city, which have fashioned an approach to volunteering, *unique* to Hull.

References

Berger, J. (1973). *Ways of seeing*. London: Penguin.

Boland, P., Murtagh, B., and Shirlow, P. (2016). Fashioning a city of culture: 'Life and place changing' or '12-month party'? *International Journal of Cultural Policy*. doi: 10.1080/10286632.2016.1231181.

———. (2018). Neoliberal place competition and *culturephila*: Explored through the lens of Derry-Londonderry. *Social and Cultural Geography*. https://doi.org/10.1080/14649365.2018.1514649.

Bourdieu, P. (1984). *Distinction: A social critique of the judgement of taste*. London: Routledge.

Cameron, D. (2010). *'Big Society Speech'* 19 July. Available at: https://www.gov.uk/government/speeches/big-society-speech [Accessed 8 Oct. 2018].

European Volunteer Centre (2006). A *Manifesto for Volunteering in Europe*. European Volunteer Centre: Brussels.

Flew, T. (2012). *The creative industries: Culture and policy*. London: SAGE.

Florida, R. (2002). *The use of the creative class: And how its transforming work, leisure, community and everyday life*. New York: Basic Books.

Goffman, E. (1969). *The presentation of self in everyday life*. Harmondsworth: Penguin.

Hardhill, I. and Baines, S. (2011). *Enterprising care: Unpaid voluntary action in the 21st century*. Bristol: Policy Press.

Information by design (2018). Hull 2017-Volunteer Programme End of Year Evaluation – Report. Information by Design: Hull.

Levitas, R. (2005). *The inclusive society? Social exclusion and new labour*. 2nd ed. Basingstoke: Palgrave.

Lowndes, V. and Pratchett, L. (2012). Local governance under the coalition government: Austerity, localism and big society. *Local Government Studies*, 38(1), pp. 21–40.

Lyons, M., Wijkstrom, P. and Cary, G. (1998). Comparative studies of volunteering: What is being studied? *Voluntary Action*, 1(1), pp. 45–54.

Massey, D. (2004). Geographises of responsibility. *Geografiska Annaler B*, 86, pp. 730–750.

Menger, P.M. (1999). Artistic labour markets and careers. *Annual Review of Sociology*, 25, pp. 541–574.

Murphy, K. (2018). How creative citizens are building hope in local communities. *Voluntary Arts Newspaper*, March. Available at: https://www.voluntaryarts.org/how-creative-citizens-are-building-hope-in-local-communities [Accessed 3 Oct. 2018].

Nichols, G. and Ralston, R. (2011). Social inclusion through volunteering: The legacy potential of the 2012 Olympic games. *Sociology*, 45(4), pp. 900–914.

Oakley, K. (2006). Include us out-economic development and social policy in the creative industries. *Cultural Trends*, 144, pp. 283–302.

Pratt, A. (2002). Hot jobs in cool places. The material culture of new media product spaces: The case of South of Market, San Francisco. *Information, Communication and Society*, 51, pp. 27–50.

Prohelvetia. (2018). *Time for cultural mediation*. Available at: https://prohelvitia.ch/app/uploads/2017/09/tfcm_o_complete_publication.pdf. [Accessed 2 Oct. 2018].

Reimer, S. (2009). Geographies of production II: Fashion, creativity and fragmented labour. *Progress in Human Geography*, 331, pp. 65–73.

Rochester, C., Payne, A.E. and Howlett, S. (2010). *Volunteering in the 21st century*. Basingstoke: Palgrave Macmillan.

Royal Institute of British Architects. (2017). Available at: www.architecture.com/whats-on/a-hall-for-hull. [Accessed 2 Oct. 2018].

Rosol, M. (2012). Community volunteering as neoliberal strategy? Green space production in Berlin. *Antipode*, 4(1), pp. 239–225.

Silva, E. (2008). Cultural capital and visual art in the contemporary UK. *Cultural Trends*, 17(4), December, pp. 267–287.

Starkey, D.J, Atkinson, D., McDonagh, B. Mckeon, S., and Salter, E. (eds.) (2017). *Hull: Culture, History, Place*. Liverpool: Liverpool University Press.

Stebbins, R.A. (2004). Serious leisure, volunteerism and quality of life. In: J.T. Haworth and A.J. Veal, eds., *Work and leisure*. New York: Routledge.

Voluntary Arts – What we do. Available at: www.voluntaryarts.org/Pages/Category/what-we-do [Accessed 1 Oct. 2018].

Warren, S. (2014). 'I want this place to thrive': Volunteering, co-production and creative labour. *Area*, 46(3), pp. 278–284.

Watson, A. (2013). Running a studio's a silly business: Work and employment in the contemporary recording studio sector. *Area*, 453.

18

POSTMODERN APPROACHES IN CURATING AND MANAGING ARTS FESTIVALS IN GLOBAL CITIES

Benny Lim

Introduction

Getz (2012) argued that a festival could be defined as a notable occurrence where the word 'notable' is interchangeable with the word 'special', making common the term 'special event' when referring to a festival. Special events are characterized by the concept of transient, which suggests that such events should not happen often, and are mostly temporary, and short-term (Gilbert and Lizotte, 1998). The limited literature on arts festivals has always focused on two directions, which seem to overlap sometimes, and yet, contradict at other times. It is reflected in many texts that festivals impact and build their respective communities. Other literature suggest that arts festivals are regarded as important aspects of the creative industries and that they contribute to the creative economy and the overall branding of the city. Quinn (2005) first identified a pressing situation in a comprehensive paper, which discussed how government in urbanized cities are more interested in the economic impact of arts festivals, and how festivals serve as a quick fix to a city's branding. In the same paper, she also highlighted that these festivals fail to celebrate and build communities.

Drawing on Quinn's research, I started visiting arts festivals since 2014, with the main intention to observe new directions in curating and managing arts festivals in urban areas, specifically in global cities. A global city is usually characterized by being the financial, media, medical, entertainment and innovation center of the state/country (Sassen, 2001). It is also where the key universities of the state/country are situated (Cunningham, 2012). Unlike other similar researches that explore interesting trends and new management styles, this research specifically delves into how the weakening of community linkages has brought about some new possibilities in curating and managing arts festivals in global cities.

In the context of Asia, Singapore, Hong Kong, Tokyo and Seoul are usually considered as global cities, although the most recent A.T. Kearney Global Cities Index 2017 includes other Asian cities such as Bangkok, Kuala Lumpur, Jakarta, Taipei, as well as a number of Chinese cities (Dessibourg and Hales, 2017). As of December 2017, non-intrusive participant observations of 15 unique arts festivals in four Asian cities, namely, Singapore, Kuala Lumpur, Bangkok and Hong Kong were conducted. In each festival, I participated in a range of the activities as an audience member, and communicated with different stakeholders informally, including other audience members and festivals' organizers. DeWalt and DeWalt (2011) recommended that researchers conducting participant observation should understand the field and connect with relevant stakeholders, be aware of the situations on the field, and learn how to listen and when to withdraw. Many arts festivals' websites also contain crucial and useful information such as artists' information, programs descriptions, and annual reports. Hence, secondary research, which included the collection and analysis of reports and other information from the websites of 30 arts festivals in these four cities, were also carried out.

This chapter discusses, drawing on the context of postmodernism, some new directions in how arts festivals in global cities are being curated and managed, with reference to case studies from four such cities in Asia. The chapter concludes with recommendations to arts managers in tackling the challenges and new directions of arts festivals in global cities.

Building communities and sense of place

The term 'festival' has its origins from traditions that celebrate festivities (Ryken, 2002). A festival differs from a 'fair' in that a fair is a gathering of tradespeople or vendors (Tribhuwan, 2003), while a festival has always been a form of celebration, where a distinctive community comes together to celebrate the special event (Getz, 2012). The festivities could involve sacred and religious elements, where communities pay respects to the supernatural forces that protect them or adhere to specific traditional practices. Hence, festivals have always played a positive role to integrate the communities and the people within them (Jepson and Clarke, 2016; Yeoman, Robertson, and Smith, 2012). The place of the festival itself contributes to the uniqueness of the community, and it offers a sense of pride to the people who reside within it. Derrett (2003) saw festivals as a long-term investment for a community to build a sense of cohesiveness, attachment, lifestyle, values, active citizenship, well-being, and new directions for future. By participating in local festivals, participants can search for authenticity, uniqueness, and familiarity of the city, and thus build up the sense of belonging and civic-mindedness (Derrett, 2004). Further thought shows that festivals also facilitate visitors from outside these communities to understand and appreciate their respective cultures. The festival becomes a place within a place for visitors to come in touch with the place and its community (Haanpää, García-Rosell, and Seija Tuulentie, 2016). Another important consideration is for the events in the festival to be executed without spoiling the quality of life of the locals and their future generations. Members within the community should be considered as key stakeholders, partners and sponsors in the development of the events and in a large number of cases, as it is them who form the majority of the festivals' participants (Jepson and Clarke, 2016). Therefore, it should be noted that a festival is not able to provide to the heart of a community unless its organizers make them culturally inclusive and the members within the community are fully invited and engaged by the event (Jepson, Wiltshire, and Clarke, 2008).

Festivals now include secular aspects such as arts festivals, which encompass a wide range of artistic activities such as performing arts, visual arts and more recently, digital arts, usually held in a specific place and curated with consideration of a specific community. Arts festivals are usually organized and presented by an association or organization, a group or a person (Tonkin and Jameel, 2016). Bourdieu (1984) has illustrated the impacts of building cultural capital as the individual's means to the enhancement of social status and distinction. The intellectual satisfaction received through participating in such cultural activities promotes individuals' creative thinking, the pursuit of arts excellence and further personal development, which in turn, build up one's cultural capital, and in the process, facilitate one's contribution to society on the whole.

Kinder and Harland (2004) also suggested that participating in the arts can influence individuals in advance learning, attitudinal and behavioral change, relationship, communication skills and psychological development. Enjoyment and engagement created in arts festivals or events influence participants' interests and thus encourage the learning of arts and self-expression. By empowering the community with the ability to appreciate arts, arts festivals can bring about cultural democratization and fulfill art education purpose of the organizing place. On a societal level, an increase in the focus on arts festivals could give rise to social awareness of issues and problems that might otherwise have remained dormant (Slater, 2016).

Arts festivals in global cities: festivalization and the disappearing communities

There is a growing number of arts festivals alongside many other different types of festivities in global cities. For instance, there is, on a monthly average, one to two arts festivals happening in Singapore and Hong Kong. Hence, the pressing issue is that some of these arts festivals are outcomes of the effects of 'festivalization', which cultural policy makers, mostly the government, adopt as a strategy to fulfill policies and economic growth. Négrier (2015) defined festivalization as "the process by which cultural activity, previously presented in a regular, ongoing pattern or season, is reconfigured to form a 'new' event, e.g., a regular series of jazz concerts is reconfigured as a jazz festival." Liu (2014) stated that arts and culture festivalization as urban policies had become a worldwide phenomenon, with aims to preserve cultural identity, promote and (re) brand the city, attract tourists, develop and rejuvenate communities, promote active citizenry, educate the public about arts and culture, exchange creative ideas, develop cultural facilities and infrastructure – the list goes on. Local politicians are becoming increasingly convinced of the potential of festivals to boost economic development and growth (Quinn, 2010; Pejovic, 2009), over and above their socio-cultural impacts to communities and their people.

Global cities are often more cosmopolitan in comparison to other urban areas, suburban or rural areas. With the over-saturation of festivals and the presence of diverse communities, each with different motivations and wants, global cities may not offer the right conditions for arts festivals to truly fulfill the celebratory function of communities and the people within, let alone building an effective sense of pride and place. It is surmised to say that the current literature on festivals and their impacts on communities seem to fit better in cities and towns that are not considered global, with lesser arts festivals, a smaller population that connects festivals and their communities. Arts festivals in global cities celebrate the intellectual, creative achievements and the aesthetics of the city. These festivals not only encourage cultural participation but also support the development of the creative industries (Ooi, 2007; Hall, 1994). In measuring the success of arts festivals, two common measurement tools are often proposed by scholars – economic impact studies and cost-benefit analysis (Bowdin et al., 2011; Williams and Bowdin, 2008). Economic impact does not just focus on the direct revenue made through sales of tickets, and other merchandise in the festival, but also the indirect and induced economic impacts generated by the existence of the festival. Cost-benefit analysis incorporates the economic impacts but also other intangible variables, such as stakeholders' engagement and sociocultural impacts to community and place, which may be considered cost or benefits depending on the nature (negative or positive) of the impact. Although cost-benefit analysis considers impacts to communities and place, the data collected have to be processed before they can be used, and non-monetary cost and benefits are often considered less important than monetary ones. In sum, socio-cultural impacts of festivals are easily sidelined in the calculations.

New directions in curating and managing arts festivals in global cities

A new cultural logic for continuity/discontinuity

Shakespeare 400 Festival was an arts festival held in Kuala Lumpur in 2016. It was timely for such a festival because 2016 marked the 400th anniversary of Shakespeare's death. Obviously, the festival was made up of theatre productions written by the bard. Considering the uniqueness of this celebration, Shakespeare 400 Festival was meant to happen only once, unlike many other festivals that usually return yearly or biannually. Despite its unique situation, Shakespeare 400 Festival triggers some further thinking in terms of continuity. One-off festivals tend to embark on a discourse in response to specific social conditions of a particular point in time and may not make any sense to have another installment in the coming year or two. For the last five years, I have been involved in organizing an annual arts festival that responds to specific socio-cultural and political happenings in Hong Kong. Though the festival returns every year in April, the continuity is disrupted by a complete change of the festival's title and focus year on year. Simply said, the same organizers put up a different arts festival every year, and therefore, each festival is one-off. Indeed, festivals serve as excellent platforms to critically reflect and respond to crucial issues. Moreover, these issues are time-based and therefore are only relevant in their immediate aftermath. One may also argue that being time-based does not mean that the issues cannot be further explored and debated. One-off arts festivals may be deemed as half-hearted in their attempt to frame a discourse. Shakespeare's works are known to be timeless. The bigger question herein lies – is there more to celebrate about Shakespeare than just his death anniversary? In fact, there are many Shakespeare Festivals around the world that return year to year to effectively bring across the timeless nature of his works. A one-off arts festival may come across as commodifying the issues it discusses in this age of consumerism.

As established earlier, festivals are special events that are celebrated by communities. Hence, the continuity of a festival ensures the ongoing opportunities for celebration, and for members of communities to be in communal settings to reinforce their sense of place. However, with the disappearing focus on communities, the continuity and survival of many arts festivals shift towards economic impacts and city branding (Ooi and Pedersen, 2010). Politicians that govern over a particular city or state would extend their support to arts festivals that contribute to the branding of the place, which in turns attracts tourists. Their support has led to a trend of major arts festivals commissioning market research agencies to assist them with economic impact studies, which would eventually become important data for state funding bodies and corporate sponsors, creating a dual-commodification process whereby economic impact studies reports would become a commodity that major arts festivals would invest in and that economically successful festivals would become products that are reproduced over and over again in the same mold. Arts festivals that subscribe to the agendas of specific political parties are also likely to receive the support for continued installments. In October 2017, I visited the second edition of Blossom Arts Festival in Kuala Lumpur. This arts festival seeks to bring a range of performing and visual arts programs to Chinese Malaysians and is organized by the Malaysian Chinese Association (MCA), which is part of the ruling Barisan Nasional (BN) party. Despite having a clear idea to build up the cultural capital of the Chinese community in Kuala Lumpur, the festival's organizer was certain that the festival must also enhance the reputation of MCA and the ruling party. With BN being voted out of power for the first time since Malaysia's independence in 1957, it is unlikely this festival would return for the third time in 2018.

Challenging the state of transient

Another unique feature of the Shakespeare 400 Festival is in its year-long programming. The events of this festival were spread over the duration of a full year in 2016, with the first theatre program in January and the final one in December. A year-long seems to challenge festivals' state of transient, but on further thinking, it might not be the case. Since this is a one-off festival celebrating a very specific moment, it makes sense to spread out the events as long as possible. It is likely that future festivals about Shakespeare similar to this one will only happen decades later on his 450th or 500th death anniversary. However, there are also arts festivals that return yearly but have their programs spread out over a longer duration. Here, I do not just refer to arts festivals that place their events only on consecutive weekends. The West Kowloon Cultural District of Hong Kong organizes Freespace Happening, which is a music and arts festival. It began in November 2014 as a 2-day Freespace Fest but the word 'Fest' was replaced by 'Happening' from 2015 onwards. Instead of a short 2-day festival, the event format was changed to one day (or two, sometimes) per month on the second weekend for six months per year. Ultimately, this festival only runs for about six to ten days, over a six-month period per year. Is this festival still a special event as defined by Getz? Perhaps the state of transient as a key characteristic of festivals is no longer valid in global cities due to the sheer number of art events and other arts and cultural activities. The public in these cities can hardly feel the unique state of the impermanence of festivals. This raises one major question – do arts festivals still make sense in global cities that are constantly filled with different kind of arts events as well as non-arts focused festivals? In hindsight, the change of name from Freespace 'Fest' to 'Happening' (as in, something that happens) foregrounds the question. From a management perspective, lengthening the festival's period does have its benefits, especially in Hong Kong, where there are shortages of arts venues. Spreading out the programs of the arts festival over a longer period means lesser pressure for the organizers to ensure a consecutive availability of venue(s).

Packaging festivals

A single, standalone performing arts or visual arts event needs to focus on its artistic vision and message. Similarly, an arts festival should have its vision and statements, but it is also made up of a number of standalone arts events, each with its own artistic message. Curators of festivals need to carefully consider the complexity of the underlying thread that links the events within the festival together. Programming philosophy serves as a guiding principle and provides a clear line of reasoning for the festival's programming team as well as the public on the choice of the arts events, artists, and venues. If well defined, the programming philosophy can definitely determine a clear existence and the 'soul' of the festival. Goldblatt (1997), in his book, *Special Events – Best Practices in Modern Event Management*, presented some key questions that must be answered in developing the core values for a special event. The first question looks at the reasons behind the event. Event organizers must be able to identify the compelling reasons for holding the event. The second question requires the identification of the various stakeholders involved, as it will influence the outcomes of the third question as to when and where the event should take place. The fourth question seeks to clarify the event's product, and in the case of the festival, it suggests that a clear statement of the festival's programming philosophy should be communicated to the public through the festival's offerings as well as other tangible cues. Finally, the last question that event organizers must address is their expected outcomes of the event. Brown and James (2004) also highlight five key design principles of events – focus, scale, shape, timing, and build – that may also affect the experience of the participants. Focus, here, aligns perfectly with Goldblatt's five key questions discussed earlier. For an arts festival, the scale is directly related to the expectations of the participants, regarding the choice(s) of programs and venues. Next, the concept of shape suggests that the layout of (or movement within) an arts festival should consider the audience psychology and expectations. The festival must also be aware of the turnaround time for different artists/arts organizations; especially if they share the same venue. Timing should also consider the participants' expectations, from the duration of the events to time needed to travel between events. Finally, there should be a fair distribution of high and low energy/impact events throughout the festival, to generate maximum impact in terms of experience for the audience. Having two high energy events one after another within the festival, for instance, will result in one event diminishing the impact of the other.

DiverseCity: Kuala Lumpur International Arts Festival was first introduced in September 2015 as a month-long post-National Day celebration event for Malaysia. In the first edition, some of the events were specially curated for the festival, while the Kuala Lumpur International Comedy Festival and the Kuala Lumpur International Jazz Festival, both with a longer history than DiverseCity, were then organized as part of the festival. These two smaller scale festivals became part of a much bigger festival, with more resources and support for publicity. It is worth clarifying that the subsuming of two smaller festivals into one big one only happens in 2015, and not in the later editions of DiverseCity. Nevertheless, the packaging of loosely organized singular events and smaller arts festivals under the umbrella of a bigger festival is highly possible, and in some ways, it creates a spectacle and indirectly contributes to the city branding. After all, it has repeatedly been mentioned in this chapter that global cities are saturated with a range of different arts and cultural events. Hence, packaging events into an arts festival also serves as a more convenient mode of operation than curating a festival from scratch. Packaging arts festivals may also mean that less thinking goes into the programming philosophy. This packaging of events into a festival should not be confused with many fringe festivals happening around the world, where any artists/arts organizations are welcomed to participate. The term 'fringe,' which suggests the broad idea of non-mainstream, is in itself a philosophy and those who participate consider their performances and activities as against or challenging the mainstream.

There is also a noticeable trend of convergence of festivals' forms and functions. Increasingly, more arts festivals are considering including different types of events that serve different functions. Some events must contribute to the financial health (big-name international acts), while some focus more on cultural democracy, giving the public more opportunities to come in touch with the arts. There are also events that transfer knowledge, such as symposiums and forums that are organized alongside arts festivals, as well as networking events within the festival for key stakeholders, such as arts markets. For the first time in 14 years, the Bangkok Theatre Festival, held between 1–18 November 2017, included a 5-day Bangkok International Performing Arts Meeting. This event offered a series of workshops and talks on specific arts forms and provided a platform for impresarios and festival directors from around the region to mingle and promote their shows.

Audience-centricity

Marketing the arts has evolved over the years, in terms of theoretical and practical perspectives, from a transactional process to a more sophisticated concept of relationship marketing (Hill et al., 2012). Within the realm of relationship marketing, there has been a clear shift from customer-focus to customer-centric (Sharma, 2011), triggering the tendency for arts festivals' organizers to map out the entire experience of the audience, which includes the non-arts aspects such as hangout spaces, food and beverages, and photo opportunities (including selfies). The advent of the digital age has brought about categorically changes to how arts festivals operate. RFID wristbands are coming into use, allowing festival-goers to leave their purses behind in safe places and store information regarding their credit card on their wristband (Thakkar, 2016). Clockenflap Music and Arts Festival is an annual 2-day arts festival in Hong Kong, which has evolved from a small and humble festival to one with 60,000 attendees. Clockenflap has effectively incorporated RFID technology into their operations, enabling the purchase of beverages and merchandise and assisting the organizers to gain some insight into the habits of the attendees that are useful for crowd control and sponsorship activation.

Technology has also shifted from being mere support (buying tickets online, acquiring information about the festivals from websites, facilitating in cashless transactions on the festivals' sites, etc.) to a medium on its own. Arts festivals in global cities are increasingly exhibiting three distinct dimensions, 'experimentation', 'spectacularization' and 'immersion', all of which offer new opportunities and challenges for the management of innovative types of work that continue to retain their separate aesthetic power (Jordan, 2016). Frew and McGillivray (2008) reiterate 'the transformational power of technology' in allowing escapism and fantasy through the design of an event. Surprises will become a theme of rising importance in arts festivals (Getz, 2015). In this digital age, participants will share these surprises on their social media platforms. The input of technology enables faster, more online, live or streamed events to be delivered and with greater use of such advanced technology (Frost, Mair, and Laing, 2015), the experience of participants, i.e., the Generation C (Sadd, 2015), can be enhanced and rapidly publicized. Even with the inevitable invasion of technology into the domain of arts festivals, several scholars believe that social meeting of events in physical spaces will still be crucial in the future (deBlanc Goldblatt, 2011; Duffy and McEuen, 2010). It is unlikely that arts festivals will completely move into the virtual sphere. A possible trend is the rise of hybrid festivals, where part of the experience is virtual while part of it needs the participants to be on site (Nolan, 2017). Festivals are also likely to popularize the use of virtual and augmented reality to enhance the layers of experience by the audience. One such festival is the Cooler Lumpur Festival in Kuala Lumpur, branding itself as a multidisciplinary celebration of culture and ideas. In the 2017 edition, the festival has incorporated a virtual reality expedition catered for children and has also invited Japanese artist Aimi Sekiguchi to showcase her virtual reality art performance.

Embracing mass culture

Arts festivals often curate events that are considered high arts, such as classical concerts, theatre productions, as well as classical and contemporary dance, as opposed to mass culture. My research suggests that some arts festivals are breaking away from only curating events that are traditionally considered as high arts. In these festivals, the divide between high and low arts is deliberately blurred, gearing towards a creative platform for a contemporary lifestyle. Freespace Happening embraces a range of different performing, visual and literary arts with handicrafts, food, digital technologies, games, pets and even skateboarding. While there are no intentions to privilege high arts, there are apprehensions that this cultural phenomenon (of blurring) leads to a public perception that the arts, and arts festivals, are therefore similar to other leisure and entertainment events. By being perceived as just one of the many leisure choices, arts festivals in global cities are likely to shift even further away from their socio-cultural benefits. Comic Arts Festival is another example of a festival embracing both events of high arts and mass culture, or a mix of both. Besides the choice of programs, the festival has always been held in a popular shopping mall in Kuala Lumpur since it was first introduced in 2013. Another noteworthy example is the

Living Arts Festival in Bangkok, which features outdoor 4D street-art creations, installation arts, and pavement arts that seek to distort pedestrians' perceptions. The festival, which only ran for two years in 2013 and 2014, was held on a pedestrian bridge in the heart of Bangkok shopping district. Cooler Lumpur Festival also renders a couple of these traits – the programs embrace a mixture of high arts and mass culture, and the festival is held in an event space within a relatively high-end shopping mall in Kuala Lumpur.

Postmodernism to blame?

'*We live in a postmodern era*' (Robinson, 2005; Janson and Janson, 2004; Ogilvy, 2002) is a common phrase used in a number of scholarly publications in the last two decades, although there seems to be a general trend of dismissing this phrase as cliché in recent times (Mestrovic, 2010). The problem lies in the (lack of) definitions of the term 'postmodern,' and its related derivations such as 'postmodernism' and 'postmodernity.' Hutcheon (2002) states that the term postmodernism is overtly abused in its association with the concepts of contemporary culture. Being a set of ideas about a particular situation in our current society, postmodernism is deemed as a condition (Holzman and Morss, 2000) and a phenomenon following the downfall of modernism (Reading and Schaber, 1993) in the late capitalist age.

Lyotard's (1984) views on the 'incredulity towards metanarratives', sometimes also known as the 'death' of metanarratives, suggests a complete rejection of absolute truths as the key characteristic of the postmodern condition. 'Incredulity' refers to disbelief or skepticism, while 'metanarrative' indicates the totalizing ideas behind the human condition. This disbelief extends to modernism, where science and progress take precedence (Capaldi and Proctor, 2012). Contemporary societies are highly computerized and capitalized, and have evolving knowledge structures, disfavoring the taking roots of metanarratives. According to Foucault, power relations play a part in knowledge dissemination, thus rejecting the idea of truths beyond the structure of power (Hannem, 2012). The discourse of festivals in relations to their community impacts could be deemed as a metanarrative in itself. In this postmodern day and age, arts festivals in global cities create a false sense of consciousness and fail to bring about impactful knowledge to communities. Moreover, it remains a big question mark whether fixed and stable communities ever existed.

Various authors have stated that in future, society will be aging but also, at the same time, ageless (Bowen, 2015; Northrup, 2015; Yeoman, Robertson, and Smith, 2012). Age may become a less important factor in attendance, and the identities of audiences in global cities will also become more complex and fluid, making the concept of communities more ambiguous. Lyotard's preference towards mini-narratives focuses on the provisional, temporary and situational in explaining the human condition. As such, the need for arts festivals to continue yearly or biannually becomes less important.

The distrust towards grand narratives has also made its way into management processes. The Industrial Revolution created new challenges for managers and business owners alike, and new management approaches were conceived to tackle these problems. In the late 19th century, Frederick Taylor came up with the Scientific Management theory, which focused on methodologies in identifying the most efficient management procedures for a given project (Schermerhorn Jr, 2009). The drive towards efficiency and effectiveness propels the evolution of Scientific Management towards Modern Management approaches, which is largely characterized by the creation of systematic management processes by the human actors. Here, management is associated closely to the processes of planning, organizing, leading and monitoring, and in the center of it all are human actors, who are believed to have the agency in controlling the management decisions and processes. Over time, these systems ironically replace the very human actors, who become commodified in the management equation (Gephart Jr, 1996). When human actors fail to control the systems, the concept of management also fails and recedes into the background, giving way to new cultural logic. This gives rise to the referencing of postmodernism to the death of individualism (Berger, 2003) or the 'unavailability of the individual style' (Jameson, 1991). In the case of arts festivals, it can also refer to a cut-and-paste curatorial style, recycling what has been successful and putting (sometimes) unrelated events together. Jameson (1991) has discussed at length on the commodification of all aspects of life in this late capitalist age, a clear shift away from the modernist critique of commodification. In this postmodern society, subscribing to the market ideology has become important and necessary, even for nonprofit sectors.

Since Enlightenment, there has been plenty of literature on the intellectual benefits of exposure to high arts. Similarly, the Frankfurt School considers high arts having the ability to project utopian visions and was critical of the rise of the commodification of the arts in the industrial age (Modleski, 1986). Jameson, on the other hand, considers Frankfurt School's view of high arts as elitist and believes that high arts and mass culture should be looked at objectively, especially when faced with capitalism (Thomas, 2013). The blurring of boundaries between high arts and mass culture is a cultural phenomenon in this postmodern age (Gloag, 2012; Huyssen, 1986). Postmodern urban spaces affirm postmodernism's plurality and multiplicity, embracing the consumption of different cultures, arts and entertainment (McClinchey and Carmichael, 2015). Many newer arts venues in global cities are built next to shopping belts and entertainment hubs. There is also the rising importance of spaces of transience, such as shopping malls, bridges, and walkways, as venues for the arts festivals. These spaces are otherwise known as non-places, a concept introduced by anthropologist Marc Augé. Buskers performing in the London Underground or New York Subway were the initial users of such non-spaces. Augé observed that places of transience are not considered significant enough to warrant the status of a particularly defined purpose (Arno and Neumann, 2012). He further argues that "in the concrete reality of today's world, places and spaces, places and non-places, intertwine and tangle together" (Augé, 1995). Interestingly, while having little anthropological past, some of these non-places in these urban cities are gaining importance in the hearts of the people, very much a part of the city's heritage. This is partly due to people spending more time in non-places. Furthermore, with the processes of gentrification going on so rapidly in urban cities, many places with rich histories and stories have to make way for urban renewal and development. By attending arts festivals in these non-places, audiences are not only exposed to a unique experience, but are also urged to reflect upon the very location in relation to the city's cultural development.

Concluding remarks

On a (postmodern) self-reflexive note, it is apt to conclude with a discussion on how managers of urban arts festivals could move forward with the scenarios and challenges mentioned in this chapter.

Growth of community arts festivals

First and foremost, the growing emphasis on city branding and creative economy suggests the further marginalization of social issues that were not represented by the arts festivals. One possible way forward is to encourage the organization of 'bottom-up' community arts festivals in global cities to counter this situation. These community arts festivals tend to focus on giving a voice to subordinated communities, such as people with disabilities, or communities that require social change (Hague, Hague, and Breitbach, 2011), that are not fully integrated into the society. The festivals are likely to be organized by the communities themselves or by NGOs and arts practitioners who work closely with the communities. In such festivals, the quality of the artwork may not be most important, but the ability to tell the stories of these subordinated communities to the public or relevant stakeholders becomes extremely crucial. Some might be concerned that this could be a form of governmental control of communities in that the people would be side-tracked in organizing and taking part in community arts festivals as a way of expressing their thoughts and opinions, rather than joining in protest meetings or marches (Bajc, 2014). Moreover, these 'bottom-up' community arts festivals could also face very stiff competition from resource-rich government agencies organizing community arts festivals from a 'top-down' approach. One such example is the PAssion Arts Festival, organized by the Community Arts section of People's Association, a government agency in Singapore. This festival prides itself to bring 'arts and culture to everyone, everywhere and every day.' Instead of being a platform for communities to voice out their stories, these 'top-down' community arts festivals sometimes focus on what the 'top' think is important, such as environmental and recycling issues, which indirectly leads back to the idea of city branding. Government agencies may support a certain community arts festival in fulfillment of their key performance indicators, such as social cohesion, and cultural democracy. Sponsors giving money to community arts festivals could be seeking opportunities for product placement and brand recognition. It is, therefore, necessary for arts managers to bear in mind the different power structures when engaging with stakeholders. Arts managers play an important role to ensure that power-sharing is way forward for such community-based festivals.

Rethinking the role of technologies in arts festivals

Given the adoption of technology into arts festivals, it is necessary for arts managers to be well equipped with technological skills and knowledge. Apart from learning how to use different technologies, arts managers need to be critical of the different approaches to incorporating technologies into arts festivals. As this chapter has highlighted, technology can be used in three ways – as a support for better service and management; as a medium of expression and co-creation; as means to enhance the entire festival experience. When making use of technologies, arts managers must consider the likely impacts and decide if it aids in achieving the mission, vision, and philosophy of the festival.

Mediation: the way forward

Arts managers need to be constantly critical of the cultural logic and resist the seduction of commodification and consumerism. Instead of the impossible task to fight the postmodern condition altogether, arts managers need to constantly navigate within the phenomenon, in search of a better environment for the arts and culture. While numbers (including economic impacts) serve as important data for decision making, arts managers should avoid being overtly obsessed with numbers in the management process. The reliance on attendance numbers as criteria for funding shifts the attention away from the process of art-making to the process of management by numbers. This shift risks the importance of the intangible benefits of the arts, such as building a more cultured and civilized society, as well as encouraging critical thinking. Moreover, the socio-cultural impacts of festivals might not be necessary at odds with the concept of city branding and economic contribution. Wee (2002) mentioned that the state support in the arts is crucial if cultural production is not to be reduced to the level of simple manufactures. He also mentioned the symbolic values of cultural productions and how they represent a larger symbolic life of the city-state. If a city wants to be successful in being culturally vibrant, the values of the arts must first be upheld. It is also worth noting that artists are currently engaging in a wide range of activities supporting the notion of place-making (Maguire, 2016) by animating public places and spaces to feed a new phenomenon which is occurring around the world, that of capturing a place's essence, through the vehicle of a festival. Maguire (2016) suggests that it would be possible to use a working prism consisting of a threefold 'people-place-purpose' in a capacity as a lens through which it could be possible to observe the unfolding of events and the constitution of various areas of work-defining self-contained spaces as place-animation, for innovation and general investigation. As Jordan (2014) argued, however, economic and tourist policymakers do not often consider this when initially formulating economic plans and policies. Managers of arts festivals should also take on the role of cultural mediators, to defend arts, to facilitate more people to come in touch with the arts through festivals, and to actively connect the relevant stakeholders, such as artists, audiences, sponsors, arts policymakers as well as city planning, economic and tourism policymakers.

References

Augé, M. (1995). *Non-places: An introduction to an anthropology of supermodernity*. London: Verso.

Arno, G. and Neumann, D. (2012). *Ear to the earth: Non-Place/Place*. Available at: www.m-i-c-r-o.net/mpld/mpldinfo/Non-place-Place_program

Bajc, V. (2014). The future of surveillance and security in global events. In: I. Yeoman, M. Robertson, U. McMahon-Beattie, E. Backer, and K.A. Smith, eds., *The Future of Events and Festivals*. New York: Routledge, pp. 187–199.

Berger, A.A. (2003). *The portable postmodernist*. Walnut Creek: Rowman Altamira.

Bourdieu, P. (1984). *Distinction: A social critique of the judgement of taste*. London: Routledge.

Bowen, A. (2015, July 22). Why more Americans would choose to stay at age 50 than 20. *Chicago Tribune*. Available at: www.chicagotribune.com/business/sc-hlth-afraid-aging-20150722-story.html

Bowdin, G., O'Toole, W., Allen, J., Harris, R., and McDonnell, I. (2011). *Events management*. New York: Routledge.

Brown, S. and James, J. (2004). Event design and management: Ritual sacrifice. *Festivals and Events Management*, pp. 53–64.

Capaldi, E.J. and Proctor, R.W. (2012). Postmodernism and the development of the psychology of science. In: G.J. Feist and M.E. Gorman, eds., *Handbook of the psychology of science*. New York: Springer Publishing Company, pp. 331–352.

Cunningham, H. (2012). Gated ecologies and 'possible urban worlds'. In: I.L. Stefanovic and S. Scharper, eds., *The natural city: Re-envisioning the built environment*. London: University of Toronto Press, pp. 149–160.

deBlanc Goldblatt, S. (2011). *The complete guide to greener meetings and events*. New Jersey: John Wiley & Sons.

Derrett, R. (2003). Making sense of how festivals demonstrate a community's sense of place. *Event Management*, 8(1), pp. 49–58.

———. (2004). Festivals, events and the destination. In: I. Yeoman, M. Robertson, J. Ali-Knight, S. Drummond, and U. McMahon-Beattie, eds., *Festival and events management: An international arts and cultural perspective*. Oxford: Elsevier, pp. 32–50.

Dessibourg, N. and Hales, M. (2017). *Global cities 2017: Leaders in a world of disruptive innovation*. Available at: www.atkearney.com/documents/20152/436055/Global+Cities+2017.pdf/f68ca227-48a0-2a74-96b9-0989ce3ce321

DeWalt, K.M. and DeWalt, B.R. (2011). *Participant observation: A guide for fieldworkers*. Plymouth: AltaMira Press.

Duffy, C. and McEuen, M.B. (2010). The future of meetings: The case for face-to-face. *Cornell Hospitality Industry Perspectives*. Ithaca: Cornell University.

Frew, M. and McGillivray, D. (2008). Exploring hyper-experiences: Performing the fan at Germany 2006. *Journal of Sport and Tourism*, 13(3), pp.181–198.

Frost, W., Mair, J., and Laing, J. (2015). The greening of events: Exploring future trends and issues. In: I. Yeoman, M. Robertson, U. McMahon-Beattie, K.A. Smith, and E. Backer, eds., *The future of events and festivals*. New York: Routledge, pp. 115–127.

Gephart Jr, R.P. (1996). Management, social issues, and the postmodern era. In D. Boje, ed., *Postmodern management and organization theory*. Thousand Oaks: Sage.

Getz, D. (2012). *Event Studies: Theory, research and policy for planned events*. New York: Routledge.

———. (2015). The forms and functions of planned events: Past and future. In: I. Yeoman, M. Robertson, U. McMahon-Beattie, K.A. Smith, and E. Backer, eds., *The Future of Events and Festivals*. New York: Routledge, pp. 44–59.

Gilbert, D. and Lizotte, M. (1998). Tourism and the performing arts. *Travel and Tourism Analyst*, 1, pp. 82–96.

Gloag, K. (2012). *Postmodernism in music*. New York: Cambridge University Press.

Goldblatt, J.J. (1997). *Special events: Best practices in modern event management*. New York: John Wiley and Sons.

Haanpää, M., García-Rosell, J.C., and Tuulentie, S. (2016). Co-creating places through events: The case of a tourism community event in Finnish Lapland. In *Managing and developing communities, festivals and events*. London: Palgrave Macmillan, pp. 34–49.

Hannem, S. (2012). Theorizing stigma and the politics of resistance: Symbolic and structural stigma in everyday life. In: S. Hannem, and C. Bruckert, eds., *Stigma revisited: Implications of the mark*. Ottawa: University of Ottawa Press.

Hague, C., Hague, E., and Breitbach, C. (2011). *Regional and local economic development*. New York: Palgrave Macmillan.

Hall, C.M. (1994). *Tourism and politics: Policy, power, and place*. London: Bellhaven.

Hill, E. et al. (2012). *Creative arts marketing*. New York: Routledge.

Holzman, L. and Morss, J.R. (2000). *Postmodern psychologies, societal practice, and political life*. New York: Routledge.

Hutcheon, L. (2002). *The politics of postmodernism*. New York: Routledge.

Huyssen, A. (1986). *After the great divide: Modernism, mass culture, postmodernism*. Bloomington: Indiana University Press.

Jameson, F. (1991). *Postmodernism, or, the cultural logic of late capitalism*. Durham: Duke University Press.

Janson, H.W. and Janson, A.F. (2004). *History of art: The Western tradition*. Upper Saddle River, NJ: Prentice Hall Professional.

Jepson, A. and Clarke, A. (2016). An introduction to planning and managing communities, festivals and events. In: *Managing and developing communities, festivals and events*. Hamsphire: Palgrave Macmillan, pp. 3–15.

Jepson, A., Wiltshire, P., and Clarke, A. (2008). Community festivals: Involvement and inclusion. In: *Council for hospitality management education: International Research Conference*.

Jordan, J. (2014). Festival policy: A typology of local urban festivals and their policy implications. *International Conference on Cultural Policy Research*.

———. (2016). Festivalization of cultural production: Experimentation, spectacularisation and immersion. *Journal of Cultural Management and Policy*, 6(1), pp. 44–55.

Kinder, K. and Harland, J. (2004). The arts and social inclusion: What's the evidence? *Support for Learning*, 19, pp. 52–56.

Liu, Y.D. (2014). Cultural event and regional development: The case of 2008 European capital of culture Liverpool. *Review of Global Politics*, 48, pp. 151–178.

Lyotard, J.F. (1984). *The postmodern condition*. Manchester: Manchester University Press.

Maguire, M. (2016). Animating places: A new festival phenomenon? In: C. Newbold and J. Jordan, eds., *Focus on world festivals, contemporary case studies and perspectives*. Oxford: Goodfellow Publishers Ltd, pp. 53–64.

McClinchey, K.A. and Carmichael, B.A. (2015). The future of local community festivals and meanings of place in an increasingly mobile world. In I. Yeoman, M. Robertson, U. McMahon-Beattie, K.A. Smith, and E. Backer, eds., *The future of events and festivals*. New York: Routledge, pp. 140–156.

Mestrovic, S. (2010). *The coming fin de Siècle: An application of Durkheim's sociology to modernity and postmodernism*. New York: Routledge.

Modleski, T. (ed.) (1986). Introduction. In: *Studies in entertainment: Critical approaches to mass culture*. Bloomington: Indiana University Press.

Négrier, E. (2015). *Festivalization: Patterns and limits*. Oxford: Goodfellow Publishers Ltd.

Nolan, E. (2017). *Working with venues for events: A practical guide*. New York: Routledge.

Northrup, C. (2015). *Goddesses never age: The secret prescription for radiance, vitality, and well-being*. Carlsbad: Hay House, Inc.

Ogilvy, J.A. (2002). *Creating better futures: Scenario planning as a tool for a better tomorrow*. New York: Oxford University Press.

Ooi, C.S. (2007). Creative industries and tourism in Singapore. In: G. Richards and J. Wilson, eds., *Tourism, creativity and development*. New York: Routledge, pp. 240–252.

Ooi, C.S. and Pedersen, J.S. (2010). City branding and film festivals: Re-evaluating stakeholder's relations. *Place Branding and Public Diplomacy*, 6(4), pp. 316–332.

Pejovic, K. (2009). Urban arts festivals: A mark on regions. In: A.M. Autissier, ed., *The Europe of festivals: From Zagreb to Edinburgh, interesting viewpoints*. Paris: Editions de lattribut, pp. 63–73.

Quinn, B. (2005). Arts festivals and the city. *Urban studies*, 42(5–6), pp. 927–943.

———. (2010). Arts festivals, urban tourism and cultural policy. *Journal of policy research in tourism*, 2(3), pp. 264–279.

Reading, B. and Schaber, B. (1993). *Postmodernism across the pages: Essays for a postmodernity that wasn't born yesterday*. New York: Syracuse University Press.

Robinson, G. (2005). *Philosophy and mystification: A reflection on nonsense and clarity*. New York: Fordham University Press.

Ryken, L. (2002). *Work and leisure in Christian perspective*. Oregon: Wipf and Stock Publishers.

Sadd, D. (2015). The future is virtual. In: I. Yeoman, M. Robertson, U. McMahon-Beattie, K.A. Smith, and E. Backer, eds., *The future of events and festivals*. New York: Routledge, pp. 209–218.

Sassen, S. (2001). *The global city: New York, London and Tokyo*. Oxford: Princeton University Press.

Schermerhorn Jr, J.R. (2009). *Exploring management*. New Jersey: John Wiley & Sons.

Sharma, S.K. (2011). *E-adoption and Socio-economic Impacts, Emerging Infrastructural Effects*. Hershey: Information Science Reference.

Slater, L. (2016). Sovereign bodies: Australian Indigenous cultural festivals and flourishing lifeworlds. In: J. Taylor, ed., *The festivalization of culture*. New York: Routledge, pp. 131–146.

Thakkar, S. (2016). *Music festival season is here: And so are these new technologies*. Available at: www.umbel.com/blog/entertainment/music-festival-season-here-and-so-are-these-new-technologies/

Thomas, C. (2013). *Ten lessons in theory: An introduction to theoretical writing*. New York: Bloomsbury Publishing.

Tonkin, A. and Jameel, S. (2016). Playing Together: Festivals and Celebrations. In: Tonkin, A. and Whitaker, J. eds., *Play in healthcare for adults: Using play to promote health and wellbeing across the adult lifespan*. New York: Routledge.

Tribhuwan, R.D. (2003). *Fairs and Festivals of Indian Tribes*. New Delhi: Discovery Publishing House.

Wee, C.J.W.L. (2002). National identity, the arts and the global city. In: D. da Cunha, ed., *Singapore in the new millennium: Challenges facing the City State*. Singapore: Institute of Southeast Asian Studies, pp. 221–242.

Williams, M. and Bowdin, A.J. (2008). Festival evaluation: An exploration of seven UK arts festivals. In: M. Robertson and E. Frew, eds., *Events and festivals: Current trends and issues*, 12(2–3). New York: Routledge, pp. 187–203.

Yeoman, I., Robertson, M., and Smith, K.A., (2012). A futurist's view on the future of events. In: S. Page and J. Connell, eds., *The Routledge handbook of events*. London: Routledge, pp. 526–534.

19

NEW ORGANISMS IN THE CULTURAL 'ECOSYSTEMS' OF CITIES

The rooting and sustainability of arts and culture organizations

Marcin Poprawski

Introduction

Since 2008 Poland has been perceived as one of the largest construction sites for arts and culture institutions in Europe. The data clearly show that the culture sector in Poland was, until recently, one of the most important consumers of EU funds allocated for numerous new buildings for cultural institutions: concert halls, museums, theatres, cultural centers and libraries, newly emplaced in modernized urban spaces. According to data provided by the STRATEG (2018) system, which is run by the Polish statistical office, there has been similar growth with other cultural institutions: in four years, almost 300 local culture centers were established. In 6 years, up until 2014, the number of museums in Poland increased by over 100. This emergent phenomenon raises a series of questions concerning the opportunities and challenges for new cultural locations and the impact on their users, audiences, employees, institution leaders, institutional competitors, local authorities, individuals or communities. These emplacements or rooting processes are challenging economic, social and cultural sustainability in cities. This study attempts to provide insight, based on empirical cases, into how to best cope with the realities of rooting and operating new venues for culture and the arts.

The point of departure is a set of findings from the research project entitled *New emplacement of public cultural institutions in the cultural 'ecosystems' of Polish cities*, conducted in 2016 and 2017 by the author's academic team, and co-funded by the Union of Polish Cities and the Polish Ministry of Culture. The researchers from the Adam Mickiewicz University in Poznan have qualitatively investigated eight carefully selected cases of newly emplaced, or rooted cultural institutions in Poland: the Gdansk Shakespeare Theatre, the location of art museum in a former mining site – the Silesian Museum in Katowice, an early Christianity memorial – the ICHOT Heritage Interpretation Centre in Poznan, the Dialogue Centre in Lodz, a public library located in a railway station – 'Stacja Kultury' in Rumia, the Philharmonic Hall in Gorzow and two cultural centers in smaller cities in central Poland: Grodzisk Mazowiecki and Wloclawek.

The research process focused on delivering the content in eight aspects:

1   The emplacement genesis
2   The new object in the context of the existing cultural 'ecosystem' of the city
3   The aesthetics and functionality of the building for cultural purposes
4   The social rooting and accessibility of the new cultural investment for the local community
5   The value, image and social reception of the new cultural site
6   The impact of the new cultural 'organism' on the city's cultural 'ecosystem'
7   The organizational cultures of the newly located cultural institutions
8   The developmental potential of the new cultural space

The qualitatively collected data bring to light the set of findings and practical recommendations aimed both at existing, newly located cultural venues, as well as the objects of future investments. In this chapter, those insights on newly emplaced cultural spaces, culture and arts venues in Poland are, at the same time, food for thought and discussion on the purpose, use and relevance of the metaphors of 'cultural ecosystem', 'rooting' in arts management studies, as well as the concept of sustainable development and the subsidiarity principle.

This is a canvas for a sequence of reflections concerning overlapping domains, where the first field of experience is *the rooting* of the new cultural organism or newly emplaced existing arts institution. This includes the social, political, urban and economic dimensions of the process. The key perspective correlated with the research objects is the one introduced as an inspiration borrowed from the metaphor and concept of the ecology of culture or *cultural ecosystems* (Holden, 2015, pp. 5–12; Markusen, 2011, pp. 8–9). Particular attention is paid here to the cultural ecosystems of cities and local urban communities.

One could ask where this will take the reader who is not familiar with the Polish or European models of financing culture and the arts, or who is not engaged in the practice of establishing and operating a public institution. There is a lesson we can learn here together, from particular stories of beginnings, as George Steiner (2010, pp. 322–326) would say, the foundational efforts of arts administration leaders, stories of attracting engagement in local communities. Again, taking Poland's case as the laboratory of socio-economic transformation, with a few local cases having universal relevance, reveals the potential of the broader applicability of such solutions.

On the threshold of the political transformation in Poland in the early 1990s, the eminent sociologist (Dahrendorf, 1990) predicted the rhythm of the change from communism and a centrally regulated economy to a democratic, free society. He used the image of three clocks of the transformation. According to his prediction, it would take six months to reform the political system, six years to change the economic system, and sixty years to bring about a revolution on the people's hearts and minds. Arts and culture organizations are basically and explicitly operating according to the tempo set by the third clock, in terms of the sphere of cultural policies, cultural education, and communities implementing the cultural regeneration processes in their playgrounds of change – their cities, towns and villages.

The study is motivated by a sequence of research questions and aims. The first one is to confront the apparent enthusiasm for the construction of new cultural facilities with the real practice and context, and the challenges and opportunities, after the initial period. Another aim is to provide an overview of how newly emplaced cultural institutions impact, influence or engage the inhabitants of their cities. Finally, the aim of the inquiry is to deliver some recommendations for the future initiators of construction projects, as well as the existing managers of new venues.

Arts and culture organizations rooted in cultural ecosystems

The primary concept adopted at the beginning of this research project on new arts and culture investments was the term *emplacement*, which aims to grasp both newly founded cultural institutions emplaced in the city space, as well as newly constructed cultural facilities for already existing institutions. In the latter case, the perception of the local residents is of importance, as they are often unaware of the formal nuances associated with the existence of a cultural object, and for whom the new space of the institution (even if it previously functioned elsewhere) becomes a new object on their 'mental map of the city', and thus is often an invigorating, attractive and intriguing object of interest.

The second reason for using the term 'emplacement' lies in its ambiguity, which is interesting for humanists and researchers in the field of social sciences. Referring, on the one hand, to the historically important 'location' of cities, which is also significant in terms of identity, and on the other hand to the concept of the 'deposits' made, and investment funds set up by, local governments, especially in the context of EU funds.

Thirdly, "emplacement" is particularly relevant for marketing activities. With this last meaning, we touch on the very complex issue of the marketing of places, and the positive or negative effects associated with the instrumentalization of cultural objects for promotional purposes and building the image of cities – for example the Basque Guggenheim Museum and the so-called Bilbao effect. In future years, could this also apply to the places investigated in these case studies? It is important, therefore, to establish new institutions as organisms that have a fresh impact on the urban environment, but on the other hand, new infrastructure investments, buildings, headquarters, locations that represent a significant opportunity (most often PR, promotional, identity, pro-development in the sense of cultural competence) but which sometimes also constitute a threat or a challenge (e.g. for the city budget in subsequent years of the institution's functioning).

The ambiguity of the notion of *emplacement* seemed to me appealing as it addresses three or four aspects in one term. One is derived from investment – funds placement, the other is derived more from branding vocabulary – cultural product placement, or place branding for city promotion, targeted at tourists or businesses – city brand placement following the opening of a new cultural venue. Finally, emplacement also relates to historical city location process or places of settlement. Rooting, however, as an alternative notion of a purely ecological origin, adapted to the social sciences, furnishes even more options due to its polysemic potential.

Indeed, according to the concept of the ecology of culture (Holden, 2015), culture is a much more complex and dynamic reality than logical processes framed in the numbers and trends forecast by economists and politicians. Culture is more of an organism than a mechanism. Holden does not concur with the privileged position of the financial and economic value of culture in relation to other values, which are more deeply rooted. Thinking by means of the metaphor of the ecosystem helps to understand the nature of the relations between cultural organisms, in the Polish context this applies above all to cultural institutions and their social environment, and ultimately leads to an improvement in the quality of cultural policies and access to cultural values.

The realm of arts and cultural activities can be defined as the reality inhabited by the following interrelated organisms: (1) subsidized cultural institutions, (2) commercial enterprises and projects, and (3) co-creative individuals, private amateur art and culture actors who are more or less ready to volunteer to help with an art organization or to create cultural artefacts in their homes or on their digital devices, either individually, or within a circle of close friends, or with total strangers who share the same interest or passion. This co-related trio is now a basic triangle of interchanges that is not regulated by monetary exchange, or simple transactions in the economic sense. All three types of players observe and learn from each other, and the third type of player, the creative individual, is at the same time the most observed and most influential for decisions taken by the other two kinds – public and commercial organizations active in the arts and culture field.

The organic approach proposed by the *ecology of culture* concept, and the metaphors of *regeneration*, *symbiosis*, *growth* and *life cycle* could bring a much more fruitful picture of the processes in the broad field of culture when they are explained in terms of cultural policy, cultural heritage and cultural management studies, and teaching and training. One example here is the *art festivals life cycle model*, which was adapted from Ichak Adizes' business studies concept by Chris Maugham (Maugham and Bianchini, 2004), who uses it to analyze festivals as growing and aging, from courtship to death. What is particularly important is, again, the perspective of the local cultural ecosystems, as the observation of crucial places where cultural activity is rooted and exposed to different conditions for growth or death. Not all Polish cities carry out advanced, conscious or strategic actions in the area of cultural policy; however, in every city we can find a cultural ecosystem, involving the natural circulation of content, value and activity in the field of culture.

Holden's ecology of culture is his name for complex interdependencies that shape the needs and processes of creating art and offers in the sphere of cultural activity. The 'ecological' attitude of researchers and decision-makers in the field of culture involves the assessment of multifaceted relations between various professional cultural entities and people involved in shaping the proposals and places for the implementation of cultural phenomena, within the scope of developing cultural competence, but also transferring funds, and rooting cultural organizations and their headquarters in the city space, which is the subject of this research project. These processes have received attention from many researchers who do not employ the ecosystem metaphor, but who are effectively seeking a way to theoretically grasp the phenomenon of planning and implementing investment processes in the field of cultural institutions (including Landry and Bianchini, 1995; Bianchini, 1996; McGuigan, 1996, 2010, pp. 39–57; Silver and Nichols Clark, 2016).

The presented study, based on eight case studies of arts and culture organizations, is an example of an inquiry which adapts and tests two ecological metaphors more intensely. One is that of *rooting* – to describe the processes activated by arts organizations; while the other is the term *ecosystem* – to describe the relations of arts and cultural organizations – coexisting organisms – sharing one city space.

An empirical study of rooting arts and culture organizations

Four of the case studies are institutional brands created from scratch, new kids in the block. The case of the Gdansk Shakespeare Theatre relates the process of how the NGO-based International Shakespeare Festival team transformed into freshly funded institution operators. It was the first newly constructed drama theatre building in Poland for over 40 years. The 7,935 square meter venue with an open roof and a full armory of stage engineering facilities was erected between 2011–2014, costing over €25 million. It employs 26 people and its total budget is around €3 million.

The Philharmonic Hall in Gorzow, a town of 100,000 inhabitants, located next to the German border in central western Poland was built in 2008–2011. The primary intention was for it to be the main element of a bigger Art Education Centre, a philharmonic venue of 6,589 square meters, integrated with new music schools for kids and adults. In the end, however, the schools were omitted. Costing over €35 million, with 65 employees and a yearly budget of over €1.6 million, the new public institution was launched.

The third case study of a newly founded culture institution is the ICHOT Heritage Interpretation Centre in Poznan, which has the combined aims of promoting city cultural tourism and commemorating early Christian heritage. The language of this place is predominantly conveyed through a set of multimedia tools. From 2010 to 2014 over €22 million were spent on the project, resulting in a 5,070 square meter cube where over 53 employees work, having an annual budget of €1.5 million.

The Browar B. Art & Culture Centre in Wloclawek, a town located in the centre of Poland, is a revitalisation and district re-cultivation project based on a former brewery. 7,000 square meters were revitalised at a cost of over €8.5 million between 2012–2014. The employees, totalling 47 people, now work for one new cultural organization, as a result of two previously existing cultural centres being merged. They share an annual budget of over €800,000.

The four other case studies focus on the relocations of existing arts or culture public institutions, or new branches.

The most impressive in size and scale is The Silesian Museum, the project involving both the construction and revitalisation of a former mining area in the centre of the city Katowice, the capital of the heavy industry region in southern Poland. Its seven floors, three of which are underground, combine three separate themes and contain an impressive art collection, as well as a narrative museum of the complex history of the Silesia region, and is the location for a theatre scenography centre. €70 million were spent in the period of 2011–2015 for the hybrid actions, providing over 25,000 square meters of new and revitalised buildings. The complex process of the rearrangement of this post-mining area is still in progress. The institution, which moved from the old headquarters, enlarged to the size of a Museum with nearly 180 employees and restarted in 2015 with an annual budget of over €7.5 million.

The new building of the Edelman Dialogue Centre in Lodz was the new emplacement for a hybrid type of culture institution – located in a housing estate area consisting of blocks of flats. Celebrating the Jewish and multicultural legacy of the city of Lodz, the Centre is funded by the contributions of the public, the municipal budget and private donors. The building consists of over 1,440 square meters and was constructed between 2008–2014 for about €3.5 million. It employs 13 people and has an annual budget of about half a million Euros.

The next example is the Art & Culture Centre in Grodzisk Mazowiecki, which is the new building for a previously existing institution. Its new space of over 3,700 square meters contains the main facilities of a culture centre, and in addition a cinema, an existing radio studio, and the headquarters of a local newspaper. Its construction in the years 2006–2008 cost €5 million. The centre has 33 employees and an annual budget of over €2 million.

The last case of rooted cultural investment is the public library branch in Rumia, named Culture Station, as it is located in a train station building. In 2016 this place was awarded an international prize, The Library Interior Design Award. In addition to its normal library function, the Culture Station became the new address for the activities of several local NGOs. It cost €1.5 million, spent from 2013 to 2014. It consists of 1,150 square meters; employs 20 people and has an annual budget of €370,000.

The research team, employing the concept of cultural ecosystems (Holden, 2015), identified various fields and characteristics of the relations created by the new public cultural institution with the urban socio-economic environment. In this regard, we were interested in both the strategic and spontaneous activities of the organization, which wants to establish itself in its new environment, as well as the local, municipal or regional self-government responsible for running a new or newly located institution.

Table 19.1 Data on selected, newly rooted arts and culture venues in Poland

Place	Emplacement context	Open	Concept/ Construct start time	Cost (aprox.) EUR	Size m²	Co-financing – EU funds (aprox.) EUR	Visitors '15 (aprox.)	Events number '15	Budget '15 (aprox.) EUR	Staff '15–16
GRODZISK MAZ. Cultural Centre	**Existing instituition – new building (constr.)**	IV 2008	2004/ III 2006	5,000,000	3,713	2,500,000	110,000	150	2,000,000	33
GORZÓW WLKP. Philharmonic Hall	**New instituition – new building (constr.)**	V 2011	1998 XII 2008	35,000,000	6,589	8,000,000	43,000	172	1,600,000	65
LÓDŹ – Edelman Dialogue Centre	**Existing instituition – new building (constr.)**	I 2014 – IV 2014	2007–2008/ IX 2008, 2009 – IX 2010, II 2013	3,500,000	1,442	–	25,000	188	500,000	13
POZNAŃ – ICHOT Heritage Centre	**Existing instituition – new brand – new location, new constr.)**	V 2014	2007/ XII 2010	22,000,000	5,070	12,500,000	108,000	11,129	1,500,000	53
WŁOCŁAWEK BROWAR B. Cultural Centre	**New instituition through merging – revitalis. of heritage/postindustrial area**	V 2014	2007/ IX 2012	8,500,000	7,000	6,000,000	20,000	120	800,000	47
GDAŃSK Shakespeare Theatre	**New instituition – new building (constr.)**	IX 2014	2008/ III 2011	25,000,000	7,935	13,000,000	81,000	777	3,000,000	26+
RUMIA – 'Culture Station' Library	**Existing Instituition (new location, interior revitalisation)**	IX 2014	2012 I 2013	1,500,000	1,150	–	7,700 (+ 6,300)	385	370,000	20–
KATOWICE Silesian Museum	**Existing instituition – new building (constr. and revitalisation of post-mining area)**	IV 2015	2004 (1950's) VII 2011	70,000,000	25,067	43,000,000	250,000 (inside) 413,000 (outside)	154 (IV – XII 2015)	7,500,000	178

Source: *New emplacement of public cultural institutions in the cultural 'ecosystems' of Polish cities*, Research Project Final Report, Poznan 2017, p. 11; table transl. by the author. http://rok.amu.edu.pl/wp-content/uploads/2013/10/Nowe-lokowanie-instytucji-publicznych-w-miejskich-ekosystemach-kultury-w-Polsce-2016-RAPORT-PDF.pdf

An important purpose of the research was to study the methods through which a new organism is rooted in the social and economic fabric of Polish cities, but also to investigate how the brands of institutions are shaped, and the impact that identity activities have on the inhabitants of the city.

In these studies, we were also interested – from a comparative perspective – in cases of previously existing institutions which have been newly located and seek, through their new headquarters, under a new address, methods for increasing their audience and strengthening their brand. On the other hand, of key importance was the functioning of new institutions and cultural locations in the context of urban cultural policies, including the appearance of an institution or a new location, the growth of new headquarters for cultural activities in the local community, and finally the cooperation with the socio-economic environment in the city.

This project has not only diagnosed the conditions that determine the functioning and impact of new cultural institutions, but also reveals a number of variables which affect the effectiveness of the strategies they implement and the cultural policies adopted towards them or with their participation (to be specific: social environment, material resources, competence resources, the social media environment, the media environment and forms of management). The project revealed areas of various potentials, opportunities and resources, but also obstacles and barriers. It described the conditions conducive to both cooperation and competition, which, when managed in an appropriate way, may become a driving force for the development of competing parties.

The research model adopted by the team, which combined on the one hand a comprehensive approach: desk research, netnography and, on the other hand, research conducted directly in (and with) the environment of the institution being studied (FGI, IDI, field studies, surveys of staff working in the institution, a survey of the institution's prospective audience) enabled an image of the institution's environment and the elements of its organizational culture to be assembled. The research project was carried out in a series of planned activities. We can divide them into three basic stages of the research process. The team employed both quantitative and qualitative methods.

Table 19.2 Empirical research in numbers

8	**Arts and culture organizations – publicly funded institutions**
8	**Fieldwork – socio-cultural research**
8	**Netnography research**
34	**Individual in-depth interviews (IDI):** directors, employees from the new and the 'old' representative institution in the city, the representatives of local authorities
91	**Focus Group Interviews with participants** – opinion leaders and cultural activists from the city being researched
153	**Questionnaires – employees**
434	**Questionnaires – prospective clients of the institutions**
712	**All the participants of the research process**

Source: New emplacement of public cultural institutions in the cultural 'ecosystems' of Polish cities, Research Project Final Report, Poznan 2017, p. 12; table transl. by the author. http://rok.amu.edu.pl/wp-content/uploads/2013/10/Nowe-lokowanie-instytucji-publicznych-w-miejskich-ekosystemach-kultury-w-Polsce-2016-RAPORT-PDF.pdf

An important element of the preliminary phase of the research was netnography – an analysis of the institutions' resources that are available on the Internet: analysis of the offer, communication-marketing models, the communication skills of the staff, and how the cultural institutions build relationships with their target audience via the Internet. The second stage of research was the case study proper – carried out in the eight institutions covered by the study, consisting of several elements and research methods (quantitative and qualitative). The innovative aspect of the research model lies in the fact that when the field researchers visited the eight institutions they were already equipped with knowledge about the given institution in the areas covered by the initial stage of research: the communication conducted between the institution and the target audience via the Internet (thanks to netnography), and an analysis of the strategic and financial documents related to cultural policies of the cities and institutions concerned.

The researchers were able to present this knowledge to the management of a given institution, and this became the starting point for further research and activities supporting the institution. During this stage of the research, the prepared tools were used in each of the institutions:

- Quantitative surveys – questionnaires tailored to the target audience and employees of the case study institution
- Qualitative research – focus group interviews with representatives of the culture-opinion making environment in each of the eight examined cities, and individual in-depth interviews in each of the eight cities with representatives of four groups of people:

  a the director of the institution,
  b key employees/management staff of the institution,
  c a director/employee from the management of the 'old' institution in the city being researched,
  d a local government officer or official responsible for the cultural policy including the activity of the case study institution.

To provide even more complete data, the research team included an element of field research. During this stage, field researchers assigned to each of the eight cultural institutions made scientific observations, photographic documentation and observational reports. During these activities, the researchers:

- Had the opportunity to take a direct look at the functioning of the newly located or new institution
- Observed the methods used in the institution
- Investigated the forms and quality of the institution's offer to the public
- Observed how the institution developed relationships with its audience
- Gathered the reactions of the target audience to the institution's offer
- Obtained data on the competences of the staff working at the institution

Field research was effective for obtaining non-declarative information and to compare declarations with reality. As a result of the qualitative part of the research project, the team collected for analysis:

- 34 individual in-depth interviews (IDI) with the most competent and knowledgeable people
- 8 focused group interviews (FGI) in which 91 people participated – the opinion and culture-forming environment of the cities studied

- 153 employee surveys
- 434 target audience surveys

In total, 712 subjects participated in research activities of the project.

The research findings – an overview

The research focused on the current place and role of new cultural institutions and new cultural locations in the cultural tissue of a given city, which could become an even stronger influence in the future. An important need for the majority of newly established institutions and the new headquarters of existing institutions is the problem of the life of the institutions after the creation of – often costly – cultural infrastructure, especially if the financing came from EU funds. Guaranteeing stable financing for these institutions and investments and ensuring a harmonious process of rooting in the socio-economic and cultural identity of the city, requires undertaking very intense, strategic actions. These actions should be a component of the institution's practice and be based on close cooperation between local or regional governments and the institution as part of the development of urban cultural policies.

An important element of the research was to tackle the important topic of coping with the real or predicted post-investment crisis of cultural institutions (including the institution successfully spending European, regional or local and its own funds on the investment, but then facing the problem of obtaining funds for ongoing maintenance of the facility and institutions in subsequent years; institutional cannibalism – i.e. other, old institutions are forced to give up some of their budgets to a new organism in the city).

Some visual representations of selected outcomes of the study are provided in Figures 19.1 through 19.6. Both employees and visitors see the new venues as having potential and better chances of convincing the local community of the value of their offer. The points of reference in this question were other, well-established arts and culture institutions in the town.

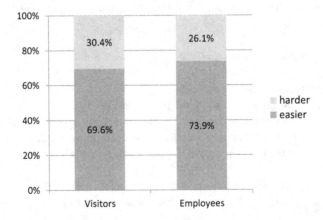

It is much easier/harder for new cultural institutions to convince members of the local community of the value of their offer

Figure 19.1   The new venue and its offer in the context of the existing cultural 'ecosystem' of the city, as seen from the perspectives of the organization's employees and visitors (*n* = 587)

Source: New emplacement of public cultural institutions in the cultural 'ecosystems' of Polish cities, Research Project Final Report, Poznan 2017, p. 51; figure transl. by the author. http://rok.amu.edu.pl/wp-content/uploads/2013/10/Nowe-lokowanie-instytucji-publicznych-w-miejskich-ekosystemach-kultury-w-Polsce-2016-RAPORT-PDF.pdf

A difference in the opinions is more noticeable in the answers to the question on the acceptance of minor failures of the newly opened venue. Here the visitors are much more generous, with over 70% expressing understanding for such situations, while only 44% of the new organizations' employees share the same attitude.

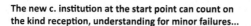

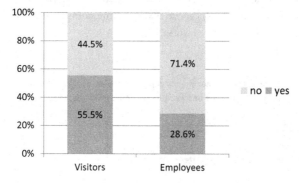

Figure 19.2 The understanding for minor failures of the newly opened culture venue, from the perspectives of visitors and employees (*n* = 587)

Source: New emplacement of public cultural institutions in the cultural 'ecosystems' of Polish cities, Research Project Final Report, Poznan 2017, p. 50; figure transl. by the author. http://rok.amu.edu.pl/wp-content/uploads/2013/10/Nowe-lokowanie-instytucji-publicznych-w-miejskich-ekosystemach-kultury-w-Polsce-2016-RAPORT-PDF

The comparison of old and new cultural venues which are present in the same city or town, aims to show the relevance of the competitive and co-operative conditions for new organisms in local cultural ecosystems from the perspective of the employees of new venues. Figure 19.3 shows the discrepancies between 8 different organisations. We can see that three of them are perceived as being in a tough, competitive or even hostile local environment. And only one out of eight sees itself as working in definitely friendly, co-operative relations.

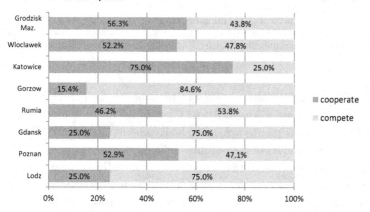

Figure 19.3 The perspective of arts and culture organizations' employees on co-operative or competitive environments (*n* = 153)

Source: New emplacement of public cultural institutions in the cultural 'ecosystems' of Polish cities, Research Project Final Report, Poznan 2017, p. 52; figure transl. by the author. http://rok.amu.edu.pl/wp-content/uploads/2013/10/Nowe-lokowanie-instytucji-publicznych-w-miejskich-ekosystemach-kultury-w-Polsce-2016-RAPORT-PDF

This perspective is well supported by other sets of outcomes delivered by all 8 organizations, when the social rooting and the accessibility of the new cultural investment for local community are finally addressed directly. The employees of the new venues are asked to indicate who the rooting process of their venue is more dependent on: their organization or its external environment. Here most of the organizations see themselves as relying on their own resources and being unquestionably responsible for their rooting process and its success. While very few rely more on others, among the latter are merely those that see more competition than cooperation in the cultural ecosystem around their organization.

Rooting of the new c. institution in the local community depends more on: activity of the new institution or openness of the social environment to the presence of the new institution – EMPLOYEES' opinions

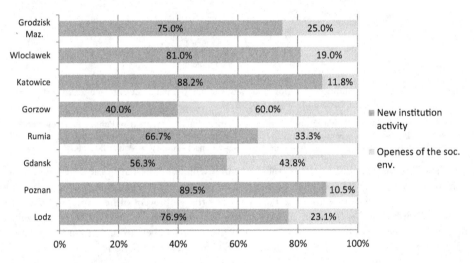

Figure 19.4 Attributing the responsibility for rooting work to the new venue or its external environment (*n* = 153)

Source: New emplacement of public cultural institutions in the cultural 'ecosystems' of Polish cities, Research Project Final Report, Poznan 2017, p. 94; figure transl. by the author. http://rok.amu.edu.pl/wp-content/uploads/2013/10/Nowe-lokowanie-instytucji-publicznych-w-miejskich-ekosystemach-kultury-w-Polsce-2016-RAPORT-PDF

The last selected graphs illustrating the outcomes of the research on the rooting process among new arts and culture venues in Poland focus on the question on the value, image and social reception of the new cultural site among both their visitors and staff. This selection shows the differences in the attitudes of the organization's clients and employees. The first outcomes concern the opinions on the impact of the new venues on the local community, with the leading positions taken by changing the city's promotional and developmental image, bringing change to the city space and increasing the access to the cultural offer in the city, and giving a feeling of pride to city inhabitants. One can see that the there is a predominance of image, symbolic and identity components.

New c. institution's influence on particular aspect of the city and its community (median for a scale 1–5)

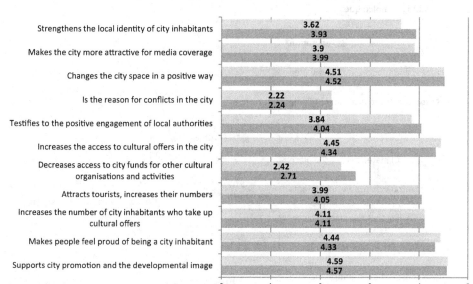

Figure 19.5 How the new arts and culture venue is influencing its city in a broad sense

Source: New emplacement of public cultural institutions in the cultural 'ecosystems' of Polish cities, Research Project Final Report, Poznan 2017, p. 117; figure transl. by the author. http://rok.amu.edu.pl/wp-content/uploads/2013/10/Nowe-lokowanie-instytucji-publicznych-w-miejskich-ekosystemach-kultury-w-Polsce-2016-RAPORT-PDF

The last figure illustrates the perspectives of both visitors and staff on the before – after effects, when it comes to impacting the particular city space in terms of the local cultural ecosystem. Both visitors and employees appreciate three aspects the most: the change of the climate and style of the place, the aesthetics of the building and the place itself, and the openness and friendly look of the area. What employees appreciated more is the place, and the reputation and popularity of the area. Visitors were much more eager to highlight 'the feeling of the clean space', the subjective feeling of security, and the improved transport facilities and communication.

The process of rooting a new cultural institution in the urban space, or a new location for a pre-existing institution, is associated with numerous dilemmas. Do the decisions made, and projects undertaken, in this area meet the needs of the residents? What narratives, reasons and ambitions are present in discussions in the public sphere. Who and under the influence of what needs decides that such an institution will be created in the city, and not another institution? What is the motive for setting up a new building for a cultural entity previously present in another place? Are many options considered in these processes, are the decisions made on the basis of a reliable analysis of the social needs of the residents? The situations from the initial phase of creating eight new locations for the institutions investigated in this project provide examples, various scenarios written by the needs and realities of the functioning of local

Crucial changes for new c. institutions visitors and employees, before and after appearance of the new building (multiple choice questions)

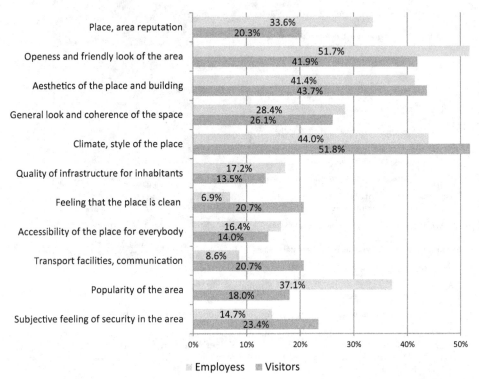

Figure 19.6   The impact of the new cultural 'organism' on the city's cultural 'ecosystem' – The rating of improvements

Source: New emplacement of public cultural institutions in the cultural 'ecosystems' of Polish cities, Research Project Final Report, Poznan 2017, p. 133; figure transl. by the author. http://rok.amu.edu.pl/wp-content/uploads/2013/10/ Nowe-lokowanie-instytucji-publicznych-w-miejskich-ekosystemach-kultury-w-Polsce-2016-RAPORT-PDF

communities in Poland. The process of locating new cultural institutions is implemented in an area already 'inhabited' by numerous organizations, institutions and environments operating in the city. In the netnographic study, deepened by qualitative research, places were recognized as attracting the cultural public and generating a magnetic field for particular environments. And a new object lands in this field – a cultural institution or its new headquarters, which must enter into relations with the existing spectrum of organizations offering cultural content and activities.

In these studies, we also devote space to the perception of cultural institutions as architectural objects that have their own visually aesthetic features, as well as functional features that are tested in use. Institutions also draw their power to influence the residents of the city and people visiting the city with these aesthetic attributes. They are architectural icons, models and reference points for other projects. It can be an architectural non-entity or a controversial idea that challenges the city's aesthetic; architectural kitsch or an incomprehensible modern masterpiece. Function-ality is purposefulness, balance, a successful investment from the perspective of those who use it – the public and employees. When a building is functionally designed, it facilitates use, helps, makes work and reaching particular places in the building easier, does not create barriers, solves problems. Aesthetics and function do not constitute opposing poles, and the best architectural and location projects create a common, non-exclusive field of values.

The empirical research brings to light several processes and shows the range of effects that accompany the rooting of new arts and culture venues in local environments. There are a few selected outcomes and general observations worth highlighting:

1   Municipalities do not hesitate to provide conditions for the development of arts and culture, or for their protection, with the use of external public funds.
2   A new culture venue is a tool for revitalizing the appearance, look and style of the cultural scene in the city, region or country.
3   A new building brings opportunities to activate new (hybrid) functions, and is the space for new fields of arts and cultural practice, which is predominantly, participative and educational.
4   A new building is a new stimulus for inhabitants to visit the arts and culture institution, even if they do not consider themselves as belonging to the cultural audience.
5   Citizens are generally proud of the aesthetic quality of these buildings and the rearrangement of the neighbourhood.
6   However, citizens do not know much about the costs already paid (and to come in the future), yet.
7   The participatory practices of newly rooted organizations are rather spontaneous projects, not strategically tailored in advance.

There are few more outcomes that address more managerial and leadership issues related to new arts and culture venues:

1   Some processes activated by the rooting of the new place raised the level of competition between arts organisations. Some are motivated to cooperate and bring about the self-improvement of organizational practices; others express indifference or attack the new venue with their biased judgments on its impact or *raison d'etre*.
2   There are both positive and negative effects of being in the spotlight (including multisource pressure on the leader & employees).
3   Another very essential effect is the real risk of *lowering the ground waters* of financial stability of the whole (eco)system of cultural institutions as organisms sharing mostly the same financial (re)sources.

Practical recommendations for the rooting of arts and culture organizations, based on an empirical study

The final section of the chapter provides a spectrum of selected recommendations for the leaders and managers of art and culture organizations, city authorities, policy and the decision-makers of local communities. These recommendations clearly illustrate the gaps in rooting processes. The list below is a direct outcome of the research discussed. The following proposals are based on the issues detected through empirical research based on the selection of public organizations freshly rooted in local cultural ecosystems. They were prepared with two areas in mind. The first is to strengthen the conditions of the leaders and staff of the newly located cultural institutions, with a view to the benefit for the local communities – the current and potential audience. The second is to draw conclusions from the experience of emplacing cultural institutions, to raise awareness of the opportunities and threats for the future rooting of this type of investment in cities.

1 There is a necessity of well-timed and well-processed public consultations and discussions with local environment representatives on the whole process of rooting new arts and culture venues.

2 There is a need for the advanced benchmarking and study visits of the organization leader, decision-makers, funders and staff representatives to the other new arts and culture venues that are already rooted.

3 Functionality is the key word – meaning, the obligation to provide enough time for consultations and workshops with the future users, including staff members.

4 Keeping control over the framework and rules of the architectural design process (all of its stages) should not be taken for granted.

5 The key task is the elaboration of the new venue's coexistence study/future relations study on the consequences of the rooting process, which result from there being a new organism in the local ecosystem. Providing the first response to the question of how the new object will change the rest of the ecosystem, with the consideration of its new functions, old and new users, new demands, costs and others impacts. The outcome of the study should contribute to the definition of the strategic role of the institution, contextualised in the cultural city and regional ecosystem, inhabited by diverse actors.

6 What is often neglected is the effort to provide access to a wide range of expertise to the rooting process leader, in the form of consultancies, experts, peer support for the rooted organization director at hand.

7 The main goal should be the construction of the new cultural space adjusted to the new trends in cultural participation and the leisure behaviours of its users.

8 There is a need for diversified talent capital among the newly rooted organization staff, people ready to respond to new challenges and demands.

9 Social rooting activities that involve the neighbourhood inhabitants are necessary right before and during the construction work. Moreover, new art and culture venues should be rooted with care for improving the material and environmental quality of the surrounding space and landscape.

10 Tailored planning, keeping just proportions, the advanced long-term programming of the new facility are security guarantees against overscaling. All the indicators should be planned carefully.

11 The rooting of the new cultural venue should be done along with the cultivation of existing organisms in the local cultural ecosystem.

12 The new rooting of an existing institution is the best, natural opportunity to improve, reconfigure or refresh its organisational culture.

13 The practice experienced by the new venue, with the use of new resources of every kind, is the best chance to share innovative solutions with the cultural 'ecosystem' actors, keeping some smaller players and projects under the umbrella of the success and visibility of the new cultural brand or its new image. This is the gate through which 'know-how' could be introduced to smaller players in the region. This is also the right moment to strenthen cooperation with partners when sharing the same cultural ecosystem.

14 Budget issues are crucial for the new venue, including the necessity of the long-term (at least biennial or triennial) budgeting and programming. The sustainability values and the perspective of the future long-term presence of the new organization in the local ecosystem requires systemic decisions from the public funders on the prevention of budget discrepancies among cultural institutions in the city or region.

15 The experience of local, municipal cultural policies, proves that the common issue is that culture, sports, and health compete in the area of public investment and the budget of subsidies. The solution for this could be an effort to indicate overlapping moments of goals and costs integration. The harmonisation of this group of disciplines and public spending could be beneficial for the cultural ecosystems in the town and regions.

16 What new venues funded from public subsidies should strive for is a clever balance between elitist and egalitarian values when programming and branding a newly funded arts and culture organization. At the same time the new organism should have the courage to be sharp and direct in communicating the value and identity of the newly rooted cultural institution. To achieve this it needs to 'speak to' a well-defined audience, who are the carriers of a variety of values, behind their behaviour as participants, in more or less organized forms of arts and culture experience.

New venues – from rooting to cultural sustainability

How do new venues impact the local cultural ecosystems, and what are the implications for cultural sustainability? To reflect on that, we shall at last approach a redefinition of sustainability in the context of cultural practice (Throsby, 1995). One of the most interesting recent research initiatives on culture and sustainability (Dessein et al., 2015) generously defined this relation with a three-dimensional perspective: culture *in* sustainability, culture *for* sustainability and culture *as* sustainability. I would like to extend the third dimension, and the newly rooted arts and culture organizations are a good basis for this.

Arts and culture organizations are faced with multiple tensions and the cultural consequences of globalization and digitalisation processes, characterised by the unlimited transmission, relatively broad accessibility and mobility of cultural objects, human artefacts, texts, meanings, symbols, narrations and interpretations. Arts and culture artefacts, as objects of curiosity and co-creation, are exposed to very hazardous, predatory competition with what is offered through comercialised communication channels. There are huge tensions in arts and culture organizations caused by marketing players that are on the opposite side in the sustainability debate.

We witness the flexible individualization that shows the real power of taste. The practices of 21st-century consumers and marketers have proved the omnipotence of the new meaning of marketing as predicted in 1963 by Sydney Levy, who wrote that marketing is a process of providing customers with "parts of a potential mosaic from which they, as artists of their own lifestyle, can pick and choose to develop the composition that for the time may seem the best" (Levy, 1963). This goes in hand with the dilemma of whether brands, as the objects of substantial aesthetic experience, will replace artworks, the main objects of such experience up till now. Or thinking ahead, whether marketing practices will replace the offers of art instititions. This is something that we are reminded of by Chris Bilton, who states that it is marketing that today provides 'open texts' which allow space for viewers, readers, and listeners to negotiate their own personal readings, even if (especially if) these readings seem to 'deviate' from, or 'resist', the encoded message of the advertiser (Bilton, 2007, pp. 155–158). The function 'patented' by the creators of artworks has been taken over by the marketers.

Open texts or *elements of the mosaic*, as mentioned earlier, co-created in the interpretations of the user or audience are recalling the rudiments of the notion of participation, which are grounded in the aesthetic theories of such philosophers as Hans Georg Gadamer. In several of his writings, including the milestone *Truth & Method* or *Actuality of Beauty*, he highlights the essence of participation and co-creation in the interpretation process, all in the frame of the universal concept of play. Art is a playground for the free activity of interpreters, where you play and are played, where play makes you a participant, integrates you into a community.

In the public realm, and in the areas of public policies, there is another important element of participation, one which has been discussed since the Middle Ages, namely the *subsidiarity principle*, referred to by such thinkers as St. Thomas Aquinas, Alexis de Tocqueville and John Stuart Mill. Here the term participation and the rooting processes of the new art and culture venues reaches the next level of reflection.

The *subsidiarity principle* is too often taken for granted in investment processes and cultural policies, but ultimately, it matters as the regulating principle for those orchestrating the construction or cultivation of a new cultural venue in town. Basically, this concept is understood as an organizing principle stating that matters ought to be handled by the smallest, lowest or least centralized, competent authority. It is the idea that a public authority like a government or a city hall should have a subsidiary function, more supportive than subordinate, performing only those tasks which cannot be performed effectively at a more immediate or local level. It is nicely summed up in the brief sentence of Reid Buckley, stating that *no public agency should do what a private agency can do better*. This is essential in the context of local community funding, or constructing an architectural object, or providing new space for arts and culture practices. Finally, this principle is the greatest law of social philosophy, as a democratic social doctrine, which aims to protect individual citizens from rising totalitarianism and exploitation (Millon-Delsol, 1992; Putnam, 1993). It was one of the key concepts for the restitution of democratic states after communism, and the decentralization of administration in countries of the former Eastern Block, such as Poland. It expresses, and organizes the response to, a desire to limit the influence of the state, where smaller communities or individuals themselves can take care of their own interests. It is the framework for rethinking practice in shaping cross-sectorial relations between the public, private and civic sectors in the cultural field.

Subsidiarity is an emergent principle in local cultural ecosystems, as a framework with local grassroots cultural organizations and individuals as its basic units and leaders of development – the most dynamic, active cultural ecosystems inhabitants and local public authorities – seriously motivated to be the stimulators, facilitators and guardians of the subsidiarity principle. The metaphor of the ecosystem again seems very appropriate for discussing sustainability, where culture and its primary playgrounds – all arts and culture organizations – are understood as organisms, and not mechanisms. This shift in metaphor is breaking through purely financial arguments and crossing or bypassing the economy – ecology – social pillars which are typical for sustainable development debate.

Play, participation and subsidiarity are, at different levels of sophistication, tools for expressing and understanding cultural sustainability. What is the content of cultural sustainability? When cultural sustainability is seen as much more than an amalgamation of the three conventional pillars, it invites the cultural notion of the transmitting dialogue between generations, where the keywords are memory, heritage and cultural identity. It engages the realms of craft, slow life patterns, localisms, it recalls the meaning of a good life, meaningful frictions, a sense of community. It emphasises the role of continuity, consistency or literacy. It highlights the roles of masters and mentors, with their skills, experience and methods of choice making, and shows that they matter (Poprawski, 2016). It is like learning to select, decide, lead and engage in the essential creative processes. Something we are missing today, enormously. Culturally-led sustainability is also the diversity which comes from settled, meaningful work with a comprehensive community; it is a balance between reflection and action, the continuity of aesthetics and ethics (Berger, 1999).

Leaders of new arts and culture venues get the role of curators of bipolar relations between the cultural institution and the social environment. The issue is what the organization is taking from its ecosystem, the city, and what it is giving back to the community of citizens. Here the subsidiarity concept returns with the domestication of new and newly rooted arts organizations. Its essential goal – and the measure of the success of the rooting – is for people to locate the new institution on their mental map, convincing them to treat it as their own, taking both responsibility and enjoyment. New arts and culture constructions sites are potentially the best participative organizations in their towns, if certain recommendations are reflected on, or not taken for granted.

References

Berger, K. (1999). *A theory of art*. Oxford: Oxford University Press.

Bianchini, F. (1996). Cultural planning: An innovative approach to urban development. In: J. Verwijnen and P. Lehtovuori, eds., *Managing urban change*. Helsinki: University of Art and Design Helsinki.

Bilton, Ch. (2007). *Management and creativity: From creative industries to creative management*. Oxford: Blackwell Publishing.

Dahrendorf, R. (1990). *Reflections on the revolution in Europe: In a letter intended to have been sent to a gentleman in Warsaw*. New York: Times Books.

Dessein, J., Soini, K., Fairclough, G., and Horlings, L. (eds.) (2015). *Culture in, for and as sustainable development. Conclusions from the COST Action IS1007 Investigating cultural sustainability*. Jyväskylä: University of Jyväskylä.

Holden, J. (2015). *The ecology of culture*. London: AHRC. Available at: https://ahrc.ukri.org/documents/project-reports-and-reviews/the-ecology-of-culture

Landry C. and Bianchini, F. (1995). *The creative city*. London: Demos.

Levy, S.J. (1963). Symbolism and life style. In: S.A. Greyser, ed., *Proceedings, American Marketing Association*, pp. 140–150.

Markusen, A. et al. (2011). *California's arts and cultural ecology*. San Francisco: James Irvine Foundation. Available at: www.irvine.org/publications-by-topic/arts/arts-ecology-reports

Maugham, C. and Bianchini, F. (2004). *Economic and social impact of cultural festivals in the East Midlands*. Report for Arts Council England. Available at: https://static.a-n.co.uk/wp-content/uploads/2016/09/Economic-and-social-impact-final-report.pdf [Accessed 15 Jul. 2018].

McGuigan, J. (1996). *Rethinking cultural policy*. Maidenhead: Oxford University Press.

———. (2010). *Cultural analysis*. London: Sage.

Millon – Delsol, C. (1992). *L' état subsidiaire*. Paris: Presses Universitaires de France.

Poprawski, M. (2016). Intergenerational transmission of values and cultural sustainability: The cultural participation of local, small town communities in Poland. *Law Social Justice and Global Development Journal*, 1(2016). Available at: https://warwick.ac.uk/fac/soc/law/elj/lgd/2016-1/

Putnam, R. (1993). *Making democracy work: Civic tradition in modern Italy*. Princeton: Princeton University Press.

Silver, D.A. and Nichols Clark, T. (2016). *Scenescapes: How qualities of place shape social life*. Chicago and London: The University of Chicago Press.

Steiner, G. (2010). *Grammars of creation*. London: Faber & Faber.

STRATEG. (2018). Available at: http://stat.gov.pl/en/topics/culture-tourism-sport/culture/ [Accessed 15 Jul. 2018].

Throsby, D. (1995). Culture economics and sustainability. *Journal of Cultural Economics*, 19, pp. 199–206.

20

THEORIZING CREATIVE CAPITAL IN CHINA

A multi-level framework

Yong Xiang and Boyi Li

Introduction

It becomes almost a cliché to suggest that cities provide favourable conditions for the cultural and creative economy. The thesis of "creative cities" (Florida, Mellander, and Stolarick, 2008; Markusen, 2006; Stolarick and Florida, 2006), for instance, taking creativity at the centre of the urban networks for entrepreneurship, regeneration, and economic competitiveness, has long been the focus of scholarly and public policy discussions (Cunningham, 2012; Florida, 2002; Hall and Hubbard, 1998; Throsby, 2010; UNCTAD, 2016). However, inquiries on the other side of this urbanity-culture relationship, particularly the question of "how does a genuine appreciation of cultural productions and the associated local communities (networks) enable an alternative imagination of urban future?", are rare and far from being well understood (Bingham-Hall and Kassa, 2017).

In the *Global Report on Culture For Sustainable Urban Future* (UNESCO, 2016), UNESCO calls for policy-makers, the business community, urban planners, and academics to place heritage and creativity at the centre of a sustainable urban future, particularly the communities of creative entrepreneurs. In a similar vein, *The Quito Papers 2016: A Manifesto For Urban Planning in the 21st Century*, by UN HABITAT III (Sennett, Burdett, and Sassen, 2018; UN-Habitat, 2016), calls for an approach to design and make urban space that not only facilitates cultural productions and cultural institutions, but also itself promotes a culture of openness, local improvisation (messyness), and public realm. This new agenda, aiming to articulate the reciprocal, more-balanced, two-way relationship between urbanity and culture, marks a paradigm shift of knowledge from the one that of a mixture of neoliberalism, industrial nationalism, and global projection of soft power, to a new one that unlocks the potential of meaningful interaction between traditionality and modernity, harmony and wellbeing, the East and the West.

For more than a decade, China has been promoting the cultural and creative industries as a new engine of growth and urbanisation (Keane, 2013; O'Connor and Xin, 2006; Xiang and Walker, 2014). The impressive growth of cultural and creative industries has been widely celebrated, albeit with mixed perceptions and judgements. This is in the context of a wider reflection upon the development since 1978 (the era of Reform and Opening-up, 改革开放), as well as the historical pitfalls of this period (notably, the environmental disasters, erosion of interpersonal trust and social morality, loss of faith, and epidemic corruption). China nowadays mobilises great efforts and resources to foster a developmental model of sustainability, in which the economy, the environment, and the society can harmoniously work for each other instead of consuming at the cost of each other. Such transformation cannot be realised without a greater emphasis upon – and a more ambitious expectation of – cultural change and social progress. Cultural and creative entrepreneurship is the pivotal point of such ambitious expectations. The changing demographic, economic, and social patterns of cities urgently require contemporary, new approaches on the planning, provision, and regeneration of urban space, in which the practices of architecture, music and museums, performance arts not only play a part, but more importantly supply new ideas and ideals, new rationale of design and regulatory rules that help reshape the imagination of future sustainable cities (Bingham-Hall and Kassa, 2017; Sennett, Burdett, and Sassen, 2018; UN-Habitat, 2016; UNESCO, 2016).

This chapter addresses this challenge of the theoretical gap connecting cultural and creative economy with future cities by theorizing the notion of "creative capital". We introduce the meaning of "capital" from the studies in economic sociology, in particular, Pierre Bourdieu's work on the analysis of relational and cultural embeddedness in the cultural production sectors (Bourdieu, 1983, 1993, 1995). The theoretical discussions on "capital", as a critical theory, are expanded in the second section. We then provide a detailed account on the theoretical framework of creative capital, highlighting the possibilities of discussing the spatiality of creative capital. The last section provides a case study of Beijing as the city is transforming itself by following the creative cities agenda.

Understanding creative capital

The notion of capital has often been narrowly defined on pure economic terms referring to the material means necessary to organize production of valuable goods for market exchange – i.e. land, machines, labour, financial assets, etc. Such conceptualization has been subject to serious critique in the field of economic sociology and cultural economy, where scholars from Max Weber, Karl Polanyi to Pierre Bourdieu and Raymond Willams suggested that social relations, and the meaning structure around which social relations are organized and instituted (family, religion, nation-state, cultural belief, etc.), constitute the essential explanations of how economic actors gain advantage over others in the economic competition of producing goods and market trade. For Bourdieu, the notion of capital needs to be defined simultaneously as economic and cultural/aesthetic terms. Capital as economic resources means it can be accounted using price signals of markets and made exchangeable with other means of production. In contrast, capital as social/cultural/aesthetic resources must be embedded socially and historically in a society where values emerge out of the common understandings – and aesthetic sensations – of certain aesthetics core, which are not immediately exchangeable but have to be learnt through living experience and education. We suggest any theoretical explanation of creative cities must have good elaborations on the non-economic forms of capital, and how such forms of capital can be appropriated, accumulated, and transformed into economic forms.

In his analysis of the Parisian circles of poetry, painting, and theatre performances of France in the late 19th century, Bourdieu reinvented the notions of 'competition', 'advantages', and 'power' in terms of the resources that economic actors manage to accumulate over time in social relations (social), educational and family background (cultural), and the symbolic values of being associated with prestigious institutions (i.e. artistic movements) (Bourdieu, 1993). He used the concept of "field" in order to make sense of the games of a power struggle between actors deploying various strategies of converting social, cultural, and symbolic resources but aiming for the same goals. Competitive advantages, in the field of cultural production, can be gained by converting values between relational, cultural, and symbolic resources, and between these non-economic and economic resources. The accumulation of these critical non-economic resources cannot be possible by purely relying on the logic of *homo economicus*, instead by the social process of studying and acting collectively towards certain abstract ideals of artistic pursuits, "the art-for-art's sake and pure theory" (Bourdieu, 1986). Bourdieu's work revealed that economic reasoning and artistic pursuit represent two opposite poles of the purpose rationality which permeates through every aspect of cultural production. This insight into economic-cultural tensions constitutes the theoretical foundation of creative capital.

We take the term 'capital' as a concept referring to the potential of cultural entrepreneurs in mobilising the relational, institutional, and cultural 'assets' to transform artistic ideas into ventures of either socio-cultural transformation or business development, or both. The theoretical root of this definition can be traced to the literature of economic sociology (Bourdieu and Wacquant, 2013; Fligstein and McAdam, 2012; Granovetter and Swedberg, 2018; Polanyi, 1957). The fundamental premise of 'creative capital' is that cultural entrepreneurs, situated in the dense networks of artists, educators and art critics, appraisal agency, collectors, and market-makers, governments, public audience and media etc., manage to accumulate capital available to them as they become embedded in the space of creative networks. Such non-economic resources (i.e. reputation, trust, aesthetic understandings, and cultural taste and cultural identity) provide the means with which the cultural entrepreneurs justify their social status of being a member of an exclusive club and can be further strengthened (reproduced) by continuously interacting with other members of society. In other words, creative capital can be approached by three forms of capital: the relational, the cultural, and the symbolic.

To handle the complexity in abstract theorizing, we hinge the essential elements of creative capital to three levels of cultural-economy practices: namely, the everyday practice (the micro-level, embeddedness analysis), the institutional arrangements (the meso-level, ecosystem analysis), and the intellectual milieu (the macro-level, historic analysis) (see Table 20.1).

The level of everyday practice asks how urban space enables or limits the process of cultural entrepreneurship by accommodating the mundane activities of networking, learning, and symbolic construction. Such inquiries are focused on the possibilities and potentials of urban space in facilitating the occurrence of the everyday practice of cultural entrepreneurs. One basic example of such possibility is to examine how easy it is for the local networks of creative-minded people to socialise (i.e. forming interest groups, surveying who's who, making collective initiatives), exchange information, and co-work in the proximate locations.

The level of institutional practice invites researchers to focus on the synergistic effects of institutional nexus surrounding creative economy. Some economic geographers referred to such synergies as the 'regime of accumulation'. The level of institutional practice asks the question of how creative capital is formed, accumulated, and re-generated in the emerging networks of institutional 'regimes of accumulation' (Markusen, 2006). Cultural and creative economy is typically characterized by the dominance of small or micro-sized, agency-type organizations networked with each other, as well as a few large corporations operating in a dynamic environment of voluntary labour, short-term projects, and temporary employment. The turnover of human resources and capital are much faster as talents are working simultaneously for more personal ambitions and more social-collective ideals (i.e., the progress of society), which, either way, means little motivation or moral justification to serve one specific business organization.[1] As a result, the personal life space of creative workers is substantially different from the modernist cities of the managerial class. This transformation of institutional structures in city space means a substantial departure of urban ideals from the late 20th century modernist view of post-industrial city (car-friendly road networks connecting suburbs with CBD, spatially and

Table 20.1 Research framework of creative capital

Levels of space	A research framework of creative capital		
	Relational capital	Cultural capital	Symbolic capital
Everyday practice (Micro-level, ethnographic)	*Social Embeddedness:* • How are the creative networks geographically distributed? How is the interpersonal trust facilitated? • What is the future urban space like where it is easy to meet and network with each other? And what does it mean to both public space (museum, university, street and traffic places, neighborhood etc.) and private space (office buildings, residential area, and family activity)? What's the mode of connection between the public and the private space?	*Cultural Embeddedness:* • The target is to have a well-educated, well-informed public in the city, from which a creative class emerge. • What are the places where people share ideas and learn from each other? Where and what art forms do creative people get inspirations from? • How to design a public space where new ideas are encouraged to be communicated and learning activities are rewarding (public library, bookshop, universities, museums etc.)?	*Cognitive Embeddedness:* • Is there a system of belief, mythology, narrative about the city's cultural life? How do cities establish and maintain a connection between their production of symbols and a unique cultural identity? • How do the cities spatially arrange socio-economic interactions through the heritage, tradition, and a specific way of framing 'good life' can be embodied? • How do the spatial arrangements address the socio-economic challenges facing the city (migration and integration, inequality, elderly/child care, leisure, environmental hazards, etc.)?
Institutional practice (Meso-level, ecosystemic)	*Institutions as mechanisms:* • What is the cultural infrastructure? Is there a structural equivalent of Triple-Helix model creative ecosystems (Government – University – Industry)? • How do cities facilitate the interactions between key institutional players? The government, the cultural institutions, and the business community? (G–Art–B)? • What's the nature of institutional collaboration in this city? • What are key interests and motivations that enable or limit the interactions and collaboration between these institutions?	*Institutions of knowledge:* • What are the roles of pivotal cultural institutions that function as the nexus of cultural production? • How do people learn the cultural capital and share the insights? How do the particular meanings of cultural tastes take shape, become influential, and eventually become the cultural legacy of the city? • How do the cultural institutions provide educational functions to the society in art and aesthetics? • What are the role of the governments in promoting art and aesthetics education? • How do business community, benefiting from the rise of creative class and art-friendly urban environment, support the activities of cultural organizations?	*Institutions as identity and heritage:* • What are the important cultural organizations, cultural events, or heritage places that give the city a distinctive identity (a city brand)? • How do the experience of living and working in the relevant networks of the city give a distinctive symbolic value to the individuals or organizations (a university degree widely recognised and recommended)? • How do the cities create a unique, local solutions to address the fundamental challenges of development (civil rights and social justice, environmental hazard, caring for the elderly and children etc.)? • Generally, how do the social and economic injustice influence the spatial reality of the city? Are there any alternative solutions/suggestions that might address these challenges?

(Continued)

Table 20.1 (Continued)

Levels of space	A research framework of creative capital		
	Relational capital	Cultural capital	Symbolic capital
Modernity and aesthetics (macro-level, historical)	*Contemporaneity of art schools:* • How do creative entrepreneurs understand and practice the notion of 'modernity' and 'good life' as aesthetic standard? What are the spatial distribution of creative networks? How do creative entrepreneurs communicate, share, and co-create new styles of art creation? • How do cultural entrepreneurs practice the idea of tradition and heritage in modern daily life?	*Forums of (post-)modernity:* • What are the core theoretical debates on modernity, contemporary art, and heritage? What are the main framework of ethics, justice, and social values that the society is striving to achieve or maintain? • What are the discourses of social critique, or art critique?	*Modernity as orthodox:* • Are there theoretical authorities setting the tones of modernity and contemporary art development? How do the cultural authorities become orthodox? (historical perspective) How do the authorities exert their symbolic power? • How do the theoretical debates between different schools impact on the ways creative entrepreneurs gain brands and credentials in their networks? • What are the emerging consensus on "culture for sustainability"? Who are the main actors in this area? How do they become influential?

chronically separating work from life), towards a post-modern paradigm of future city with physical and cultural infrastructure for the 'space of flows' (Castells, 2004). Most importantly, we aim to elaborate the concept of creative capital in the light of modernism and its contemporary discourses in Chinese context. This level of analysis will focus on the historical debates around ideas of modernity and aesthetic ideals, and how these debates become embodied in the actions of contemporary creative networks, institutional relations and creative communities, from which an image of creative cities can be seen.

Relational capital

The relational capital refers to the capability that actors gain by being well-connected in clusters of social ties, to the extent that they can leverage the positions of high centrality, connectivity (transitivity), or "structural holes" as means to achieve desirable ends – the behaviour Fligstein and McAdam (2012) referred to as the "strategic agency" (Fligstein and McAdam, 2012). The propensity to gain power and influence is high when actors occupy key *positions* in social networks, which can be seen by applying structural analysis (for example, by the network graph theories or complex network theories). While the modelling of tie structures is straightforward, given a universal definition of tie, the determination of key positions can be complicated and tricky in real-world social analysis, because the meanings of ties vary in different contexts and are notoriously hard to define on measurable terms.

The benefits of relational capital can be materialized by two categories of social mechanisms: interpersonal trust and cross-sectional synergy. The former is the basic condition for the formation of any social community. Relational capital in the form of interpersonal trust is accumulated and preserved on the basis of everyday life as community members share the same space of social interaction, work, and living struggles. The effects of high relational capital can take the form of embedded 'solidarity', where individual members of a community assume general interpersonal trust with each other and are motivated to collectively protect the community from behaviour of opportunism, malfeasance, or other kinds of anti-social behaviour. Such community structure is characterized by close-knit clusters of interpersonal relationships, which leads to the rise of sharing culture among its members. It has been argued that the urban conditions of cultural and creative economy in contemporary cities should place great emphasis on the community-buildings efforts between the artists, the business community, and other stakeholders, for example, by designing public spaces consciously promoting the culture of openness and transparency. The development of cultural and creative economy benefits from the urban conditions conducive to the general accumulation of relational capital of society, so that actors who manage to broker across different clans of social networks are capable of facilitating innovation the draw upon the ideas, talents and trust across the range of sectors, disciplines, and other institutional silos (phenomena referred to as the cross-sectional synergy, or the *Medici Effect*). Modern cities that place culture at the centre of its future development strive to become the space for complex social networking and for shaping a consensus/identity of artistic and moral ideals, rather than the space for arms-length marketplace, industrial 'growth poles', gentrification and social inequality (Harvey, 1992, 2013).

In the Chinese context, the studies of "guanxi" highlighted the complicated, subtle, situated interpretations of ties in Chinese society, which are impossible to be reduced to universal definitions and thus subject to structural analysis (Luo, 2008; Redding, 2013). The purpose of studying guanxi is not just to confirm the statement that the leverage of social ties can lead to competitive advantages of individuals or groups in economic terms, which probably can be found in all human societies. Instead, the studies of guanxi cultures reveals a set of distinctive rituals, norms, contingencies, and personal strategies in Chinese society to generate the relational capital as well as to safeguard the investment of social labour, emotions, and time as the maintenance of relations. Such rituals, norms, contingencies, and strategies are functional not just in the sense of celebrating cultural identities, but in the sense that they provide a cover of meaning over the embarrassing consideration of money or other economic returns, and thereby conceal the purpose of economic reasoning. We know that, from existing studies of Chinese business networks, guanxi cultures have positive effects on the accumulation of relational capital because interpersonal trust is generally assumed, facilitated and accumulated through these rituals and norms. However, we don't know whether, empirically or theoretically, guanxi cultures can be obstacles or facilitators to the development of Medici Effects in Chinese fields of cultural production.

Empirically, we have yet to see research that reveals how cultural entrepreneurs manage to leverage the relational capital of guanxi by playing the rules of the distinctive rituals, norms, and strategies in Chinese society. Examples can be found in DiMaggio's study of art consumers, social stratification, and networks of cultural entrepreneurs in the US (DiMaggio and Useem, 1978; DiMaggio, 1982, 2011), as well as the American film industries 1895–1929 by Mezias and Kuperman (2001). The latter study discovered and explained the pivotal roles of social networks formed in an entrepreneurial community of Hollywood and revealed how the success of risky film ventures depends on the combination of the quality of artistic creations and management of "value chains", both of which are highly embedded in close-knit social networks.

Cultural capital

The cultural capital refers to the capability of individuals or organizations to interpret and communicate the meanings of aesthetic experience on sophisticated and theoretical levels. The definition of cultural capital stresses the tacit capabilities of people, organizations, and communities living in the urban space, which differs from the economists' understandings[2] (Throsby, 2010) and is not about any tangible or intangible asset to directly generate values of any kind. Possessing cultural capital means that the cultural entrepreneurs can (1) discover those opportunities of new or refreshed aesthetic perspectives that was invisible to those lacking such cognitive capabilities, and (2) develop a coherent and convincing account of art theories (article, talk, interview, lecture, etc.) that help others partake in this novel and transcendental experience of aesthetics. In his seminal paper "The Artworld", Danto argued that the very existence of art depends on the epistemic communities of theorists and art critics and the intellectual ways they extract aesthetic meaning from the material objects. Danto (1964, p. 581) used Andy Warhol's Brillo Box as an example to highlight the crucial connections between 'cultural capital', epistemic communities (relational capital), and artistic values:

> What in the end makes the difference between a Brillo Box and a work of art consisting of a Brillo Box is a certain theory art ... without the theory, one is unlikely to see it as art, and in order to see it as part of the artworld, one must have mastered a great deal of artistic theories as well as considerable amount of history of New York paintings.

Cultural capital can be in the form of natural talent or human knowledge learnable and transferable across time and space and is best (co-)produced and shared in a close-knit community of artists, educators, critics, public audiences that develop a common identity of aesthetic movement. Like tacit knowledge or craftsmanship, the development of cultural capital takes time, patience, and most importantly, the space for everyday practice and interaction with people of the same worldview and sense of belonging.

Gaining cultural capital is a tacit, interactive, social learning process. It is common sense that when some ideas emerge from the creative landscape (writing genres, film styles, musical performances, etc.), the importance of theories and cultural theorists (gurus) is evident since it is necessary, for the sake of market logic, to explain what is going on, how to appreciate the creative value, and how to capture and reproduce the discovered values in appropriate manners. Such necessity and demand further drive the re-use and re-creation of cultural values (i.e. the effect of standing the giants' shoulders), which in turn generate more opportunities for business development (i.e. the periphery effect of cultural products, the network effects, the long tail, etc). Cultural capital is an important resource of creative entrepreneurship which is simultaneously existing on the level of individuals, the level of communities, and the level of regions (cities). Cultural capital is accumulated when there is a dynamic social process of teaching and research-ing, networking, relationship-building, and tacit knowledge sharing. None of these social pro-cesses is possible without the existence of appropriate spatial conditions that accommodate the social life of actors and institutions in these interactive networks, in particular, the institutions of education and knowledge production. Inquiries on the spatial conditions that make possi-ble such dynamic process of cultural capital accumulation – the conditions of possibility – are not new in the manufacturing and technological innovation sectors (Amin and Robins, 1990; Cooke, Gomez Uranga, and Etxebarria, 1997; Saxenian, 1994). Recent discussions on "creative cities" also shed lights on the spatiality of cultural entrepreneurship, particularly the US cities (Stolarick and Florida, 2006; Throsby, 2014). Little is known on the spatial conditions of creativ-ity in Chinese cities.

Symbolic capital

Symbolic capital refers to the capabilities of individuals and organizations to create or re-discover new associations between symbols and cultural meanings, to the extent that such associations become widely unchallenged, almost taken for granted, even ritual (if not religious), things of the mundane yet taken for granted among members of communities. Anthropologists have long argued that the cognitive capability of creating and interpreting symbols is human nature and that human society is constituted by historical layers of symbolic meanings (belief, ritual, lan-guage, art, etc.). In cultural production fields, symbolic significance such as reputation, fashion brands, school of art/thoughts, academies or universities, is often equivalent to social status, and thereby of paramount importance to actors operating in the fields. As we previously argued, the uncertainty in determining artistic values is relatively high, in comparison to other economic sectors, due to the nature of the evaluation process that is highly dependent on 'cultural capital' of epistemic communities (i.e. social movements) with common theories and interpretations of history. To tackle such uncertainty, economic actors usually reply on the 'social structures' of art communities to proxy the potential values of art objects: the higher status of recognition an artist or a work of art gains in the communities, the higher values being conferred upon this person or work. Symbolic capital functions to display and communicate social status in a delib-erately unequal way that serves to indicate the potentials of cultural productions convertible to economic values.

On one hand, symbolic capital, as the means and medium of signaling and representing cultural capital and artistic ideas, can help keep the fields of cultural production economically efficient and accessible to outsiders (not just market speculators, but also public audience with genuine cultural interests), because one does not always need to fully understand or appreciate the meanings of culture (or quality of cultural products) before making decisions to participate, to invest one's time, money, or collaborative labour. Symbolic capital, typically exemplified by academic qualifications, are functional instruments to indicate quality, trustworthiness, risks, and considerations which are essential to business decision-making. On the individual and organization level, the accumulation of symbolic capital can bring benefits to the brand values and positive recognitions from the society, which can be converted into opportunities of economic profits. On the regional level, such benefits can be in the forms of cultural heritage and cultural identity. Symbolic capital can be seen as the objectified interface, the medium of conversion between cultural capital and economic capital, which provides what Bourdieu referred to as the "profits of unconsciousness". For example, as the travel industry demonstrates, the attractiveness of travel products is most likely to be associated with the symbolic values objectified by those buildings and places of historic figures, residences and palaces, places of art collections, and landscapes, all of which are organized by a grand narrative about the historical change of politics and artistic tastes.

On the other hand, since symbolic capital is capable of reproducing itself symbolically as long as the message it contains can be apprehended by human beings, it gives rise to the vicious circle of self-referential, inflationary self-promotion, to the extent that the symbolic message becomes detached from the substantial meanings it claims to represent.[3] Symbolic capital is not something cultural entrepreneurs create out of thin air but instead is rooted in the accumulation of cultural capital being communicated and maintained by cultural networks. Critical theorists have long used the concept of 'symbolic violence' to discern the injustice in modern society (whether in gender and feminism issue, the religious freedom issue, or Marxist class-struggles), where schemes of cognitive categorisation, dominated and controlled by a certain group or class of social elites, are used to justify the dominance of their social power. It can be equally argued that those social groups of little power, the underdogs, can also strategically deploy symbolic means to shape the cognitive schemes of society, in order to achieve social justice, as much Marxist literature tends to suggest (Harvey, 1992, 2013). In the cultural and creative landscape, this can be seen when cultural entrepreneurs or artists use means of aesthetic experiences (writing, drama, film, painting, photographer) and novel business models (digital media, social enterprise, for example) to publicise the alternative ways of cognitively understanding reality, to create new social movements that address contemporary problems of injustice (for example, the movement of street graffiti artists often exemplified by the work of Banksy). In summary, symbolic capital is closely associated with the hierarchies of social power and how actors consciously struggle to resist symbolic dominance and create alternative ways of cognitive understandings. The production of symbolic capital means cultural entrepreneurs and artists are fully engaged in the power struggle of their societies and the ability to offer alternative means of interpretation.

Beijing as a creative city

In this section, we present a case study of Beijing as the city is undertaking a significant transformation towards a new urbanism by culture and creative economy. In the light of the conceptual framework of creative capital, we assess the potential of Beijing's urban space of creativity in terms of how it can mobilize those heritage resources embedded in its spatial structures and historical narratives (cultural, relational, symbolic), by analysing the structure of creative capital on three levels of urban space (everyday practice, institutional practice, and modernity/aesthetics theories). We then draw lessons of what we find on each level of Beijing's creative capital, and suggest implications for future theoretical development and policy-thinking on creative cities – which is a paradigm shift of urbanism from the old pure economic point of view that takes creative economy as an industrial engine of growth to a new perspective that appreciates the historical continuation of aesthetics traditions and the community-institutional mode of cultural production, and manages to convert these embedded creative capital into unique advantages of future economic development and urban regeneration.

In recent years, Beijing set ambitious targets to become a global city with a focus on the cultural and creative economy. In the contemporary era of Reform and Open-Up, the city has extensively urbanised itself and sprawled into rural peripheries. Today the capital is the biggest metropolis in China – leading the table of so-called Tier 1 cities (Beijing, Shanghai, Guangzhou, Shenzhen). Such growth, however, has placed enormous pressure on the urban fabric of living space, cultural heritage, wellbeing and health, and environment (especially, under the threats of desert expansion, extreme weather, water shortage, and air quality). In order to cope with the urbanisation challenges, the municipal government of Beijing has been campaigning for more support resources (capital investment, water reservoir and canals, infrastructure and building space, etc.), including legislative measures to control the influx of migration. These efforts were largely counterproductive and produced serious moral and constitutional backlashes.

After the 18th CPC (Communist Party of China) Congress in 2012, a series of pivotal, long-term decisions were made in the sense that Beijing, as the way it has always been, should be transformed from being an economic centre to a metropolis of culture and creativity. Under the grand strategy of President Xi, Beijing aims to distribute the economic and industrial functions into the periphery regions, in particular forging a closer economic partnership with the Tianjin City and the Hebei Province, the latter of which remains one of the least-developed provinces in China ironically at a proximate distance to Beijing. In the context of wider sustainable development pledges and planning, the president's grand strategy for Beijing includes setting up a completely new future city outside Beijing (*Xiong'An*), which is supposed to not just host the ministerial and state organs but also set the benchmark of what a sustainable, wellbeing-oriented future city should be. The grand strategy also includes the emigration of Beijing's Municipal Government from the inner city to the suburb towns (the re-defined Beijing-Tianjin-Hebei Metropolis). According to the new plan of regional integration, the city of Beijing shall return to the status as the capital of culture, civilisation, and creativity, just like the way it has always been for many centuries.

Since Beijing is set to be the capital of culture and creativity, the business and investment of cultural and creative industries in the periphery regions – and indeed possibly the whole country – have become even more agglomerated and centralized in the new creative space in the downtown of Beijing. Institutionally, Beijing's Capital Cultural Industry Association and the counterparts of Tianjin and Hebei are set to become more institutionally integrated from 2015, as the three agencies joined efforts in workshops and seminars, annual industrial expos. The new institutional arrangement of regional coordination provides policy and economic impetus to the growth of the cultural and creative economy, mostly in the form of new industrial districts. The purpose of these institutional efforts is to create a clear cultural identity for the metropolis region of Beijing.

Globally, Beijing provides a world-class infrastructure of cultural communication and exchange, in terms of its geographic proximity of pivotal cultural institutions (universities-museum-media), and the advantageous access to global connections. Hosting a rich list of public libraries, museums, theatres, architectural heritage, Beijing is globally recognised as the place of best exemplifying China's rich heritage of literature, music, architecture and craft, and folk art. The city is listed by the UNESCO as a member of Creative Cities Networks with a cultural identity of the "City of Design", recognizing the city's great potential in combining Chinese cultural heritage with the country's contemporary achievement in industrial manufacturing. After the Olympics in 2008, Beijing has substantially transformed its cultural landscape with the aspiration of becoming a truly global city for culture. Recent projects of urban space regeneration such as the Olympic Stadium Park (Bird's Nest and Water Cube), and the Grand National Theatre have added great value to the city's contemporary cultural identity. As China is making unprecedented commitments to globalization and sustainable development in recent years, the city is making great efforts to become the place of cultural exchange and global connections, especially as the meeting place for setting a global development agenda (i.e. the Belt and Road Summit, the UNESCO Centre for Creativity and Sustainability, the Asia Infrastructure Investment Bank, the Creative Cities Network Summit etc.).

From networks to modernity: encountering creative capital in Beijing

So how do we approach the 'creative capital' embedded in the potentials of Beijing as the city transforms itself towards a future of culture, harmony, and sustainability? With the lens of the multi-level framework (Table 20.1), we find the incredible foundations of creative capital in the spatial and historical fabrics of the city. As the capital city of China for more than 800 years, Beijing remains one of the central places of Chinese civilisation for nearly ten centuries, displaying remarkable resilience against political disasters, waves of foreign invasion and cultural shock, migration and demographic change, climate and environmental deterioration. The contemporary spatial foundation of Beijing was master-planned and built between Yuan and Ming dynasties (13th–14th century, AD). For nearly 800 years, the city has been designed, maintained, and used as an imperial capital, not just of a nation but of a central place of civilisation which accommodate different cultures, ethnicities and religions, while conforming to the *dao* of living (as modern Chinese decide to name the country, 中国 "Central State" or "the State of the Medium or the Middle-Way"). The Chinese civilisation has consistently emphasized the wisdom of harmony between human society and the nature (天人合一, from the book of *I Ching*, 1000–750 BC), which is symbolically shrined in rituals of "emperor" traditions and the imperial residential city. The city of Beijing is supposed to be a living testament to such civilizational belief.

On the level of modernity and aesthetics theories, the fact that the city's historic resilience, as an imperial and intellectual capital of Chinese civilisation in defiance of dynastic change and foreign invasion, reveals many facets of heritage on the philosophical and aesthetic meanings of modern life in a Chinese city, and its mirrored projections in contemporary China. According to Confucianism, to take responsibility for the society (shè jì, "社稷") by serving in the civil service – hence, the emperor – is priority of the educated members of society, commonly referred to as the "*shi*" (士), or gentleman class (*jūn zi* 君子). Theorists of Confucianism and Daoism, both originating from the book of *I Ching*, established that the ruling legitimacy of the state comes from the ways the ruler (who is to be assisted by the cascading class of wise gentlemen) understands and practices the constant of the nature (tiān dào, the Dao of the Celestial, 天道). Confucianism does not define the class of gentleman by blood, property or wealth, but instead on the depth of intellectual education and the capability of independent thinking, and that it is the ruler's responsibility to find and foster these capable men and to listen to their wisdom with patience. Generations of Chinese intellectuals, rich or poor, lived and worked in this imperial city with a deep sense of pride and self-esteem, most of whom were cherry-picked by the imperial court through a sophisticated, competitive examination system. It is clear that meritocracy and social mobility is deeply embedded in the heritage of Chinese society, and Beijing is the city where these miracles of social mobility actually take place. The imperial examination system is itself a heritage institution that dates back to the Sui and Tang dynasties (the 7th century, AD), which ensures the authority and efficiency of the mandarin system of the empire. The backbones of this institutional heritage can be still seen today as the country's twin elite universities

(Peking and Tsinghua, literally located next to each other) remain the place where the country's most-respected intellectuals and academically elite students live and work. The north-west corner of the city, the district of Haidian today, where universities, academies, and research institutes are next door to each other, still maintain intimate relationships with the power centre of the country, the inflows of ideas, politics, and intellectual labour.

It is important to note that the cultural heritage of Beijing, the spatial and institutional patterns of how intellectuals cope with the epochal change, breeds the ideal of modernity in the early 20th century that fundamentally re-shaped China as a modern state. After the 1911 Republican Revolution, Beijing became a city with an emperor still living in the forbidden city, stripped of political power yet with formidable symbolic power. Everything has changed yet nothing has been changed. So how has China taking on modernity? Open forums, public debates, private salons, and academic seminars organized by the networks of intellectuals and students take place regularly and intensively within the campus of Peking University (Bêi Dà, 北大), or in proximate locations. These debates and continuous discussions between the Confucian conservatism (the royalists), the republicans, the social democrats, the neo-revolutionists (communists), and the anarchists etc., consequentially shape the discourses and re-construct the meta-narratives about China, Chinese civilisation, and Chinese modernity, when the military juntas and warlords took turns to preside over short-lived and powerless central governments amid paralysed projects of political institutionalization.

The historical significance of such intellectual milieu of Beijing, in the cultural forms of lectures, books, proses, newspaper comments or other publications by scholars and public intellectuals working for Peking, Tsinghua, and similar local institutions in 1910s–1930s, remain the central points of intellectual debates in China today. Most of these debates focus on the subjects of cultural identity of China and its critique (Lû Xùn 鲁迅, Liáng Qichao 梁启超), history of Chinese philosophy (Feng Youlan 冯友兰, Jin Yuèlín 金岳霖), the civilisations and history of the West (Wang Guowei 王国维), social justice (Lî Dàzhāo 李大钊, Chén Dúxiu 陈独秀), the art of poetry (Chen Yanque 陈寅恪) and painting (Feng Zikai 丰子恺), modern literature (Hú Shì 胡适), and architecture (Liáng Sichéng 梁思成), university and education (Cai Yuánpéi 蔡元培). The intellectual achievement of this period becomes the sources of ideas and ideals about Chinese modernity that drive the transformation of China in the 20th century.[4]

Historians now refer to this period of Chinese culture and art movements as the "New Culture Movement", a major shift of Chinese cultural life marked by the replacement of classical prose by everyday mundane language (bái huà wén 白话文) in literature. A notable example is the periodical called *The New Youth* (新青年), edited by then Peking professor Chen Dúxiù (who was the dean of the Humanities Faculty), created the communication space where students and scholars talk about art, philosophy, and political thoughts using everyday language that is accessible to the wider society. The periodical is later recognised as the focal communities of scholars and students who orchestrated the *May 4th Movement* in 1919 (五四运动), which eventually lead to the founding of the CPC in 1921, and subsequent events of historical magnitudes. Theories on contemporary art and aesthetics were gradually formed in this rich and diverse intellectual milieu of Beijing. These emerging aesthetic theories were built upon the concepts of progress, justice, and self-esteem. These concepts, to various degrees, remain the foundation of contemporary Chinese aesthetic and modernity theories. Any imagination of Beijing's future cities and its connection with the cultural and creative economy is impossible without taking into account this rich intellectual legacy of Chinese modernity in the early 20th century. In other words, the creative capital is embedded, symbolically and culturally, in the ways people of Beijing interpret, embody, and mobilize these legacy thoughts in the everyday life of today's city life, which stresses upon the ideal of sustainability.

At the risk of simplifying this complex and dynamic historic period unfolding in the urban space of Beijing, the concept of modernity in China has come to somehow a rather *inconclusive* consensus, an ongoing project with open possibilities, the one that is about being open to and learning from the great examples of the Western civilisation, particularly the institutional structures and technical rationality, while remaining deeply divided over the Confucian heritage and its modern values. The latter became the antecedents of Cultural Revolution in the 1970s when the politics of anti-Confucianism and anti-intellectualism peaked and wreaked havoc for ten years, which took its inspirations and initiatives from the student movements in Beijing's Tsinghua campus in 1966, the neighbour institution of Peking. The point we try to make here is to highlight that the creative capital of Beijing must be approached by associations with the city's intellectual struggles between accommodating modernity and cultural heritage at the same time, which, by no means coincidently, touches the nerve centre of China's modernisation project, the *RealPolitik in* Zygmunt Bauman's sense (Bauman, 1988). In other words, the spatiality of Beijing, as it is changing today, carries great symbolic, cultural, and relational significance as it has the potential to (re-)define the meaning of Chinese modernity, which itself is heritage concept from China's state-state-building experience in the 20th century.

On a relational level, one can find the structural resemblance of creative and cultural networks in contemporary Beijing that characterized the city of "New Cultural Movement" in the 1910s–1930s. These creative and cultural networks are anchored by the institutional ties in universities, cultural industries (media, publisher, film, antique, performance art, etc.), museums and national academies. These creative networks share similar ideals of art standards which can be traced into a common sense on the question of "what is Chinese modernity" and how it is to be lived in contemporary city life. Artists, cultural entrepreneurs, students, and mandarins are co-located in the same space where reviews and communication channels are made. Cultural tastes are shaped and magnified by business and political interests. Institutionally, the city hosts the clusters of universities, think tanks, international organizations, and the government research bodies which had developed sophisticated networks of information flows and knowledge sharing, to extent that it has an indisputable regional identity as the modernised Chinese way of life, as the example of living thick cultural heritage into modern life within the context of global connections. The recent establishment of UNESCO International Centre for Creativity and Sustainability in Beijing is just another endorsement on this regional identity of Heritage-Modernity, the East and the West.

Symbolically, the city is recognised as the place where ideas of Chinese modernisation are shared, debated, and decisions are made; the open space where intellectuals, activists, political parties, and foreign powers meet and share the same time and space for communication, debates, and association. The co-presence of elite universities, research institutes, think tanks, artistic and intellectual heavyweights, ministerial mandarins in the western and north-western part of the city create the high-level place with the support of cultural infrastructures to make ideas being articulated, mediated, and being listened by the people of influence. The city's institutions of memories, enshrined in the forbidden city, the museums, the libraries, the theatres, and the academies, become the silent context and stage where innovations on art forms and content can be proposed and put into practice. A detailed analysis of Beijing's creative capital can be expanded into the network structures of creative ecosystems, and how these creative ecosystems can be supported or limited by the institutional structures that characterize the regional culture of Beijing.

Conclusion

How can we draw lessons from the analysis of Beijing's creative capital? The critical point is that a theory of creative capital is about the content and the forms of cultural production activities at the same time. The discussion on the content of artistic productions, such as the cultural/aesthetic meanings, the social values, the economic values etc., have been often separated by the forms of art (literature, film, painting, poetry, design, music, etc.), which creates a constant dilemma for the theorizing project of art management – either to focus on the cultural meaning (pure theory, the art-for-art's sake), or on the process of cultural production (the business management side, the industry, the intellectual property and its associated value chains, the ecosystems etc.). An analysis on the creative capital potential of Beijing reveals that the forms of artistic productions can be universally synthesised by understanding the philosophical core of what modernity is and how art expressions articulate such meanings of modernity in economic and industrial terms. Such synthesis should address the challenges of heritage and modernity that are enshrined in the daily life of creative cities, and provide an important opportunity to theorize 'creative cities' in the line of Danto's 'artworlds', Bourdieu's sociology of taste, and Becker's thesis of "Art as Collective Actions" (1974). This analysis can only be done by developing a multi-level framework on the activities of cultural productions: the everyday practice, the institutional nexus, and the modernity reflections. Secondly, the development of creative city is not just about policies that incentivise cultural entrepreneurship or creating new industrial parks that contribute to the competitiveness of cities. Rather, the thesis of creative city focuses strategically on the quality and wellbeing of city life, which is predominantly about the cultural progress of learning, networking community building, and social movements, about how the future cities can provide infrastructure that is focused on the content of aesthetic meanings. The theory of creative capital provides an opportunity for urban planners, policy-makers, and practitioners (1) to address the practical challenges of urban regeneration by tapping into the strength of art and aesthetics; (2) to appreciate the historical legacy of the urban culture by bridging the past with the future.

The theoretical framework of creative capital can be regarded as the beginning of continuous research efforts to uncover the significance of creative cities for future cities. Future research should aim to address a number of important questions whose answers remain largely unclear. For example, we still know little about the patterns of social ties in the space of creativity in Chinese cities, and how such patterns of social networks are associated with the institutional structures in the Chinese space of creativity, and the Chinese ways of interpreting modernity. We know little about the corresponding relationships between the patterns and meanings of social ties (social relations), the institutional arrangements (regional systems of creativity?), and the abstract level aesthetic ideals of artistic and cultural productions, or whether such corresponding relationship can change across time and places, in China or other countries. These theoretical curiosities will be the future research agenda of creative capital, and we look forward to generating more insightful understandings on the space of creativity, and ways to contribute to the discourses on contemporary critique of modernity.

Notes

1 In response, many business corporations nowadays are investing resources and efforts to become more mission-driven, instead of profit- or share-shareholder driven. Corporations successful at retaining a large pool of talents and human capital tend to be those elite groups that have clearly articulated their agenda of "changing the world into a better place" (The Silicon Valley groups like Google, Facebook have been particularly strategic in combining such mission with business success). The trend can be interpreted as an adaptive tactic of the business world to accept the fact that in a future economy of innovation and creativity, corporate loyalty is in crisis unless the employees believe the value they create stretch far beyond the accounting books and stock market dynamics.

2 For example, a prominent cultural economist David Throsby (2010) defined cultural capital as "an asset, tangible or intangible, which embodies or yields cultural value in addition to whatever economic values

it embodies or yields". We believe this definition of capital is a bit narrow in the sense that it is too much objectified perhaps in measurement of economic/monetary terms, to the extent that it overlooks the dynamic historic process of accumulation and the social structure that give rise to the particular potentiality of change (Bourdieu, 1986) that is the intrinsic value of capital.

3 In fact, the detachment of symbol from the meanings it claims to represent is exactly the point made explicit and artistically re-created by the postmodernist culture, which has no universal doctrine of aesthetic theories but are unified in criticizing the fallacy of "the project of modernity" and its associated "metanarratives" (Bauman, 1988; Habermas, 1983; Harvey, 1990). A further exploration on the impact of postmodernism on the formation and function of creative capital is relevant and highly interesting for understanding the relationship between culture and future cities, yet beyond the scope of this paper.

4 It is notable that Mao Zedong worked as a librarian in the Peking University in 1910s, living and working at the heart of the intellectual milieu of the "New Cultural Movement". He was influenced by Li Dazhao, professor at PKU, the translator of '*Das Capital*' into Chinese, and the leading founder of CPC in 1921.

References

Amin, A. and Robins, K. (1990). The re-emergence of regional economies? The mythical geography of flexible accumulation. *Environment and Planning D: Society and Space*. https://doi.org/10.1068/d080007

Bauman, Z. (1988). Sociology and postmodernity. *The Sociological Review*. https://doi.org/10.1111/j.1467-954X.1988.tb00708.x

Becker, H.S. (1974). Art as collective action. *American Sociological Review*. https://doi.org/10.2307/2094151

Bingham-Hall, J. and Kassa, A. (2017). *Making cultural infrastructure*. London: Theatrum Mundi. Available at: http://eprints.lse.ac.uk/85683/1/Bingham-Hall_Kaasa_Making cultural infrastructure.pdf

Bourdieu, P. (1983). The field of cultural production, or: The economic world reversed. *Poetics*. https://doi.org/10.1016/0304-422X(83)90012-8

———. (1986). The forms of capital. In: J. Richardson, ed., *Handbook of theory and research for the sociology of education*. New York: Greenwood. https://doi.org/10.1002/9780470755679.ch15

———. (1993). *The field of cultural production*. Columbia University Press. https://doi.org/10.1111/b.97814 44331899.2011.00023.x

———. (1995). *The rules of art: Genesis and structure of the literary field*. https://doi.org/10.4324/9780 203131527

Bourdieu, P. and Wacquant, L. (2013). Symbolic capital and social classes. *Journal of Classical Sociology*. https://doi.org/10.1177/1468795X12468736

Castells, M. (2004). Space of flows, space of places: Materials for a theory of urbanism in the information age. In: R. LeGates and F. Stout, eds., *The cybercities reader*. London: Routledge, pp. 82–93.

Cooke, P., Gomez Uranga, M., and Etxebarria, G. (1997). Regional innovation systems: Institutional and organisational dimensions. *Research Policy*. https://doi.org/10.1016/S0048-7333(97)00025-5

Cunningham, S. (2012). The creative cities discourse: Production and/or consumption? In *Cities, Cultural Policy and Governance*. https://doi.org/10.4135/9781446254523.n8

Danto, A. (1964). The artworld. *Journal of Philosophy*, 61(19), pp. 571–584.

DiMaggio, P. (1982). Cultural entrepreneurship in nineteenth-century Boston: The creation of an organizational base for high culture in America. *Media, Culture & Society*. https://doi.org/10.1177/016344 378200400104

———. (2011). Cultural Networks. In: J. Scott and P.J. Carrington, eds., *Sage handbook of social network analysis*. London: Sage Publications.

DiMaggio, P. and Useem, M. (1978). Social class and arts consumption. *Theory and Society*. https://doi.org/10.1007/BF01702159

Fligstein, N. and McAdam, D. (2012). *A theory of fields*. https://doi.org/10.1093/acprof:oso/978019985 9948.001.0001

Florida, R. (2002). Bohemia and economic geography. *Journal of Economic Geography*. https://doi.org/10.1093/jeg/2.1.55

Florida, R., Mellander, C., and Stolarick, K. (2008). Inside the black box of regional development – Human capital, the creative class and tolerance. *Journal of Economic Geography*. https://doi.org/10.1093/jeg/lbn023

Granovetter, M. and Swedberg, R. (2018). *The sociology of economic life*. 3rd ed. https://doi.org/10.4324/9780429494338

Habermas, J. (1983). Modernity – an incomplete project. In: H. Foster, ed., *The anti-aesthetic: Essays on postmodern culture*. Seattle, WA: Bay Press, pp. 3–15.

Hall, T. and Hubbard, P. (1998). *The entrepreneurial city: Geographies of politics, regime and representation*. Hoboken, NJ: John Wiley & Sons.

Harvey, D. (1990). *The Condition of Postmodernity: An Enquiry Into the Origins of Cultural Change*. Oxford: Blackwell Publishing.

———. (1992). Social justice, postmodernism and the city. *International Journal of Urban and Regional Research*, 16(4), pp. 588–608. https://doi.org/10.1111/j.1468-2427.1992.tb00198.x

———. (2013). *Rebel cities. from the right to the city to the right to the urban revolution*. New York, London: Verso. https://doi.org/10.4067/S0250-71612014000100013

Keane, M. (2013). *China's new creative clusters: Governance, human capital and investment*. London: Routledge. https://doi.org/10.4324/9780203124505

Luo, Y. (2008). The changing Chinese culture and business behavior: The perspective of intertwinement between guanxi and corruption. *International Business Review*, vol. 17(2), pp. 188–193.

Markusen, A. (2006). Urban development and the politics of a creative class: Evidence from a study of artists. *Environment and Planning A*. https://doi.org/10.1068/a38179

Mezias, S. and Kuperman, J. (2001). The community dynamics of entreprenurship: The birth of the American film industry, 1895–1929. *Journal of Business Venturing*, 16(3), pp. 209–233.

O'Connor, J. and Xin, G. (2006). A new modernity?: The arrival of "creative industries" in China. *International Journal of Cultural Studies*, 9, pp. 271–283. https://doi.org/10.1177/1367877906066874

Polanyi, K. (1957). *The Great Transformation: The Political and Economic Origins of Our Time*. Boston, MA: Beacon Press. https://doi.org/10.1057/palgrave.ejis.3000454

Redding, G. (2013). *The spirit of Chinese capitalism*. Berlin: Walter De Gruyter.

Saxenian, A. (1994). Inside-out: Regional networks and industrial adaptation in silicon valley and route 128. *Cityscape*, 2, pp. 41–60. https://doi.org/10.2307/3158435

Sennett, R., Burdett, R., and Sassen, S. (2018). *The Quito papers and the new urban agenda*. London: Routledge. https://doi.org/10.4324/9781351216067

Stolarick, K. and Florida, R. (2006). Creativity, connections and innovation: A study of linkages in the Montréal Region. *Environment and Planning A*. https://doi.org/10.1068/a3874

Throsby, D. (2010). *The Economics of Cultural Policy*. New York: Cambridge University Press. https://doi.org/10.1017/CBO9780511845253

———. (2014). Investment in urban heritage conservation in developing countries: Concepts, methods and data. *City, Culture and Society*, 7(2), pp. 81–86. https://doi.org/10.1016/j.ccs.2015.11.002

UN-Habitat. (2016). Quito Declaration on Sustainable Cities and Human Settlements for All. *Habitat III Issue Papers*. https://doi.org/10.3389/fmicb.2015.00023

UNCTAD. (2016). *CREATIVE ECONOMY OUTLOOK AND COUNTRY PROFILES: Trends in international trade in creative industries*. *UNCTAD Publications*. https://unctad.org/en/PublicationsLibrary/webditcted2016d5_en.pdf

UNESCO. (2016). *CULTURE URBAN FUTURE: GLOBAL REPORT on CULTURE for SUSTAINABLE URBAN DEVELOPMENT*. Paris, France. https://doi.org/10.1016/j.jcin.2009.09.017

Xiang, H.Y. and Walker, P.A. (2014). *China Cultural and Creative Industries Reports 2013*. Beijing: Springer.

PART IV

Arts organizations
Strategic management, marketing, and fundraising

21

TRACING THE EVOLUTION OF MARKETING IN ARTS ORGANIZATIONS

From 'third wheel' to protagonist of the arts scene

Marta Massi and Chiara Piancatelli

Introduction

Traditional arts organizations, such as museums and theatres, have historically held a negative view of marketing principles and techniques (Hill, O'Sullivan and O'Sullivan, 1995), and many of them have often been oriented towards what can be defined as the 'marketing-does-not-work-philosophy' (Diggle, 1986). Mainly owing to its market orientation, marketing has been regarded as a practice that is not "honorable" for the higher mission of arts organizations (Raymond and Greyser, 1978, p. 130). Therefore, in the arts context, marketing has often played the role of the 'third wheel' in the relationship between the artists/arts organizations and the arts consumers, for a long time regarded as the only actors in the arts consumption process.

How could the art world, based on the romantic assumption of the artistic autonomy and the sacredness of art (Diggle, 1976; Kolb, 2000) be enslaved to the market-centric orientation representing the foundations of marketing? The same term 'arts marketing,' introduced by Diggle in 1976, sounds like an oxymoron-based expression produced by postmodern dedifferentiation. For these reasons, arts marketing has often represented a number of approaches aimed at solving an orientation dilemma (Lee, 2005), that is the antinomy between the artist's sovereignty and autonomy, and the market orientation.

The main argument against the *tout-court* application of marketing to the arts, raised by artists and arts practitioners, is that products cannot be made to meet customer needs since arts products refrain from satisfying preexistent needs of a market segment (Colbert, 2003). The history of arts marketing is, therefore, an attempt to conciliate two opposite orientations: that towards the content itself (the arts) and that towards the market. In order to conciliate the two opposites, it is not sufficient to broaden the concept of marketing (Kotler and Levy, 1969; Kotler, 1972) – which is nevertheless a necessary phase – but marketing needs to abdicate from a part of itself so that a new discipline is founded.

Over time, the discipline has gradually evolved from the status of "functional tool" (mainly aimed at developing audience) to that of "business philosophy and strategy" (Boorsma and

Chiaravalloti, 2010, p. 298), and an increasing number of arts organizations have begun to recognize the added value that marketing could bring in terms of building a strong brand identity and engaging customers. Brands such as Guggenheim and Piccolo Teatro di Milano are typical examples of arts organizations that have embraced such a philosophy and have capitalized on introducing marketing as an active part of their management.

This chapter will examine the evolution of the role of marketing in the arts sector and review the literature on 'marketing of arts organizations' (Lee and Lee, 2017), i.e., how arts organizations develop marketing strategies in order "to maximize revenues and meet the organization's objectives" (Byrnes, 2009, p. 373).

The chapter starts with the identification of the different arguments used by arts organizations against the marketing concept and will proceed with a review of the evolution of arts marketing, including an analysis of the definitions of arts marketing and of excerpts from semi-structured interviews conducted with museum managers in Italy and Australia.

Building on previous literature reviews (e.g., Colbert and St-James, 2014; Fillis, 2011; Bradshaw, 2010; Lee and Lee, 2017), this chapter will guide the reader through the transition from traditional marketing approaches for arts organizations to modern forms of arts marketing which also take advantage of digitalization and social media, and value co-creation practices.

The authors will illustrate, through a series of case studies, how the role of marketing has been shifting from that of 'third wheel' between the artists and the audience to a more leading role in the arts scene. In particular, they will emphasize what marketing can do for the arts and what role marketing can have in arts organizations. By providing a comprehensive review of the literature on arts marketing, this chapter will lay the ground for identifying future directions for research in arts marketing.

Can we market arts organizations as soap? a broadened concept of marketing

In 1951, Wiebe was wondering whether an abstract idea, such as brotherhood, could be sold like soap. The author meant that marketing mainly deals with tangible products that are put on the market for profit by businesses. What about products that do not originate from businesses or that are not conceived for profit, such as ideas, people and services, including the arts, or arts organizations themselves? With this in mind, Kotler and Levy (1969) opened the door to the so-called broadening of the concept of marketing.

The marketing concept was first conceived in the early 1950s as the business ability to do what corresponds to the customer's interests (McKitterick, 1957). Marketing, when defined this way, has been broadly applied to the for-profit sector and to physical or tangible products. However, according to Kotler (1972, p. 46), one of the signs of the well-being of a discipline is its capacity to "re-examine its own focus, its own techniques and goals" in accordance with social shifts and the emergence of new issues. The interpretation of the marketing concept as a prerogative of the for-profit sector appears, therefore, to be limited, because it relegates its application to the concepts of market transactions and business products and services (Kotler, 1972).

The first reference to the application of the marketing concept to organizations whose main purpose is other than profit is in the *Journal of Marketing* by Kotler and Levy (1969). By broadening the concept of marketing, the authors state that the discipline basic principles may also be applied to any organization potentially involved in non-business activities, e.g., political parties, universities, arts institutions such as museums.

However, such organizations are usually ignored by marketing scholars, since their actions are reductively considered as public relations activities. In contrast, Kotler and Levy (1969) claim that marketing is a socially pervasive activity that could also be applied to a broader number of sectors, inaugurating "the marketing of people, ideas and organizations."

The consequence of the broadening of the concept of marketing is that not only physical products such as soap but also ideas, arts institutions, and services can become involved within marketing processes (Kotler, 2005). Kotler and Scheff (1997) described many cases of arts organizations such as theaters, ballet companies, and orchestras capable of attracting both large audiences and donors. Thus, if brotherhood can be marketed as soap, arts organizations can be marketed too.

Arts marketing: oxymoron or reality?

The first definitions of the concept of marketing (e.g., McKitterick, 1957), with their emphasis on the correspondence between products and consumer needs, and on the satisfaction of consumer *desiderata*, are in contrast with the romantic assumption of the creative autonomy of the artist (Bhrádaigh, 1997; Colbert, 1994; Evrard, 1993). Based on a romantic view, the artistic creation process, indeed, reveals itself as a spontaneous and unconditional expression of the until then unexpressed potential of a genius artist.

Therefore, given that the creation of an artwork is independent from the satisfaction of the preexistent needs of a market segment (Colbert, 2003), the basic premise of marketing appears to be inapplicable to the arts sector. In fact, many scholars agree that an excessive focus on the needs of consumers would correspond to "downgrading the artistic product or, worse, ignoring the creative expression of the artist" (Bhràdaigh, 1997, p. 208).

The greatest challenge of the application of the marketing concept to the arts sector is in the assumption that products are made to meet customers' needs (Bhràdaigh, 1997). The idea that marketers could decide which products should be placed on the market is, therefore, the main argument that arts practitioners use against the application of marketing to the arts (Kolb, 2000). This is also the main reason why the marketing concept has been deemed inappropriate for the arts sector, as well as the most glaring difference between an arts organization and a profit-driven company (Hill, O'Sullivan, and O'Sullivan, 1995).

Under this perspective, the notion itself of arts marketing seems to be an oxymoron, i.e., a contradiction between two opposite *weltanschauung*: that of the artist, who is not giving up on his/her creative independence and that of the market that is driving the business production process. As a consequence, arts organizations find themselves facing an "orientation dilemma" (Lee, 2005, p. 295): either indulging in the market orientation, typical of modern businesses (Avlonitis and Gounaris, 1999) by denying the concept of the autonomy of the arts or preserving the creative independence of the artist without considering the market (Andreasen, 1985; Lee, 2005).

On the one hand, some scholars (e.g., Boorsma, 2002; Hirschman, 1983) have identified the limitations associated with a *tout-court* application of the marketing concept to the sacral world of art (Kolb, 2000). On the other hand, others (Colbert, 1994; Diggle, 1976, 1994; Melillo, 1983) have tried to develop models and theories able to solve or evade such an antinomy between arts and marketing, trying to find common ground between the two. However, such a strain between the market orientation and the artistic autonomy is anything but resolved in arts organizations and represent a fundamental instance affecting their management and strategies. In the following paragraph, the reasons why arts organizations are so idiosyncratic and adverse toward marketing are outlined.

The traditional idiosyncrasy of arts organizations towards marketing

The marketing orientation concept is the foundation of the marketing concept (Avlonitis and Gounaris, 1999) and has been adopted by a growing number of companies. Two main definitions of the notion have been developed: (1) market orientation as a business attitude (Deshpande and Webster, 1989; Drucker, 1954) and (2) marketing orientation as a philosophy (Houston, 1986).

As a philosophy of the company, market orientation is characterized by three priorities: (1) consumers, (2) making marketing a prevailing culture, and (3) adapting the product on the basis of market requirements and needs (Avlonitis and Gounaris, 1999). Although market orientation has been recognized as a fundamental approach in the context of business enterprises, other organizations, such as those operating in the arts sector, have been showing a certain reluctance in adopting and applying marketing strategies (Diggle, 1976; Kolb, 2000)

Arts organizations have traditionally held a negative view of the marketing principles and techniques (Hill, O'Sullivan, and O'Sullivan, 1995). In fact, marketing has often been regarded as a "dangerous technology" capable of getting individuals to purchase products or services that they do not need (Kotler and Levy, 1969). In addition, arts organizations often refer to marketing as a synonym for advertising and promotion, and it may still be called 'audience development,' 'audience outreach,' or 'audience engagement' instead. Such an attitude towards marketing has led to an absence of professionalism (Raymond and Greyser, 1978). Looking at the reasons of such an idiosyncrasy and aversion of arts organizations toward marketing, some main arguments can be identified, including (1) the alleged superiority of the arts over marketing; (2) marketing as a profit-driven activity; (3) reluctance to use the marketing terminology; marketing as a waste of the limited resources of arts organizations; marketing as an intrusive and manipulative activity; marketing as an activity typical of the commercial sector and the popular culture.

The alleged superiority of the arts over marketing

The traditional concept of marketing, based on which the satisfaction of customer needs is the *raison d'être* of making a product, cannot be applied to arts products (Hirschman, 1983), which have their *raison d'être* in themselves (Colbert, 2003), considering that they do not satisfy any need other than the self-fulfillment of the artist.

The arts, indeed, are regarded as sacral activities which are inspired by God (Diggle, 1986), and, therefore, superior to any other commercial activity. According to Diggle (1994, p. 18), the application of marketing strategies to arts sector has always been opposed by the "religious school of thought that held art to be sacred, that audiences were made by God and that any attempt to improve their sizes was profanity." As a process originated in the context of commercial enterprises, marketing is deemed unworthy to be in the sight of the arts. For instance, the former Marketing Director of the Piccolo Teatro di Milano stated:

> The sacredness of the artistic choice must remain intact. In a theater, there is a sacred place, which is the stage, and it is only thanks to the stage, the creativity and the artistic choices that the marketing function can have a role. The work of the production of a theatrical work is purely artistic: the authors and the directors propose and outline the performances interpreted by the actors. In this way, the Management of the theater defines the program and provides the guidelines for the season of a theater. At this point, marketing takes over, providing from time to time the most appropriate promotion and communication tools aimed at reaching the public.
>
> *(Marketing manager, 2016, interview, 5 May)*

Very often, in the arts sector, art is conceived of as a sacral activity, created by God and not by humans and any interference with this divine process is as pointless as "asking the sky to stop raining" (Diggle, 1986, p. 22). Consequently, arts organizations tend to reject marketing and its focus on the consumer and believe that priority should be placed on the artistic content (Massi and Harrison, 2009).

Marketing as a profit-driven activity

According to Diggle (1986), the reason of such an inbred aversion of arts organizations lies in the incorrect view that the arts sector has on the business world, which appears to be caused by movies and television portraying the whole business as a "Big business" (Diggle, 1986, p. 27). Diggle states that the reasons why many people in the arts sector refuse to approach marketing are expressed by confusing syllogisms such as: "Marketing is about profit making. Profit is evil. Ergo, Marketing is evil" or "Marketing is about profit making. Art is not about profit making. Ergo, arts do not need to deal with marketing".

Reluctance to use the marketing terminology

Many arts practitioners do not like to use marketing terms with reference to arts and culture. Firstly, the word "product" (Diggle, 1986) – which refers to a serial production in the commercial sector – does not identify the unique and authentic artistic creation. Further, the term "marketing" itself belongs to a group of anglicisms, particularly mistrusted by the arts people. Owing to its link to the economic dimension – reductively associated to the logic of profit – the business terminology is regarded as antithetical to art, science and culture (Jalla, 2001). A typical example of such an aversion of arts organizations regards the use of the word 'brand,' which is very common in the business sector. For instance, at Company B, an Australian theatrical organization, they try to avoid talking about brand:

> We believe in the importance of our values. I think we, we kind of quite actively shy away from talking about that in terms of a brand. I also think you've got to, because a lot of what we do is about taking artistic risk, you've got to be very careful. You know, you've got to give yourself enough room to try to go in new parts artistically. And I think if you're too brand conscious um, that can, that can stymie you a bit. Particularly because you know, like our brand is not associated with being risky and edgy. That's not, that might come into it pretty low down. But it's not kind of in the forefront of what we are.
>
> *(Communication manager, 2008, interview, 10 June)*

In general marketing terms are unpopular within the art world. For the Conservator of the Modern Art Gallery in Milan, the term 'consumers' should be replaced by 'visitors.' Similarly, the former Marketing Director of the Piccolo Teatro stated:

> English marketing terminology can appear to be an end in itself; sometimes it sounds redundant to employ Anglo-Saxon terms such as 'marketing plans' or 'redemptions': why talk about redemption if we can talk about sales results/promotional campaigns? I prefer to call it 'service to the public' rather than theatrical marketing; anyway, whatever the term adopted, the important thing is that marketing is a means and that the

marketing tools available are used to reach the primary objective, which is to better communicate the show by making it understood and respecting always the public.

(Marketing manager, 2016, interview, 25 February)

Marketing as a waste of the limited resources of arts organizations

Kolb (2000, p. 68) claims that the reason for this aversion is the belief that marketing is an inappropriate use of funds and an unnecessary investment of the already limited resources of arts organizations. Often, arts organizations have to live without a marketing budget for a long time, as stated by the Marketing Director of Sydney Opera House in 2008:

> I've finally got a market research budget back in my hands. So that's very exciting because I haven't had that for a few years. So that would enable us to do some of that market testing and research into those sorts of things, that we haven't been able to, over the last few years. I'm finding out that conversion, I'm finding out you know what triggers people to purchase and all those sorts of things.
>
> *(Marketing manager, 2008, interview, 5 March)*

Marketing as an intrusive and manipulative activity

According to Bhràdaigh (1997), the reluctance to apply marketing to the arts sector lies in the fear that the influence of market forces and the implementation of marketing techniques could damage the artistic product (Bhràdaigh, 1997). Such a circumspect attitude towards marketing is real and has been found, for instance, in some British non-profit cultural organizations (Bennett, 1998: Clutterbuck and Dearlove, 1996). The ostracism towards the application of marketing strategies often comes from specific stakeholders (e.g., donors, government agencies, board members, politicians, employees), for whom the arts organization should be focusing on the artistic mission rather than devoting itself to marketing or public relations (Raymond and Greyser, 1978).

Marketing as an activity typical of the commercial sector and the popular culture

Arts operators have specifically chosen not to work in the for-profit sector and consequently refuse the idea of an intermingling of art and culture with anything that could be considered commercial and related to the so-called popular culture (Kolb, 2000). A circumspect attitude, together with an unclear understanding of what marketing is, and a substantial lack of training make it difficult for the marketing discipline to be accepted in the field of arts. A mix of ignorance, prejudice, and superstition (Jalla, 2001) prevents many arts organizations from approaching marketing principles, increasing the belief that the expression "arts marketing" is an unsolvable and impossible oxymoron. Despite a certain reluctance of arts operators and the criticism of academics, the broadening of the concept of marketing (Kotler and Levy, 1969) has paved the way for the application of the discipline to the arts sector.

Birth and evolution of arts marketing

Introduced in the late 1960s (Colbert, 2017), arts marketing was initially interpreted as an operational tool, a "collection of techniques" to increase the participation of the public (audience development) (Lee, 2005, p. 292). The focus was on the use of marketing research designed to obtain demographic information, i.e., the so-called bums-on-seats research (Reiss, 1974) about art and culture consumers, while little attention was paid to understand the audience's motivations and needs (Kolb, 2000). The first authors to link the marketing discipline to the arts are Diggle (1976), Newman (1977) and Reiss (1974), all of them with a background in the management of arts organizations.

However, Diggle (1976) was the first to propose a full arts marketing definition in his pioneering text *Arts Marketing*. According to Diggle, the main purpose of marketing of the arts is to bring an appropriate number of people to an appropriate contact with the artist. Thus, the main purpose of arts marketing is an artistic purpose, since art is an end in itself and does not have to provide an economic return. In his following books *Guide to Arts Marketing* (1986) and *Arts Marketing* (1994), Diggle completed the definition of arts marketing, stressing how the art audience of the art has to crosscut social and income classes, as well as age groups.

Diggle's interpretation of arts marketing is, according to Bhràdaigh, restricted because, by putting the focus on promoting arts to the public, it ignores other fundamental aspects of marketing, such as segmentation and market research and, in the long term, could damage the arts organization because consumers will not feel involved or "feel they have received value in exchange for their investment" (Bhràdaigh, 1997, p. 211).

The eighties were characterized by a rapid expansion of the number of arts organizations, particularly in the United States (Kolb, 2000), as well as a growing interest in marketing techniques and principles (Lee, 2005). Especially the unwinding of government funding pushed arts organizations to rely on marketing and, at least at the beginning, the spread of marketing was dictated by the system of financing under pressure from the government (Lee, 2005). In these years, the literature on arts marketing used to include both academic texts (e.g., Mokwa et al., 1980; Melillo, 1983), and practical manuals. According to Mokwa et al. (1980), the role of marketing is not to suggest to the artist how to create a work of art, but to facilitate the meeting between artistic creations and the appropriate public.

In the nineties, arts marketing experiences a significant development. The first evolution is terminological: no more is it marketing of the arts or marketing applied to art, but it is "arts marketing" (Lee, 2005), i.e., the expression coined by Diggle in 1976. The second evolution is the creation of the first marketing departments in arts organizations, and the introduction of specialized courses, seminars, and conferences dedicated to marketing increased (Rentschler and Shilbury, 2008).

According to Hill, O'Sullivan, and O'Sullivan (1995), at this stage, a tactical orientation prevails and, therefore, an emphasis on two of the 4Ps: promotion and pricing. The most important text of these years is, without a doubt, Francois Colbert's *Marketing culture and the arts*. According to Bhràdaigh (1997), the definition of arts marketing that Colbert (1994, p. 14) provides in this text is more comprehensive than any previous one: *the art of reaching those market segments likely to be interested in the product while adjusting to the product the commercial variables (price, place and promotion) to put the product in contact with a sufficient number of consumers and to reach the objectives consistent with the mission of the cultural enterprise.*

Besides defending the independence of the artistic creativity, this definition recognizes a more active role of the public and stresses the need to promote the communication with consumers whether they be "customers, visitors, members of the public or participants" (Bhràdaigh, 1997, p. 211). This definition is more complete than the Diggle's because it has the product as the starting point, but it also considers the consumer's point of view (Bhràdaigh, 1997).

According to Colbert (2003, p. 31), arts products do not exist to satisfy market needs. In contrast to traditional marketing, arts marketing does not start from the market or from the study of consumer's needs, but from the product itself, and passing through the information systems it reaches the relevant market segment. Through the information collected about the prospect customer's profile, the arts organization can act upon the so-called residual marketing residual mix, i.e., price, distribution and promotion, without compromising the essence of the artistic product or its mission (Colbert, 2003).

Recently, however, we are witnessing a shift from a supply-based to a customer-oriented view of arts marketing (Colbert and St. James, 2014). Many artists are challenging the romantic view of the sacredness and autonomy of the arts to pursue commercial objectives (Kubacki and Croft, 2011). At the same time, arts organizations are continuously innovating their offerings in order to keep their audiences interested (Voss and Voss, 2000).

Marketing in the 2000s: what can marketing do for the arts?

Despite the apparent opposition between those that seem to be parallel worlds, arts and marketing can, therefore, undergo a reconciliation. Many authors (see Colbert, 1994; Diggle, 1986, 1994; Evrard, 1993; Kolb, 2000; Lee, 2005) agree that it would be impossible to apply the marketing tenets to arts and culture without adapting them to the idiosyncratic characteristics of arts products and organizations. Therefore, the history of arts marketing may be interpreted as a series of attempts to circumvent the antinomy inherent in the concept of arts marketing itself and to solve such a "orientation dilemma" (Lee, 2005).

The recent history of arts marketing allows for identifying a number of advantages of arts applied to marketing. Many arts institutions have started adopting marketing strategies to achieve their mission. Things that marketing could do for arts institutions include: (1) build identity; (2) segment customers and identify target markets; (3) position or reposition an arts organization; (4) engage customers; and (5) verify customer satisfaction; create and build customer loyalty. In the next sections, such functions will be outlined.

Build identity

A typical marketing tool is the brand, which is not only a hallmark, a signal aimed at unequivocally identifying an organization and its products, but also the very essence of the organization, its mission, and values. However, despite the importance of brand management being widely recognized in commercial enterprises, in the arts sector branding processes have received little attention and can be considered a "new phenomenon" (Colbert, 2005, p. 67). The few studies on this topic dealt with museum branding (Caldwell, 2000; Caldwell and Coshall, 2002), the concept of "cultural brand equity" (Camarero, Garrido, and Vicente, 2010; Camarero, Garrido, and Vicente, 2012), artists as brands (Schroeder, 2005) and brand art (Baumgarth, 2018).

However, the importance of brand management cannot be underestimated, not even in the arts field. A strong brand allows for identifying an arts organization/product. Given the growing competitiveness of the market in which they operate (leisure market), arts organizations need to differentiate their identity, in order to obtain a distinctive and differentiated positioning in the mind of the consumer (Ries and Trout, 1986; Nantel and Colbert, 1992). In particular, appropriate brand management can enable arts organizations to attract more consumers and to survive in a turbulent market where competition takes place both at the level of the allocation of scarce state funds, and at the level of participation of the audience (Colbert, 2003, p. 31). The construction of a solid brand strategy is, therefore, a resource, not only for the business world but also, and especially, for the arts sector.

Many arts organizations have employed branding to redefine their identity. An interesting example is that of Museum Victoria, Australia's largest public museum organization. Starting in 2003, Museum Victoria went through a massive rebranding process in order to clarify its identity, which was not clear for the audience and the stakeholders, owing to the incoherent and multifaceted variety of sub-brands that characterized the organization in the past, including Melbourne Museum, Scienceworks, Immigration Museum, Melbourne Planetarium, Royal Exhibition Building, IMAX Melbourne. Described as a networked organization, Museum Victoria aimed to operate as "a single Museum organization capable of realizing its full potential" (J. Patrick Greene, former CEO of Museum Victoria, 2005). For this reason, the entire branding process can be seen as an attempt to recast and classify the clutter – which characterized the previous brand concepts – and to reduce the ambivalence and confusion generated by that multitude of different brands (Figure 21.1).

The rebranding helped identify the various sub-brands as a family of brands, hierarchically organized and clearly related to each other (Figure 21.2). Each brand represents a different concept and experience. For instance, the brand values of Museum Victoria include knowledge, respect, accessibility, memorability, and commitment; Scienceworks is family-minded, stimulating, surprising, educational, and interactive; the Immigration Museum is empathetic, inspiring, touching, personal, and relevant.

Branding has proved to be a successful strategy for arts organizations that are playing in an increasingly competitive market. However, an excessive brand orientation can be detrimental for arts organizations. For instance, the Guggenheim Museum has been criticized for being the "Starbucks of the art world" (Butler, 2000) and for being too commercial as a brand. In general, any time an arts brand gets out of the arts context, new issues arise. Brand "Caravaggio" is a good example of an arts brand that is often used in contexts other than the arts (e.g., labels of wine products or Trussardi clothing), thus entailing a more superficial reality of Caravaggio's life and works (Drummond, 2006).

Figure 21.1   Museum Victoria before rebranding

Source: Used with permission.

MASTER LOGO

VENUE LOGOS

SUB-VENUE
LOGOS

MV EXPERIENCE
BRANDS

Figure 21.2 The new brand identity of Museum Victoria

Source: Used with permission.

Segment audience and reach the right target market

Arts marketing is basically a marketing of the supply (Evrard, 1993) designed to reach those market segments that can potentially be interested in the product, adapting the commercial variables (price, distribution and promotion), i.e., the residual marketing mix, to the product, in order to put it in contact with a sufficient number of consumers (Colbert et al., 1994). Thus, it is crucial that the right segments be identified in order to reach out to them with customized residual marketing mixes. The 2018 marketing campaign of Museo Egizio in Turin, Italy, is a great example of arts marketing because the communication is directed to a specific target market, i.e., Arabs living in Italy (Figure 21.3).

Moreover, segmentation and customer profiling can be developed further thanks to digitalization, which favors audience development not only by broadening the customer base but also by deepening the relationships with the different publics, which are increasingly profiled and targeted (Colombo, 2018).

The digitization process and data analytics have also influenced the way that art is consumed and has contributed to making arts consumption more interactive and dynamic. Many arts organizations are now involved in a new digitalization process; an evolution that has allowed them a presence on the web with an interface that looks to the future more engagingly.

The revolution of art in the digital age also involves the creation of digital applications (apps) that offer virtual tours. New digital technologies have also entered art galleries and museums, with the introduction of tools that make art much closer to users. The Louvre Museum app, for example, is a visual experience where visitors can consult more than 100 works in the museum. Further, the Magnus app, which is akin to a 'Shazam for Art', allows customers to get all the information related to artworks and their price, simply by taking a picture of the artwork and uploading it to the app. By promoting continuous interaction with the customer, digitalization allows for new ways of segmenting and profiling customers.

Reposition an organization

Sometimes the positioning of an arts organization does not correspond with the identity of the organization itself. Positioning is the image that the arts organization occupies in the

Figure 21.3 The 2018 advertising campaign of Museo Egizio di Torino
Source: Used with permission of Museo Egizio.

mind of consumers (Ries and Trout, 1986). Arts organizations often struggle with positioning themselves based on their values, mainly because such values or even the vision are not clear to the employees and the management. This is the case with the Sydney Opera House (SOH), the Australian institution that is known all around the world for its iconic building. In 2008, the management realized that people were not getting the correct positioning of Sydney Opera House, often ignoring that SOH is a complex of theatres with its own theatrical company. In order to reposition itself, SOH developed a new positioning statement expressed by the payoff 'Live performance everyday':

> The Business DNA of the company has the performance at the center, while keeps the iconic location peripherally. We kind of look to what is business DNA and looking at it from a sort of a circular diagram, really kind of thinking this . . . this is kind of almost like the outside of the building. We are – there's no doubt that the Sydney Opera House is an iconic destination. I think it's pretty clear. This is about – I think it's recognized by about four billion people word wide. The next kind of layering, as you're actually getting closer to the Opera House, you get the sense that you can browse, you can walk around the outside, there's some notion of hospitality. You can have drink, you can have dinner here, is then there's tours and there's also shopping and then when you finally get towards the middle, I guess, is that you get a notion of performing arts and it's not really until you walk through the doors that you get, oh, it is about performance.
>
> *(Marketing manager, 2008, interview, 5 March)*

Another interesting example of repositioning is that of the Jewish Museum of Berlin, that launched an advertising campaign aimed at changing people's perceptions of the museum in 2002. During the visit, many visitors were scared by the empty spaces and the so-called voids of the museum that resembled the tragic of the Holocaust experience. Therefore, the museum management aimed to change the negative visitor perceptions related to the iconic building projected by Daniel Liebeskind and launched an innovative advertising campaign.

Developed by the Berlin office of the international advertising agency, Scholz & Friends, this campaign included nine quasi-surreal photographs in 2,500 locations in eight German cities. The signature image featured a scallop shell staged to appear to sit on the ocean floor, yawning surprisingly to reveal a fried egg (Chametzky, 2008). The payoff for the campaign read 'Nicht das, was Sie erwarten'. Not what you are expecting (Figure 21.4).

Figure 21.4 The Jewish Museum of Berlin advertising campaign

Source: Used with the permission of the Jewish Museum of Berlin © Scholz & Friends Berlin.

Obviously, a campaign like this could have the side effect of making people perceive the museum as a commercial entity and not so much as an arts institution. What would be the difference between an ad for soap and an ad for a museum in this case? However, many organizations are using advertising to reposition themselves as more of commercial entities. For instance, the Australian Ballet has managed its brand so to broaden its audience and include the younger segments:

> We have tried to position the company as a "more commercial entity" ... we are trying to change the perception of the ballet as a form of art, making it a little more athletic and positioning it as a serious and commercial activity at the same time.
>
> *(Marketing manager, 2008, interview, 10 February)*

Engage customers

The final aim of an arts organization is to build a relationship with its customer and to do so, it is fundamental that the customer is engaged. Artists and arts organizations are increasingly marketing their work by introducing active arts practices, to give the consumer the chance to participate with and co-create their artwork. Brown, Gilbride, and Novak (2011) published a framework that describes the different ways participatory arts programs work. The Audience Involvement Spectrum is a five-stage model that shows a development from "spectating" to the point where the audience is the artist. While the audience is receptive in the stages "spectating" and "enhanced engagement," they are participatory in the stages "crowd sourcing," "co-creation," and "audience-as-artist." In the "crowd sourcing" stage the participants level of creative control is curatorial so that the audience can contribute towards an artistic product. When the audience functions as co-creator they have an interpretative level of creative control, they contribute something towards an artistic experience that is curated by an artist. In the stage with the highest participation by the audience, they become artists themselves. They take control of the artistic experience; the product is no longer the focus of the installation, but the process of creation is.

Measure customer satisfaction

Museum managers have recently started looking at visitor satisfaction as a key component of the museum experience. Satisfaction drives visitor intention to recommend the museum experience to their peers and friends, and the intention to revisit the museum itself. Satisfaction affects loyalty and post-purchase behaviours, such as intention to recommend and revisit (Chen and Chen, 2010).

A research conducted in 2017 on a sample of 1,051 visitors of Museo del Novecento, Italy, allowed for identifying the downfalls of the visit experience. For instance, the feature that received the lowest score in terms of satisfaction was the presence of places to stop and rest (3,31/5): Many visitors complained about the difficulty of stopping by during the visit, outlining the need to include more benches in the museum rooms. The survey showed that people could not appreciate the collection or the exhibits because they did not want to spend too much time in a place that was not comfortable for them. Fatigue came out as a factor that pushed the public to abandon the museum even without having visited the whole place.

Marketing the arts also means to look at customer needs regarding the experience. This approach to marketing aims to broaden the definition of arts product through a breakdown of the product itself into a main part (core) – which cannot be changed – and a secondary or additional part (augmented) on which managers can intervene with changes (Bhrádaigh, 1997;

Boorsma, 2002; Colbert and St. James, 2014; Kolb, 2000; Kotler and Kotler, 1998). Keeping the core of the product intact, i.e., not changing the nature of the exhibit or a show, would allow for preserving the artistic mission of the organization. For instance, such peripheral services have been found critical to affect repurchase intentions in the performing arts (Hume and Mort, 2010). In this sense, an arts product – such as a visit to a museum – can be understood as a package "that includes entertainment, learning experience, social experience, an annual ritual and/ or an adventurous event" (Kolb, 2000, pp. 78–79). Satisfaction can, therefore, be measured on different aspects of the arts product.

Build trust and make customers loyal

Building trust, i.e., "the willingness of a party to be vulnerable to the actions of another party based on the expectation that the other will perform a particular action important to the trustor" (Mayer, Davis, and Schoorman, 1995, p. 712) is crucial when it comes to arts organizations. Owing to the uncertainty about an arts product or service, such as a theatrical play or a museum exhibit consumer tend to be skeptical and only trust organizations that are perceived as reliable. In this sense, established brands, such as Louvre or Teatro Alla Scala, can count on a high level of perceived trustworthiness because consumers have positive expectations about the behavior of these organizations.

For instance, the former Marketing Director of Teatro La Fenice stated that, due to its peculiar nature, the theatrical product represents a sort of unknown, as the public can not verify its quality if not *in fieri*, that is at the moment of the staging of the theatrical work. From this point of view, the theatrical product can be compared to services with which it shares the characteristic of intangibility:

> For a lyrical theater and for what we do, it is essential to focus on the brand, because you must sell a product a year in advance. You sell a product on paper. And as if you sold an apartment without having seen it before, because we cannot get to a week from the beginning or the beginning of a symphonic or lyrical production without having a full theater. . . . People buy on trust and, if there is trust, we can sell.
>
> *(Marketing manager, 2008, interview, 10 July)*

Figure 21.5   Piccolo Card

Source: Used with the permission of Piccolo Teatro di Milano.

Consumer trust has been found to be an antecedent of loyalty. The importance of brand loyalty has been widely recognized in the marketing literature (Howard and Sheth, 1969). According to Aaker, in particular, brand loyalty generates value, as it reduces the costs of marketing and gaining new customers. Furthermore, brand loyalty leads to a positive word of mouth in relation to products and services represented by the brand and to a greater resistance of consumers to competitors (Dick and Basu, 1994).

Loyalty is so crucial to arts organizations that they are implementing loyalty policies based on what businesses do. For instance, Piccolo Teatro di Milano looked at airline companies and supermarkets when they developed their loyalty cards that allow spectators to collect points through the purchase of tickets and subscriptions (Figure 21.5). While this strategy has been certainly successful, such an approach could appear too marketing oriented to a more conservative audience.

Conclusion

Recently introduced to the art world, marketing has increasingly conquered a role as protagonist, proving to be an essential resource for arts organizations. Originally emerged as a new *locus* where the artist autonomy is safeguarded based on a withdrawal, that of marketing from the market sovereignty, arts marketing has gradually evolved to increasingly adopt a relational 'customer orientation' (Voss and Voss, 2000).

Indeed, arts works need to be communicated and spread in order to get out of the private and particularistic sphere – from which they originated – and to have access to the public sphere where the consumption takes place. Marketing facilitates the diffusion of the artistic value within the organization while preserving intact the "solitary" nature of the artwork (Botti, 2000).

The arts can no longer be considered as far removed from the social and cultural context in which they are conceived, and marketing can play a role in helping the arts to reach to the public in more innovative and interactive ways. Arts consumers are provided with new value co-creation opportunities blurring the distinction between the artist who creates the artwork and the individual who consumes it. Especially, the Internet and social media have become a new alternative environment where art can be consumed, discussed, known, and even purchased. Marketing can help this process by offering more open experiences to the active participation of consumers.

Marketing represents, therefore, a means of intermediation between the artist and the arts consumer because it creates the opportunities for the meeting of the artwork and its public. Marketing enables arts organizations to make their mission visible in order to attract the attention of the "right" public, i.e., the market segment potentially interested in the arts organization's products/goods/services. It makes it possible for arts organizations to develop and communicate a distinctive and recognizable identity, and to position themselves in an increasingly competitive leisure time market. It also allows for measuring customer satisfaction and build loyalty-based relationships with customers.

This does not mean that marketing should take precedence over the mission of arts and culture organizations, but it implies that arts organizations will increasingly look at marketing as a philosophy more than an actual orientation. In the future, arts and culture organizations will need to open up to the broader community, including customers, donors and other stakeholders, taking into account their needs and opinions. Especially organizations such as museums can no longer focus exclusively on their curatorial and expositive activities but will have to look at customers as active co-creators in the arts production process. In this process, marketing could offer a valid support. Far from being the 'third wheel' in the relationship between the artists/arts organizations and the arts consumers, marketing will eventually conquer a more leading role in the arts scene.

References

Andreasen, A.R. (1985). Marketing or selling the arts: An orientational dilemma. *Journal of Arts Management and Law*, 15(1), pp. 9–20.

Avlonitis, G.J. and Gounaris, S.P. (1999). Marketing orientation and its determinants: An empirical analysis. *European Journal of Marketing*, 33(11/12), pp. 1003–1103.

Baumgarth, C. (2018). Brand management and the world of the arts: Collaboration, co-operation, co-creation, and inspiration. *Journal of Product & Brand Management*, 27(3), pp. 237–248.

Bhràdaigh, E.N. (1997). Arts marketing: A review of research and issues. In: M. Fitzgibbon and A. Kelly, eds., *From maestro to manager: Critical issues in arts and culture management*. Dublin: Oak Tree Press, pp. 207–219.

Bennett, T. (1998). *Culture: A reformer's science*. London: Sage.

Boorsma, M. (2002). Arts marketing and the societal functioning of the arts: The case of the subsidized dramatic arts in the Netherlands. *International Journal of Cultural Policy*, 8(1), pp. 65–74.

Boorsma, M. and Chiaravalloti, F. (2010). Arts marketing performance: An artistic-mission-led approach to evaluation. *The Journal of Arts Management, Law, And Society*, 40(4), pp. 297–317.

Botti, S. (2000). What role for marketing in the arts? An analysis of arts consumption and artistic value. *International Journal of Arts Management*, 2(3), pp. 14–27.

Bradshaw, A. (2010). Before method: Axiomatic review of arts marketing. *International Journal of Culture, Tourism and Hospitality Research*, 4(1), pp. 8–19.

Brown, A.S., Gilbride, S., and Novak, J. (2011). Getting in on the act: How arts groups are creating opportunities for active participation. Available at: www.irvine.org/images/stories/pdf/grantmaking/Getting-in-on-the-act-2011OCT19.pdf [Accessed 29 Jul. 2018].

Butler, P. (2000). By popular demand: Marketing the arts. *Journal of Marketing Management*, 16(4), pp. 343–364.

Byrnes, W. (2009). *Management and the arts*. New York: Elsevier.

Caldwell, N.G. (2000). The emergence of museum brands. *International Journal of Arts Management*, 2(3), pp. 28–34.

Caldwell, N. and Coshall, J. (2002). Measuring brand associations for museums and galleries using repertory grid analysis. *Management Decision*, 40(4), pp. 383–392.

Camarero, C., Garrido, M.J., and Vicente, E. (2010). Components of art exhibition brand equity for internal and external visitors. *Tourism Management*, 31(4), pp. 495–504.

———. (2012). Determinants of brand equity in cultural organizations: The case of an art exhibition. *The Service Industries Journal*, 32(9), pp. 1527–1549.

Chametzky, P. (2008). Not what we expected: The Jewish Museum Berlin in practice. *Museum and Society*, 6(3), pp. 216–245.

Chen, C.F. and Chen, F.S. (2010). Experience quality, perceived value, satisfaction and behavioral intentions for heritage tourists. *Tourism Management*, 31(1), pp. 29–35.

Clutterbuck, D. and Dearlove, D. (1996). *The charity as a business. directory of social change*. London: Directory of Social Chang.

Colbert, F. (2003). Entrepreneurship and leadership in Marketing the arts. *International Journal of Arts Management*, 6(1), pp. 30–39.

———. (2005). The piccolo Teatro of Milan: Theatre of Europe. *International Journal of Arts Management*, 7(3), pp. 66–73.

———. (2017). A brief history of arts marketing thought in North America. *The Journal of Arts Management, Law, and Society*, 47(3), pp. 167–177.

Colbert, F. and St-James, Y. (2014). Research in arts marketing: Evolution and future directions. *Psychology & Marketing*, 31(8), pp. 566–575.

Colbert, F., Nantel, J., Bilodeau, S., and Rich, J.D. (1994). *Marketing culture and the arts*. Chair in Arts Management.

Colombo, M.E. (2018). Musei e digitale. Intervista a Chiara Bernasconi. *Artribune*, 3 Jan. Available at: www.artribune.com/progettazione/new-media/2018/01/intervista-chiara-bernasconi-moma-new-york/ [Accessed 29 Jul. 2018].

Deshpande, R. and Webster Jr, F.E. (1989). Organizational culture and marketing: Defining the research agenda. *The Journal of Marketing*, 53(1), pp. 3–15.

Dick, A.S. and Basu, K. (1994). Customer loyalty: Toward an integrated conceptual framework. *Journal of the Academy of Marketing Science*, 22(2), pp. 99–113.

Diggle, K. (1976). *Marketing the arts*. London: City University.

———. (1986). *Guide to arts marketing. The principles and practice of Marketing as they apply to arts.* London: Rhinegold

———. (1994). *Arts marketing.* London: Rhinegold.

Drucker, P.F. (1954). *Management by objectives and self-control.* Practice of Management.

Drummond, K. (2006). The migration of art from museum to market: Consuming Caravaggio. *Marketing Theory*, 6(1), pp. 85–105.

Evrard, Y. (1993). *Le management des entreprises artistiques et culturelles.* Paris: Economica.

Fillis, I. (2011). The evolution and development of arts marketing research. *Arts Marketing: An International Journal*, 1(1), pp. 11–25.

Hill, L., O'Sullivan, C., and O'Sullivan, T. (1995). *Creative arts marketing.* Oxford: EO Hill.

Hirschman, E.C. (1983). Aesthetics, ideologies and the limits of the marketing concept. *The Journal of Marketing*, 47(3), pp. 45–55.

Houston, F.S. (1986). The marketing concept: What it is and what it is not. *The Journal of Marketing*, 50(2), pp. 81–87.

Howard, J.A. and Sheth, J.N. (1969). *The theory of buyer behavior.* New York: Wiley.

Hume, M. and Sullivan Mort, G. (2010). The consequence of appraisal emotion, service quality, perceived value and customer satisfaction on repurchase intent in the performing arts. *Journal of Services Marketing*, 24(2), pp. 170–182.

Jalla, D. (2001). *Standard e qualità per i musei italiani,* Il Sole24 ore.

Kolb, B. (2000). *Marketing cultural organisations: New strategies for attracting audiences to classical music, dance, museums, theatre and opera.* Dublin: Oak Tree Press.

Kotler, P. (1972). A generic concept of marketing. *Journal of Marketing*, 36(2), pp. 46–54.

———. (2005). The role played by the broadening of marketing movement in the history of marketing thought. *Journal of Public Policy and Marketing*, 24(1), pp. 114–116.

Kotler, N. and Kotler, P. (1998). *Museum strategy and marketing: Designing missions, building audiences, generating revenue and resources.* San Francisco: Jossey-Bass.

Kotler, P. and Levy, S.J. (1969). Broadening the concept of marketing. *Journal of Marketing*, 33(1), pp. 10–15.

Kotler, P. and Scheff, J. (1997). *Standing room only: Strategies for marketing the performing arts.* Boston: Harvard Business School Press.

Kubacki, K. and Croft, R. (2011). Markets, music and all that jazz. *European Journal of Marketing*, 5(5), pp. 805–821.

Lee, H. (2005). When arts met marketing: Arts marketing theory embedded in Romanticism. *International Journal of Cultural Policy*, 11(3), pp. 289–305.

Lee, J.W. and Lee, S.H. (2017). Marketing from the art world: A critical review of American research in arts marketing. *The Journal of Arts Management, Law, and Society*, 47(1), pp. 17–33.

Massi, M. and Harrison, P. (2009). The branding of arts and culture: An international comparison. *Deakin Business Review*, 2(1), 19–31.

Mayer, R.C., Davis, J.H., and Schoorman, F.D. (1995). An integrative model of organizational trust. *Academy of Management Review*, 20(3), pp. 709–734.

McKitterick, J.B. (1957). *What is the marketing management concept.* Chicago, IL: Taylor & Francis.

Melillo, J. (1983). *Market the arts.* Brooklyn: Arts Action Issues.

Mokwa, M.P., Dawson, W.M., Prieve, E.A. and Permut, S.E. (1980). *Marketing the arts.* New York: Praeger.

Nantel, J.A. and Colbert, F. (1992). Positioning cultural arts products in the market. *Journal of Cultural Economics*, 16(2), pp. 63–71.

Newman, D. (1977). *Subscribe now!: Building arts audiences through dynamic subscription promotion.* New York: Theatre Communications Group.

Raymond, T.J.C. and Greyser, S.A. (1978). The business of managing the arts. *Harvard Business Review*, 56(4), pp. 123–132.

Reiss, A.H. (1974). *The arts management handbook.* New York: Law-Arts Publishers.

Rentschler, R. and Shilbury, D. (2008). Academic assessment of arts management journals: A multidimensional rating survey. *International Journal of Arts Management*, 10(3), pp. 60–71.

Ries, A. and Trout, J. (1986). Marketing warfare. *Journal of Consumer Marketing*, 3(4), pp. 77–82.

Schroeder, J.E. (2005). The artist and the brand. *European Journal of Marketing*, 39(11/12), pp. 1291–1305.

Voss, G.B. and Voss, Z.G. (2000). Strategic orientation and firm performance in an artistic environment. *Journal of Marketing*, 64(1), pp. 67–83.

Wiebe, G.D. (1951). Merchandising commodities and citizenship on television. *Public Opinion Quarterly*, 15(4), pp. 679–691.

22

ALIGNMENT

The nexus of effective strategic planning

Rebekah Lambert

Introduction

How do we make sure our next strategic plan does not sit on a shelf and get dusty? That is a bit of a cliché, but it is a still a very good question, frequently asked by arts leaders. Too often, strategic planning processes result in documents that fail to meet the needs of nonprofit arts organizations. They sit on that proverbial shelf, getting dusty literally or figuratively, and business continues without a shared sense of direction or a clear understanding of the goals and objectives needed to move forward. Even worse, skepticism can emerge, limiting prospects for a more effective process that results in a useful plan.

These common problems can be avoided if strategic planning begins with an acknowledgment that it is an evolving process. Strategic thinking, which needs to precede planning, recognizes that there is a need for organizations, plans, and processes to be responsive, concurrent with the ever-changing world we live in and with the concept of a learning organization that grows and adapts in an increasingly competitive business environment. There is a recognition that, even within a rigorous intellectual planning framework, each process and plan needs to be reflective of the individual organization, its mission, community, and its place in that community. This calls for strategy that is "adaptive," "emphasizes learning," and "reclaims the value of strategic thinking for the world that now surrounds us" and for leaders who are "continuously asking [themselves] . . . questions about [their] organizations, programs, and initiatives" (O'Donovan and Flower, 2013).

Strategy and strategic planning

At its core, strategy is simply about making decisions about the right things to do. (In the author's experience, some apprehensive or skeptical arts organization leaders occasionally need to be reminded of this.) It is a "plan of action to achieve a goal or goal set" (Rollinson and Young, 2010). It answers fundamental and essential questions like: "Who are we? Where are we? Where do we want to go? How are we going to get there?" By inference, then, strategy is also about making decisions about what an organization does not want to do.

Good strategy is also about identifying an arts organization's competitive advantage – its ability to engage the attention and resources of talented artists, dedicated volunteers, committed donors, like-minded program collaborators, and others – in order to put the organization in a stronger, more sustainable position, better able to fulfill its mission and serve its stakeholders. It answers the questions: "What do stakeholders think of and feel about the arts organization? What are their needs? What are the impacts that they seek? Why does the community need this organization?" In *Good Strategy/Bad Strategy: The Difference and Why It Matters,* Richard Rumelt writes that the "most basic idea of strategy is the application of strength against weakness . . . or strength applied to the most promising opportunity" (Rumelt, 2011).

Therefore, strategic planning is understood to be the process through which an arts organization clarifies and affirms its vision (what does the organization ultimately want to accomplish?), mission (what does the organization do, who does it serve and how?), and values (what does the organization stand for?), as well as its goals (aims), strategies (priorities), and objectives (actions) for some set timeframe into the future. Keep in mind that a strategic plan is different from an operational or tactical plan, which translates the organization's strategic plan goals and strategies into the "how," the specific actions required for implementation.

A funder is often the impetus when starting a strategic planning process. While an organization meeting certain eligibility criteria for grant-funding may indeed be important, there are far more profound and long-lasting reasons for an arts organization to recognize the need for an effective strategic plan. Planning is connected with overall organizational effectiveness. A national survey of nonprofit 501(c)3 organizations, conducted by the Association for Strategic Planning (ASP) in 2012, found that "successful organizations make strategic planning a consistent/routine periodic process, and not just something they do in times of crisis, or because a funder requires it" (McNerney, Perri, and Reid, 2013). Strategic planning also helps organizational leaders prioritize and allocate scarce resources and understand the distinction between what is urgent and important versus what is simply urgent.

Because this chapter focuses on the characteristics of an effective strategic planning process, it is helpful to acknowledge upfront some of the challenges that can make a process ineffective. Randall Rollinson sets forth five pitfalls for organizations to avoid for the successful implementation of their strategic plans. (Rollinson, n.d.) Recognizing that managing the development and implementation of a strategic plan is a significant endeavor for any organization, Rollinson first reminds leaders of the risk of failing to acknowledge the importance of the "necessary preparatory steps" in the planning process. This critical early stage will be discussed in detail in the section on Alignment.

Second, in a "rush to define strategy," many organizations fail to build a "common information base upon which sound strategic decisions can be made." (The information gathering process is covered in this chapter under Discovery.) The third misstep that Rollinson points out is the "failure to successfully engage in 'team-based' strategic thinking." Rather than relying on an "all knowing leader," Rollinson advocates that "all levels of leadership be involved throughout the process – continuously." Among other benefits, using this team approach builds commitment to the plan and enhances the likelihood of successful management and implementation of the plan once underway. Suggestions for ensuring that multiple stakeholders have input into the planning process are included here in Alignment, Discovery, and Action.

The fourth challenge in a strategic planning process is to not "use a balanced set of performance measures to monitor execution and make mid-course corrections." Rollinson recommends that organizations deploy a diverse portfolio of success metrics that recognize the multiple facets of organizational and operational success. Finally, the fifth obstacle is a lack of execution. Execution of strategy takes considerable organizational resources and attention. Rollinson points out that implementation is "long-term and continuous" (p. 5). It requires deliberate attention and ongoing oversight from the boards and executives of arts organizations to "ensure the [right] work gets done" (p. 5). Both execution and measurement are incorporated in Action below.

Strategic planning as a cycle

The development of a strategic plan is not a standalone endeavor. Rather, strategic planning can be thought of as a cycle that flows from the development of the plan, to plan implementation, to evaluation, and back to planning as incremental revisions are made, or the plan is refreshed and updated. The cycle is represented as an ongoing process of Alignment, Discovery, Diagnosis and Decision which finally leads to Action (see Figure 22.1) and will be outlined in detail in this chapter.

In doing so, this chapter will focus on two representative arts organizations, briefly introduced in Table 22.1.

Alignment

Alignment embodies the recognition of Rollinson's "necessary preparatory steps." Alignment has two familiar definitions – the first, an arrangement of items in "correct relative positions," and the second, "a position of agreement or alliance." There is also an interesting lesser-known usage of alignment as the "route or course of a railway or road" (Oxford University Press, n.d.). It is helpful to keep the following three definitions in mind in the context of designing a pragmatic strategic planning process.

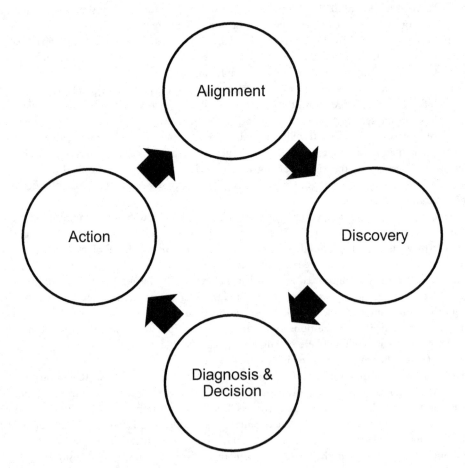

Figure 22.1   Strategic planning cycle

Table 22.1 Organization overview

	Historical Museum	*Orchestra*
Location	Small rural town (population approximately 25,000)	Large city (population between 500,000–750,000)
Annual Budget	Less than $500,000	Approximately $4 million
Mission	To preserve and interpret the history of the people, cultures, and commerce of our county as well as the natural history and fine arts of the region	To serve our community through extraordinary musical and education experiences
Program Snapshot	Exhibits and collections in cultural and natural history, quarterly newsletter, programs for adults, students, and families	Eight-concert masterworks series, holiday and pops presentations, summer parks concerts, school programs and other educational programs for children and adults
Personnel	Three paid staff members, including an executive director, plus a large pool of dedicated volunteers	Fully professional artistic, executive, and administrative staff; professional orchestra musicians under a collective bargaining agreement with the American Federation of Musicians

As items in relationship to each other, the first definition, Alignment requires an assessment of whether an organization is truly ready for strategic planning. Is there a shared sense of urgency and prioritization for this effort? Strategic planning requires a significant commitment of organizational resources – temporal, creative, intellectual, and likely financial – and this can be daunting to many arts organization executives and board members. For example, 43% of respondents to the ASP survey identified "lack of time to plan" as a challenge during plan development (McNerney, Perri, and Reid, 2013).

It is also important to recognize that it may not be a good time to undertake strategic planning if there are other significant initiatives underway that sap organizational attention and resources. Table 22.2 provides examples of those time-consuming initiatives for the Museum and the Orchestra. Other examples might encompass the opening of a significant exhibition, completion of a major commissioning project, or negotiation of a collective bargaining agreement or facility lease.

With the second definition of Alignment understood as agreement or common purpose, it is important to understand and agree on who should be engaged in guiding the strategic planning effort. In nonprofit arts and culture organizations, particularly those in the United States, the responsibility for strategic management of the institution is shared between the board and executive/artistic leadership. The board should have a more significant role in setting the overall strategic direction of the organization, and the staff should have the greater role in operationalizing and implementing the strategic plan. Both parties must have responsibility for measurement and evaluation (see Figure 22.2). As such, the most effective strategic planning processes are shared learning and decision-making efforts by board and staff, led by a strategic planning committee or task force made up of board members and senior executive and artistic staff. When appropriate, key volunteers and artists, such as musicians, curators, actors, and others closely engaged with programming the organization, are also included on that core committee. Table 22.3 shows how leadership of the strategic planning process is shared at the Museum and the Orchestra.

Table 22.2 Significant initiatives

	Historical Museum	Orchestra
Significant initiatives	The museum's annual gala, which takes a considerable amount of volunteer effort and is the museum's primary revenue generator, is in the fall. As a result, the museum decided to do its planning work in the spring.	The orchestra chose to delay strategic planning so that it could hire its new executive director before starting the planning process. The orchestra's board of directors believed it was important for the new executive director to be involved in and have a voice in the process, rather than to inherit a plan done before his or her arrival to the organization. The board understood that being engaged and invested in the strategic planning process would prepare the executive director to commit to and act on strategic plan implementation, with full ownership in the future direction and actions of the organization.

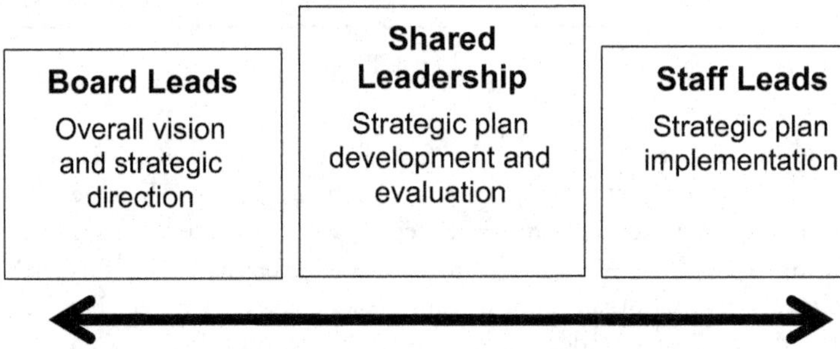

Board Leads
Overall vision and strategic direction

Shared Leadership
Strategic plan development and evaluation

Staff Leads
Strategic plan implementation

Figure 22.2 Shared leadership of strategic management

Table 22.3 Leadership of the strategic planning process

	Historical Museum	Orchestra
Who guides the planning effort	The executive committee of the museum delegated responsibility for organizing its planning effort to a small ad hoc committee, comprised of the board chair, the chair of the volunteer committee, and the executive director.	The executive committee and the executive director chose a large strategic planning committee in order to include a diversity of internal stakeholders: several board members, representatives from the volunteer guild and the orchestra, the music director, the executive director, and staff department heads.

As a route or course, Alignment in its third definition constitutes deciding upon the full scope of the strategic planning effort, including timeframe, budget, and extent of research and information gathering at the start of the process. How is the organization going to get from its starting point to the result it wants? Any thoughtful planning process requires some additional commitment of intellectual, financial, and temporal resources regardless of the size and scope of the organization, and that process must be designed simply and clearly with the organization's mission, vision, values, culture, and context in mind. Further, as the process unfolds, the organization may learn something that leads to a change in the process. New information, for example, about demographic changes in the school system might stimulate interest in gathering data on "best practice" school arts programs for a certain student age or demographic. Hearing that the local college is exploring the possibility of building a new student union with a recital hall may indicate a need for additional stakeholder interviews or research on the likelihood and impact of such an effort.

As arts organizations increasingly recognize that cultural equity is critical to their long-term sustainability, alignment must also include clarification of what diversity and inclusion mean to the organization in the context of its mission, vision, and values, as well as strategic planning. Americans for the Arts states:

> Cultural equity embodies the values, policies, and practices that ensure that all people – including but not limited to those who have been historically underrepresented based on race/ethnicity, age, disability, sexual orientation, gender, gender identity, socioeconomic status, geography, citizenship status, or religion – are represented in the development of arts policy; the support of artists; the nurturing of accessible, thriving venues for expression; and the fair distribution of programmatic, financial, and informational resources.
>
> *(Americans for the Arts, 2015)*

Each arts organization, by necessity, will regard diversity and inclusion differently, so this will require discussion and transparency from the start of the planning process. A strategic planning committee should review the organization's statement on cultural equity, or equivalent if such a document exists, and then ensure that the strategic planning process is in alignment with that statement. If an organization does not have such a statement, the strategic planning committee should still have a discussion about how the planning process will engage a broad representation of the stakeholders that the organization aims to serve. There are several ways, then, that this might be reflected in the process, such as:

- Making a community engagement survey multilingual so that community members may respond in the language they are most comfortable with, e.g., English, Spanish, or Chinese
- Having paper copies of an e-survey available at community locations for stakeholders who may not have computer/internet knowledge or access
- Scheduling town hall meetings or focus groups in various neighborhoods around the community, rather than expecting people to come to the gallery or the concert hall

This concept of Alignment then leads to the understanding that the breadth of a strategic planning process for the Museum with a relatively small staff and budget in a small rural town will likely differ from that for the much larger Orchestra, given the differences in their size, scope, artistic focus, programming goals, communities, and so forth (see Table 22.4).

This difference in the breadth of the strategic planning process, however, is easier said than done. An April 2017 board governance and planning survey distributed and administered by the management consulting firm Arts Consulting Group, Inc. to arts and culture organization executives and board members throughout North America, found only one-third rated their

Table 22.4 Summary of the scope of the strategic planning process

	Historical Museum	*Orchestra*
Scope of planning process	1-day summit for board, staff, and key volunteers	In-depth process over 6–8 months, facilitated by an external strategic management consultant
Goal	Identify top organizational priorities for the next 2 years	Develop a multi-year strategic plan, articulating the orchestra's strategic direction, goals, strategies, timeline, financial impacts, assumptions, and performance measures

organization's effectiveness at "aligning strategy and organizational culture" as extremely effective or very effective (Lambert, 2017). In this context, organizational culture encompasses the following:

- Consistent, observable patterns of behavior within an organization
- Jointly held beliefs, shared awareness, and understanding of the organization
- Shared values, 22 beliefs, and stories that bring people together in the organization

(Watkins, 2013)

Discovery

The Museum or Orchestra will have to decide what information is needed to make good decisions about its plans and priorities. An effective strategic planning process is grounded in Discovery – the gathering of quantitative and qualitative information about the organization's strategic environment – that informs planning discussions and decision-making. Among the findings of the ASP survey is that "high success nonprofits are far more likely to engage in [multiple discovery activities] including looking at industry trends and their external environment" (McNerney, Perri, and Reid, 2013).

There is an emphasis on looking at the external environment. One hallmark of a well-rounded strategic planning process is that it looks outward for input and information, as well as inward through a process that is appropriately scaled for the organization. Management consultant Bruce D. Thibodeau notes that

> Issues today in the arts and culture sector require examination from a cross-functional and multi-dimensional perspective, thus touching on every aspect of how internal and external stakeholders are involved in an institution's stability, growth, and community service. . . . The most successful cultural organizations have discovered that a strategic process focused on stakeholder participation can demonstrate how an organization plays a central role in the cultural, educational, social, and economic development of your community. A complete trends analysis – social, technological, environmental, economic, political, legal, and ethical – is needed to understand what may influence future strategies.
>
> *(Thibodeau, 2012)*

Just as in Alignment above, the Discovery phase must be scaled appropriately in the context of organizational resources, capacity, programs, and community (see Table 22.5). With that in

Table 22.5 Discovery process

	Historical Museum	Orchestra
Existing internal information reviewed	• Mission, vision, and values • Summary from the prior planning summit • Recent board meeting packets which include minutes, program updates, and financial statements	• Mission, vision, and values • Prior strategic, operating, and program plans • Current budget and projections, prior year financial statements, audit • Past, current, and future program information • Ticket sales reports and trends • Fundraising reports and trends • Key policy documents/agreements, including bylaws, facility lease, and collective bargaining agreement • Organizational chart • Resumes of artistic/executive leadership • Board meeting packets and membership information
New internal information gathered	• Board self-assessment survey results	• Board self-assessment survey results • Focus groups with board alumni and volunteers • Town hall meeting with musicians
New external information gathered	• The mayor, the executive director of the Chamber of Commerce, and the principal of County High School were each asked to come to a board meeting prior to the summit to talk about their perspectives on community priorities and needs	• Findings from confidential interviews with external stakeholders, including funders, business and civic leaders, partner organizations, educators, guest artists, etc. • Patron survey (in Spanish and English) • Benchmarking of comparable organizations • Market and demographic information • Industry trends and best practices

mind, among other things, what might the Orchestra and the Museum include in their Discovery process? What information might their respective strategic planning committees want to gather to inform their learning and decision-making process?

Diagnosis & decision

In *Good Strategy/Bad Strategy*, Richard Rumelt also writes that good strategy contains, among other things, "a diagnosis that defines or explains the nature of the challenge" (Rumelt, 2011). Once all that information about the organization's strategic environment is gathered and analyzed during the Discovery phase, a diagnosis must be made. Indeed, "a great deal of strategy work is trying to figure out what is going on. Not just deciding what to do, but the more fundamental problem of comprehending the situation." To illustrate what is meant by a diagnosis:

Challenge: A theatre company is struggling to recruit and retain new board members.
Diagnosis: The possible explanations for that problem might include the following.

Possible recruitment issues:

• The Governance Committee is disorganized and ineffective. It does not meet regularly and does not have a plan of action.

- There are many long-term board members who are retired and no longer well-connected and engaged in the community. They struggle to identify potential candidates for board membership, beyond their social circles which are getting smaller every year.

Possible retention issues:

- The organization does not have an effective board orientation process. There is no mentoring of new board members. They do not even have a board manual.
- Board meetings are not well organized and not well attended. Board discussions are not interactive or strategic. There are a lot of reports and not a lot of dialogue. It is not very interesting or engaging.

An organization may choose to employ one of many analytical models and tools to encourage critical thinking and to support decision-making based on what it learned from the Discovery phase. Many organizations that the author has worked with find that engaging in a strengths, weaknesses, opportunities, and threats (SWOT) analysis is useful to create and update organizational objectives. A **SWOT Analysis** is a "clear-cut and effective strategic planning tool that quickly identifies areas to build upon, challenges to remedy, opportunities to prioritize, and threats to address" (Lambert and Mraz, 2017). Table 22.7 shows how the Museum might bring together information from its Discovery phase into its Diagnosis and Decision phase, using a SWOT analysis.

Other organizations may need or desire an additional or different analytical framework to help their strategic planning committees assess the information from the Discovery process. The next several paragraphs demonstrate two strengths-based frameworks. These can be particularly appealing and effective, given the distinct characteristics of nonprofit arts and culture organizations that often rely on the passion and drive of volunteers and donors while striving for excellence in artistic practices. Building on strengths helps to "[link] strategy and execution closely together by creating distinctive, complex capabilities that set . . . [arts organizations] apart" (deSousa, Kauffeld, and van Oss, 2017). An arts organization can use one of these frameworks to understand those capabilities which add the most stakeholder value, as well as those that the organization must continue to develop in order to grow and maintain its competitive advantage with patrons, donors, board members, artists, partners, and others.

Building on strengths is perhaps best exemplified by Jim Collins's **Hedgehog Concept** in which an organization focuses on the intersection of three concentric circles representing (1) what the organization is most passionate about, (2) what drives the organization's resource engine (time, money, brand, etc.), and (3) what the organization can uniquely contribute to its stakeholders and community. The key strategic idea behind the Hedgehog Concept is to articulate that which truly moves the organization forward and then "[to exercise] the relentless discipline to say 'No thank you' to opportunities that fail the Hedgehog Test." Collins writes that

> the most critical step in the Hedgehog Concept is to determine how best to connect all these three circles so that they reinforce each other. An organization must be able to answer the question, 'How does focusing on what we can do best tie directly to our resource engine, and how does our resource engine directly reinforce what we can do best?'
>
> *(Collins, 2005)*

The **Core Competencies framework** is similar in spirit to Collins's hedgehog. Developed by C. K. Prahalad and Gary Hamel, this approach recognizes that "organizations develop key areas of expertise that are distinctive to their business and critical to long-term growth" (Rollinson and Young, 2010). The core competencies framework can help an arts organization home in on and build those unique attributes that both help the organization advance its mission and are most valued by stakeholders, whether that means valued by buying a ticket or valued by contributing. Similar to Collins' advice to say "no" to those things that fail the Hedgehog Test, this framework also helps an arts organization distinguish those things that are outside of its core.

Putting either of these frameworks into action means that an organization has to incorporate fully the information gathered in the Discovery process. An organization is not using either of these frameworks appropriately if it relies solely on discussions amongst internal stakeholders about what it thinks it does best or what it thinks donors and ticket buyers "should" support. Here are two hypothetical examples to illustrate:

1   A chamber music festival used the "hedgehog" framework as a tool to understand and collate quantitative and qualitative data from the Discovery process to affirm its mission.

    Hedgehog: Quality performances of rarely performed works

    Information from the Discovery process:

- In meetings and interviews, board members, the artistic director and executive director, musicians, and staff uniformly expressed curiosity about, enjoyment of, and commitment to the presentation of rarely performed works. They love finding and bringing these works "to life." *(What is the organization passionate about?)*
- A market scan of chamber music presenters and festivals in the region showed that those other organizations generally programmed better-known repertoire with standard instrumentation (i.e., string quartets, piano trios). *(What can the organization uniquely contribute to the people it touches?)*
- Focus groups with ticket buyers revealed that they value the unusual experience of repertoire new to them and that they are willing to buy tickets from this particular festival, with which they associated this repertoire/knowledge/expertise. *(What drives the organization's resource engine?)*

2   A professional chorus used the "core competency" framework as a tool to understand and collate quantitative and qualitative data from the Discovery process and to prioritize an aspect of its education program for expansion.

    Core competency: Professional development and training of young artists

    Information from the Discovery process:

- Young artists bolster the ranks of the professional chorus for large works, and they are also engaged in a significant number of outreach activities for the chorus to schools and community organizations. *(Does this competency contribute to the organization's long-term growth? Does it strengthen more than one program/aspect of its work?)*
- The chorus has the only young artist program for singers in its region of the country. The Artistic Director has connections with and does master classes and workshops at major conservatories. These relationships facilitate the recruitment of top talent to the chorus's young artist program. *(Is this hard for others to provide to stakeholders? Is it unique to the organization?)*
- In focus groups, current young artists, as well as alumni, talked about how extraordinary the program is for their artistic and professional development. In feedback surveys, schools and community organizations responded positively and indicated that they would continue to invite the young artists. Interviews with current funders showed

alignment with their interests and values and a desire to see the program grow. *(Is this valued by stakeholders? Does this contribute directly to serving the organization's stakeholders?)*

As articulated in a recent *Forbes* article, using a strengths-based framework can help an arts organization realize a "strong and sensible" nonprofit strategy that "is built on existing capabilities," "ignites the passions of those who must implement it," and "is aligned with stakeholders who care enough to open their wallets" (Latham, 2016).

There are other analytical frameworks that an arts organization may choose to deploy during the Diagnosis & Decision phase. Briefly, among these is the **Balanced Scorecard**, which is particularly helpful when an organization wants to ensure a process that provides a cohesive set of strategies across multiple aspects of the organization and emphasizes the linkage between the strategic plan and execution. This scorecard focuses on four strategic perspectives – customer or stakeholder, internal processes and operations, learning and growth, and financial or stewardship – and defines strategic objectives and performance measures for each (Rollinson and Young, 2010). Again using the information gathered in the Discovery phase, this would lead an organization to identify at least one objective for each perspective, such as the following which might be appropriate for a regional museum:

- Stakeholder Perspective: astound visitors with compelling interactions, including objectives including to upgrade learning experiences and increase use of technology in the visitor experience
- Internal Processes and Operations: enhance internal capacity to achieve the organization's mission, including objectives to implement a new collections plan and better use of technology to disseminate content
- Learning and Growth: build leadership for the future, including objectives to recruit board members who reflect the diversity of the region and build a volunteer program
- Stewardship: ensure future financial stability, including objectives to maintain the financial discipline to continue operating in the black and ensure proper ongoing maintenance of the building and grounds

The **MacMillan Matrix,** developed by Ian MacMillan of the Wharton School of Business, is especially useful if an organization needs to make strategic decisions among an array of programs and how well each aligns with organizational mission, skills, and resources (Straughan, 2003). A community arts center with multiple overlapping programs serving youth might use this matrix to understand which among those many programs (1) has the stronger fit with the center's mission, (2) has the better match with the skills and capacity of the center's teaching artists, (3) is most likely to attract financial resources (tuition, donations, grants), and (4) is unique in its community (that is, other organizations are not providing the same or a similar program). The matrix then would allow the arts center to strategically and wisely prioritize limited resources in the growth of some programs, while also perhaps identifying a handful of other programs to phase out (see Table 22.6).

Regardless of the model chosen, as illustrated in Table 22.6, an effective planning process is well-served by the use of an analytical framework to support strategy prioritization and decision-making,

> As the organization completes the Diagnosis and Decision part of the planning cycle,
> it should reaffirm its vision, mission, and values, in the context of everything it has
> learned and discussed throughout the process. With heightened understanding, as the

Table 22.6 MacMillan Matrix for two of the community arts center programs

Program	Mission Fit?	Skills Fit?	Resources?	Unique?	Decision?
Arts & literacy for 4th–6'h graders	YES	YES	YES, but limited	NO – public library has a similar after school program	Start referring kids to the library, talk to library about partnership opportunities
Dance fitness for middle school students	YES	YES	YES	YES – most "fitness" programs for this age group are sports-related	Continue, and explore possibility of adding a program for younger children

organization begins to make decisions about its strategic priorities, it returns to the questions: "What is the vision for the organization? Does the mission support this vision? How are values manifested internally and externally? Do programs align with the mission, vision, and values?"

While vision, mission, and values are not discussed in detail in this chapter, it is important to point out the role that values can play in the process of strategy prioritization. Values can serve as a filter for the selection of organizational strategies and can also help ensure that strategy selection is in alignment with an organization's highest ideals (Lambert, 2016). About the planning process at the Jerome Foundation, Ben Cameron writes that "before we tackled the questions or strategies, goals, programs, initiatives, and so on, we stopped to ask ourselves, 'Within this universe of need and urgent advice, what do we want to stand for?' 'What, in essence, are our core values?' Rather than letting our mission and goals set the framework for our programs, we believed that our value and values should set the framework from which our mission and goals would arise" (Cameron, 2018). See Table 22.7 for an example of how values and strategic decisions can align.

Connecting Discovery to Diagnosis & Decision

Now, by way of example, to put Discovery and Diagnosis & Decision together, let's assume that the two representative organizations both identify declines in earned revenue as a concern (admissions for the Museum, ticket sales for the Orchestra). Rather than setting a goal to increase admissions or ticket sales, each organization needs a thorough diagnosis of the nature of the challenge to determine the actions to take in response. Each must ask and answer: "What is really going on here? Moreover, what can be done about it, given the organization's resources and capabilities?"

Table 22.7 provides a simplified illustration of how the Discovery and Diagnosis & Decision phases might result in the selection of strategies and actions for the Museum and the Orchestra, recognizing their differences in mission, values, program, capacity, and community. The result of these processes is to reach decisions about actionable strategies that will be used when the plan is implemented.

The final step of the Diagnosis & Decision phase is to pull this all together into a planning document, again as appropriate for the scale of the organization.

An arts organization's strategic plan should be focused and uncomplicated. The organization is more likely to be successful in advancing its mission and implementing its strategic plan if it

Table 22.7 Simplified outcome of the discovery and diagnosis & decision phases, with selected strategy and actions

	Historical Museum	*Orchestra*
Issue	Decline in admissions	Decline in ticket sales
Relevant information gathered during discovery phase	The mayor and the executive director of the chamber of commerce both said that they are often not aware of what is going on at the museum The high school principal said that one of his goals is to develop more school/business partnerships to expand on the educational opportunities available to students in the classroom	In the patron survey, approximately three-quarters of respondents identified the soloist/guest artist as being important to their decision to attend a performance. This was the ranked the highest among several options, including ticket price, familiarity with repertoire, etc.
Diagnosis	The museum needs to be more present and visible, out-and-about in the community	Selection of the guest artist is critical to patron buying decisions. We need to pay more attention to this
Analytical model	A SWOT analysis helped to Board match an opportunity – partnership with the school – with strengths that the museum could build on to respond to that opportunity – a unique skill set in the community in the area of exhibit curation and underutilized exhibit space	The Hedgehog Concept helped the strategic planning committee recognize part of what drives their resource engine – patrons and donors respect the Music Director and trust her artistic choices – and that they uniquely touch guest artists who report that they love working with the Music Director and the orchestra.
Values alignment	Learning Community	Musical excellence Creative collaborations
Decision about strategy & actions	Priority: develop a partnership with County High School for an annual exhibit of student artwork to bring students and their families to the museum and to build visibility and community relevance Desired timing for first exhibit: next spring Who's responsible: Executive Director First step: meeting with school principal to suggest the idea, goal to schedule that meeting within two weeks of the summit and report back at the next board meeting	The orchestra prioritizes bringing extraordinary guest artists to enhance the artistic experience for both musicians and audience members Specific objective (among several): Program at least two young artists making regional or national debuts, or recent winners from prominent competitions, each season

focuses on only two or three prioritized strategic initiatives, rather than attempting to tackle a laundry list of every new goal or opportunity unearthed during the Discovery phase of the process. The organization should also keep in mind that whatever is in the strategic plan is above and beyond the ongoing general operations of the organization, requiring that organizational capacity to take on new initiatives must be considered. Finally, the strategic plan should be considered as a working document that will be periodically revised as progress is evaluated, lessons are learned, and new opportunities emerge. Of the managers who responded to the ASP survey, 60% noted that one key to success in plan development is to "focus on making the goals, objectives, and other content concise and making them understandable for planning participants" (McNerney, Perri, and Reid, 2013).

As a result, the Museum may find a plan consisting of a summary of the summit discussion, with an outline of the school partnership and one or two other priorities useful and adequate (see Figure 22.3). Given its programs, capacity, and resources, the Orchestra's strategic plan will likely be a far more detailed document that sets forth the organization's vision, mission, values, goals, and strategies, together with performance measures, a timeline, and financial impacts.

Action

The Action phase is particularly challenging because it asks arts leaders to simultaneously manage the busy day-to-day operations and needs of their organizations while also keeping a focus on long-term goals and priorities. Rollinson reminds organizational leaders that "acting on strategy requires much more time, commitment, and resources than the planning process ever consumes" and that "the competencies required for implementation and ongoing management are just as complex and demanding as those required for planning" (Rollinson, n.d.). Most strategy implementation also depends on the efforts of many people, requiring each of those individuals to understand and commit to the organization's strategic direction. Getting back to the question at the beginning of this chapter, how then can an arts organization ensure the strategic plan moves into Action, instead of sitting on that dusty shelf? Beyond ensuring that the plan has focus and discipline in recognizing organizational capacity, here are three recommendations.

Historical Museum Strategic Priorities 2018–2020	**Mission:** To preserve and interpret the history of the people, cultures, and commerce of our county as well as the natural history and fine arts of the region.	
	Vision: Our Historical Museum honors the rich and unique history of our county, celebrates its present, and imagines its future.	
Approved by the Board of Directors on May 23, 2018	**Values:** Learning, Community, Stewardship, Integrity	
	Priority 1: Strengthen our connection to and relevance in our county.	Develop a partnership with County High School for an annual high school art exhibit – Executive Director and Education Committee
		Become an active member of the Chamber of Commerce tourism committee – Executive Director
	Priority 2: Prioritize board and volunteer development.	Do a better job of matching volunteer skills and interests with volunteer jobs – Volunteer Committee
		Implement a board orientation and mentoring program – Governance Committee
	We will monitor progress on these priorities through monthly reports at board meetings.	

Figure 22.3 Historical museum strategic priorities

First, Action starts with accountability. One can look beyond the nonprofit sector for data on this topic. Based on survey research drawn from more than 26,000 people in 31 companies, among those companies that are successful in strategy execution, 71% of individuals agreed with the statement: "Everyone has a good idea of the decisions and actions for which he or she is responsible." In companies that are weak in strategy execution, that percentage dropped to 32% (Neilson, Martin, and Powers, 2008). In arts organizations, overall accountability for ensuring that the strategic plan is acted upon is rightly shared between the board and staff leadership. This accountability then needs to cascade down within the organization, regardless of its size and scope, so that department heads, volunteer committee chairs, staff teams, and individual staff members all understand their roles in the implementation of specific objectives.

How is this cascading accomplished? Most arts organizations find it helpful to translate the long-term goals and strategies into plans for implementation, action, or operations. Such plans provide a practical roadmap for the concrete steps required to turn strategy into action and results. This topic is worthy of a chapter of its own, but here are a few recommendations:

- Keep these plans simple
- Engage the staff members who will do the work in plan development
- Break the plan onto doable chunks
- Be clear about the timeline, roles, responsibility, and metrics
- Be flexible to allow for learning and revisions along the way

(Harvard Business Essentials, 2005)

Second, accountability requires measurement. An arts organization needs metrics by which it can measure action and progress on and learn from its strategic plan. These metrics need to be relevant, understandable, simple to measure, and multi-dimensional. For example, in addition to the prioritization of guest artists, the Orchestra, wanting to address that decline in ticket sales, might identify objectives around the growth and diversification of its audience with three metrics to track: (1) overall increase in paid audience (i.e., 2% in the first year of the plan), (2) development of new partnerships/collaborations with business and community organizations, (i.e., two new group sales partnerships per season), and (3) results of a pilot "Invite a Friend" initiative to engage the connections of current patrons (i.e., 50 "Invite a Friend" coupons redeemed and qualitative feedback from patrons). Such metrics demonstrate both mission impact (serving more of the community) and resource effectiveness (increased ticket sales through a diversity of marketing tactics to meet the needs and interests of ticket buyers).

Third, Action recognizes that "strategy is not a matter of immaculate conception, where you get a single answer and forever rule out other options. . . . You need to think about your strategy as an open, living thing. You start out by defining who you are as a company. But then you try it out, and discover that it's not working so well, so you adjust it" (Favaro and Kleiner, 2013). There needs to be a set process for routine check-in, evaluation of progress, and revision of the plan when new information is learned or when unanticipated opportunities or challenges emerge. The findings of the ASP survey "[indicate] that high success Nonprofits are more disciplined in conducting systematic implementation practices. . . . [S]taff and board leaders must put reasonable processes for assessment and reporting into place, and keep in mind that highly successful Nonprofits do this 3 to 4 times per year" (McNerney, Perri, and Reid, 2013). It is important that the plan not get stale; periodic updates and changes as circumstances change should be expected.

Returning to the Museum and the Orchestra one last time, Table 22.8 shows how strategies and outcomes, along with accountability, metrics, and evaluation, can be systematically put into Action at the Museum and the Orchestra.

Table 22.8 Overview of strategy & outcomes put into action

	Historical Museum	*Orchestra*
Strategy & outcomes	The museum will develop a partnership with County High School for an annual exhibit of student artwork to bring students and their families to the museum and to build visibility and community relevance	Program at least two young artists making national debuts, or winners from nationally and internationally renowned competitions, each season
Accountability	Executive Director, who sets up a Project Committee with the Exhibits Curator, the Chair of the Education Committee, and the County High School art teacher	Music Director and Director of Artistic Operations
Cascade from strategic plan	Project plan – a one-page document that includes key dates, assignments, and a project budget	Artistic plan – a multi-year document that is updated annually and identifies long-term artistic projects and goals; timelines for finalizing dates and repertoire and for selection/contracting guest artists; detailed budget and projections, etc.
Metrics	Increased communication and connection with school leadership Successfully implementing the exhibit Number of student artists and pieces of art Number of people who attend the opening of the exhibit Local news coverage	Number of young artists or competition winners each season Increased patron engagement in social media and pre/post-concert activities with artists Single tickets sold for these concerts Feedback on artists from reviews, audience comments, and surveys
Evaluation	The Executive Director will provide monthly progress reports to the Board, and a project report after the exhibit closes. The school principal and art teacher will be involved in a post-exhibit debrief to assess success of the event, whether both parties want to continue the partnership, and what might be done differently in the future	The Strategic Planning Committee will meet twice a year to monitor progress on the plan and to recommend any additions, changes, or extensions

Alignment revisited

Ultimately, the planning cycle returns to Alignment. It then becomes clear that the mark of an effective strategic planning process, and its resulting strategic plan – that nexus – is that *it is in Alignment, with itself, the organization, and the community.*

Consider the alignment that emerges through the Museum's planning process. The community, as manifest through the input received from the high school principal during the Museum's discovery process, voiced an interest in more programs to serve young people. This community need aligns with the Museum's values of "learning" and "community," and the Museum has capacity within the expertise of its staff (exhibit curation) and the resources of its facility (underutilized exhibit space) to support a new program or initiative to help meet that need.

Figure 22.4 Alignment as nexus

These come together in the Museum's plan with the priority to develop a partnership with County High School for an annual exhibit of student art.

An effective strategic planning process – one that results in a useable plan that moves the organization forward – requires that the right people, engaged at the right time, take ownership of a process that is well-articulated and appropriate for the organization's size and sophistication. Then, an appropriately scoped Discovery process looks inward and outward by soliciting input from internal and external stakeholders and by gathering information about the organization's external environment and market trends. The data and research from that process inform a greater understanding of customer value and the world in which the organization operates. From there, a cogent critical thinking framework helps the organization understand the issues at hand and provides a structure for the selection of goals and actions that flow logically from vision, mission, and values, and are congruent with each other as well as with organizational capabilities and resources. That process then results in a usable strategic plan that is straightforward and compellingly stated and takes into account the organizational capacity to take on new projects while continuing with busy daily operations. It includes a prioritized set of strategic initiatives that logically advance the organization and can be cascaded into concrete action plans that allow for flexibility and continuous improvement.

Clear-headed in its diagnosis and aligned with the culture and resources of the organization and its community, a good strategic planning process results in a plan that makes common sense – a plan which (literally or figuratively) sits dog-eared on a staff member's desk, rather than untouched on a forgotten shelf. From there, the three definitions of Alignment cited earlier in this chapter now provide insights into three recommendations for the effective ongoing strategic management of the organization:

- An arrangement of items in relationship to each other leads an arts organization to focus on strengths
- Agreement on a common purpose demands that arts leaders should always be asking themselves why the world needs their arts organization (Favaro and Kleiner, 2013)
- The route of a road or railway, the image of the connection between the here and now to there and then, means keep it simple

References

Alignment. (n.d.) In: *Oxford living dictionary* [online] Oxford: Oxford University Press. Available at: https://en.oxforddictionaries.com/definition/alignment [Accessed 22 Apr. 2018].

Americans for the Arts. (2015). *Statement on cultural equity.* [online] Available at: www.americansforthearts.org/about-americans-for-the-arts/statement-on-cultural-equity [Accessed 22 Apr. 2018].

Cameron, B. (2018). Organizational Planning: Beyond Mission. *GIA Reader*, 28(1). Available at: www.giarts.org/organizational-planning-beyond-mission [Accessed 22 Apr. 2018].

Collins, J. (2005). Good to great and the social sectors: A monograph to accompany good to great. Jim Collins, pp. 17–23.

deSousa, I., Kauffeld, R, and van Oss, D. (2017). 10 Principles of strategy through execution. *Strategy + Business*, [online] Spring 2017, (86). Available at: www.strategy-business.com/article/10-Principles-of-Strategy-through-Execution?gko=7f785 [Accessed 22 Apr. 2018].

Favaro, K. and Kleiner, A. (2013). The thought leader interview: Cynthia Montgomery. *Strategy + Business*, [online] Spring 2013, (70). Available at: www.strategy-business.com/article/00163?gko=f0c49 [Accessed 22 Apr. 2018].

Harvard Business Essentials. (2005). *Strategy: Create and implement the best strategy for your business.* Boston: Harvard Business School Press, p. 89.

Lambert, R. (2016). Leveraging values to strengthen your organization. *Arts Insights*, Arts Consulting Group. XV(1). Available at: http://artsconsulting.com/wp-content/uploads/2018/03/Arts-Insights-Volume-XVI-Issue-1-Leveraging-Values-to-Strengthen-Your-Organization.pdf [Accessed 22 Apr. 2018].

———. (2017). Alignment, diagnosis, and hedgehogs: Characteristics of an effective strategic planning process. *Arts Insights*. Arts Consulting Group. XVII(7). Available at: http://artsconsulting.com/arts-insights/alignment-diagnosis-and-hedgehogs-characteristics-of-an-effective-strategic-planning-process/ [Accessed 22 Apr. 2018].

Lambert, R. and Mraz, P. (2017). Effective summits: Turning away for greater understanding and capacity. *Arts Insights*. Arts Consulting Group. XVII(10). Available at: http://artsconsulting.com/arts-insights/effective-summits-turning-away-for-greater-understanding-and-capacity/ [Accessed 22 Apr. 2018].

Latham, A. (2016). 8 Signs of a great nonprofit strategy. *Forbes*, [online]. Available at: www.forbes.com/sites/annlatham/2016/05/15/8-signs-of-a-great-non-profit-strategy/#44f7f3236b56 [Accessed 22 Apr. 2018].

McNerney, D., Perri, M., and Reid, M. (2013). Strategic planning practices in high performing nonprofit organizations (501c3). Research results from national survey sponsored by Association for Strategic Planning (ASP) with University of Arkansas. Presented 23 April 2013, ASP National Conference. Atlanta, GA. Available at: https://c.ymcdn.com/sites/www.strategyassociation.org/resource/resmgr/Docs/ASP_Article_Higher_Performin.pdf [Accessed 22 Apr. 2018].

Neilson, G., Martin, K., and Powers, E. (2008). The secrets to successful strategy execution. *Harvard Business Review*. June 2008. Available at: https://hbr.org/2008/06/the-secrets-to-successful-strategy-execution [Accessed 22 Apr. 2018].

O'Donovan, D. and Flower, N.R. (2013). The strategic plan is dead. Long live strategy. *Stanford Social Innovation Review*, [online] 10 January 2013. Available at: https://ssir.org/articles/entry/the_strategic_plan_is_dead._long_live_strategy [Accessed 25 May 2018].

Rollinson, R. (n.d.). Why strategic plans fail. *LBL Strategies*. [online] Available at: https://lblstrategies.com/wp-content/uploads/2016/10/5-Reasons-Why-Strategic-Plans-Fail.pdf. [Accessed: 22 April 2018].

Rollinson, R. and Young, E. (2010). Strategy in the 21st century: A practical strategic management process. Chicago: Looking Glass Publishing, 13, pp. 141–142, 266–268.

Rumelt, R. (2011). Good strategy/bad strategy: The difference and why it matters. New York: Crown Business, 9, Crown Business, Ch. 9, pp. 77, 79.

Straughan, B. (2003). *Managing in hard times. Institute for conservation leadership and the environmental support center*, pp. 39–41. Available at: www.icl.org/product/macmillan-matrix/ [Accessed 8 Jul. 2018].

Thibodeau, B. (2012). Community building in the arts & culture sector. *Arts Insights*. Arts Consulting Group. XII(10).

Watkins, M. (2013). What is organizational culture? And why should we care? *Harvard Business Review*, [online] 15 May 2013. Available at: https://hbr.org/2013/05/what-is-organizational-culture [Accessed 22 Apr. 2018].

23

DIVERSITY, EQUITY, AND INCLUSION IN THE ARTS IN AMERICA

Strategies and practices

Jean E. Brody

Introduction

During the latter half of the twentieth century American society began to collectively acknowledge its long history of discrimination based on culture, race, ability, gender, gender identity, sexual preference or expression, and more. Americans have been challenged to question ideas of what constitutes art, who makes art, and how art is funded in recent decades. Understanding the history of structural racism, of inequities in opportunity, and in recognition of cultural expression have become pressing issues for the entire arts and culture sector in the twenty-first century.

For the arts manager, issues surrounding diversity, equity and inclusion demand attention on many levels. Managers carry experiences, expectations, and biases into their work, and these can affect which art is chosen to be created or presented, the people selected to work with artistically, who may be on a board of directors and staff, and interactions with members of the community. While many cultural workers and organizations have begun to address these issues, this is work that cannot be completed easily or quickly, but instead requires an ongoing and persistent effort.

Defining diversity, equity, and inclusion (DEI)

Diversity most often refers to who is present, and which specific groups can be identified as members of an organization, an audience, and a public. Many arts and cultural organizations wish to increase the diversity of their audiences, their staff and board, their volunteers, and participants in their programs.

It is important to note that diversity encompasses many different categories. Racial diversity is nearly always the first to come to mind, due to the history of discrimination based on perceived racial and cultural identity. Overcoming societal biases is both an everyday and long-term effort: centuries of bias built into language and culture are difficult to tear down. Science tells us that there's no such thing as race (Chou, 2017). However, because bias, discrimination, and racism are quite real, much of the work to be done on diversity has to do with overcoming a history of as well as current racially discriminatory behaviors. The fact that race itself is not biologically real does not obviate the need to counteract racism and its effects.

At the same time, arts organizations have increasingly acknowledged the need to expand notions of inclusivity beyond race by considering whose identities, artwork, and cultural expressions have not been sufficiently represented, or in some cases not represented at all. Concerted efforts are being made to include more artistic and cultural expression by women, by people of differing abilities, and by gender non-conforming and transgender artists. Grantmakers in the Arts, for example, has chosen to focus specifically on racial equity and uses the acronym NALAA to encompass Native American, Latinx, Asian, and Arab-American artists (Grantmakers in the Arts, 2018). There is an increased sensitivity to representing the experiences of non-Christians, particularly Muslims. The Museum of Fine Arts Houston's Islamic Worlds Initiative committed ten years of exhibitions to present the art of various Islamic cultures (Museum of Fine Arts, Houston, 2017).

There are also varying levels of awareness of what has come to be called "intersectionality" – the overlapping of a variety of identities in each individual (Tatli and Özbilgin, 2012). A person whose appearance indicates she is a white female might also be lesbian or may have a disability that's not immediately apparent and therefore, self-identification becomes crucial. Knowing who is present and working to increase the representation of underrepresented groups, is often the first step in addressing diversity.

Equity, or cultural equity, refers to the equitable treatment of all groups, cultures, races, abilities, and so forth. Equity includes correcting for institutionalized racism, building more accessible programs and facilities, and correcting for inequities in funding, both public and private, that have long favored European-based art forms and institutions over those created to promote the works of people of color, of women, and of people with disabilities.

Americans for the Arts defines cultural equity expansively:

> Cultural equity embodies the values, policies, and practices that ensure that all people – including but not limited to those who have been historically underrepresented based on race/ethnicity, age, disability, sexual orientation, gender, gender identity, socioeconomic status, geography, citizenship status, or religion – are represented in the development of arts policy; the support of artists; the nurturing of accessible, thriving venues for expression; and the fair distribution of programmatic, financial, and informational resources.
>
> *(Americans for the Arts, 2018)*

Cultural equity efforts interrogate institutions and institutional behavior and seek ways to change societal structures that favor one group over others. One important piece of the work of addressing equity has been the examination of how the philanthropic sector still overwhelmingly favors arts institutions that are primarily run by, and present the work of, white Americans and people of European descent (Sidford, 2011; Grantmakers in the Arts (GIA, 2018).

Inclusion/Inclusiveness. An inclusive organization is one in which all members can participate fully. *Inclusion* and *Inclusiveness* are used variously by different authors but typically describes an internal culture that promotes acceptance, an appreciation that everyone can learn from those whose experiences may be different from theirs and uses that multiplicity of perspectives to strengthen the organization. Inclusiveness efforts may cover everything from interpersonal behaviors, organizational habits or structures that may erect barriers to full inclusion and re-examining how the arts and cultures of a broad array of communities and identities are valued.

According to the Denver Foundation's Inclusiveness Project, "Inclusive organizations . . . not only have diverse individuals involved but, more importantly, they are learning-centered organizations that value the perspectives and contributions of all people, and they incorporate the needs, assets, and perspectives of communities of color into the design and implementation of universal and inclusive programs. . . . [I]nclusive organizations recruit and retain diverse staff and volunteers to reflect the racial and ethnic composition of the communities they serve" (Denver Foundation, 2018).

The LA County Arts Commission's Cultural Equity and Inclusion Initiative's report explains, "While a truly 'inclusive' group is necessarily diverse, a 'diverse' group may or may not be 'inclusive'" (Dang, Hernandez, and Jackson, 2017, p. 11).

A brief history of DEI in the U.S. arts and cultural sector

In the United States, the great majority of art forms, arts institutions, and arts and cultural history has been based on aesthetics and expectations derived from European arts traditions. While many of these art forms have a great deal to offer, this history has resulted in regular patterns of exclusion, discrimination, and inattention to large segments of the population. Several recent studies offer insights into the history of exclusionary attitudes and practices.

Los Angeles County Arts Commission's report identifies two main periods of interest in what was once called affirmative action or multiculturalism: the 1970s and the 1990s (Dang, Hernandez, and Jackson, 2017, p. 4). Early in the history of the National Endowment for the Arts, many "multicultural" organizations were supported through the Expansion Arts program (Coleman, 2016). In the early 1990's, publications by Samuel Gilmore (Gilmore, 1993) and by Clement Alexander Price (Price, 1994) offered reviewed the history of exclusion of works by women, African Americans, Latinos, Native Americans, and Asian Americans.

A report by the DeVos Institute traces the history of African American and Latin American performing arts groups and the lack of recognition and financial support that has frequently kept these artists and arts organizations from flourishing (DeVos, 2015). Many arts service organizations have made efforts to look back at works by women and artists of color that did not receive the attention they deserved in their time. An excellent example of this is the Legacy Leaders of Color Project created by Theatre Communications Group, presenting video interviews with key leaders of color in the theatre world.

Arts managers find themselves working within a funding ecosystem built upon a history of structural inequities. Artists and arts organizations that have had unequal access to funding and other resources may not survive or may continue to struggle for recognition and organizational stability. There is a shared responsibility first to acknowledge those inequities and then work actively to make organizations, arts communities, and society more just and equitable.

Why diversity, equity and inclusion now?

Issues of diversity, equity, and inclusion belongs to all arts managers regardless of how they self-identify, not just to the people who are members of an underrepresented group. Many artists, arts managers, and leaders seek to have a positive impact on their communities and see the arts experiences offered by their organization as contributing to building a better, more equitable society. Many organizations that have a longer history find there is a need to respond to the changes in society in order to stay relevant and continue to attract audiences, contributors, and broad community support. Numerous broad societal pressures have led to an urgency to make change happen as quickly as possible.

Racial Diversity. For decades, American society has grown more racially diverse, with an increasing majority of the population belonging to what has been considered a "minority" group. Many major metropolitan areas are already demographically majority "minority" (Berg,

2012). The U.S. Census Bureau predicts that by 2060 non-Hispanic whites will constitute just 43.6% of the U.S. population as a whole (Colby and Ortman, 2015, p. 9). Despite these realities, many arts and cultural organizations continue to be predominantly white in their boards, staffing, senior leadership, and audiences.

Culture, Country of Origin, Language. There is an increasing diversity of culture and country of origin. The Immigration and Naturalization Act of 1965 expanded the number of countries from which the U.S. accepts immigrants, resulting in decades of people arriving from all around the globe, and bringing with them a wealth of linguistic diversity and cultural expression (Price, 1994; Ngai, 2004).

Generational Change. Baby boomers, born from 1946–1964, are entering their retirement years. Numerous arts organizations will see a change in leadership, as well as changing roles for experienced artists and arts leaders. At the same time, Gen X-ers (born 1965–1980) and Millennials (born 1981–1997), as well as even younger generations, have changing expectations about inclusiveness, patterns of interpersonal behavior, and institutional norms of inclusiveness (Ono, 2016). Emiko Ono's report for the Hewlett Foundation focuses on California but is applicable nationally. She finds that Millennials and Gen X-ers have an expectation that leadership can and should be shared, and that arts organizations will welcome and support diversity amongst staff, board, and audience. The report suggests solutions such as distributed leadership, as well as addressing the continuing lack of diversity in senior leadership and on boards (Ono, 2016).

Gender, Gender Identity, and Sexual Orientation. Although women have strong representation in the cultural workforce, there are still imbalances in leadership and board membership. Recent decades have seen an increasing openness regarding sexual orientation, and gender identity and expression. In 2015 the Supreme Court made gay marriage legal following decades of public controversy. The depiction of gay characters and gay relationships in the arts, whether in paintings, on television, in film, or on stage, is increasingly common. Public conversation in recent years has brought about an increasing acceptance of transgender and gender non-conforming people. Despite these advances, there is more progress needed to achieve equity in pay, opportunity and artistic representation for all of these groups.

Welcoming People with Varying Abilities. The Americans with Disabilities Act (ADA) was passed in 1990, and arts organizations have gradually been changing facilities and programs to better comply with ADA requirements. Among arts and cultural organizations, there is an increasing awareness of the need for ADA compliance, including both the legal and moral obligation to include the disability community. A guide to ADA compliance for arts and cultural organizations is available on the website of the National Endowment for the Arts as well as VSA Arts on the Kennedy Center website.

Beyond compliance, many arts organizations have welcomed people with disabilities as arts creators, arts appreciators, arts managers, board members, and supporters. Some organizations have seen reaching out to the disability community as a marketing opportunity, a chance to reach a new demographic. For example, the Theatre Development Fund (TDF) has promoted sensory-friendly performances and provides services for people with a variety of accommodation needs.

Potential barriers to DEI in the arts

While many arts organizations seek to improve their track record in DEI, there are also factors that make progress potentially more difficult.

Income Inequality. While the Occupy Wall Street movement highlighted this issue beginning in 2011, recent decades have seen a growing gap between the very wealthy and the rest of the population. Income inequality has an impact on arts organizations' audience development efforts, their desire to diversify their staffs, and to diversify their donor base. If only the wealthiest can afford to attend the programs or join an organization, an organization's audience and donor pool will be missing potential small and mid-level donors.

Professionalization of the Sector and the Demand for Formal Training. The field of arts and cultural management has become more professionalized since the mid-twentieth century, resulting in an increased demand for job candidates with bachelor and master's degrees (Laughlin, 2017; Green, 2017; Kreidler, 1996). There has been a proliferation of arts administration programs, both graduate and undergraduate, growing from just nine in 1975, to more than 80 by 2013 (Varela, 2013; Laughlin, 2017). This growth has created a potential barrier for aspiring arts managers who may not have had access to formal training due to the increased cost of higher education (Green, 2017; Garcia, 2018). For those who do earn degrees, it is also resulting in increased student debt, making it less likely that a candidate can afford to work for the historically low salaries that are common at the entry level in the sector.

Unpaid Internships. Another potential barrier is the assumption that a young person entering the field will be able to complete an unpaid or low paying internship in order to gain experience. While some families can support this intermediate career step, for others this is not financially realistic. This problem is particularly acute in the museum world, where young people who must support themselves may be effectively shut out of the sector. Making funding available for paid internships and fellowships should be a priority for arts and cultural organizations when developing fundraising plans.

Inequities in Funding. Researchers of cultural philanthropy find a clear pattern of inequities in funding, which disadvantage arts and cultural organizations arising from racial and cultural minority art forms and artists (Price, 1994; Gilmore, 1993). In "Fusing Arts, Culture and Social Change," Holly Sidford provides clear data showing the historical discrepancy in funding for communities of color and culturally specific organizations (Sidford, 2011). Sidford's initial report shows that just two percent of arts organizations received more than 50 percent of total revenue in the sector and that these institutions predominantly focus on Western European-based art (Sidford, 2011, p. 5).

A subsequent report in 2017 by Sidford's research firm, The Helicon Collaborative, found that these inequities persist, they are pervasive both locally and nationally, and the situation has worsened from the first to the second report. Helicon faults the lack of diversity amongst philanthropic leaders, especially on boards, for policies and practices that result in structural, sector-wide inequities (Helicon, 2017). Foundations that support the arts, for example, should build more diverse boards, and re-examine structures and policies that may disadvantage artists and arts organizations of color.

DEI efforts need a multi-pronged approach

An organization wishing to embark on a comprehensive diversity, equity, and inclusion program should assume that a multi-pronged approach will be necessary, including making change on an organizational level and contributing to sector-wide efforts.

Advancing Sector-Wide Changes. To contribute to sector-wide efforts, arts managers can learn about current research DEI issues and how other organizations are addressing it. Numerous arts service organizations have issued statements on diversity, equity, and inclusion, and recent studies have been conducted to collect data on the diversity of the arts and cultural workforce. Research on the state of diversity efforts has been issued by the American Association of Museums, the Andrew W. Mellon Foundation, by the Los Angeles County Arts Commission, the New York

City Department of Cultural Affairs, by Grantmakers in the Arts, and many more. Examples of existing networks that arts managers can connect with include Museum Hue, founded in New York City by museum workers of color, and the Arts Administrators of Color, founded in Baltimore, Maryland which supports arts managers of color.

Arts organizations can join in these efforts by creating a formal DEI or Equity statement, adding their voice to existing advocacy efforts, supporting efforts to prepare young people for careers in the arts, and understanding where inequities can be found in funding for arts and cultural organizations and entities.

Committing to DEI through Formal Public Statements. Many organizations in recent years have created diversity, equity, and inclusion statements, and have revised internal policies to make sure that they are matching their actions with stated policies. Americans for the Arts has published extensive information about its DEI initiative and has created an editable document that any organization can use as a model to begin to build its own statement. Links to examples of DEI statements are included in the Resources section at the end of the chapter.

When creating a public statement about DEI, organizations will need to consider:

- Who will be involved in developing the statement? What will be the process?
- What terminology will be used?
- Will the focus be on addressing inequities that affect all groups, or will certain groups be chosen as the primary focus?
- Will the priority be on certain areas of artistic and management practice?
- Will there be a statement of purpose and an action plan?

Joining with Others as an Advocate. As noted, arts advocacy organizations such as Americans for the Arts, and arts service organizations serving specific segments of the arts and cultural sector, are excellent resources. Arts managers can add their voices to advocacy efforts already underway within their arts discipline or geographic region.

Contributing to a More Inclusive Pipeline. Among the key factors contributing to staffing inequities in the arts and cultural sector is the limited access based on racial, socioeconomic, educational, linguistic, and disability status. Arts managers can identify existing internship and mentorship programs that reach out to underrepresented groups and participate in these efforts. If none exist, cultural organizations can build a network in their region or within a discipline and establish programs to encourage potential new members of the field who.

Connecting to organizations that offer internship programs could be a productive way for arts managers to tap into potential job applicants for future openings in their organization. Examples of internships can be found at Wolf Trap Performing Arts Center, which offers a Multicultural Diversity Initiative internship, and an Economic Diversity Initiative. On a national level, Theatre Communications Group offers the Spark Leadership Program and the Rising Leaders of Color program to mentor rising leaders of color in theatre. The Bloomberg Arts and Culture Internship program reaches out to high school students to introduce them to a variety of careers and institutions in arts and culture in New York City, Philadelphia, and Baltimore.

Self-Assessments by Arts Managers. Along with these large societal and sector-wide efforts, arts managers need to examine their assumptions and behaviors as an essential part of supporting the change process. Here are few key areas where arts managers can focus their attention.

Implicit Bias. Implicit bias is the unconscious bias we absorb from the society around us. Whether that involves assuming that a "director" must be male, or that a person of color may have less education than a white person, people are often unaware of the assumptions they make based on what they think they know about people. Studies of implicit bias have shown that conscious beliefs and values are not always reflected in the actions people take due to these unconscious forces (Jost et al., 2009). However, understanding that biases are absorbed from social and cultural environments only underscores the shared personal responsibility that all arts and cultural workers must accept in order to counteract the impact of these pervasive and often invisible forces.

Acknowledging Privilege. What is privilege? It is anything that makes it easier for someone to do things on a daily basis and in their lives. Privilege is not limited to race: it also includes gender, culture and language, sexual orientation, education, economic background, and whether or not someone has a disability or health challenge. Many elements of privilege are things that the individual has little to no control over, such as whether your parents are married, what their education levels are, and what economic circumstances an individual grew up in. Most people carry different forms of privilege, which they may not be aware of until there is a realization, for example, not everyone can run, not everyone was encouraged to express themselves artistically, and not everyone grew up in a house full of books. Privilege may be economic, or it may simply be a lack of barriers.

Taking Personal Responsibility. Responsibility does not equal guilt: this does not mean that each person is personally guilty for all of the wrongs of society. It does mean that each individual needs to commit to understanding their privilege and biases, and to changing what they can. Acting on this awareness may involve pursuing implicit bias training, listening to others' experiences and perspectives, and monitoring internal thoughts and assumptions to try to heighten awareness and modify one's own attitudes and behaviors.

Organizational strategies to reflect DEI goals

The most common areas of organizational practice requiring DEI efforts will include planning, programming, audience development, community engagement, staffing, and board development. Organizations must first determine where they are in the DEI process, make a plan that reflects clear priorities and actions, and then continue to modify practices and monitor progress to work on key areas needing improvement.

Internal Awareness, Assessment, and Planning. An arts manager cannot make progress alone, but needs staff and the board buy-in, acknowledging that the organization can do better when it comes to addressing diversity, equity, and inclusion. Without recognizing the need for change, DEI efforts will feel imposed from the outside or from above and will be less likely to succeed. Conversations about diversity, equity, and inclusion can often be uncomfortable, so although this step may seem unnecessary, it is important to begin with acknowledging the organization's shortcomings. Everyone needs to become accustomed to the discomfort these conversations may entail and recognize this discomfort can be productive.

An arts manager may need to conduct some initial research to make sure there is an understanding about what areas most urgently need attention. An internal audit of the organization's programming and practices, ideally conducted by an outside consultant, will help identify specific areas for improvement. Specific, actionable, and measurable goals and tactics should be incorporated into the organization's strategic plan. Even if changes have already been made in some areas, it is likely there is more to be done. For example, there may be a good balance of gender and race/culture, but the audit may reveal there is little economic diversity, or the organization may not offer ready access to people with disabilities.

In Philadelphia, the Greater Philadelphia Cultural Alliance has undertaken a multi-year initiative to examine its practices; it developed an actionable plan which created internal change as well as resources for the arts and culture sector in the region. This process involved the board, staff, a consultant, and constituents in the arts and culture sector, with significant efforts to reach out to community members who may not already be connected with the Cultural Alliance (Greater Philadelphia Cultural Alliance, n.d.).

Along with publishing their DEI statement and action plan, all of the Cultural Alliance's working documents are publicly available on their website. Chief Strategy Officer Michael Norris, who has been leading this effort, explained that the organization realized that all aspects of DEI are connected. The Cultural Alliance's plan reflects the reality that DEI efforts must be long-term, must include strong partnerships with others in the community, and must operate within the organization's limitations of funding and staff time (Michael Norris, 2017, interview with the author, December 7).

Programming. Many organizations will state as a goal of DEI that they want to reflect the communities they serve. A good starting point would be to ask if the programming is reflective of, and appealing to, the broad demographics of the local community? Does the organization have certain populations ghettoized into certain times of the year, such as only showing works by African American artists during Black History Month, or works by women artists during Women's History Month? Is the audience primarily older, wealthier adults, and is it possible to make programming choices more varied and appealing? If this seems financially risky, an arts manager can set aside a certain amount of funding in future budgets designated for artistically (and financially) risky new choices.

While it is essential to consider what the public programming says about the organization's identity, and who is welcomed into its space and to its programs, change does begin at home, within the organization. The arts manager will need to consider who is on the staff and board, who holds key leadership roles, the composition of the volunteers and donor corps, and how hiring and human resources policies and practices may impact the organization's ability to sustain internal diversity.

An excellent example of an organization that made changes to increase its inclusivity is the Samuel S. Fleisher Art Memorial in Philadelphia. Their process is described in a report from the Wallace Foundation, "Staying Relevant in a Changing Neighborhood" (Harlow, 2015). The Fleisher staff observed that many of the more recent immigrant groups in their neighborhood did not attend their programs, and the demographics of their student body (they primarily offer visual arts education programs) were not reflective of the demographics of their neighborhood. Through a combination of research efforts, developing relationships with specific communities, planning programs with community partners, and planning programs designed to welcome all, the Fleisher has changed its relationship with its neighborhood (Harlow, 2015; Magda Martinez, 2015, interview with the author, February 2).

Disrupting the Locus of Artistic Control. Because so many arts organizations are founded to serve the artistic vision of a single visionary artistic leader, it can be difficult to re-envision how artistic and programmatic decision-making could be made differently. Some organizations have found ways to bring the staff, volunteers, and community into the decision-making process. Sharing authority and authorship with people whose knowledge and lived experiences may be different from the staff's can enhance an organization's ability to more effectively reach the community.

For example, Yerba Buena Center for the Arts in San Francisco has made numerous changes to their operations to diffuse control and put more decision-making in the hands of more people. Just one of these changes involves the YBCA 100, a list of influential people released annually by the organization, around which a variety of programming is designed. This list is developed through a process that allows all staff at every level to nominate and advocate for people who they find inspiring (Deborah Cullinan, 2017, interview with the author, December 22).

Similarly, People's Light and Theatre Company in Malvern, Pennsylvania has changed its season development process to include input from employees at all levels (Abigail Adams, 2015, interview with the author, September 4).

Some organizations are experimenting with turning over a portion of their programming to audience choice. Jacob's Pillow Dance Festival gives audience members a vote through their Chance to Dance competition. "The Chance to Dance contest is a crowd-sourced online competition that allows dance fans from all around the world to have a say in who gets to perform as part of the Festival 2018 Inside/Out Performance Series" (Jacobs Pillow Dance Festival, 2018). The Joplin Little Theatre in southwest Missouri turned a full season over to audience choice, allowing audience members to nominate plays to be produced. Nominated plays were evaluated based on the company's financial and artistic capacity, and a reduced list of the top 20 choices was put to an online vote open to any audience member (Nicholas, 2017).

Another potential disruption would be to invite an artist or community group whose perspective is not represented by the artistic leadership or recent programming to curate a portion of the season or to add a new program offering. As a result of long-term community engagement activities, the Fleisher Art Memorial responded to the local Mexican American community's request to work together to create an annual Día de los Muertos, or Day of the Dead, celebration. Because this idea was initiated within the community, it was also embraced by that community (Magda Martinez, 2015, interview with the author, February 2).

Audience Development and Community Engagement. An excellent reference and source of inspiration for building diverse audiences can be found in Donna Walker-Kuhne's "Invitation to the Party," which is based on her work building audiences for The Public Theatre in New York (Walker-Kuhne, 2005). Two recent publications by the Wallace Foundation, "The Road to Results" and "Staying Relevant in a Changing Neighborhood" provide examples of organizations that studied their local communities and adjusted their programming to better serve their local population (Harlow, 2014, 2015).

Organizations may think first about their audience: who is attending events, subscribing to the seasons, attending classes, or joining as members? It's just as important to ask who is *not* participating in the programs. Are there demographic groups in the local community who could be more effectively included and welcomed? Do the programming choices and marketing messages convey inclusivity or exclusivity? Developing real relationships with existing community groups can result in programming that is relevant to those groups.

Staff. An internal audit of who is already present within an organization may be able to reveal the diversity that's already present. However, even in a small organization, staff leadership may not know how everyone self-identifies. Arts organizations have had to build better tools for asking their audience, staff, and board to voluntarily identify themselves as belonging to one or another group while still respecting privacy. DataArts, which has been collecting data on the arts and culture community since the mid-1990s, has developed a demographic survey that can serve as a model for building an anonymous tool that offers respondents many options for identifying themselves (Sullivan, 2018).

Another area to assess is how authority is distributed in the organization: who is making decisions, representing the organization to the public, and implementing programs? A more diverse staff can bring a broader perspective to organizational and programming decisions and increases the likelihood that an arts manager will notice when someone is being misrepresented or left out altogether. For example, is the staff organized in a way that it keeps some voices silent, while others dominate? It may be necessary to build deliberate practices into staff meetings and decision-making processes to make sure that everyone is heard.

Hiring/Recruiting Practices and Policies. While some arts organizations may already have a staff that is highly diverse, many are challenged to increase staff diversity. For smaller organizations, there may be only occasional hiring opportunities. Having a deliberate policy of considering each staff opening as an opportunity to increase diversity can help to guide decisions in the hiring process. Chapter 24 "Strategic Staffing in the Arts" in this book offers a more thorough review of best practices to hire, recruit, and retain employees.

Senior Leadership. Along with looking at who is in the organization as a whole, organizations should examine the distribution of diversity across types of roles. For example, there may be a disparity between the top leadership and those in entry-level and mid-level positions. In some cases, that top leadership may include the founder or other long-time leaders, who are often older, male, and white. If these individuals are not yet ready for retirement, but the organization wants to find a way to empower younger or newer staff, then it might be worth considering increasing the number of senior management positions in order to promote a promising leader from within who can add diversity as well as expertise. It may also be worth considering the concept of distributed leadership, which redistributes authority so that all members of the staff can contribute to key leadership roles and decision-making. This idea is proposed in Emiko Ono's "Moving Arts Leadership Forward," mentioned above (Ono, 2016).

Building from the Ground Up. Increasing diversity can be easier when building a new team or rebuilding an existing team. When everyone is new, it can be easier to deliberately recruit for a diverse mix of people. An example of this can be found in two arts groups in Philadelphia.

The Pennsylvania Academy of Fine Arts (PAFA) in Philadelphia knew that it needed to change a public misperception of the institution as old, stuffy, and not fully inclusive. As part of a larger campaign to address diversity, equity and inclusion, then-human resources director James Gaddy replaced the gallery security guards with a Visitor Experience Team that would become one of the museum's key interfaces with the public. Gaddy recruited an entirely new team of mostly young, recent college graduates, who were charged with welcoming gallery visitors and engaging with them about the art, while still maintaining necessary security for the art in the galleries. This team was deliberately built to reflect Philadelphia's diverse local population. Gaddy used hiring criteria such as knowledge of a non-English language and knowledge of the arts to build a diverse, welcoming team (James Gaddy, 2015, interview with the author, August 28).

Jeri Lynne Johnson, founder and Artistic Director of Black Pearl Chamber Orchestra, tells the story of being inspired by the election of President Barack Obama to create a chamber orchestra that would showcase talented, highly trained, and diverse musicians. As an African American woman, she refused to be restricted by other people's preconceptions of what a conductor should look like. Because Johnson built her ensemble from scratch, she was able to be very deliberate in recruiting talent who also supported her vision of classical music performers that reflect local Philadelphia audiences. Johnson describes an ensemble that is well balanced between African American, Latin American, Asian American, and Caucasian American musicians. Johnson speaks eloquently about the importance of embodying her belief that classical music is for everyone:

> For me, creativity is as much a human right as is education, as is health, liberty, the pursuit of happiness. The ability to create is what makes us human. And so, to deny people that, or to impede that, or restrict it, or oppress it in some way is not right, to me.
>
> (*Jeri Lynne Johnson, 2017, interview with the author, December 18*)

Boards. Arts and culture boards are often older and predominantly white, and can be homogeneous in terms of ability, income level, and gender. A recent report by the American Alliance of Museums shows that 89.3% of museum board members are non-Hispanic white, and 30% of boards are 100% white (BoardSource, 2017). An NEA report on arts boards showed that "On average, 91 percent of board members were white, 4 percent were African-American or black, 2 percent were Hispanic, and 3 percent were in the "Other" category. . . . Fully 58.7 % of the boards had only white, non-Hispanic members" (Ostrower, 2014).

Some of the obstacles to diversifying boards have to do with board members' limited familiarity with people who are demographically different from the current board membership. There is also an inclination to want to surround oneself with people with whom one feels comfortable: i.e., people like oneself. If an arts organization's board is predominantly one demographic, then it is highly likely that it will replicate itself when recruiting new board members. This tendency can only be overcome by making a deliberate choice to seek more diverse candidates and reach outside of comfortable social circles.

Some organizations maintain a board policy of deliberately recruiting for diversity across a range of categories. In conversations with the Philadelphia Museum of Art (PMA) and the Pennsylvania Academy of Fine Arts (PAFA), both mentioned that board recruitment practices prioritize diversity goals while also taking into consideration other desired characteristics of prospective board members, such as knowledge of a particular area of art or art history, or connections with galleries or collectors (Gail Harrity 2015; James Gaddy, 2017, interviews with the author).[1] The PMA works with a detailed matrix of desired board member characteristics to identify gaps in current membership as part of its board recruitment strategy (Harrity, 2015, interview with author).

It is also important to note that what constitutes diversity may vary from one organization to another. Jeri Lynne Johnson of Black Pearl Orchestra noted that some organizations of color might need to recruit older white board members to achieve a better balance (Jeri Lynne Johnson, 2017, interview with author).[2]

Many organizations use their volunteer committees as a potential source of new board members. Seeking diversity of background and expertise in committees will increase the likelihood that there will be someone already dedicated to the organization who can add board diversity.

Inclusivity practices and policies

In an organization's efforts to increase diversity (who is there), it is all too easy to assume that once a new hire has been made or a new board member has been recruited, the diversity efforts are done. However, an arts manager may be mystified when a recently hired young black man quits after just a few months, or when a woman who just joined the board, and who uses a wheelchair, does not attend the organization's events. The reason may be that the arts organization has not yet created a culture of inclusivity. While there are many ways to address this, a few suggestions are described below for building a more inclusive organizational culture.

Inclusivity Audit. An internal inclusivity audit seeks feedback from the people who know best whether the organization's internal culture feels inclusive. This audit should include staff on all levels, part-time or contract artists and other employees, students, parents, board members, and volunteers. An anonymous survey can ask about key areas of that make up inclusivity. Is the space adequate? (do nursing moms have a private place to go?); is the language inclusive (do you know what pronouns everyone prefers, and does everyone use them?); and is the informal culture inclusive? Are meetings sometimes scheduled in locations that are not physically accessible to all? Is everyone comfortable requesting time off for religious holidays they observe? Does everyone feel their voice is heard, and their perspective is valued? Ideally, this kind of audit would be carried out by an outside consultant, but it can also be developed internally. Once the have results have been assessed, the arts manager needs to be open to learning from them.

Formal Diversity/Sensitivity Training. Experts can be hired to offer training for boards and staff to increase their understanding of and sensitivity to a variety of inclusion issues. Some training may focus on racism and racial bias, others on gender, sexual orientation, and disability. Larger arts organizations may be able to fund DEI training through their HR budgets, but smaller organizations may need to seek special funding or may look for other small organizations to partner with in order to afford the experts.

Avoiding Tokenism. A person joining the staff or board and who is the first of any under-represented group should not be considered the first and last. Each new person joining an organization provides an opportunity to broaden the diversity and variety of perspectives of the organization's board, staff, and volunteers.

Not a Spokesperson. A person who is the sole representative of her/his group should not be asked to speak for the entire group. Each individual brings a set of experiences and perspectives with them, but they can't be expected to know what all members of a particular identity group think, believe or like.

Creating Space to Listen. Arts managers should also review internal processes and procedures to see if they reveal where it is possible to increase the variety of voices that are being heard. For example, if the board agenda is set only by a small Executive Committee or a Board Chair, and are there opportunities for other board members to request that a topic be discussed or debated? Within staff meetings, do all staff have the opportunity to speak and to be heard? How do people who do speak up know whether their concerns raised have been heard and addressed? It is important to build in more ways for more people to have a voice, and for everyone to become more practiced at listening within the organization.

Policy Review. Organizations should have diversity, equity and inclusion policies that all employees are familiar with. Employees, volunteers, and board members need to know what compliance looks like, and what the consequences of non-compliance will be. Employees should not only know what the national, state and local law may require, but they should also understand the importance of following the spirit of equity-related policies, which are intended to create a positive work environment for all.

Final thoughts

The imperative for action on DEI encompasses the artistic, moral, legal, and financial elements of an arts organization. Programming that is based on the genuine needs and interests of the communities being served can provide a greater range of arts and cultural experiences that increase cultural knowledge and sensitivity. Arts organizations can broaden their base of support, attracting more diverse patrons and donors and strengthen their long-term financial viability. Arts organizations can go beyond compliance with legal requirements to truly valuing difference and the contributions of a much wider range of people and backgrounds than currently is the case.

Successful DEI efforts will directly and deliberately address changes in programming, staff and boards, relationships with a broader portion of the community, and through building genuinely inclusive organizations. With planning, clear focus and a long-term commitment, it is possible to build and rebuild institutions to create a more just and equitable arts and culture sector, one that values the cultural expressions of everyone in the community, that helps all voices to be heard, and where all are welcome.

Resources for DEI in the Arts

Americans for the Arts maintains a list of arts-oriented DEI resources and consultants: www.americansforthearts.org/

Arts Administrators of Color is based in the Mid-Atlantic region: www.aacdmv.org/

ArtEquity offers training to DEI facilitators as well as consulting services. www.artequity.org

DataArts'Demographic Survey Tool: www.culturaldata.org/pages/demographicslandingdemo

Denver Foundation Inclusiveness Project: www.nonprofitinclusiveness.org/

D5 Coalition offers resources to the philanthropic sector: www.d5coalition.org/International Association of Blacks in Dance – Equity Project: www.iabdassociation.org/page/Equity Project

The League of American Orchestras Resource Center: www.americanorchestras.org/learning-leadership-development/diversity-resource-center.html

Museum Hue: www.museumhue.com/ National Association of Latino Arts and Culture: www.nalac.org

Examples of DEI or Cultural Equity Statements

American Association of Museums: www.aam-us.org/programs/diversity-equity-accessibility-and-inclusion/

Americans for the Arts Statement on Cultural Equity, with a link to a statement you can adapt: www.americansforthearts.org/about-americans-for-the-arts/statement-on-cultural-equity

Chamber Music America: www.chamber-music.org/statement-commitment

Grantmakers in the Arts: www.giarts.org/racial-equity-arts-philanthropy-statement-purpose

Native Arts and Cultures Foundation: www.nativeartsandcultures.org/

Theatre Communications Group: www.tcg.org/TheNext50Years/EDIInitiative.aspx

Understanding Implicit Bias, Privilege, and White Privilege

Implicit Bias: Explanation of Implicit Bias: https://perception.org/research/implicit-bias/ Take the test here: https://implicit.harvard.edu/implicit/.

Understanding Privilege: Video visualization of the privileges we may live with: www.youtube.com/watch?v=awGctTODPBk.

Understanding White Privilege: www.tolerance.org/magazine/fall-2018/what-is-white-privilege-really

Resources for Accessibility and Access

National Endowment for the Arts: Accessibility Planning and Resource Guide for Cultural Administrators: www.arts.gov/accessibility/accessibility-resources/publications-checklists/accessibility-planning-and-resource

Theatre Development Fund: www.tdf.org/nyc/33/TDFAccessibilityPrograms

VSA Arts at the Kennedy Center: www.kennedy-center.org/pages/accessibility/services

Notes

1 Interview Gail Harrity 2015 and the author, October 4, 2017; and James Gaddy, 2017, interview with the author, 14 December.
2 Interview with Jeri Lynne Johnson, 2017. Month and day not recorded.

References

Americans for the Arts. (2016). *Statement on cultural equity* [Online]. Available at: www.americansforthearts. org/about-americans-for-the-arts/statement-on-cultural-equity. [Accessed 7 Nov. 2018].

Berg, N. (2012). *U.S. metros are ground zero for majority-minority populations*. Available at: www.citylab.com/ equity/2012/05/us-metros-are-ground-zero-majority-minority-populations/2043/ [Accessed 12 Feb. 2018].

BoardSource. (2017). *Museum board leadership 2017: A national report*. Available at: www.aam-us.org/.

Chou, V. (2017). How science and genetics are reshaping the race debate of the 21st Century. *Science in the News* (blog). 17 April 2017.

Colby, S.L. and Ortman, J.M. (2015). *Projections of the size and composition of the U.S. population: 2014 to 2060*. Available at: www.census.gov/library/publications/2015/demo/p25-1143.html [Accessed 9 Nov. 2018].

Coleman, E. (2016). *The growth of community arts*. Available at: http://gardfoundation.org/2016-symposium/. [Accessed 17 Mar. 2018].

Dang, T., Hernandez, H., and Jackson, M.R. (2017). *LA county arts report: Cultural equity & inclusion initiative*. Available at: www.lacountyarts.org [Accessed 1 Jan. 2018].

Denver Foundation Inclusiveness Project. (2018). *Definitions of inclusiveness and inclusive organizations*. Available at: www.nonprofitinclusiveness.org/definitions-inclusiveness-and-inclusive-organizations [Accessed 14 Oct. 2018].

DeVos Institute of Arts Management at University of Maryland. (2015). *Diversity in the arts: The past, present, and future of African American and Latino museums, dance companies, and theater companies*. Available at: http://devosinstitute.umd.edu/What-We-Do/Services-For-Individuals/Research%20Initiatives/ Diversity%20in%20the%20Arts [Accessed 8 Nov. 2018].

Garcia, L. (2018). Representation of Latinx arts administration leaders in San Diego, California. MS Thesis, Drexel University.

Gilmore, S. (1993). Minorities and distributional equity at the national endowment for the arts. *Journal of Arts Management, Law & Society*, Summer 93, 23, p. 137.

Grantmakers in the Arts. (GIA). (2018). Racial equity in arts philanthropy. *GIA Reader*. March 2015, rev. March 2018. Available at: www.giarts.org/racial-equity-arts-philanthropy. [Accessed 6 Jun. 2018].

Greater Philadelphia Cultural Alliance (n.d.). *Diversity, equity and inclusion page*. Available at: www.philacul ture.org/dei. [Accessed 12 Dec. 2018].

Green, P.M. (2017). Increasing the presence of African Americans in the arts administration field: Models from the for-profit sector. MS Thesis, Drexel University. Available at: https://idea.library.drexel.edu/ islandora/object/idea%3A7684

Harlow, B. (2014). *Staying relevant in a changing neighborhood*. Available at: *The Wallace Foundation*: www. wallacefoundation.org/knowledge-center.

———. (2015). *The road to results*. Available at: www.wallacefoundation.org/knowledge-center.

Helicon Collaborative (2017). *Not just money: Equity issues in cultural philanthropy*. Available at: http://heli concollab.net/our_work/not-just-money/ [Accessed 9 Nov. 2018].

Jacobs Pillow Dance Festival (2018). *Festival*. Available at: www.jacobspillow.org/festival/ [Accessed 9 Nov. 2018].

Jost, J.T. et al. (2009). The existence of implicit bias is beyond reasonable doubt. *Research in Organizational Behavior*, 29, pp. 39–69.

Kreidler, J. (1996). *Leverage lost: The nonprofit arts in the post-ford era*. Available at: www.inmotionmagazine. com/lost.html [Accessed 6 Jul. 2018].

Laughlin, S. (2017). Defining and transforming education: Association of arts administration educator. *The Journal of Arts Management, Law, and Society*, 47(1), pp. 82–87. DOI: 10.1080/10632921.2016.1278186

Museum of Fine Arts, Houston. Press release 25 July 2017. Available at: www.mfah.org/press/art-of-the- islamic-worlds-initiative-at-the-museum-of-fine-arts-houston [Accessed 7 Nov. 2018].

Ngai, M. (2004). *Impossible subjects: Illegal aliens and the making of modern America*. Princeton: Princeton University Press.

Nicholas, C.J. (2017). *Engaging arts audiences through technology*. MS Thesis, Drexel University. Available at: ProQuest Dissertations & Theses Global.

Ono, E.M. (2016). *Moving arts leadership forward: A changing landscape*. Available at: https://hewlett.org/library/moving-arts-leadership-forward-a-changing-landscape/ [Accessed 9 Nov. 2018].

Ostrower, F. (2014). *Diversity on cultural boards: Implications for organizational value and impact* (working paper). Available at: https://repositories.lib.utexas.edu/handle/2152/61737 [Accessed 21 Oct. 2018].

Price, C.A. (1994). *Many voices many opportunities: Cultural pluralism & American arts policy*. New York: American Council for the Arts.

Sidford, H. (2011). *Fusing arts, culture and social change*. Available at: http://heliconcollab.net/our_work/ [Accessed 15 Aug. 2014].

Sullivan, A. (2018). Identity in the cultural workforce. *GIA Reader*, 29(1). Available at: www.gia.org/ [Accessed 14 Aug. 2018].

Tatli, A. and Özbilgin, M. (2012). Surprising intersectionalities of inequality and privilege: The case of the arts and cultural sector. *Equality, Diversity and Inclusion: An International Journal*, 31(3), pp. 249–265. https://doi.org/10.1108/02610151211209108.

Varela, X. (2013). Core consensus, strategic variations: Mapping arts management graduate education in the United States. *Journal of Arts Management, Law & Society*, 43(2), pp. 74–87.

Walker-Kuhne, D. (2005). *Invitation to the party: Building bridges to the arts, culture and community*. New York: Theater Communications Group.

24

STRATEGIC STAFFING IN THE ARTS

Brea M. Heidelberg

Introduction

The best time to read and reflect on a chapter about hiring is before the information is needed. Organizations that routinely engage in critical self-reflection of the methods used to gather data about the work being done, recruitment and selection processes, and the ways in which new hires are welcomed into the organization always have access to important staffing information. These organizations are not caught off guard when there is a sudden departure or if there is an unexpected opportunity to grow. This chapter provides some considerations for how organizations can engage in the staffing process strategically and equitably.

There are many reasons why organizations bring on new staff members. Whether it is because the organization has recently let someone go, someone deciding to pursue employment with another organization, retirement, or organizational expansion the need to hire someone is an exciting and challenging opportunity. The ideal situation is to have the right person doing the right work.

This chapter begins with information about rightsizing or determining the correct number of people needed for the organization to achieve its strategic goals. Next, this chapter provides a blueprint for identifying the amount and type of work each position requires – a process known as job analysis – as well as how to assess the current organizational culture through exit interviews. Together, job analyses and exit interviews provide the background information needed to successfully navigate the more commonly known aspects of the hiring process: writing a position description, position advertisement, applicant assessment, interviews, and presenting the employment offer.

The importance of effective hiring practices

Hiring is often looked at as a daunting task that is largely dependent upon luck. Many people working in arts organizations are surprised when they find themselves responsible for hiring someone to work within their organization. There are countless resources available that discuss hiring in general (Pynes, 2009; Word and Sowa, 2017), but what about hiring specifically for arts organizations? Is it different? While there are many universal elements in the hiring process, hiring in arts and cultural organizations can require additional considerations. These considerations include a desire for three distinct types of knowledge: knowledge of a subject matter area (e.g. finance, marketing, or development), knowledge of a particular art form (e.g. dance, theater, or visual art), and knowledge of the operational context of the hiring organization (e.g. non-profit, funding institution, or for profit). The need to account for these additional considerations, coupled with the fact that there is often not much training in human resources in general (Varela, 2013), let alone hiring as a specific subset of human resources, means that many arts and cultural managers are left without the resources they need to ensure that they are doing what is best for their organization.

Hiring the wrong person can negatively impact an organization in a number of ways. First, the process can be a drain on current employees. The process of recruiting, selecting, and onboarding a new employee takes current employees from their primary tasks. While this is a necessary part of hiring someone new, getting it right the first time minimizes the impact on current employees. If the initial attempt is unsuccessful, current workers are taken away from their work to engage in the hiring and onboarding process repeatedly. Furthermore, continuously having to let the wrong person go and re-engaging in the hiring process will negatively impact the organization's reputation with potential workers, funders, and the general public. In addition to wasting employee's time and damaging the organization's reputation, ineffective hiring practices, especially practices that are unethical and discriminatory, can result in costly lawsuits. Finally, the continued presence of ineffective workers could undermine an organization's effectiveness, preventing the achievement of strategic goals for an indeterminate amount of time, draining resources like money and time while also negatively impacting less-tangible resources, like its reputation. Organizations that choose to employ strategic hiring practices can save valuable resources and avoid all of the aforementioned calamities that may befall an organization that does not hire wisely.

Chapter overview

Hiring is a strategic function that can help organizations achieve their mission. This chapter focuses on the earlier phases of the hiring process, beginning with figuring out exactly how many people are needed to reach organizational goals, also known as rightsizing. The next step is figuring out what each person should be doing. This process, known as job analysis, provides the specific information required to craft a position description – one of the initial steps in the recruitment process. Recent investigations into the arts and entertainment industry workforce have noted the lack of diversity present at all organizational levels (Cuyler, 2015; DeVos, 2015; Schonfeld, Westermann, and Sweeney, 2015). This research indicates a need for not only an informed hiring process that will result in the right hire but also an equitable hiring process that encourages a diverse applicant pool and removes barriers that have created systemic inequities within the field.

Beginning the strategic staffing process

Strategic staffing is a process Bechet (2008) framed to help organizations create both short- and long-term staffing strategies that can be implemented even without a completed or up-to-date strategic plan. This approach accounts for changes to the overall workforce and can be adapted to address the needs of small, mid-sized, and large for- and nonprofit organizations. This approach is particularly useful because it champions making data-informed decisions. To that end, the process starts by identifying staffing needs.

Identifying staffing needs

How many people are needed for an organization to operate effectively? Simply sticking with the number of employees currently on staff, or – if the staff is majority part-time workers – the current number of working hours, without taking a critical and strategic look at whether or not the current way of working is best for the organization both now and in the near future may prevent an organization from ever working at full capacity.

Strategic staffing includes the process of identifying the number of workers or the number of hours current employees work and comparing it with the workforce that will allow the organization to reach strategic objectives. This process is common in other industries. Accounting firms tend to hire more workers and authorize more working hours from current employees during tax season. Restaurants that expect an increase in the number of customers during a holiday will shift schedules around to account for the increased need for servers. Almost all retail companies hire additional help and stay open additional hours in the time between Thanksgiving and Christmas in order to reap the financial benefits of holiday shopping. Each of these industries engages in gathering information about what their organizations need to accomplish and how many people it needs to achieve those goals in order to determine the number of people that need to be hired and how many hours each employee needs to work.

Working in an organization that does not have the optimal number of people working, or that does not account for the number of hours needed from each employee to accomplish strategic organizational tasks can have negative results:

- Burnout – when employees are overworked and end up less productive as a result. Employee burnout is often directly related to turnover.
- Absenteeism – when employees regularly call out of work, despite not having a medical or personal need for doing so. Absenteeism results in decreased productivity.
- Excessive turnover – when employees consistently leave the organization, often after only a short period of working, requiring the organization to be engaged in the hiring process continuously.

Proactively aligning an organization's human resources and its talent management strategies with the organization's strategic plans is particularly important if there are issues with productivity, morale, or a need to account for an increase in responsibility due to a new grant or initiative. This process may require shifts in departmental structures, reorganization of employee responsibilities, identification of new roles that need to be filled, and changes in who reports to whom.

Subtract the optimal number of employees or working hours from the current number of employees or working from the hours to identify an organization's staffing gap or surplus. An organization that currently employs five people but has identified the need for ten total employees has an obvious staffing gap. A staffing gap may be addressed by shifting positions from part-time to full-time or increasing the number of hours a part-time individual works each week. From a hiring perspective, if there is a gap in the number of employees needed, then this is the number of individuals you should look to hire in the near future. Conversely, an organization with ten employees, but with an identified need for only five total has a staffing surplus and should consider rightsizing in order to avoid wasting resources. A staffing surplus may be addressed by shifting some full-time employees to part-time, reducing the number of hours part-time employees work, or by eliminating positions that do not serve the organization's strategic goals.

In many cases, financial constraints can prevent arts and cultural organizations from being able to fully right size. However, gathering rightsizing data can help leaders make strategic staffing decisions, equipping them with a list of workforce priorities to guide hiring as resources become available.

After determining the workforce needed to operate at full capacity, the next step is gathering information about an organization's culture and working environments. One of the most efficient ways of doing this is conducting exit interviews and staff surveys.

Exit interviews

It may seem odd to begin the recruitment and selection process with exit interviews. However, starting at the end is a great way to identify any barriers to effective hiring and retention before they arise in the hiring process, a time where there is an audience, and it is more difficult to make changes. Exit interviews are conversations designed to provide the organization with information about what it is doing well and areas for improvement from a departing employee's perspective.

There are many different ways of conducting an exit interview. While it may be done via a survey – either online or on paper – it is best if the exit interview is conducted in person during the last few days of the employees' tenure with the company. Face-to-face exit interviews are much more likely to yield candid information, which is the most important outcome. Ideally, someone that can be as neutral as possible conducts exit interviews. Often, this results in the HR department conducting the exit interview. Unfortunately, many small and mid-sized arts organizations do not have dedicated HR departments. In organizations without a HR department, some companies have a departing employee's direct supervisor conduct the exit interview. While this is an understandable impulse, it is not the best option. The direct supervisor may be one of the reasons, and potentially the main reason that the employee is leaving. If this is the case, then the exit interview is unlikely to yield any useful information, as many employees would not feel comfortable being completely honest in that situation. If there is no HR department, a supervisor that is one level removed from the employee should conduct the exit interview. For example, if the departing employee is a marketing assistant, then the Executive Director should conduct the exit interview – rather than the Marketing Manager (the Marketing Assistant's direct supervisor). Likewise, if the Marketing Manager were the departing employee, then the Board Chair (a representative of the Board of Directors – the equivalent of the Executive Director's direct supervisors) should conduct the exit interview. This allows some space for the departing employee to identify any significant issues with their direct supervisor and the working environment they created for junior staff. If it is not possible to have an objective individual conduct the exit interview, another option is a post-turnover survey. This method presents a former employee with a questionnaire one to six months after their departure. This separation of time allows the former employee to reflect on their time with the organization. It also allows current employees to process the feedback more objectively and productively. This option also alleviates the anxiety that may accompany the prospect of a face-to-face exit interview.

There is some concern that employees interested in having a good reference may not provide the type of information needed in order to initiate organizational change – especially in arts and cultural ecosystems that are small and interconnected, where one's reputation is arguably almost as important as their tangible skills. In some cases, what is left unsaid in exit interviews coupled with other contextual information provides the most insight. If the Development Assistant position is experiencing consistent turnover but exit interview responses about the

Development Manager or Director are vague, this may indicate a supervisory-level issue that should be investigated.

The information gathered during an exit interview or post-turnover survey can be important on many levels. Therefore, it is best when there are multiple people involved in developing the exit interview questions. The data needs of direct supervisors may differ from the data needs of the HR department, executive-level staff, and the board of directors, especially if they are a working board. Each of the levels above should be given the opportunity to weigh in on exit interview policy and questions. While the particular data needs of the organization and the individuals involved will alter the number and type of exit interview questions asked, questions typically fall into one of five categories: (1) reasons for departure, (2) satisfaction with the working environment and position tasks, (3) compensation satisfaction (i.e., salary/pay, benefits, and work/life balance), (4) interpersonal aspects of the job (i.e., relationships with supervisors and coworkers), or (5) any general feedback about the organization and the working environment and culture.

A team comprised of whoever conducted the interview, the departing employee's direct supervisor, and any other directly concerned parties should review the data gathered during an exit interview. When analyzing positive feedback, note if the beneficial aspects of the organization are purposefully done within the organization – or if they are 'accidental assets?' If the departing employee is complimentary about purposeful and strategic workplace practices or norms, then those initiatives should continue. There may also be instances where the benefits of a particular working environment are not intentional. For example, if a departing employee cites a low salary as their reason for leaving but highlights their work/life balance because the offices are close to their apartment, this does not indicate that the organization is good at helping employees maintain a healthy work/life balance. Instead, it may indicate a need for additional information from remaining employees. If a departing employee identifies issues that negatively impacted their experience with your organization, then you need to investigate the source of those issues and determine a plan of action for addressing them prior to beginning the search for a new employee. If there are remaining questions after a series of exit interviews, a useful follow-up tool is an employee satisfaction survey. They serve a similar purpose as the exit interviews, except they are for current employees (Allen, Bryant, and Vardaman, 2010).

Determining what the new hire will do

A common mistake organizations can make when hiring is assuming that they simply need a new person to do whatever tasks their predecessor did. Much like people, organizations evolve and so should organizational structures and the various roles within those structures. One way to determine what is needed of a new hire is through a job analysis. Job analysis is the process of determining what people do at work, helping to identify gaps or redundancies throughout the organization to maximize efficiency. There are many reasons to conduct a job analysis, including designing jobs and teams, classifying jobs, determining training and job safety requirements, and establishing employee evaluation processes. Conducting a job analysis as part of the hiring process helps organizations hire the right person to do the work needed for the organization to thrive.

Job analysis methods range from simple to complex with regard to the time commitment and labor intensity required. There are three main categories of job analysis methods: work-oriented, worker-oriented, and hybrid. Work-oriented methods focus on analyzing the work that is being done, whereas worker-oriented methods focus on the workers completing the work. Hybrid methods seek to analyze both the work being done and the workers doing the work simultaneously. For an in-depth conversation about all of the methods available see the *Job Analysis Handbook* (Brannick, Levine, and Morgeson, 2007; Breaugh, 2017; Landau and Rohmert, 2017; Moscoso et al., 2015). While the task inventories method is often used within larger organizations, it can easily be adapted for use in small and mid-sized organizations – those organizations that are least likely to have a dedicated and specifically trained Human Resources Department.

Task inventories

A task inventory is a listing of tasks associated with a particular position. This task list is often constructed by looking at the various objectives or goals of a specific position and breaking those goals down by the tasks required to achieve them. Ideally, a task inventory questionnaire would be developed and administered by a trained job analyst. For some arts and cultural organizations, hiring a job analyst would be cost-prohibitive – but those organizations can conduct their own task analysis. Starting with internal documents such as previous position descriptions and informal interviews with staff can provide much of the background information necessary to begin constructing a task inventory. Another useful tool would be O∗NET, a website run by the U.S. Department of Labor that houses a wealth of information about various occupations (www.onetonline.org). Additionally, smaller organizations could reach out to other arts organizations and create a collective among staff with similar positions across organizations in order to gather information and insight. For an accessible discussion of how to go from inventory construction to analysis, see Highhouse et al. (2016).

Once the task inventory is constructed, job incumbents and their supervisors assess whether or not the listed task is done in the position specified. This is important as there are many organizations where a task is assigned to one person but done by another. This can happen for a number of reasons, including a mismatch of skills and abilities (e.g. the staff member responsible for completing a task is unable to do so because they lack the skills, so another staff member with the required skillset takes on the task), an error in the way the task was originally assigned, or it can be a function of employee preference (e.g. if it is the secretary's job to walk to the mailroom, but a junior staffer enjoys the walk, so the junior staffer may take responsibility for getting the mail each day). Regardless of how or where the task has migrated it needs to be accounted for during the task inventory process. Once all of the tasks under the purview of the identified position are identified, they are each rated on the difficulty of completing the task, the difficulty of learning how to accomplish the task, and how often the task is required.

Task analysis not only provides information on the everyday tasks associated with a particular position, but it also can also provide useful information for organizations looking to hire staff that will operate in a managerial capacity. Many managerial tasks are difficult to observe and analyze with traditional job analysis methods. In order to account for the nuanced and often semi-specialized mental work of managerial-level staff, Page (1988) developed the Management Position Description Questionnaire (MPDQ). The MPDQ takes roughly 2.5 hours to complete and provides information about the requirements of the managerial role in questions with the use of a Likert-scale ranging from 0 (Definitely not a part of the position) to 4 (Crucial significance to the position) (Page, 1988, p. 864). Asking current or recently departed managers to complete the MPDQ can yield insights about the accuracy of current managerial position descriptions.

Results from task analyses are also useful in determining the appropriate title of a position. For example, regardless of whether the Marketing Associate works in a theater company, dance company, or museum – the fact that they are a marketing associate comes with certain duties that can be expected across organizations. While there will certainly be some variations based on organizational context, size, and structure – the role of job classification and titling is to allow potential applicants the ability to have some reasonable assumptions about the kind of tasks required in a specific role. Mistitling a position can have a profound impact on an individual's career – especially when considered from an equity perspective. Organizations sometimes will arbitrarily label something a "manager" role when the work being done is more in alignment with that of a "director." Much more than being a semantic choice, this difference in the title may negatively impact someone's career path – as many who are hiring look at previous titles more than they look at the bullet points on the resume that explain what was done in the role. Organizations or departments working within the confines of a government or higher educational structure may not have many choices for the position title – as certain titles come with required responsibilities, clearance levels, salary ranges, and prior approval. Even outside of stricter organizational structures titles are often used as a justification for pay ranges – for example, managers routinely make less than directors. Organizations should be prepared to adjust titles (and compensation!) to reflect better the role individuals play.

Writing position descriptions

Position descriptions are an organization's first and best chance of getting potential applicants to apply. While some applicants will have previous experience with an organization from their community programming, shows, or even as a volunteer, it is the position description that will serve as a primary point of contact for many. It is very important to make a good first impression.

When organizations fail to make a good impression on potential applicants, it results in a less diverse and often less qualified candidate pool. A well-crafted position description not only attracts the right kinds of applicants (those that are qualified and interested), but it also discourages the wrong kinds of applicants. This can save an organization a significant amount of time reviewing applications. Position descriptions can vary greatly depending on industry standards, national and local legal requirements, and cultural norms, but there are some consistent elements: a header and organizational introduction, a list of the responsibilities/tasks required of the position, a list of qualifications, compensation information, and finally any equity or employment statement the company may have adopted.

Header and organizational introduction

Most organizations will post their position descriptions on a job board of some sort, many of which require a subject line. This is usually the very first thing that potential applicants see. Similar to a subject line in an email, your position description header should be a pithy summary of what you are looking for. The formula that is most often used is: organizational descriptor + seeks a(n) + adjective + position title: ABC Dance Company seeks a dynamic leader to serve as Executive Director.

The organization introduction should be a condensed organizational profile that provides enough information for readers to determine if the organization's mission is one they want to support. To avoid overloading potential applicants, some organizations provide direct links to specific web pages and social media outlets that demonstrate the organization's mission in practice.

Tasks/responsibilities

Ideally, there should be 5–12 tasks or responsibilities listed for a typical job (Brannick, Levine, and Morgeson, 2007; Moscoso et al., 2015). If it is determined that more than 12 tasks are of top priority for this position, then it is likely that there needs to be more than one hire. While including too many tasks in position descriptions is something that can happen accidentally, many organizations purposefully overload their position descriptions hoping that they will get someone that can do as many of the tasks as possible. This is problematic because "add-on" tasks are often not directly related to the position they seek to fill, outside the scope of the associated position title, and not in alignment with the knowledge, skills, and abilities required. Most importantly, overloaded position descriptions serve as a deterrent for otherwise qualified applicants who see the laundry list of tasks and fear they will be overworked. There may also be applicants who do not feel qualified to apply because they are only comfortable with a subset of the tasks and responsibilities listed.

Qualifications

For some art organizations, especially those embedded within colleges and universities or public arts agencies that are run as government entities, qualification requirements are established by a separate office. For all other organizations, it is the organization's responsibility to determine the required qualifications for each position. Many qualifications pitfalls occur because arts organizations are looking at the position descriptions of peer institutions. Despite the seemingly innocent way that qualifications are recycled throughout the field, the inclusion of unnecessary qualifications reifies systems of inequity. Organizations often confuse qualifications, a term that – when used by itself – usually connotes a requirement, with *desired* or *preferred* qualifications. This mistake creates unnecessary barriers to entry that causes organizations to miss qualified applicants. For example, a position working in the box office for a theater organization may list a Bachelor's degree as a requirement. However, an applicant with an Associate's degree in Accounting may also be qualified for the position. While an organization may *prefer* someone who has completed a Bachelor's degree, the skills required for the job could be acquired with an Associate's degree. Qualifications should focus specifically on the knowledge, skills, and abilities (KSAs) needed to complete job tasks (i.e., the ability to use accounting software, or reconciling sales at the end of each performance), rather than relying on the shorthand of a degree name to convey the organization's intent. Many organizations struggle with to articulate requirements for a position without relying on pre-established notions of education that are built on systems of iniquity. Having a frank conversation within the organization about qualification equivalencies is important: is there an amount or type of experience that could be considered equivalent to a Bachelor's degree? Conversely, some organizations still struggle with the idea of the professionalization of the field – which has seen a significant increase in the number of arts/cultural management programs offered, and a steady increase in the number of students pursuing a formal education in a field that was built on limited or no formal training. In those instances, is there a degree type (e.g. Associate's or Bachelors) and area of study (Arts Management or Finance) that could be considered the equivalent of a specific type or amount of experience? When looking for a Marketing Associate, that kind of bullet point would look like the following:

Required qualifications:

- Bachelor's degree in Arts Management or related field (e.g., Marketing) *OR* 3 years' experience working on social media marketing

In the preceding example, the "or" is italicized to emphasize the fact that potential applicants could meet the required qualification with either the degree or three years' experience – as some applicants might miss the very important "or" among the rest of the text.

Another common pitfall with qualifications is mistaking the skills that are required at the time of hire with those that can be learned on the job. An entry-level development position may require knowledge of Tessitura (a specific audience engagement and box office software program) – but the organization should think about whether or not Tessitura knowledge is something that is needed on the first day of the job, or if it is something that can be learned after someone is hired. If there is room for someone to be trained to use Tessitura after they are hired, then the position description should focus on other qualifications, especially skill sets that are needed immediately or are not as easily teachable within the working context.

Working conditions

A "Working Conditions" section should be included when there are elements of the position outside the scope of assumed working conditions for a given position. If an employee needs to be able to lift 40 lbs as a regular part of their position, that requirement should be mentioned in a Working Conditions section. However, the necessity of these kinds of requirements should be carefully considered as they may preclude someone with a physical disability from applying – when they may be otherwise qualified for the position.

A growing number of positions within arts and cultural organizations require workers to leave the office in order to communicate directly with community partners, to coordinate performances, or to meet with donors and other constituents. These types of requirements should also be listed a Working Conditions section so that applicants may decide if the position is a good fit for them. Allowing potential candidates to determine if they could be successful in a position given the working contexts prevents awkward, and potentially illegal, conversations about a candidate's personal life during the interview phase – as the applicant will have already determined their willingness to travel as required for the position.

Red flag phrases

In position descriptions, there are some common phrases that organizations use to help potential applicants get a sense of how it is to work within the organization. However, many commonly used phrases have become euphemisms for problematic working contexts or behaviors and are red flags to jobseekers. There are blog posts, listserv notices, and affinity group discussions highlighting phrases to look out for in position descriptions – especially among underrepresented groups. Here are examples of a few phrases to avoid and a brief explanation of their negative associations.

"Multitasker" and "Fast-paced"; "Ability to work under pressure"

The combination of "multitasker" and "face-paced" indicates that the workflow is not organized. That combination and "ability to work under pressure" convey that the organization is constantly under heavy deadlines and there is no consideration for work-life balance.

"Willing to help out across the organization"

It is assumed that this phrase means that the organization is understaffed and that there is no plan in place to rectify that situation. This most likely means that individuals are asked to do the work of a few people – and there is no guarantee that those jobs will be in the same function area (e.g., doing work tasks that are all related to marketing or development).

"Hit the ground running"; "Thrown in the deep end"; "Self-starter"

These phrases indicate that there will be no onboarding process and little to no training. It is assumed that new employees will have to learn everything on their own and under pressure.

"Sense of humor required"

This phrase is often used in situations where nothing is funny, and laughter is supposed to be used to either diffuse a tense situation, or you need to laugh in order to avoid crying. Either way, it is not good.

Phrase or concept repetition

This signifies that you and your organization has recently suffered from some internal issue and are trying to make sure you do not repeat past mistakes with this new hire. However, it leads potential applicants to ask what was wrong behind the scenes that prompted such an anxious position description.

"We're a family/like a family"

Over time, this phrase has come to be associated with negative and emotionally abusive behavior that employees must grin and bear because "we're a family" and family, for most people, means that you forgive behaviors that you would not normally allow or forgive from strangers or coworkers. Another negative connotation with this phrasing is the assumption that it is a close-knit group that may be unwelcoming for newcomers. Starting a new job can be an intimidating social experience, and the thought of having to insert oneself into an exclusionary social group can be daunting.

"Benefits: making a difference"

This phrase, or any other "feel good" information inserted where information about compensation is supposed to go, is inappropriate. This is not the place the be witty. Compensation is a serious part of the equation for many applicants. Additionally, given the wealth of information available about how most salaries in the arts and culture can lag behind other sectors – rest assured that those who choose to pursue a career in the arts know that there is an element of altruism involved when it comes to compensation.

"Salary commensurate with experience"

This particular phrase is problematic because it is a sneaky way to avoid inputting specific salary range information. Part of the decision-making process when individuals are applying for jobs includes determining if they can afford to take the job, should it be offered. Providing applicants with all of the information they need to make an informed decision to apply should be the main goal of creating a position description.

Encouraging a diverse applicant pool

Many organizations are increasingly interested in attracting a diverse applicant pool as efforts to create a more diverse and equitable sector continue to flourish. In the past decade, organizations have come to understand that a diverse staff is integral to attracting diverse audiences and better financial performance (Hunt, Layton, and Prince, 2015). Recruiting a diverse applicant pool requires some additional work in determining where and how to advertise open positions. Organizations that advertise new positions in the same ways and places they have advertised all of their other positions will attract the same kind of people they have always attracted.

Ensuring a diverse applicant pool for any open position requires ongoing relationship building. Opportunistically tapping into "diverse networks" to advertise a position sends the message that the organization is more interested in engaging in tokenism than in shifting its organizational culture and truly embracing diversity.

Some ways to recruit a diverse applicant pool:

- Reach out to identity-specific affinity groups and community groups
- Complete a search for local print or online outlets that serve racial/ethnic minorities, the LGBTQ community, and networks that support individuals with cognitive or physical disabilities
- Seek out connections with Hispanic-Serving Institutions, Historically Black Colleges and Universities (HBCUs), and Native American-Serving Nontribal Institutions
- Reach out to identity-based professional development groups at Predominantly White Institutions (PWIs).

There are also a number of groups in the United States that exist at various organizational levels, from Facebook groups to established 501(c)(3) arts service organizations, that focus specifically on advocacy, opportunities, and mentorship for artists and arts administrators of color such as:

- Arts Administrators of Color (www.aacdmv.org/)
- Women of Color in the Arts (WOCA) (www.womenofcolorinthearts.org/)
- National Association of Latino Arts and Cultures (www.nalac.org/)

Another plan to increase diversity within the organization is through internship and volunteer programming. Diversifying these aspects of an organization is another way to build a network of potential applicants that are already familiar with, and dedicated to, an organization.

In addition to the preceding suggestions, it is important to consider relationships outside of the arts/arts organizations. Are there local community centers serving specific cultural groups or members of the disability community? Are there chambers of commerce that serve underrepresented communities? Developing ongoing relationships with an array of partners will increase organizational reach and provide a network to advertise positions as they become available.

Requesting and reviewing materials

It is common practice to request a cover letter and a resume from job applicants. Some organizations may request a writing sample or something that demonstrates specialized knowledge if it aligns with the advertised position. Organizations that ask for a lot of materials quickly regret it, as they then have to review all of those materials.

Many larger organizations have stopped requesting salary history information as a part of their application process. Basing current pay on what someone has made in the past reifies inequities in compensation for women and minorities – two groups that are routinely underpaid. Instead, companies are opting to base salary and benefits on what each position calls for and what they require of people upon hire. Unfortunately, smaller organizations are often slow to create systemic change and are more likely to continue discriminatory practices such as requiring a salary history or engaging in interview questions that are in poor taste (Hunt, Layton, and Prince, 2015), often because of the desire to hire "like" individuals and the general lack of oversight that exists within smaller organizations.

Despite some resistance to the work of creating and maintaining equitable hiring practices, the past decade has seen more organizations become increasingly aware of how implicit bias may play a role in the way they review application materials. Research has identified implicit bias against "ethnic sounding names" (Kang et al., 2016), a higher penalty for typos in application materials for women and minorities, and a bias against experience that is not articulated in implicit cultural or industry norms – even when those industry norms are not universally accepted across an entire sector (Hunt, Layton, and Prince, 2015). A discussion of how implicit bias can work against DEI initiatives is covered in chapter 23, *Diversity, Equity, and Inclusion in the Arts in America.*

Interviews

Deciding who should be involved in the interview process can be tricky. Some organizations opt for quicker interview sessions that only involve the position's direct supervisor and sometimes that person's supervisor. This gives applicants a good overview of the position and the supervisory context but does not give them a true feel for the entire organization and how their work would fit into the overall structure. This has prompted many organizations to hold longer interview sessions that include a tour of the organization and meetings with each department as well as community partners. Exposing applicants to a variety of institutional stakeholders gives those making the decision information about the applicant from multiple vantage points. For the sake of equity, if a longer form interview with multiple stakeholders is done, it is important to try and give each candidate the same type of interview experience. Uniform applicant evaluation materials should also be used to gather information about the candidate post-interview.

Prepping those that will be a part of the interview day is an important step that many organizations miss. Applicants are also using the interview to determine if the organization will meet both their personal and professional needs. Therefore, it is important that all interviewers be aware that candidates use the behavior of those they encounter during the interview process as an indicator of important organizational characteristics like leadership style, communication style, and the overall culture of the organization.

Specific interview questions, especially those that provide insight into how each candidate thinks and works, will vary depending on the organization and the position. However, the types of questions utilized by arts and cultural organizations tend to be behavioral and competency based. Behavioral questions ask candidates to provide information about past behaviors and choices, while competency questions ask candidates to connect past behaviors and decisions to job competencies. These types of questions have the highest predictive validity rates and have come to be industry standard – at the expense of questions like "What kind of superhero would you be?" or opinion-based questions. Unfortunately, there are many organizations, especially small and mid-sized ones, that still ask questions (either directly or indirectly) about an applicant's race or national origin, religion, gender, gender identity, or sexual orientation, pregnancy status or number of children, age, disability status, genetic information (e.g. HIV/AIDS status), or citizenship status. These types of questions are unnecessary, inappropriate, and illegal in the United States. Organizations asking these questions often go unchecked because candidates are in a vulnerable position and those within the organization who might not agree with the tactic say nothing against it. These organizations may not be held accountable in an official forum, but they are discussed at length within networks (both in person and online), and their applicant pools do tend to shrink for subsequent jobs, whether or not they are aware of it.

Notifying candidates

Organizations that map out the entire hiring process at the onset are those that are most likely to get their top choice candidate. Some organizations do not account for how busy organizational decision makers can be, especially if their decision must be approved at the executive or board-level. Organizations that have long delays between position posting and the initial candidate outreach or between the interview stage and making offers may find that their top choice candidates are not willing or able to wait. After all, interviews are conducted, it is important to get decision makers into a room and while information about the candidates is fresh. As a courtesy, organizations should let people know if they were not selected as early as possible. As the number of applicants per opening has steadily increased, it has become increasingly common for job seekers to apply and never receive a response. The time it takes to draft a general response for unsuccessful applicants at the initial screening or interview phase and a more personalized note for those who were interviewed but were not chosen is a small price to pay in order to maintain a positive reputation among job seekers.

A final note

While this chapter focused on the lesser-known elements of the strategic hiring process, the more common aspects, such as making a final selection and making an offer, should also be considered carefully for how they can be both strategic and equitable. Organizations that figure out ways to address both needs are best equipped to choose candidates that suit the organization's needs, avoid dysfunctional turnover, and achieve organizational goals while creating or maintaining a good reputation within the field for being a good place to work. This is especially important as word of mouth is one of the best recruitment tools.

Conclusion

Arts and cultural organizations have made important strides away from exclusionary hiring practices such as relying solely on personal networks created from systemic iniquities. Additionally, succession planning is becoming a strategic practice for use throughout the organization (Groves, 2007; Griffith et al., 2018). The creation and significant growth of both undergraduate and graduate programs in arts and cultural management (Redaelli, 2016), calls for diversity, equity, and inclusion within all aspects and levels of arts and cultural institutions (Arts Consulting Group, 2017), and the continued diversification of individuals seeking careers in this sector (Cuyler, 2015) have resulted in significant changes at the entry- and mid-levels in the field. These factors have impacted the labor market by increasing the labor supply and have, in many cases, created a more educated and diverse pool of applicants. However, these changes have largely missed the executive level. There are some notable exceptions as some organizations, such as the National Assembly of State Arts Agencies and the National Endowment for the Arts, have welcomed their first non-male or person of color Executive Director. There is still a long way to go toward making sustained change in the makeup of executive-level staff in the arts and cultural sector. Even with the growing number of arts-focused consulting agencies, who specialize in executive leadership searches (usually for larger organizations with big budgets), the pool of "viable" applicants, and those ultimately chosen by the board of directors is still usually male. Even when gender diversity exists, racial, ethnic, and class diversity often does not.

As the field strives to become more equitable and healthier, there is a noticeable divide between organizations who have adapted to create and improve upon equitable hiring practices in order to diversify their board and staff and those organizations who have not. Likewise, organizations that have problematic, toxic, or discriminatory organizational cultures are experiencing excessive turnover as employees no longer put up with the behavior that was considered a normal a decade ago. While all organizations are trying to do more with fewer resources, it is the organizations who engage strategic staffing principles and have a functional organizational culture that succeeds in times of smaller budgets, more competition for funding, and the need to nimbly navigate both internally and externally induced organizational change.

References

Allen, D.G., Bryant, P.C., and Vardaman, J.M. (2010). Retaining talent: Replacing misconceptions with evidence-based strategies. *Academy of Management Perspectives*, 24(2), pp. 48–64.

Arts Consulting Group. (2017). *Inclusion, diversity, equity, and access: Why now in the arts and culture sector?* Arts Insights. B. Thibodeau and W. Lynch-McWhite, vol. XVII, Issue 12.

Bechet, T.P. (2008). *Strategic staffing: A comprehensive system of effective workforce planning.* 2nd ed. New York: American Management Association.

Brannick, M.T., Levine, E.L., and Morgeson, F.P. (2007). *Job and work analysis: Methods, research, and applications for human resource management.* London: Sage.

Breaugh, J.A. (2017). The contribution of job analysis to recruitment. *The Wiley Blackwell Handbook of the Psychology of Recruitment, Selection and Employee Retention*, pp. 12–28.

Cuyler, A.C. (2015). Exploratory study of demographic diversity in the arts management workforce. *Grantmakers in the Arts Reader*, 26(3), pp. 16–19.

DeVos Institute of Arts Management. (2015). *Diversity in the Arts: The Past, Present, and Future of African American and Latino Museums, Dance Companies, and Theater Companies.* Washington, DC: DeVos Institute of Arts Management.

Griffith, J.A., Baur, J.E. and Buckley, M.R. (2018). Creating comprehensive leadership pipelines: Applying the real options approach to organizational leadership development. *Human Resource Management Review*, 29(3), pp. 305–315.

Groves, K.S. (2007). Integrating leadership development and succession planning best practices. *Journal of Management Development*, 26(3), pp. 239–260.

Highhouse, S., Doverspike, D., and Guion, R.M. (2016). *Essentials of personnel assessment and selection.* 2nd ed. New York: Routledge.

Hunt, V., Layton, D., and Prince, S. (2015). *Diversity matters.* New York: McKinsey & Company. Available at: www.mckinsey.com/~/media/mckinsey/business%20functions/organization/our%20insights/why%20diversity%20matters/diversity%20matters.ashx

Kang, S.K., DeCelles, K.A., Tilcsik, A., and Jun, S. Whitened resumes: Race and self-presentation in the labor market. *Administrative Science Quarterly*, 61(3), pp. 469–502.

Landau, K. and Rohmert, W. (eds.) (2017). *Recent developments in job analysis.* Vol. 24. Taylor & Francis.

Moscoso, S., Vilela, L.D., and García-Izquierdo, A.L. (2015). Work analysis for personnel selection. In: I. Nikolaou and J.K. Oostrom, eds., *Employee recruitment, selection, and assessment.* Hove: Psychology Press, pp. 21–38.

Page, R.C. (1988). Management position description questionnaire. In: S. Gael, ed., *The job analysis handbook for business, industry, and government.* Vol. II. New York: Wiley, pp. 861–879.

Pynes, J.E. (2009). *Human resources management for public and nonprofit organizations: A strategic approach.* 3rd ed. New York: John Wiley & Sons.

Redaelli, E. (2016). American cultural policy and the rise of arts management programs: The creation of a new professional identity. In: J. Paquette, ed., *Cultural policy, work and identity.* London: Routledge, pp. 159–174.

Schonfeld, R., Westermann, M., and Sweeney, L. (2015). *Art museum staff demographic survey*. New York: The Andrew W. Mellon Foundation.

Varela, X. (2013). Core consensus, strategic variations: Mapping Arts Management graduate education in the United States. *The Journal of Arts Management, Law, and Society*, 43(2), pp. 74–87.

Word, J.K.A. and Sowa, J.E. (eds.) (2017). *The nonprofit human resource management handbook: From theory to practice*. New York: Routledge.

25

ARTISTIC INTERVENTIONS FOR ORGANIZATIONAL DEVELOPMENT

Case studies from Italy

Chiara Paolino and Daniela Aliberti

Introduction

This chapter is an examination of how artistic interventions can contribute to organizational development and innovation in the workplace, through a reflection on a set of informative experiences focused on integrating art within the dynamics of the organizational life.

An artistic intervention can be defined as a group of people, practices or products coming from the world of the arts, entering the business organization with the aim to benefit the organization itself (Berthoin Antal, 2009; Schiuma, 2011). For example, it could consist of an artist entering the organizational spaces with the idea to disrupt working routines by stimulating an active debate and collaboration in the creation of an artefact, or of an artistic performance, sharing creative techniques and different values. Generally, artistic interventions in the workplace are aesthetic experiences that allow for the engagement of all employees' senses, enabling them to develop a new perspective, guiding their decisions and actions (Berthoin Antal, 2013).

From the seminal work of Lotte Darsø in "*Learning Tales of Arts in Business*" (2004), the discussion around the role of art to improve the organization now encompasses the capacity of art to enhance employees' strategic thinking, their ability to learn and opportunity to innovate within the organization. Indeed, the practice and research in this field started in management learning and education, and it has moved towards broader topics, such as the role of art to shape new leadership capabilities (e.g., Adler, 2006; Taylor and Ladkin, 2009; Taylor, 2002; Sutherland and Purg, 2010).

The urgency and the importance to reflect on the meaning of the role of art at the workplace can be traced back to the question of Purg and Sutherland (2017, p. 382) about management education: 'Why should we care about the arts in management education? Why are the arts part of reforms in developing future professionals? What is the fundamental value of the arts for developing tomorrow's manager-leaders?' More generally, the answer revolves around the power of art to allow employees and managers to look for new meaning in their actions – to pause, reflect and question what art can bring to the workplace.

In order to contribute to this important debate, this chapter focuses on how artistic interventions at the workplace can help people in organizations in their search for meaning for their actions by focusing on three main issues. First, we explore and exemplify how an artistic intervention can help employees to think differently about their professional identity and to rebuild a positive relationship with their organization. Second, we discuss the topic of how artistic interventions can contribute to enhancing learning during training in organizations. Our third goal is to debate how artistic interventions can foster product innovation at the workplace. In concluding this chapter, we highlight the implications of artistic interventions for the role of the arts manager within an organization.

Our examples of artistic interventions will focus on cases in Italy. In particular, we will refer to the artistic interventions organized by the Fondazione Ermanno Casoli (FEC since now). The FEC[1] is a non-profit institution that promotes artistic interventions at the workplace; its mission is to encourage companies to welcome artists and their works within the organization to promote opportunities for innovation and renewal. We will present how foundations, like FEC, need the professional profile of an arts manager, rather than a curator or a pure manager, to promote and organize effectively artistic interventions at the workplace.

We will first present the role of FEC as an intermediary between the artist and the companies in artistic interventions. Then, we will analyze the relationship between artistic interventions, individual identity, learning dynamics and innovation opportunities at the workplace. We will conclude with recommendations on how companies can manage successful interventions, and we will underline the possible risks a company can go by implementing artistic interventions.

Artistic interventions and the dynamics of identity and organizational identification

The concept of professional identity captures the essential features believed to be central, enduring, and distinctive of an individual as a professional (Albert and Whetten, 1985; Cole and Bruch, 2006). Organizational identification reflects the specific ways in which individuals define themselves in terms of their membership in an organization (Mael and Ashforth, 1995); the strength of organizational identification is believed to benefit individuals, workgroups, and the organization as a whole (Ashforth and Mael, 1989; Riketta, 2005).

A change in professional identity and organizational identification occurs when the opportunity is offered to employees to participate in a new sensemaking and sensegiving process. The process of sensemaking around professional identity allows employees to articulate a revised conception of their role in the organization; this revision demands disconfirmation of the existing interpretative scheme about one's role, and it requires a revised one to take place (Poole, Gioia, and Gray, 1989). After disconfirmation and replacement occur, a new vision of the relationship with the organization can be formalized and disseminated through the process of sensegiving. This process implies that a new meaning of the relationship between the workers and the company is established in the organization (Gioia and Chittipeddi, 1991).

Artistic interventions can create a disruption in the usual way of thinking and feeling of individuals at the workplace, such that they might be able to rethink their professional identity and identification with their organization (Barry and Meisiek, 2010). The discussion of the role of artistic interventions in the identification process is particularly important when we think about phenomena such as layoffs or downsizing within organizations; the same holds for all those things which create instability and break the usual way individuals think about their roles in their organization and the company (Adler, 2015). In addition, the disruptive potential of artistic interventions is fundamental when we think about the need for continuous innovation and ideas' generation to support company performance.

Artistic interventions generate a discontinuance by creating the conditions which cause people to perceive their job differently: when people take part in an artistic intervention, they make an effort to re-discover themselves in artistic contents. The arts rely on tools and beliefs that encourage employees 'seeing more and seeing differently' (Barry and Meisiek, 2010, p. 3), which stands for an opportunity to look at the organizational context in a new and original way, functional to more innovative decision making. Indeed, artistic interventions often involve the creation of a new story to tell through a process of context shifting. Through context shifting, employees gain a different vision of the place they work in, which allows questioning the status quo. If we take the example of corporate art collections, previous studies indicate they are able to intrigue employees, inciting new questions about their professional and personal role (Barry and Meisiek, 2010). When viewing the art, employees have the chance to ask themselves if the work is accurately reflecting organizational values, and their professional and their identity. The presence of the artist can strengthen this process by allowing closer collaboration, continuous interaction and discussion with the artist and among the employees.

This process can be exemplified by the artistic intervention that the artist Danilo Correale[2] did in three companies in Italy, thanks to the promotion and sponsorship of FEC. Danilo Correale organized an artistic performance, lasting six months, named 'The Game',[3] which was an occasion for employees' and artist's self-expressions, in order to share thoughts and feelings related to the ideas of precariousness and instability the companies were experiencing at that moment. In addition, 'The Game', now included in the permanent collection of MADRE museum in Naples, created the opportunity to substitute this sense of precariousness with different values, by encouraging workers to reflect upon their condition in their company and to cope with the crisis their company was living.

'The Game' consisted of a soccer game played by the teams of three companies from the Sienese territory (Tuscany, Italy). It was described by the artist as an 'acting and reacting' platform: each company had a team and participated in a soccer match with three doors, in accordance with a new set of rules, where the values of creativity, generosity, and collaboration had to substitute the values of competition and individualism (e.g., employees donated their free time to discuss and implement the project). The pitch was hexagonal, and each team was assigned to two opposite sides of it. The match was made not of two, as expected for a soccer game, but of three rounds and the final score of each team was based on the conceded goals, rather than on the scored ones. Victory could not be achieved based on how many goals one team scored but in terms of the creative and collaborative actions of participants. Indeed, the last third of the match consisted in a moment of celebration for all teams, regardless of the number of goals achieved. In addition, beyond the soccer match, the intervention consisted of important preparatory phases to plan the design of the soccer field, to produce the uniforms of the three teams, and to provide the set of objects needed for the final performance (posters, anthems, festoons, etc.). The most important part was the set of several encounters between the teams and the artist, which required some months and long hours for effectively sharing thoughts, building empathy and listening to each other's opinions. The teams not only discussed the way and rules the game should have been performed but mostly shared their ideas about the message they wanted the match to transmit.

This artistic intervention needs to be contextualized with respect to the perception the workers have had of their role in their organization, which was threatened by a feeling of loss, inadequacy, and uncertainty about the future. These feelings could be traced back to the fact that the companies and the entire industry had gone through a crisis and that they had experienced a lay off in some cases. The awareness of this condition represents the first phase of the artistic intervention, the moment in which the artist invites the workers to pause and to reflect on their condition, which resulted in a claiming possible threat with respect to their identification in the company (see Phase 1, Table 25.1).

Table 25.1 How the artistic intervention helps to revisit identity and organizational identification: an example based on 'The Game'

Phase 1: awareness of a new condition	Phase 2: art creates a disruption	Phase 3: sensemaking of a new identity and new identification	Phase 4: potential for sensegiving
Workers' professional identity and their sense of identification with their companies are threatened because of recent layoffs and the feeling of instability and uncertainty these events bring	The artistic intervention is organized and presented to the workers, creating a moment of disruption: they can participate to the realization of an art work with a living artist and can borrow from the art world new meanings and metaphors to interpret their current condition	The preparation of the soccer match (discussing, crafting, reflecting among the workers, and between the workers and the artist) and the soccer match itself provide workers with the opportunity to revisit their identity and identification with their company, by relying on the values of team-working, collaboration reciprocal help, and freedom to voice their opinions and concerns	Thanks to the involvement of the companies' top management who supported and endorsed the project, this new meaning of the workers' identity has the potential to be spread out in the companies themselves, especially through all the artifacts (videos, drawings, uniforms) that the artistic interventions has generated

'The Game' helped employees overcome the sense of frustration and alienation connected to this precarious condition, and to find in the values of solidarity and collaboration new ways to reconnect their personal and professional life to that of their organizations. The artist guided the employees, mainly workers, to engage in something unusual that allowed them to express their opinions and concerns about their current condition. This part stands for the phase of disruption (Phase 2, Table 25.1) corresponding to the moment in which the art effectively entered organizational routines. In this phase, the participants borrowed new meaning from the art world to interpret their condition. The workers had the chance to discuss among themselves and with the artist the meaning of this unusual soccer match (where the creativity of each team, rather than its athletic and technical superiority, was going to be rewarded) and to use this soccer game to reevaluate their condition of workers. They had the chance to craft all the materials needed to play the match, to be involved in a creative production relevant to reshaping the meaning of teamwork, and to reflect on their organizational identity (i.e., each team for each company had to decide a name for the team and to create the uniforms). This moment of reflection corresponds to the phase of sensemaking of a new identity (see Phase 3, Table 25.1). The match, in the form of a performative event, took place in December 2013, in a stadium adapted to the three-door structure of the game. The process of preparation and the entire match were filmed and became a medium-length film, presented to the public in the same stadium the year after. The event, the video and the realization of other artifacts were possible thanks to the support and the endorsement by top management; this mechanism contributed to the phase of sensegiving (see Phase 4, Table 25.1).

The artist, who had already realized art works with workers and that had already reflected on the meaning of precariousness connected to the nature of a routinized job, was able to organize a complex intervention where the moments of discussion, of collective reflection and of crafting were as important as the soccer match itself.

The day of the match, nobody won 'the Game', as the main intent of the artistic intervention was not to elect any winner but to stimulate a new reflection on the nature of the relationship between the workers and their company through the expedient of a game. The described process is summarized in Table 25.1.

Artistic interventions and the learning process at the workplace

The role of art in management education has been theorized and investigated for a long time, and training was one of the first areas where art entered different organizational settings, including private and public institutions (e.g., Ladkin, 2008; Austin and Devin, 2003; Taylor, Fisher, and Dufresne, 2002). These contributions have been particularly important to support the presence of art in HR training strategies and to explain how art can support the development of strategic capabilities for the success of a company.

The topic has been considered so important by the academic and business community that more recent contributions have been dedicated to shedding light on how art can foster learning in organizations (Antal, 2013; Purg and Sutherland, 2017). In particular, Antal, Woodilla, and Sköldberg (2016) have specified that artistic interventions can operate by affecting learning at individual, group and organizational levels. Through art, at an individual level, people learn new competences for abstracting, conceptualizing and prototyping ideas, together with a new ability for reflecting on organizational action through the exercise of critical thought. At the team level, people learn how to experience organizational spaces together, and which become places for debating, criticizing and sharing ideas. Artistic interventions allow the development of a new mindset for innovation, strategic thinking and the revitalization of organizational values and culture.

In this paragraph, we integrate literature from training and learner-centered approaches (Keith and Frese, 2005), from aesthetics in organizations (Strati, 2007) and from management education (Adler, 2015; Taylor, Fisher, and Dufresne, 2002) to discuss how to organize an artistic intervention to foster knowledge creation and exchange. This integration is useful to make sense of three pillars that, according to the experience and data we have been collecting so far, are important to explain how artistic interventions can contribute effectively to learning at the workplace. These three pillars to be considered when organizing a training section with an artistic intervention are: relying on positive error framing, building an aesthetic experience, and providing the opportunity for a re-composition of relationships at the workplace.

Positive error framing in training design implies that the learning experience is built in such a way that mistakes are encouraged rather than being punished. The main assumption of this approach is that mistakes are useful to provide information to the learners about how to improve the learning performance. In this way, the learners' autonomy and ability to plan are improved since permitting mistakes increases their ability to explore by themselves the issue at hand; finally, encouraging mistakes can be important to arouse curiosity (Keith and Frese, 2005).

Artistic interventions can be important tools to introduce positive error framing in the training strategy of an organization since the artistic process offers the opportunity to have more than one possibility to perform a certain task in the creation of a work of art. Mistakes have been very often theorized as an integral part of the artistic process, as it allows the artists to investigate their own poetry more deeply and to communicate with their audience more effectively (Vettese, 1996, 2012). As a consequence, the artistic processes characterized by induced mistakes and reflections are able to allow for new idea generation. As such, the presence of the artist during a training session could be an ideal way to introduce a new approach where errors can be considered as an integral part of effective decision making within the organization.

When considering the dimension of the aesthetic experience and aesthetic knowledge, it is relevant to point out that aesthetic knowledge is derived from the senses and particular situations and experiences (Ewenstein and Whyte, 2007, p. 691). It comes from practitioners understanding the look, feel, smell, taste, and sound of things in organizational life. Aesthetic knowledge exists in organizational symbols, as expressions through non-verbal signifiers, and in feelings, sensitivity, and corporal experiences. Artistic interventions are extremely suitable activities to introduce aesthetic knowledge and reflexivity within training since they are able to encourage inductive reasoning above and beyond the usual deductive scheme adopted in the decision making within organizations. Furthermore, artistic interventions assume that the artist, in collaboration with the organizational members, presents physical experiences, especially thanks to their crafting and making activities. The artist brings into the company a heightened opportunity for sensorial perceptions thanks to a wide set of stimuli from music, painting or photographing. Finally, artists help employees to reflect on this sensorial experience and its link with their individual and professional life.

The last dimension to understand the peculiar value of artistic interventions is their potential to recompose and rebuild relationships within the organization. The artistic intervention can be the chance for discovering new ground to explore in working and personal relationships at the workplace since the interventions introduce something that is completely new to the company. It is a new work of art, not seen before, neither by the artist nor by the organization; something unique, and that requires the active contribution of the organizational members for its realization. The production of a work of art helps people who had never collaborated before to meet and to create something distinctive and original together. The participation in this artistic experience has the disruptive potential to create the opportunity to rethink working routines and relationships and to inspire the search of a deeper meaning.

These three concepts can be exemplified by the artistic intervention, named 'VITRIOL',[4] that the artist Andrea Mastrovito[5] designed and implemented within an Italian pharmaceutical company with the sponsorship and the support of FEC. VITRIOL consisted of seven mural 'paintings' the artist realized together with a hundred employees of the company on the company's walls. However, 'painting' is not the right term to describe this collective activity, even though the effect the murals produced looked like they were painted. The artist and the employees first made a drawing on one of the walls in the company; then the wall was not properly painted, but 'peeled off' by the employees till a layer of the wall itself emerged, showing a particular color. The outcome was a drawing tinted and filled with color belonging to the different layers of the wall itself. The drawings represented a subject related to the identity of the company and its business, so they all revolved around the topic of chemistry and alchemy. The drawings were as big as the wall of a manufacturing plant or a conference room. The intervention required one week and around 100 employees working on different shifts. The goal of the company was to organize this artistic intervention within a training initiative aimed at transmitting the concept that an effective result required a team effort and the constant work of each team member.

The artistic intervention was organized so that each team assigned to each wall had a general view of the drawing, and each team member had a particular task to perform. In terms of positive error framing, this activity was particularly powerful: each team member had a task, but the time constraints and the huge size of the work to be realized forced everyone to immediately express their difficulties, delays or mistakes, since this was the only way to get help and to achieve the final goal. The artist and his assistants persisted in this way of working, (which is consistent with the artist's poetry, attitude and execution methods, where trials and errors are an integral part of the artistic process), never punishing any mistakes, but encouraging more of this openness and disposition to voice difficulties immediately. This 'try-and-see-what-happens' approach helped the employees participating in the intervention without any fear and to transfer then this ability to admit mistakes in their daily life. The artistic intervention gave employees the chance to observe that when dealing with a challenging task, the most appropriate strategy was to discuss their own mistakes immediately.

When considering the aesthetic dimension of the training experience to foster learning, it is important to note that VITRIOL generated multiple chances for employees to experience a different way to make decisions and engage in actions. This artistic intervention was physically demanding and required an intense effort on the part of numerous people over a week to be realized. The employees had the chance to experience different feelings, from frustration to satisfaction, and to engage in this experience with their senses fully since the activity required that they touched the wall, that they changed it and that they had both a global and particular view of the drawing they were realizing. In addition, many among the employees worked on the drawing, even doing an extra-shift and not wearing their working clothes, even though they were still within the boundary of their organization. All this set of stimuli provided them the opportunity to know whether the work was done or not and to decide what to do, not only on the basis of the usual routine but also by making reference to their sensorial experience and non-verbal cues. Finally, when considering the importance of restoring a positive climate among people, VITRIOL can work as a suitable example. The artist, the company, and the FEC agreed to build teams with members having different tenure, status, and organizational position. This choice created the feeling that coordination and communication among people do not encounter any barrier, such as hierarchy, during the artistic intervention. In addition, competition between people and individualism would have been completely dysfunctional for the realization of the work of art. In such a context, the artistic intervention became the opportunity for reshaping some relationships and finding new ways of communicating with others for a common goal rather than competing or being stuck due to the obstacles that status rules might create.

Thus, VITRIOL, for its ability to embrace mistakes, to create a sensorial experience and to give people the chance to experiment a new way of communicating and thinking about their relationships, was able to deliver an effective training experience, reflecting the original goal of the company. In the words of one employee: 'during this experience nobody ever explained to me formally that I was been taught about the relevance of individual contribution to teamworking. But I immediately realized by myself that I would have never finished my part without the physical and psychological support from the others . . . someone said 'I can't do it, please you do it for me'. At the workplace, it is not easy to say that you cannot do something, but as another employee acknowledged, when you admitted it, you found the help you needed and 'it was evident that a big task, carried out by a numerous teams, with small details and small mistakes by everyone, resulted in a beautiful thing. In big projects, it is likely to miss the value of the individual contribution, but this was not the case, it was clear to everyone that each of us did his part' (Paolino, Smarrelli, and Carè, 2018, pp. 80–81). The aim of the artistic intervention was to deliver a training experience able to create reflection on the way of working; an employee concluded: 'I discovered how to combine the artistic experience and the scientific knowledge characterizing my job. . . . Now, anytime I join a project, I try to give value to this artistic part' (Paolino, Smarrelli, and Carè, 2018, p. 83).

Artistic interventions to foster innovation

Next, we discuss how artistic interventions can be organized within a company to sustain and encourage innovation by referencing an artistic residency supported by FEC in an Italian company, which can be considered a source of inspiration for product innovation.

The fact that the introduction of art in the company setting can reinforce lateral and creative thinking has been analyzed by the literature focused on art and its connections with individual and organizational learning (e.g., Berthoin Antal, 2013). However, in extant literature, there is also a more direct reference to the link between art and innovation at the workplace, when, for instance, we consider the contributions about the concept of studio or *atelier*, when introduced in organizational settings (Barry and Meisiek, 2015; Meisiek and Barry, 2016). 'It is from the Enlightenment in the 16th century that the studio concept became fully articulated, distinctively combining intellectual curiosity, craft skills, aesthetic expression, and artisan-style production. . . . For both art and design, studios are places for an inquiry into the pernicious problems of business and society, and for creatively expressing the results of the inquiry process' (Barry and Meisiek, 2015, p. 154). In the organizational setting, studios have been created as dedicated and private spaces where employees can experiment and explore ideas and problem-solving issues, by relying on the artistic practices (e.g., for the visual arts, on drawing, filming, painting).

We want to discuss the role of the artistic studio in organizational contexts, such as a permanent residency of an artist in a company. This focus on the residency is important to understand how the creation of a dedicated space for the artists within the company and the continuous interaction between them and the company's employees can be crucial to foster innovation. Indeed, residencies are not usually spent within a company setting, but within an artistic institution. The residency is company-based when an artist works within the organization to complete a full project that the artist and the company agreed upon. In doing so, the artists use company materials and interact with the members of the organization, on a topic of mutual interest.

The relationship between this type of artistic interventions and organizational innovation can be explained in the light of the stream of research based on materiality (e.g., Leonardi, 2012), where materiality represents a whole set of physical and digital spaces and objects encountered in an organizational context. This stream of research is particularly relevant to discuss innovation processes and innovative decision making (Stigliani and Ravasi, 2012), since it assumes that, beyond language, discourses and interpretation, the objects we are surrounded by are vital to articulate new thoughts, formulate new concepts, and propose new courses of action within the organization. Artifacts, such as notes, product prototypes, powerpoint documents, sketches, have been theorized to be protagonist for knowledge creation process and forward thinking and innovation, especially in the design field (e.g., Hargadon and Sutton, 1997). Artifacts are effective ways of storing knowledge, they create the chance for leveraging a company's product history, and they constitute means through which concepts and ideas can be rearranged and projected into the future.

Also, artistic interventions, especially when in the form of a long residency, might generate objects that are useful to rethink through a company's processes and to reorganize previous notions to get inspiration for new strategic thinking, new prototypes, and products. During a residency, an artist introduces a wide range of artifacts, from the preparatory materials (sketches, drawings, prototypes, raw materials, and artist's tools) to the final output of the artistic process. With respect to the usual objects created during production phases in a company setting, the artifacts produced during the artistic residency, while intertwined with the core business of the company, have a deep bond with the art world. We argue that being their nature is so complex, they can work as an even more powerful source of innovative thinking with respect to traditional artifacts.

This concept can be exemplified by the residency the artist Sissi[6] spent in Elica, an Italian company producing kitchen range hoods. As one of the artistic interventions conducted by FEC for Factories, the residency gave birth to three art works, named by the artist 'Aspiranti Aspiratori'[7] (2012). During the residency, the artist was constantly present within the company and was in an ongoing exchange with the participants of the artistic intervention who consisted of technicians in charge of prototyping the hoods before they went into the production phase. The artist created her studio on the shop floor of the company, in the corner of the prototyping room; the studio was made of materials from the production process, and it was meant as a space of both private composition and exchange between the artist and the technicians. For this residency, the artist was required to reflect upon the concept of purification, since the company was thinking of entering a new area of business related to air purification. During the residency, the artist produced numerous artifacts, many of them created by changing and intervening on the shape and on the purpose of tools and objects that already existed at the shop floor. For instance, the artist drew her models of air purifiers on the original documents the technicians used to develop the prototype of a kitchen hood, changing the nature and the purpose of these plans. In addition, while doing this, the artist asked for constant information and feedback to (and from) the technicians, often resulting in them working with their tools in ways that were unrelated to their original functions and in a completely different way with respect to the usual working routines.

Beyond thinking, drawing, and sketching, the artist created from scratch three purifiers out of the ten she had envisioned. To do this, she used materials from the shop floor, again by relying on something that was familiar to the company but completely changing the shape, the look, and the function of these objects. These purifiers were later displayed inside the company, so they could be visible and appreciated as part of the legacy of this artistic intervention. Furthermore, the artist created a video and a book that documented the whole process of ideation, prototyping, selection, and production of the purifiers. These products represented the artifacts where the company and the artist met metaphorically since they collected all the relevant steps the artist did at the shop floor to create her purifiers. On one hand, the book stood for the narrative the artist gave back to the company, as a sensemaking activity she did to document and to build an interpretation of how, where and when her art and poetry had been intertwined with the organizational life. On the other, the video described the aspirators' creation. The artifacts can leave organizational spaces to enter artistic institutions; previous studies show museums are often involved in the final phase of artistic interventions, with both the organization and the artists involved (Berthoin Antal, 2012). In this case, the book was presented at MAMbo – Museo d'Arte Moderna di Bologna, within the IX edition of the Bologna Artelibro Festival 2012; while the artist's personal exhibit was presented the Aike-Dellarco Gallery in Shanghai, in 2013.

These artifacts were not all created by the artist with the explicit purpose of stimulating innovation or knowledge exchange. However, these artefacts were disseminated and made available while the artist was operating, relying on the collaboration of company employees, and they became a source of reflection for the organization. In the words of one the technicians: 'the artist took out our blueprints and she drew on them with her stuff, making shapes that were unusual for us, to design her own sketches for the purifiers. She was using the blueprints in a completely different way from us, the blueprints, they are believed to be 'sacred' materials for prototyping. I was surprised and pushed to see our usual and familiar tool in a different way' (Paolino, Smarrelli, and Carè, 2018, p. 100). This spontaneous reflection, coupled with the availability of the artist and her objects, stimulated a different way of thinking about the company's production processes and about company products themselves. Indeed, after the residency was over, even though the purifier could not be launched as a new line of product, a kitchen hood designed with a mirror was launched by the company. The 'mirroring purifier' was one of the three purifiers the artist decided to realize within her studio and that was also made available in the main building of the company, ultimately acting as a source of inspiration for new product development.

The role of the arts manager in the artistic interventions

Artistic interventions open a new space within art foundations, within business organizations and arts organizations for the role of the arts manager, who should be in charge of conceiving and managing the interventions, of negotiating the conditions and the applications of these collaborations, and in enhancing the integration of art within companies.

The state of the research in the field has highlighted there is a potential role to be filled to make the presence of art and artistic interventions more frequent, more structured and effective at the workplace and promote the presence of the works of art produced with the interventions in public arts institutions. A research carried out on 160 corporate art collections in Italy (Paolino and Bodega, 2016) has illustrated that almost 70% of these art collections are not managed by a full-time employee or a dedicated team, whose background is consistent with the goal of integrating art within the workplace. Most of the time, individuals in charge of the art collection, and all the activities referred to it, are managers in the company officially with a role in corporate communication and marketing, and who are lent part-time to the management of the collection (or they are external consultants, generally trained as art advisors). While the work of these managers has been extremely precious to enhance the role of art in the workplace dynamics, the research has also illustrated that the best-managed collections were those that had a dedicated team or a full-time employee in charge. In these cases, managers in charge of the collections and of the artistic activities of the company were permanent and long-tenured employees either with a background in arts administration or in the humanities, and always identifiable as strongly aware of the processes and history of the company. To improve the effectiveness of art at the workplace, these results pinpoint the importance of a stable managerial role, socialized within the organization, and who is an expert in the art field and in the administrative processes the artistic production requires to be managed and promoted better.

In addition, as previously described and scrutinized, another research stream has specifically clarified the role of 'intermediaries' in artistic interventions, meaning with 'intermediaries' those organizations and individuals 'seeking out artists and organizations, matching them and making contractual arrangements; helping specify the focus of the project; assisting in finding funding; providing a framework to structure the process; addressing conflicts that may emerge; communicating with authorities and the media locally and beyond; monitoring progress; evaluating results and; stimulating cross-fertilization between projects' (Berthoin Antal, 2012, p. 53). It was observed that for corporate art collections, these intermediaries also were usually separated from the organization that requires the artistic interventions.

However, given the strategic values of the activities they carry out and the potential impact they have on the organization, the opportunity for internalizing them and for creating 'arts manager' positions for these activities can be easily envisioned. This internationalization of the intermediaries' activities could be meaningful both for traditional companies and for arts institutions that promote and organize artistic interventions.

When we look at traditional companies, based on the experiences analyzed in this chapter, the role of arts manager at the workplace can go far beyond the previously listed activities of matching, funding, organizing, and communicating. A broader role can be designed for arts managers in organizations investing in art and artistic interventions; this role can include the strategic task of keeping the memory of the interventions, spreading the knowledge coming from them to the whole organization and sustaining innovation and continuous change.

When we look at arts organizations, artistic interventions can be become a part of the institutional activity of a theatre or a museum, to promote and spread art and to raise funding. Examples in Italy can be found in the experience of some extremely important theatres, such as Teatro Litta in Milan, which provides team building activities for companies. While team building could not be properly considered, in the light of the FEC activities we discussed in the chapter, as an authentic artistic intervention, this is a sign that there could be attempts from arts institutions to expand their activities to improve companies' workplace through arts and that this new field will require arts management abilities.

So, either if internalized within a company or an arts organization, or if included within the professions of an intermediary such as a foundation, we propose that beyond the activities Berthoin Antal (2012) specified, the following responsibilities can be referred to the arts manager organizing artistic interventions:

- Integrating art and artistic interventions within the knowledge management process of the company where the artistic intervention takes place: art works within an art collection or produced during artistic interventions should not be left stored in places that are detached from the normal routine of the working life and the daily processes of the organizations. These artefacts, including the prototypes and the documenting materials (books, videos, pictures) should be organized so that they can be available as much as the artefacts from the traditional production process or the history of the company. The responsibility of the arts manager should be that of promoting the presence of artefacts and documents within the formal places and channels through which the organization normally gathers, stores, and changes critical information and knowledge.

- Negotiating the conditions of the arrangement between organizations, artists and other institutions: the organization of an artistic intervention requires various phases and meetings of the parties that may be managers with a different background, employees, artists and other artistic entities. The role of an arts manager in shaping the conditions of a contractual arrangement is crucial; for this reason, the arts manager should help the communication of needs and the relative arrangements among the parties involved in the artistic intervention. Thanks to arts and the business background, the arts manager can make contractual arrangements that meet all involved parties' needs as an intermediary (Berthoin Antal, 2012).

- Being in charge of the company storytelling: artistic interventions have been highlighted as important to change the storytelling around the company for its external and internal audiences (Berthoin Antal, 2012). While this task is usually delegated to the communication department, it is important that the storytelling of artistic interventions be created and narrated by the arts manager, the most knowledgeable and reliable employee to create a narrative of art at the workplace. The main responsibility is that of integrating this storytelling within the history of the company. At the same time, the arts manager needs to understand when it is important to innovate the storytelling and to propose a new trajectory for the company values and identity through different interventions. Last, the arts manager needs to create, when possible, continuity among artistic interventions, so that the deep intents and principles of the company to organize them can always be understood and clear. When considering the artistic interventions organized by arts organization, the storytelling has to be also developed internally. In Italy, the management side of arts is still in its infancy when we look at its application in our institutions. To start artistic interventions could be even a disruptive for the organizing institutions and deserves to be contextualized concerning its missions, values, and audience.

Managerial implications and the 'dark side' of artistic interventions

In this chapter, we have discussed and presented how artistic interventions can be particularly beneficial to organizational development and performance by highlighting how they can impact the nature of the relationship between the employee and the organization, the learning processes within a company, and how they can foster innovation. We illustrated the case of artistic interventions, supported and sponsored by one of the main Italian private foundations, FEC, whose mission is spreading the value of contemporary art to support company identity, forward thinking and performance.

In Table 25.2, we illustrate the recommendations to guide the managerial actions when thinking and organizing artistic interventions at the workplace. These recommendations are generally valuable when artistic interventions take place in the organization, but we try to connect them with the three particular issues we discussed in the chapter. Given the increasing interest of organizations in achieving the benefits of artistic interventions (e.g., Purg and Sutherland, 2017), the growing participation of artistic institutions in the promotion of the outputs, and the development of stronger networks bridging different actors involved, we first address general recommendations for the organization aiming to undertake an artistic intervention, and we later specify the role of the arts managers to support identification processes, learning and innovation by referring to different phases characterizing their implementation.

Table 25.2 shows that, in order to support identification processes, the organization should first reflect upon its current values and future needs; the role of the arts manager in this first phase is to contribute to the selection of an artistic project that can challenge the people in the organization to reflect on a currently relevant issue. The second row shows the recommendations to include an artistic intervention aimed at supporting learning. In a first phase, the organization includes within the HR training an intervention that is coherent with the latest trends in management and adult learning. The role of the arts manager in this phase is to contribute to the selection and the structuring of the proper training intervention, by integrating its competences from management and the arts and by involving an artist open to embrace mistakes during the process. Later, while the artist should be allowed to create dissonance, the role of the arts manager is to mediate the actors involved and to act as a role model in embracing the creation of dissonance at the workplace. Last, with respect to artistic interventions with the aim to support innovation, the crucial part is the creation of an artistic residency within the organizational walls; the role of the arts manager is to share the need for innovation and change by inviting and sustaining the discussion on relevant business issues and by selecting the artist that is more capable of introducing groundbreaking innovation through the arts. Once the residency has started, the role of the arts manager is to manage these organizational spaces by integrating the needs of the artist with organizational practices. As summarized in the last column of each intervention presented in Table 21.2, the arts manager should always be in charge of the storytelling not only inside the organization but also with external institutions.

Beyond the implications and advantages discussed so far, extant research and practice has also highlighted the possible risks and negative effects that artistic interventions can produce at the workplace. The drawbacks can be summarized in three main categories:

1. The foundation/the company/the arts organization organizes artistic interventions without positioning them within the broader picture of the corporate values and performance. One of the main implications is that artistic interventions are interpreted by employees as outdoor or team building activities, meant more to generate an immediate sense of affection toward the organization or a team, than for developing strategic capabilities. In this

Table 25.2 Recommendations to support an effective implementation of artistic interventions, to foster identification, learning and innovation

	The company values system	Long term approach	The promotion of a 'sensorial' experience
To support identification processes **The role of the arts manager to support identification processes**	Before articulating the artistic intervention, the organization should reflect upon its current values and how and whether they are going to change in the future. This reflection is fundamental to select an artistic project that can challenge the organizational population. The aim is to make them think about the new values and the new course of action the organization wants to take and to build a sense out of them. To contribute to the selection of an artistic project that is able to challenge the people in the organization to reflect on a current relevant issue.	After the artistic intervention, it is important not to push for an immediate check of the outcome of the intervention in terms of identification (for instance through the results of the organizational climate survey, in terms of commitment and willingness to stay in the company). The stimuli the artistic intervention can provide to substitute the current values with new and alternative ones need time to consolidate and to be spread across the company. Especially in crisis times, pushing for an indicator to check the effectiveness of the intervention would only emphasize a utilitarian approach and being detrimental to the elaboration of new values. To be in charge of the storytelling inside the company and with external institutions, without pushing to immediately check an economic outcome. When the artistic intervention is organized by an art organization, this long term approach has to be nurtured also internally to give the organization the time to grasp the implications of this project for the theatre/museum life.	The artistic intervention has to propose a different way of processing information, stimulating aesthetic reflexivity and knowledge creation. This implies that, instead of deductive reasoning and traditional rational decision making, the artistic intervention stimulates an
	The approach to errors in the poetry of the artist	**The creation of dissonance**	
To support learning **The role of the arts manager to support learning**	It is important that, when the artistic intervention is included within the HR training, the structure of the intervention includes a dialogue about the recent trends in management and adult learning. The acceptance of mistakes during training has been demonstrated to foster the acquisition of complex competences and to be more effective for the transfer of	To foster learning by introducing a new way of thinking in the organization, it is fundamental that the artistic intervention creates a dissonance – a break in the organizational population language, objects, processes the organizational population is used to. So, the objects, the words, the concepts the artist is going to rely on need to create a disruption, a 'messy' area, which can later support the involvement in the artistic experience and the experimentation of new frames and new styles of reasoning.	

inductive process, relying on data collection approaches based on the five senses stimulation.

these competences on the job. Thus, if the company is aiming to reflect and transfer competences, such as team dynamics and project organization, it is recommended that the artist is open to embrace mistakes in its poetry and work and to accept them authentically.

The arts manager need to be both an expert in training processes and to be able to understand how the research of one artist could be more or less suitable for discussing errors, dissonance and promoting an aesthetic experience.

To support innovation
The role of the arts manager to support innovation

Opportunity to intervene on a relevant business/organizational issue

If process or product innovation is the goal of the company, the artist should be invited to work on a precise and relevant business issue. For example, the brainstorming for the launch of a new product or the renewal of a particular production/ideation phase rather than, for instance, working on more general and organizational issues such company identity or training strategies.

Being located in this area, the artist intervention could be focused on a specific matter and contribute to it more explicitly.

To share the need for innovation and change by inviting and sustaining the discussion on relevant business issues.

To contribute to the selection of an artist whose poetry includes the discussion of change and innovation.

The artistic residency/the art studio format

The residency is the ideal format to contribute to process/product innovation, since it implies a long stay of the artists within the company and the opportunity for them to intervene on company spaces and objects, in a mutual exchange and in a process of slow and reciprocal familiarization between the artist and the organizational population.

To manage the organizational spaces in which the residency is taking place, by integrating the needs of the artists with organizational practices.

The material production

The format of the residency and of the studio are important because they generate the chance to create multiple and intermediate artefacts at the interspace between the world of art and the organizational settings.

These artefacts are essential to leave a 'heritage' of the artist intervention that can be a source of reflection and inspiration to organize new ideas and concepts eventually.

To build the storytelling around the artefacts, inside and outside the company.

way, the employees miss the value of artistic interventions as the chance to look at and to think about their organization in an unedited way and to propose an initiative to change and improve their work processes. In particular, Berthoin, Debucquet, and Frémeaux (2017) have shown how the lack of visible support from top managers and of sensemaking orientation generate interventions of little added value.

2. The artistic interventions can generate a feeling of *muteness* (Taylor, 2002). It might happen that the art process and the artist do not manage to connect with employees' work and daily activities; or that employees do not manage to articulate the meaning of the artistic intervention, remaining metaphorically *mute*. The art work and the process are too distant to be perceived as powerful means to reflect upon the organizational life and employees find it impossible to interpret the experience and its implications. In these cases, it is likely that this impossibility to articulate their thinking on the artistic intervention is followed by a reinforcement of the 'old' stereotype of the relationship between art and daily work, seen as opposite and pertaining to the different realms of creativity and standardization.

3. Once the artistic intervention is over or the art work is removed from the organizational space, this absence can generate a sense of emptiness. This is especially true when artistic interventions had the chance to change the organizational physically, to influence the patterns of interpretation employees were used too, and to change the contents of their conversations and the way they approached their daily working tools. Both in the case of muteness and emptiness, the role of the arts manager, as depicted in the previous paragraph, can be crucial to support employees' interpretation and to create a feeling of continuity between interventions.

In this chapter, we explored the nature of artistic interventions with the aim to highlight their benefits and the possible criticalities for organizations; therefore, we framed the role of the art manager for the implementation and the success of these interventions and we provided recommendations and made a list of the possible drawbacks.

We hope this chapter will contribute to stimulating interest in introducing artistic intervention in organizations. Indeed, it is important to create opportunities for accumulating more evidence about the implications of artistic interventions, in order to advance our knowledge about how these interventions should be implemented at the workplace. Finally, we believe that a more extensive use of artistic interventions could enlarge the role of arts managers both in the for-profit and in non-profit organizations.

Notes

1 For a full view of the activities of the foundation: www.fondazionecasoli.org/
2 For a full profile of the artist and of his work: www.danilocorreale.com/
3 For a full description of 'The Game': www.danilocorreale.com/the-game/; 'The Game', Artist Book, 2014, produced by FEC
4 For a full view of the project VITRIOL: www.andreamastrovito.com/index2.php?pagina=works&id_cat=0013&id_prod=00000167; VITRIOL, Artist book, 2016, produced by FEC
5 For a full profile of the artist and of his work: www.andreamastrovito.com/index.php
6 For a full profile of the artist and her work: https://cargocollective.com/sissi
7 Aspiranti Aspiratori' means literally: 'aspiring aspirators'. The artist was asked by the company to work on the concept of air purification and she decided to name the all project with this pun. For a complete review of 'Aspiranti Aspiratori': www.fondazionecasoli.org/attivita/fec-for-factories/fec-for-factories-aspiranti-aspiratori-di-sissi-2012/.

References

Adler, N.J. (2006). The arts & leadership: Now that we can do anything, what will we do? *Academy of Management Learning & Education*, 5(4), pp. 486–499.

———. (2015). Finding beauty in a fractured world: Art inspires leaders – leaders change the world. What inspires the academy: Book reviews and beyond? *Academy of Management Review*, 40(39), pp. 480–494.

Albert, S. and Whetten, D.A. (1985). Organizational identity. *Research in Organizational Behavior*, 7, pp. 263–285.

Antal, A.B. and Strauß, A. (2013). Artistic interventions in organizations: Finding evidence of values-added. *Creative Clash Report, WZB*.

Ashforth, B.E. and Mael, F. (1989). Social identity theory and the organization. *Academy of Management Review*, 14(1), pp. 20–39.

Austin, R.D. and Devin, L. (2003). *Artful making: What managers need to know about how artists work*. Pearson Education Inc., publishing as Financial Times Prentice Hall, Upper Saddle River, NJ.

Barry, D. and Meisiek, S. (2010). Seeing more and seeing differently: Sensemaking, mindfulness, and the workarts. *Organization Studies*, 31(11), pp. 1505–1530.

———. (2015). Discovering the business studio. *Journal of Management Education*, 39(1), pp. 153–175.

Berthoin Antal, A. (2009). *A research framework for evaluating the effects of artistic interventions in organizations*. Gothenburg: TILLT Europe.

———. (2012). Artistic intervention residencies and their intermediaries: A comparative analysis. *Organizational Aesthetics*, 1(1), pp. 44–67.

———. (2013). Art-based research for engaging not-knowing in organizations. *Journal of Applied Arts & Health*, 4(1), pp. 67–76.

Berthoin Antal, A., Debucquet, G., and Frémeaux, S. (2017). When top management leadership matters: Insights from artistic interventions. *Journal of Management Inquiry*. doi: 1056492617726393.

Berthoin Antal, A., Woodilla J. and Sköldberg, U.L. (2016). *Artistic interventions in organizations*. In: U.L. Sköldberg, J. Woodilla and A. Berthoin Antal, eds., *Artistic interventions in organizations: Research, theory and practice*. Abingdon: Routledge, pp. 3–17.

Cole, M.S. and Bruch, H. (2006). Organizational identity strength, identification, and commitment and their relationships to turnover intention: Does organizational hierarchy matter? *Journal of Organizational Behavior: The International Journal of Industrial, Occupational and Organizational Psychology and Behavior*, 27(5), pp. 585–605.

Darsø, L. (2004). *Artful creation: Learning-tales of arts-in-business*. Samfundslitteratur; UK ed. edition.

Ewenstein, B. and Whyte, J. (2007). Beyond words: Aesthetic knowledge and knowing in organizations. *Organization Studies*, 28(5), pp. 689–708.

Gioia, D.A. and Chittipeddi, K. (1991). Sensemaking and sensegiving in strategic change initiation. *Strategic Management Journal*, 12(6), pp. 433–448.

Hargadon, A. and Sutton, R.I. (1997). Technology brokering and innovation in a product development firm. *Administrative Science Quarterly*, 42(4), pp. 716–749.

Keith, N. and Frese, M. (2005). Self-regulation in error management training: Emotion control and meta-cognition as mediators of performance effects. *Journal of Applied Psychology*, 90(4), 677.

Ladkin, D. (2008). Leading beautifully: How mastery, congruence and purpose create the aesthetic of embodied leadership practice. *The Leadership Quarterly*, 19(1), pp. 31–41.

Leonardi, P.M. (2012). Materiality, sociomateriality, and socio-technical systems: What do these terms mean? How are they different? Do we need them. In: P.M. Leonardi, B.A. Nardi, and J. Kallikinos, eds., *Materiality and organizing: Social interaction in a technological world*. Oxford: Oxford University Press, pp. 25–42.

Mael, F.A. and Ashforth, B.E. (1995). Loyal from day one: Biodata, organizational identification, and turnover among newcomers. *Personnel Psychology*, 48(2), pp. 309–333.

Meisiek, S. and Barry, D. (2016). Organizational studios: Enabling innovation. In: *Artistic interventions in organizations: Research, theory and practice*/[ed] Ulla Johansson Sköldberg, Jill Woodilla, Ariane Berthoin Antal, Abingdon: Routledge, pp. 225–238.

Paolino, C. and Bodega, D. (2016). *Corporate Collecting in Italy*. Unpublished research report.

Paolino, C., Smarrelli, M., and Carè, D. (2018). *Innovare l'impresa con l'arte: Il metodo della Fondazione Ermanno Casoli*. Milano: EGEA.

Poole, P.P., Gioia, D.A., and Gray, B. (1989). Influence modes, schema change, and organizational transformation. *The Journal of Applied Behavioral Science*, 25(3), pp. 271–289.

Purg, D. and Sutherland, I. (2017). Why art in management education? Questioning meaning. *Academy of Management Review*, 42(2), pp. 382–396.

Riketta, M. (2005). Organizational identification: A meta-analysis. *Journal of Vocational Behavior*, *66*(2), pp. 358–384.

Schiuma, G. (2011). *The value of arts for business*. Cambridge: Cambridge University Press.

Stigliani, I. and Ravasi, D. (2012). Organizing thoughts and connecting brains: Material practices and the transition from individual to group-level prospective sensemaking. *Academy of Management Journal*, 55(5), pp. 1232–1259.

Strati, A. (2007). Sensible knowledge and practice-based learning. *Management Learning*, 38(1), pp. 61–77.

Sutherland, I. and Purg, D. (2010). Arts-based leadership development at the IEDC-Bled School of Management. *Business Leadership Review*, 7(4), pp. 34–40.

Taylor, S.S. (2002). Overcoming aesthetic muteness: Researching organizational members' aesthetic experience. *Human Relations*, 55(7), pp. 821–840.

Taylor, S.S. and Ladkin, D. (2009). Understanding arts-based methods in managerial development. *Academy of Management Learning & Education*, 8(1), pp. 55–69.

Taylor, S.S., Fisher, D., and Dufresne, R.L. (2002). The aesthetics of management storytelling: A key to organizational learning. *Management Learning*, 33(3), pp. 313–330.

Vettese, A. (1996/2012). *Capire l'arte contemporanea: dal 1945 ad oggi*. Umberto Allemandi eamp, C.; Prima edizione (First Edition), Torino, Italy.

26

EXPLORING INTERNATIONAL FUNDRAISING FOR THE ARTS – CROSS-BORDER PHILANTHROPY FOR CULTURAL ORGANIZATIONS

Renate Buijze

Introduction

Under the influence of globalization, international transactions of goods, services, and capital have increased. The activities of arts organizations and their audiences are not exempted from this trend. Tourists travel from far and abroad to visit the world's heritage sites. Collections of renowned museums travel abroad for exhibits and so do performing arts companies. This increase in international activities has an effect on the financing of arts organizations, as their audience, and thus their potential donors, stem from different countries.

It is vital for many arts organizations to attract gifts, as the income they generate from ticket sales and other commercial activities is too limited to finance their activities. Therefore, arts organizations solicit other sources of income. One of the various sources of income for arts organizations is individual donations (Pommerehne and Frey, 1990). The individual donors are found both in the own country of the arts organization, as well as abroad. However, how do arts organizations reach these foreign donors?

Focus lies on raising philanthropic gifts among individuals, where 'philanthropic gifts' refers to voluntary financial donations (Bekkers, Schuyt, and Gouwenberg, 2015). Throughout the chapter, 'donation' and 'gift' are used interchangeably to refer to the act of making a contribution in cash or in kind with a value that is disproportionately large compared to the tangible benefits for the person who makes this contribution. Furthermore, the benefit must go beyond one's own family, which characteristic I derive from the definition of 'charitable giving' by Bekkers and Wiepking (2011).

Fundraising for the arts

Research has mainly focused on donors, and far less attention has been paid to fundraising (Breeze and Scaife, 2015). This is despite the fact that we know that the majority of donations is in response to a solicitation; the more opportunities an individual has to give, the more likely they are to give (Bekkers and Wiepking, 2011, p. 23; Breeze and Scaife, 2015, pp. 607–609).

Based on older research from the 1980s and 1990s, we know that effort put into fundraising pays off well for museums, with ratios varying from 1:2 to 1:7 (Heilbrun and Gray, 2001, pp. 212–213). This underlines the importance of solicitation and fundraising. Luckily, the sector recognizes this, and fundraising is becoming more professional and professionalized (Breeze and Scaife, 2015, p. 587).

Prerequisite for philanthropy is that individuals are aware that there is a need. Non-profit organizations and their fundraisers, as well as the media, have an important role to play here (Bekkers and Wiepking, 2011, pp. 20–23). According to Dietz and Keller (2016), the four fundamental issues donors care about, and thus key to successful fundraising, are that:

1 Donations are spent correctly
2 The organization is reputable
3 The organization's mission is sound
4 Contributions make a difference

What it mainly boils down to, therefore, is trust in the organization (Breeze and Scaife, 2015, p. 590). When it comes to raising funds abroad, the question is of course, how to ensure donors have trust in the organization if they are not in the proximity of the organization?

Most arts organizations provide their donors with a range of benefits (Heilbrun and Gray, 2001, p. 264). These benefits can increase donations, as shown by a study on gifts to the English National Opera (Buraschi and Cornelli, 2002), but also engaging donors with the organization helps increase loyalty. 74% of a representative sample of US donors say that attending an event, has a positive effect on their likelihood to donate (Dietz and Keller, 2016). Around the world, hosting events is one of the most frequently used methods to raise funds (Breeze and Scaife, 2015). Volunteering for an event has a similar effect to fundraising events, and 73% of volunteers stated that it increased their likelihood to donate (Dietz and Keller, 2016). Both organizing events for potential foreign benefactors, as well as engaging them as volunteers is more challenging than when an organization focusses on its local community to attract benefactors.

This chapter explores the significance of international fundraising as one of the sources of income. It explores which strategies arts organizations use when they try to attract foreign benefactors. Other questions that are answered are the following. Do arts organizations engage in international fundraising? How does an arts organization set up international fundraising?

Methodology

As part of a larger research on cross-border giving to the arts and more specific the tax incentives involved, a first exploratory research was conducted on international fundraising among arts organizations (Buijze, 2017). Thirty-six case studies were made (see Appendix 1), in order to obtain insight in cross-border fundraising, its specific context, complexity and particular nature (Bryman, 2008, pp. 52–53, 697; Yin, 2003, pp. 1–9). The case studies consist of document analysis of annual reports, websites and media coverage of arts organizations and semi-structured interviews with the person(s) responsible for international fundraising at the arts organizations.

The organizations were selected through a non-probability sampling strategy, to ensure a variety of organizations was included. The organizations vary according to (1) discipline, (2) type of organization, (3) size and (4) location. All organizations, however, are of some international relevance and knowledge is available among employees of the arts organization on cross-border philanthropy. The organization has either received donations from abroad or made a serious attempt to raise funds abroad. All selected arts organizations are public benefit organizations in their country of residence. The organizations are located in Austria, Denmark, France, Germany, Italy, the Netherlands, the United Kingdom, and the United States. Table 26.1 displays the sample according to discipline and type of organization.

Table 26.2 depicts the sample according to the size of the organization, with the annual budget as its main indicator. The articles by Chang (2010) and Frey (1998) served as anchor points to group the arts organizations included in this research according to their size.

The strand of literature on cross-border fundraising is limited. Therefore, the main source of information to gain insight in the practice, context and particular nature of international fundraising were the semi-structured interviews. Key informants were employees of arts organizations responsible for fundraising among (foreign) private donors. These persons work with foreign donors and, therefore, are the persons within the arts organizations with the most knowledge on international fundraising. The function of those responsible for fundraising among private donors differs across arts organizations. The majority of arts organizations have a fundraiser or development department, but in some arts organizations, the managing director is responsible for raising funds. Job titles varied from 'director', 'manager friends', 'membership consultant', 'head of funding', 'coordination of international friends', 'head of development', 'associate development officer' to 'senior deputy director of external affairs'. For the sake of readability, the job titles were limited to two categories: 'director' and 'fundraiser'. Regardless of the job title and responsibilities, the interviewees were always those within the organization responsible for individual cross-border donations. In a few cases, multiple people within the organization were interviewed. Each employee of an arts organization who provided information was assigned the number of the arts organization in order to anonymize them. If there were multiple respondents from one organization with the same function, an affix was added.

In total, 47 employees from 36 different arts organizations were interviewed.[1] All interviews were recorded and transcribed according to the 'system for simple transcription' (Dresing, Pehl,

Table 26.1 Arts organizations by type

	Fixed location	Festival	Network organisation	Mobile organisations	Total amount organisations
Fine arts	3, 4, 8, 10, 13, 14, 18, 19, 22, 23, 24, 25, 29, 30, 32, 33, 34, 36	21	16		20
Performing arts	28	5, 27, 35		2, 7, 9, 12, 15	9
Cultural heritage	1, 6, 11, 26		17, 20, 31		7
Total amount	23	4	4	5	37

Table 26.2 Survey organizations by annual budget size

	Annual budget	Cases of arts organisations	Total amount of organisations
Small	<EUR 5,000,000	2, 4, 11, 14, 16, 17, 19, 26, 29	9
Medium	EUR 5,000,0000–EUR 19,999,999	1, 3, 5, 6, 8, 12, 15, 23, 24, 31, 33	11
Major	EUR 20,000,000–EUR 49,999,999	7, 13, 18, 20, 21, 30, 35	7
Superstar	>EUR 50,000,000	9, 10, 22, 25, 27, 28, 32, 34, 36	9

and Schmieder, 2015). They were analyzed with the software for qualitative analysis, 'Atlas TI'. Pragmatic coding resulted in 889 codes, which were clustered into specific topics. Later interpretation rounds uncovered patterns. Reoccurring observations, as well as remarkable observations, were described and form the basis of this chapter.

The significance of international fundraising for arts organizations

The majority of arts organizations only receive incidental gifts from abroad and do not actively engage in international fundraising. For those organizations that do engage in international fundraising, it is something their organization either engages in alongside domestic fundraising or the organization does not distinguish between domestic and international fundraising and it receives income from both domestic and foreign donors. None of the 36 arts organizations researched engage in international fundraising without engaging in domestic fundraising. In this sense, international fundraising a relatively small phenomenon in comparison to philanthropy as a whole, as it is not a primary source of income, but an additional source of income. Still, even those organizations that do not actively aim at international fundraising are faced with donations coming from abroad.

Even though arts organizations do not proactively raise funds abroad, they may still receive donations from abroad. Often this concerns incidental gifts or annual gifts by one or a few foreign donors. A large number of arts organizations in the sample receive only incidental gifts from abroad. Fundraiser 18 explains that the majority of the foreign donors live in the city where the arts organization is located. She, however, does not see any use in proactive international fundraising among individuals. She says, "Well, because actually, we do not see why people who do not live here would support us." For other organizations, it is a matter of a lack of capacity within the organization, as In-house accountant 33 says when she's asked, why they do not pursue more international donors, after receiving a major gift from abroad: "Unfortunately, that was a single occurrence and we do not have anyone within our organization that solicits gifts from individuals in other countries."

Despite arts organizations not proactively raising funds abroad, they might have structures in place that facilitate foreign donors who spontaneously give with a tax benefit. Arts organizations 6, 23, 24, and 25 are examples of other arts organizations that do not actively raise funds in the US, but all have a structure that allows American taxpayers to donate to them with a tax benefit. The arts organizations either have an American friends organization or they are registered with an intermediary charity. These structures were mainly initiated upon the request of a spontaneous donor or in response to a cross-border donation received. Now that the structures exist, the arts organizations receive incidental donations through these structures of anywhere from USD 5,000 to 30,000 a year, but there is no steady flow of income. Arts organization six, for example, does not actively engage in activities in the US but receives USD 20,000 a year on average through its American friends organization.

Initial steps in international fundraising

For some arts organizations, the existence of a structure that solves the barriers to cross-border giving becomes a reason to start proactively raising funds abroad. If they see that spontaneous gifts are made via the structure, this is an indication for them that it might pay off to make an effort for international fundraising. Arts organization 24, for example, established an American friends organization for a gift that it received from the US. After several years of just maintaining the American friends organization, arts organization 24 decided to actively raise funds in the US.

The exploration time between the initial thought of raising funds abroad and the actual act of raising funds abroad is rather long. Fundraiser 34B specified this for international corporate fundraising. He started exploring the opportunity of raising funds among international corporations in 2009. Only after two years, in 2011, arts organization 34 established an international corporate support group. For some arts organizations it is also a matter of waiting for the right opportunity to come along. Among the fundraisers of arts organization ten, the idea of raising funds abroad was present long before they started raising funds abroad. They waited until some of the artworks of arts organization ten travelled abroad before setting up international fundraising.

For fundraiser 21, an opportunity arose when his organization hired an artistic director with working experience in various countries. The artistic director had a group of curators from around the world to advise her, each with their network of people interested in the topic of the organizations among which fundraiser 21 could raise funds. He sent out a letter to these people, in which he explained that he was searching for supporters. This resulted in eight memberships, after which a second letter was sent out in which it was announced that an international circle of friends had been established and people were invited to join. This led to substantial growth in the number of memberships.

The plans to raise funds abroad are often much more ambitious than what is eventually done. Fundraiser 15, for example, says, "and so we have tried to set up an international friends circle in each of these cities. From [home country], this is extremely difficult, because it is so far away. Singapore . . ., Saint-Petersburg, New York and we were eager to go to Sao Paulo. What is left of these plans is that we said: we will create opportunities to give international [donors opportunities], but we will not do it per city." Fundraiser 15 now focusses on New York, since the arts organization has a large circle of people it knows in New York.

There are more arts organizations within the sample that want to raise funds abroad. However, not all of them are currently doing so. This stems from different reasons. Some arts organizations first want to better establish themselves before raising funds abroad, such as the relatively young arts organization 14, which was established three years before the interview was held. Other arts organizations first want to cultivate potential local donors. Arts organization three, for example, wanted to develop its local and national support further and streamline the development department − which had only been established three years before the time of this research − before raising funds abroad. Finally, raising funds abroad is not a straightforward task without challenges. It requires investment before funds can be attracted. Therefore, it does not seem to be the first option for organizations that want to increase funding. If funds can be gathered more easily, arts organizations usually do not proceed with their idea of raising funds abroad.

Reasons for arts organizations to raise funds abroad

The main reason arts organizations start raising funds abroad is that they are in need of an alternative or additional source of income. Cross-border donations can compensate for a decrease in domestic funding from individuals, corporations or the government, but also for a decrease in other sources of income. When there is, for example, an economic downturn in one country but other countries are doing well, cross-border fundraising can provide interesting opportunities.

As European governments decrease their subsidies and arts organizations become more independent of governments, arts organizations search for alternative sources of income. This makes them more dependent on private funding. Several Dutch arts organizations explicitly mention in their annual report that support from these friends organizations is vital as they face subsidy cuts in the Netherlands. Arts organization 24 sees its American friends organization as a new way of obtaining funds to compensate for the budget cuts on arts and culture by the government and to supplement the income it receives from the government, foundations, and companies in its own country. For arts organization 12, subsidy cuts were not the reason to start raising funds among individuals. The arts organization had already decided to start raising funds among individuals before the subsidy cuts started. The subsidy cuts, however, increased the urgency of fundraising among individuals and was a push factor to start raising funds among foreign individuals.

International fundraising is not solely a response to a decrease in government subsidies; interviewees also report that it is an alternative to corporate support. The weakening of the economy in the residence country of arts organization 34 in 2008, due to the financial crisis, led to a decrease in corporate support. In 2009 arts organization 34 started looking at stronger economies. In these countries, the arts organization started to raise funds in order to compensate for the decrease in domestic corporate support.

A risk of the fast implementation of international fundraising in response to a decrease in another source of income is that it leads to *ad hoc* decisions and a lack of long-term strategy. A downside of sudden subsidy cuts is that fundraising among individuals is suddenly implemented in an unprofessional manner. Fundraiser 12 mentions that because of the unprofessional implementation of fundraising among individuals, a large number of counter-benefits are offered. This threatens the long-term benefit of individual fundraising.

International fundraising is also used as an additional source of income. Arts organization 28 started to raise funds abroad because its general manager wanted to launch a new initiative and the organization had to increase its income to realise the new initiative. For fine arts organizations, special projects such as exhibitions abroad or exhibitions of foreign artists, often create the need and desire to raise additional funds. When domestic sources are exhausted, and additional funding is necessary, foreign funding can provide a solution. However, when other sources of income are available that require less of an investment, these are preferred.

During the process of recruiting interviewees, I quite frequently came across fundraisers who wanted to raise funds abroad, but in the end, they did not engage in it. When I spoke with a fundraiser in the fall of 2014, for example, she was preparing for an exhibition of an American artist. She mentioned that she wanted to raise funds in the US for this exhibition. A year later, the exhibition was held. When I then asked her about the fundraising in the US, she replied that in the end, she did not raise funds abroad for this exhibition, as she found a main corporate sponsor in the home country.[2] I also came across several cases where fine arts organizations had exhibitions abroad, but refrained from raising funds abroad, as the profit margin on their foreign exhibitions were large and there was no urgency to attract additional funds.[3] Arts organization eight is one such museum. When an exhibition travelled to the US, Japan, and Italy, the organization decided not to raise funds in Italy, as the exhibition was there for only ten weeks and there was a large profit margin on the exhibition. This made it unnecessary to raise funds in Italy. In the US and Japan, however, the organization did make an effort to raise funds. Arts organization eight came upon several challenges, especially in Japan, where its fundraising efforts did not turn out to be successful.

In exceptional cases, a domestic donor incentivises arts organizations to raise funds abroad. Arts organization 31 had a major donor who supported it for ten years in a row with ten million USD annually. One of the requirements of the donor was that the arts organization matched his grant with foreign funds, whether private, governmental or corporate funding. After ten years, however, when the grant expired, there was no replacement for the major donor. Fundraiser 31 says, "And ideally we would have said, in years five to ten we would have been busy to replace it, but inevitably, I don't know. . . . That was kind of beyond my role. But it was a little baffling to me why yeah . . . I think it was a little bit challenging to the organization."

Strategies used when raising funds

Arts organizations that raise funds abroad use different strategies to attract foreign benefactors. Among the arts organizations researched, three strategies can be distinguished: (1) embracing grassroots initiatives by foreign donors; (2) arts organizations focus on one or a few foreign countries and set up friends circles in these countries; and (3) arts organizations have a friends circle at their home location specially-dedicated to international supporters from all over the world.

One arts organization may use a combination of these strategies for different countries. Arts organization 20, for instance, raises funds in France through grassroots initiatives, as well as focussing on several other specific countries where it set up friends circles.

Embracing grassroots initiatives by foreign donors

Spontaneous cross-border gifts received by arts organizations, as discussed earlier, illustrated that it is not always the arts organization that takes the initiative to attract cross-border gifts. Instead, foreign donors sometimes find the organization, are eager to contribute and are even occasionally willing to take the initiative to raise funds for the foreign arts organization. Often it concerns donors with a strong involvement in the content of the arts organization or with a close relationship with the location of the arts organization.

Arts organization 20, for instance, has a donor in France who wanted to start the French friends of arts organization 20. Arts organization 20 was, however, reluctant to embrace this initiative. The underlying reason was that arts organization 20 in the US and the UK experienced that having a formal foreign friends organization is labour intensive. Instead, arts organization 20, together with the French donor, decided to set up an association and first see how this would develop. The arts organization made an effort to advertise it on its website and to facilitate the French donor with the necessary information. The donor managed to attract a modest group of members. If it turned out to be a successful initiative, arts organization 20 would commit to further formalising the French friends. As it was only set up three months before the interview, the fundraisers of arts organization 20 could not yet evaluate it. Earlier, arts organization 20 had collaborated with Swiss donors in a similar manner. There, some people wanted to set up an organization to support arts organization 20. They arranged everything themselves, even coming up with the needed amount of CHF 50,000 to set up the legal entity in Switzerland.

Yet another example is that of the Swiss friends of arts organization seven. That was initiated by two befriended couples who originate from the home country of arts organization seven but moved to Switzerland. When they were still living in the home country of arts organization seven, they were regular attendants of its concerts. After moving to Switzerland, they remained in touch with the fundraiser of arts organization seven. During one of their conversations, the topic of establishing a support group in Switzerland came up. They organized an event, and these Swiss fans of arts organizations established the legal entity. Since then, the Swiss friends of arts organization seven has grown into a group with 60 major donors. One strategy is thus to collaborate with foreign benefactors and enthusiasts for the arts organization to set up a friends organization abroad.

Foreign friends circles in specific countries

Other arts organizations do not await the initiative of donors to raise funds abroad. Instead, they take action to raise funds abroad. Arts organizations use a strategy in which the focus lies on one or a few specific countries, which are selected with care. In these countries, the arts organizations actively try to create a group of benefactors by establishing (often formal) friends circles in these countries. At the location of these friends circles, activities are undertaken to build the relationship with the foreign benefactors and thank them for their support. From the interviews, it came to light that the majority of arts organizations initially focus on one country. Later on, they might add several countries to this selection. The maximum number of countries on which an arts organization in this research focussed on was five. In the selection of countries, arts organizations tend to look at the countries where there is a large support base for the arts organization, but also at countries with which the organization has some relationship based on which it can justify the fundraising abroad and create a case for support.

Foreign countries where a large support base is expected are selected based on the size of the audience from the specific country. Furthermore, arts organizations tend to look at the existing network of contacts with peers and potential donors. The presence of emigrants and expatriates from the home country of the arts organization are also taken into account to determine the size of the support base.

Countries with which an arts organization has a certain relationship, often based on the content of the art it produces or presents, are also potential focus countries. Furthermore, activities abroad are perceived as opportunities to create a case for support. When arts organization 24 decided it wanted to raise funds in the US, it even arranged an exhibition in the US to create a strong case for support. Arts organization 8 had a similar approach. According to its 2013 annual report, the exhibition of some of its superstar artworks in the US and accompanying events – a cocktail party and a dinner – led to an increase in the number of members of the American friends organization and a gift of USD 100,000 for the arts organization. Activities in collaboration with foreign arts organizations are also used as a justification to raise funds in a specific foreign country. Fundraiser 8, for example, used the exhibition of a US arts organization that would be held at arts organization 8 as an argument to raise funds in the US.

Other aspects that are taken into account when selecting a country are the historical and geopolitical relationships with a specific country and the philanthropic traditions in a country. These are additional justifications for an arts organization's presence in a foreign country.

Fundraiser 34 summarises the factors in a matrix when deciding on which countries to focus in international fundraising. The fundraiser puts countries on the one axis and possible links, such as existing contacts in the network, number of visitors from that country, revenue from that country, programmatic links, the level of individual giving in the country, the competition of local arts organizations and local prosperity on the other axis. The more links and the heavier the weight of these factors in the matrix, the higher the fundraising potential in that country.

Once a country is selected, a friends circle can be established in that country, and the solution to obtain a tax benefit on the cross-border donation is usually established. The friends circle is typically established by identifying a few key persons who can mobilise their networks and local relationships. Peer pressure, as well as the exclusive character and prestige of these friends circles, are used to attract persons to the friends circle abroad. Arts organization 11, for example, has developed a system that it employs in every country it focusses on. In each of these countries, there is a chairperson of the friends circle. This person is responsible for gathering a certain minimum number of donors for its friends circle. Each of these donors pledges a gift for five years in a row to join the friends circle, and the chairperson gives double the amount of the donors. Key persons to attract donors can also be local representatives of the home country.

Some arts organizations decide to join efforts and to raise funds together in a specific country by setting up a joint friends circle there. A common denominator, such as a common country of origin, seems to be required to make this into a success. The potential donors of arts organizations from one country are likely to overlap, as often there are a limited number of individuals who have a strong bond with a specific country, are wealthy enough to engage in philanthropy and have an interest in the arts. The collaboration allows the arts organizations to gather additional funds from these potential foreign donors while sharing the overhead costs. This can make collaboration in international fundraising into an efficient effort. Mutual trust between the organizations, however, is required.

Global friends circles at the home organization

Only a few arts organizations that raise funds abroad do not select specific countries, but instead, target foreign donors in general. This approach is used by highly specialised arts organizations and superstar arts organizations with international stature. Instead of establishing friends circles in specific countries, these arts organizations have friends circles at the home organization. Arts organizations 10, 13, 28 and 34 have friends circles specifically targeting international donors. Arts organizations 16, 17, 18 and 21 do not have separate circles targeting international donors. In these organizations, the international donors join the circles that are also available for domestic donors.

Arts organization 16 is small and is one of these highly specialised arts organizations. It specialises in visual art from a specific region and era. In its international fundraising, arts organization 16 aims at people interested in this specific type of art who are spread across the world. Enthusiasts – who are often art collectors – find arts organization 16, and vice versa, through the mutual love for this specific fine art and their relationship is based on this joint interest. The majority of the art collectors got to know arts organization 16 by word of mouth or via its website. The donors are usually people who have been collecting for a long time and actively use the website of arts organization 16 to gain knowledge and then reach out to the organization to get in touch with curators.

Among superstar arts organizations there are also a few examples of organizations that target international donors in general. Superstar arts organization 36 is one of those, as it has admirers in all corners of the world. It targets the wealthiest supporters among those admirers, instead of a specific country. Superstar arts organization 28 also targets international donors in general. It uses the visitor database to approach wealthy foreign visitors. The arts organization sends out personalized invitations once a year to those who bought tickets in a high-price section and with a foreign address to join its international friends circle. Every year, there are two or three visitors who join this circle, which requires a significant level of giving.

A strategy the fundraisers of highly specialised arts organizations use to recruit foreign donors is strategic networking. They search for opportunities in the networks of people that surround them. The fundraisers rely on the artistic staff of the arts organization, who have an (international) network of people who share their passion for art. Fundraiser 21, for example, got in touch with curators from around the world through the artistic director of his organization. These curators opened their network to him so that he could raise funds among those interested in the type of art exhibited by arts organization 21. This resulted in an international group of patrons.

Another strategy used is the advertisement of the international friends during events abroad. Arts organization 10 used the loan of one of its superstar artworks to several foreign arts organizations as an occasion to arrange fundraising events abroad. With these fundraising events, it aimed at advertising its circle for international donors. A variation on this strategy is that of arts organization 36. It specifically targets people with a connection to a certain region where it develops programmes. It invites these people to join friends circles surrounding these regions at their home organization. The Middle East is one of these regions. Collectors of art from the

Middle East (who may be resident in the home country of arts organization 36, but also foreign benefactors) are joined in a friends circle at arts organization 36. Together, they acquire artworks for the museum and support programming and exhibitions that involve art from the Middle East. Following the success of the Middle East support group, arts organization 36 is now starting a Latin American support group.

Connections with private collectors across the world are of high importance for highly specialised fine arts organizations because, first, the collectors give works and loans; second, because the arts organizations can exchange knowledge with them; and third because collectors might be potential donors. The exchange of knowledge and raising support abroad go hand in hand for arts organizations. Therefore, arts organizations that target potential international donors in general also use the exchange of knowledge to attract donors. Private collectors are important not only as beneficiaries but also as a network to gain knowledge for arts organizations. Director 16 visits international art fairs, together with a curator, so that they can approach art collectors and art traders and reach them through the knowledge and interest on this specific topic. Arts organization 32 gets in touch with art collectors who collect in its area of expertise when it organises international loan exhibitions. Following these exhibitions, art organization 32 builds a relationship, and the art collectors then become instrumental in negotiating loans for the arts organization and helping find funders for exhibitions. Arts organization 22 also has foreign donors who have similar collections as arts organization 22, and also know the curators because of their shared interest. The same holds for arts organization 36. It has a group of international collectors who are very interested in the art world and want to learn at the same time. The curators of arts organization 36 provide this group with presentations on art, even including information on what to buy. When there is an important art fair in town, contributors to the arts organization get a guided tour with the curator of the arts organization. The employees, during these visits, share their expertise on collecting art. Fundraiser 36 says: "And when they are here at the . . . art fair they walk around the fair with a curator. So they have an opportunity, you know, for a very educated eye. So that is part of the reason why they [contribute to the arts organization]."

Conclusion

The majority of arts organizations do not raise funds abroad. For some of these organizations, it is a deliberate choice not to engage in raising funds internationally. Other arts organizations wish to raise funds abroad, but it is not a priority for them and, therefore, they do not actively invest money and time. Despite inactivity in raising funds abroad, arts organizations still might receive spontaneous gifts from foreign benefactors. Transforming incidental cross-border donations into a steady stream of income requires a large investment and commitment. It can take a while before an arts organization turns its wish to raise funds abroad into action.

Those organizations among the sample studied that do raise funds abroad use different strategies. Some arts organizations select specific countries on which they focus when raising funds abroad. This strategy is very suitable for arts organizations that have a strong tie with a specific country, for example, because the organization has regular activities in the country, it has a large audience in the country or because there are (historical) ties between the organization and the country. The giving potential and size of the potential donor base in that country are important factors to take into account. A second strategy that is best used by superstar arts organizations and highly specialised arts organizations is to raise funds abroad without focussing on a specific country. Instead, potential donors from across the world are drawn to the arts organization, and a circle for international friends is created at the home organization. Other organizations might best embrace the initiatives by foreign donors. They can provide the organization with a network to draw from and build upon to create friends circles there.

Usually, the increasing need for funds and the lack of other funding is the reason to transform the wish to raise funds into actual international fundraising. However, when other sources of income are available that require less fundraising effort, these are preferred. International fundraising is mostly considered an additional source of funding or an alternative source of funding in case the regular income of an arts organization decreases. Instead of pursuing international gifts when another source of income decreases or disappears, it would be more fruitful if arts organizations with a potential international donor base include international fundraising into their regular mix of funding sources.

Literature shows that the majority of donations is done in response to solicitation (Bekkers and Wiepking, 2011, p. 23; Breeze and Scaife, 2015, pp. 607–609). Soliciting the international potential donor base would allow arts organizations to cultivate their international donor base, which is now largely left untouched. Furthermore, by diversifying the sources of income, arts organizations become less dependent on one (or few) sources of income, such as government funding or sponsorship. An additional advantage of international fundraising in this regard is that it not only spreads risk across multiple sources of income, it also creates a geographical spread, making the organizations less vulnerable to economic downturns in a specific geographic region. Adding international fundraising to the sources of income can thus contribute to a healthy and durable funding base for arts organizations.

Notes

1 See Appendix 1 for the full list of arts organizations and interviewees.
2 Since this organization had no experience in cross-border fundraising, they were not interviewed, nor was a document analysis performed of their annual report and media coverage.
3 Large sums of money are involved in travelling exhibitions. Costs for producing exhibitions, as well as transportation, insurance and protection of the artworks are expensive. But still, there is a large demand for exhibitions and some organizations are willing to pay a high fee to have a certain exhibition. Fees for travelling exhibitions of EUR 1.5 to 4 million were reported by the interviewees. Although travelling exhibitions are costly, producing them can also be very profitable due to the high entrance fees paid by visitors.

References

Bekkers, R.H.F.P., Schuyt, T., N.M., and Gouwenberg, B. (eds.) (2015). *Geven in Nederland 2015. giften, legaten, sponsoring en vrijwilligerswerk*. Reed Business: Amsterdam.

Bekkers, R.H.F.P. and Wiepking, P. (2011). A literature review of empirical studies of philanthropy eight mechanisms that drive charitable giving. *Nonprofit and Voluntary Sector Quarterly*, 40(5), pp. 924–973.

Breeze, B. and Scaife, W. (2015). Encouraging generosity: The practice and organization of fund-raising across nations. In: P. Wiepking and F. Handy, eds., *The Palgrave handbook of global philanthropy*. New York: Springer, pp. 570–596.

Bryman, A. (2008). *Social research methods*. Oxford: Oxford University Press.

Buijze, R. (2017). *Philanthropy for the arts in the era of globalisation: International tax barriers for charitable giving*. Rotterdam: Erasmus University Rotterdam.

Buraschi, A. and Cornelli, F. (2002). *Donations*. Centre for Economic Policy Research Discussion Paper. Available at: http://papers.ssrn.com/sol3/papers.cfm?abstract_id=331485.

Chang, W.J. (2010). How "small" are small arts organizations? *The Journal of Arts Management, Law, and Society*, 40(3), pp. 217–234.

Dietz, R. and Keller, B. (2016). *Donor loyalty study*. Austin: Abila.

Dresing, T., Pehl, T., and Schmieder, C. (2015). *Manual (on) transcription. transcription conventions, software guides and practical hints for qualitative researchers*. (3rd English Edition ed.). Marburg: Self published.

Frey, B.S. (1998). Superstar museums: An economic analysis. *Journal of Cultural Economics*, 22(2–3), pp. 113–125.

Heilbrun, J. and Gray, C.M. (2001). *The economics of art and culture*. Cambridge: Cambridge University Press.

Pommerehne, W.W. and Frey, B.S. (1990). Public promotion of the arts: A survey of means. *Journal of Cultural Economics*, 14(2), pp. 73–95.

Yin, R.K. (2003). *Case study research: Design and methods*. 3rd ed. Thousand Oaks, CA: Sage Press.

Appendix 1
ARTS ORGANIZATIONS

#	Location	Interviewee	Discipline	Type	Size	FFO*	EA**
1	NL	Fundraiser 1	Cultural heritage	Fixed location	Medium		
2	NL	Fundraiser 2	Performing art	Company	Small		
3	NL	Fundraiser 3	Fine arts	Fixed location	Medium		
4	NL	Director 4	Fine arts	Fixed location	Small		
5	NL	Fundraiser 5	Performing art	Festival	Medium		
6	NL	Director 6	Cultural heritage	Fixed location	Medium	V	
6	NL	Fundraiser 6	Cultural heritage	Fixed location	Medium	V	
7	NL	Fundraiser 7	Performing art	Company	Major	V	
8	NL	Fundraiser 8	Fine arts	Fixed location	Medium	V	
9	NL	Fundraiser 9	Performing art	Company	Superstar		
10	NL	Fundraiser 10A	Fine arts	Fixed location	Superstar		
10	NL	Fundraiser 10B	Fine arts	Fixed location	Superstar		
11	NL	Fundraiser 11	Cultural heritage	Fixed location	Small		
12	NL	Fundraiser 12	Performing art	Company	Medium		
13	NL	Fundraiser 13	Fine arts	Fixed location	Superstar		
14	NL	Director 14	Fine arts	Fixed location	Small		
15	NL	Fundraiser 15	Performing art	Company	Medium	V	
16	NL	Director 16	Fine arts	Network organisation	Small		
17	NL	Director 17	Cultural heritage	Network organisation	Small		
18	BE	Fundraiser 18A	Fine arts	Fixed location	Major		
18	BE	Fundraiser 18B	Fine arts	Fixed location	Major		
18	BE	In-house lawyer 18	Fine arts	Fixed location	Major		
19	CH	Fundraiser 19	Fine arts	Fixed location	Small	V	
20	IT	Fundraiser 20A	Cultural heritage	Network organisation	Major	V	
20	IT	Fundraiser 20B	Cultural heritage	Network organisation	Major	V	
20	IT	Fundraiser 20C	Cultural heritage	Network organisation	Major	V	
21	DE	Fundraiser 21	Fine arts	Festival	Major		
22	FR	Fundraiser 22A	Fine arts	Fixed location	Superstar	V	
22	FR	Fundraiser 22B	Fine arts	Fixed location	Superstar	V	
23	BE	Director 23	Fine arts	Fixed location	Medium		

(Continued)

(Continued)

#	Location	Interviewee	Discipline	Type	Size	FFO*	EA**
24	DK	Fundraiser 24	Fine arts	Fixed location	Medium	V	
25	UK	Fundraiser 25	Fine arts	Fixed location	Superstar	V	
26	BE	Director 26	Cultural heritage	Fixed location	Small		
27	AT	Fundraiser 27	Performing art	Festival	Superstar	V	
28	US	Fundraiser 28	Performing art	Fixed location	Superstar		
29	BE	Director 29	Fine arts	Fixed location	Small		
30	FR	Fundraiser 30	Fine arts	Fixed location	Major	V	
31	US	Fundraiser 31	Cultural heritage	Network organisation	Medium		V
32	US	Fundraiser 32A	Fine arts	Fixed location	Superstar		
32	US	Fundraiser 32B	Fine arts	Fixed location	Superstar		
32	US	In-house lawyer 32	Fine arts	Fixed location	Superstar		
33	US	Fundraiser 33	Fine arts	Fixed location	Medium		
33	US	In-house accountant 33	Fine arts	Fixed location	Medium		
34	US	Fundraiser 34A	Fine arts	Fixed location	Superstar		
34	US	Fundraiser 34B	Fine arts	Fixed location	Superstar		
35	FR	Fundraiser 35	Performing art	Festival	Major		
36	US	Fundraiser 36	Fine arts	Fixed location	Superstar		V

 * Foreign friends organisation
** Legal entity abroad with charitable activities

27

TURNING CROWDS INTO PATRONS

Democratizing fundraising in the arts and culture

Marta Massi, Piergiacomo Mion Dalle Carbonare, and Alex Turrini

Introduction

Defined as an organizational activity aimed at collecting financial resources and identifying the main sources of funds (Andreasen, Kotler, and Parker, 2008), since the 1990s fundraising has gradually evolved as a strategic activity aimed at ensuring the sustainability of organizations (Andreasen, Kotler, and Parker, 2008; Frumkin, 2010; Gallagher, Gilmore, and Stolz, 2012).

Fundraising is particularly crucial for arts and culture organizations. Recent government cutbacks on public funding in many countries including Australia (Meyrick and Barnett, 2017), the US (Greenblatt, 2017) and Europe (Cuccia, Monaco, and Rizzo, 2017), and the decrease of private donations to arts and culture have pushed arts organizations to look for alternative ways to fund themselves. Further, digitalization and the emergence of social media have enabled arts organizations to reach new audiences, including younger generations, and particularly potential donors, more easily.

In addition, owing to the aging of their historical donor base, which is not being "replaced by a new and younger generation of support" (Holter, 2018), arts organizations, such as museums and theatres, have been experiencing the need to replace their traditional donors with random "patrons with $100 donations" (Holter, 2018) and to diversify their donor base (Jung, 2015).

As a result, arts and culture organizations are slowly realizing that their funders are not only wealthy patrons or angel investors, but also individuals who want to participate in a project, contributing to it by offering their financial support. Often these people are extremely motivated to support an organization or a project because they share the value system or the mission of the organization or they are simply motivated by the need to belong to a community.

That being so, fundraising can no longer be considered as a mere "request for money, based on the philanthropic motives", but rather should be regarded as an activity aimed at exchanging value with donors and meeting donor needs (Andreasen, Kotler, and Parker, 2008).

Based on these premises, this chapter describes the gradual evolution of fundraising from an elitist and individual activity, which has been, for many years, a prerogative of few wealthy people (i.e., mecenatism and patronage), to a participated and more democratic process in which anyone can contribute (i.e., crowdfunding).

The authors will make the case for the use of more democratic types of fundraising in the arts and culture, by illustrating successful cases of alternative types of fundraising. First, the rationale for fundraising in arts and cultural organizations will be explained in order to provide context. Second, a review of the different approaches to fundraising in the international context will be provided, identifying country-based idiosyncrasies. Third, the different fundraising options will be classified in order to outline the pros and cons. The taxonomy will be supported by cases exemplifying the different options. Finally, managerial implications and future directions for fundraising will be outlined.

Why fundraising?

Most institutions operating in the arts and culture sector are either public institutions or non-profit organizations needing the funding support of private donors or the government. As a strategically managed activity, fundraising can guarantee sustainability to organizations who increasingly need to diversify their sources of funds.

The financial survival of many arts and culture organizations is, indeed, severely threatened by the changes of donor priorities from arts and culture to more 'worthy causes' (Scheff and Kotler, 1996a), including religion, education and human services (Giving USA, 2018). In the US, giving to arts, culture and humanities has increased by 6.4 percent since 2016 (Giving USA, 2018), even if the amounts donated by small and medium donors has decreased (Rooney, 2018). In many European countries, donations from private individuals investing in arts and culture have decreased since 2012 (Edgar, 2012).

Not only have arts and cultural organizations had to compete with each other to attract the largest number of customers, but they also rival for receiving the increasingly scarce funds from both the governments and the private donors or corporations (Kotler, Kotler, and Kotler, 2008; Colbert, 2003).

In addition, arts and culture organizations, such as museums and theatres, cannot rely on their traditional donor base, which is aging and not been replaced by younger generations, such as Millennials, who are more interested in other social causes than arts and culture (American Alliance of Museums, 2013). All these conditions have prompted arts organizations to undertake more systematic practices of fundraising to sustain themselves.

Fundraising can, indeed, provide opportunities for creating relationships with donors (Burnett, 1992; Sargeant, 2001) and making them share the mission and the values of the organization (Sacco, 2006). In this sense, fundraising can serve to creating relationships between the organization and its donors (Lindahl, 2009).

In sum, fundraising is not only an activity which can guarantee sustainability to art and culture organizations but also a philosophy, embracing the whole organization, that can contribute to communicating systems of values, motivations and skills (Sacco, 2006, p. 19). By spreading their values to the broader community, arts and culture organizations can gain legitimacy within their communities turning them into future patrons (Carroll and Stater, 2008; Lindqvist, 2012; Jung, 2015). In the long term, fundraising can allow arts and culture organizations to raise their public profile and reputation (Najev Čačija, 2013).

Fundraising: a taxonomy

This section provides a classification of the types of fundraising and identify its main concepts, as well as discuss the Constituency Model (Rosso, 1991) as a reference to raise funds for arts and culture organizations. It is possible to identify various types of fundraising activities and different approaches which characterize the constituencies to refer to when organizing a fundraising campaign (Rosso, 1991; Tempel, Seiler, and Burlingame, 2016), namely

- Individuals
- Corporations
- Public administrations
- Not-for-profit organizations and Foundations

These four segments can support the activities of arts and culture organizations in different ways, but the combination of all of them ensures the sustainability of the fundraising efforts (Lewis, 2009; Epstein and McFarlan, 2011). Individuals can provide money and time, while corporations usually provide in-kind gifts, cash donations, sponsorship or volunteering opportunities for their employees (Herbst and Norton, 2012). Traditionally, public funding has been typified in terms of provisions to the demand (e.g., bonus) or the supply (e.g., subsidies) or direct allocations or tax concessions (Towse, 1997), while not-for-profit organizations and foundations work through project-based funding and grant-making (Sargeant and Jay, 2014).

Therefore, the four segments have different weights in the fundraising efforts of arts and culture organizations, based on the business models adopted and the context in which they are based. While in European countries there is a higher impact of public funding, in the US- and UK-based art organizations the role of private companies is critical for the sustainability of the organization and the development of projects (Sargeant and Jay, 2014). The role and opportunities of the different segments will be discussed further.

Despite the variety of the segments available for a fundraising campaign, it is important to consider that the fundraising is an exchange of value between a donor and a recipient. "People give to people to help people" (Weinstein and Barden, 2017, p. 1) is a quote that is often used to describe what fundraising is and how it works. This statement shows how the decision on giving is made by individuals and the reason behind it is a philanthropic action in supporting someone else's need. Hence, with reference to donors, it is possible to identify some specific characteristics and requirements.

As highlighted by Rosso (1991), the level of interactions that donors have with the arts and culture organizations need to be identified and measured. Therefore, it is critical to think about possible donors as stakeholders, taking into account their proximity with the institution itself. The closer they are to the activities of the arts and culture institution, the higher is their willingness to donate and contribute to its growth (Rosso, 1991). In particular, if we envisage a series of concentric circles representing the stakeholders with the institution at the very center, the ones closer to the center are those who participate directly to the activities of the organization (i.e., the management, members of the board and major donors). In the outer circles are those stakeholders who are either active in the organization (albeit with a decreasing level of involvement) or close to the organization.

The inner circle represents the heart of the organization and includes those stakeholders with the highest commitment and dedication towards the organization and those who can influence the other circles and set the pace for the fundraising campaign. It is fundamental to have them on board in order to kick-start the fundraising and take their "energy" to the outer circles. However, it is necessary to consider also a degree of fluidity within the model. In fact, those in the inner circle today might be the former donors of tomorrow and vice-versa. Interests, priorities, and availability may change over time. Therefore, it is of utmost importance to maintain stable relations with all the rings of the circle to ensure sustainability of the fundraising activities and the creation of a strong reputation among donors (Rosso, 1991; Tempel, Seiler, and Burlingame, 2016).

Fundraising practitioners should be ready to dedicate time and effort in developing their constituencies and giving them value (Rosso, 1991; Tempel, Seiler, and Burlingame, 2016) while conducting research on their needs and wants in to maximize the exchange of value (Nudd, 1993; Somerville, 2015).

Individual giving: from patronage to crowdfunding

The shrinking size of public budgets for art and cultural activities over the past decades has increased the need of arts and culture organizations to find innovative practices in funding their activities as well as to increase private giving, becoming centers for managerial innovation and excellence (Lampel and Germain, 2016).

In order to attract donors is important first to understand what drivers support their willingness to donate. Motivations to donate can be either intrinsic, extrinsic, or reputational (Bertacchini, Santagata, and Signorello, 2011).

A donor is moved by intrinsic motivations when he/she does not receive any reward for the donation but the activity itself (Deci, 1975). In fact, elements such as civic duty, moral codes and the reward of giving are driver for donations. Intrinsic motivations have proved to be assurance for better quality as well, compared to the monetary incentives to donate (Titmuss, 1970). In the case of donations to arts and culture organizations, four elements shall be considered as positively related to the willingness to donate: (1) previous consumption; (2) previous donations; (3) sense of civic duty and (4) the willingness to preserve for the future generations. The first factor is the addictive effect created by the consumption of cultural products, which lowers the costs of access while increasing the benefits of consumption (Becker and Murphy, 1988). A second critical element is the 'warm glow' effect proved in the previous donations experience, which drives to replicate the giving (Andreoni, 1988). Lastly, the willingness to preserve the heritage and making it accessible to both present and future generations as well as the sense of belonging to the community in which the arts and culture organizations operate (Titmuss, 1970; Throsby, 2001; Wheatley and Bickerton, 2017).

When the extrinsic motivations for giving are taken into consideration, it is critical to consider the cost-benefit analysis done by rational individuals before giving (Bertacchini, Santagata, and Signorello, 2011). Extrinsic motivations include economic incentives, benefits and rewards, including tax rebates. Lowering the opportunity cost of engaging in pro-social activities through tax rebates or exemptions, for example, must be supplied to an optimal level to outweigh the costs and to be considered effective. Another limitation of the intrinsic benefits in supporting donations is due to "bribe effect" (Frey and Oberholzer-Gee, 1997; Coccia and Benati, 2018), which economic incentives might create in the individuals' perception. Individual donors' extrinsic motivation might be crowded out by the economic incentives, reducing the impact of the civic duty motivation.

The last form of motivation that drives individual donations is the reputational one. Individuals who choose to donate are moved by the social recognition they will receive in return and the status they will achieve once the donation is recognized by the community (Glazer and Konrad, 1996). This last factor is quite important when the evolution of the characteristics of individual donors and donations are taken into account, from a smaller number of wealthy individuals (Maecenates) to the crowdfunding approach, with more donors but smaller contributions. Since acquiring reputation through donations is strictly related to the visibility of the donations itself, arts and culture organizations make a large use of the donors' desire to show their donations, and this may be used to set an example for other potential donors as well, supporting their willingness to contribute (Bertacchini, Santagata, and Signorello, 2011). Text

Box 27.1 illustrates the example of FAI (Fondo Ambiente Italiano), an organization that makes of individual fundraising its main form of funding.

Box 27.1   The case of FAI – Italian National Trust

FAI – Fondo Ambiente Italiano (Italian National Trust) is one of the main arts and culture organizations in Italy with the mission of protecting and promoting the historical, artistic and landscape heritage in Italy. Since 1975, FAI restores and takes care of special places in Italy so that present and future generations from all over the world may enjoy a priceless legacy. As of October 2018, FAI involves more than 7,500 volunteers each year and manages 58 heritage sites across Italy (FAI Annual Report 2017).

Since its foundation in 1975, FAI has increased year by year its members reaching more than 170,000 individuals in 2018, who every year contribute to the activities of the foundation. In 2017 FAI collected 68% of its funding from private individuals (FAI Annual Report 2017), thanks to the network of volunteers spread all around Italy. The most important events of fundraising are represented by the so-called Giornate FAI (FAI days) which are organized two times a year over the weekend (in Spring and Fall each year).

Giornate FAI represent an opportunity for communicating the work done by the foundation and raising funds for supporting the organization. In these days (Giornate FAI), FAI members have a reserved entrance and in some cases some heritage sites are open only to them, providing a simple yet important recognition for the trust and support they give. Another aims of Giornate FAI is to raise funds for the work of the foundation and spreading its mission and activities. Allowing nonmembers to access palaces, heritage sites, libraries, archives and private houses which are usually closed to the public ensures a higher participation of visitors thus the opportunity to establish more contacts with individuals. During these days the volunteers are involved in the opening of private or public properties that are usually closed to the public and characterized by a distinct beauty and value for the local community. These distinctive factors (*presence of volunteers and access to places that otherwise would be closed to the public*) support the willingness to donate and participate, while identifying FAI as an important actor for the preservation and protection of the heritage in the very community.

FAI is able to support itself thanks to the work of the thousands of volunteers around Italy and the support of its members. Communication and transparency are important but a key component for its sustainability is the mix of membership opportunities offered to individuals. FAI offers *individual membership, couple membership* (considering a couple as two people willing to share the same mailing address), *families* (two adults and two children) as well as special offers for young people and first-time members. The different memberships allow a customized approach to possible members, addressing the different needs and allowing better pricing and higher involvement.

If arts and culture organizations want to rely on crowdfunding (both online and offline) they should, therefore, apply a clear communications plan to transfer the value they generate, the activities they carry out and the benefits produced to the individuals. Communication is not the only variable to be taken into consideration. Research shows how the level of social capital (Coleman, 1988) and engagement of the target population affects the results of the fundraising efforts. It is interesting to note that territorial social capital – that is shared within a given territory – does not have a clear impact on the ability of the organization to raise funds. This represents good news for members-based art and culture organizations.

On the contrary, it may create some negative impacts on online crowdfunding platforms. A study by Giudici, Guerini, and Rossi Lamastra (2013), for instance, shows how the territorial social capital ensures that projects can be easily funded and creates the collateral effect of perceiving those projects listed in crowdfunding platforms as the one with a lower quality hence less appealing to donors.

See Text Box 27.2 for an example of successful crowdfunding platform, which is completely dedicated to funding arts projects.

Box 27.2   Crowdfunding in the arts: The BeArt case

Launched in 2015, BeArt (www.beartonline.com/) is the first crowdfunding platform completely dedicated to contemporary art. BeArt offers artists, museums, foundations, curators, galleries, academies and fairs the opportunity to raise funds and create projects, involving an international and potentially unlimited web community. One of the founders of Beart, Jessica Tanghetti describes the platform as "the virtual meeting place between art players and art lovers". BeArt's mission is to offer an innovative, easy and user-friendly way to find funding for the realization of art projects, while providing the possibility of involving art lovers who can support art projects and obtain exclusive rewards, which are proportional to the size of their donation, including artworks and special experiences. The vision of BeArt is instead very ambitious, i.e., to contribute to the creation of a new online art community, through the meeting between art professionals and users. For Tanghetti "crowdfunding is the 2.0 patronage". The evolution from classical patronage is represented by the broadening of the audience and the consequent democratization. BeArt allows anyone to play the role of patron regardless of the breadth of economic availability. BeArt makes it possible to support projects starting from a donation of only 2 euros

---

Managers of arts and culture organizations must therefore clearly consider the drivers of individual donations and adapt their communication campaigns and donors' packages to the meet expectations of donors. A critical determinant is the presence of social capital in the territory, but this is not enough to ensure the long-term sustainability of the art and culture organizations. It is important to establish a continuous dialogue with the constituencies and adapt to the ever-changing needs and expectations of donors (Giudici, Guerini, and Rossi Lamastra, 2013).

Corporate giving: sponsorships and other programs

Arts and business can at first appear as an oxymoron representing two antithetical worlds (Martorella, 1990). For many years, the traditional view of the relationship arts/business has been often regarded as a "one-way affair" where corporations can fund arts organizations, but the arts cannot offer anything to a businesses (Schiuma, 2011).

In fact, this relationship has evolved quite significantly so that nowadays there are many points of contact between the two (Carlucci and Schiuma, 2017). It is only in the 1980s and

1990s that businesses have started looking at arts organizations not "just a passive beneficiary, but rather act as business partners" (Lewandowska, 2015, p. 33; Holt, 2006).

The decrease in public funding to the arts contributed to changing the approach of private companies to the artistic-cultural investment, broadening the type of projects funded, moving from a logic based exclusively on the sponsorship to a more philanthropic and patronage-based approach (Radbourne and Watkins, 2015). This type of collaboration has been beneficial not only for artists and the companies involved, but also for the community, which has benefited from a rich and lively cultural offer (Harris and Howarth, 2014).

Over the past few decades, companies have realized their need to convey a set of values, in addition to marketing their products and services. Their awareness of the potential of art and culture in expressing this philosophy has been growing more and more (Martorella, 1990, 1996) and to date they represent a strategy for legitimation within the society, within the widest range of actions and projects related to Corporate Social Responsibility (CSR) (Moir and Taffler, 2004).

In this context, corporate art programs are defined as "initiatives financed by private companies and aimed at funding the art and culture, which are not directly related to the company's commercial activity" (Turrini, 2017, p. 6). Such initiatives can include activities which are extraordinarily different from each other: from the purchase of works of art for exhibition, to the conservation and restoration of buildings with high artistic value; from the opening of company galleries and the establishment of awards and scholarships for artists, to the creation of foundations, to the support of artistic-cultural institutions. Although most of the projects foresee an economic-financial support, in-kind contributions such as donations of artworks are not excluded (Martorella, 1990).

Corporate art programs are not addressed only at employees, but also at the community (in terms of positive impacts on the artists' career, on quality and quantity of the cultural offer, etc.). They create a favorable context for the support of art and culture, favoring this type of investment also by other organizations (both public and private). Corporate art programs can include corporate philanthropy or patronage, and sponsorships (Lewandowska, 2015).

Philanthropy is defined as in-kind donation or economic aid that an organization can confer to a person or entity (Wu, 2002). The concept of patronage has taken on different forms and meanings over the centuries; however, the characteristics of generosity and gratuity related to patronage have remained unaltered. Developed as a prerogative of the Church and wealthy individuals, patronage has then spread within the corporate culture. The first forms of philanthropy appeared in the late 1800s, even if it is difficult distinguish between individual and business philanthropy (Carroll, 2008).

In the 1920's UK and US corporations and CEOs started to use patronage to show their economic and financial power. Furthermore, support to local artists by corporations has been widely regarded as a form of active citizenship, or commitment to the community (Swengley, 2004). Patronizing the arts allowed companies to improve their image and strengthen their corporate identity (Alexander, 1996; Le Clair and Gordon, 2000).

In some cases, the commission of artworks and donations to arts organizations derive from an authentic passion for the art of top management and represents the intent of the company to give back to the territory and the local community (Martorella, 1990). In Italy, for instance, Pirelli has created Pirelli Hangar Bicocca in 2004 through the reconversion of an industrial plant into an institution dedicated to the production and promotion of contemporary art. With its 15,000 square meters, Hangar Bicocca is one of the largest exhibition spaces in Europe and each year presents important personal exhibitions by Italian and international artists (www.hangarbicocca.org).

Works of art do not just have an aesthetic function. Corporate involvement in artistic projects can also develop employee creativity and create a stimulating work environment. In this sense, corporate patronage also contributes to the improvement of the working environment, stimulating creativity and commitment of employees, and helps the company attract qualified personnel (Le Clair and Doornbosch, 1995; Woolnough, 2002). Given its characteristics, very often patronage fits into broader programs of corporate social responsibility, which embrace ethics, the environment, and human capital.

Unlike patronage, sponsorship implies a "do ut des" approach between sponsor and sponsee and is characterized by a relationship that involves some form of promotion, that the company receives in exchange for its support to the artist or cultural institution. It is a sort of "strategic philanthropy" (Rich, 2001) based on a trade agreement, according to which an organization supports economically a second part in exchange for direct or indirect benefits (Klincewicz, 1998). For instance, the agreement between TODS and the MIBAC (the Italian Ministry of Cultural Heritage) for the restoration of the Colosseum (that cost 25 million euros) granted TODS the right to the exclusive use of a logo depicting the Colosseum.

In the past, businesses were inclined to sponsor mostly sporting events, as they were considered the only ones able to generate significant media exposure. Art, in contrast, was considered too elitist. More recently, however, also due to the reduction of public funds destined for art and to culture, an increasing number of private companies have decided to contribute to support the arts and culture (Quester and Thompson, 2001).

The renovation of historic buildings, urban regeneration actions, support to museums, and the organization of exhibitions or awards for young talents are just some of the main actions sponsored in the artistic-cultural field by companies. The choice of the single initiative usually responds to a specific investment strategy, in line with the corporate objectives and values (Finkel, 2010).

Public funding

Public funding mechanisms have been traditionally typified in terms of provisions to the demand (i.e. vouchers) or the supply (i.e. subsidies) or of direct allocations and indirect tax concessions (Towse, 1997). However, recent trends in the public funding to culture at an international level have renewed the ways in which public administration support the arts financially (Katz-Gerro, 2015).

Recently, new factors have come into the game, including the decentralization of public spending (Bertelli et al., 2014), the tension on allocating funds based on the excellence of artistic production (Feder and Katz-Gerro, 2015) and the governance/brokering mode of intervening in the arts by the State (Turrini, 2009). As a result, nonprofit organizations can no longer enjoy the traditional stickiness of public funding distribution but are pushed to competing more and more among themselves.

From this perspective we might categorize different public funding mechanisms according to the different degrees of competition they might introduce among arts organizations (see Figure 27.1). In the following we will therefore briefly describe the different mechanisms at hand according to this continuum.

Demand subsidies/vouchers

The provision of demand subsidies or vouchers in the arts and cultural field has not seen a major adoption in the arts and cultural domains (Dalle Nogare and Bertacchini, 2015). In the last decade however, some national and local governments have proposed this type of scheme (either

Type of beneficiary/Level of competitiveness among NPOs	Low	High
Individuals (i.e. users or citizens)	Demand subsidies	Voucher
Donors/sponsors		Tax concessions
Arts organizations	Tax concessions Direct public subsidies	Matching and Reverse grants

Figure 27.1   Categorization of public funding mechanisms in the arts

in the form of direct provisions of money users might spend for going to museums or buying a book or in the form of vouchers). When adopted, demand subsidies have enabled arts institutions to increase their revenues; they have been introduced as tools to empower the freedom of choice of citizens and targeted users (typically younger generations), they have pushed arts institutions to compete for better service quality replicating for the arts the benefits of competitive markets. Demand-side subsidies have encountered some negative drawbacks relative to enforcement of mechanisms to ensure that the consumption of arts is effectively enjoyed by the recipients of the subsidy and not by someone else (this occurs when vouchers are not nominal). Some other more evident negative drawbacks have been related to the difficult or expensive implementation of these type of demand-side mechanisms.

The Slovak Republic is an example of nation where these vouchers have been employed. In this country, the Ministry of Culture distributes vouchers through elementary and secondary schools. Students or teachers can use them to pay for admission to a cultural institution including theatres, museums, galleries, or to pay for cultural services in libraries or other cultural centers (Ministry of Culture of the Slovak Republic, 2018).

Tax concessions for donors

As O'Hagan (2012) noted, calls for the introduction of taxation measures aiding the donations for the arts have been increasing in the last decades in countries where public funding does not rely on tax expenditures as in the United States (see Text Box 27.3 for the Italy Arts Bonus mechanism). The debate around the effects of this type of measures is still lively. On the one side, income tax deduction places the decision-making power over the support of arts institutions in the hands of those with higher incomes (O'Hare and Feld, 1984). On the other side in countries where government play a relevant role, democratizing and enlarging the bases of donors to the arts might be an achievable goal when tax concessions schemes are introduced (Mulcahy, 2006).

Box 27.3   *Art Bonus* in Italy

The *Art Bonus* was launched in 2014 by the Ministry of Cultural Heritage and Activities and Tourism of Italy with the aim of increasing the fundraising opportunities for Italian public art and culture organizations through a new favorable tax regime for those who support culture with charitable donations. The *Art Bonus* is a tax credit equal to 65% of charitable contributions that individuals or companies and organizations make in favor of public cultural heritage. The Art Bonus grants a tax

---

credit to individuals, to nonprofit organizations and businesses for charitable contributions destined to the (1) maintenance, protection and restoration of public cultural works (i.e. monuments, historic buildings, works of art), (2) support of public cultural institutions (i.e. museums, libraries, archives, archaeological areas and parks), opera/symphonic foundations and traditional theater and other entertainment organizations as required by the law; and (3) realization, restoration and upgrading of facilities of public institutions dedicated to performances.

Public art and culture institutions can upload their project on a dedicated platform (www.art bonus.gov.it) and donors can read the specifics of the project and choose to which one to donate. Once the project is identified, donors can directly contact the institution to which they want to donate and agree upon the details of money transfer (through a bank, post office, debit or credit and debit cards, bank checks).

According to ALES – the in-house company of the Ministry of Cultural Heritage and Activities and Tourism that manages the Art Bonus platform – since 2014 there has been more than 1,200 public institutions registered, 1400 project proposals and more than 7,500 donors. The Art Bonus contributed to fundraise 245 million Euros.

Direct public subsidies, tax concessions to nonprofits, matching and reverse grants

The provision of subsidies or tax concessions (like the VAT concessions) to arts organizations has been one of the most traditional ways to support the art and cultural sector especially in continental Europe (O'Hagan, 2012). Dalle Nogare and Bertacchini (2015) have distinguished between direct measures administered by local or national governments and arms' length systems of subsidization, which implies the action of an independent public agency which decides quite independently about the distribution of public funding allocated by the government and/or its political bodies. This type of systems has provided a fertile ground for the development of matching grants/reverse grants type of subsidies. Box 27.3 exemplifies this type of mechanism (focusing the attention on the matching grants system implemented by the National Endowment for the Arts in the US).

Interestingly enough this public funding systems introduce a higher degree of competition among nonprofit organizations applying for the grants. Arts institutions do not compete only in proposing the best project relative to artistic quality or outreach capacity but also in being able to crowd in more and new funding from different sources, above all when the amount of the grant requested or awarded is relatively small (Borgonovi and O'Hare, 2004).

Empowering donors: the democratization of fundraising

Fundraising has been shifting from an activity that was once a prerogative of wealthy people to a participated process that can involve millions of people (i.e. crowdfunding). Once arts projects and artists were funded mainly by the aristocracy, popes, and the royalty, while now we are witnessing a fragmentation of the traditional patronage paradigm, which is spread out to different patrons who have an interest in the project (Brabham, 2017).

Information technology and digitalization have disrupted traditional fundraising models and obliged organizations to review their processes for raising funds. Probably, the most disruptive process being introduced in this context has been crowdfunding, i.e. a process whereby "an entrepreneur raises external financing from a large audience (the 'crowd'), in which each individual provides a very small amount, instead of soliciting a small group of sophisticated investors" (Belleflamme, Lambert, and Schwienbacher, 2014). While the classic concept of patronage involves a process where "the rich exchange their material resources for a share of that intangible good, cultural credibility" (Rothfeld, 2015, p. 1), crowdfunding functions as a more inclusive form of fundraising, leading to a democratization process. As stated by the mission of Indiegogo, one of the first crowdfunding platforms, there is a need to "democratize fundraising to empower everyone across the world to fund their passions". New forms of fundraising such as crowdfunding "empower people to control their own destiny since everyone has an equal shot" (Roseman, 2013, p. 12).

While fundraising is going towards donor empowerment and democratization, some arts operators are still skeptical about this democratization process (Olson, 2014; Tugend, 2014; Erb, 2015). The main resistance is based on the lack of control that characterizes crowdfunding processes. Owing to their intangible and informal nature, hardly any crowdfunding process can be managed through traditional models of fundraising (Valeri, 2017, p. 122), thus introducing a degree of uncertainty, which cultural operators would rather avoid.

However, there are also examples of crowdfunding by established arts organizations, e.g., the Louvre campaigns. The Louvre Museum has managed to finance the purchase of the painting *Le Tre Grazie* involving more than fifty thousand people in raising a million euros (Brunello, 2014). Indeed, digitalization and crowdfunding enable arts organizations to reach new audiences, and particularly new donors. The importance of more democratic forms of fundraising becomes evident in times when the historical donor base is shrinking.

Therefore, arts organizations, such as museums, may soon be urged to build "personal and emotional connections with a new base" (Holter, 2018).

The future of fundraising: implications for managers

Today's art and culture organizations must face important societal changes, including the consequences of the so-called networked society which allows individuals to freely "choose their own personalized network of connections and influences" (Miller, 2009, p. 365) due to higher levels of education, class and gender equality and widening opportunities for travels. These changes have brought about higher levels of sophistication and confidence in consumers, impacting the management of organizations, including art and culture ones. In particular, one of the most important shifts is the reaction on the individuals to mass marketing and communication. Individuals, whether they are customers or visitors, are looking for exclusive experiences and a dedicated relationship. In this context, the role of fundraising, as a tool to establish relations and build engagement (Spirer, 2014; Gelles, 2014; O'Neil, 2014; Saratovsky and Feldmann, 2013; Erb, 2015; Valeri, 2017) has become critical.

Arts managers should look at fundraising activities as a process aimed not only at building a relationship between the organization and its donors but also at engaging donors making them feel active part of the organization itself. They should give preeminence to tools able to create donor engagement and participation. Traditional means such as direct mailing, calls or mass campaigns may not be as effective as in the past decades. Because of the rapid growth of the Internet and the connectedness of society, donors want to have clear understanding of where their money goes and are looking for convenient ways to donate (Grace and Wendroff, 2001; McPherson, 2007).

Relationship marketing (Rentschler et al., 2002) can help arts organizations build these relationships with customers and create loyalty by cultivating long-term relationships with existing and prospective donors.

The support of the marketing and public relations area is fundamental for successful fundraising (Byrnes, 2014). The link between fundraising and marketing is particularly true when the organizational structure and the proximity between the marketing and fundraising department are taken into consideration, which often depends on the same manager.

In this sense, marketing has become crucial for attracting potential donors and funders. It is not random that crowdfunding is also employed as a marketing and communication tool to boost brand awareness, provide exclusive distribution and explore and validate new markets (Valeri, 2017). Marketing can also be used to segment donors and offer targeted fundraising options. While major donors are already loyal to the organization in that they share and agree on the brand values, prospect donors are the most challenging to attract, especially younger customers who do not belong to the historical donor base and are keener on using social media and the Internet to donate. Research has shown that younger donors prefer to fund causes which they can relate to (O'Neil, 2014) and how they request to know where the money goes and what the impact of the fundraising campaign is (Johnson Grossnickle Associates, 2011). Museum managers should, therefore, look at fundraising options that are appealing to young generations and that can raise interest in the specific cause.

Arts managers must invest effort not only in attracting their donors but also in retaining them, to ensure the highest possible value. A possible support in doing so, by leveraging on the sense of community which is highly valued by the modern society, should be the use of the online fundraising as a tool to customize the offer and make it visible to the relevant community. In other words, arts and culture organizations must be able to gain visibility in donors' daily activities and habits, by making donations easy to access and establishing relations in familiar environments (i.e. social media and internet platform).

Increasingly donors are looking for ways to connect to the organizations they support (Saratovsky and Feldmann, 2013).

A good example could be DonorBox, a tool to bring organizations closer to the possible donors by customizing the access to the donations and giving multiple opportunities for performing the donations. Consumers who donate through social media feel like "part of the solution, a sort of ambassador for supporting the cause" and are also incentivized by the ease of the process: "no need to register or go through lengthy processes" (Interviewee 1, 2018, pers. comm., 8 May).

Socialization and accessibility are key determinants for the success of fundraising campaigns and the use of the Internet is critical to achieving them. Fundraisers seeking higher impact will probably need to change their perspectives and introduce tools to customize their outreach and empower their donors.

Donors are no longer keen on playing a passive role in the giving process (Grace and Wendroff, 2001) and express the need to know the longer-term outcomes and impacts on beneficiaris"(Lloyd, 2006, p. 20).

Arts managers should keep in mind that empowering customers is particularly crucial in times when individuals are constantly looking for authenticity, a dimension that relates to 'having authority or control over' (Trilling, 1972). Thus, empowering customers, making them an active participant in the artistic project and, therefore, authors, allows them to regain control over the value creation process (Prahalad and Ramaswamy, 2004). Through crowdfunding, customers can actively participate in all the phases of the fundraising project, thus co-creating it by a progressive cession of power and control from the providers and a redefinition of the roles. By focusing on projects that have measurable outcomes and making the goals of the funding campaign evident from the start (Saratovsky and Feldmann, 2013), online crowdfunding emerges as an appealing fundraising option.

References

Alexander, D.V. (1996). From philanthropy to funding: The effects of corporate and public support on American art museums. *Poetics*, 24(2–4), pp. 87–129.

American Alliance of Museums (2013). *Trendswatch 2013: Back to the Future*. Available at: www.aam-us. org/wp-content/uploads/2018/04/trendswatch2013.pdf [Accessed 5 Nov. 2017].

Andreasen, A.R., Kotler, P., and Parker, D. (2008). *Strategic marketing for nonprofit organizations*. Upper Saddle River, NJ: Pearson/Prentice Hall.

Andreoni, J. (1988). Privately provided public goods in a large economy: The limits of altruism. *Journal of Public Economics*, 35(1), pp. 57–73.

Becker, G.S. and Murphy, K.M. (1988). A theory of rational addiction. *Journal of Political Economy*, 96(4), pp. 675–700.

Belleflamme, P., Lambert, T., and Schwienbacher, A. (2014). Crowdfunding: Tapping the right crowd. *Journal of Business Venturing*, 29(5), pp. 585–609.

Bertacchini, E., Santagata, W., and Signorello, G. (2011). Individual giving to support cultural heritage. *International Journal of Arts Management*, 13(3), pp. 41–54.

Bertelli, A.M., Connolly, J.M., Mason, D.P., and Conover, L.C. (2014). Politics, management, and the allocation of arts funding: Evidence from public support for the arts in the UK. *International Journal of Cultural Policy*, 20(3), pp. 341–359.

Borgonovi, F. and O'Hare, M. (2004). The impact of the national endowment for the arts in the united states: Institutional and sectoral effects on private funding. *Journal of Cultural Economics*, 28(1), pp. 21–36.

Brabham, D.C. (2017). How crowdfunding discourse threatens public arts. *New Media & Society*, 19(7), pp. 983–999.

Brunello, A. (2014). *Il manuale del crowdfunding: Ovvero come realizzare le tue idee grazie ai nuovi strumenti di finanziamento online*. LSWR, Milan.

Burnett, K. (1992). *Relationship fundraising*. London: White Lion Press.

Byrnes, W.J. (2014). *Management and the arts*. Waltham, MA: Focal Press.

Carlucci, D. and Schiuma, G. (2017). An introduction to the special issue. The arts as sources of value creation for business: Theory, research, and practice. *Journal of Business Research*, 85, pp. 337–341.

Carroll, A.B. (2008). A history of corporate social responsibility: Concepts and practices. In: A. Crane, A. McWilliams, D. Matten, J. Moon and D. Siegel, eds., *The Oxford handbook of corporate social responsibility*. Oxford: Oxford University Press, pp. 19–46.

Carroll, D. and Stater, K.J. (2008). Revenue diversification in nonprofit organizations: Does it lead to financial stability? *Journal of Public Administration Research and Theory*, 19(4), pp. 947–966.

Coccia, M. and Benati, I. (2018). Rewards in public administration: A proposed classification. *Journal of Social and Administrative Sciences*, 5(2), pp. 68–80.

Colbert, F. (2003). Entrepreneurship and leadership in marketing the arts. *International Journal of Arts Management*, 6(1), pp. 30–39.

Coleman, J.S. (1988). Social capital in the creation of human capital. *American Journal of Sociology*, 94, pp. 95–120.

Council of Europe. (2018). *Culture Vouchers*. Ministry of Culture of Slovak Republic. Available at: www. coe.int/en/web/culture-and-heritage/-/culture-vouchers [Accessed 5 Nov. 2018].

Cuccia, T., Monaco, L., and Rizzo, I. (2017). Are less public funds bad? New strategies for art providers. In: V. Ateca-Amestoy, V. Ginsburgh, I. Mazza, J. O'Hagan and J. Prieto-Rodriguez, eds., *Enhancing participation in the arts in the EU*. Cham: Springer, pp. 357–369.

Dalle Nogare, C. and Bertacchini, E. (2015). Emerging modes of public cultural spending: Direct support through production delegation. *Poetics*, 49, pp. 5–19.

Deci, E.L. (1975). *Intrinsic motivation*. New York, NY: Plenum Press.

Edgar, D. (2012). Why should we fund the arts? *The Guardian*. 5 January. Available at: www.theguardian. com [Accessed 28 Nov. 2018].

Epstein, M.J. and McFarlan, F.W. (2011). *Joining a nonprofit board: What you need to know*. New York: John Wiley & Sons.

Erb, E.K. (2015). *Crowdfunding the museum: Fad or future.* Doctoral dissertation, University of Texas.

Feder, T. and Katz-Gerro, T. (2015). The cultural hierarchy in funding: Government funding of the performing arts based on ethnic and geographic distinctions. *Poetics,* 49, pp. 76–95.

Finkel, R. (2010). Re-imaging arts festivals through a corporate lens: A case study of business sponsorship at the Henley Festival. *Managing Leisure,* 15(4), pp. 237–250.

Frey, B.S. and Oberholzer-Gee, F. (1997). The cost of price incentives: An empirical analysis of motivation crowding-out. *The American Economic Review,* 87(4), pp. 746–755.

Frumkin, P. (2010). *The essence of strategic giving: A practical guide for donors and fundraisers,* University of Chicago Press, Chicago.

Gallagher, D., Gilmore, A., and Stolz, A. (2012). The strategic marketing of small sports clubs: From fundraising to social entrepreneurship. *Journal of Strategic Marketing,* 20(3), pp. 231–247.

Gelles, D. (2014). Wooing a new generation of museum patrons. *New York Times,* 19 March. Available at: www.nytimes.com. [Accessed 5 Nov. 2018].

Giudici, G., Guerini, M., and Rossi Lamastra, C. (2013). Why crowdfunding projects can succeed: the role of proponents' individual and territorial social capital. *SSRN.* Available at: https://ssrn.com/abstract=2255944 [Accessed 6 Nov. 2018].

Giving USA (2018). *The annual report on philanthropy for the year 2017.* Available at: https://givingusa.org/see-the-numbers-giving-usa-2017-infographic/. [Accessed 5 Sep. 2018].

Glazer, A. and Konrad, K.A. (1996). A signaling explanation for charity. *The American Economic Review,* 86(4), pp. 1019–1028.

Grace, K.S. and Wendroff, A.L. (2001). *High impact philanthropy: How donors, boards, and non-profit organizations can transform communities.* New York City, NY: John Wiley & Sons, Inc.

Greenblatt, A. (2017). Should government support artistic and cultural expression? *CQ Researcher.* Available at: www.cqpress.com [Accessed 5 Nov. 2018].

Harris, P. and Howarth, S.R. (2014). *A celebration of corporate art programmes worldwide.* London: Wapping Asts Trust.

Herbst, N.B. and Norton, M. (2012). *The complete fundraising handbook.* 6th ed. London: Directory of Social Change.

Holt, G.E. (2006). Corporate sponsorships. *The Bottom Line: Managing Library Finances,* 36(5), pp. 689–705.

Holter, E. (2018). *We help museums to grow and change.* Available at: https://cuberis.com/should-museums-brand/. [Accessed 5 Sep. 2018].

Johnson Grossnickle Associates (2011). *Millennial donors report 2011.* Available at: https://d3n8a8pro7vhmx.cloudfront.net/jfn/pages/1774/attachments/original/1502140394/millennial_donors_2011_report.pdf?1502140394. [Accessed 5 Nov. 2018].

Jung, Y. (2015). Diversity matters: Theoretical understanding of and suggestions for the current fundraising practices of nonprofit art museums. *The Journal of Arts Management, Law, and Society,* 45(4), pp. 255–268.

Katz-Gerro, T. (2015). Introduction – cultural policy and the public funding of culture in an international perspective. *Poetics,* 49, pp. 1–4.

Klincewicz, K. (1998). Ethical aspects of sponsorship. *Journal of Business Ethics,* 17(9–10), pp. 1103–1110.

Kotler, N.G., Kotler, P., and Kotler, W.I. (2008). *Museum marketing and strategy, designing missions, building audiences, generating revenue and resources.* San Francisco: Jossey Bass.

Lampel, J. and Germain, O. (2016). Creative industries as hubs of new organizational and business practices. *Journal of Business Research,* 69(7), pp. 2327–2333.

Le Clair, M.S. and Doornbosch, K. (1995). Corporate acquisitions of fine art: Measuring the underlying motivations. *Managerial Finance,* 21(6), pp. 1–15.

Le Clair, S.M. and Gordon, K. (2000). Corporate support for artistic and cultural activities: What determines the distribution of corporate giving? *Journal of Cultural Economics,* 24(3), pp. 225–241.

Lewandowska, K. (2015). From sponsorship to partnership in arts and business relations. *The Journal of Arts Management, Law, and Society,* 45(1), pp. 33–50.

Lewis, T. (2009). *Management accounting for non-governmental organizations.* Oxford: Mango.

Lindahl, W.E. (2009). *Principles of fundraising: Theory and practice.* Sudbury, MA: Jones and Bartlett Publishers.

Lindqvist, K. (2012). Museum finances: Challenges beyond economic crises, *Museum Management and Curatorship,* 27(1), pp. 1–15.

Lloyd, T. (2006). *Cultural giving: Successful donor development for arts and heritage organizations.* London: Directory of Social Change.

Martorella, R. (1990). *Corporate art.* New Brunswick: Rutgers University Press.

———. (1996). *Art and business. An international perspective on sponsorship.* Westport, CT: Praeger.

McPherson, R.C. (2007). *Digital giving: How technology is changing charity.* Lincoln, NE: iUniverse.

Meyrick, J. and Barnett, T. (2017). Culture without "world": Australian cultural policy in the age of stupid. *Cultural Trends,* 26(2), pp. 107–124.

Miller, B. (2009). Commufundraising 2.0 – the future of fundraising in a networked society? *International Journal of Nonprofit and Voluntary Sector Marketing,* 14(4), 365–370.

Moir, L. and Taffler, R. (2004). Does corporate philanthropy exist? Business giving to the arts in the UK. *Journal of Business Ethics,* 54(2), pp. 149–161.

Mulcahy, K. (2006). Cultural policy. In: B. Peters and J. Pierre, eds., *Handbook of public policy.* London: Sage, pp. 265–279.

Najev Čačija, L. (2013). Fundraising in the context of nonprofit strategic marketing: Toward a conceptual model. *Management: Journal of Contemporary Management Issues,* 18(1), pp. 59–78.

Nudd, S.P. (1993). Thinking strategically about information. In: H.A. Rosso, ed., *Achieving excellence in fund raising.* San Francisco: Jossey-Bass, pp. 349–365.

O'Hagan, J. (2012). Tax expenditures: Pervasive, 'hidden' and undesirable subsidies to the arts. *Homo Oeconomicus,* 29(3), pp. 329–359.

O'Hare, M. and Feld, A.L. (1984). Indirect aid to the arts. *The Annals of the American Academy of Political and Social Science,* 471(1), pp. 132–143.

O'Neil, M. (2014). *Lifestyles, attitudes, and technology are shaping millennials' giving,* 16 June 2014, *The Chronicle of Philanthropy.* Available at: www.philanthropy.com. [Accessed 5 Sep. 2018].

Olson, E. (2014). Soliciting funds from the crowd? Results will vary. *The New York Times,* 19 March. Available at: www.nytimes.com. [Accessed 5 Sep. 2018].

Pirelli HangarBicocca (2004). Available at: www.hangarbicocca.org/pirelli-hangarbicocca/ [Accessed 5 Nov. 2018].

Prahalad, C.K. and Ramaswamy, V. (2004). Co-creation experiences: The next practice in value creation. *Journal of Interactive Marketing,* 18(3), pp. 5–14.

Quester, G.P. and Thompson, B. (2001). Advertising and promotion leverage on arts sponsorship effectiveness. *Journal of Advertising Research,* 41(1), pp. 33–47.

Radbourne, J. and Watkins, K. (2015). *Philanthropy and the arts.* Melbourne: Melbourne University Publishing.

Rentschler, R., Radbourne, J., Carr, R., and Rickard, J. (2002). Relationship marketing, audience retention and performing arts organisation viability. *International Journal of Nonprofit and Voluntary Sector Marketing,* 7(2), pp. 118–130.

Rich, J.D. (2001). Sponsorship. In: F Colbert, ed., *Marketing culture and the arts.* Montréal: Chair in Arts Management, pp. 184–194.

Rooney, P.M. (2018). Giving by small and medium donors: What can we do about it? Nonprofit quarterly. *Nonprofit Quarterly,* 21 November. Available at: www.nonprofitquarterly.org. [Accessed 21 Nov. 2018].

Roseman, E. (2013). How to raise money by crowdfunding. *Toronto Star,* 25 June. Available at: www.thestar.com. [Accessed 5 Sep. 2018].

Rosso, H.A. (1991). *Achieving excellence in fund raising: A comprehensive guide to principles, strategies, and methods.* San Francisco: Jossey-Bass.

Rothfeld, B. (2015). Will crowdfunding outpace old-fashioned arts patronage?, 3 March 2015, *Hyperallergic.* Available at: www.hyperallergic.com [Accessed 5 Sep. 2018].

Sacco, P.L. (2006). La nuova centralità della cultura e le prospettive del fundraising culturale. In: P.L. Sacco, eds., *Il fundraising per la cultura.* Milano: Meltemi Editore, pp. 9–23.

Saratovsky, K.D. and Feldmann, D. (2013). *Cause for change: The why and how of nonprofit millennial engagement.* New York: John Wiley & Sons.

Sargeant, A. (2001). Relationship fundraising: How to keep donors loyal. *Nonprofit Management and Leadership,* 12(2), pp. 177–192.

Sargeant, A. and Jay, E. (2014). *Fundraising management: Analysis, planning and practice.* London: Routledge.

Scheff, J. and Kotler, P. (1996a). Crisis in the arts: The marketing response. *California Management Review,* 39(1), pp. 28–52.

Schiuma, G. (2011). *The value of arts for business.* Cambridge: Cambridge University Press.

Somerville, M.M. (2015). Building fundraising momentum: Message, relationship, and alliance essentials. *Proceedings of Re-think it: Libraries for a New Age,* Grand Valley State University, 10–12 August.

Spirer, G. (2014). *Crowdfunding: The next big thing.* North Charleston, SC: CreateSpace.

Swengley, N. (2004). Masterpieces meet minibars. *Weekend Financial Times*, 19 June, p. W6.

Tempel, E.R., Seiler, T.L., and Burlingame, D.F. (2016). *Achieving excellence in fundraising*. New York: John Wiley & Sons.

Throsby, D. (2001). *Economics and culture*. Cambridge: Cambridge University Press.

Titmuss, R.M. (1970). Developing social policy in conditions of rapid change: The role of social welfare. In: B. Abel-Smith and K. Titmuss, eds., *The philosophy of welfare: Selected writings of Richard M. Titmuss*. London: Allen and Unwin, pp. 254–268.

Towse, R. (1997). *Baumol's cost disease*. Cheltenham: Edward Elgar Publishing.

Trilling, L. (1972). *Sincerity and authenticity*. Cambridge, MA: Harvard University Press.

Tugend, A. (2014). The effect crowdfunding has on venerable nonprofits raises concern. *New York Times*, 7 February. Available at: www.nytimes.com [Accessed 5 Sep. 2018].

Turrini, A. (2017). Corporate art program in Italia: il contributo delle imprese Altagamma, Report Master in Arts Management and Administration, SDA Bocconi School of Management – Fondazione Altagamma.

Turrini, A. (2009). *Politiche e management pubblico per l'arte e la cultura*. Milan: EGEA.

Valeri, A. (2017). Crowdfunding in arts and culture: From funding to engagement. *Economia della Cultura*, 1, pp. 121–130.

Weinstein, S. and Barden, P. (2017). *The complete guide to fundraising management*. New York: John Wiley & Sons.

Wheatley, D. & Bickerton, C. (2017). Subjective well-being and engagement in arts, culture and sport. *Journal of Cultural Economics*, 41(1), pp. 23–45.

Woolnough, R. (2002). Corporate imagination: Companies are increasingly commissioning artworks to make a mission statement. *The Guardian*, 21 October. Available at: www.theguardian.com. [Accessed 5 Nov. 2018].

Wu, C.T. (2002). *Privatising culture: Corporate art intervention since the 1980s*. London: Verso.

28

FUNDRAISING FOR CLASSICAL MUSIC

Case studies from Hong Kong and Macao

Meggy Cheng, Rebecca Wai In Chou, and Benny Lim

Introduction

Classical music developed substantially in Europe in the last 450 years. The Baroque era (1600–1750) laid the very foundations for different musical genres, including opera, which we still enjoy in theaters and concert halls around the world today. The Classical period (1750–1820) clarified and polished the way music was structured and expressed, while the Romantic era (1780–1850) saw the attempts of musicians to balance between their artistic self-expression and the strict rules of music making laid down during the Classical period. Since the last century, some composers (such as Igor Stravinsky and Frederick Delius) have attempted to experiment and adopt a 'think out of the box' approach towards music making, often breaking out of the prescribed norms (Yudkin, 2005). Notwithstanding the evolution, one thing remains fairly constant in classical music – the concept of giving. In the 17th and 18th century, musicians were often supported by patrons, made up of the aristocracy. In return, musicians performed their compositions for the nobles and royalty (Campbell, 1999). The concept of arts patronage still exists today, though it has evolved quite substantially.

The concept of fundraising works alongside giving: in order for sponsors or funders to give, there must be efforts on the artists' part to promote the cause, establish relationships, and seek the support of the patrons. It is no secret that Mozart's eventual downfall was very much due to the alienation of the very patrons who once supported him (Harris, 2002). For one, the art has benefits that make apparent the support towards it. Listening to classical music, for instance, has been known to be an intellectual exercise (Johnson, 2002), and at the same time, offers pleasure and relaxation (Lowe, 2007). Successful fundraising campaigns lead to more performances being offered at subsidized prices, and in the process, create better access to the benefits of classical music.

This chapter introduces the reader to the current state of classical music fundraising in Hong Kong and Macao, which are also known as Special Administrative Regions (S.A.R.) of China. Under the "One country, two systems" policy, both cities are part of China, yet they retain autonomy on their economic and administrative systems. To a large extent, both cities develop and manage their arts and cultural policies independent of influences from Mainland China. It should also be noted that Hong Kong was still a colony of the United Kingdom before 1997, and Macao was a Portuguese colony up till 1999, which explain both cities' Western influences.

The chapter also discusses the current challenges and future possibilities of classical music fundraising in these two East Asian cities.

Types of fundraising in the arts

Government grants and private foundations

Government grants are subsidies awarded by the federal, state or local government to eligible arts organizations (Kaiser, 2015). Generally, government bodies are likely to offer different types of grants, each with clear procedures for application, as well as review and evaluation processes. Such grants are funded by tax money, suggesting the need for stringent compliance and reporting measures to ensure that the money is well-spent and accounted for (Brustein, 1991). According to Foundation Center based in New York, private foundations are non-governmental, nonprofit corporations or charitable trusts that are established by specific individuals, families or corporate companies, with the purpose of making grants available to organizations, institutions or individuals in specific geographical areas, for the sake of scientific, educational, cultural, religious or other charitable causes (Foundation Center, n.d.). Some foundations may also run activities alongside their giving programs.

Corporate sponsorship: cash and in-kind

The National Council of Nonprofits states that "corporate sponsorship is the financial payment by a business to a nonprofit to further the nonprofit's mission, with an acknowledgement that the business has supported the nonprofit's activities, programs, or special event" (Corporate Sponsorship, n.d.). Some companies may view sponsorships to the arts as a form of corporate social responsibility. Corporate sponsorships are also sometimes based on the concept of 'reciprocity', where their support to the arts becomes a form of marketing communication tool, and arts groups are required to ensure some form of advertising outreach for their sponsors (McDonnell and Moir, 2013). In-kind sponsorships refer to the sponsors' provision of goods or services, such as venues, equipment, F&B, and marketing platforms, instead of giving cash directly. More often than not, the goods and services provided are aligned to the sponsors' business offerings, such as a hotel providing free rooms for international guest artists of an orchestra. In-kind sponsorships may sometimes be deemed as less impactful than actual cash sponsorships. Nevertheless, in-kind sponsorships contribute to cost-cutting and are especially beneficial to smaller arts organizations.

Equity financing and selling IP rights

Equity financing is a fundraising method through selling shares of the arts organization or specific arts productions to the public, financial institutions, or venture capitalists (Walter, 2015). Investors provide the arts organization or productions with the necessary capital to sustain and develop, in exchange for dividends on shares or return of investments through ownership percentage. Intellectual Property (IP) are original creations, which offer the creators rights and protections under the law (Cantatore and Crawford-Spencer, 2018). These include rights for artistic, musical, film and literary works, as well as the creation of symbols, designs, and inventions. Due to the legal protections, creators of the IP can sell the rights to other individuals or corporations for monetary exchange. The producer of a classical music concert can sell partial

IP rights, such as the broadcast rights of the concert to a TV station, in return for funds to produce the performance in the first place.

Donations and crowdfunding

Donation activities could either be ad hoc–based or carefully planned. Arts organizations could simply place a PayPal donation button on their websites to solicit donations all year long. On the other hand, arts organizations could also plan specific donation drives/events, such as a costume ball, a silent or live auction, an annual dinner, etc. where staff and volunteers interact with donors and build visibility at the same time. Crowdfunding is an outcome of the advent of sharing in the digital age, where arts organizations rely on collecting small contributions from a substantial number of backers (Scholz, 2015). Crowdfunding can be donation-based, where there is no financial return to the backers of donation-based crowdfunding. Rewards-based crowdfunding gives backers some form of incentives in return for the monetary support, which may include free tickets or VIP passes to performances. Equity-based crowdfunding works similarly to equity financing, where contributors receive a financial return on their investment in the form of dividends (Pazowski and Czudec, 2014).

Case study – Hong Kong

As Asia's World City, Hong Kong's cultural influence stems from its mixed heritage of Chinese culture and Western colonization (Carroll, 2007). Since the return to China in 1997, the Hong Kong S.A.R. government has been the largest funding body and cultural presenter. Due to the 'high arts' status attached to the art form and its audience profile, corporate sponsorship has been a norm in the fundraising of classical music (Kolb, 2005). Scalable music organizations that have already attained a recognized level of artistic excellence and reputation, such as the Hong Kong Philharmonic Orchestra (HK Phil), seem to be more successful in raising revenue through sponsorships, funding, and donations.

People in Hong Kong are not in the habit of financially supporting the arts. The HKSAR government has invested in 'cultural hardware', such as the West Kowloon Cultural District, a HK $29 billion (US $3.72 billion) project started 20 years ago with the vision to create a new vibrant cultural quarter on a cinematic harbor front. Being the major supplier of arts creation, arts organizations (big or small) are 'cultural software' essential to the success of the government's investment in this world-class architecture. The government expects cultural organizations to be relevant to the communities that they operate in (and there is no greater endorsement than financial support from the citizens), and that the cultural organizations are capable of managing the donations they receive and delivering what the supporters expect. This is rapidly professionalizing the industry.

In the next section, the fundraising practice of two distinctively different organizations is explored and discussed. The case of HK Phil demonstrates how corporate endorsement transcends into a commitment beyond being just a sponsor. The case of Music Lab, a relatively smaller music organization, demonstrates how fundraising can be achieved through innovative means, including its artistic positioning.

HK Phil and the Swire Group

HK Phil is the flagship arts organization in Hong Kong, with 96 full-time musicians and 37 staff members, presenting more than 150 concerts over a 44-week season, and attracting 200,000 music lovers annually. Originally named the Sino-British Orchestra, it was renamed the Hong Kong Philharmonic Orchestra in 1957 and became professional in 1974. As a registered charitable organization, HK Phil receives a significant subsidy of over HK $74 million (US $9.5 million) per year from the HKSAR government through the direct subvention for the nine Major Performing Arts Groups. Other sources of income include long-term financial support from The Swire Charitable Trust, the Hong Kong Jockey Club Charities Trust, and other supporters. Funding, donations, and sponsorships make up approximately 79% of the total operating cost of HK Phil annually.

The Swire Group, or Swire, a company established two centuries ago in the United Kingdom, is well known in Hong Kong and East Asia as the property giant with a range of businesses including Cathay Pacific Airlines and as Coca-Cola franchisee. Swire has been the principal patron of the HK Phil since 2006, contributing about HK $14.7 million (US $1.9 million) to HK Phil yearly. Swire endeavors to promote artistic excellence, fosters access to classical music, and stimulates cultural participation in Hong Kong. Then, the *giver/receiver* hierarchy was obvious. Traditional sponsor entitlements are VIP tickets, media exposure and ticket discounts for the sponsored programs.

Eventually, Swire and the HK Phil begin to strategically bond at various levels and operate as a tight partnership. Every single piece of publicity material the orchestra produces is contractually required to carry the logo of Swire on a parallel level to the HK Phil's logo. Even when there is a third party sponsoring a specific programme, Swire's logo will still share the 'stage' with HK Phil. Such sharing of space likens the marriage of the two brands on equal and mutually beneficial terms. Each season, four dedicated series are branded under Swire, with programs tailored for different target segments: *Swire Maestro Series* consisting of masterpiece programs; *Swire Denim Series* for young urbanites; *Swire Sunday Family Series* for kids and families and *Swire Classic Insights* for university-level inspiration. On top of the series, Swire's *Symphony Under the Stars* is an annual free concert held at the Central Harbourfront, attracting over 18,000 audience members on a single evening. This event, which is co-presented by both Swire and HK Phil, is regarded as a mega concert contributing to Hong Kong's brand as an international cosmopolitan city with excellence in its arts.

A senior Swire representative sits on the HK Phil's board and contributes to the governance of finance and artistic development of the orchestra. Such an assimilated partnership at the executive management level implies mutual trust and the sharing of risks and responsibilities. This is a solid commitment of a corporate patron rarely seen in any other art organization in Hong Kong. One might argue that Swire's overwhelming presence may undermine other potential corporate sponsors' (especially those of similar business nature) desire to be affiliated with HK Phil. This puts the orchestra at risk of over-reliance on one principal patron, which could lead to catastrophic impacts to HK Phil if funding from Swire were to be withdrawn due to any changes in Swire's leadership, philanthropy direction, and business performance. Through its patronage, Swire has empowered HK Phil to make strategic plans with less financial constraint, and at the same time, enables the orchestra to take creative risks in achieving its artistic mission. Swire's generous contributions over the last 11 years, and it anticipated future support, will help ensure the orchestra's legacy as a premiere arts organization in Hong Kong.

Planned giving as another opportunity

In order to encourage individual giving through alternative means, HK Phil diversifies its fundraising efforts by capitalizing on its long history and connections with their patrons over the last 45 years. In 2018, the orchestra introduced a bequest programme, namely, *The Continuo Circle*, asking patrons to leave a legacy to secure HK Phil's future. Death has always been a taboo in Chinese society and is seldom being discussed publicly. The bequest programme is a planned giving campaign centered in this sensitive context. The design of the bequest programme has to go beyond the negative connotations of death and to be anchored on the idea of future continuity. The words used in the publicity materials are meticulously chosen and crafted. Strategically targeted on donors and patrons with the longest connections with the HK Phil, the bequest programme invites a dedicated group of patrons to become a Continuo Circle member by including the orchestra in their will as a gift. The gift enables the patrons' passion towards HK Phil to be remembered, shared and carried onto future generations as the orchestra flourishes through their ongoing support.

The bequest programme had a monumental start with Mr. Daniel Ng's family bequeathing a still-life oil painting by the Flemish artist Edwaert Collier to the orchestra. Ng was a board member of HK Phil between 2006 and 2013. Music and visual art lover, Ng remembered the HK Phil in his estate with a gift that reflects his passion for both art forms. His family and the HK Phil are celebrating the legacy of Mr. Ng and proceeds of his gift will be invested in a fund to support the education outreach of the orchestra. Planned giving is not uncommon in the western contexts, but it is a concept unfamiliar in Hong Kong, especially amongst the local Chinese. However, since HK Phil has a long history and a loyal following, it has been able to create a bequest programme which has provided a means for the most dedicated long-term patrons to express their devotion to the orchestra.

Music lab

Founded in 2013, Music Lab is a nonprofit arts organization that serves as a collaborative platform to unite artists and promote diversity to the Hong Kong's arts scene. Music Lab positions its contemporization of classical music making as "pouring old wine into new bottles". Their programs make age-old classical music relevant to the current society through the exploration of societal issues and cultural meaning. Kar Jing Wong, or KJ, is the founder of Music Lab. His name is popularized after a documentary, *KJ – Music & Life* (2009), was made on his passion, pursuits, and ideals in music. The documentary has received rave reviews and awards, including the 'Best Documentary' award at the Golden Horse Film Festival in 2009. Breaking the pilgrimage status of conventional classical music, KJ's passion and visions of 'Classic; Timeless; and Original' was shared by many young musicians, as well as people beyond the classical music scene. KJ has also successfully established himself a key opinion leader of contemporized classical music on social media, where he accumulates a wide pool of supporters and fans. With his rising popularity, Music Lab has utilized an unconventional fundraising means for classical music – crowdfunding for the *Music Lab Festival*.

> Music Lab Festival celebrates Hong Kong's best talents to present a series of concerts of the highest originality, dynamism and artistic quality. Centred on classical and original music by local artists, Music Lab Festival aims to display the originality of the city's young music-makers, compose the new sound of tomorrow, and reimagine Hong Kong itself. (*Music Lab Festival's* crowdfunding website)

Music Lab Festival appeals in particular to the younger crowd which celebrates localism and its boldness. A critical feature of the festival is the crowdfunding project running on its website since it first started in 2016. For *Music Lab Festival 2018*, they set a target to fundraise HK $100,000 (US $12,821) by offering three tiers of reward-based crowdfunding – HK $1,200/$800/$650 (US $154/103/83). Supporters receive tickets to the festival and merchandises such as CDs, posters, postcards, and others, depending on their level of contribution. In just 27 days, HK $102,600 (US $13,154) was raised from 68 patrons. Music Lab's success is not just about the ability to reach their fundraising target. Rather, they have successfully engaged their publics to participate in making the festival possible via the collective fundraising effort. The social media engagement and dialogues induced by this act create an invaluable return on investment for the brand. The idea to fundraise for tangible and intangible return, as well as the return on social engagement through the crowdfunding process, is opening up more fundraising possibilities for arts organizations.

Case study – Macao

Macao is a located on the southeast coast of Mainland China with a mere total land area of 30.8 square kilometers. Before the return to China in 1999, Macao was the colony of Portugal for over 400 years since the mid-16th century. According to Macao's Statistics and Census Service (2018), the city has a population of 653,100 and a GDP per capita of approximately US $76,000 in 2017. Macao's economy relies heavily on the tourism, gaming and hospitality industries, which contribute to a major portion of GDP and government spending. Despite the small population, Macao is a city full of nonprofit associations, and many music organizations are established as nonprofit associations. The proliferation of associations has affected how fundraising in Macao works, as most of the subsidies and grants are only applicable to these associations.

According to the Macao Music Yearbook 2014, there were over 200 concerts or music events in the city that year, of which over 90% were classical music concerts. There is only one professional orchestra in the city, Macao Orchestra, which is directly under the purview of the Cultural Affairs Bureau (CAB) of the Macao S.A.R. Government. Around a dozen from the hundreds of music associations are considered active, and they are the major organizers of concerts in Macao. They include the Macau[1] Strings Association, Macau Band Directors Association, Macao Youth Symphony Orchestra Association, Macau Piano Association, and Macao Percussion Association, to name a few. Besides holding regular concerts and activities annually, these associations also provide music training to those interested

Fundraising for the arts and culture in Macao

Fundraising in Macao can be attributed to two major sources – government funding and foundation funding. Only a small percentage of financial support to the arts comes from private donations and corporate sponsorships. Government funding is available from different governmental departments depending on the nature of the arts activities. For instance, an organization may apply for subsidies from the CAB for classical music concerts or from the Education and Youth Affairs Bureau for educational concerts. Where relevant, arts organizations may even apply for funding from the Civil and Municipal Affairs Bureau or the Tourism Government Office. The Office of Secretariat for Social Affairs and Culture may sometimes award funding to special projects, such as the touring of arts activities out of the city.

Amongst all the governmental department, CAB has a more comprehensive subsidy programme for local nonprofit associations to apply. The subsidy programme is classi-fied into three different categories – Financial Support for Local Associations (Activities and Cultural Projects); Talent Training Programme in Arts Management; Community Arts Projects Support Programme. Subsidy amounts range from MOP5,000 (US $610) to MOP250,000 (US $30,500) for a single project. The Talent Training Programme in Arts Management offers a yearly subsidy for associations to hire full-time or part-time art administrators for the day-to-day operations of the association. The Bureau also offers subsidies for groups or individuals going overseas for cultural exchanges and competitions. Hence, most of the associations rely on annual subsidy programs to finance their music projects and hire arts administrators.

Funding from foundations is extremely important in Macao. Macao Foundation, one of the major foundations, is a public organization comprising of the Trust Committee,

Executive Committee and Board of Advisors. The major source of funds comes from the tax income of the gaming industry, where it is mandatory for gaming companies to contribute 1.6% of their gross income into the foundation every year. Including other government funding and private donations, the Macao Foundation raised more than MOP42.09 billion (US $5.13 billion) worth of funds in 2017, of which MOP159 million (US $19.4 million) was allocated to art organizations and cultural events. Henry Fok Foundation and Oriental Foundation are two other foundations that contribute enormously to the cultural activities.

Macao orchestra

Macao Orchestra is the only professional orchestra in Macao, set up as a chamber orchestra in 1983, and developed into a double winds orchestra by the government in 2001. As of October 2018, the orchestra has over 60 musicians from more than ten countries and regions. The orchestra runs an 11-month concert season from September to July every year, offering over 90 concerts and outreach programs to the public each season. Operating under the auspices of CAB's Performing Arts Development Department, the orchestra is fully funded by the government, providing all the necessary resources that the orchestra needs through an annual budget, as well as the support of the performance venue. Indeed, the orchestra has to undertake the responsibility, adhere to regulations being the government's entity, and encounter several limitations in its operations and management. This means they lack flexibility when compare to other major privatized orchestras in the world.

Due to the direct link to the Macao government, Macao Orchestra is not in any position to fundraise for cash through other foundations, private donations, or corporate sponsorships. Nevertheless, the orchestra is allowed to seek in-kind support from corporations. In recent years, the orchestra has actively sought in-kind support from hospitality corporations or the tertiary education institutes, with the hope to expand the influence and better promote the orchestra to the public and tourists on the one hand, and on the other, solve the critical issues that the orchestra is facing. One such issue is the lack of venues in Macao. Currently, the only professional performance venue is the Macao Cultural Centre, in which there is a multi-purpose grand auditorium for the performances in Macao. In-kind support from the University of Macau has enabled the orchestra to use the rehearsal space and the University Hall for concerts, in return for some free concerts for the university's students as part of their general education programme. Another example venue support is The Venetian Macao, an integrated luxury resort of leisure and entertainment, with a handful of theatres and performance venues within the resort. The orchestra has partnered with the resort in recent years on projects such as multimedia concerts or festivity concerts such as the Valentine's Day Concert. Again, these collaborations between Macao Orchestra and corporations do not involve direct cash support, yet they encourage corporations to support the arts, and open doors to other art organizations seeking for direct cash sponsorships.

Macau band directors association

Macau Band Directors Association is a nonprofit music association founded in 1996, with aims to promote wind music activities and its development. Their members include wind band conductors, instruments instructors, and students. With around 150 active members, the association organized around 30 wind music activities every year, of which the major activity is the annual Macau Band Fair. Many experienced wind band conductors, wind soloists, and educators join their performances and deliver master classes in the fair. The Association is also a member of the Asia Pacific Band Directors' Association since 1998, and they had hosted the *14th Asia Pacific Band Festival* and *Asia Pacific Band Directors' Association Conference in Macau* in 2006. Being one of the leading music associations in Macao, their main sources of revenue include the CAB, Education and Youth Affairs Bureau, and the Macao Foundation. With funds from the above entities, the association can fully finance its annual activities and the operations, as well as to purchase instruments. Besides direct cash funding, the association also seeks in-kind support from the government, churches, and the Oriental Foundation, mainly for subsidized or free performance venues.

Macau strings association

Macau Strings Association is a nonprofit music association set up in 2011, with aims to create a platform for performances, information, and training for strings musicians. In order to enhance the capabilities and professional techniques of their members (around 300), the association organizes around ten concerts and regular workshops. The association also partners with high schools to deliver instrumental training classes. The fundraising situation of Macau Strings Association is similar to Macau Band Directors Association in that both organizations receive funding from the CAB and the Macao Foundation. Moreover, Macau Strings Association also seeks in-kind support for performance venues, such as the Macao Cultural Centre and Dom Pedro V Theatre. Nevertheless, there are also some crucial differences. A private donation, including a venue, was offered to Macau Strings Association to set up the association in 2011, and this has remained as a major source of funds for the association. The Historic Centre of Macao has been listed on the UNESCO's World Heritage List since 2005. The association has also made use of heritage sites for small music concerts, bringing about extraordinary and enjoyable experiences to audiences at the world heritage sites. With the approval from CAB, the Macau Strings Association do not have to pay for the use of these heritage sites.

Fundraising for classical music – present and future

Having presented the current state of classical music fundraising in Hong Kong and Macao, this section focuses on some critical issues of the current development and attempts to offer some thoughts on future possibilities of fundraising in these two cities.

Governmental vs. non-governmental giving

From the discussions thus far, one observation is the reliance of public money for classical music organizations in both Hong Kong and Macao. This reliance on public money could be interpreted in two ways. First, the organizations *receive* public funding, which covers a large percentage of their total expenditure. This is especially evident in Macao case studies. When public funding is deemed sufficient, organizations become less motivated to raise funds via other means, such as ticket sales. Organizations might, therefore, cut down the number of performances and have a lesser drive to develop new audiences. The second approach suggests that organizations *expect* public funding to cover a large part of the expenses, but in reality, public funding is often a moderate percentage of what they need. This funding scenario is more common in the case of Hong Kong (and the rest of the world). In Hong Kong, there is a clear divide between performing arts organizations (MPAOs; HK Phil included), and other small- and medium-sized ones. While MPAOs are not fully funded by the government, they do receive a sizeable amount of public money and can devote a budget for fundraising efforts. Smaller organizations receive projects or yearly grants from the Hong Kong Arts Development Council (HKADC), an independent statutory body of the government. However, HKADC operates with a very limited budget, and it struggles to meet the demands of the smaller organizations that lack the resources to implement fundraising strategies if any at all.

While there is some evidence of corporate sponsorships in classical music, the current trend of giving seems to be directed towards the major organizations in the two cities. Moving forward, the government of Hong Kong and Macao needs to rethink its strategies to encourage further non-governmental giving (such as corporate sponsorships) directed towards the arts, and special considerations must be given smaller and medium-sized groups. Since 2016, HKADC has rolled out the Matching Fund Scheme (MFS) to stimulate non-governmental giving towards arts organizations, especially small and medium ones. Under MFS, eligible organizations could receive up to 1.5 times of matching fund for cash sponsorships received. Moreover, the minimum sum of sponsorship is set at HK $30,000 cash (US $3823). The MFS, though helpful, does not quite address the root of the problem. While arts organizations may work harder to seek for donors, the existence of a matching grant from the government does little to boost donors' motivation towards giving to the arts. Furthermore, smaller arts organizations may be further marginalized in the process, as donors, especially corporate companies, may be keen to give to organizations with higher visibility.

On a yearly basis, HKADC presents the Award for Arts Sponsorship to several donors who have provided financial support to the development of the arts in Hong Kong. In 2017, only four companies were given this award, and their impacts were not significant. A case-in-point for both governments to explore is the Patrons of the Arts Award initiated by Singapore's National Arts Council in 1983. This award is given to individuals or corporate companies who have supported arts organizations either in cash or in-kind. Non-cash sponsorships that lead to arts organizations reducing their real cost of operations are accepted. This encourages a whole new paradigm of sponsorship activities for arts organizations of all sizes and scales. For smaller arts organizations, they may benefit from office and rehearsal spaces sponsored by corporate companies with extra rooms in their buildings. Support could also come from technology firms, providing free hardware and software for daily operations (such as computers and web servers). Across the board, arts organizations benefit from in-kind sponsorships in printing, hotel accommodations, flight tickets, and the list goes on.

Another highlight of the Patron of the Arts Award is in its tiered system with three categories of award. With different amounts of sponsorships, starting from a minimum of SGD $10,000 (HK $57,200 or US $7300) for individual donors SG $50,000 (HK $286,000 or US $36,500) for corporate donors, one may receive a Friend of the Arts Award, a Patron of the Arts Award, or a Distinguished Patron of the Arts Award. To attain the highest giving level, sponsorship amounts must reach at least SG $100,000 (HK $572,000 or US $73,000) for individuals and SG $1.5 million (HK $8.59 million or US $1.09 million) for corporate donors. With a tiered system, corporate donors (especially) are keen to reach high levels to reflect their excellent corporate citizenry. The final highlight of this award lies in the capitals generated in its entire organization. The annual award ceremony is held in the presence of a special guest, usually the President of the Republic of Singapore, and the minister for Culture, who gives out the awards to the patrons (cultural and symbolic capital for the donors). Arts organizations and artists (recipient of the economic capital) are also invited to the ceremony, with a reception for further networking (social capital for the arts organizations/artists). Usually, the event will be well reported in the local news media, often with a full list of awardees mentioned in the national newspaper (more symbolic capital for the donors). In 2017 alone, 302 donors in Singapore supported the arts with SG $51.6 million (HK $295.2 million or US $37.6 million) worth of cash and in-kind sponsorships.

Revisiting crowdfunding

Crowdfunding for classical music is not a common practice in the two cities studied. In Macao, crowdfunding for the arts is almost non-existent, likely due to the generous public funding. In Hong Kong, on the other hand, crowdfunding seems to be a more popular option for choral music and acapella performances, both targeting seemingly younger audiences. One possible explanation lies in the public perception of classical music. Many deem classical music as an art form for the rich, by the rich. It is not surprising to receive occasional remarks that orchestras are very well endowed. In fact, it might seem weird or even degrading for orchestras or other classical music organizations to raise funds through crowdfunding. Moreover, research has shown that classical music audiences are generally more affluence and have better social status (Gibson and Connell, 2016; Sawyer, 2012). While they have the means to support the orchestra, these audiences are likely to prefer other modes of engagement with the organization, such as attending fundraising galas and subscribing to meet-the-musicians' sessions.

Classical music organizations ought not to exclude crowdfunding from the list of fundraising strategies too quickly. Increasingly, there are more organizations that fuse classical and contemporary music, seeking to push forward a new look and feel for classical music and attracting wider support from younger people. These organizations, such as Music Lab, could make use of crowdfunding and the impacts of going viral on social media to raise funds. Through reward-based crowdfunding, organizations could secure audiences for their performances, where backers receive tickets to the performances for contributing to the production cost. The direct access to backers also mean that crowdfunding could even be an opportunity for organizations to establish good relationships with their supporters, with constant updates of the creation and rehearsal process. Conventional classical music organizations could also adopt crowdfunding for specific projects or activities beyond their musical cause, such as building an archive for educational purposes or making music accessible to subordinated communities.

Generating IPs as a fundraising strategy

The nonprofit nature of most classical music organizations in Hong Kong and Macao meant that equity financing would be a less adopted approach. While the performing arts is categorized as part of the creative industries in both cities, there has never been clear evidence of how the performing arts in these two cities contribute to the economy, other than the simplified explanation of the multiplier effect. Nevertheless, there are opportunities for performing arts to work towards generating IPs that would eventually contribute to the creative economy. An artistic product, such a classical music concert, has the potential to create multiple IPs that could contribute to the fundraising process of an organization. A concert, once recorded, can be stored in a medium for further distribution and sales. Immediately, this opens up a new opportunity for classical music fundraising. One such example is HK Phil's live recording of the four-part *Wagner's Ring Cycle*, which is available for sale on CD/Blu-ray. Partial IPs of upcoming concerts can also be pre-sold to arts-related TV channels and cinemas with performing arts programming anywhere in the world to raise funds to cover the costs of production. With more advanced technology, including high definition screens, it is even possible for concerts to be streamed live, reaching out to more audiences in the process. For instance, a concert in Hong Kong or Macao can be broadcast live to another group of classical music audiences in Beijing and Shanghai at the same time. All the preceding possibilities mean that the income generated from audience attendance can increase exponentially, breaking away from the two major limitations of a conventional live performance – a fixed number of seats at a fixed time.

Conclusion

The chapter has discussed the current state of classical music fundraising in both Hong Kong and Macao, through the case studies of five organizations. This section extends the fundraising discourse into the performing arts in general. Assuming that government funding for the performing arts in both cities is going to continue for many years to come, organizations should still work towards developing multiple sources of funds from multiple corporate sponsors, as well as other avenues, such as crowdfunding and selling partial IP rights. Definitely, it might be an impossible task for performing arts organizations directly under the purview of the government (such as Macao Orchestra) to accept other sources of funding. For the majority of other nongovernmental arts organizations, having multiple funding sources would gradually reduce their reliance on government funding. The additional financial resources from the government could be redirected to support other small and medium arts organizations with good potential, or be injected into infrastructural development for the performing arts. Policies should also allow and encourage performing arts organizations to develop strong endowment fund, to better prepare themselves for any major reduction or cuts of funding due to unforeseen circumstances. For instance, funding policies may change significantly when the "One country, two systems" policy comes to an end in Hong Kong and Macao by 2047 and 2049 respectively. At this stage, it is impossible to predict what will exactly happen to the state of public funding for the arts then.

Note

1 'Macao' is the official English name of the city, while 'Macau' is the official Portuguese name and sometimes used by organizations as their registered name.

References

Brustein, R.S. (1991). *Reimagining American theatre*. New York: Hill and Wang.
Campbell, M. (1999). Masters of the baroque and classical eras. In: R. Stonewell, ed., *The Cambridge companion to the cello*. Cambridge: Cambridge University Press.
Cantatore, F. and Crawford-Spencer, E. (2018). *Effective intellectual property management for small to medium businesses and social enterprises: IP branding, licenses, trademarks, copyrights, patents and contractual arrangements*. Irvine: BrownWalker Press.
Carroll, J.M. (2007). *A concise history of Hong Kong*. Lanham, MD: Rowman & Littlefield Publishers.
Corporate Sponsorship. (n.d.). Available from: www.councilofnonprofits.org/tools-resources/corporate-sponsorship [Accessed 14 Sep. 2018].
Foundation Center. (n.d.). *What is the difference between a private foundation and a public charity?* Available at: https://grantspace.org/resources/knowledge-base/private-foundations-vs-public-charities/ [Accessed 27 Sep. 2018].
Gibson, C. and Connell, J. (2016). *Music festivals and regional development in Australia*. London and New York: Routledge.
Harris, R. (2002). *What to listen for in Mozart*. New York: Simon and Schuster.
Johnson, J. (2002). *Who needs classical music?: Cultural choice and musical value*. New York: Oxford University Press.
Kaiser, M.M. (2015). *Curtains?: The future of the arts in America*. Waltham, MA: Brandeis University Press.
Kolb, B.M. (2005). *Marketing for cultural organisations: New strategies for attracting audiences to classical music, dance, museums, theatre & opera*. London: Cengage Learning EMEA.
Lowe, M. (2007). *Pleasure and meaning in the classical symphony*. Bloomington and Indianapolis: Indiana University Press.
McDonnell, I. and Moir, M. (2013). *Event sponsorship*. London and New York: Routledge.
Music Lab Festival 2018. (n.d.). Available at: https://musicbee.cc/project/music-lab-festival-2018 [Accessed 12 Oct. 2018].
Pazowski, P. and Czudec, W. (2014). Economic prospects and conditions of crowdfunding. In: *Management Knowledge and Learning International Conference*, pp. 1079–1088.
Sawyer, R.K. (2012). *Explaining creativity: The science of human innovation*. New York: Oxford University Press.
Scholz, N. (2015). *The relevance of Crowdfunding: The impact on the innovation process of small entrepreneurial firms*. Wiesbaden: Springer Gabler.
Walter, C. (2015). *Arts management: An entrepreneurial approach*. New York and London: Routledge.
Yudkin, J. (2005). *Understanding music*. Upper Saddle River, NJ: Pearson Prentice Hall.

29

FUNDING FORWARD

Stable funding for museums in an unstable world

Julianne Amendola, Kaywin Feldman, and Matthew Welch

Introduction

After the global economic recession that began in 2008, nonprofit arts leaders waited anxiously for their world to "return to normal." Instead, it has become clear that we live in a new reality that entails constant change and uncertainty. In addition to economic and philanthropic changes, societal shifts are increasingly altering our audiences' behavior and worldview. Like it or not, we must adapt or risk a slow but inevitable demise.

The pace of change has never been faster and cultural organizations now exist in a world of digital connectivity that brings information, opportunity, distractions, and threats in equal measure. After the end of the Cold War, the U.S. Army College described the new context in which the world operates in terms of four distinct challenges, referred to as VUCA, an acronym for **V**olatility, **U**ncertainty, **C**omplexity, and **A**mbiguity (U.S. Army Heritage and Education Center, 2018)

The business world quickly adopted this concept to describe their external operating environment. To thrive in a VUCA world necessitates being agile, flexible, and always open to multiple scenarios. While an organization's objective should be clear, there may be equally multiple paths to reach that goal.

In a volatile world, change is constant but unpredictable, requiring the ability to pivot quickly. Agility, therefore, becomes more important than ever before. Added to the volatility is uncertainty, making it hard to hypothesize about any kind of linear future. This world is complex and full of interdependencies, making it more difficult to achieve anticipated outcomes. Ambiguity means that there may be several different ways to understand and resolve a situation.

The physical impressiveness of museum buildings, the extensive collections, the weight of their histories, and the loftiness of their missions can give the impression that cultural organizations are immune to external societal changes. Of course, museums are hardly inured to the challenges of a VUCA world as market volatility, and global uncertainties impact endowment earnings, foundation and corporate support, and even patron contributions, and as the complex new demographics of our communities impact our audiences and the knowledge, perspective, and expectations they bring to their museum visits and to philanthropy.

Despite the volatility of our operating environment, art institutions are rarely quick to innovate or to risk untested tactics, especially when it comes to financial support. Most innovation capital comes from private donors and foundations, which can mean a lengthy process of research and cultivation, solicitation, confirmation, and gift receipt. Arts philanthropy tends to be conservative and backward-looking, resting more comfortably on approaches that reflect proven behaviors of the past, often with known or anticipated outcomes. Increasingly, venture innovation funders (applying the venture innovation funding model to support social good) have entered the philanthropic mix, but these donors tend to work more closely with organizations that tackle difficult social problems, and not within the arts sector (Cobb, 2002).

Arts institutions grew substantially during the 20th century. For example, the Museum of Fine Arts Boston had four major expansions (1915, 1928, 1970, 1981) and in 1999 embarked on a master planning process that would drive two additional expansions in 2006 and 2010 (Museum of Fine Arts Boston, 2018). The Museum of Fine Arts Houston has had four major expansions (1953, 1958, 1974, 2000) with a campus-wide refresh and expansion anticipated to be completed in 2020 (Museum of Fine Arts Houston, 2018). The Virginia Museum of Fine Arts expanded in 1954, 1970, 1976, and 1985, and unveiled its largest expansion to date in 2010 (Virginia Museum of Fine Arts, 2018). Moreover, the Minneapolis Institute of Art has undergone four major expansions since its opening in 1915 (1927, 1974, 1998, 2005) (see Figure 29.1).

Already grand buildings, these and many more across the country were enlarged to accommodate more visitors and growing collections. With each expansion designed by a notable architect, these institutions were a source of civic pride and identity – physical indications that American ingenuity, productivity, and wealth could provide its citizens with a rich and varied cultural life.

In the 21st century, museum leaders increasingly grapple with this unbridled growth. How sustainable is the prospect of even larger campuses with more and bigger buildings to house and display ever-increasing collections? At what point will institutions buckle under the financial expense of maintaining, heating, cooling, operating, and securing such vast facilities? For example, the Metropolitan Museum of Art currently overwhelms visitors with some 633,100 square feet of gallery space stretching a quarter mile along Fifth Avenue and deep into Central Park, the result of some twenty building expansions. Maintenance, utilities, and security alone cost a daunting $103,584,000 in 2016 (Metropolitan Museum of Art, 2017).

Figure 29.1   Minneapolis Institute of Arts (showing three architectural styles of its five major expansions, 2018)

Source: Minneapolis Institute of Art

At the same time, the visiting public's expectations for a cultural experience are changing. Immersive experiences and direct participation are supplanting passive learning (Schwab, 2016). Programmatic offerings that have relevance to visitors' lives and reflect the realities of their diverse communities are replacing the monolithic narrative of a colonial worldview (Olsen, 2018). Opportunities for engagement with others and contemporary, relevant community issues are an increasing driver of attendance.

Frequently, however, the existing physical, programmatic, and organizational structures in historic cultural institutions are rooted in an older vision. Museums and arts organizations must change these structures to fit new, more dynamic and agile approaches. Moreover, in order to fund this direction, ways must be found to work with both existing and new donors – to engage them with new ideas, to inspire their long-term support and loyalty, and to meet their often-competing needs. In truth, as museum audiences' expectations have changed, so have the needs and interests of many of our donors. U.S. ice hockey player Wayne Gretzky famously stated that to score, he "needed to skate to where the puck is going to be, not where it has been." But where do you go when there are multiple pucks, all headed in different directions?

This chapter will provide an overview of issues museums face, now and in the future, with special emphasis on changing demographics, visitor expectations, and philanthropic giving to the arts. The latter half of the chapter will posit how our offerings and programs must change to meet the expectation of new, younger donors and granting agencies, while also keeping traditional donors engaged. Finally, the chapter will offer recommendations for systemic changes in how museums fundraise that will better position them for a stable financial future in the midst of an increasingly unstable world.

Figure 29.2   *Resistance, Protest and Resilience* exhibition at Mia, Nov. 5, 2016–April 2, 2017, tapped into the zeitgeist of civic unrest after the last presidential election

Source: Minneapolis Institute of Art

Scanning the horizon: where are we and where are we going?

The Minneapolis Institute of Art (Mia) was incorporated in 1883 as the Minneapolis Society of Fine Arts and opened the doors of a newly built museum in 1915. Since then, the museum has grown through successive expansions to over 425,000 square feet (approximately 160,000 square feet of gallery space), with an encyclopedic collection of some 90,000 objects. For much of its history, the permanent collection has been free and open to the public, and this tradition continues today, thus delivering on the museum's mission to enrich the community by making accessible the art works that it collects and preserves. In recent years, the museum has heightened its national and international reputation through ambitious exhibitions and initiatives intended to further the field (e.g., Museums as Site for Social Action and the Center for Empathy in the Visual Arts). At the same time, improvements in the visitor experience, including enhanced amenities, easily understood gallery didactics, online resources, and provocative programming have served to push annual attendance to record levels (891,206 in FY2017).

The museum's strategic plan begins with an environmental scan. While it is imperative that we think broadly and conduct extensive research, it is also important to determine a manageable list of contemporary trends and behaviors that the institution will monitor closely.

Mia's Strategic Plan 2021 highlights ten contemporary societal tendencies (Minneapolis Institute of Art, 2016). We have identified these trends as having the greatest potential impact on the museum, our audience, and our fundraising opportunities:

- Changing population demographics (current and projected) in Minnesota and across America
- Rise of big data and analysis; enhanced understanding of consumer behavior and personalization ("show me you know me")
- Increased need for people to slow down, disconnect from media, and connect with humanity in the face of a noisy, digital, and distracted world
- Changes in philanthropic behavior and the generational transfer of wealth
- Enhanced need for relevance and attention to social justice
- Economic uncertainty and the need for stronger sustainability through new financial models
- An audience that includes passionate cultural omnivores who maintain a much broader definition of arts and culture than ever before
- Greater competition for leisure time, coupled with an increasing number of visitors who arrive at the museum feeling stressed
- The rise of the experience economy
- New opportunities for formal and informal learning

These important trends can be summarized into four broad areas that merit closer examination for their impact on arts fundraising: changing demographics, customer expectations, the experience economy, and the philanthropic landscape.

Changing demographics

Changing demographics will radically impact the future of arts organizations in America. The Census Bureau currently projects that people of color will constitute the majority of the American population by 2045 (see Figure 29.3).

Two trends are causing this change: between 2018 and 2060 the population of people of color will grow by 74% through higher birth rates and immigration, while the white population

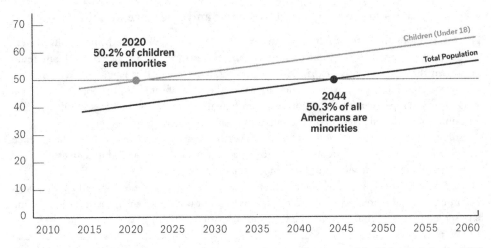

Figure 29.3 Non-Hispanic whites may no longer comprise over 50 percent of the U.S. population by 2044

will decline through aging and lower birth rates. The populations with the largest projected increases include people of mixed race, Asians, and Latinos. Minority groups are younger than white groups, and it is projected that as early as 2020 the majority of people under the age of 18 will be people of color (Frey, 2018).

America's diverse population will consist of future voters, consumers, tax-paying citizens – and active arts participants and philanthropists. It is imperative that arts organizations diversify their staff and boards so that they can better understand and attract arts and cultural programming seekers from among this increasingly diverse population. According to the 2015 Mellon Foundation report, only 16% of senior staff members (leadership, curators, educators) in American art museums are people of color (Schonfeld, Westermann, and Sweeney, 2015). Museum boards, too, are sorely lacking in diversity.

In recent years, Mia has experienced significant growth among younger (under 45) and more diverse visitors as we have broadened our programmatic offerings, connected through social media, and placed more emphasis on online resources (see Figure 29.4).

Historically, the museum's largest visitor segment has been comprised of "loyal traditionalists," people who are older (over 60), largely white, and who enjoy traditional programming. Given that the majority of our current funders fall in this loyal traditionalist's category, keeping them engaged and feeling valued while also ensuring that the organization's programming, marketing, and events meet the needs of a younger and more diverse audience is a significant challenge. Loyal traditionalists will sometimes walk away from an organization that they feel disregards them and their needs by prioritizing younger and more diverse audiences. It is difficult but important to strike a balance so that we engage new audiences while maintaining our more traditional – and more philanthropic – base. Indeed, loyal traditionalists are largely comprised of baby boomers who have time and financial capacity; as well, many are at the point in their lives when they are thinking about their legacies and potential planned financial gifts to arts organizations with whom they have longstanding relationships (Samuel, 2017).

Another challenge for arts organizations is the expectation of young and diverse audiences that their arts organizations demonstrate relevancy by engaging in contemporary issues, such as gender equality, racial equity, social justice, and environmental concerns – the very issues that they track via online news feeds and social media (Devos, 2018). Retailers are being held to the

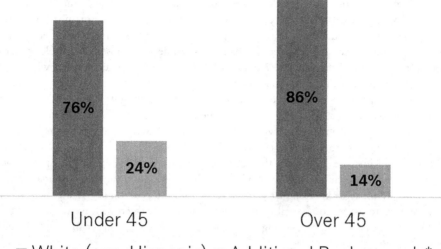

Under 45   Over 45

■ White (non-Hispanic) ■ Additional Backgrounds*

*Additional backgrounds include American Indian/Alaska Native, Asian/Pacific Islander, Black/African American/African, Middle Eastern/North African, Multi-Racial/Multi-Ethnic, Spanish/Hispanic/Latino, and an option to self-describe.

Figure 29.4 Younger visitors are more racially and ethnically diverse

Source: Minneapolis Institute of Art, Annual Visitor Study: 2018 Audience Report (page 8). Used with permission

same standards (Cone, 2017). We need to garner support for these new topical approaches to our collections and interpretation; however, this is difficult because many of our current philanthropists are loyal traditionalists who grew up in an overwhelmingly white world (78% of people age 65 and older are white) when cultural organizations were perceived to be a refuge from pressing problems of the day (Bryant-Greenwell, 2017).

Customer expectations: data and personalization

Consumer research has been integral to the retail sector since its beginnings in the 1920s. Gathering and interpreting consumer data is just as important to cultural organizations. Our audience comprises sophisticated consumers who expect us to understand their needs and behaviors. At Mia, the area of greatest staffing growth in the last three years has been audience research, with the addition of team members who can help us design studies and gather, analyze, and interpret data. Armed with this data, we can make more accurate predictions of visitor and donor behavior, thereby anticipating and improving their experiences and engagement with the museum. This engagement includes how and when they want to hear from us; how often they visit and what types of experiences they prefer; how they might like to be solicited and which parts of our program would be of greatest interest; and how much or little attention they want.

Robert Stephens, former Mia trustee and founder of The Geek Squad, a company that offers various computer-related services (merged with Best Buy in 2002), notes that, in the world of data capture and usage, "there is a fine line between creepy and cool – and you always want to be on the cool side" (R. Stephens 2018, personal communication, 1 September). Mia strives to find and keep this balance. For example, at the acquisition of a new member, we send an email asking after their interests – from youth programs to talks and films to local artists. Then, when we send monthly program-related emails, we include only those content blocks for the programs they have said they are interested in. Additionally, we provide members with person-alized digital dashboards, allowing them to track their activity with us, to update their contact information and preferences, and to express their interests and insights. These dashboards, only recently launched by Mia, will evolve based on member feedback, allowing us to tailor future communications to enhance their awareness of museum activities that match their expressed interests – hopefully, a "cool" case in point.

At the same time, we know that the visitor experience can be negatively impacted when we get it wrong. For example, it is "creepy" to a visitor if we go outside the boundaries of our social media. While it is expected that we post exhibition information to our sites that they fol-low, if we were to tag visitors' social media handles directly with content we think they might find interesting, that would be crossing a "creepy" line that would impact the potential future relationship.

Studies have shown that consumer engagement with cultural organizations has changed substantially, especially among younger audiences. Many museums have seen a decline in annual memberships and many performing arts organizations have witnessed flagging season subscrip-tions. It is not that the arts are out of style, it is that our modes of engagement are outmoded. As described in Culture Track, younger audiences are cultural omnivores; they consume lots of culture, but they do it in their own way and on their own schedule (La Placa Cohen, 2017; National Endowment for the Arts, 2015).

To address this changed behavior, at Mia we have added a free membership level with the goal of opening lines of communication with a larger pool of people interested in art. Given that accessibility is our most important value, why not offer everyone who self-selects the oppor-tunity to be "under the tent"? With more people in the membership pool, providing us with more information about their interests and needs, we can do a better job of creating compelling programs and optimizing their experience. Over time, this approach also allows us to personalize our relationships with members and donors and to identify those who are truly prospects for higher levels of philanthropic engagement.

Part of Mia's new approach to membership is to emphasize that paid membership levels represent philanthropy rather than simple financial transactions to receive a member magazine, tickets, catalogs, event invitations, and so forth. At its core, this model allows us to pose the ques-tion, "how much do you value the museum, its collections, and programs?" Inevitably, members contribute more in this scenario than in a transactional one, and the average gift from con-tributing members has increased by more than 25% since the launch of the new membership approach (based on a comparison of the average gift received from contributing members prior to the launch, and at the close of the fiscal year ending June 2018).

It is important to stress that this is a strategy for entry-level members and not high-level donors; high-level philanthropy will always be high touch. As museums have learned, entry-level membership is rarely a path to major giving (Axelrad, 2014). A better revenue strategy for mem-bership is more targeted engagement with members that demonstrate the institution's value to the community and quality of civic and social life. As organizational consultant Simon Sinek states, "People don't buy what you do; they buy why you do it. And what you do simply proves what you believe" (Sinek, 2009). This entails working to convey the passion we feel about the collection, its preservation, meaning, and accessibility. Ultimately, this strategy should enhance members' perception of the institution and lead to more visits, ticket sales, event registrations, social media promotion, and store visits – likely, a more robust financial relationship overall that is rooted in deeper engagement and shared investment in the museum's mission.

The experience economy

Many of America's large arts organizations were founded in the early 20th century. As our urban centers grew up, civic leaders looked to Europe as a model and recognized that all great cities could boast of a library, an art museum, a symphony, a zoo, and so forth. (Rodini, 2018) These civic institutions defined a civilized, cultured, and democratic society and their growth was a dominant theme in the United States for much of the 20th century. For art museums, the rallying cry was "more space to show the public more art." We were part of a service economy, offering intangible benefits by enabling visitors to see and learn about art through our ever-expanding collections.

Throughout the last century, art museum officials and their patrons have passionately acquired, conserved, and displayed growing collections, attracting visitors by advertising the breadth and depth of these collections ("something for everyone") and, periodically, unveiling new buildings filled with more art. Moreover, we have convinced "loyal traditionalist" donors to support this work financially.

During the 21st century, cultural organizations have begun to move into the "experience economy." "An experience occurs when a company intentionally uses service as the stage, and goods as props, to engage individual customers in a way that creates a memorable event. Commodities are fungible, goods tangible, services intangible, and experiences memorable" (Pine and Gilmore, 1998). For example, a recent traveling exhibition of Yayoi Kusama's installation art has been a sold-out blockbuster in every location of the tour. Museums are rushing to work with artists who create large-scale immersive environments that are memorable, in part, because they stimulate multiple senses (see Figure 29.5).

Research indicates that learning and memory imprint more strongly when more than one sense is involved in a given activity. (Shams and Seitz, 2008) At the same time, immersive installations encourage visitors to document their experiences within a unique environment by taking selfies – a means to preserve the experience further and to share it with others. Because an encyclopedic art museum like Mia cannot only show large immersive contemporary artwork, how do we replicate the exciting and delightful experiences that younger audiences crave within our more traditional and static collections? Moreover, how do we fund this innovative new work?

In 2015, Mia celebrated its centennial. To dissociate the museum with all of the black-tie self-laudatory notions that a "centennial" implies, we named it "the birthday year" and created a surprising event or program each week, calling them "birthday surprises." The "surprises" ranged from small (100 artist-created jack o'lanterns on the steps of the museum on Halloween) to large (water towers around the city wrapped in vinyl reproductions of famous works in the museum's collection) (see Figure 29.6).

The museum positioned these experiences as "birthday gifts" to our community in recognition of 100 years of support. In raising money for the year, a few of our loyal traditionalists disdained the entire endeavor as frivolous and not core to our mission. In one case, a donor generously contributed the gift we requested, but specifically asked that it not be used to fund the year's surprise experiences ("frivolous"), but instead to fund a specific exhibition ("real" museum work).

Figure 29.5   Power and Beauty in China's Last Dynasty at Mia, February 3–June 10, 2018. Immersive installation designed by theatrical producer and designer, Robert Wilson

Source: Minneapolis Institute of Art

For the most part, our traditional donors still consider us a part of the service economy; we have trained them to fund the things that we need (equipment, collections, buildings) in order to provide the visiting public with a service (viewing works of art). How do we move these patrons – and entice new ones – to help us fund our work in offering experiences?

The challenge of fundraising for the creation of experiences, instead of the tangible things indicative of the service economy model, will become ever more pressing as museum curators and artists struggle to stage immersive installations, programs, and events in aging museum facilities not designed for such use. At Mia, we have developed a facility master plan that will require a significant capital campaign, but that does not feature the traditional elements of such a campaign: i.e., more art and more galleries.

Our project plan is to remedy past building mistakes (confusing labyrinthian galleries) that were designed to maximize display space at the lowest cost. In addition, we will add more of the elements that guests in an experience economy crave, such as beautiful places to pause and to enjoy natural light and views of the outdoors; a greater variety in types of galleries; more space for social interaction; new kinds of flexible spaces that allow for performance and participatory experiences; and more opportunities to refresh with coffee or a glass of wine. Our traditional donors struggle to understand this plan, as it is not focused on buying more art or building more gallery space; however, if we are to thrive in the coming decades, our focus must be on effectively using our collections and physical spaces to create memorable, enjoyable and impactful experiences for new and diverse audiences. Indeed, the visitors of tomorrow will expect such experiences and will seek them out elsewhere if the museum fails to provide them.

Figure 29.6 Water tower wrapped with reproduction of Frank Stella's *Tahkt-I-Sulayman Variation II* as part of the Minneapolis Institute of Art's 100th anniversary "birthday surprises"

Source: Minneapolis Institute of Arts

The philanthropic landscape

No less impactful than the shifts in audience demographics, consumer behavior, and programmatic expectations are the changes in philanthropic behavior affecting museums in the 21st century.

Traditional patronage from corporate sponsors and arts foundations is becoming a thing of the past. Corporations, buffeted by shifts in the worldwide economy since 2008, are re-centralizing their historic focus on profitability and shareholder return. While overall corporate giving has seen recent slight increases, giving to arts and culture within this sector is not keeping pace (Giving USA, 2018). Much of the tradition behind corporate philanthropy was a method for building communities – for creating the great civic institutions described earlier in this chapter, which would help make the community a better place in which to live and work. In 1976, 23 Minnesota companies launched The 5% Club (now called the Minnesota Keystone Program) to encourage charitable giving, recognizing corporations based in the state who agreed to set aside 5% of their pretax income for philanthropic purposes. Created out of a shared appreciation for the common good, as well as a practical approach to attracting good talent, the Twin Cities has long displayed a history of healthy peer pressure in the corporate giving sector (MPLS Regional Chamber, 2018).

With the rise of globalization and a VUCA world, our experience is that new corporate leaders recruited from outside the community do not feel the same commitment to the place in which they are headquartered, as evidenced by decreased giving and reduced participation on local nonprofit boards. Additionally, the rise of cause-related marketing and the need to connect corporate philanthropy to core business objectives is moving corporate funding toward major social issues such as hunger and homelessness, economic development and equity, education, climate change, and health care. The Twin Cities, long a bastion of corporate philanthropy and called "the Emerald City of giving" by the *New York Times*, due in part to the number of major international corporations based here, hosts many examples of these shifts – Target's recent philanthropic focus on health and wellness, Thrivent's support for housing and economic development, 3M's priority for science education, Medtronic's philanthropic shift toward world health issues (Nocera, 2007). All are logical and appropriate strategies aligned with their core businesses – yet have a significant impact on the arts and cultural institutions that have historically benefitted from their largess and the C-level involvement of corporate leaders.

Government foundation sources, such as the National Endowment for the Arts (NEA), the National Endowment for the Humanities (NEH), and Institute of Museum and Library Services (IMLS), continue to provide important funding for museums, in particular for exhibition development. Not surprisingly, however, this is one of the most unstable areas of potential revenue, given the increasingly partisan nature of funding for arts and culture. While there are international examples of museums largely supported through government funding, it is increasingly rare in the United States, and subject to the shifting directives of the divided federal government, state legislatures, and city councils (Stubbs, 2012).

The authors have observed locally that private and community foundations, similarly, continue to realign their giving priorities to meet pressing community needs, as well as to allow a new generation of foundation leaders and board members to drive philanthropic strategy. The generational transfer of wealth is not just evident at the individual level but through the presence of a new generation of family and board members in the foundation sector. Many of these children no longer live in the same communities as their parents and grandparents who started these foundations and often maintain very different philanthropic interests than their predecessors. Many of our civic "legacy" institutions, created at the turn of the last century, no longer hold the same importance for their founder's descendants.

Consequently, individual giving is the most significant revenue source for arts organizations, and it is expected to remain so far into the future. Individual donors have the most philanthropic impact on museums, in particular when it comes to gifts for capital projects, art acquisition, and endowment. However, while overall giving trends show growth in this area, it is notable that this growth is driven by large gifts from a small, but significant, number of major individual donors (Giving USA, 2018). The proportion of smaller gifts from a broader pool of individual donors shows signs of diminishing and may be further influenced by the potential impact of the 2018 Tax Cuts and Jobs Act. The increase in the standard deduction is likely to take the charitable deduction out of reach for many taxpayers and may serve to reduce the number of annual contributors further (National Council of Nonprofits, 2018). This is a wake-up call for museums to explore and implement ways to increase the number of donors contributing at all levels.

The intersection of strategy and fundraising: what does it all mean for funding?

In the face of this new landscape and ongoing pace of change, strategy is king; not just fundraising strategy, but a broad strategy that guides the institution, and articulates the key goals and priorities. This must be visionary and future-focused – it is, indeed, this vision that is critical to driving significant philanthropy and branding the museum as vital, relevant, and imperative. Donors are motivated to make a difference and want to hear about our vision and ideas in a way that illustrates change (O'Reilly, 2015). Big dreams drive big philanthropy, and this is truer than ever.

Regardless of the scale of the vision, certain fundamental fundraising principles will continue to be inviolable in the years ahead:

- The strategic plan clearly articulates key institutional priorities
- The fundraising strategy is in alignment with the strategic plan and guides the allocation of resources
- Leadership across all institutional divisions supports the strategic plan and corresponding fundraising strategy
- Dedicated staff (Advancement team) details and implements the fundraising strategy and monitors the funding landscape for new opportunities
- While being responsive to new ideas and funding opportunities, the focus remains on the strategic plan and identified fundraising strategy
- Fundraising for strategic new initiatives is balanced with fundraising for ongoing operational costs
- Advancement staff builds long-term relationships with donors on growing loyalty while also managing short-term funding needs
- All key staff play a role in fundraising as vital connectors to potential donors and should be engaged in not just solicitation, but also the key steps of donor research and cultivation
- Trustees are notable partners in fundraising strategy, making the museum their own highest philanthropic priority, being ambassadors for the museum and its goals, telling the museum's story throughout the community, opening doors to new funders, and supporting the staff's work to engage both longstanding and new donors

Implementing strategy with a focus on the future

To increase financial sustainability, successful implementation of a future-focused strategy requires blending the information gained from our environmental scan with the sound principles above and focusing on what we have to offer, who we are offering it to, and how we can best accomplish this in our new and rapidly changing environment.

What are we offering?

Museums of the future must change their programmatic and content approach to align with the public's concerns and interests. For most of their histories, American museums have collected, preserved, and interpreted their objects in a manner that reflected the interests and expertise of their professional staff. Visitors, for their part, understand museums to be bastions of "culture" where exposure to great works of art of the past served to elevate and enlighten them – and transport them, however briefly, from the realities of their lives. Going forward, it will be increasingly important for museums to understand the public zeitgeist, and to stage exhibitions and interpret their collections in a manner that not only acknowledges the public's concerns, but that provides a forum for discourse. Human rights, environmental concerns, and cultural appropriation dominate this present moment, and museums are responding with exhibitions that place these issues within a historic context, while also offering contemporary responses from today's artists. For example, an exhibition titled "Art and Healing: In the Moment," recently staged at Mia, featured works produced by community artists that memorialized Philando Castile, a young African-American man who was killed by a police officer during a traffic stop in a suburb of St. Paul (see Figure 29.7).

Figure 29.7 Visitors to *Art and Healing: In the Moment*, June 17–July 29, 2018, an exhibition featuring community artwork commemorating Philando Castile, an African-American man killed by a police officer

Source: Minneapolis Institute of Art

As the title suggests, the exhibition focused on the role art can play in the wake of trauma, and programming included discussions about conflict resolution, appropriation, and art-making as a form of resistance.

Mia also recently installed a temporary exhibition of works created by students as part of a project called "Your Story, Our Story." The exhibition displays the art of students from a high school in St. Paul, Minnesota, which serves some 250 young newcomers to the United States from several dozen countries (see Figure 29.8).

Their individual works, powerfully reflecting on the experience of their immigration or migration stories, put a face and a place on today's timely debates over this subject, and will be followed by a series of special exhibitions and related programs focusing on Vietnam and the topic of migration.

The challenge for museums, with their lengthy exhibition development cycles, is to be predictive and agile enough to respond to the public's collective psyche in a meaningful and timely manner. The ability to read and adapt to coming trends will be a vital qualification for museum leaders. "The notion of zeitgeist might be intangible, but the risks of contextual insensitivity are concrete. If you can't read the business landscape, you risk leading your organization in the wrong direction . . ." (Mayo and Nohria, 2005).

At the same time, cultural institutions embedded within communities must be sensitive and responsive to local concerns. As demographics change, museums must work to ensure that their collections and programming reflect the diversity and interests of their proximate communities – in all likelihood vastly different from when the museum was founded (see Figure 29.9).

Figure 29.8   Young artist represented in the exhibition *Your Story, Our Story*, June 22–September 27, 2018, at the Minneapolis Institute of Art

Source: Minneapolis Institute of Art

Figure 29.9 Visitor to the exhibition *"I Am Somali": Three Visual Artists from the Twin Cities,* August 19, 2017–May 27, 2018, at the Minneapolis Institute of Art

Source: Minneapolis Institute of Art

In instances where distance and perception thwart community participation, museums might consider off-site programming within target communities. The Los Angeles County Museum of Art is currently planning for one or two satellite campuses in South Los Angeles as part of a larger statement about national initiatives around social justice. Supported in part by a grant from the Ford Foundation, Darren Walker said of the project, "By going right into the community, this turns the traditional, elitist museum model on its head. It's about democratizing our idea of a museum's mission" (Finkel, 2018).

In addition to addressing what we offer, museums must better articulate our ideas and projects; not just how we will implement them, but what need they will serve, why they are critical and relevant, what impact they will have, and what change will result. Building a case applies to formal grant requests as well as to ongoing conversations with individual donors. This rigorous practice should become part of every arts organizations messaging for new and innovative initiatives, as well as our core work of exhibitions, interpretation, and programming so that we have a consistent and thorough fundraising case that is articulated across our institutions. Needs that are operational, such as keeping the lights on, staff salaries, and art conservation, become much more palatable to donors when bundled into a case for innovative programming and research that is rooted in our galleries, collections, and expertise.

Just as traditional donors looked to museums to fulfill their needs for collection quality and gallery space, the donor of today is looking for the museum to demonstrate impact and relevance. How does our collection and its display and interpretation impact visitors' lives and represent all of our diverse visitors and their cultural histories? How do our learning programs build empathy and an understanding of our increasingly interdependent world? How does the museum serve as a welcoming and dynamic physical resource for our community and our neighborhood in particular?

Museums must be able to articulate responses to these questions and track and measure impact. Historically, museums have excelled at demonstrating activity, such as the number of school children served; the number of tours led; and the number of visitors to an exhibition (see Figure 29.10). However, true impact is deeper, and analyzing and reporting outcomes and

Figure 29.10　Facilitated visits to art museum yield educational benefits for school children

Source: Minneapolis Institute of Art

impacts needs to illustrate how the lives of our visitors and community members are changed by our work. A recent impact study prepared for the National Art Education Association (NAEA) and the Association of Art Museum Directors (AAMD), which addresses the effects of facilitated single-visit art museum programs on students in grades 4 through 6, can serve as a good example. The rigorous study, funded by ILMS and the Samuel H. Kress Foundation, demonstrates that a facilitated visit to an art museum yields a variety of educational benefits for schoolchildren (National Art Education Association, 2018).

Increasingly, donors have the expectation of a much deeper evaluation of our effectiveness that helps them determine if their philanthropic dollars are being well used. In short, we must show how we serve critical community needs and prove a return on investment.

Who are we offering it to?

Building a solid and robust case is foundational, as it guides the important next steps of donor research and qualification. A donor-centric approach is critical, as long-term fundraising success based on trust and loyalty will only result from building and deepening relationships that meet a donor's needs and interests. The new venture innovation approach to fundraising requires that museums develop greater internal capacity to research and find donors who may want to support and invest in our innovative new work.

The greatest opportunity for future fundraising growth for the arts lies primarily with individual donors. Multiple sources cite the unprecedented and impending transfer of wealth from the baby boomer generation. While dollar estimates vary, those older than age 50 currently hold 80% of America's household wealth. (Carlozo, 2017) Not surprisingly, many of the arts' loyal traditionalists are baby boomers. We must be prepared to find and cultivate the next generation of donors and meet their needs.

New and younger donors, in particular, those who have accumulated wealth through growing industries such as technology and investments, are driving new forms of philanthropic financing and venture capital funding (Janus, 2017). These approaches are well suited to support special museum initiatives that strive to meet specific interests and societal needs. For example, at Mia, we have found success in securing funding for projects like Museum as Site for Social Action (MASS Action), an industry-wide initiative to explore new methodologies for museums to engage in social justice work within their communities (MASS Action, 2018) (see Figure 29.11).

Our funding for this was secured through two donors, both of whom have some history of support for the museum, but who we identified for this project through research into their support for other related social justice work. Additionally, through our prior relationship with them, we knew of their openness to innovative ideas and interest in helping Mia to launch new initiatives. We have also launched The Center for Empathy and the Visual Arts (CEVA), a first-ever initiative in the museum field to conduct scientific research, test, and launch new approaches to building empathy through engaging with art (Minneapolis Institute of Art, 2018). Funding to implement the first phase of this project was secured by way of a major foundation grant from a partner who historically has provided support for the collection and curatorial work; however, they were compelled through speaking with us about the opportunity, through this project, to utilize the collection in a greater way, as a catalyst for empathy and to affect change in society.

Major grantmakers are taking a proactive stance to drive change in the area of diversity, equity, and inclusion, as witnessed by the recent partnership between The Walton Family Foundation and Ford Foundation, each committing $3 million over three years to support creative solutions to diversify management and curatorial staff at art museums around the country. Through this

Figure 29.11   MASS Action (Museums as a Site for Social Action) convening at the Minneapolis Institute
    of Art, October 10–12, 2018

Source: Minneapolis Institute of Art

initiative, Mia has received a major grant to support the launch of a robust fellowship program for college students of diverse cultural backgrounds, to help strengthen the pipeline of art museum leadership positions for those who have been historically underrepresented. "For museums to be truly inviting public spaces, they must better reflect the communities they serve. Achieving diversity requires a deeper commitment: To hire and nurture leaders from all backgrounds. This initiative creates the opportunity for museums to build a more inclusive culture within their institutions," said Alice Walton, board member of the Walton Family Foundation and founder and Board Chair of the Crystal Bridges Museum of American Art (Ford Foundation, 2017).

As valuable as these new funding approaches are, they offer challenges to the nonprofit sector and arts institutions in particular. Our traditional methods of programming and evaluation and the relatively slow pace at which cultural organizations adjust to change do not meet the needs of younger, business-oriented donors who are accustomed to operating in a world that is defined by speed, innovation, experimentation, return on investment, and immediately quantifiable results.

A particular challenge in working with new donors is to articulate and engage them with the pressing needs arts organizations have for shorter-term operating support. Museums, by our nature, consist of large physical spaces that have significant ongoing operating costs, including the maintenance of gallery spaces, the utility needs for the care and preservation of our collections, and staffing costs for art handling, display, and security. As much as these can be outlined as core program needs, they do not provide the alluring and innovative case for support that an affluent, young tech entrepreneur may be seeking.

Cultural institutions must also look to build a new base of donors, rooted in the changing demographics of our audiences. These new donors, from diverse cultural backgrounds, are often new to the cultural sector and traditional concept of philanthropy. Since they come to museums for different reasons – often for community engagement or for specific programs that speak to their interests – museums need to be diligent about planning and communicating such programs on a more consistent basis. Though attracted to the idea of more engagement with the museum, concepts of "membership" and "annual giving" often do not resonate. Their use of traditional benefits, which have been the historic core of museum cultivation and stewardship programs, is very different. Membership cards and donor circles hold little allure. Instead, these new donors anticipate greater social opportunities and personalization.

Their loyalty is not a given, and their perspective on loyalty is very different from traditionalists. For those without a cultural or familial basis for arts philanthropy, we need to test new ideas and fundraising messages, such as preserving heritage for future generations, supporting the museum as a space for community gathering, and giving as a way for the museum to remain vital to everyone, regardless of background. An important tool for this exercise is to utilize surveys and focus groups. These communities know best what their priorities are, and because museum staff may not be directly reflective of their audience profile, engaging them directly in conversation can be the best way to learn more accurately what may help engage them in giving to the museum.

How do we offer it?

In addition to changing our programming, messages, and communications to reach a new audience of younger and increasingly diverse individual donors, museums must also invest the additional effort and resources required to research, cultivate, and solicit them. We must provide for more services to support expanding teams, in particular, to provide research into the museum's data and other sources to identify and qualify those with the greatest potential to have a fundraising impact in this new environment.

We need to look carefully at how we recruit, train, manage, and engage new fundraising talent. Enhanced skills at research, social media, and technology are increasingly important as we embrace a new donor audience of digital natives, whose expectations for communication and information are very different from our traditional donor base. For example, Mia stopped publishing a member magazine about seven years ago. The decision was not inspired by a desire to save money on printing costs but by the need to communicate with donors in a more agile and accessible manner. The museum still prints materials that are mailed to donors, but we deliver information in a more timely, efficient, and effective manner. Ironically, even though we hesitated to discontinue the magazine out of fear of disgruntled donors, we only received one complaint. Arts organizations are often more constricted by their assumptions about donors than are the donors themselves.

There are far too few people of color working in the cultural fundraising profession, and the field has done a poor job of working to make itself attractive to these candidates. As our audiences change, our staff members will also need to change, as donors expect to see themselves represented in museum advancement offices. We must work to develop and mentor new professionals, starting with students in high school and college. Adding these new members to our teams will not only support donor cultivation, but it will also impact the financial success of our museums overall.

> Most important, we found that the most diverse enterprises were also the most innovative, as measured by the freshness of their revenue mix. In fact, companies with above-average total diversity, measured as the average of six dimensions of diversity (migration, industry, career path, gender, education, age), had both 19% points higher innovation revenues and 9% points higher EBIT margins, on average.
>
> *(Lorenzo and Reeves, 2018)*

In addition to current research on the benefits of diversity in the private sector, this enables nonprofits to deliver on their mission as well, through better decision-making, more creativity, and an increased ability to listen to our audiences (Rahman, 2017).

We need to be open to new ways of networking with potential donors. This is where diversifying museum staff and boards is especially important, to introduce the museum to new audiences, who can then help open doors to others throughout the community. The support and endorsement of new "champions" is critical for reaching a new, younger, and diverse audience, more reliant on the feedback of their social networks than any loyalty to an organization or brand.

We must cultivate an environment in which we are willing and able to test new approaches with agility, analyze results, and make change. Email and direct mail solicitations should involve multiple audience segments and A/B message testing to see which fundraising appeals work with different audiences. While this work requires short-term investment, the gains of establishing benchmarks to support future data-driven decisions will have an increasing impact in the long term.

Conclusion

The role of cultural organizations is changing in our communities, with an increased focus on community engagement, diversity and inclusion, empathy and global understanding, and relevance. Our institutions exist in an increasingly volatile, uncertain, complex, and ambiguous world, and we must address the challenges and opportunities presented by this new environment. This new climate includes significantly changing audience demographics, increasingly sophisticated customer expectations, and the rise of the experience economy. Equally evolving is the nature of the philanthropic landscape in the U.S. and for the arts sector.

Building a robust institutional and fundraising strategy in this new environment is more critical than ever, one with clear roles across the museum and a balance that can support funding both short and long-term needs. We must focus on changing what we offer through our collections, interpretation, programs, and events to address our new environment, and then appropriately build a case for fundraising support that articulates our relevance and impact.

Once the strategy is established and aligned, our organizations must focus on not only reaching out to our loyal and core audiences, engaging and inspiring them with new initiatives, but also identifying and cultivating new, younger, and diverse audiences that are attracted to the arts and their vital community role. We must increase the diversity of our staff and boards to help reflect and reach these new audiences and continue to test innovative fundraising messages and approaches to identify what leads to success in this changing environment.

The arts must have an increasingly agile approach that articulates the institution's vision and anticipated impact and that addresses the complexities of our new environment, and meets donor needs for outcomes and engagement. Understanding and maintaining this balance is the key to finding stable funding in a highly unstable world.

References

Axelrad, C. (2014). Yes the donor pyramid is really dead: An open response to Andrea Kihlstedt. *GuideStar Blog*, blog post, 8 July. Available at: https://trust.guidestar.org/blog/2014/07/08/yes-the-donor-pyramid-is-really-dead-an-open-response-to-andrea-kihlstedt/. [Accessed 30 Oct. 2018].

Bryant-Greenwell, K. (2017). The 21st century museum: A think-tank for community. *Museum iD: The #FutureMuseum Project*, blog post. Available at: http://museum-id.com/the-futuremuseum-project-what-will-museums-be-like-in-the-future-essay-collection/. [Accessed 30 Oct. 2018].

Carlozo, L. (2017). Will millennials be ready for the great wealth transfer? *U.S. News & World Report*, July 18. Available at: https://money.usnews.com/investing/articles/2017-07-18/will-millennials-be-ready-for-the-great-wealth-transfer. [Accessed 10 Oct. 2018].

Cobb, N.K. (2002). The new philanthropy: Its impact on funding arts and culture. *The Journal of Arts Management, Law, and Society*, 32(2). Available at: www.americansforthearts.org/sites/default/files/Cobb.pdf [Accessed 9 Nov. 2018].

Cone (2017). *2017 Cone Gen Z CSR Study: How to Speak Z.* Available at: www.conecomm.com/research-blog/2017-genz-csr-study. [Accessed 29 Oct. 2018].

Devos, L. (2018). How understanding post-millennials will help your museum. *Team Works Media*, blog post. Available at: www.teamworksmedia.com/museums/understanding-post-millennials-will-help-museum/. [Accessed 29 Oct. 2018].

Finkel, J. (2018). Lacma seeks to expand its footprint into South Los Angeles. *The New York Times*, 24 January. Available at: www.nytimes.com/2018/01/24/arts/design/lacma-south-los-angeles-michael-govan.html. [Accessed 10 Oct. 2018].

Ford Foundation (2017). *Ford foundation and Walton family foundation launch $6 million effort to diversify art museum leadership*, November 28. Available at: www.prnewswire.com/news-releases/ford-foundation-and-walton-family-foundation-launch-6-million-effort-to-diversify-art-museum-leadership-300562243.html. [Accessed 10 Oct. 2018].

Frey, W. (2018). *The US will become 'minority white' in 2045, census projects.* Brookings: The Avenue, blog post, 14 March 2018. Available at: www.brookings.edu/blog/the-avenue/2018/03/14/the-us-will-become-minority-white-in-2045-census-projects/. [Accessed 10 Oct. 2018].

Giving USA, a public service initiative of The Giving Institute (2018). *See the numbers – Giving USA 2018 Infographic.* Available at: https://givingusa.org/see-the-numbers-giving-usa-2018-infographic/ [Accessed 10 Oct. 2018].

Janus, K.K. (2017). Innovating philanthropy. *Stanford Social Innovation Review*, November 1. Available at: https://ssir.org/articles/entry/innovating_philanthropy. [Accessed 10 Oct. 2018].

La Placa Cohen (2017). *Culture track 2017.* Available at: http://2017study.culturetrack.com/. [Accessed 10 Oct. 2018].

Lorenzo, R. and Reeves, M. (2018). How and where diversity drives financial performance. *Harvard Business Review*, January 30. Available at: https://hbr.org/2018/01/how-and-where-diversity-drives-financial-performance. [Accessed 10 Oct. 2018].

Mayo, A.J. and Nohria, N. (2005). Zeitgeist leadership. *Harvard Business Review*, October Issue. Available at: https://hbr.org/2005/10/zeitgeist-leadership. [Accessed 10 Oct. 2018].

MASS Action (2016). *MASS action home page*, Minneapolis Institute of Art. Available at: www.museumaction.org/. [Accessed 9 Nov. 2018].

Metropolitan Museum of Art (2017). *Annual Report 2016–17: Report of the Chief Financial Officer*, 14 November 2017. Available at: www.metmuseum.org/-/media/files/about-the-met/annual-reports/2016-2017/annual-report-2016-17-report-of-the-chief-financial-officer.pdf. [Accessed 30 Oct. 2018].

Minneapolis Institute of Art (2016). *Strategic Plan 2021: Executive Summary*, July 2016. Available at: https://staging.artsmia.org/wp-content/uploads/2016/07/Exec-Summary_2021.pdf. [Accessed 30 Oct. 2018].

———. (2018). *Center for empathy and the visual arts.* Available at: https://new.artsmia.org/empathy. [Accessed 9 Nov. 2018].

MPLS Regional Chamber (2018). *Minnesota keystone program.* Available at: www.mplschamber.com/minnesota-keystone-program/. [Accessed 30 Oct. 2018].

Museum of Fine Arts Boston (2018). *Architectural history.* Available at: www.mfa.org/about/architectural-history. [Accessed 30 Oct. 2018].

Museum of Fine Arts Houston (2018). *The MFAH: An architectural history.* Available at: www.mfah.org/about/mfah-architectural-history/. [Accessed 30 Oct. 2018].

National Art Education Association (2018). *NAEA-AAMD Research study: Impact of art museum programs on K-12 Students*, September 25. Available at: www.arteducators.org/research/articles/377-naea-aamd-research-study-impact-of-art-museum-programs-on-k-12-students. [Accessed 10 Oct. 2018].

National Council of Nonprofits (2018). *Tax cuts and jobs act, H.R. 1: Nonprofit analysis of the final tax law*, 5 April 2018. Available at: www.councilofnonprofits.org/sites/default/files/documents/tax-bill-summary-chart.pdf. [Accessed 30 Oct. 2018].

National Endowment for the Arts (2015). *A decade of arts engagement: Findings from the survey of public participation in the arts, 2002–2012.* January. Available at: www.arts.gov/sites/default/files/2012-sppa-jan2015-rev.pdf. [Accessed 10 Oct. 2018].

Nocera, J. (2007). Emerald city of giving does exist. *The New York Times*, 22 December. Available at: www. nytimes.com/2007/12/22/business/22nocera.html. [Accessed 10 Oct. 2018].

Olsen, C. (2018). How art museums can remain relevant in the 21st century. *Artsy*, 15 June 2018. Available at: www.artsy.net/article/artsy-editorial-art-museums-remain-relevant-21st-century. [Accessed 10 Oct. 2018].

O'Reilly, B. (2015). Major gifts fundraising 101: It's not about us. It's about them! *Network for good: The nonprofit marketing blog*, blog post, 17 December. Available at: www.networkforgood.com/nonprofitblog/major-gifts-fundraising-101-its-not-about-us-its-about-them/. [Accessed 30 Oct. 2018].

Pine II, B.J. and Gilmore, J.H. (1998). Welcome to the experience economy. *Harvard Business Review*, July-August Issue. Available at: https://hbr.org/1998/07/welcome-to-the-experience-economy. [Accessed 10 Oct. 2018].

Rahman, A. (2017). Diversity and inclusion: Essential to all non-profits. *Huffington Post*, 7 August. Available at: www.huffingtonpost.com/entry/diversity-and-inclusion-essential-to-all-non-profits_us_5988c06 ce4b0f25bdfb31ecb. [Accessed 30 Oct. 2018].

Rodini, E. (2018). *A brief history of the art museum*, 10 July 2018, Smarthistory. Available at: https://smart history.org/a-brief-history-of-the-art-museum/. [Accessed 30 Oct. 2018].

Samuel, L.R. (2017). *Boomers 3.0: Marketing to baby boomers in their third act of life*. Santa Barbara, CA: Praeger/ABC-CLIO, p. 62.

Schonfeld, R., Westermann, M., and Sweeney, L. (2015). *Art museum demographic survey*, 28 July 2015, The Andrew W. Mellon Foundation. Available at: https://mellon.org/programs/arts-and-cultural-heritage/art-history-conservation-museums/demographic-survey/. [Accessed 10 Oct. 2018].

Schwab, K. (2016). Art for Instagram's sake. *The Atlantic*, 17 February 2016. Available at: www.theatlantic.com/entertainment/archive/2016/02/instagram-art-wonder-renwick-rain-room/463173/. [Accessed 10 Oct. 2018].

Shams, L. and Seitz, A.R. (2008). Benefits of multisensory learning. *Cell Press*, 12(11), pp. 411–417. Available at: https://doi.org/10.1016/j.tics.2008.07.006. [Accessed 10 Oct. 2018].

TED Talks (2009). *Simon Sinek: How great leaders inspire action*, YouTube video, September 2009. Available at: www.ted.com/talks/simon_sinek_how_great_leaders_inspire_action?language=en [Accessed 3 Dec. 2018].

Stubbs, R. (2012). Public funding for the arts: 2021 update. *Grantmakers in the Arts Reader*, 23(3). Available at: www.giarts.org/sites/default/files/23-3_Vital-Signs.pdf. [Accessed 30 Oct. 2018].

U.S. Army Heritage and Education Center (2018). *Who first originated the term VUCA (Volatility, Uncertainty, Complexity and Ambiguity)?* 16 February 2018. Available at: http://usawc.libanswers.com/faq/84869. [Accessed 26 Sep. 2018].

Virginia Museum of Fine Arts (2018). *History of the museum*. Available at: www.vmfa.museum/about/museum-history/. [Accessed 30 October 2018].

INDEX

Note: Page numbers in *italics* refer to figures, whereas page numbers in **bold** refer to tables.

461

Printed in the United States
by Baker & Taylor Publisher Services